THE PAPERS
OF
JOHN MARSHALL

Sponsored by
The College of William and Mary
and
The Institute of Early American History and Culture
under the auspices of
The National Historical Publications and Records
Commission

UNITED STATES CAPITOL

The North, or Senate, wing of the U.S. Capitol, where the Supreme Court met beginning in 1801. Watercolor by William R. Birch, 1800. *Courtesy of the Library of Congress*

THE PAPERS
OF
JOHN MARSHALL

Volume VI

Correspondence, Papers, and Selected Judicial Opinions
November 1800–March 1807

CHARLES F. HOBSON, *Editor*

FREDRIKA J. TEUTE, *Associate Editor*

LAURA S. GWILLIAM, *Editorial Assistant*

The University of North Carolina Press, Chapel Hill
in association with the
Institute of Early American History and Culture
Williamsburg, Virginia

The Institute of Early American History and Culture
is sponsored jointly by The College of William and Mary in Virginia
and The Colonial Williamsburg Foundation

*The ornament on the title page is based upon John Marshall's personal seal, as it appears on a
gold watch fob that also bears the seal of his wife, Mary Willis Marshall. It was drawn by
Richard J. Stinely of Williamsburg, Virginia, from the original, now owned by the Association
for the Preservation of Virginia Antiquities, Richmond, Virginia, and is published with the
owner's permission.*

Library of Congress Cataloging-in-Publication Data
(Revised for volume 6)

Marshall, John, 1755–1835.
    The papers of John Marshall.
    "Sponsored by the College of William and Mary and the Institute of Early American History
and Culture under the auspices of the National Historical Publications Commission."
    Includes bibliographical references and indexes.

    CONTENTS: v. 1. Correspondence and papers, November 10, 1775–June 23, 1788. Ac-
count book, September 1783–June 1788.   v. 2. Correspondence and papers, July 1788–December 1795. Account book, July 1788–December 1795.—[etc.]—v. 6. Correspondence, papers,
and selected judicial opinions, November 1800–March 1807 / Charles F. Hobson, editor.
    1. Marshall, John, 1755–1835—Archives.   2. Statesmen—United States—Archives.
3. Judges—United States—Archives.   4. United States—Politics and government—Revolution,
1775–1783—Sources.   5. United States—Politics and government—1783–1865—Sources.
6. Judicial opinions.   I. Johnson, Herbert Alan, ed.   II. Cullen, Charles T., 1940–   ed.
III. Institute of Early American History and Culture (Williamsburg, Va.)   IV. Title.
E302.M365   347.73'2634   347.3073534   74-9575
                        ISBN 0-8078-1233-1 (v. 1)
                        ISBN 0-8078-1302-8 (v. 2)
                        ISBN 0-8078-1337-0 (v. 3)
                        ISBN 0-8078-1586-1 (v. 4)
                        ISBN 0-8078-1746-5 (v. 5)
                        ISBN 0-8078-1903-4 (v. 6)

To the memory of
WILLIAM F. SWINDLER

The publication of this volume has been assisted by grants from the William Nelson Cromwell Foundation, the Virginia Law Foundation, the Earhart Foundation, the National Historical Publications and Records Commission, and the National Endowment for the Humanities.

CONTENTS

NOVEMBER 1800—MARCH 1807

1800

1801

1803

1804

1806

ILLUSTRATIONS

Preface

Volume VI of *The Papers of John Marshall* is the first of approximately five or six volumes that will present a documentary record of John Marshall's years as chief justice of the United States. This volume resumes the chronological format of the first four volumes, a format that will be adhered to for the remainder of the series. It begins where Volume IV ended, in November 1800, with Marshall in the midst of a brief term as secretary of state in the administration of John Adams. While the electoral defeat of the Federalists in the fall of 1800 cut short his career as the president's principal officer, that event conspired with other circumstances to place Marshall within a few months at the head of the judicial branch. Commissioned as chief justice on 31 January 1801, he retained that office until his death on 6 July 1835.

No new developments in foreign affairs occurred during the last four months of the Adams administration. Marshall continued to implement policies and forward negotiations already in progress. News of a convention with France, reported by the American commissioners in their dispatch of 4 October 1800, reached Washington in December. Negotiations with Great Britain to resolve differences over the construction of article 6 of the Jay Treaty—relating to the recovery of pre-Revolutionary debts owed to British merchants—were at a less advanced stage, though prospects were favorable for an eventual settlement. Relations with Britain commanded Marshall's principal attention. Of particular concern was the increasing number of American merchant ships captured and condemned as prizes in British vice-admiralty courts. British affairs was one of three pressing problems that Marshall singled out for urgent attention by his successor. The other two were relations with the Barbary states and with Spain.

While attending to his official duties as head of the State Department, Marshall at the same time acted as President Adams's confidential adviser. The president entrusted him with chief responsibility for drafting his message to Congress, delivered at the November 1800 session, the first to be held in the city of Washington. He also relied heavily on Marshall's counsel in making the numerous judicial appointments that marked the final days of his presidency. In response to his own appointment as chief justice, Marshall wrote Adams: "This additional & flattering mark of your good opinion has made an impression on my mind which time will not efface" (4 February 1801).

Marshall viewed the impending change of administration with

gloomy apprehension. While the issue was in doubt whether Thomas Jefferson or Aaron Burr would be the next president, Marshall at first leaned toward the latter as the lesser of two evils. Although persuaded by Alexander Hamilton that Burr posed the greater danger, Marshall continued to feel "almost insuperable objections" to Jefferson, whose "foreign prejudices seem . . . totally to unfit him for the chief magistracy." Jefferson, moreover, appeared "to be a man who will embody himself with the house of representatives. By weakening the office of President he will increase his personal power. He will diminish his responsability, sap the fundamental principles of the government & become the leader of that party which is about to constitute the majority of the legislature" (to Hamilton, 1 January 1801). On the day of Jefferson's inauguration, Marshall confided to a fellow Federalist his prognosis for the "new order" of democratic rule: "The democrats are divided into speculative theorists & absolute terrorists: With the latter I am not disposd to class Mr. Jefferson. If he arranges himself with them it is not difficult to foresee that much calamity is in store for our country—if he does not they will soon become his enemies & calumniators" (to Charles Cotesworth Pinckney, 4 March 1801).

Within a short time the new political majority began to assert its power, directed particularly at the judiciary, where Federalism still prevailed. One of the first acts of the Republican Congress was to repeal the judiciary law enacted by its lame-duck predecessor in February 1801, thereby abolishing in one stroke the host of new judgeships that had been filled by Adams's appointees. In the mind of the chief justice, the repeal raised a serious constitutional issue. The 1801 law had created separate judges for the circuit courts, relieving the Supreme Court justices of circuit duty. Now, with the restoration of the former system, they were being ordered to ride circuit again. Believing the Constitution required distinct commissions for circuit court judges, the chief justice doubted the repeal's validity and polled his brethren to ascertain their sentiments. With the exception of Samuel Chase, the associate justices considered the question already settled by the practice of riding circuit between 1789 and 1801. Chase set forth at length his view that the repeal law was void, chiefly on the ground that it unconstitutionally deprived sitting circuit court judges of their offices (to Marshall, 24 April 1802). Whatever his own views on this question, Marshall considered himself bound to follow the majority of his colleagues in acquiescing in the repeal. He had no doubt "that policy dictates this decision to us all" (to William Paterson, 3 May 1802).

The repeal of the Judiciary Act of 1801 was but one of a series of political tempests that swirled about the judiciary during the early years of Marshall's leadership of the Supreme Court. Before the repeal occurred, the court, in December 1801, had received an application from one William Marbury for a writ of mandamus commanding the secretary of state to deliver Marbury's commission as justice of the peace for the District of Columbia. The outcome of this application was the decision in *Marbury* v. *Madison* at the February 1803 term, in which the chief justice set forth his view that delivery of this commission was a legal duty, not a matter of political discretion. Republican partisans denounced the opinion as a thinly veiled attack on the president and an unwarranted judicial intrusion into the province of the executive department. In a retaliatory mood, the House of Representatives in the spring of 1804 adopted articles of impeachment against Justice Chase, who was notorious for using his circuit court grand jury charges as a platform for giving vent to his own highly partisan Federalist views. To Marshall, these impeachment proceedings were "sufficient to alarm the friends of a pure & of course an independent judiciary, if among those who rule our land there be any of that description" (to James M. Marshall, 1 April 1804).

The trial of Justice Chase early in 1805, at which Marshall himself testified (16 February), ended in his acquittal by the Senate. That outcome reflected the triumph of moderate Republicans in Congress and introduced a period of accommodation, if not harmony, between the judicial and political branches of the government. Tension remained and conflict would break out again, but the concept of an independent judiciary had more or less gained acceptance.

Paradoxically, perhaps, these dramatic events in the public history of the Supreme Court do not loom large in the personal papers of the chief justice. To be sure, much of Marshall's correspondence has been lost or destroyed, and the surviving remnant may not accurately reflect either the range or priority of his daily pursuits during these years. Yet it cannot be doubted that the most extensively documented of his activities from 1801 to 1807 was in fact his primary preoccupation. This was the writing of *The Life of George Washington*, a massive life and times of the late general. Marshall undertook this project out of a sense of duty and a hope of handsome remuneration (to help finance his purchase of the Fairfax estate). Published by the Philadelphia publisher Caleb P. Wayne, the work appeared in five large volumes between 1804 and 1807. The story of the publication of the *Life*, as it unfolds in the author's letters to his publisher, occupies center stage throughout this volume.

Marshall produced his voluminous history in five years while presiding over the Supreme Court and attending his circuits twice a year in Richmond and Raleigh—an extraordinary display of self-discipline and fluency with a pen. Writing the *Life* caused Marshall no little vexation. Under constant pressure from Wayne to meet publication deadlines, he fretted over infelicities of style, errors of diction, and prolixity that unavoidably resulted from hasty composition. The hardest volume to write was the last, a history of the "civil administration" from the close of the war to Washington's death. There was simply too much ground to cover, the materials too abundant, to be crammed into one volume. Moreover, as the narrative moved closer to the present day, Marshall found it more difficult to maintain the stance of a dispassionate historian. He correctly predicted that his account of the partisan conflicts of the period would provoke party passions. Putting down his pen in the summer of 1806, the author prepared to meet the animus of hostile readers:

> With respect to myself, I have reason to fear that the imprudent task I have just executed will draw upon me a degree of odium & calumny which I might perhaps otherwise have escaped. I should never have undertaken it but in the hope, certainly a very fallacious one, that the author would forever remain totally unknown. But having undertaken it I have endeavoured to detail the events of a most turbulent & factious period without unnecessarily wounding the dominant party, but without a cowardly abandonment or concealment of truth. What may be the consequences of having ventured to offend those whom truth however moderately related must offend, it is not difficult to divine (to John Adams, 6 July 1806).

Acknowledgments

The editors take pleasure in recognizing those persons and institutions who assisted in preparing this volume. The staffs of the Earl Gregg Swem Library and the Marshall-Wythe Law Library provided prompt and courteous service in response to our numerous requests. Margaret Cook, Curator of Manuscripts and Rare Books at Swem Library, deserves special thanks for her help.

Research on John Marshall and his milieu requires frequent visits to the Virginia State Library in Richmond. Among its many rich collections are the records and papers of the U.S. Circuit Court, district of Virginia, over which Marshall presided from 1802 to 1835. Conley Edwards and Minor Weisiger of the Archives Division of the State Library greatly facilitated access to this indispensable collection. Henry Grunder of the General Library Division generously provided a photocopy of the *Maps* to Marshall's *Life of George Washington*.

E. Lee Shepard of the Virginia Historical Society kindly provided copies of documents from his institution and shared his great knowledge of Virginia legal history. The editors are grateful to Linda Stanley of the Historical Society of Pennsylvania for enabling them to inspect the originals of a number of Marshall letters in that repository, alerting them to newly accessioned manuscripts, and supplying copies of documents. The staff of the University of Virginia Library, Rare Books, provided advice on and access to multiple sets of Marshall's *Life of George Washington*. Christine Jordan of the Documentary History of the Supreme Court, 1789–1800, Celeste Walker of the Adams Family Papers, Willie Parker and his co-workers at the Colonial Williamsburg Foundation, and Sara Dunlap Jackson and her staff at the National Historical Publications and Records Commission provided information and documents concerning specific topics arising in this volume.

Mark A. Mastromarino, a graduate student in the history department at William and Mary, has been associated with the project since 1986 as part-time research assistant, executing a variety of editorial tasks with great diligence. Another graduate student, Suzanne E. Coffman, also performed skillfully in this capacity during the later stages of the volume.

From July through December 1988 the editors profited from the presence at the project of L. J. ("Bill") Priestley, judge of the Court of Appeal of New South Wales, Sydney, Australia. On sabbatical leave, Judge Priestley chose to spend it pursuing a scholarly interest in John Marshall. Bill took part in all aspects of the editorial process and provided helpful suggestions and professional insight as he read over the judicial documents.

Two institutions, the College of William and Mary and the Institute of Early American History and Culture, sponsor this editorial enterprise. The college, through an appropriation from the Virginia General Assembly, supplies principal funding. The National Historical Publications and Records Commission also provides continuing financial aid. While this volume was in preparation, the project was the recipient of a generous award from the National Endowment for the Humanities. Grants from the Earhart Foundation, the William Nelson Cromwell Foundation, and the Virginia Law Foundation also contributed timely assistance.

The Plan of the Volume
and
Editorial Policy

Volume VI is composed of 250 documents published in full and another 370 documents that are either calendared or listed. The bulk of the documents fall into two broad categories, correspondence and judicial papers, which together chronicle Marshall's public and private activities through March 1807. As chief justice, Marshall sat not only on the Supreme Court but also on the U.S. Circuit Courts for Virginia and North Carolina. When not attending his various courts, he was busily engaged in writing a history of the life and times of the late George Washington.

CORRESPONDENCE AS SECRETARY OF STATE

Continuing the policy announced in Volume IV, the editors have not attempted to reproduce the great mass of documents that emanated from the State Department during Marshall's secretaryship. They have selected for printing in full only those letters that deal with issues and policies that occupied Marshall's primary attention. To convey a sense of the variety of matters, foreign and domestic, that came before Marshall and of the routine nature of the office, the editors have prepared calendar summaries of a large portion of his official correspondence, particularly letters addressed to him. Calendared correspondence, however, has been separated from the main body and placed in an appendix, a departure from previous editorial practice (see Appendix I). Still another class of routine official correspondence has been listed. It consists of diplomatic dispatches addressed to Marshall by U.S. consuls (and ministers in some cases), most of which were received at the State Department after or at the very end of his term of office and were not acted on by him (see Appendix II). Other routine letters and documents, such as requests to the secretary of the treasury for warrants, commissions and letters enclosing commissions, and documents countersigned by Marshall, have been omitted entirely.

PRIVATE CORRESPONDENCE

In contrast to his official correspondence as secretary of state, which is preserved nearly intact in the public archives, large portions of Marshall's personal correspondence have been lost or destroyed. What survives does not form a continuous record and consists overwhelmingly of letters Marshall wrote to others. Seventy percent of the correspondence published in full in this volume (official as well as private) consists of letters from him. While writing the *Life*, Marshall corresponded frequently with Caleb P. Wayne, his Philadelphia publisher. What is known about this work's publication derives largely from the happy accident that Wayne saved letters from Marshall and Bushrod Washington and wrote drafts of his replies on the blank spaces of their letters. In the mid-nineteenth century, probably after Wayne's death in 1849, this correspondence passed into the hands of James H. Castle, a Philadelphia attorney, according to Henry Flanders in his "Preface" to volume II of *The Lives and Times of the Chief Justices of the Supreme Court of the United States* (1858; Buffalo, N.Y., 1971 reprint from 1881 ed.). Ferdinand J. Dreer, a nineteenth-century autograph collector, subsequently acquired the collection and gave it to the Historical Society of Pennsylvania, where it is currently preserved. These letters between author and publisher form a central theme of Volume VI. In telling the particular story of Marshall's efforts to bring his history from manuscript to bound volumes, the correspondence with Wayne also illuminates the larger story of book publishing in the early republic.

Marshall's other surviving letters for this period are distributed among numerous recipients, with rarely more than one letter addressed to the same correspondent. Family correspondence in this volume consists of just two letters to Mrs. Marshall ("Polly"), one to his son Thomas, and four to his brother James M. Marshall. The letters to James are important for Marshall's business and legal affairs, notably those arising from their purchase of the former Fairfax estate. Although letters concerning the inner workings of the Supreme Court are disappointingly few, one notable series occurring during this early period has been spared loss or destruction. In the spring of 1802 the chief justice solicited the opinions of his colleagues on the constitutionality of the repeal of the Judiciary Act of 1801. Volume VI marks the first publication in full of this important exchange of correspondence.

JUDICIAL PAPERS

Over the course of his long judicial tenure, Marshall delivered nearly seven hundred reported opinions in the Supreme Court and in the U.S. Circuit Courts for Virginia and North Carolina. From 1801 on, judicial opinions constitute an ever-increasing proportion of the documentary record of his career. The editors have adopted the following policy with respect to this voluminous material.

This edition is not a documentary history of the Supreme Court from 1801 to 1835. Nor does its scope entail reproducing all 550 opinions Marshall delivered on the Supreme Court. This is rendered unnecessary by the ready availability of these opinions in the official *United States Reports*. Moreover, the original drafts of the great majority of his opinions have not survived, which precludes rendering more accurate texts than we now have. Only 88 of Marshall's manuscript opinions (16 percent of the total) are extant, most of them dating from his last years in office. Yet omission altogether of so large and important a group of documents from this edition of his papers is not intended. The plan is to publish in full the 30-odd constitutional opinions and a small but representative selection of nonconstitutional opinions. In addition, the editors will supply calendar entries for all the opinions given by the chief justice during the years covered by a volume. (See Appendix III for a list of the opinions from 1801 through 1807.)

Selecting from the huge mass of nonconstitutional opinions presents an editorial problem that admits of no fully satisfactory solution. Even eliminating many relatively insignificant cases that were disposed of in a brief opinion still leaves a sizable body of judicial literature. From this corpus the editors have attempted to provide a sampling of Marshall's jurisprudence in the several fields that occupied the major share of the court's attention, including procedure, real property, contracts and commercial law, admiralty, and international law. With this general purpose in mind, they have flexibly applied several other criteria to shorten the list of potential choices. Priority is given to opinions that illuminate Marshall's broader views on politics, society, and economy; that reflect an important public issue or policy of the time; and that can be amply documented from the official case file and other sources, especially if the supplementary materials provide new information about the case not found in the printed report. Another important consideration is the availability of the original manuscript opinion, though this criterion will not often come into play until the latter years of Marshall's chief justiceship. There is, to be sure, an unavoidable element of arbitrariness in the selection process. For every opinion chosen for inclusion, many others could equally suffice as examples of the chief justice's style, mode of reasoning, and learning in a particular field of law.

Besides formal opinions, Marshall produced another group of judicial papers while presiding over the Supreme Court. These are his unpublished notes of arguments in cases heard at various terms of the Supreme Court, most of them in the last five years of his tenure. These notes, which will be published in full, show Marshall's judicial mind in action and cast light on the working methods of a justice during the hearing of a case. A fuller description of the sources documenting Marshall's Supreme Court career is provided in the editorial note under date of 4 February 1801.

While only a small fraction of the Supreme Court opinions will be published in full, Marshall's cases in the U.S. Circuit Courts for Virginia and North Carolina will be documented as completely as is possible. Marshall spent much the greater part of his judicial life on circuit, yet this side of his career is relatively unknown and the documents less accessible. His circuit court papers include more than sixty autograph opinions delivered in the Virginia court. These manuscripts along with other opinions available only in printed form will be fully reproduced in this and subsequent volumes. The one previous edition of these opinions, prepared by John W. Brockenbrough in 1837, is extremely rare. Although Brockenbrough's reports have been reprinted in *Federal Cases*, the alphabetical arrangement of that work scatters Marshall's opinions over many volumes. The editors believe that bringing the opinions together in the present edition serves a sound documentary purpose. By comparison with the Virginia materials, Marshall's judicial papers from the North Carolina court are scanty. They include eighteen briefly reported opinions given between 1802 and 1806, which are reprinted in this volume from a collection of North Carolina cases published in 1806 by John Haywood. Marshall's circuit court papers are described more extensively in the editorial notes preceding the opinions of 9 December and 31 December 1802.

MISCELLANEOUS AND OMITTED PAPERS

This volume includes some documents that do not fit into either of the two principal categories of correspondence and judicial papers. Among these are Marshall's draft of President Adams's message to Congress, his reported testimony in the impeachment trial of Justice Samuel Chase, and bills in chancery, depositions, and other papers relating to the purchase of the Fairfax estate. One document that has been excluded is the five-volume *Life*, whose publication is chronicled in the correspondence with Wayne. With the exception of two surviving autograph drafts of passages from the biography, none of Marshall's original manuscript survives. The two fragments are presented along with the finished versions in order to illustrate the process of composition. The volume also reprints Marshall's preface to the *Life*, which is of interest for its statement of the author's intentions in undertaking the work and for its discussion of the sources used in composing his narrative of the colonial period of American history.

As a general editorial policy, routine documents arising from Marshall's financial transactions—bills of exchange, promissory notes, bank drafts, and the like—are omitted entirely, though they may be referred to in the annotation. In the earlier volumes, deeds for the sale or lease of lands have been calendared and sometimes printed in full. Beginning with this volume, such documents will in most instances not rate even a calendar entry. The editors, however, have brought together in a single list more than fifty deeds executed by Marshall to the former tenants of South Branch Manor between 1800 and 1806. Collectively, these deeds document Marshall's most important private pursuit during these years, namely, his efforts to raise money to pay the final installment on the purchase of the Fairfax estate (see Appendix IV).

Editorial Apparatus

Editorial Method

The editors have applied modern historical editing standards in rendering the texts of documents. Transcriptions are as accurate as possible and reflect format and usage as nearly as is feasible, with the following exceptions. The first letter of a sentence is capitalized, and redundant or confusing punctuation has been eliminated. Superscript letters have been brought down to the line, and thorns ("ye," "yt," "yn") have been expanded. Words abbreviated by a tilde (˜) have not been expanded, but the tilde has been omitted and a period added. Layout and typography attempt to replicate the appearance of the originals. However, the location of the dateline in letters has been standardized, placed on the first line of the letter, flush to the right margin. The salutation has been set flush to the left margin. The complimentary closing has been run into the last paragraph of letters. Signatures, regardless of whether they are autograph, have been set in large and small capital letters and indented one space from the right margin. Other names at the foot of a document (for example, those of witnesses, sureties, and pledges) are rendered in the same distinctive type as signatures and are placed approximately where they appear in the originals.

Obvious slips of the pen, usually repeated words, have been silently corrected, as have typographical errors in printed sources. Words or parts of words illegible or missing because of mutilation are enclosed in angle brackets; letters or punctuation added by the editors for clarity's sake are set off by square brackets. If the editors are uncertain about their rendition, the words are enclosed within brackets followed by a question mark. If a portion of the manuscript is absent, this is shown by ellipsis points within angle brackets. Undecipherable words or phrases are indicated by the word "illegible" set in italics within angle brackets. Official and corporate seals are designated by the word "seal" set in capital letters and enclosed within square brackets. Wafer, or signature, seals are denoted by the initials "L.S." (*Locus Sigilli* ["place of the seal"]) within square brackets.

This volume retains some changes in format that were introduced in Volume V. Footnotes follow immediately at the end of the document, and identification of the source occurs in an unnumbered provenance note (referred to as "n." in cross-references) preceding the first numbered footnote. This note also supplies information on other copies, endorsements, dating, description, or peculiarities of

the original. The provenance contains a full citation for the source of
each document, except that National Union Catalog Symbols for depositories are used throughout. Elsewhere the editors have employed
abbreviated titles for the most frequently cited public collections of
manuscripts and secondary sources. These appear below in the lists
of symbols and short titles. For other publications, a full citation is
given in the first footnote and a shortened reference used thereafter.

For books, periodicals, and articles, the editors follow the style of
citation used in standard academic history. Reports of cases, however,
are given in legal citation form. The name of the case is followed by
the volume number and abbreviated title (usually the reporter's last
name); the page number on which the case begins; and, if needed,
the court and year within parentheses. For the old English cases, the
volume number and page of the reprint of the case in *The English
Reports* (abbreviated "Eng. Rep.") are also given. Full titles of all reports cited in this volume are provided in the short-title list. References to statutes also follow the historical style. In citing English statutes, the editors use the standard abbreviated form giving the regnal
year, chapter and section (if appropriate), and year of enactment (if
not otherwise indicated). For example, 13 Edw. I, c. 31 (1285); 4 and
5 Anne, c. 3, sec. 12 (1705).

Annotation consists of footnotes to the documents and occasional
editorial notes preceding a document or group of documents. The
guiding principle is to supply enough information and explanation to
make the document intelligible to the general reader. The editors
prefer to let the documents speak for themselves as much as possible.
This laissez-faire policy is more easily followed in the case of personal
correspondence. Legal materials by nature require denser annotation. Without presuming any knowledge of law on the reader's part,
the editors attempt to strike a balance between too little and too much
commentary.

The provenance note is followed, if needed, by one or more numbered footnotes that address matters arising immediately from the
document: identifications of persons, places, technical words and
phrases, statutes, authorities, cases, pamphlets, newspaper articles,
and the like. If the information is available in a standard reference or
secondary work, the note is brief, often no more than a citation to
that source. Three standard reference works are not cited: *Dictionary
of American Biography*, *Dictionary of National Biography*, and *Biographical
Directory of Congress*. If the source is a manuscript collection or archival record group that is relatively inaccessible, the information derived from it is reported in greater detail. Cross-references to other
documents or notes in the same volume are kept to a minimum,
leaving it to the index to bring them all together. Editorial notes

provide more extensive information or interpretation than can be conveniently included in footnotes. They serve to introduce documents of unusual significance or important subjects or episodes that are reflected in a number of documents.

Textual Notes

Two kinds of documents receive special editorial treatment in this volume. These are Marshall's manuscript drafts of opinions given in the U.S. Circuit Court for Virginia and his draft passages of the *Life*. With these documents, Marshall's intent as author takes on additional importance, for he meant them to be officially promulgated or published. In his opinions and the biography, Marshall made many deletions and insertions, which reveal his thought process at work; his choice of words and redrafting of phrases show a careful consideration of meaning. The final result was what he intended the public to hear or read, and in keeping with that object, the editors have followed their standard rules of transcription and editorial method in presenting nearly clear texts of these documents as the main entries. However, in order to provide an inclusive list of all of Marshall's alterations in the manuscript, they have appended a set of textual notes, following the annotation, to each of these autograph opinions and drafts. By this means, a genetic text can be reconstructed, and a complete record of Marshall's revisions is preserved.

Marshall made changes in his text in a variety of ways: he struck through words, erased them, wrote over them, added words above the line, or indicated by means of a superscript symbol an addition to be inserted from the margin or a separate sheet. In recording Marshall's alterations, the editors have not distinguished among his various modes of deleting words, or between words inserted above the line as opposed to altered on the line. Marshall made many of his changes on the line, indicating that he revised as he was writing. In his judicial manuscripts, Marshall appears to have made all of his revisions as he was drafting his opinions; he delivered them orally and did not intend them to be subsequently printed. The editors believe that the alterations were part of his process of refining his opinions and that he incorporated them into his final statement from the bench. He did not go back later and improve upon his opinion as originally delivered. Similarly, Marshall wrote each of the draft fragments for the *Life* in a brief span of time. Because of this contemporaneity of the alterations, the methodology employed in the textual notes is meant to reveal Marshall's rephrasings and elaborations, rather than the exact manner by which he made them.

Deletions are indicated by canceled type (~~case~~), and insertions are surrounded by up and down arrows (↑court↓). Deleted punctuation will appear below the strike-through rule (~~, appeal~~). Illegible erasures or deletions are denoted by "*erasure*" within square brackets. Uncertain renderings are followed by a question mark within square brackets. Insertions within insertions are not indicated, but deletions are. Insertions within a deletion appear in canceled type and are set off by arrows.

Characteristically, in changing a preposition, article, indefinite pronoun, or verb ending, Marshall wrote over the end of the existing word to alter it to a new form. For instance, he transformed "that" to "this" by writing "is" over "at" and "on" to "in" by writing "i" over "o." Rather than placing internal marks within words to replicate Marshall's process of altering them, the editors have represented the change in substance by entering complete words. Canceled type shows his first version; up and down arrows indicate his substitution. Thus, a change from "that" to "this" will appear in the text notes as ~~that~~ ↑this↓, rather than ~~that~~ ↑is↓. Although this method sacrifices the exact recording of how Marshall entered a change, it does make clear the alteration of the content of what he wished to say. Marshall's intentions are not always self-evident; irregularities in pen, ink, and manuscript preclude certainty in some instances. Sometimes it is not possible to know whether he added or erased a word or whether he had crowded words on a line or blotted a drop of ink. Where Marshall inadvertently repeated a word or words, the repetition is left out in the main text but is recorded verbatim in the textual notes.

All deletions and insertions, as the editors have been best able to determine from appearance and context of the manuscript, are listed by paragraph and line numbers of the printed document. (Paragraph numbers appear in the margin of the main text to facilitate use.) A word or two before and after the alteration are included to aid the reader in finding the phrase and following the change. The succeeding designations indicate alterations made in places other than in the middle of the text: "Title," in the title of an opinion; "mar.," in a marginal note; "footnote," in a note at the bottom of the manuscript page; "beg.," at the beginning of a paragraph before the first word of the main text. To avoid confusion, footnote numbers in the document have been dropped from words appearing in the textual notes.

Descriptive Symbols

AD	Autograph Document
ADf	Autograph Draft

ADfS	Autograph Draft Signed
ADS	Autograph Document Signed
AL	Autograph Letter
ALS	Autograph Letter Signed
Df	Draft
DS	Document Signed
JM	John Marshall
LS	Letter Signed
MS, MSS	Manuscript, Manuscripts
Tr	Transcript

All documents in an author's hand are designated as autograph items (e.g., ALS). If the attribution of autograph is conjectural, a question mark within parentheses will follow the designation. Documents can be in the hand of someone else but signed by persons under whose names they are written (e.g., DS). If the signature has been cropped or obliterated, the "S" appears within square brackets (c.g., AL[S]). Copies are contemporary replications of documents; if they are made by the author, the type of document will be indicated by one of the above symbols followed by "copy" or "letterbook copy" within parentheses. For instance, an unsigned copy of a letter retained by the writer will be described as AL (copy). Thomas Jefferson's letterpress copies are designated as ALS (press copy). Transcripts are transcribed versions of documents made at a later time by someone other than the author.

Location Symbols

CSmH	Henry E. Huntington Library, San Marino, Calif.
CtHi	Connecticut Historical Society, Hartford, Conn.
CtY	Yale University, New Haven, Conn.
DeHi	Historical Society of Delaware, Wilmington, Del.
DLC	Library of Congress, Washington, D.C.
DNA	National Archives, Washington, D.C.
GEpFRC	Federal Records Center, East Point, Ga.
ICHi	Chicago Historical Society, Chicago, Ill.
ICN	Newberry Library, Chicago, Ill.
MB	Boston Public Library, Boston, Mass.
MdHi	Maryland Historical Society, Baltimore, Md.
MH	Harvard University, Cambridge, Mass.
MHi	Massachusetts Historical Society, Boston, Mass.
MoSW	Washington University, St. Louis, Mo.
MWiW	Williams College, Williamstown, Mass.

N   New York State Library, Albany, N.Y.
NbO   Omaha Public Library, Omaha, Nebr.
Nc-Ar   North Carolina State Department of Archives and
               History, Raleigh, N.C.
NHi   New-York Historical Society, New York, N.Y.
NIC   Cornell University, Ithaca, N.Y.
NjMoHP   Morristown National Historical Park, Morristown, N.J.
NjP   Princeton University, Princeton, N.J.
NjR   Rutgers–The State University, New Brunswick, N.J.
NN   New York Public Library, New York, N.Y.
NNC   Columbia University, New York, N.Y.
NNPM   Pierpont Morgan Library, New York, N.Y.
NSchHi   Schenectady County Historical Society, Schenectady, N.Y.
PHi   Historical Society of Pennsylvania, Philadelphia, Pa.
PP   Free Library of Philadelphia, Philadelphia, Pa.
PPAmP   American Philosophical Society, Philadelphia, Pa.
P.R.O.   Public Record Office, London, England
ScC   Charleston Library Society, Charleston, S.C.
Vi   Virginia State Library, Richmond, Va.
ViHi   Virginia Historical Society, Richmond, Va.
ViU   University of Virginia, Charlottesville, Va.
ViW   College of William and Mary, Williamsburg, Va.
Wv-Ar   West Virginia Department of Archives and History,
               Charleston, W.Va.

Record Groups in the National Archives

RG 21   Records of the District Courts of the United States
RG 36   Records of the Bureau of Customs
RG 42   Records of the Office of Public Buildings and Grounds
RG 45   Naval Records Collection of the Office of Naval Records
               and Library
RG 53   Records of the Bureau of the Public Debt
RG 59   General Records of the Department of State
RG 76   Records of the Boundary and Claims Commissions and
               Arbitrations
RG 233   Records of the United States House of Representatives
RG 267   Records of the Supreme Court of the United States

Abbreviations for Court and Other Records

App. Cas.	Appellate Case RG 267, National Archives
F.O.	Foreign Office Papers Public Record Office
T.	Treasury Group Papers Public Record Office

U.S. Cir. Ct., Va.
    Ord. Bk.
    Rec. Bk.
    Rule Bk.
	U.S. Circuit Court, Va.
	    Order Books
	    Record Books
	    Rule Books
	Virginia State Library

U.S. Cir. Ct., N.C.
    Min. Bk.
	U.S. Circuit Court, N.C.
	    Minute Book
	RG 21, National Archives

U.S. Sup. Ct.
    Minutes
    Dockets
	U.S. Supreme Court
	    Minutes
	    Dockets
	RG 267, National Archives

Va. Ct. Ap. Ord. Bk.	Virginia Court of Appeals Order Books Virginia State Library

After the first citation of legal papers in a case, the court reference is omitted, and the suit record is designated simply by the names of plaintiff v. defendant. The exception is the provenance note, where complete depository information will be given for the document printed.

Abbreviations for English Courts

Ch.   Chancery
C.P.   Common Pleas
Ex.   Exchequer
K.B.   King's Bench
N.P.   Nisi Prius

Short Titles

The expanded titles for the English reports are taken chiefly from W. Harold Maxwell and Leslie F. Maxwell, *A Legal Bibliography of the British Commonwealth of Nations: Volume I, English Law to 1800* (2d ed.; London, 1955).

Annals of Congress
> Debates and Proceedings in the Congress of the United States, *1789–1824* (42 vols.; Washington, D.C., 1834–56).

ASP
> *American State Papers. Documents, Legislative and Executive, of the Congress of the United States* . . . (38 vols.; Washington, D.C., 1832–61).

Atk.
> John Tracy Atkyns, *Reports of Cases Argued and Determined in the High Court of Chancery, in the Time of Lord Chancellor Hardwicke [1736–1754]* (3d ed.; London, 1794).

Beveridge, *Life of Marshall*
> Albert J. Beveridge, *The Life of John Marshall* (4 vols.; Boston and New York, 1916–19).

Black. H.
> Henry Blackstone, *Reports, Courts of Common Pleas and Exchequer Chamber, 1788–1796* (2 vols.; London, 1791–96).

Blackstone, *Commentaries*
> William Blackstone, *Commentaries on the Laws of England* (4 vols.; 1765–69; London, 1966 reprint, from 1st ed.).

Brock.
> John W. Brockenbrough, *Reports of Cases Decided by the Honourable John Marshall . . . in the Circuit Court of the United States for the District of Virginia and North Carolina, from 1802 to 1833 [1836] Inclusive* (2 vols.; Philadelphia, 1837).

Burr.
> James Burrow, *Reports, King's Bench, 1756–1772* (5 vols.; London, 1766–80).

Call
> Daniel Call, *Reports of Cases Argued and Adjudged in the Court of Appeals of Virginia* (6 vols.; Richmond, Va., 1801–33). Beginning with vol. IV, the title reads: *Reports of Cases Argued and Decided.* . . .

Cranch
> William Cranch, *Reports of Cases Argued and Adjudged in the Supreme Court of the United States, 1801–1815* (9 vols.; New York and Washington, D.C., 1804–17).

CVSP

William P. Palmer et al., eds., *Calendar of Virginia State Papers and other Manuscripts* . . . (11 vols.; Richmond, Va., 1875–93).

Dall.

Alexander J. Dallas, *Reports of Cases Ruled and Adjudged in the Several Courts of the United States, and of Pennsylvania* . . . (4 vols.; Philadelphia, 1790–1807).

Doug.

Sylvester Douglas, *Reports, King's Bench* (London, 1782).

Dy.

J. Dyer, *Ascuns Nouel Cases. Les Reports des divers select Matters and Resolutions* (London, 1585).

East

E. H. East, *Reports of Cases in the Court of King's Bench* (16 vols.; London, 1801–14).

Eng. Rep.

The English Reports (176 vols.; reprint of all the early English reporters).

Eq. Ca. Abr.

General Abridgment of Cases in Equity Argued and Adjudged in the High Court of Chancery . . . (2 vols.; London, 1732–56).

Esp.

I. Espinasse, *Reports of Cases at Nisi Prius, King's Bench and Common Pleas, 1793–1807* (6 vols. in 3; London, 1796–1811).

Evans

Charles Evans, ed., *American Bibliography* . . . *1639* . . . *1820* (12 vols.; Chicago, 1903–34).

Haskins and Johnson, *Foundations of Power*

George Lee Haskins and Herbert A. Johnson, *The Oliver Wendell Holmes Devise History of the Supreme Court of the United States. Volume II. Foundations of Power: John Marshall, 1801–15* (New York, 1981).

Haywood

John Haywood, *Cases Adjudged in the Superior Courts* . . . *of North Carolina* (2 vols.; Halifax and Raleigh, N.C., 1799–1806).

Hening, *Statutes*

William Waller Hening, ed., *The Statutes at Large; Being a Collection of All the Laws of Virginia, from the First Session of the Legislature* (13 vols.; 1819–23; Charlottesville, Va., 1969 reprint).

Hutchinson, *Papers of Madison*

William T. Hutchinson and William M. E. Rachal et al., eds., *The Papers of James Madison* (15 vols. to date; Chicago and Charlottesville, Va., 1962—).

Jones, W.

Sir W. Jones, *Les Reports de divers Special Cases cy bien in le Court de Banck le Roy, come le Common Banck, Angleterre* (London, 1675).

Life

John Marshall, *The Life of George Washington, Commander in Chief of the American Forces, during the War Which Established the Independence of His Country, and First President of the United States. Compiled under the Inspection of the Honourable Bushrod Washington, from the Original Papers Bequeathed to Him by His Deceased Relative, and Now in Possession of the Author. To Which Is Prefixed, an Introduction, Containing a Compendious View of the Colonies Planted by the English on the Continent of North America, from Their Settlement to the Commencement of That War Which Terminated in Their Independence* (5 vols.; Philadelphia, 1804–7).

All textual references in this volume of *PJM* are based on copy 2, signed William Holliday, at the University of Virginia Library.

Life (1805 ed.)

John Marshall, *The Life of George Washington, Commander in Chief of the American Forces . . . and First President of the United States . . .* (5 vols.; Philadelphia, 1805–7).

All textual references in this volume of *PJM* are based on the set signed Jno. McClelland at the University of Virginia Library.

Life (1832 ed.)

John Marshall, *The Life of George Washington, Commander in Chief of the American Forces . . . and First President of the United States . . .* (2d ed. rev.; 2 vols.; Philadelphia, 1832).

Maps

[John Marshall], *The Life of George Washington. Maps and Subscribers' Names* (Philadelphia, 1807).

All observations of the plates in this volume of *PJM* are based on copy 2 (bookplate, Westmoreland Club) at the Virginia State Library.

Naval Documents: Quasi-War

Naval Documents Related to the Quasi-War between the United States and France (7 vols.; Washington, D.C., 1935–38).

Park.

T. Parker, *Reports of Cases concerning the Revenue, Court of Exchequer* (London, 1776).

Pet.

Richard Peters, Jr., *Reports of Cases Argued and Adjudged in the Supreme Court of the United States, from 1828 to 1843, Inclusive* (17 vols.; Philadelphia, 1828–43).

PJM

    Herbert A. Johnson et al., eds., *The Papers of John Marshall* (6 vols. to date; Chapel Hill, N.C., 1974—).

PMHB

    Pennsylvania Magazine of History and Biography.

P. Wms.

    W. Peere Williams, *Reports of Cases, Court of Chancery, and of Some Special Cases, King's Bench* (3 vols.; London, 1740–49).

Raym. Ld.

    Robert, Lord Raymond, *Reports, King's Bench and Common Pleas* (2 vols.; London, 1743).

Rutland, *Papers of Madison: Sec. of State*

    Robert A. Rutland et al., eds., *The Papers of James Madison: Secretary of State Series*, I: *4 March–31 July 1801* (Charlottesville, Va., 1986).

S

    Ralph R. Shaw and Richard H. Shoemaker, eds., *American Bibliography . . . 1801–1819* (22 vols.; New York, 1958–66).

Salk.

    William Salkeld, *Reports of Cases in the Court of King's Bench, with Some Special Cases in the Courts of Chancery, Common Pleas and Exchequer . . .* (London, 1717–24).

Senate Executive Journal

    Journal of the Executive Proceedings of the Senate of the United States of America . . . , I (Washington, D.C., 1828).

Shepherd, *Statutes*

    Samuel Shepherd, ed., *The Statutes at Large of Virginia, from October Session 1792, to December Session 1806, Inclusive* (3 vols.; 1835; New York, 1970 reprint).

Shower K.B.

    Sir B. Shower, *Reports, King's Bench* (London, 1718–20).

Skeel, *Weems*

    Emily Ellsworth Ford Skeel, ed., *Mason Locke Weems: His Works and Ways in Three Volumes* (New York, 1929).

Str.

    J. Strange, *Reports of Cases in the Courts of Chancery, King's Bench, Common Pleas and Exchequer* (2 vols.; London, 1755).

Syrett, *Papers of Hamilton*

    Harold C. Syrett et al., eds., *The Papers of Alexander Hamilton* (26 vols.; New York, 1961–79).

T.R.

    C. Durnford and E. H. East, *King's Bench Reports* (8 vols.; London, 1787–1800).

Tucker, *Blackstone's Commentaries*
> St. George Tucker, *Blackstone's Commentaries: With Notes of Reference, to the Constitution and Laws, of the Federal Government of the United States; and of the Commonwealth of Virginia* (5 vols.; Philadelphia, 1803).

U.S. *Statutes at Large*
> *The Public Statutes at Large of the United States of America, 1789–1873* (17 vols.; Boston, 1845–73).

Vent.
> P. Ventris, *Reports in Two Parts* (London, 1696).

Vern.
> Thomas Vernon, *Cases Argued and Adjudged in the High Court of Chancery* (2 vols.; London, 1726–28).

Ves. jun. or Ves. (after vol. 2)
> Francis Vesey, Jr., *Reports of Cases Argued and Determined in the High Court of Chancery* (20 vols.; London, 1795–1822).

VMHB
> *Virginia Magazine of History and Biography.*

Wash.
> Bushrod Washington, *Reports of Cases Argued and Determined in the Court of Appeals of Virginia* (2 vols.; Richmond, Va., 1798–99).

Wils. K.B.
> G. Wilson, *Reports, King's Courts at Westminster* (2 vols.; London, 1770–75).

WMQ
> *William and Mary Quarterly.*

MARSHALL CHRONOLOGY
1 November 1800–31 March 1807

1800

November–December	At Washington.

1801

January–4 March	At Washington.
20 January	Nominated to be chief justice.
27 January	Confirmed as chief justice.
4–10 February	Attends Supreme Court.
18 March	At Richmond.
ca. 1 April	Travels to Buckingham County and then to Winchester.
4–12 August	At Washington, attends Supreme Court.
Late August–September	Visits Winchester and Martinsburg.
8–31 December	At Washington, attends Supreme Court.

1802

January–April	At Richmond.
ca. 15 April	Travels to Washington to settle accounts as secretary of state.
May–July	At Richmond.
August–September	Trip to Winchester, Martinsburg and the Allegheny.
29 September	Awarded honorary LL.D. by College of New Jersey.
22 November–10 December	At Richmond, holds first session of U.S. Circuit Court for Virginia.
30 December–31 December	At Raleigh, holds first session of U.S. Circuit Court for North Carolina.

1803

1–5 January	At Raleigh, attends U.S. circuit court.
8 February–2 March	At Washington, attends Supreme Court.
11 February	Birth of Charles William Marshall.
24 February	Delivers opinion in *Marbury* v. *Madison*.

23 May–7 June	At Richmond, attends U.S. circuit court.
15–21 June	At Raleigh, attends U.S. circuit court.
October	Death of Charles William Marshall.
22 November–13 December	At Richmond, attends U.S. circuit court.
29–31 December	At Raleigh, attends U.S. circuit court.

1804

1–3 January	At Raleigh, attends U.S. circuit court.
6 February–6 March	At Washington, attends Supreme Court.
22 May–8 June	At Richmond, attends U.S. circuit court.
11 June	Volume I of *Life* published.
15–20 June	At Raleigh, attends U.S. circuit court.
ca. 20 July	Sets out for upper country.
10 August	At Front Royal.
ca. 16–31 August	Travels to the Allegheny.
September	At Front Royal.
3 September	Volume II of *Life* published.
ca. 1 October	Returns to Richmond.
November–13 December	At Richmond, attends U.S. circuit court.
26 November	Volume III of *Life* published.
31 December	At Raleigh, attends U.S. circuit court.

1805

1–5 January	At Raleigh, attends U.S. circuit court.
13 January	Birth of Edward Carrington Marshall.
5 February–6 March	At Washington, attends Supreme Court.
16 February	Testifies at impeachment trial of Samuel Chase.
22 May–7 June	At Richmond, attends U.S. circuit court.
17–20 June	At Raleigh, attends U.S. circuit court.
July–September	At "the mountains."
12 August	Volume IV of *Life* published.
26 September	Returns to Richmond.
Late September–ca. 20 October	Sick with "bilious intermittent."

23 November–16 December	At Richmond, attends U.S. circuit court.
31 December	At Raleigh, attends U.S. circuit court.

1806

1–2 January	At Raleigh, attends U.S. circuit court.
3 February–4 March	At Washington, attends Supreme Court.
22 May–17 June	At Richmond, attends U.S. Circuit Court.
Late June	Confined to home by illness; misses term of U.S. circuit court at Raleigh.
10 July	Sets out for Sweet Springs and Sulphur Springs.
21 August	Awarded honorary LL.D. by Harvard College.
October	Returns to Richmond.
22 November–19 December	At Richmond, attends U.S. circuit court.
29–31 December	At Raleigh, attends U.S. circuit court.

1807

1–2 January	At Raleigh, attends U.S. circuit court.
2–28 February	At Washington, attends Supreme Court.

CORRESPONDENCE, PAPERS,
AND
SELECTED JUDICIAL OPINIONS

November 1800–March 1807

To Rufus King

Private
Sir   Washington Novr. 4th. 1800
    Colo. Beriah Norton has a claim on the british government for
supplies furnishd their army during their war with the United States
as he says on contract, & which he also says has been acknowledgd &
in part paid.[1] The demerit of having furnishd these supplies is considerably diminishd by the situation of the persons from whom they
were drawn.
    The inhabitants of Marthas vineyard were I understand considerd
as excuseable for remaining in a state of neutrality & thereby rescuing
themselves from that ruin the british army coud so readily inflict &
from which the American government coud not protect them.
    Being thus circumstancd the President will be well pleasd at pay-
ment being made to their agent Colo. Norton & if your inofficial
countenance can assist them in obtaining payment, he coud wish that
aid to be afforded. But he does not mean that there shoud be any
application in your public character or that the nation shoud be
considerd as in any degree supporting the claim.
    He recommends no aid either of a pecuniary or any other sort but
that which is abov[e] expressd. I am Sir with very much respect, your
obedt. Servt.

                                                    J MARSHALL

ALS, CSmH. Marked "private" by JM and addressed by him to King, "Minister
plenipotentiary &c/of the United States/London." Endorsed as received 17 Mar. "No
Duplicate received." Cover also has notation "N 55 Threadneedle Street."

    1. On Norton's claim, see *PJM*, IV, 231–32 and n. 3, 255, 276.

To John Jay

Sir   Department of State, Washington Novr. 5th 1800
    I enclose you several documents which have been transmitted to
this Department by the Minister of his Britannic Majesty Mr Liston
accompanied with a Letter in which a wish is manifested that for the
purposes of Justice, Thomas Jameson now in prison in the district of
Montreal may be demanded by the United States in order to be tried
for a forgery alledged to have been committed in the State of New
York.[1] The President is of opinion that as the offence is against the
State of New York and is only punishable by its laws it would be
improper for him to direct the requisition to be made but on the

application of the injured Government. The papers are therefore forwarded to You. If Sir you shall wish the aid of the Government of the United States you may be assured that every proper attention will be paid to the request. With the most respectful consideration, I remain Sir your most obt. Servant

                    (signed)   J MARSHALL

Letterbook copy, N.

1. Liston to JM, 25 Oct. (*PJM*, IV, 333–34 and n. 4). Copies of the enclosures are entered in the letterbook. For further developments concerning Jameson's extradition, see Jay to JM, 15 Nov.; JM to Jay, 28 Nov.; JM to Robert Shore Milnes, 28 Nov. 1800.

From St. George Tucker

Dear Sir,   Williamsburg. Nov. 6. 1800.

Our former friendship which on my part, and I flatter myself on yours also, has suffered no diminution, from political difference of opinion, will I hope serve as an Apology for a letter which I write in behalf of a man whom I never saw, nor ever had the smallest intercourse or communication with until the last Evening when I got a letter from him on a subject which suggested to my mind the expedient of addressing myself to you. The letter however has not the most remote connexion with such an address, nor am I sure that I shall oblige him by writing it: On the contrary I am induced to believe if he could guess at my present intention he would be displeased.

The person I allude to is Callender.[1] I am told he is advanced or advancing in life—He is doomed to confinement in the Richmond Jail, a mansion of whose wretchedness you can not fail to have a just Idea, for the whole of the approaching Winter. I dare not ask a favour for him, nor would I for myself on any account. But I have read Fenno's attack on Mr Adams, in a pamphlet published in New york some months ago: And I have also read Mr Hamiltons late attack upon him.[2] If there is any thing in the *prospect before us* more virulent, more bitter, more injurious to Mr Adams's feelings as a Man or more derogatory to his Character as chief magistrate of the union, than is contained in both those publications I have not been able to find the passages. Whether a prosecution against either or both has been ordered or will be instituted it is not for me to enquire. But should it happen that Callender should expiate his offence by a severe imprisonment and no notice be taken of more conspicuous and influential persons under similar or more provoking circumstances it might produce a reflection too painful for repetition to you.

I am far from being anxious that Mr Adams should do a *popular* act, but I should be gratified that he would do an *humane* one. And tho I am in truth incapable of saying any thing which maybe considered as offering Incense to the President of the United States, I have no hesitation in declaring to My friend John Marshall, that I should feel myself obliged to HIM for his humane interposition in behalf of a man, whom I cannot but consider as suffering an unconstitutional punishment.[3]

Excuse, My friend, this letter: if it displeases you burn it—and forget it, but remember with your usual kindness one who most cordially regards you. Your friend &c.

S: G: TUCKER.

ALS (copy), Tucker-Coleman Papers, ViW. Endorsed: "Copy/Letter to Jno. Marshal/Novr. 6. 1800."

1. James Thomson Callender, whose pamphlet *The Prospect before Us* had led to his trial and conviction under the Sedition Act the preceding June at the U.S. Circuit Court, Virginia District. He was fined two hundred dollars and sentenced to nine months in jail. For a full account of this celebrated trial, see James Morton Smith, *Freedom's Fetters: The Alien and Sedition Laws and American Civil Liberties* (Ithaca, N.Y., 1956), 334–58.

Callender had written to Tucker, a judge of the Virginia General Court, on 4 Nov. In this letter he denounced the Sedition Act as unconstitutional and requested Tucker to release him from confinement by issuing a writ of habeas corpus. In his reply of 6 Nov. Tucker, after explaining the procedures necessary to follow under Virginia's habeas corpus act, advised Callender not to pursue this course since the writ seemed to be confined to cases occurring before conviction (Callender to Tucker, 4 Nov. 1800 [with draft of Tucker's reply], Tucker-Coleman Papers, ViW).

2. The reference is to John Fenno's *Desultory Reflections on the New Political Aspects of Public Affairs in the United States of America, since the Commencement of the Year 1799* (New York, 1800) and to Alexander Hamilton's *Letter from Alexander Hamilton, concerning the Public Conduct and Character of John Adams, Esq. President of the United States* (New York, 1800). For the latter pamphlet, see Syrett, *Papers of Hamilton*, XXV, 169–234.

3. Eventually pardoned by President Jefferson, Callender later turned his journalistic guns on the new administration when he failed to obtain an office (Dumas Malone, *Jefferson the President: First Term, 1801–1805* [Boston, 1970], 207–12).

To Edmund Randolph

Sir   Department of State, Novr. 12th 1800

I receivd a few days past your letter of the 1st. of October[1] requesting

1st. The accounts renderd by Mr. Thomas Pinckney, & any letter which he may have written on the subject of some bills to the amount of £1600 sterling in consequence of a letter which you wrote to him.

2d. Any inteligence of Heissell the consul whose appointment was submited to Colo. Humphries, which may have been receivd in this department.

3d. Any inteligence which may have been receivd concerning the bill on Longueman which Mr. Gouverneur Morris receivd.

4th. A copy of the bankers accounts in Holland during the years 1794, 1795, & 1796.

1st. Mr. Pinckneys accounts were, while Colo. Pickering was Secretary of State, taken out of this office by himself in order to arrange them for final settlement.

2d. I have causd the office to be searchd for information concerning Heissell. No other inteligence respecting him is to be found than is containd in a letter written by my predecessor on the 29th. of May 1798, to the comptroller of the treasury, & its inclosures, of which one copy was transmited by the comptroller to the Attorney of the district, & one other he says to you. Lest this shoud have miscarried I woud now have inclosd you the information it contains had not the comptroller authorizd me to say that Mr. Nelson² was at liberty to show you that which he has recievd, & to permit you if such shoud be your wish to take a copy. Mr. Nelson on seeing this letter will not hesitate to comply with this agreement.

3d. There is in this office no account of any bill on Longueman recievd by Mr. Morris, nor any letter from you to him on the subject. As there are however two letters which relate to a bill on Longueman which may be important to you I have directed them to be copied & I now inclose them.

4th. I send you the bankers accounts for the years 1794, 1795, & 1796. I am Sir very respectfully, your Obedt. Servt.

J MARSHALL

ALS, U.S. v. Edmund Randolph, U.S. Circuit Court, Va., Ended Cases (Restored), 1804, Vi. Endorsed by Randolph, "General Marshall."

1. Letter not found. JM's letter was filed as an exhibit in the suit brought by the U.S. against Edmund Randolph for the recovery of funds expended during his tenure as secretary of state. For a summary of the case, which began in 1797 and was not concluded until 1804, see John J. Reardon, *Edmund Randolph: A Biography* (New York, 1974), 355–57.

2. Thomas Nelson, Jr., U.S. attorney for the Virginia district.

From John Jay

Sir   Albany 15th Novr. 1800
   I was this moment favoured with your letter of 5 instant enclosing
certain Documents from which it appears that a certain Thomas
Jameson, alias Charles Splendor alias Charles Holland stands charged
on oath with a forgery by him done & committed within the Jurisdiction of this State and that he hath fled and now remains at Montreal
in the Province of Canada and the Dominion of his Britannic Majesty
and informing me that the President is of opinion that as the offence
is against the State of New York and is only punishable by its laws it
would be improper for him to direct a requisition to be made but on
the application of the injured Government. I take the earliest opportunity therefore to return these documents lest you should not have
copies of them and to request that a requisition be made by the Government of the United States to the person administering the Government of the King of Great Britain in Canada for the delivery of
the said Fugitive from the Justice of this State to such agent as the
Governor of this State shall appoint and send to receive him & bring
him to this State to the end that he may be here dealt with according
to Law. Be pleased Sir to return the Documents with the requisition
and be assured of the great respect & consideration with which I have
the honor to be, Sir your most obt Servant
                           (signed)   JOHN JAY

Letterbook copy, N; ADf, Jay Papers, NNC.

Draft of President's Speech

                                              [ca. 15 November 1800][1]
Gentlemen of the Senate
     &
Gentlemen of the house of representatives
   I felicitate my country on meeting you at the place, which, in pursu-
ance of the constitution, has been selected for the permanent resi-
dence of the government of the United States.[2]
   This event is the more important, as exclusive legislation within the
ceded territory, may be exercisd by you.
   Neither the policy nor feelings of a great nation, subdivided into
States in many respects sovereign, coud permit the government of
the whole to continue, in any degree, dependent on the legislature of
a part. However strong the reasons for being more than satisfied with

the conduct of those within whose Jurisdiction your deliberations have been heretofore held, a laudable respect for our national dignity, & a just desire to possess equal influence where all have an equal interest, coud not fail to produce in a people, anxious for the future as well as the present, an earnest wish to see those to whom the great concerns of our common country are entrusted, exempt from the possibility of other control, than that which is imposd by the general will.

Under these impressions the voice of America has requird that their government shoud be fixd, where the representatives of the whole might exclusively legislate.

Guided by this voice, the wisdom of the nation & that venerated patriot whose name it bears have chosen the spot where we are now assembled.

Its central position & its great natural advantages have undoubtedly led to the choice.

It is with you Gentlemen to consider whether the local powers over the district of Columbia vested by the constitution in the congress of the United States, are immediately to be exercisd. If such shall be your opinion, then to your wisdom is confided the important trust of framing those rules which shall constitute the fundamental principles of its government. In performing a duty worthy of the representatives of the American people, you cannot fail to take into view the future probable situation of the territory for the happiness of which you are about to provide. You will consider it as the capital of a great empire, advancing, with a rapidity heretofore unexampled, in arts, in commerce, in wealth, & in population; & possessing within itself those energies & resources which, if not thrown away or lamentably misdirected, place its destinies in its own hands, & secure to it a long course of prosperity & self government.[3]

Such gentlemen are the prospects of our common country; and it is for the Metropolis of such a country, in which you are to exercise exclusive legislation, that fundamental rules are to be framd.

But whatever may be the future grandeur of the United States, let us offer up our fervent prayers to that BEING whose providential care we have so often & so signally experiencd, that we may be still more preeminently distinguishd for virtue, moderation, rational liberty, & happiness than for power.[4]

The malignant disease with which some of our commercial cities have been for several years afflicted, has in the course of the last summer again made its appearance.[5]

While we bend with due humility beneath this aweful dispensation of a providence whose ways are inscrutable, all human precautions ought to be taken to prevent the return of so destructive a calamity.

If the powers vested in the general government shall enable you still further to aid the state authorities in the promotion of this desirable object no recommendation from me will be requisite to induce their full exertion.

In all other respects the interior of our country remains prosperous & we have still abundant reason to be grateful for the numerous blessings we possess.

The commerce of the United States tho unjustly harassd by the belligerent powers of Europe continues to flourish & to extend itself.

The island of St. Domingo having been restord to a situation which renders safe a renewal of its commercial intercourse with this country I have deemd it expedient & for the interest of the United States to remit & discontinue for the time being with respect to that island the restraints & prohibitions imposd by the act intitled "an act further to suspend the commercial intercourse between the United States & France, & the dependences thereof," except so far as respects the ports for which vessels may clear out from the offices of the United States.[6]

The differences concerning the construction of the 6th: article of our treaty of Amity, commerce & navigation with Great-Britain, are not yet adjusted. The negotiations on this subject are still depending.[7]

I regret much that it is not yet in my power to inform you that our efforts to effect an accomodation between the United States & France have met with a success proportiond to the sincerity & earnestness with which they have been so often repeated.

The Envoys extraordinary & ministers plenipotentiary of the United States were receivd by the first Consul as the representatives of an independent republic & three persons with equal powers were appointed to treat with them. At the date of the last inteligence they were yet in Paris. The negotiation had not terminated.[8] If an accomodation on terms approaching justice & compatible with the honor & safety of the United States be attainable they will obtain it. To other terms neither the Government nor the people of America can allow themselves to submit.

While our best endeavors for peace will continue to be usd, it ought not to be conceald that the temper of the belligerent powers towards each other & their conduct towards the United States admonish us of the insecurity of trusting too confidently to the success of those endeavors.[9] If the many lessons furnishd by the experience of others can have faild to instruct us, our own experience must have impressd deeply on the bosom of every American the solemn truth, *that on ourselves exclusively must we rely for the protection of our best interests & the preservation of everything desirable to Man.*

To maintain in our own hands the direction of our own affairs, we must prove that no foreign interference can benefit the intruding nation; & to maintain this direction in peace we must stand prepard firmly to repel every aggression unequivocally hostile. This preparation can best be made & can only be effectually made, in the American mind. A high sense of national honor & of national character, a just degree of self respect, a reciprocal & liberal confidence in each other & in those to whom the public voice shall commit the public affairs, & above all, a perfect conviction that our interests can only be consulted by ourselves, will lead to measures best calculated to preserve peace, or, if the violence & injustice of others shall render peace impracticable, to preserve the nation.

With confidence Gentlemen may our country rely on the wisdom & patriotism of Congress for a steady adherence to such a system as will, under every aspect of our affairs, best promote the public welfare.[10]

ADf, Adams Papers, MHi. Endorsed by Adams, "Mr. Marshall."

1. This draft is filed immediately after JM's note to Adams of 17 Nov., which in MHi is placed under date of ante 22 Nov. 1800. The preceding September Adams had asked the heads of departments to submit their suggestions for his speech to the next session of Congress. They replied during the first two weeks of November: Benjamin Stoddert, 5 Nov.; Oliver Wolcott, 11 Nov.; Charles Lee, 12 Nov.; Samuel Dexter, 13 Nov. (Adams Papers, MHi). JM no doubt wrote his own undated draft about this time. The department heads then met to digest a final version, which JM submitted to the president on 17 Nov. Adams delivered the address on 22 Nov. 1800.

2. This sentence is similar to the first sentence of the second paragraph of the final draft (printed as an enclosure to JM to Adams, 17 Nov. 1800).

3. Most of this paragraph was embodied in the fifth paragraph of the final draft.

4. Similar to the third paragraph of the final draft.

5. This reference to the recurrence of yellow fever was omitted in the final draft.

6. See JM to Adams, 6 Sept. 1800 (*PJM*, IV, 262 and n. 7). This information was dropped from the final draft.

7. Similar to the first two sentences of the ninth paragraph of the final draft.

8. This and the preceding paragraph were embodied in the tenth paragraph of the final draft.

9. Similar to the first sentence of the eleventh paragraph of the final draft.

10. Immediately following this document in the Adams Papers is a sheet containing two drafts of a message to the Senate submitting a treaty for ratification. The drafts, one of which was prepared by JM, were apparently for the message transmitting the convention with France, which President Adams sent on 15 Dec. (Adams Papers, [Nov.–Dec. 1800?], MHi).

To John Adams

Munday morning [17 November 1800?][1]

The Secretary of State respectfully submits to the President, the draft of the Speech to Congress as digested finally by the heads of departments.

The necessity of placing it immediately under your consideration will, he trusts, apologize for his not detaining it for the purpose of making a fair copy.

[Enclosure]

Gentlemen of the Senate
    &
Gentlemen of the house of representatives[2]

Immediately after the adjournment of Congress at their last session in Philadelphia, I gave directions, in compliance with the laws, for the removal of the public offices, records, & property. These directions have been executed; & the public officers have since resided, & conducted the ordinary business of the government, in this place.

I congratulate the people of the United States on the assembling of Congress at the permanent seat of their government; & I congratulate you gentlemen on the prospect of a residence not to be changd. Altho there is cause to apprehend that accomodations are not now so complete as might be wishd, yet there is great reason to beleive that this inconvenience will cease with the present session.

It woud be unbecoming the representatives of this nation to assemble for the first time in this solemn temple, without looking up to the supreme ruler of the universe & imploring his blessing.

May this territory be the residence of virtue & happiness! In this city may that piety, & virtue, that wisdom & magnanimity, that constancy & self government, which adornd the great character whose name it bears, be for ever held in veneration! Here & throughout our country, may simple manners, pure morals, & true religion flourish forever![3]

It is with you gentlemen to consider whether the local powers over the district of Columbia, vested by the constitution in the Congress of the United States, shall be immediately exercisd. If in your opinion this important trust ought now to be executed, you cannot fail, while performing it, to take into view the future probable situation of the territory, for the happiness of which you are about to provide. You will consider it as the capital of a great nation, advancing, with unexampled rapidity, in arts, in commerce, in wealth & in population, & possessing within itself those energies & resources which, if not thrown away or lamentably misdirected, secure to it a long course of prosperity & self government.

In compliance with a law of the last session of Congress the officers & soldiers of the temporary army have been dischargd. It affords real pleasure to recollect the honorable testimony they gave of the patriotic motives which brought them into the service of their country by the readiness & regularity with which they returned to the station of private citizens.[4]

It is, in every point of view, of such primary importance to carry the laws into prompt & faithful execution, & to render that part of the administration of justice which the constitution & laws devolve on the federal courts, as convenient to the people as may consist with their present circumstances, that I cannot omit, once more to recommend to your serious consideration, the Judiciary system of the United States. No subject is more interesting than this to the public happiness, & to none can those improvements which may have been suggested by experience, be more beneficially applied.

A treaty of amity & commerce with the King of Prussia has been concluded & ratified. The ratifications have been exchangd, & I have directed the treaty to be promulgated by proclamation.[5]

The difficulties which suspended the execution of the 6th. article of our treaty of amity, commerce, & navigation with Great Britain, have not yet been removd. The negotiation on this subject is still depending. As it must be for the interest & honor of both nations to adjust this difference with good faith, I indulge confidently the expectation that the sincere endeavors of the government of the United States to bring it to an amicable termination, will not be disappointed.

The Envoys extraordinary & ministers plenipotentiary from the United States to France, were receivd by the first consul with the respect due to their character, & three persons with equal powers were appointed to treat with them. Altho at the date of the last official inteligence the negotiation had not terminated, yet it is to be hoped that our efforts to effect an accomodation will, at length, meet with a success, proportiond to the sincerity, with which they have been so often repeated.

While our best endeavors for the preservation of harmony with all nations will continue to be usd, the experience of the world, &, our own experience, admonish us of the insecurity of trusting too confidently to their success. We cannot, without commiting a dangerous imprudence, abandon those measures of self protection which are adapted to our situation, & to which, notwithstanding our pacific policy, the violence & injustice of others may, again, compel us to resort. While our vast extent of sea coast, the commercial & agricultural habits of our people, the great capital they will continue to trust

on the ocean, suggest the system of defence which will be most beneficial to ourselves; our distance from Europe & our resources for
maritime strength, will enable us to employ it with effect. Seasonable
& systematic arrangements, so far as our resources will justify, for a
navy adapted to defensive war; & which may, in case of necessity, be
quickly brought into use; seem to be as much recommended by a wise
& true economy, as by a just regard for our future tranquility, for the
safety of our shores, & for the protection of our property commited
to the ocean.[6]

The present navy of the United States, calld suddenly into existence by a great national exigency, has raisd us in our own esteem, &
by the protection afforded to our commerce, has effected, to the
extent of our expectations, the objects for which it was created.

In connection with a navy ought to be contemplated the fortifica-
tion of some of our principle seaports & harbors. A variety of considerations which will readily suggest themselves, urge an attention to
this measure of precaution. To give security to our principle ports,
considerable sums have already been expended, but the works remain incomplete. It is for Congress to determine whether additional
appropriations shall be made, in order to render competent to the
intended purposes, the fortifications which have been commencd.[7]

The manufacture of arms within the United States still invites the
attention of the national legislature. At a considerable expence to the
public, this manufactory has been brought to such a state of maturity
as, with continued encouragement, will supercede the necessity of
future importations from foreign countries.[8]

Gentlemen of the house of representatives

I shall direct the estimates of the appropriations necessary for the
ensuing year, together with an account of the public revenue & ex-
penditure to a late period, to be laid before you. I observe with much
satisfaction, that, the product of the revenue, during the present year,
has been more considerable, than during any former equal period.
This result affords conclusive evidence of the great resources of this
country, & of the wisdom & efficiency of the measures which have
been adopted by Congress for the protection of commerce & preservation of public credit.[9]

Gentlemen of the Senate & Gentlemen of the house of representatives

As one of the grand community of nations, our attention is irre-
sistably drawn to the important scenes which surround us. If they
have exhibited an uncommon portion of calamity, it is the province of
humanity to deplore, & of wisdom to avoid, the causes which may
have producd it. If turning our eyes homeward, we find reason to
rejoice at the prospect which presents itself; if we perceive the interior of our country prosperous, free, & happy; if all enjoy in safety,

under the protection of laws emanating only from the general will, the fruits of their own labor, we ought to fortify & cling to those institutions which have been the source of such real felicity, & resist with unabating perseverance the progress of those dangerous innovations which may diminish their influence.

To your patriotism gentlemen has been confided the honorable duty of guarding the public interests, & while the past is, to your country, a sure pledge that it will be faithfully dischargd, permit me to assure you that your labors to promote the general happiness will receive from me the most zealous cooperation.

AL and enclosed ADf, Adams Papers, MHi (filed under date of ante 22 Nov. 1800).

1. Presumably this was the Monday preceding the president's address, which was delivered on Saturday, 22 Nov.

2. JM compiled the final version of the address from the various drafts (including his own) and suggestions submitted by the heads of departments. See Draft of President's Speech, ca. 15 Nov. 1800 and n. 1. The speech was printed by order of Congress as *Speech of the President of the United States, . . . 22d November, 1800* [Washington, D.C., 1800; Evans #38906]. See also *Annals of Congress*, X, 723–25, and *ASP, Foreign Relations*, I, 53–54.

3. This paragraph is derived from Stoddert's draft of 5 Nov. (Adams Papers, MHi).

4. This and the succeeding paragraph (dealing with the judiciary) were suggested by Charles Lee in his letter of 12 Nov. (ibid.).

5. See *PJM*, IV, 303 and n. 9.

6. Much of this paragraph is based on Stoddert's draft of 5 Nov. (Adams Papers, MHi).

7. The substance of this paragraph was supplied by Samuel Dexter's letter of 13 Nov. (ibid.).

8. Derived from Oliver Wolcott's letter of 11 Nov. and Dexter's of 13 Nov. (ibid.).

9. This passage was supplied by Wolcott in his letter of 11 Nov. (ibid.).

To St. George Tucker

Dear Sir   Washington Novr. 18th. 1800

I receivd with much pleasure yours of the 6th. inst. I wish with all my soul that those with whom I have been formerly in habits of friendship, woud like you, permit me to retain for them that esteem which was once reciprocal. No man regrets more than I do, that intolerant & persecuting spirit which allows of no worth out of its own pale, & breaks off all social intercourse as a penalty on an honest avowal of honest opinions.

Fennos attack on Mr. Adams I never saw & that of Genl. Hamilton I wish for his sake had never been seen by any person. I have no doubt that it wounds & irritates the person at whom it is directed infinitely more than the Prospect before us,[1] because its author is worthy of attention & his shaft may stick. Whether it is as properly the subject of judicial enquiry is a question on which I have no opinion because I have only given it one hasty reading & that not with a view to such an object. Be this as it may the proceeding, or omiting to proceed against him, can make no impression respecting the character of the executive because that is a subject over which the President exercises no control. The laws are made, & those who violate them are prosecuted by the proper officer without the knowledge or direction of the President. With respect to Mr. Callendar I am mistaken if you & all the world, so far as the circumstances of the case are known, do not concur in the opinion, that nothing can render him an improper object for the punishment of the law but his being below its resentment. On that principle & on that only coud he I think, with any sort of propriety, be recommended for mercy. On that account my own private judgement woud have been against his being prosecuted, but I am not quite sure that it is a sufficient reason for interposing & arresting the course of the law. However this may be I do not think Mr. Adams woud take any step in the case while the election is uncertain. These acts are so often attributed to other than the real motives, that unless there were stronger reasons for them than exist at present, it woud not be adviseable to do any thing til the choice of future President shall be over.

The unconstitutionality of the law, cannot be urgd to the President because he does not think it so. His firm beleif is that it is warranted by the constitution. This opinion is confirmd by the judgement of the courts & is supported by as wise & virtuous men as any in the Union. Of consequence whatever doubts some of us may entertain, he who entertains none, woud not be & ought not to be influencd by that argument.

There will be a house of representatives to day. I beleive confidently that an accomodation has taken place with France tho we have as yet no official account of it. I think it is time for peace to be universal. I am dear Sir with much esteem & regard, yours &c.

J MARSHALL

ALS, Tucker-Coleman Papers, ViW. Addressed by JM to Tucker in Williamsburg and franked; postmarked Washington, 21 Nov.

1. *The Prospect before Us* was the title of Callender's pamphlet.

To Wilhelm Anton Lendemann

Sir,   Department of State, Novr. 20th. 1800

Your letter of the 6th. of August has just been received.[1] You judge rightly Sir, of the sentiments of the government of the United States, when you suppose that it feels the importance of that peace which has been hitherto maintained with his Danish Majesty. Be assured that nothing to disturb the good understanding which has ever subsisted between the two governments will be intentionally done on our part.

The most serious and explicit instructions are given to the armed cruizers of the United States to respect the flag of all neutral nations, and Lieutenant Maley of the Experiment has been dismissed the service, principally on account of his inattention to these instructions.[2] With very much respect, I am Sir &c &c.

J MARSHALL

Letterbook copy, RG 59, DNA.

1. Lendemenn was governor-general of the Danish West Indies (Virgin Islands). His letter of 6 Aug. (not found) complained of the capture of the ships *Mercator* and *Charming Betsey*, the property of Jared Shattuck, a native of Connecticut but then a subject of Denmark. The *Mercator* had been taken by Lt. William Maley of the *Experiment* in May 1800 on a voyage from St. Thomas to St. Domingo. The *Charming Betsey*, bound for Guadaloupe in July 1800, had been captured by a French vessel and then recaptured by Capt. Alexander Murray of the *Constellation*. These captures ultimately led to two cases that came before JM on the Supreme Court (*Naval Documents: Quasi-War*, VI, 45, 139, 548–49; Stoddert to JM, 25 Nov. [App. I, Cal.]; JM to Richard Söderström, 26 Nov.; Murray v. Charming Betsey, 2 Cranch 64 [1804]; Maley v. Shattuck, 3 Cranch 458 [1806]).

2. On Maley's misconduct, see *Naval Documents: Quasi-War*, VI, 41–45, 157, 293–99, 373–74.

To Charles Cotesworth Pinckney

Dear Sir   Washington Novr. 20th. 1800

I wrote to you a few days past[1] & was then confident that Maryland woud give six federal votes. The gentlemen from whom I receivd this information were mistaken. The electors from the two districts not then certainly known are both antifederal. This is not yet officially known but comes in such a way as to gain universal credit. The vote therefore of Maryland is six to four—the anti's having the majority.

The members of Congress think the New England vote except Rhode Island will be indisputably right. It is beleivd that Rhode Island will vote federally, but this is uncertain & from thence you will probably receive by water earlier information than I can give you.

I beleive the Senate of Pennsylvania will maintain their ground. This however will not do for us if Mr Jefferson gets any votes in South Carolina. It is not impossible that a compromise between the two branches may be made in which case I expect the house of representatives may obtain 9 to 6. This will exclude Mr. Jefferson provided he gets no vote in South Carolina. But it is now reducd to an absolute certainty that any success in your state elects him. We have not yet a Senate. I am dear Sir with much esteem, your Obedt. Servt.

J MARSHALL

ALS, Pinckney Family Papers, DLC. Addressed by JM to Pinckney in Columbia and franked; postmarked Washington, 20 Nov. Endorsed by Pinckney.

1. Letter not found.

From John Adams

Washington Nov 21st 1800

The President presents his kind regards to Gen Marshall, & requests the favor of him to look into the dispatches of Gen. Pinckney, which gave an account of his rejection by the Executive directory & of Mr. Barras's speech to Mr. Monroe on his taking leave & mark the day when that news was first received. It must have been in the month of march 1797.[1] The President wishes to be furnished with this date as exactly as may be.

Letterbook copy, Adams Papers, MHi.

1. Charles C. Pinckney related his rejection by the French Directory in his dispatch of 20 Dec. 1796. In a subsequent dispatch, dated 6 Jan. 1797, he mentioned the speech by M. Barras, president of the Directory, delivered on 30 Dec. 1796 to James Monroe, the departing minister plenipotentiary (ASP, Foreign Relations, II, 5–8, 10, 12; PJM, III, 175 and n. 51).

To John Adams

[ca. 21 November 1800]

The Secretary of State presents most respectfully to the President a volume containing the Letters from Genl. Pinckney.

That of the 20th of Decr. 97 was receivd on the 23d of March 98 & that on the 6th. of Jany 98, on the same day.[1]

The letter of the 15th of Jany. was receivd on the 4th. of April &

that of the 24th. of Jany. on the 18th. of May. The letter of the 20th. of Decr. shows the rejection of Genl. Pinckney & contains the speech of Barras.

AL, Adams Papers, MHi.

1. JM was mistaken as to the dates. Pinckney wrote on 20 Dec. 1796 and 6 Jan. 1797.

To Charles Cotesworth Pinckney

Dear Sir   Washington Novr. 22d. 1800
   I write to tell you that neither my first nor last account of the vote of Maryland was correct. The State is precisely divided. No doubt is entertaind but that the federal electors will vote for both the federal Gentlemen. At least no man with whom I have conversd doubts it.
   I was much pleasd at the honorable testimony given by your fellow citizens of the respect & attachment they still retain for you.[1] We hope & the democrats fear that the legislature will testify the same sentiments. On your legislature I beleive depends absolutely the election. The Pennsylvania Senate has maintaind their ground. My letters say & I beleive they will maintain it. We look out anxiously for inteligence from Rhode Island. If the federal ticket succeeds in that State I think it almost certain that both the federal gentlemen will be elected—if it fails I cannot say what may happen.
   Congress met yesterday & the speech was deliverd to day.[2] With much respect & esteem I am dear Sir, your Obedt.

                                                        J MARSHALL

ALS, Collection of Frank G. Tiesen, San Diego, Calif. Addressed by JM to Pinckney in Columbia and franked; postmarked Washington, 22 Nov. Endorsed by Pinckney.

1. Pinckney had been elected to the state senate (Marvin R. Zahniser, *Charles Cotesworth Pinckney: Founding Father* [Chapel Hill, N.C., 1967], 224).
2. The speech of President Adams, which JM drafted.

To [William Nelson]

Dear Sir   Washington Novr. 25th. 1800[1]
   I have to reproach myself for not having mentiond earlier to you the subject of this letter.
   Under the expectation that you woud be appointed to the command of the 2d. Brigade of Virginia militia I was applied to last

summer to mention Major Richardson to you for the office he now fills.[2]

I coud not wish or expect that any recommendation from me shoud induce you to retain this gentleman against your inclination, but as my omiting to mention him might imply some dissatisfaction with him, which is very far from being the fact, I promisd to do so.

Of his capacity you can judge as well as myself. I need only assure you that I have ever found him an honorable faithful & obliging officer. I am persuaded he will continue to merit this character. With much respect & esteem, I am dear Sir your Obcdt. Servt

J MARSHALL

ALS, Marshall Papers, ViW.

1. The address leaf is missing, but the recipient was almost certainly William Nelson (see n. 2).

2. JM had recently resigned as brigadier general of the Second Brigade of the Virginia militia. The General Assembly elected William Nelson on 17 Dec. to succeed JM (Gov. James Monroe to Speaker of House of Delegates, 8 Dec. 1800, Executive Communications, Vi; *Journal of the House of Delegates of the Commonwealth of Virginia [Dec. 1800]*, 27–28). Major Richardson was probably William Richardson, an officer of the Nineteenth Regiment (*CVSP*, VIII, 491; IX, 31).

From Charles Young

Sir,   Richmond 25th. Novemr. 1800

Since writing you last evening[1] through the medium of Mr. Patton, I have seen Mr Randolph who am sorry to say informs me there is the greatest danger from the complexion the writ of Error has assumed from the mistakes of the Clerk & the nonappearance of Counsel last August Term as represented in Mr Tilghmans Letter to Donald & Burton.[2] Mr. Randolph has desired me in the most earnest manner *to procure directly* the papers undermentioned; and if it is not giving you too much trouble, I must entreat you will forward to him whatever depends upon you relative to Counsel being engaged yourself in the first place and that you engaged Mr. Lewis[3] afterwards, with the reasons of your assuring Mr Patton[4] it could not certainly come on last Supreme Court. Any other service you can render in this illfated business I calculate upon, confiding in your doing every thing you can to relieve me as they expect to have the Clerks Certificate so as to make the motion next Tuesday at all events, this I hope you'll attend to as far as possible & as soon. I am respectfully, Sir, Your Mo. Obt. Servt

CHA YOUNG

Papers wanted
Certificate from the Clerk the Supreme Court the US
    of the pending of the Writ of Error; or if it be dismissed
    of the reason of dismission; and of the time
    when the Record got to hand.
    ───────
    that the Record is so lengthy as to prevent him from
    transcribing it under   days.
Do. from General Marshall of his having been employed
    and of his having engaged Mr Lewis;
    of the reason it did not come to Issue last Court in Augt.[5]

ALS, Blaine v. Ship Charles Carter, Appellate Case No. 80, RG 267, DNA. Enclosed
in JM to Clerk of Supreme Court, ca. 30 Nov. Addressed to JM in Washington; postmarked Richmond, 25 Nov.

1. Letter not found.
2. Charles Young was attorney in fact for Thomas Blane, a London merchant, whose
case was then pending in the Supreme Court. The case, styled Blaine v. The Ship
Charles Carter and Donald & Burton and Others, Claimants, originated in the federal
district court of Virginia in Jan. 1798. Blane libeled the *Charles Carter*, owned by Alexander Macaulay of Yorktown. At the same time, Alexander Donald & Robert Burton,
London merchants, who had obtained judgments against Macaulay in the federal circuit court at Richmond, levied execution against the ship. The court had to decide
which of Macaulay's creditors—Blane or Donald & Burton—would receive the proceeds of the sale of the vessel. The district court ruled for Blane, but the circuit court
reversed this decree and dismissed the libel in Dec. 1799.
    The case was removed by process of appeal to the Supreme Court, which in Feb.
1800 dismissed the suit on the ground that the removal of suits from the circuit court
to the Supreme Court had to be by writ of error, as provided in section 22 of the
judiciary act. Blane's attorney, Edmund Randolph, then obtained a writ of error, which
however was quashed at the Aug. 1800 term for procedural irregularities. "Mr. Tilghman" was either William or Edward Tilghman, the Philadelphia lawyers who frequently argued cases in the Supreme Court (Blaine v. Ship Charles Carter, 4 Dall. 22
[1800]; 4 Cranch 328 [1808]; App. Cas. No. 80; Blane v. Ship Charles Carter, App. Cas.
No. 76; Blane v. Donald & Burton, U.S. Sup. Ct. Dockets, App. Cas. No. 80).
    3. William Lewis, a Philadelphia lawyer and member of the Supreme Court bar. JM
had previously appeared for and against Blane in cases heard in the federal circuit
court (*PJM*, V, 534–35 and n. 4). See also JM's opinion in Blane v. Drummond, 9 Dec.
1803.
    4. Robert Patton, a Fredericksburg merchant (*PJM*, II, 330 n. 4).
    5. A new writ of error was issued in June 1801, and the case remained on the docket
until Aug. 1803, when by order of the plaintiff the circuit court decree was affirmed.
In the meantime, Blane took his cause back to the circuit court by means of a bill of
review, which was filed at the June 1803 term. The case again was removed to the
Supreme Court by writ of error in Aug. 1804. Final disposition did not take place until
Mar. 1808, when the court upheld the decree of the circuit court (Blaine v. Ship
Charles Carter, App. Cas. No. 80; U.S. Sup. Ct. Dockets, App. Cas. Nos. 80, 183; U.S.
Cir. Ct., Va., Ord. Bk. IV, 255, 325; 4 Cranch 328).
    For a discussion of the procedural aspects of this case, see Goebel, *Antecedents and*

Beginnings, 796–98nn. The substantive merits are discussed in Haskins and Johnson, *Foundations of Power*, 491–92.

To Richard Söderström

Sir,   [26 November 1800][1]

I have received your letters of the 24th and 25th instant, accompanying one from the governor general of the Danish West India Islands, bearing date the 6th of August last.[2]

Be assured, sir, that the government of the United States respects as it ought to do, the friendship and flag of his Danish majesty, and will not intentionally commit an act which may insult the one, or diminish the other. If in any instance our cruizers have violated a really neutral flag, they have in doing so, departed from the instructions under which they sail.

It is not however to be disguised, that means have been devised by which the Danish flag has been used in the West Indies, for purposes which we believe his Danish majesty would not countenance.

I have communicated the letters from yourself and the governor general of the Danish West India Islands, to the secretary of the navy. He informs me that lieut. Maley has been dismissed the service principally on account of the improper manner in which he has conducted himself towards neutrals.[3]

With respect to the particular case of the Mercator, it is certainly advisable to prosecute an appeal. If she was really a neutral bottom, she will not it is presumed be condemned. Without deciding absolutely that the United States will or will not consent, when the case shall be ultimately decided, to pay for the vessel and cargo if confiscated, we are certainly not sufficiently informed at present to take any responsibility on ourselves, in the event of an unfavorable issue of that affair.[4]

Printed, *Message from the President . . . Transmitting a Report of the Secretary of State Complying with the Resolution of the Senate . . . April 2d, 1810* (Washington, D.C., 1810; S #21739), 5–6.

1. Söderström was Swedish consul general to the U.S. and also represented the Danish government. This letter was printed as part of a report of Secretary of State Robert Smith, communicated to Congress on 30 Mar. 1810. The report reproduced extracts from the correspondence of the secretary of state with the Danish minister concerning the case of the *Mercator*. It is also printed in *ASP, Foreign Relations*, III, 344–47.

2. See JM to Lendemenn, 20 Nov. These letters have not been found and were not in

the State Department at the time of Secretary Smith's report in 1810 (Robert Smith to James Madison, 29 Mar. 1810, ibid., 344).

3. Stoddert to JM, 25 Nov. (App. I, Cal.).

4. After Lieutenant Maley captured the *Mercator*, a British privateer recaptured her and had her condemned as a prize at the vice-admiralty court in Jamaica. In 1804 Shattuck exhibited a libel in the federal district court of Pennsylvania, seeking restitution for the loss of his vessel and cargo. The district court dismissed the libel, but the circuit court reversed the decree in 1805. Maley appealed to the Supreme Court, which affirmed the sentence of the circuit court in 1806 (Maley v. Shattuck, 3 Cranch 458–92).

To Toussaint Louverture

Sir,   Department of State, Washington Novr. 26. 1800

I have received your letter of the 4th. Messidor in the 8th. year of the French Republic one and indivisible,[1] and Mr. Meade has communicated to me the articles you wish to purchase.[2]

The principles which direct the Government of the United States do not permit its executive to engage in commercial enterprizes; of consequence from that source the articles you wish cannot be furnished. It is by individuals only that you can be supplied. No law exists which prevents the exportation from this Country to St Domingo, of any article of commerce which can be received there, and of course Mr. Meade or any other citizen is at perfect liberty to engage in the business on his own account.

Be assured, Sir, of our sincere desire to preserve the most perfect harmony and the most friendly intercourse with St. Domingo, and that we shall rejoice at every occasion of manifesting this disposition compatible with those fixed principles, which regulate the conduct of our Government. With very sincere & respectful consideration, I am, Sir, Your obedt. svt.

J MARSHALL

Letterbook copy, RG 59, DNA. Original enclosed in JM to Edward Stevens, 26 Nov. (App. I, Cal.).

1. Toussaint's letter of "4th. Messidor" (22 June 1800) has not been found.

2. Richard W. Meade (1778–1828), son of prominent Phildelphia merchant George Meade (1741–1808). The younger Meade entered his father's business and in 1796 went to St. Domingo, establishing a business on his own account. He returned to Philadelphia in 1801. Soon thereafter Meade set up a commercial house in Cádiz, moving there with his family in 1804. In 1806 he was appointed U.S. naval agent at Cádiz. No letter from Meade to JM has been found.

To St. George Tucker

Dear Sir   Washington Novr. 27th. 1800

I had the pleasure a few days past of receiving a pamphlet written by you on the question how far the common law is the law of the United States for which I thank you.[1] I have read it with attention, & you will perhaps be surprizd at my saying that I do not suppose we shoud essentially disagree.

In political controversy it often happens that the precise opinion of the adversary is not understood, & that we are at much labor to disprove propositions which have never been maintaind. A stronger evidence of this cannot I think be given than the manner in which the references to the common law have been treated. The opinion which has been controverted is, that the common law of England has not been adopted as the common law of America by the constitution of the United States. I do not beleive one man can be found who maintains the affirmative of this proposition. Neither in public nor in private have I ever heard it advocated, & I am as entirely confident as I can be of any thing of the sort, that it never has been advocated. This strange & absurd doctrine was first attributed to the judiciary of the United States by some frothy news paper publications which appeard in Richmond something more than twelve months past, but I never suspected that an attempt woud be made to represent this as a serious opinion entertaind by respectable men, until I saw the argument containd in the report of a committee of the house of Delegates in Virginia.[2] You will pardon me for saying that notwithstanding the respectability of the author of this report I coud not read the part of it respecting the common law without being reminded of a ludicrous story told by Mr. Mason in the house of delegates in Williamsburg of a ram who amusd himself by taking such a position as to cast his shadow on a wall & then but at it as at a real enemy. So this report has gratuitously attributed to certain gentlemen an opinion never entertaind & has then very gravely demonstrated that the opinion is founded in error.

What the precise opinion entertaind on this subject may be I do not profess to know but I beleive that in the general definition of the principle sensible men of the two parties woud not disagree very materially. In the application of principles there woud perhaps be more difference than in their definition.

With respect to the case of Isaac Williams which you have mentiond in a note, I cannot beleive that you & Judge Ellesworth (if I understand that case rightly) woud disagree. Isaac Williams was prosecuted on two separate indictments—the one for privatiering under a french commission against the British & the other for privatiering under the same commission against his own Country men. He was found guilty on both indictments. In the one case he was guilty of an offence against a public treaty of the United States & in the other of an offence against the United States on the high seas. I beleive it is not controverted that both these crimes are clearly punishable in the federal courts. The defence set up, so far as I understand it, was that by taking a commission in the service of France which was itself a crime, Isaac Williams withdrew himself from the cognizance of our courts by ceasing to be an American citizen. I mistake your opinions very much if you woud have countenancd this defence.[3]

In the case of Williams the common law was not relied on as giving the court jurisdiction, but came in incidentally as part of the law of a case of which the court had complete & exclusive possession.[4] I do not understand you as questioning the propriety of thus applying the common law, not of England, but of our own country.

My own opinion is that our ancestors brought with them the laws of England both statute & common law as existing at the settlement of each colony, so far as they were applicable to our situation. That on our revolution the preexisting law of each state remaind so far as it was not changd either expressly or necessarily by the nature of the governments which we adopted.

That on adopting the existing constitution of the United States the common & statute law of each state remain as before & that the principles of the common law of the state woud apply themselves to magistrates of the general as well as to magistrates of the particular government. I do not recollect ever to have heard the opinions of a leading gentleman of the opposition which conflict with these. Mr. Gallatin in a very acute speech on the sedition law was understood by me to avow them.[5] On the other side it was contended, not that the common law gave the courts jurisdiction in cases of sedition but that the constitution gave it.[6] I am dear Sir yours truely

J MARSHALL

ALS, Marshall Papers, DLC. Identity of recipient based on internal evidence noted below.

1. The reference is to Tucker's pamphlet, *Examination of the Question, "How Far the Common Law of England Is the Law of the Federal Government of the United States?"* (Richmond, Va., [1800]). Tucker reprinted the essay in his *Blackstone's Commentaries*, I (pt. 1), app., 378–433.

2. James Madison wrote the report of the committee defending the Virginia resolutions of 21 Dec. 1798 opposing the Alien and Sedition Acts. It had been published early in 1800 as *Report of the Committee to Whom Was Committed the Proceedings of Sundry of the Other States, in Answer to the Resolutions of the General Assembly, of the [21st] Day of December [1798]* (Richmond, Va., [1800]; Evans #38961).

3. On the case of Isaac Williams, tried at the federal circuit court in Connecticut in

Sept. 1799, see *PJM*, IV, 207, 223, 225; Francis Wharton, *State Trials of the United States* . . . (1849; New York, 1970 reprint), 652–58. See also Tucker, *Blackstone's Commentaries*, I (pt. 1), app., 379n.

4. Chief Justice Ellsworth, who presided at Williams's trial, stated that "the common law of this country remains the same as it was before the Revolution." His opinion concerned the legal effect of evidence that Williams had expatriated himself (Wharton, *State Trials*, 653–54).

5. The reference may be to Gallatin's speech in the debate of 23 Jan. 1800 (which JM attended) on the repeal of the Sedition Act (*Annals of Congress*, X, 421–22).

6. On the federal common law of crime, see Kathryn Preyer, "Jurisdiction to Punish: Federal Authority, Federalism and the Common Law of Crimes in the Early Republic," *Law and History Review*, IV (1986), 223–65; Robert C. Palmer, "The Federal Common Law of Crime," ibid., 267–323; Stephen B. Presser, "The Supra-Constitution, the Courts, and the Federal Common Law of Crimes: Some Comments on Palmer and Preyer," ibid., 325–35. See also the exhaustive treatment by Stewart Jay, "Origins of Federal Common Law: Part One," *University of Pennsylvania Law Review*, CXXXIII (1985), 1003–1116; "Part Two," ibid., 1231–1333. Jay reprints JM's letter to Tucker and comments on JM's views (1326–33).

From Robert Liston

Philadelphia, 27th November 1800.
R. Liston presents his respects to General Marshall, Secretary of State.

His Majesty's Packet Boat, the Mary, lately arrived from Falmouth, and which was to have sailed on Thursday next with the December mail from this Country, has been seized by the principal Officers of the Customs at New York on account of the fraudulent landing of certain merchandize by some of the crew; and the vessel is considered as liable to confiscation, pursuant to the Revenue Laws of the United States.

By the enclosed statement of the business, in a letter addressed to me by Mr. Barclay, His Majesty's Consul General at New York, it appears that the Captain of the Packet was not only free of all participation in the irregular transaction, but would have been happy to prevent it, had it been in his power.[1]

The common interest of nations seems to require that Vessels employed in carrying on the general correspondence should be regarded as sacred, and be exempted from the usual process of law in cases of contraband trade: and His Majesty's Packets are in fact in the enjoyment of this species of immunity in Lisbon, and (as far as my information goes) in the other ports of Europe, with which a periodical communication is carried on by their means.

Should any doubts exist with respect to the expediency of granting to these vessels the same privilege in the territories of the United

States, or should the federal Government think it requisite to enter into explanations with that of Great Britain on the necessity of taking effectual measures to prevent the crews of the Packets from attempting the irregular introduction of merchandize in time to come, I hope, Sir, that you will at all events be pleased to use your interest to induce the President to authorize, through the Secretary of the Treasury, the release of the Packet Mary, that she maybe enabled to proceed on her voyage as soon as may be after the time fixed for the dispatch of the mail.

AL, RG 59, DNA; copy, F.O.5/29 A, P.R.O. Enclosure: copy of Thomas Barclay to Liston, 25 Nov. 1800.

1. Barclay informed Liston that the *Mary* "was seized on an information that twenty one pieces of second broad Cloth had been clandestinely landed."

To Thomas FitzSimons

Dear Sir   Washington Novr. 28th. 1800
   I receivd your letter of the 18th. instant[1] too late to give you any advice which coud affect your conduct in respect of the Genessee lands & have therefore postpond writing in the hope that I might receive some information on the subject from Mr Morris.[2] I have not however mentiond it to him nor he to me.
   I coud wish to know what defect exists in the deeds which the gentlemen allude to. If I coud learn what is relied on I coud be a better judge of the danger to be apprehended from it. At present I perceive none—but a lawyer of New York is more capable than myself of deciding that question. I think the defect can only be in the manner of recording the deed. Of this the laws will not enable me to judge but you can very easily ascertain it.
   I perceive Mr. Morris acknowledgd the deed before a Judge of the United States. Was it recorded on that acknowledgement singly or on other proof? If on that acknowledgement is there an act of the State of New York authorizing a court to receive probat of deeds & record them on the certificate of a Judge of the United States? I fear there is not. If there was other proof what was it?
   The laws of New York direct mortgages to be enregisterd in a separate book from absolute conveyances. Is it the practice to record deeds of trust with mortgages or with absolute deeds?
   These are the only difficulties which in my opinion exist in the case. I fear that by absolute negligence our deed may be good for nothing. If this is not the case I have no apprehension from the Judgement &

sale which has been made under it. If our deed has been properly recorded I think a suit in chancery ought immediately to be instituted in the federal court in New York.[3] I will write to you again after seeing my brother. I am dear Sir with much respect, your obedt

J MARSHALL

There may be something wrong in the manner of sealing or indenting the deed. Do the laws of New York require that a deed shoud be actually indented & if so was this indented? Will a scrowl suffice as a seal or must there be an actual seal? If an actual seal be necessary was the deed seald?

ALS, Collection of Henry N. Ess III, New York, N.Y., and James G. Stahlman, Nashville, Tenn. Addressed by JM to FitzSimons in Philadelphia and franked; postmarked Washington, 28 Nov. Endorsed by FitzSimons as received 2 Dec. MS consists of two sheets, separated from each other. Ess owns main text of letter; Stahlman owns address leaf, with postcript on verso.

1. Letter not found. FitzSimons was a prominent Philadelphia merchant.

2. Robert Morris, father-in-law of JM's brother James, was then in debtors' prison in Philadelphia. In Feb. 1798 Morris had conveyed 110,000 acres of his Genesee lands (Ontario County, N.Y.), in trust, to FitzSimons, Joseph Higbee, and Robert Morris, Jr., to secure payment of debts enumerated in the deed of trust (Barbara Ann Chernow, *Robert Morris: Land Speculator* [New York, 1978], 80–81).

3. This was apparently the genesis of the suit that eventually came before the Supreme Court as FitzSimons and Others v. Ogden and Others, 7 Cranch 2 (1812). See also JM to James M. Marshall, 7 Feb. 1803 (App. I, Cal.); JM to FitzSimons, 28 Apr. 1805 (App. I, Cal.). JM had further correspondence with FitzSimons concerning this case in 1809, 1810, and 1811.

To John Jay

Sir   Department of State, Novr. 28th. 1800
In compliance with the request containd in your letter of the 15th. instant the President has directed a requisition to be made to the Governor of lower Canada for the delivery of Thomas Jamieson, alias, Charles Splendor, alias Charles Johnston to such person as you may authorize to receive him.[1]

I have the honor to transmit herewith the requisition together with the documents on which it is founded & to assure you that with great respect & consideration, I am your most obedt. Servt.

J MARSHALL

ALS, MWiW; letterbook copy, N.

1. See JM to Robert Shore Milnes of this date.

To Robert Shore Milnes

Sir,   Department of State Washington Novr. 28th. 1800[1]
It has been communicated to this Government by Mr. Liston the Minister Plenipotentiary of His Britannic Majesty to the United States, that a certain Thomas Jameson alias Charles Spendor, alias Charles Holland, who is charged on oath with forgery by him done and committed in the State of New York one of the United States, and is a fugitive from justice, is now detained in prison at Montreal.

I am directed by the President to request that in pursuance of the 27th. article of the treaty of amity commerce and navigation between the United States of America and his Britannic Majesty, You will please to order the said Thomas Jameson alias Charles Spendor, alias Charles Holland to be delivered up to such agent as the Governor of New York may authorize to receive him, that he may be dealt with according to law.[2] I am sir, with great respect &c. &c.

J. MARSHALL

Letterbook copy, RG 59, DNA.

1. The recipient was governor-general of Lower Canada. This letter was enclosed in JM to Jay, 28 Nov.

2. Article 27 of the Treaty of 1794 (Jay Treaty) provided for the extradition of persons charged with murder or forgery.

To Elias B. Caldwell

[ca. 30 November 1800]
The inclosd letter relates to the case of the Charles Carter which I am told was dismissd at the last Aug. term of the supreme court for non appearance.[1] I shall be very much obligd if you will certify what is requird in the letter so far as relates to your office & send it by the mail this evening to Robert Patton in Alexandria. I am Sir your Obedt

J MARSHALL

ALS, Blaine v. Ship Charles Carter, Appellate Case No. 80, RG 267, DNA.

1. See Charles Young to JM, 25 Nov.

To Robert Liston

Sir,   Department of State Decr. 2nd 1800

Your note of the 27th ulto. requesting the release of His Britannic Majesty's Packet Boat the Mary, seized for a breach of the Revenue Laws of the United States, was received last night; and I hastened to manifest my sollicitude to comply with any request you might make, by an immediate application for the discharge of the vessel.

The Secretary of the Treasury writes today to the officers of the Revenue at New York, instructing them to liberate the Mary, and to dismiss the prosecution against her.

I am inclined to believe that the regulations of the United States respecting Ships of war and publick packets have escaped your attention. We suppose them to be as liberal as those of any other commercial country whatever. You will perceive it in the 4th volume of the Acts of Congress page 331.[1] We require no report and rely on the nation owning the vessel to enforce its own prohibition to carry on commerce but if smuggling be detected, it would seem that a nation whose revenues depend principally on duties on imports, must enforce penalties calculated to prevent the mischief.[2] I am Sir with great respect and consideration &c

(signed)   J. MARSHALL

Copy, F.O.5/29 A, P.R.O. In hand of Edward Thornton. Enclosed in Thornton to Lord Grenville, 6 Dec. 1800.

1. JM referred to the 1799 act to regulate the collection of duties on imports and tonnage. Section 31 stipulated that foreign ships of war and vessels engaged in carrying mail and public dispatches (which by the laws of the country were prohibited from carrying on commerce) did not have to file reports of entries with the customs officers (*U.S. Statutes at Large*, I, 651). JM cited a contemporary imprint, *The Laws of the United States of America. In Four Volumes. Volume IV* . . . (Philadelphia, 1799; Evans #36523).

2. Liston left Philadelphia on this day to return to England. JM's letter was received by Edward Thornton, chargé d'affaires. In his first dispatch to Lord Grenville on 6 Dec., Thornton noted that he had received JM's letter on 5 Dec., commenting that "it would be doing injustice to the prompt and handsome manner, in which Mr Marshall has interfered on this occasion not to inclose a copy of his letter." Thornton added: "The Secretary of State does not however enter into the question, how far a Packet ought to be considered as a public Ship, and in that character to be exempt from seizure or detention; but by his manner of referring to the 31st Section of an Act passed in the month of March 1799 . . . by which the Commander of Ships of war and publick packets, *not employed in the transportation of merchandize*, are excused from making the usual entries required from other vessels, he seems rather to justify the general right of seizing such publick vessels, when they are detected in transgressing the Revenue Laws" (F.O.5/29 A, P.R.O.).

To Samuel Sitgreaves

Dear Sir,   Department of State, Decemr. 2d. 1800[1]
 I have had the pleasure of receiving your letters to the 29th. of September and among them that of the 23d. inclosing a copy of your letter of the 22d. of April, the original of which had unfortunately miscarried.[2]
 It is probable that before this can reach you, the negotiation respecting the 6th. article of our treaty of amity commerce and navigation with Great Britain will have terminated, and that Mr. King will have come to some agreement with Lord Grenville, or will be able to state precisely the ultimata of the British Cabinet on this subject. Should it, contrary to our expectation remain open, the President is of opinion, that informal explanations may be received in lieu of the articles required, provided sufficient assurances accompany them that the Commissioners on the part of his Britannic Majesty will, in the true spirit of conciliation, conform to those explanations.[3]
 The idea suggested to Lord Grenville by Mr. King, of sending over confidential characters to the United States with power to make arrangements for facilitating the just and impartial execution of the treaty, and with an eventual appointment as commissioners, is a valuable one. If no positive agreement can be made which will enable us to enter again on the execution of the 6th. article without submitting to injurious and disgraceful imposition, this idea may perhaps be so improved as to become the foundation of a reasonable accommodation. It is certainly recommended by the probabilities you have suggested.
 If the system of informal explanation should be adopted and a new board be constituted in the mode intimated by Lord Grenville there will undoubtedly be considerable difficulty in agreeing on rules which shall guide its proceedings, and in obtaining security that these rules will not be departed from. The explanatory articles which before your departure were digested by this government and committed to you, are believed to be a liberal as well as just construction and would be therefore with reluctance receded from: indeed there are among them some from which we never ought to recede.[4] Such, for example as that to charge the United States, the British Creditor must bring his case completely within the treaty; and not require that the United States should furnish evidence to discharge themselves from every claim which may be at present, or, on the signature of the treaty of amity, may have been unpaid. Such a construction appears to us so totally unreasonable, that we should never have deem'd it necessary to guard against it, had not the principle been already asserted, and it is of course a construction to which we never can and

never ought to submit. Other principles were insisted on which seem to us not less objectionable. But if it shall be found that a new Board is to be resorted to, it will become necessary to revise the instructions which have been given, and to modify them so far as a proper respect for justice and our own character will permit.

The President allows your return to the United States as soon as the negotiation shall have taken a turn which in your opinion may render your longer continuance in England unnecessary, or so soon as you shall have communicated fully to Mr. King all the ideas on the interesting subject of your mission, which your intimate acquaintance with it has enabled you to acquire. With very much respect & esteem, I am Sir, &c. &c.

J MARSHALL

Letterbook copy, RG 59, DNA.

1. This letter is printed in *ASP, Foreign Relations*, II, 388–89, along with all the correspondence relating to the Convention of 1802, communicated by President Jefferson to the Senate on 29 Mar. 1802.

2. Letters not found. Samuel Sitgreaves, a Pennsylvania lawyer, had served as one of the American members of the commission appointed under article 6 of the Jay Treaty. This commission heard claims of British creditors for recovery of pre-Revolutionary debts owed by Americans. After the work of this commission was suspended, Sitgreaves went to London early in 1800 to assist in new negotiations (Pickering to King, 31 Dec. 1799 [*ASP, Foreign Relations*, II, 385]; Moore, *International Adjudications*, 21, 350).

3. For a summary of the negotiations leading to the convention, see Moore, *International Adjudications*, 350–56. JM's major statement of the American position is his letter to King of 23 Aug. 1800 (*PJM*, IV, 233–38).

4. The explanatory articles were communicated by Secretary of State Pickering to King on 31 Dec. 1799 (*ASP, Foreign Relations*, II, 384–85).

From Charles Cotesworth Pinckney

Dear Sr: Columbia Decr: 2d: 1800.

The antifederal Tickett has been succesful 87 to 69. I wrote you a few days ago that I thought the Election would be lost to us.[1] I did not however think they would have carried it by such a majority. Had the Federalists been succesful Mr: Adams would have had full as many votes as myself. The Antifederal Electors are to vote equally for Mr: Jefferson & Coll: Burr. I remain with great regard & esteem, yrs. very sincerely

CHARLES COTESWORTH PINCKNEY

ALS, Adams Papers, MHi.

1. See Pinckney to JM, 29 Nov. (App. I, Cal.).

To Rufus King

No. 9.[1]

Dear Sir   Department of State Decr. 4th. 1800

Your letters to No. 85 inclusive have been receivd.[2]

In my No. 2[3] I stated to you the opinion of the President, that an adjustment by explanatory articles, of the differences which arose in executing the treaty with Great-Britain, was preferd to the stipulation of a sum in gross to be paid in lieu of the compensation to creditors demandable from the United States.

This opinion is still retaind. But it has been suggested that, however unreasonable the principles asserted by the british commissioners may be, it will be difficult, perhaps impossible, to induce the british cabinet formally to abandon them. That the same thing may probably be obtaind in an informal way, which woud be withheld if requird in the shape of a solemn public stipulation.

Under the impression that this may be the fact, the President directs me to inform you that an informal agreement, provided it be perfectly understood, will be satisfactory to this government.

If however on any such agreement a new board shoud be constituted, it is of the last importance that the persons appointed to act as commissioners, shoud possess dispositions inclind to conciliation, & characters which impress you with a favorable opinion of the impartiality to be expected in their decisions. These are requisites the materiality of which we have been taught by experience, & on them must greatly depend our assent to another board.

If you have brought the negotiation to a conclusion respecting the sum in gross mentiond in a former letter; or if it is in such a train that no change can, without embarassment, be made; it is not intended to derange, or unsettle the business. But if no agreement has been concluded; or has progressd so far as to pledge the United States, it is decidedly the judgement of the President that it will be most adviseable to execute the treaty in the manner originally agreed on; provided satisfactory tho informal assurances can be obtaind, that we shall not be subjected by a majority of the board, to an enormous burthen not imposd by the original contract.

If persons coud be deputed to make arrangements here for facilitating the execution of the treaty, with an eventual appointment as Commissioners, some difficulties might perhaps be surmounted which at present appear very considerable, & the business might be greatly expedited.

As we cannot know the precise state of the negotiation, it is impossible to do more than to communicate in general terms, the course which the President most wishes it to take. Having done this to your judgement it must be submitted.

The most desirable plan of accomodation is by public explanatory articles placing the treaty on its true principles in terms not easily to be misunderstood.

Second to this is the system of informal explanation by which we may be enabled without great injustice, to execute the treaty in the mode originally designd.

If in neither the one way nor the other a new board can be so constituted as to comply with the engagements we have made according to their real import, without exposing the united States to the immense losses threatend by that which has been dissolvd, then the stipulation for a sum in gross will be deemd more eligible than to permit things to remain in their present unsettled situation.

We are surprizd that at the date of your No. 85 no letter on this subject had been receivd from this department.[4] With the most respectful esteem, I am Sir your Obedt. Servt.

J MARSHALL

ALS, PP; LS (duplicate), RG 59, DNA; letterbook copy, RG 59, DNA. ALS endorsed by King as received 16 Mar. 1801 "Pr. Wm. Penn."

1. This letter is printed in *ASP, Foreign Relations*, II, 389, along with other correspondence relating to the Convention of 1802. JM's dispatch to King of 24 Oct. was also labeled "No. 9" (*PJM*, IV, 333).

2. King's dispatch No. 85 was dated 7 Oct. (*PJM*, IV, 321).

3. 23 Aug. 1800 (erroneously transcribed in *PJM*, IV, 233, as "No. 4").

4. At the time King wrote on 7 Oct., he had not yet received JM's letter of 23 Aug. That letter did not reach him until 14 Nov. (*PJM*, IV, 233 n. 5).

To Charles Cotesworth Pinckney

My dear Sir   Washington Decr. 6th 1800
I write altho I can give you no inteligence which you do not already possess.

Altho the federal ticket has succeeded in Rhode island it is feard that you may lose one vote there. I hope the fear will not be realis'd. Pennsylvania you know votes 8 & 7. Maryland has given 5 & 5—a fair federal & antifederal vote. It is feard that North Carolina will also throw away one vote. Shoud South Carolina vote for Mr. Jefferson he will be the President according to present appearances. Our last letters from your state are unfavorable & of consequence we are a good deal alarmd. We expect however every day to receive a line from some of our federal friends which may dispel the doubts with which the election is at present overcast. I am dear Sir Your

J MARSHALL

Photostat of ALS, Pinckney Family Papers, DLC. Addressed by JM to Pinckney in Columbia and franked; postmarked Washington, 6 Dec. Endorsed by Pinckney.

From Augustine Davis

Dear sir,   Richmond, Decr. 7th. 1800

The Portsmouth ship of War arrived at Norfolk last Friday evening direct from France, with Governor Davie on board, one of our Ambassadors, who has brought with him the Treaty of Amity and Commerce entered into with the French Republic.[1] This news may be relied on, there being a letter received here last night which mentions it, and which cannot be doubted. As the last Mail from Norfolk cannot convey any information of the Arrival of the Portsmouth there, it having left Norfolk on Friday Morning last, I do myself the honor of communicating the News to you, in order that Government may get the earliest information possible. As there can be no further intelligence receieved here by Mail from Norfolk until Tuesday evening next, it is probable an Express may arrive here some time to night with dispatches for Government, it [sic] there should, they will certainly be forwarded to morrow morning. I have the honor to be, Dr Sir, Your Most Obe Servt

AUGUSTINE DAVIS

ALS, Adams Papers, MHi.

1. Davie was one of the three commissioners (Ellsworth and Murray the others) who negotiated the Convention of 1800. See American Envoys to JM, 4 Oct. 1800 (*PJM*, IV, 315–19). Augustine Davis was publisher of the Richmond *Virginia Gazette, and General Advertiser*. A notice of Davie's arrival appeared in his paper of 9 Dec.

From Tobias Lear

Dear Sir,   Walnut Tree Farm,[1] December 12th: 1800

You will receive herewith a trunk containing sundry books and papers, (as per inclosed list) relating to the late General Washington. The key of the trunk is also inclosed.

It has not been in my power to make out so full a list of these

TOBIAS LEAR

Pastel on paper attributed to James Sharples, ca. 1800. *Courtesy of an anonymous owner*

documents, with notes, as I intended. And it is with pain I must add, that I fear it will not be in my power to make that arrangement of the late General's papers &c, preparatory to writing the history of his life, which I suggested to you, when I had the pleasure of seeing you in the City. My own affairs are in that deranged state as to occupy all my thoughts and all my time, in endeavouring to put them in such a situation as will enable me to do equal justice to my Creditors, so far as may be in my power.

I find by the Bankrupt Law, that no person can receive the benefit of it, unless he was actually engaged in trade on the first of June last.[2] This was not my case; for I quitted commerce more than two years ago, upon the dissolution of the Copartnership of Lear & Company. My late partners have taken the benefit of the insolvent law of Maryland; and as I have been a resident in this State, I presume I cannot follow the same course. I have no wish to make the reservation of a cent to myself, either directly or indirectly, out of any property which I possess. My only desire is to do *equal* justice to all to whom I am indebted, as far as my property will go; and to have my person and future earnings secure from these demands; leaving it in my own breast to make full payment at a future day, if I should ever be able; and in that case, I trust my honest inclinations would prompt me to do it.[3] Upon a fair and equitable valuation, I have no doubt but I possess and have interest in property enough to make full payment; but where a sale is forced, it is well known that property will not sell for its value. And, to have incumbrances of this sort hanging upon a person, deprives him of all energy in new pursuits. I cannot, therefore, in justice to yourself and Judge Washington, undertake to bear a part in preparing the History of the General's life, lest, in my present situation, I should be interrupted in the pursuit, without a possibility of my preventing it. If, however, it should be in my power to give any collateral aid in this business, it shall be most readily done; but without an idea of compensation. And at all times, you will find me most ready and willing to give any information which I possess that may be useful towards accomplishing so desireable a work.[4]

I should have had the pleasure of seeing you before this time; but I have lately had a judgement and Execution against me for two thousand dollars, which is yet unsatisfied; and I therefore, conceive that I ought not to leave the State for an hour.

As I never before felt embarrassments of this kind, I am ignorant of the steps which I ought to pursue; and I have no friend at hand sufficiently acquainted therewith to give me advice. As to calling upon a friend for aid, where he may become responsible, it is out of the question with me. If I fall, I will fall alone.

You will pardon me for troubling you with this detail of my affairs, which I should not have ventured to have done, had I not thought it my duty to be candid in explaining the reason for declining a part in a work which it will give me the greatest happiness to see executed with justice; and to aid in which, the whole energy of my soul should have been given, were I free from my present embarrassments. With very great Respect & Regard, I am Dear Sir, Your most obedient Servant

TOBIAS LEAR.

A List of Papers, Books &c. belonging to the late General Washington, contained in a trunk sent to General Marshall, in the City of Washington.[5]

One bundle of papers—Genealogical Tables &c of the Family &c of General George Washington.[6]

One bundle of Parchment, containing old Commissions, and a Journal of a Voyage to Barbadoes.[7]

One bundle of Original Papers relating to the War in 1755 &c. &c.[8]

Four Volumes of Letters and Orders written in 1754, 5, 6, 7 & 8.[9]

One Volume of do—and—do written in 1755 & 6.

One Volume of Letters written from 1767 to 1775.

One Volume of Letters written from 1778 to 1785.

Five Volumes of Letters written from 1785 to 1790.

Fourteen Diaries from No. 1 to No. 14.[10]

Five—ditto—broken numbers.

One—ditto—in loose Sheets.

Twenty two Almanacks, containing various memoranda.[11]

Eight manuscripts, Extracts from several Authors.[12]

*Five small books containing Letters &c. from 1755 to 1758.

    *(N.B. The 4 Vols. first mentioned contain transcripts of these)[13]

Six manuscripts of Arithmetic, Geometry &c.[14]

TOBIAS LEAR.
Mt. Vernon Decr. 10th: 1800

The foregoing are of the earliest dates found among the papers of the late General Washington.

The letters and papers of the General from 1775 to 1783, relating to the Revolutionary War, are in Trunks & Boxes by themselves.[15]

The Official Letters and Records of the Presidency of General Washington, from 1789 to 1797, are also by themselves.[16]

The Diaries are broken & interrupted (much to be regretted).

The Almanacks contain Memoranda which may be useful. Many of them are for that period of the General's life, in which there seems to have been fewer documents than in any other.

The manuscript Extracts are monuments of his Industry and accuracy.

From many of the foregoing but little information is to be expected;
but it was thought best to send them, as some hints, with respect to
dates, occupations &c, may be collected.

T. L.

ALS, Marshall Papers, ViW; ADfS, Benjamin Lincoln Papers, MHi. Cover missing.
There are minor variations between ALS and draft copy. See Lear to JM, 13 Aug.
1803.

1. In his will George Washington gave Walnut Tree Farm as a life estate to Tobias
Lear (1762–1816). It was a part of the larger River Farm, one of the divisions of the
Mount Vernon estate. Washington had bequeathed all of River Farm to his grand-
nephews George Fayette and Charles Augustine Washington, who were also the step-
sons of Lear. They were to come into possession of Walnut Tree Farm upon Lear's
death (Last Will and Testament, 9 July 1799 [John C. Fitzpatrick, ed., *The Writings of
George Washington* (39 vols.; Washington, D.C., 1931–44), XXXVII, 287, 289–90];
Charles W. Stetson, *Washington and His Neighbors* [Richmond, Va., 1956], 93, 138; John
Alexander Carroll and Mary Wells Ashworth, *George Washington*, VII: *First in Peace*
[New York, 1957], 589).

2. See "An Act to establish an uniform System of Bankruptcy throughout the United
States," sec. 1 (*U.S. Statutes at Large*, II, 19–21). The act was passed on 4 Apr. 1800 and
repealed on 19 Dec. 1803 (ibid., 248).

3. In 1793 Lear gave up his position as George Washington's private secretary, which
he had held since 1786, in order to begin a mercantile venture in the District of
Columbia. The firm of Lear and Company purchased several lots, a site for a wharf
and warehouse on the Potomac near the mouth of Rock Creek, and a square in
Georgetown. The company was engaged in the import-export business and for a while
prospered before the collapse of 1797. At the time of its liquidation in 1798, the firm
consisted of Lear, Tristam Dalton, Jonathan Hobson, John Coles, and Robert E. Grif-
fith, the last three of whom were nonresidents of the Federal City. James Greenleaf,
land speculator in the District of Columbia, had also been a partner at the outset. Lear
overcommitted his capital resources with involvement in the Potomack Company and
land transactions at Harper's Ferry, as well as in his company. In 1797, with a balance
of only ninety-eight dollars in the Bank of Alexandria, Lear appealed to George Washington for a loan of three thousand dollars. Washington replied that he could offer
him only a thousand. A year later, Lear resumed his position as aide and private
secretary to Washington. By 1799 Lear's financial difficulties caught up with him and
he defalcated. Hoping to recoup his losses, Lear in the spring of 1801 embarked on a
new career in the consular service under Jefferson's patronage (Douglas Southall Freeman, *George Washington, A Biography*, VI: *Patriot and President* [New York, 1954], 52;
Carroll and Ashworth, *Washington*, VII, 95, 479 and n. 97, 527; Wilhelmus Bogart
Bryan, *A History of the National Capital . . .*, I: *1790–1814* [New York, 1914], 220–21,
221–22 n. 3, 415 and n. 1; Constance McLaughlin Green, *Washington: Village and Capi-
tal, 1800–1878* [Princeton, N.J., 1962], 3, 20, 36; Ray Brighton, *The Checkered Career of
Tobias Lear* [Portsmouth, N.H., 1985], 113–14, 120–23, 141, 146–52, 155–59, 176–81;
Lear to James Madison, 29 May 1801 [Rutland, *Papers of Madison: Sec. of State*, I, 237];
Lear to Benjamin Lincoln, 5 June 1803, Benjamin Lincoln Papers, MHi).

4. Bushrod Washington's original plans for publishing a biography of George Washington included Tobias Lear's participation. In his capacity as private secretary, Lear
had a detailed knowledge of Washington's manuscripts. As the general lay dying, he
had instructed Lear to "'arrange and record all my late military letters and papers.
Arrange my accounts and settle my books, as you know more about them than any one

else.'" Lear spent the day of 24 Dec. 1799 "in looking over & arranging papers in the General's Study." Two days later Bushrod Washington proposed to him that they jointly write a biography of the general, Lear to organize the papers and prepare the manuscript and Washington to participate in the later stages of the work (*Letters and Recollections of George Washington . . . With a Diary of Washington's Last Days, Kept by Mr. Lear*, ed. by Louisa Lear Eyre [New York, 1906], 133, 141; Lear to Alexander Hamilton, 16 Jan. 1800 [Syrett, *Papers of Hamilton*, XXIV, 198–99]; Carroll and Ashworth, *Washington*, VII, 586–87, 623; The Library of Congress, *Index to the George Washington Papers* [Washington, D.C., 1964], "Introduction," by Dorothy S. Eaton, viii and n. 19). For the inclusion of JM in Bushrod's project, see *The Life of George Washington*, editorial note (preceding Preface, [ante 22 Dec. 1803]).

5. This list was made on a separate folded sheet.

6. The George Washington Papers, ser. 4, at the Library of Congress contains a short Washington family chart in George Washington's hand, docketed by him, "Genealogy of the Washington Family in Virginia." A date of 1753 has been attributed to it in the series of the collection.

7. Military commissions are found ibid., ser. 6A, DLC; Washington's journal of his voyage to Barbados in 1751–52 is ibid., ser. 1B, DLC, and has been printed in facsimile in Donald Jackson and Dorothy Twohig, eds., *The Diaries of George Washington* (6 vols.; Charlottesville, Va., 1976–79), I, 38–117.

8. Military papers relating to the French and Indian War are in the Washington Papers, ser. 6A, DLC; Washington's general correspondence, sent and received, along with some other autograph documents including military papers, is arranged chronologically in ser. 4. Washington's papers are being published in the series *The Papers of George Washington* (Charlottesville, Va., 1983–), ed. by W. W. Abbot et al., in three separate chronological sets: *Colonial Series* (Charlottesville, Va., 1983–); *Revolutionary War Series* (Charlottesville, Va., 1985–); and *Presidential Series* (Charlottesville, Va., 1987–).

9. See below where Lear identifies these as transcripts. They are copies of Washington's letters and orders from Aug. 1754 through the end of 1758. These letterbooks are in ser. 2, vols. I, III, IV, and V, and are copies transcribed by one of Washington's private secretaries at a later time from Washington's original, contemporaneous letterbooks, only two of which are extant. For a description of the original and transcript letterbooks and their provenance, see Abbot, *Papers of Washington: Col. Ser.*, I, xvii–xix, 236–40.

10. Most of the extant diaries are in the Washington Papers, ser. 1B, DLC. A few other journals or fragments are located in other depositories or in printed sources. All the presently known diaries are printed in Jackson and Twohig, *Diaries of Washington*. For a current list with locations of the originals, see ibid., I, xliv–xlvi. Included in these are the "Almanacks," listed below, in which Washington at different periods in his life kept his diaries. Washington's first journal is of his journey across the Blue Ridge Mountains on a surveying trip in Mar.–Apr. 1748 for Lord Fairfax (ibid., 6–23). His last diary entry was made on 13 Dec. 1799, the day before his death (ibid., VI, 378–79). For some of the intervening years no diaries exist. They either are missing or were never kept. Because of careless handling of Washington's papers from the time of his death until George Corbin Washington sold them in 1834 and 1849 to the federal government, an exact correlation of the number of extant diaries with the total of forty-two listed here by Lear is impossible. The diaries and other papers passed through the hands of a series of caretakers, beginning with Lear and Martha Washington, then Bushrod Washington, JM, Jared Sparks, and finally George Corbin Washington. During this period numerous letters, pages, and fragments were extracted from Washington's papers and handed out to relatives, friends, autograph collectors, and former correspondents of Washington seeking missing copies of their own letters.

Jackson and Twohig list fifty-one separate diaries or fragments; John C. Fitzpatrick in his edition of the diaries over sixty years ago arrived at the number of forty-four. Deducted from both counts should be the 1754 journal of Washington's military expedition to the Ohio against the French, who published Washington's captured manuscript, along with other documents, in 1756. The original of Washington's journal has been lost since then and would not have been among those diaries sent by Lear to JM. Roughly, the periods covered by known diaries are the 1760s and early 1770s to mid-1775, the 1780s, and the retirement years of 1797–99. By Washington's own comment, he appears not to have kept a journal during the Revolutionary War years until the closing months in 1781. The times during his presidency for which there are no diaries are Feb.–Sept. 1789, mid-1791 to Apr. 1795, except for one brief journal, and the second half of 1796 (*Index to Washington Papers*, viii–xv; Jackson and Twohig, *Diaries of Washington*, I, xli–xlvi, 166–73; III, 338, 356; John C. Fitzpatrick, ed., *The Diaries of George Washington, 1748–1799* [4 vols.; Boston, 1925], I, xv–xviii; see Lear to JM, 13 Aug. 1803; JM to Benjamin Lincoln, 21 Nov. 1803).

JM definitely received some journals for the presidential years. He quoted Washington's diary entry from 16 Apr. 1789, upon his leaving Mount Vernon to assume his position as president (*Life*, V, 154). And JM's son John Marshall practiced his signature on the endpapers of the 30 Sept.–20 Oct. 1794 journal (concerning Washington's journey with the militia to western Pennsylvania to suppress the Whiskey Rebellion). The boy also used some of the blank pages of that journal as an exercise book, into which he copied Latin passages (Washington Papers, ser. 1B, DLC).

11. Beginning in 1760 Washington began to interleave entries in the *Virginia Almanack*, published annually in Williamsburg, and he continued this practice until 1775. From 1795 through 1798 he resumed using almanacs, the *American Repository of Useful Information* (Philadelphia) and *Brigg's Virginia and Maryland Almanac* . . . (Alexandria) (Fitzpatrick, *Diaries of Washington*, I, xv–xviii; Jackson and Twohig, *Diaries of Washington*, I, xli–xlii; VI, 199).

12. Washington Papers, ser. 8D, DLC. These are Washington's notes and extracts, taken primarily from treatises on husbandry. Washington also made an abstract of the first volume of Guillaume T. F. Raynal, *A Philosophical and Political History of the Settlements and Trade of the Europeans in the East and West Indies*; extracts from LePage du Pratz, *The History of Louisiana*; and a copy of James Madison's "Notes on Ancient and Modern Confederacies" (see Rutland, *Papers of Madison*, IX, 3–22 and n.).

13. See n. 9.

14. Washington Papers, ser. 1A, DLC. There are now three bound schoolwork copybooks, the earliest manuscripts among Washington's papers, ca. 1744–48. They contain exercises in mathematics and surveying and examples of a variety of forms. For a description, see Abbot, *Papers of Washington: Col. Ser.*, I, 1–4.

15. Apparently not sent to JM at this time but probably included in what Bushrod Washington forwarded to JM in the summer or fall of 1801. On 21 Nov. 1801, Washington informed Alexander Hamilton, "I sent to Richmond about four months ago all the trunks of papers which I received from Mount Vernon except two" (Syrett, *Papers of Hamilton*, XXV, 432–33; see also JM to Benjamin Lincoln, 21 Nov. 1803). The trunks of Revolutionary War papers would have contained the Varick transcripts of George Washington's letters and orders (Washington Papers, ser. 3, DLC), made under the supervision of Lt. Col. Richard Varick during the war, and the originals of these as well as incoming correspondence, other documents, and military papers (ibid., ser. 4, 5, and 6, DLC; see *Index to Washington Papers*, v–vi; Abbot, *Papers of Washington: Rev. Ser.*, I, xvii–xx).

16. Washington Papers, ser. 2, 4, and 7, DLC. Not sent to JM at this time. He told his publisher, Caleb P. Wayne, on 23 [22] Dec. 1803 that "the trunks containing the papers relative to the civil administration have reachd me only this week."

To Charles Cotesworth Pinckney

My dear Sir   Washington Decr. 18th. 1800

According to our present inteligence Mr. Jefferson & Mr. Burr have an equal number of votes & of consequence the house of representatives must chuse between them. It is extremely uncertain on whom the choice will fall. Having myself no voice in the election, & in fact scarcely any wish concerning it, I do not intermeddle with it, but I hear what is said by others, & witness the anxiety of parties. Once more I suspect the contest (shoud one be made) will be decided by South Carolina. So far as I am enabled now to conjecture I think the person for whom your state votes will be President. Indeed if it shoud be decidedly for Mr. Jefferson I doubt whether Mr. Burr will not surrender so far as he can surrender all his pretensions to the office.

In the chagrin which I experiencd under our late defeat I had drawn much consolation from the opinion that the federalists throughout the continent had been faithful to themselves & to each other. I am extremely mortified to learn that this has not been completely the case. I beleive a Mr. Manton of Rhode Island threw away a vote.[1] This is attributed in the letters from that State to Genl. Hamiltons pamphlet—but certainly the cause did not justify the effect.

The treaty with France is before the Senate. Many of that body appear to be by no means satisfied with it. I greatly suspect that an unconditional ratification will not be advisd.[2]

Mr. Ellsworth has resignd his seat as chief justice & Mr. Jay has been nominated in his place. Shoud he as is most probable decline the office I fear the President will nominate the senior Judge.[3]

I shall return to Richmond on the 3d. of March to recommence practice as a lawyer. If my present wish can succeed so far as respects myself I shall never again fill any political station whatever.

Present me respectfully to Mrs. Pinckney. I am dear Sir with much esteem & affection, your obedt. Servt

J Marshall

ALS, Pinckney Family Papers, DLC.

1. This was apparently Simeon Martin, a Federalist merchant from Newport. He threw away his vote for Pinckney (on the Federalist ticket with Adams), apparently voting for John Jay (David Hackett Fischer, *The Revolution of American Conservatism: The Federalist Party in the Era of Jeffersonian Democracy* [New York, 1965], 281; Manning J. Dauer, *The Adams Federalists* [Baltimore, 1953], 257 [Table 12]).

2. President Adams submitted the convention with France on 15 Dec. The Senate advised a conditional ratification on 2 Feb. See *ASP, Foreign Relations*, II, 295–345.

3. The "senior Judge" was William Cushing.

To John Jay

Sir   Department of State Decr. 22d. 1800

The President, anxious to avail the United States of your services as chief Justice, has nominated you to the senate for that important office, now vacant by the resignation of Mr. Ellesworth.

In the hope that you may be prevaild on to accept it, I feel peculiar satisfaction in transmitting to you the commission. With very much respect & esteem, I am Sir your obedt. servt.

J MARSHALL

ALS, ICN. Endorsed by Jay. Copy of enclosed commission, dated 19 Dec. 1800, RG 59, DNA.

From Robert Craig

Dear sir   Manchr. 22d Decmr 1800

I have been told you are very disireous of disposing of your Buckingham Land & negroes, should that be the Case—I am willing to give you an Exchang for property in Richmond & manchester which Commands an anuall rent of £600—& I will venture to say as advantagausly Situated as any property on Either Side of the River. I shall say nothing further respecting my own property untill, I know if it will be agreable to you to make the Exchange. I can recomend you to Wm Claiborne Esqr in Manchester[1] to give you the nessary information respecting the Vallue of my property & the Situation of it—be good Enough to say on receipt of this, what you think respecting it.[2] I am Dear sir, your most Ob Svt

ROBERT CRAIG

ALS, ViHi. Addressed by Craig to JM in Washington; postmarked by hand "Manchs/ Decr 23."

1. This was apparently the William Claiborne (d. 1809) whose son, William C. C. Claiborne, later became governor of the Mississippi Territory (Richmond *Enquirer*, 5 Oct. 1809).

2. JM forwarded this letter to Edward Carrington on 28 Dec. On JM's Buckingham land, see also Bill in Chancery, 28 Jan. 1803; JM to William Bernard, 8 Sept. 1803, 17 Jan. 1804.

To John Adams

Sir   Decr. 24th 1800
   I have been requested to make to you the application of Mr. DAmbrugeac to provide for him a passage to France. He says that he has not been furnishd with money by Genl. Toussaint for that object.[1]
   I set out to wait on you but have been stopt til it is too late. As he wishes to set out tomorrow I communicate his request in writing.
   I do not pretend to express any opinion on the subject but think it my duty to lay the request before you. With the most entire respect, I remain Sir, your obedt. Servt.

                                                          J MARSHALL.

ALS, Adams Papers, MHi.

   1. Dambrugeac carried dispatches from Toussaint to the French government. His passage was delayed until Mar. 1801 (*Naval Documents: Quasi-War*, VII, 141, 147).

From Timothy Pickering

(private)
Dear Sir,   Easton[1] Decr. 27. 1800.
   On my return lately from the Woods, I found, among other letters received in my absence one dated the 22d. of April, from Mr. King, which tho' marked "private and personal" I think it proper to transmit to you: The *subject* being wholly of a public nature. I must nevertheless presume, that after hearing of my removal, he must have written a similar letter to you; seeing the contents were designed for the President's information. But however this may be, I must request you, agreeably to Mr. King's desire, "not to consider his letter to me as belonging to your office; or in any respect as a public communication."[2] I have the honor to be with great respect & esteem, Dear Sir, Your obt. servant

                                                          TIMOTHY PICKERING.

ADfS, Pickering Papers, MHi.

   1. Pickering and his family had temporarily settled in Pennsylvania.
   2. For the letter from King, see *PJM*, IV, 136–37. JM returned the letter on 18 Jan. 1801.

To John Quincy Adams

Sir   Washington Decr. 28th. 1800

I am requested by the family of Mr. Littlepage an American who has excited some attention both in Europe & the United States, to transmit you the inclosd & to ask the favor of you to make some enquiries concerning him.[1]

No certain inteligence from him has I beleive been receivd since the King of Poland was deposd. The general conjecture has for some time been that he is dead. Shoud this be the fact it is desirable that it shoud be known.[2] With very much respect & consideration, I am Sir your Obedt. Servt

J MARSHALL

ALS, Adams Papers, MHi. Addressed by JM to Adams in Berlin. Endorsed by Adams as received 16 Apr. and answered 18 Apr. 1801. Sent by way of Hamburg and endorsed by U.S. consul Joseph Pitcairn, "Recd opend."

1. Enclosure not with the letter. Lewis Littlepage (1762–1802) was a soldier of fortune, who in 1786 became chamberlain to King Stanislaus of Poland. His family in Virginia had presumed him dead and was suing for his portion of the family estate (Curtis Carroll Davis, *The King's Chevalier: A Biography of Lewis Littlepage* [Indianapolis, Ind., 1961], 366–91; Nell Holladay Boand, *Lewis Littlepage* [Richmond, Va., 1970], 268–90).

2. In his reply of 18 Apr. (received by James Madison), Adams reported that Littlepage was about to embark for home (Rutland, *Papers of Madison: Sec. of State*, I, 104).

To Edward Carrington

Dear Sir   Washington Decr. 28th. 1800

I am extremely desirous of selling my Buckingham land for the purpose of enabling me to raise money to pay for the Fairfax purchase.[1]

It is divisible into two parts each of which may again be subdivided into two parts. Eppersons plantation comprehending the land south of bear branch & of snoddys spring branch contains about 1600 acres. For this my price is 50/ per acre. For the whole tract I will take 40/ per acre.[2]

I inclose you a proposition receivd from Mr. Craig.[3] I have referd him to you. I hope you will excuse this trouble. Mr. Hopkins[4] on whose friendship I am accustomd to rely for things of this sort is in a state of distress which disinclines me to apply to him. As I shall have to sell the property again, its selling price must be regarded in any exchange which may be made. Copland[5] is in possession of a bond given by my brother & myself for £3800 payable with interest from the date in three years. If he woud purchase any of the property with that bond I woud consider it as cash. You will much oblige me by writing on this subject.

It is understood that the votes for Mr. Jefferson & Colo. Burr are equal—tho there is a report that New York has given Burr a majority of two votes.

In the event of equality it is extremely doubtful who will be the President. I take no part & feel no interest in the decision. I consider it as a choice of evils & I really am uncertain which woud be the greatest. So far as I can learn however from what passes around me I really think the probability in favor of Burr. It is not beleivd that he woud weaken the vital parts of the constitution, nor is it beleivd that he has any undue foreign attachments. These opinions incline many who greatly disapprove of him yet to prefer him to the other gentleman who is offerd to their choice.

I have only to wish that the best for our common country may be done but I really do not know what that best is.

I hope it will be practicable for me to be in Richmond in February but I am not certain that I shall not be compeld to remain til the 3d. of march at this place. I am dear Sir with much esteem & affection, your Obedt. Servt.

J MARSHALL.

ALS, Pequot Library Collection, CtY. Addressed by JM to Carrington in Richmond and franked.

1. On the Fairfax purchase, see *PJM*, II, 140–49.
2. JM is listed on an 1800 Buckingham County tax list as having one white male tithable (his son, Jacquelin A.) and as owning nine horses, ten slave tithables, and two slaves between the ages of twelve and sixteen. The list indicates that this information was reported by "Apperson," probably John Epperson (Edythe Rucker Whitley, *Genealogical Records of Buckingham County, Virginia* [Berryville, Va., 1984], 37, 133–34).
3. Craig to JM, 22 Dec. and n. 2.
4. John Hopkins, a Richmond merchant and law client of JM's (*PJM*, V, 534–35).
5. Charles Copland, a Richmond attorney.

From Thomas Jefferson

Sir   Washington Dec. 28. 1800.

I have the honor to inform you that a list of the votes for President & Vice-president of the US. has come to my hands from every state of the union; and consequently that no special messenger to any of them need be provided by the department of state.[1] I have the honor to be with great respect Sir, Your most obedt. humble servt

TH: JEFFERSON

ALS (press copy), Jefferson Papers, DLC. Endorsed by Jefferson on verso: "Marshall John. Dec. 28. 1800."

1. Jefferson alluded to the 1792 law concerning the election of the president and vice president. Section 4 provided that if a list of votes had not been received at the seat of government by the first Wednesday in January, then the secretary of state was to send a special messenger to the district judge (who was to keep such a list) in each of the states (*U.S. Statutes at Large*, I, 240).

To Alexander Hamilton

Dear Sir   Jany 1st. 1801

I receivd this morning your letter of the 26th of Decr.[1] It is I beleive certain that Jefferson & Burr will come to the house of representatives with equal votes. The returns have been all receivd & this is the general opinion.

Being no longer in the house of representatives, & consequently compeld by no duty to decide between them, my own mind had scarcely determind to which of these gentlemen the preference was due. To Mr. Jefferson whose political character is better known than that of Mr. Burr, I have felt almost insuperable objections. His foreign prejudices seem to me totally to unfit him for the chief magistracy of a nation which cannot indulge those prejudices without sustaining deep & permanent injury. In addition to this solid & immoveable objection Mr. Jefferson appears to me to be a man who will embody himself with the house of representatives. By weakening the office of President he will increase his personal power. He will diminish his responsability, sap the fundamental principles of the government & become the leader of that party which is about to constitute the majority of the legislature. The Morals of the Author of the letter to Mazzei cannot be pure.[2]

With these impressions concerning Mr. Jefferson I was in some degree disposd to view with less apprehension any other character, & to consider the alternative now offerd us as a circumstance not to be entirely neglected.

Your representation of Mr. Burr with whom I am totally unacquainted shows that from him still greater danger than even from Mr. Jefferson may be apprehended.[3] Such a man as you describe is more to be feard & may do more immediate if not greater mischief.

Beleiving that you know him well & are impartial my preference woud certainly not be for him—but I can take no part in this business. I cannot bring my self to aid Mr. Jefferson. Perhaps respect for myself shoud in my present situation deter me from using any influence (if indeed I possessd any) in support of either gentleman. Altho no consideration coud induce me to be the secretary of State while there was a President whose political system I beleivd to be at variance with my own, yet this cannot be so well known to others & it might be suspected that a desire to be well with the successful candidate had in some degree governd my conduct.

With you I am in favor of ratifying our treaty with france tho' I am far very far from approving it. There is however one principle which I think it right to explain.

Our Envoys were undoubtedly of opinion that our prior treaty with Britain woud retain its stipulated advantages & I think that opinion correct. Was our convention with any other nation than France I shoud feel no sollicitude on this subject. But France, the most encroaching nation on earth, will claim a literal interpretation & our people will decide in her favor. Those who coud contend that a promise not to permit privatiers of the enemy of France to be fitted out in our ports amounted to a grant of that privilege to France woud not hesitate to contend that a stipulation giving to France on the subject of privatiers & prizes the privileges of the most favord nation placd her on equal ground with any other nation whatever. In consequence of this temper in our own country I think the ratification of the treaty ought to be accompanied with a declaration of the sense in which it is agreed to.[4] This however is only my own opinion. With very much respect & esteem, I am dear sir your Obedt

J MARSHALL

ALS, Hamilton Papers, DLC. Endorsed by Hamilton.

1. Letter not found.

2. JM alluded to Jefferson's letter to Philip Mazzei, 24 Apr. 1796, which the recipient, after translating it into Italian, published in a Florence newspaper; the Paris *Moniteur* then printed a French translation of the Italian version. An English translation from the *Moniteur* eventually appeared in American newspapers, provoking much partisan commentary. In the letter Jefferson spoke of "'an Anglican monarchical, & aristocratical party . . . whose avowed object is to draw over us the substance, as they have already done the forms of the British government'" (see Dumas Malone, *Jefferson and the Ordeal of Liberty* [Boston, 1962], 267–68, 302–7). JM commented on the Mazzei letter in the appendix to the last volume of the *Life* (vol. V, app., 36). The letter was published with a more extensive commentary in the second edition (vol. II, app., 23–32).

3. Hamilton was writing to a number of Federalists at this time urging them to support Jefferson over Burr (Syrett, *Papers of Hamilton*, XXV, 258n).

4. JM referred to article 6 of the convention, which stipulated that the vessels of the

two nations, and their privateers as well as prizes, should be granted most-favored-nation status. By the Treaty of 1794 with Great Britain, on the other hand, it was unlawful for foreign privateers to be armed and provisioned in the ports of either country. That treaty further provided that while the two countries remained friendly, neither party would make any treaty inconsistent with the article concerning foreign privateers (Miller, *Treaties*, 262). On this point, see American Envoys to JM, 4 Oct. 1800 (*PJM*, IV, 319).

President Adams had submitted the convention to the Senate on 15 Dec. without comment, having decided not to use the draft of a message prepared by JM. The draft reads: "I understand it to be a principle of the law of nations universally understood, that, if in a subsequent treaty, there be stipulations contradictory to those containd in a prior treaty, those subsequent stipulations are to be considerd as containing a reservation of the rights previously granted to another nation. Altho this be a general rule yet it appears most safe to express it, & therefore if the senate should advise its ratification without modification I shall deem it proper to explain the sense in which the agreement is formd." Adams did make this point in a subsequent message to the Senate on 21 Jan. (draft of message, [Nov.–Dec. 1800], Adams Papers, MHi; *ASP, Foreign Relations*, II, 295).

To Unknown

[Washington, 2 January 1801]

Mr. Foster[1] has transmitted to me a certificate of the select men of the town of Springfield concerning John Gardener an impressed American Seaman which had been inclosed to him by you.[2]

To succeed in the application for his liberation it is necessary to produce an affidavit or affidavits stating his birth & describing his person so that the identity of the individual whose liberation is demanded may appear.

Being truly sollicitous to render as early as possible every service in my power to our impressed seamen, I take the liberty to give you this information in the hope that you will aid in furnishing the necessary documents.

Printed, Thomas F. Matigan, Inc., Catalog (New York, n.d.). Dated 2 Jan. 1800 in catalog (probably so dated in original) but should be 1801. Described as one-page ALS.

1. Probably Sen. Dwight Foster of Massachusetts.

2. The name of a John Gardiner was on the list of impressed seamen enclosed in JM to Benjamin Lincoln, 30 Oct. 1800 (*PJM*, IV, 335).

From John Jay

Sir   albany 2 Jany. 1801
   I recd. Yesterday the polite Letter wh. you did me the Honor to write on the 22d. ult: enclosing a Commission whereby the Presidt., with the advice and Consent of the Senate, has been pleased to appoint me ch. Justice of the United States. I am very sensible of the Honor done me by this appointmt. but (independent of other Considerations) the Incompetency of my Health to the fatigues incident to the office, forms an insuperable objection to my accepting it.[1] With Sentiments of Respect & Esteem I have the Honor to be Sir, your most obt. Sevt

P.S. I return the commission herewith inclosed.

  AL (copy), ICN. Endorsed by Jay.

   1. In a letter to President Adams the same day, Jay set forth the "other Considerations" preventing him from accepting the appointment—namely, the unlikely prospect of a reform of the judiciary (Adams Papers, MHi).

To Rufus King

Dear Sir: Department of State, Washington Jan'y 3rd. 1801
   This will be presented to you by Mr Curwen[1] the agent of Mr Stephen Gerard who goes to England for the purpose of expiditing the Trial of an appeal from a sentence of the court of Vice Admiralty in Halifax condemning the brig Sally and her cargo as being enemy property. This extraordinary sentence turns on the character of Mr Gerard who was born a frenchman. He became however a citizen of the United States before our Treaty with Great Britain which acknowledged our independence and was an inhabitant of our country before that independence was declared. This case therefore appears to be so entirely free from all those circumstances which could be disputable, that I know not how to doubt its issue. Mr Gerard is particularly anxious for dispatch. Any aid you can give him consistently with propriety will be an acceptable service to your country.[2] I am, etc.

J MARSHALL

  Letterbook copy, RG 59, DNA; copy, Girard Papers, PPAmP.

   1. Joseph Curwen (L. H. Butterfield, ed., *Letters of Benjamin Rush* [2 vols.; Princeton, N.J., 1951], II, 1082 n. 3).

2. King presented Girard's case to Lord Hawkesbury on 6 Mar 1801 (Charles R. King, ed., *The Life and Correspondence of Rufus King* [6 vols.; New York, 1894–1900], III, 397–98).

To David Humphreys

(No. 4.)

Sir   Department of State Jany 5th. 1801

In my letters on the subject of depredations commited by Spanish privatiers on american commerce I have as much as possible avoided mentioning particular cases.[1] I have been inducd to observe this line of conduct by the opinion, that his Catholic majesty coud not hesitate to accede to the proposition for appointing a board of commissioners with powers to ascertain the amount of these depredations; & that the government of Spain woud pay the sums so ascertaind.

This opinion is still entertaind. If the claims of justice are to be attended to, or if a good understanding with the United States be worth preserving, Spain cannot be inattentive to our remonstrances on this subject.

As however there may be some delay in agreeing on the mode of a general settlement of claims, it is thought not improper to ask your attention to some particular cases provided they can be attended to without impairing the force of the application for an arrangement which may embrace the whole, & afford compensation for the long catalogue of injuries of which we have complaind.

The case of Mr. Preble owner of the ship Eliza is so well known to you as to render it unnecessary for me to give a statement of it.[2]

The case of the Messrs. Fishers is also well known to you.[3]

These gentlemen have applied for the interposition of government in a particular manner in their favor, & their cases seem to us of such a complection as to render it impossible to decline this interposition.

These captures & condemnations, as well as very many others, seem to us entirely without apology, & such as only a state of open war coud excuse.

I have therefore to request that you will render to these claims all the support in your power; & endeavor without impeding an arrangement for a general settlement, to obtain compensation for the losses they have sustaind.[4] I am Sir with very much respect your obedt Servt

                                                J MARSHALL

ALS, Collection of André de Coppet, NjP; letterbook copy, RG 59, DNA. ALS endorsed by Humphreys, "Ansd. March 3d."

1. See JM to Humphreys, 8 Sept., 23 Sept. 1800 (*PJM*, IV, 266–73, 298–302).
2. Henry Preble to JM, 2 Jan. 1801 (App. I, Cal.).
3. Samuel and Miers Fisher to JM, 23 Dec. 1800 and n. 1 (App. I, Cal.).
4. Humphreys acknowledged receipt of JM's letter in a postscript (dated 3 Mar. 1801) to his dispatch of 2 Mar. 1801 (App. II, List).

To Benjamin Williams

Sir   Dept. of State Jany. 5th. 1801

I have just receivd your letter of the 27th. of Decr.[1] inclosing the copy of a resolution of the General assembly of North Carolina with respect to the extension of the boundary line between that State & the Indians.

As the subject to which this resolution & your letter relate, does not belong to the department of State, but to that of war it is not in my power to act decisively on the case. So soon as a Secretary of war shall be appointed in the place of Mr. Dexter,[2] I will deliver to him your letter with its enclosure, & will with much satisfaction, give any aid which it may be in my power to give, towards promoting the wishes of the State of North Carolina.

Your letter to my predecessor was transmitted to the department of war by him. Had it remaind in this office be assurd Sir I shoud not have neglected it. With very much respect I am Sir, your Obedt. Servt

J MARSHALL

ALS, Nc-Ar. Addressed by JM to Governor Williams in Raleigh and franked; postmarked Washington, 6 Jan.

1. Williams to JM, 27 Dec. (App. I, Cal.).
2. Samuel Dexter, formerly secretary of war, had been appointed secretary of the treasury in place of Wolcott. Roger Griswold of Connecticut was confirmed as Dexter's replacement on 3 Feb. (*Senate Executive Journal*, I, 363–64, 375).

From George Mathews

Dear Sir,   Chilicothe January 10th. 1801

Waiting Six or Seven weeks for Letters from the New England Mississippi Land Company the Severe weather has prevented me setting out for the Natches until April, together with my attending to my

Lands in the Northwestern Territory which is at low merket when sold for taxes, not giving more than a Cent per Acre. If so much time can be Spared from the duties of your Office as to inform me of the fate of Mr. Wickham's Attachment and Mr. Nelson's Appeal,[1] it will much oblige me; and whether you intend to remain in Office under Mr. Jefferson, and what effect his appointment appears to have on his adherents. You will much oblige me by informing me what prospect there is of the State of Georgia ceding her Lands to Congress, and if the Commissioners have reported on the Claims of the Companies.[2]

Shoud Governor Sergeant not be thought of to be reappointed to the government of the Mississippi Territory, the appointment will be grateful to me; and I have full confidence in your wishes to serve me: and Surely the real republica will respect the Service of a man that has devoted eight years of the prime of his life to the Service of his Country, and bled from five Wounds, to say nothing of private losses.[3] I am, Dr. Sir with much esteem, Your real Friend

GEO MATHEWS

N.B. Please direct to Danville Kentucky any Letters you may send.

ALS, RG 59, DNA.

1. John Wickham and William Nelson were Richmond lawyers. One of the cases mentioned may be the chancery suit between Robert Bunn, surviving partner of John Hyndman & Co., and Sampson Mathews and others (including George Mathews) in the U.S. circuit court at Richmond. A decree was rendered in this suit at the Nov. 1800 term (U.S. Cir. Ct., Va., Ord. Bk. III, 430–32).

2. JM had recently been appointed a commissioner under a 1798 act for settling limits with the state of Georgia and authorizing the establishment of government in the Mississippi Territory. Under this act commissioners appointed by the U.S. were to meet with commissioners appointed by Georgia to determine the interfering claims of the U.S. and that state and to receive proposals for the cession of the whole or part of the territory claimed by the state (*U.S. Statutes at Large*, I, 549–50; *Senate Executive Journal*, I, 356).

3. Mathews (1739–1812) was born in Augusta County. After serving as an officer in the Virginia line of the Continental army, he moved to Georgia in the 1780s, becoming governor in 1787 and representing the state in the First Congress, 1789–91. He again served as governor from 1793 to 1796 at the time of the Yazoo land scandal. President Adams nominated him as the first governor of the Mississippi Territory in 1798 but later withdrew his name.

From Edward Thornton

Sir,   Washington 12th January 1801.

About the month of August last, a British Ship called the *Ranger* (the real name of which was the *Three Brothers*) arrived in the port of Alexandria, having been piratically carried off by the Captain from the legitimate owner, Mr Barlow of Gibraltar; and on account of the defect of her papers and other suspicious appearances was seized in that port by the Collector of the Customs. The circumstances of the piratical capture were proved in the Court of Admiralty on the institution of a libel against the vessel by a Citizen of the United States, who had some claims against the Captain:[1] and since the dismission of the libel, the details of which I understand have been transmitted to you, Sir, by the Attorney of the United States for the district of Virginia, the Ship has remained in the hands of the Collector until some legal claimant shall appear.

As the true proprietor has no representative in this country, it becomes my duty to request that you will have the goodness to procure an order through the Secretary of Treasury to the Collector, for the delivery of this vessel and her tackle to James Patton Esqre. acting at Alexandria under the orders of His Majesty's Consul for Virginia, that she may be disposed of for the benefit of the lawful owner. And I take the liberty of adding my hope that this may be done with as little delay as practicable; as the expences that have been incurred since her seizure are now accumulating to such a sum, that a very little time will render it a matter of prudential consideration with His Majesty's Consul, whether he ought to burthen himself with a property, the sale of which will perhaps scarcely re-imburse the charges incurred, and from which consequently the proprietor will derive little or no advantage. I have the honour to be with perfect truth and respect, Sir, Your most obedient, humble servant.

                                        EDWD. THORNTON.

ALS, RG 59, DNA. Endorsed by JM.

1. The captain of the ship was Elihu Marchant, who at the Nov. 1800 term of the U.S. circuit court in Richmond was indicted and found guilty of piracy. Sentenced to imprisonment for two years, Marchant was later pardoned by President Jefferson (U.S. Cir. Ct., Va., Ord. Bk. III, 427, 429, 442; Rutland, *Papers of Madison: Sec. of State*, I, 321–22 and n. 1).

To Roger Griswold

Sir   Department of State Jany. 15th. 1801

In compliance with your wish I now submit to you the estimate on which so large an appropriation on account of fulfilling the engagements of the United States with the mediterranean powers, was requested for the year 1801.[1]

Our consul at Algiers states that the annuity payable to that Regency is now in arrear two years, & the third will become due in the course of the year 1801. The annuity has been calculated at eighty thousand dollars.

In addition to this it is usual to make a biennial present of about the value of ten thousand dollars which present is to be receivd in the course of the present year.

We were too on the 8th. day of October 1800 indebted to the Bacris a commercial house at Algiers, in the sum of $38,886.51.

On the change of a consul presents are made to the amount of about twenty thousand dollars. Mr. O'Brine has demanded his recall in positive terms. Shoud he persist in this demand the consul who takes his place must carry with him the presents usual on such occasions.[2]

To complete the stipulated Regalia to Tunis will require thirty thousand dollars.

There may then be necessary for the year 1801

Three years annuity to Algiers at $80000—	$ 240 000
The biennial present—	10,000
Due the Bocris—	38,886.51
	288,886.51

I have not included in this sum the Consular present because I am not certain that it will be requird, nor the debt to Tunis because the former appropriations unexpended will leave no very considerable part of it unsatisfied.

I am not sure that good policy requires absolute punctuality with Algiers, but I beleive the annuities ought not to accumulate too considerably & that the government ought to be in a situation to act in this respect as circumstances may make necessary.

Under this impression I have beleivd that the appropriation of a less sum than has been requested coud not safely be askd for.[3] I am Sir with very much respect, your Obedt. Servt.

J MARSHALL

ALS, CtY. Cover missing but recipient identified by depository as Griswold (see n. 1).

1. Griswold, a member of Congress from Connecticut, was then chairman of the House Ways and Means Committee and soon to be named secretary of war. On 5 Jan. he presented an appropriations bill for the support of government (*Annals of Congress*, X, 877–78).

2. Richard O'Brien remained consul until Nov. 1803.

3. Congress appropriated $256,000 for "fulfilling the engagements of the United States with the Mediterranean powers" (*U.S. Statutes at Large*, II, 120).

From Timothy Pickering

Dear Sir,   Philadelphia Jany. 15. 1801.

Mr. Joseph Iznardy, acting-consul for Cadiz, has desired me to express to you my sentiments concerning his official conduct.

The complaints against him being numerous, I was sometimes apprehensive that they could not be wholly unfounded. Yet it was evident enough that many of them proceeded from the enmity of Mr. John M. Pintard, whose projects Mr. Iznardy had thwarted. And Chandler Price,[1] an intelligent merchant of this city, who resided some time at Cadiz, bore such honourable testimony of the rectitude, diligence and zeal of Mr. Iznardy, as removed, at the time, every unfavourable impression concerning him.

Many American captains, *in these modern times,* have been too apt to expect & demand unreasonable attentions and indulgences; and a Consul having firmness enough to resist their demands, would not fail to incur their displeasure. These repulses would naturally excite in such men, a deportment *not very courteous*; and when manifested toward a consul of much sensibility (or, as Mr. Iznardy says of himself, having a good deal of "*pepper*" in his constitution) would unavoidably produce asperities, and perhaps mutual reproaches.

Mr. Iznardy's resolution in coming to America, to face the complaints of his Accusers, is a strong evidence of his innocence; and upon the whole, I am disposed to believe him worthy of the station he has filled, during the absence of his son, the Consul.[2] I have the honour to be, with much respect & esteem, Dear Sir, your obt. servant,

TIMOTHY PICKERING

ADfS, Pickering Papers, MHi.

1. On Chandler Price, see Price to JM, 20 Jan. 1801 and n. 1 (App. I, Cal.).

2. Yznardy acted in place of his son, Joseph M. Yznardy, who had been appointed U.S. consul at Cádiz in Feb. 1793. On 18 Feb. President Adams nominated Henry Preble as consul at Cádiz, but the Senate did not act on the appointment. The consul-

ship remained unfilled until Jan. 1802, when President Jefferson appointed the elder Yznardy (*Senate Executive Journal*, I, 131, 381, 403; Rutland, *Papers of Madison: Sec. of State*, I, 31, 32 n. 2).

To Samuel Dexter

Sir   Washington Jany. 16th. 1801
    The right of Arnold Henry Dohrman to one town ship of land accrued under a resolution of Congress which passd the 1st. of October 1787.[1]
    Concerning his title there is not I beleive a single doubt.
    It does not however appear to have been the sense of the legislature that the executive coud issue patents in cases not directed by an act of Congress. There have therefore been particular acts directing patents in all cases where titles have accrued under the present Government. In the case of the society of the United Brethren for propagating the gospel among the heathen, which strongly resembles this, it was deemd necessary to pass a particular act authorizing the issuing a patent.[2]
    As there is I beleive no instance in which the President has issued a patent by virtue of his general executive authority & as there is no law authorizing him to issue one in this case I think it necessary that an act for that purpose shoud pass. I am Sir with much respect, your Obedt. Servt

J MARSHALL

ALS, RG 233, DNA. Cover missing but addressee identified by internal evidence (see n. 1).

1. This letter and other papers relating to Dohrman's claim were transmitted on 19 Jan. by treasury secretary Samuel Dexter to Nathaniel Macon, chairman of the House Committee on Claims (RG 233, DNA).

2. Macon presented a bill for the relief of Dohrman on 23 Feb., which was approved on 27 Feb. In 1817 Congress granted further relief to Dohrman's widow (*Annals of Congress*, X, 1050, 1552; *ASP, Claims*, 508–14).

To Rufus King

(No 10)
Dear Sir,   Department of State, Jany 18. 1801
    On the surrender of Curraçoa to the English, there were in that port several American vessels, whose owners complain heavily of the treatment they have experienced.

It is certain that the property and the place were saved from the French by the exertions of two ships of war belonging to the United States, and by the crews of some American merchant-men, who were willing to encounter the hazard of war in order to obtain ultimately security for their lives and their property from the dangers to which both would have been exposed had the French invaders succeeded. These exertions have put into the possession of the English the Island of Curaçao—for themselves the merchant-men only wished and expected to be protected by the new government, and to be permitted to complete the commercial transactions they were engaged in, as if the Island had never been attacked.

Instead of being gratified in this reasonable expectation, salvage has been claimed by the English Captain to whom Curraçao surrendered, from all the American vessels found in that port, and two the George belonging to Mr. Patterson of Baltimore and the Maria belonging to a Mr. Biays have been taken possession of, and I believe detained from their owners.[1]

The George I understand was taken for the purpose of carrying dispatches to England, and the Maria was employed between Curraçao and Kingston.

I hope there will be no necessity of formal complaints in this case. The vessels taken will I trust be returned or paid for and in case of their being returned compensation will be made for the service they have rendered.

The court of Vice Admiralty I hope will frown on this disgraceful claim of salvage and the vessels seized in port, because their cargoes were in part oznabrigs, will, I flatter myself, be given up.

Yet I thought it not improper to give you notice of these facts, that you may, if you think proper, take occasion to mention them incidentally. I hope they will not become subjects of national remonstrance.

The Congress are probably about to pass a bill reorganizing our judicial system. The principal feature in the new bill is the separation of the supreme from the circuit courts.

The Senate is yet employed on our late convention with France. That instrument encounters, as I am told, considerable opposition. With very much respect &c. &c.

J MARSHALL

Letterbook copy, RG 59, DNA.

1. The island of Curaçao had capitulated the preceding September to Capt. Frederick Watkins of H.B.M. Ship *Nereid*. U.S. consul Benjamin H. Phillips reported the seizure of the *George*, owned by Baltimore merchant William Patterson, in his dispatch to JM of 18 Oct. The pretext for seizing the *George* was that its cargo of oznabrig (osnaburg), a coarse linen, was declared to be contraband because it could be used to

make sails. Capt. Thomas Truxton wrote Patterson that "Watkins calls oznabrigs (only suitable for negro cloathing, and other purposes, of that sort) Sail cloth" (*Naval Documents: Quasi-War*, VI, 337–41, 481–82, 508–9).

To Timothy Pickering

Dear Sir   Jany. 18th. 1801
I now return you the letter which you were so polite as to transmit me. Its contents have been communicated & as you do not wish it to remain in the office it cannot I presume be more properly placd than in your possession. With much respect & esteem, I am your Obedt
                                                                    J MARSHALL

ALS, Pickering Papers, MHi.

To Unknown

Dear Sir[1]   Jany. 23d. 1801
I have receivd your letter of yesterday communicating the wish of Governor Trumbull to know how many packets of proposals for printing *facsimile* copies of letters from Genl. Washington to Sir John Sinclair on agricultural subjects had by that Gentleman been sent into the United States.[2]
He has sent in nineteen packets, one to the President one to the Vice-President, one to the Governor of each state & one to the Governor of the Northwestern territory. I am Sir with the highest respect & esteem, Your Obedt. Servt
                                                                    J MARSHALL

ALS, CtHi.

1. The recipient may have been Oliver Wolcott or a member of the Connecticut congressional delegation.
2. *Letters from His Excellency George Washington . . . to John Sinclair, . . . on Agricultural, and Other Interesting Topics . . .* (London, 1800).

From John Adams

Dear Sir   Washington Jan. 28. 1801

As it has been the practice of this Government to Summon the Senate of the United States to meet on the fourth of March after a new Election of a President and Vice President, and as various considerations render it probable that it will be at least as necessary this year as it ever has been at any former period, I request you to prepare Summons's for all the Senators, who are to serve after the third of March next, to meet at the Capitol in the Chamber of the Senate in Congress on the fourth day of March 1801, to receive such communications and Act on Such Executive Business of the United States as the public service may require. The form of the former Summons's or Proclamations, you will find in the office. There is no time to be lost. I am, sir with great Esteem and regard, your most obedient servant

JOHN ADAMS

ALS, RG 59, DNA; letterbook copy, Adams Papers, MHi.

From William Tazewell

Dr. Sir,   Williamsburg Jany 28th. 1801.

I fear your patience with me begins to be almost threadbare. I certainly should not have again troubled you, but that on accurate examination, I find the statement of my Acct. as forwarded from your office too incorrect to be settled in its present state.[1]

The charge, for loss of money & Clothes to the amount of dols. 226.44.Cs which is certainly to be looked upon as part of the expense of my Captivity, & which I could have supported on my arrival in Phila., had the thing been required, by the most respectable evidence (several of the passengers, that were taken at the same time that I was, continued with me till my arrival in the U. States) is entirely omitted. I think you will not hesitate to admit the justice of its insertion in the true statement you now receive.

As to the credits they are correct except the last Item, which instead of dols 283.50Cs. should have been dols. 272 only, as will fully appear, reference being had to my note of hand to Col. Pickering, dated Philadelphia April 12th. 1799. This note Coll. Pickering required of me in consequence of his having undertaken to discharge John Bulkeley & Sons draft. As the United Statets will have had the use of the money that shall be finally determined my due, from March 30th. 1799, indeed of the greater part, from a much earlier period, I hope there will be no difficulty in allowing me interest from that date up to the date of final settlement.

Should the statement now sent, meet your approbation you will please have the interest added or not as you think just, & return it to me that a proper affidavit & receipt may be annex'd.[2] In the mean while please pay yourself the £50 sterling I am indebted to you with interest from the date of my receipt, & accept my most grateful acknowledgments for the long indulgence I have received at your hands. With every sentiment of esteem & gratitude, I remain yr. Obt.

WILLIAM TAZEWELL

ALS, RG 59, DNA. Addressed by Tazewell to JM in Washington and franked. Endorsed by JM.

1. For the earlier history of Tazewell's attempts to settle his accounts as secretary to special envoy Elbridge Gerry in 1798 and 1799, see *PJM*, IV, 113, 118–20, 126–27, 162–63, 229–30.

2. Tazewell's account is filed with his letter. It bears an endorsement in his hand: "Acct. allowed by Genl. Marshall forwarded from the Secy. of State's office." On 27 Mar. Tazewell sent a revised account to James Madison, who on 10 Nov. 1801 requested Secretary of the Treasury Gallatin to issue a warrant for the balance in Tazewell's favor, $942.21. Interest apparently was not allowed (Rutland, *Papers of Madison: Sec. of State*, I, 54; Madison to Gallatin, 10 Nov. 1801 [filed with account and auditor's report, 14 Nov. 1801], RG 53, DNA).

To John Adams

Sir   [ca. 29 January 1801]

Inclosd is the answer of the secretary of the Senate to a request that he woud furnish the department of State with the names of the Senators.[1] There being no official certainty of the Senators newly elected to serve after the 3d. of March may produce some doubt respecting the propriety of a summons addressd to them individually.

There is not to be found on the files of this department any copy of the summons heretofore issued to the members. That having been a Presidential act is I presume to be lookd for among the papers in the keeping of the President. If Mr. Shaw will furnish a copy the proper number of summonss shall immediately be made out.[2] I am Sir with the utmost respect, Your Obedt. Servt

J MARSHALL

ALS, Adams Papers, MHi.

1. The enclosed answer from the secretary of the Senate (Samuel A. Otis) has not been found.

2. William Shaw was the president's personal secretary. The summonses went out the following day.

From John Adams

Dear Sir   Washington January 31. 1801

I request you would cause to be prepared Letters for me to Sign to the King of Prussia, recalling Mr John Quincy Adams as Minister Plenipotentiary from his Court. You may express the Thanks of the President to his Majesty for the obliging Reception and kind Treatment this minister has met with at his Court and may throw the Letter into the form of leave to return to the United States.¹ You will look into the forms in your office of former Instances of recall. I wish you to make out one Letter to go by the Way of Hamburgh another by Holland a third by France a fourth through Mr King in England, and a fifth if you please by the Way of Bremen or stettin or any other Channel most likely to convey it soon. It is my opinion this Minister ought to be recalled from Prussia. Justice would require that he should be sent to France or England if he should be continued in Europe. The Mission to St James's is perfectly well filled by Mr King, that to France is no doubt destined for Some other Character. Besides it is my opinion that it is my duty to call him home. With great regard, I am, sir your most obedient servant

JOHN ADAMS

ALS, RG 59, DNA; letterbook copy, Adams Papers, MHi.

1. A copy of Adams's letter to the king of Prussia (Frederick William III), 31 Jan., is in RG 59, DNA. See also JM to John Quincy Adams, 3 Feb. 1801.

Commission as Chief Justice of the Supreme Court of the United States

[31 January 1801]

JOHN ADAMS, President of the United States of America,

To all who shall see these Presents,—GREETING:

KNOW YE, That reposing special Trust and Confidence in the Wisdom, Uprightness and Learning of JOHN MARSHALL, of Virginia, I have nominated, and by and with the advice and consent of the Sen-

ate DO appoint him CHIEF JUSTICE OF THE SUPREME COURT OF THE
UNITED STATES, and do authorize and empower him to execute and
fulfil the Duties of that Office according to the constitution and Laws
of the said United States; and to HAVE and to HOLD the said Office,
with all the powers, privileges and Emoluments to the same of Right
appertaining unto him the said JOHN MARSHALL during his good
behaviour.[1]

   IN TESTIMONY WHEREOF, I have caused these Letters to be
[L.S.] made Patent, and the Seal of the United States to be here-
   unto affixed. GIVEN under my Hand at the City of Wash-
   ington the Thirty first day of January, in the year of our
   Lord one thousand Eight hundred and one; and of the
   Independence of the United States, the Twenty Fifth.

               JOHN ADAMS

Copy, RG 59, DNA.

1. Adams nominated JM on 20 Jan., and the Senate confirmed the appointment on
the twenty-seventh (*Senate Executive Journal*, I, 371, 374). On the politics of the appointment, see Kathryn Turner, "The Appointment of Chief Justice Marshall," *WMQ*, 3d
ser., XVII (1960), 143–63.

From Philo-Historia

Sir   1 Feby 1801[1]
 Having already determined to intrude, apologies, if apologies were
necessary, would be impertinent. I might, in the language of Swift,
"complain to you in the name of all the learned and polite persons of
America and Europe, that there are no means of obtaining anything
like a complete Historical knowledge of this Country.["][2] There is no
man who, when he views the causes and consequences of the American revolution, will not aknowledge it one of the most important
events in the History of the World. The discovery, therefore, the
settlement, the progress of population, the government, and all that
long train of causes which led to a final seperation from Great Britain, are objects of the greatest Magnitude; and every man, but particularly every American must sincerely regret the total want of any
thing like a complete History of these events. Dr Robertson,[3] it is
true, has given us some valuable information on some of these subjects, but his History only embraces a particular period of our existence as a Country, and, even in this, he confesses and regrets that he
has had access only to a part of the necessary documents in Spain. Dr
Ramsay,[4] it is presumed, only intended to give an epita⟨ph⟩ of the

History and events of the Revolution. As to Gordon,[5] Stedman[6] &ca &ca. their books may be considered as small aids to so⟨me⟩ future Historian. The cause of this disgraceful deficiency in history is obvious: There are no materials for the composition of such an History within the reach of any individual. They are deposited in the cabinets of Spain, of England, of France, of Holland, of Prussia, of Sweeden, of Denmark, of Russia. And had we a Thucidydes, a Livius, a Guicciardini, a Hume, a Gibbon, or a Robertson, without these materials their talents would only reflect disgrace on their Country. Under present circumstances, no man of talents would think of writing such an History even though he had fortune, enterprize and patriotism sufficient to carry him all over Europe in pursuit of materials (a combination of circumstanc⟨es⟩ not likely to occur) for by the time his collection was made his life would be drawing to a period. Mr Adams, in a letter to L'abbé de Mably, when he had thoughts of writing a general History of this Country, tells him that "Il faudroit la vie entiere & la plus longue, a commencer des l'age de 20 ans, pour assembler de toutes les Nations & de toutes les parties du monde, dans lesquels ils sont deposes, les documents propres a former une Histoire complette de la Guerre Americaine, parce que c'est proprement l'Histoire du Genre humain de toute cette epoque."[7]

In the same letter he tells the Abbé that "La plupart des docum⟨ents⟩ & materiaux etant encore secrets" and again "Il m'est impossible de vous dire si le Gouvernment de ce pays Souhaiteroit de voir quel⟨que⟩ ouvrage profondment ecrit &c—Il est question d'exposer des princip⟨es⟩ de gouvernment, si different de ce qu'on trouve en Europe &c &."

I have quoted this letter because it contains all the reasons that could be urged against the writing of a complete history at that time. But, however forcibly they might have operated at that time, they have now ceased to exist. Our own administration have now no revolution-secrets; and the principles of our Government have devoloped themselves so fully that European Countries will gain no further information by their publication in the form of an History. The present period is certainly auspicious. We are at peace with all the world, except France, and on such terms with the European powers, that none of them would refuse us a reasonable request. Under all these considerations I will suggest to you, Sir, the expediency of taking some measures under the sanction of Government, to obtain these inestimable materials. The labor would be great, but the expense insignificant: the object contemplated, of the first national magnitude. Harley did not deem the improvement of the English language an object below his attention, and Swift, Bolingbroke, Pope Arburthnot and Addison volunteered to accomplish so glorious an undertaking. France pensioned, or offered pensions to the Litterati of the whole world in order to effect the same object. How infinitily more important is it to procure the very vitals of History, than merely to labor at embellishment!

I know that, if this collection of documents should be undertaken at the expense of Gover[n]ment, it will not be made an object of emolument; a genteel support is all that will be allowed, and that is enough; and I know persons who would glory in the task on that condition. It will certainly reflect honor on that administration under which it is commenced, and for this, and a thousand other reasons it is desireable it should be ag[r]eed on (if at all) before the fourth of March.

If the subject be worth your consideration, it is immaterial by whom it is suggested: If not, it is also of no consequence. In the first case, however, it would be extremely gratifying to me to know your sentiments upon it.

PHILO-HISTORIA

Should you think it worth while to write, a letter dire[c]ted to my fictitious signature, enclosed in one to Robert Pearson Esqr. to be left at Negus's ferry Philada. will reach me.

ALS(?), RG 59, DNA. Angle brackets enclose letters obscured in margin.

1. The writer has not been identified. One possible candidate for "Philo-Historia" is Ebenezer Hazard (1744–1817), an early advocate for preserving and publishing the archival records of the U.S. He had previously published two volumes of *Historical Collections* (Philadelphia, 1792–94). See Boyd, *Papers of Jefferson*, I, 148n.

2. This placement of the close quotation is conjectural. The source of the quotation (more likely, a paraphrase) has not been identified.

3. William Robertson's *The History of America* was originally published in 1777 (2 vols.; London) and contained books I–VIII, covering the discovery of America and the conquest of Mexico and Peru. *The History of America, Books IX. and X. Containing the History of Virginia to the Year 1688; and of New England to the Year 1652* (Philadelphia, 1799, from 1796 London ed.) was published posthumously in 1796. The eighth edition was the first to contain all ten books (3 vols.; London, 1800).

4. David Ramsay, *The History of the American Revolution* (2 vols.; Philadelphia, 1789).

5. William Gordon, *The History of the Rise, Progress, and Establishment, of the Independence of the United States of America . . .* (4 vols.; London, 1788).

6. Charles Stedman (1753–1812), a British loyalist who had served in the British army under Sir William Howe. After the war he wrote *The History of the Origin, Progress, and Termination of the American War* (2 vols.; London, 1794).

7. John Adams's letter to Mably, 15 Jan. 1783, was originally published in French in the appendix to the first volume of his *A Defence of the Constitutions of Government of the United States of America* (3 vols.; Philadelphia, 1787–88; Evans #20176), I, 386, 387. The English version is in C. F. Adams, ed., *The Works of John Adams* (10 vols.; Boston, 1856), V, 492–96. See also L. H. Butterfield, ed., *The Diary and Autobiography of John Adams* (4 vols.; Cambridge, Mass., 1961), III, 102.

To William Paterson

Dear Sir   Washington Feby. 2d. 1801
I had this instant the pleasure of receiving your letter of the 26th. of January.[1]

For your polite & friendly sentiments on the appointment with which I have been lately honord I pray you to accept my warm & sincere acknowledgements.

I regret much that you cannot attend this session of the supreme court & still more the cause which detains you from us. I hope it will be of short duration & that the other members will be present. As yet however I have only seen Judge Cushing.

The question on the judicial bill will probably be taken in the Senate tomorrow, & we hope it will pass. It is substantially the same with that of the last session. Its most essential feature is the separation of the Judges of the supreme from those of the circuit courts, & the establishment of the latter on a system capable of an extension commensurate with the necessities of the nation.[2] With great respect & esteem I am dear Sir, your obedt. Servt

J MARSHALL

ALS, Paterson Papers, NjR; Tr, NN. Addressed to "The Honble William Patterson" in New Brunswick, N.J., and franked; postmarked Washington, 2 Feb. Transcripts at NN copied in Dec. 1879 from originals in possession of William Paterson, Perth Amboy, N.J.

1. Letter not found.
2. The judiciary act passed the House on 20 Jan. and the Senate on 7 Feb. (*Annals of Congress*, X, 734, 742). For JM's participation in this legislation, see *PJM*, IV, 117–18. JM alluded to section 11 of the 1801 act, which significantly enlarged the jurisdiction of the circuit courts. These courts were to have jurisdiction over all cases in law and equity arising under the Constitution, laws, and treaties of the U.S., exempting such cases from the jurisdictional amount (now reduced from five hundred to four hundred dollars) required in other cases. And in disputes involving the title or bounds of land, jurisdiction would not be restricted by reason of the value of the land (*U.S. Statutes at Large*, II, 92). See Kathryn Turner, "Federalist Policy and the Judiciary Act of 1801," *WMQ*, 3d ser., XXII (1965), 3–32.

Memoranda on Foreign Affairs

[February 2. 1801.][1]
Memoranda
The state of our affairs with the Barbary powers generally & with Tripoli in particular requires immediate attention. They are disclosd in the letters from our consuls & in a very late letter from Mr.

Humphries. It will be seen that there is cause to expect some mischief from Tripoli.

The present mode of paying the stipulated annuity to Algiers is not only extremely burthensome but exposd to considerable frauds. I have written to Mr. OBrien requesting him to endeavor to commute it from the specified articles of the treaty to a sum of money & have mentiond 30,000 dol. It woud be a good bargain to fix it at twice that sum.[2] The mode of procuring the articles has been by special contracts made with various persons by the secretary of State. I have changd it so far as to conduct the whole business through the Purveyor & had I continued in Office shoud have requird it to be conducted through the secretary of the treasury.

The state of our affairs with Spain will command the very serious consideration of this department.

I have notice that complaints in regular form will be made by our merchants against the lately increasd depredations of Britain. When they appear they will speak for themselves & the late letters from Mr. King will deserve consideration. What has been said by this department to our minister will appear on the book of correspondence & woud certainly have taken a very earnest shape had it not been proper to avoid any step which might in any degree anticipate the system which the administration about to conduct the affairs of the U.S. may deem most advantageous to our country. I beg leave however to recommend the most prompt attention to the negotiation concerning our differences under the 6th. art. Its commencement will be seen in my letter to Mr. King No. 2.[3] & its state at the date of our last inteligence in some of Mr. Kings last letters. I fear the subject is concluded. I say I fear so because it is very much my wish that it shoud be found in a situation to be abandond or pursued as shall in the opinion of the administration be most conducive to the public interest, & it is for this reason I recommend the most immediate attention to the subject. What producd the letter No. 2 will be perceivd by adverting to the letters receivd from Mr. King some short time previous to its date.

Justices—Job Wall[4]

AD, RG 59, DNA. Endorsed: "Judge Marshall's Minutes."

1. JM did not date his memoranda, but someone wrote in the dateline: "file February 2. 1801." The actual date may be later in the month, however. Note the reference to the "very late letter from Mr. Humphries." This probably refers to the letter and enclosures of 7 Nov. 1800, received 26 Feb. 1801 (App. I, Cal.).

2. See JM to O'Brien, 29 July 1800 (*PJM*, IV, 193). By the 1795 Treaty with Algiers,

the dey of Algiers agreed to abide by the articles on consideration of an annual payment by the U.S. of twelve thousand Algerine sequins (twenty-one thousand dollars) in maritime stores (Miller, *Treaties*, II, 303). See also *PJM*, IV, 152–53, 159–60.

3. See JM to King, 23 Aug. 1800 (*PJM*, IV, 233–38, erroneously docketed "No. 4").

4. The reference to "Justices" may refer to the making out and delivery of the commissions of justices appointed under the new judiciary act. Job Wall was U.S. consul at St. Bartholomew. JM had written to him on 12 Jan. 1801 (App. I, Cal.) about the protest of his bills and the necessity of settling his accounts.

To John Quincy Adams

Sir   Department of State Feby. 3d. 1801
The objects of your mission to Berlin having been entirely accomplishd the President is of opinion that you may be permited to return to the United States. He therefore wishes you to sollicit from his Prussian Majesty an audience for the purpose of delivering the letter which communicates this intention & of taking leave. In doing this the President requests that you will, in terms fitted to the occasion, express his sense of the obliging manner in which the Minister of the United States has been receivd by his Prussian Majesty, & his sincere desire for the continuance of that harmony & friendship which at present so happily subsists between the two nations.[1] With very much respect I am Sir, Your Obedt Servt

J MARSHALL

ALS, Adams Papers, MHi; letterbook copy, RG 59, DNA. ALS endorsed by Adams, "4 May recd: (Dup.)." Filed with ALS are LS and copy of John Adams to king of Prussia, 31 Jan.

1. A copy of this letter was received by Adams on 26 Apr., and on 28 Apr. he wrote James Madison of his intention to leave soon for Boston (Rutland, *Papers of Madison: Sec. of State*, I, 124–25).

To Edward Thornton

Sir,   Department of State Feb. 3rd 1801.
The increasing complaints of our citizens respecting depredations made by British Cruizers on our commerce have rendered indispensable very serious remonstrances on this subject to your Government. We shall reluctantly abandon the hope that the representations which have been so often repeated, concerning the conduct of the British

Cruizers in the American Seas and of the Courts of Vice-Admiralty in the British American Colonies, will at length produce such a change of system as may comport with justice, and with the Continuance of that harmony which we very sincerely believe to be essential to the interests of both nations.

While we wait the result of these representations, we assure ourselves that no proper exertion on your part will be wanting to prevent, so far as you can prevent, any of those irritating injuries which good men of both nations must ⟨ . . . ⟩.

Under this impression I take ⟨the⟩ liberty to solicit your attention to the case of ⟨the⟩ brig Ruby and cargo, owned by Mr Chandler ⟨Price,⟩ a merchant of Philadelphia.¹

His case is particularly prese⟨nted⟩ to you in the hope that by interposing your ⟨good⟩ offices previous to the trial, its circumstances may receive a degree of attention which otherw⟨ise⟩ might not be afforded them.

The brig Ruby is understood ⟨to be⟩ an American vessel, laden with a cargo entirely ⟨the⟩ property of an American Citizen, and without ⟨an⟩ article on board, which can even be alleged to b⟨e⟩ Contraband.

I am informed that she is de⟨tained⟩ under a suspicion produced by a letter found ⟨on⟩ board another vessel, which was addressed by ⟨Mr⟩ Price to a Mr Morgan,² and which in speaking ⟨of⟩ the brig used the expression "our vessel," ther⟨eby?⟩ indicating that she was jointly owned by them. This Mr Price states to have been an accid⟨ental⟩ expression, produced by the habit of using it ⟨in?⟩ writing to his partner. But independent of this satisfactory explanation, it certainly cannot be imagined that, if Mr Morgan really possessed a joint interest with Mr Price in both the vessel and cargo, such joint ownership could be a cause of capture.

New Orleans being in fact as well an American as a Spanish port, our citizens will very probably settle there, and the trade from any of our ports on the Atlantic to New Orleans will unquestionably be as lawful, although citizens of the United States residing at each place may be concerned therein, as the trade between Philadelphia and Charleston. But Mr Morgan does not reside at New Orleans. He is accidentally there for the benefit of his health.

The capture of vessels bound up the Mississippi is the more to be complained of in consequence of the agreement between the two nations respecting that river. The stipulation for its free navigation is illusory indeed, if vessels bound up it are to be captured on account of their destination.

I do not, Sir, pretend to conjecture how far you may interpose your good offices ⟨in a⟩ case depending before one of the Vice-Admiral⟨ty⟩

Courts of your nation. Mr Price states this interposition to have been on a former occasion effectually made by Mr Liston.

If according to your own convi⟨ction⟩ of propriety you can present this subject to ⟨the⟩ Judge or other constituted authorities at Halifax[3] in such a manner as to promote ⟨a⟩ decision conforming to the justice of the cas⟨e,⟩ I am entirely persuaded that it will be unnecessary for me farther to urge my req⟨uest⟩ that you will, so far as may be consistent wit⟨h⟩ right, aid the claim of Mr Price.[4] With great and respectful consideration I am &c

(signed)   J. MARSHALL.

Copy, F.O.5/32, P.R.O. In Thornton's hand. Enclosed in Thornton to Lord Grenville, 5 Feb. Angle brackets enclose letters obscured in margin.

1. On the case of the *Ruby*, see Chandler Price to JM, 20 Jan., 28 Jan. 1801 (App. I, Cal.).

2. As Price explained in his letter to JM of 20 Jan., Benjamin Morgan was his "Partner in general Transactions" but had no interest in the *Ruby* or her cargo. He also pointed out that Morgan was an American who was temporarily in New Orleans for his health.

3. In the margin, someone wrote "New Providence." The case of the *Ruby* was before the vice admiralty court at New Providence in the Bahamas, rather than at Halifax.

4. In his covering dispatch to Lord Grenville on 5 Feb., Thornton observed that with the relaxation of tensions between the U.S. and France, complaints against British armed vessels "are likely to be more loud and vehement, and the irritation of the public opinion more acrimonious." This circumstance, he continued, may explain why JM in his letter seemed "to discover more personal feeling, than he has ⟨been⟩ accustomed to exhibit on former occasions of ⟨this⟩ nature." Thornton went on to say that the case of the *Ruby* "appeared hard" and that he had written to the British governor of the Bahamas that in this instance the principles of capture may have been too harshly applied.

The Supreme Court

EDITORIAL NOTE

On 4 February 1801, a quorum of justices assembled in a "half-finished Committee room, meanly furnished," on the first floor of the Capitol. This was the first session of the Supreme Court held in the city of Washington. The new chief justice, John Marshall, presented his commission and then "took the oath prescribed by Law." After granting motions for continuances, admitting several attorneys to practice, and hearing arguments in one case, the court adjourned on 10 February.[1] Three days later Congress passed a new judiciary act, which among other things provided for separate justices of the Supreme and circuit courts and changed the terms of the Supreme Court to June and December each year. Because the new law took effect after the

August term of that year, the court met three times in 1801. In 1802, however, the court did not hold a single session, owing to repeal of the 1801 act. The act of 1802 restored the February term but restricted the August term to procedural orders and motions presided over by the associate justice resident in the fourth circuit (Samuel Chase). Beginning in 1803 the Supreme Court met once each year on the first Monday in February; in 1826 the term was moved to the second Monday in January.[2] In the early years the average session of the court lasted about a month, gradually increasing in length to three months by the end of Marshall's chief justiceship in 1835.

The most immediate and obvious change that Marshall instituted was the abandonment of seriatim opinions in favor of a single "opinion of the court," usually pronounced by the chief justice. Through the 1807 term Marshall delivered seventy-three opinions in reported cases, nearly three-fourths of the total.[3] Although most of the original drafts have been lost, the surviving material indicates that Marshall undertook the major burden of writing as well as delivering the opinions of the court. In time, with the steady increase in the number of cases coming before the court, the labor of composing opinions had to be more widely shared with other justices. Up to the end, nevertheless, Marshall's output was prodigious. During his last eight terms, he gave the opinion in approximately one-third of the cases. In 1834 he delivered thirty-two opinions (about half the total), the largest number given at any term during his lengthy tenure.[4]

As explained in the statement of editorial policy (xxvii), this edition will publish selected Supreme Court opinions, including all those involving a constitutional question. The original manuscript, where it exists, constitutes the text. Of approximately 550 opinions delivered by the chief justice on the high court, only 88 of his autograph drafts survive. These include six constitutional opinions: *Osborn* v. *Bank of the United States* (1824), *American Insurance Company* v. *Canter* (1828), *Foster and Elam* v. *Neilson* (1829), *Weston* v. *Charleston* (1829), *Willson* v. *Blackbird Creek Marsh Company* (1829), and *Worcester* v. *Georgia* (1832). Seventy-five manuscript opinions date from 1828 or later and belong to five of Marshall's last eight terms: 1828, 1829, 1832, 1834, and 1835. For these terms, a complete set of drafts appears to exist, not counting brief opinions he delivered orally without committing to writing. The thirteen autograph opinions of an earlier date are distributed among five terms: 1808 (one), 1812 (one), 1816 (seven), 1817 (three), and 1824 (one).

Loss of the great bulk of the original opinions is not surprising since there was no attempt to preserve them as part of the official archival record until 1834. In that year the Supreme Court adopted a rule ordering original opinions to be filed in the clerk's office after the reporter had published the report. The practice up to that time had been to give the opinion to the reporter after it was read.[5] Once the opinion was set in type, the reporter must in many instances have destroyed the original or made no special effort to preserve it. By good fortune, Richard Peters, Jr., who became reporter in 1828, kept a number of Marshall's opinions and eventually turned them over to the clerk. All the extant autograph opinions (except for one that is privately owned) are in the National Archives, Record Group 267, Records of the Supreme Court of the United States.[6]

WILLIAM CRANCH

Oil on canvas by John Cranch, 1845. *Courtesy of U.S. District Court for the District of Columbia (Photography courtesy of the National Museum of American Art, Smithsonian Institution)*

In the absence of a manuscript, the text of the opinion in most instances is taken from the printed reports of William Cranch, Henry Wheaton, and Richard Peters, Jr. For the years covered by this volume, Cranch, a judge (later chief judge) of the U.S. Circuit Court for the District of Columbia, undertook the task of reporting Supreme Court cases. He published his first of nine volumes of *Reports of Cases Argued and Adjudged in the Supreme Court of the United States* (1804–17) in June 1804, covering the 1801 and 1803 terms. As of May 1809 Cranch had published four volumes reporting cases through the 1808 term. In the preface to his first volume, Cranch noted that he was "relieved from much anxiety, as well as responsibility, by the practice which the court has adopted of reducing their opinion to writing, in all cases of difficulty or importance." He thus compiled his reports of opinions directly from the written drafts supplied by the court.[7]

If a report was first published in the newspapers, that source provides the text of the opinion. Cranch's report of *Marbury* v. *Madison* appeared in the Washington newspapers less than a month after the decision and fifteen months before his volume containing that case was published. In *Marbury* and in the two opinions in *Ex parte Bollman and Swartwout*, the editors have collated the newspaper text with the "official" report and noted any significant variations.

This edition will also present Marshall's unpublished notes of arguments in twenty-odd cases heard at various terms of the Supreme Court (mostly during his last five years on the bench). The notes are preserved in collections at the National Archives, Columbia University, Pierpont Morgan Library, and Historical Society of Pennsylvania. The provenance of these manuscripts can be traced to the reporters Wheaton and Peters. An eight-page manuscript of Marshall's notes on six cases heard at the 1831 term, for example, was given to the National Archives in 1966 after being found in the law library of the Prudential Insurance Company in Newark, New Jersey. That company obtained them in 1890 from a Newark citizen who received them from the man to whom Peters had given them years earlier.[8]

The earliest notes of this kind in Marshall's hand are of a case argued at the 1803 term, *Fenwick* v. *Sears*, found among the papers in the appellate case file at the National Archives.[9] Notes of arguments occasionally turn up in case files, and more such documents in Marshall's hand may turn up as editorial work proceeds. The file of another early case, *Hepburn and Dundas* v. *Ellzey*, contains a lengthy set of notes (kept by Justice William Johnson) on that and five other cases argued at the 1805 term.[10] Another type of document commonly found in the case papers is the official judgment or decree of the court. The text of the decree in *Murray* v. *Charming Betsey*, published in this volume, is taken from Marshall's autograph draft in the appellate case file.[11]

Case papers, besides supplying an occasional autograph document, are a valuable source for researching Marshall's cases. A typical appellate file contains the writ of error, a transcript of the record of the case in the court below, exhibits, correspondence, and other documents that shed light on the controversy and identities of the parties. Also useful are the minutes and dockets of the Supreme Court, which survive nearly intact for these years and form part of Record Group 267 at the National Archives. Newspapers, particularly the Washington *National Intelligencer*, occasionally provide details about the proceedings of a particular case that are not revealed either in the case papers or in the printed report.

1. Benjamin H. Latrobe to James Madison, 8 Sept. 1809 (John C. Van Horne et al., eds., *The Correspondence and Miscellaneous Papers of Benjamin Henry Latrobe*, II [New Haven, Conn., 1986], 765); U.S. Sup. Ct. Minutes, 4–10 Feb. 1801; Haskins and Johnson, *Foundations of Power*, 80–82.

2. *U.S. Statutes at Large*, II, 89, 156; IV, 160.

3. See Appendix III for a calendar of Marshall's opinions, 1801–7.

4. Nineteen of JM's drafts for that term survive. Many cases, of course, were disposed of briefly and did not require a written opinion.

5. Order, 14 Mar. 1834 (8 Pet. vii); Anonymous, 3 Pet. 397 (1830).

6. See *Index to the Manuscript and Revised Printed Opinions of the Supreme Court of the United States in the National Archives, 1808–1873* (Washington, D.C., 1965).

7. 1 Cranch iv–v.

8. *Newark Sunday News*, 3 Apr. 1966.

9. See Notes on Arguments, 18–19 Feb. 1803.

10. See Opinion, 25 Feb. 1805, n. 1.

11. See Opinion and Decree, 22 Feb. 1804.

To John Adams

Sir   Feby. 4th. 1801
I pray you to accept my grateful acknowledgements for the honor conferd on me in appointing me chief Justice of the United States.

This additional & flattering mark of your good opinion has made an impression on my mind which time will not efface.

I shall enter immediately on the duties of the office & hope never to give you occasion to regret having made this appointment. With the most respectful attachment, I am Sir your Obedt. Servt.

J MARSHALL

ALS, Adams Papers, MHi.

From John Adams

Dear Sir   Washington Feb. 4. 1801
I have this moment received your Letter of this morning and am happy in your acceptance of the office of Chief Justice.

The Circumstances however of the times render it necessary that I should request and Authorise you, as I do by this Letter, to continue to discharge all the Duties of Secretary of State, untill ulteriour Arrangements can be made. With great Esteem, I have the Honor to be, sir your Sincere Friend

JOHN ADAMS

ALS, RG 59, DNA; letterbook copy, Adams Papers, MHi.

From Edward Thornton

Washington Wednesday 4 Feby 1801

Mr Thornton presents his respectful compliments to General Marshall, and has the honour of transmitting to him two letters for New Providence, of which if Mr Price does not intend to deliver them in person, he shall be very happy to furnish him with duplicates.

Mr Thornton takes this opportunity of returning to General Marshall the papers relating to Mr Price's vessel.

AL, RG 59, DNA.

From Elihu Hall Bay

Sir,   City of Washington 8th. Feby 1801.

In consequence of the hint you gave me the other day, I avail myself of this opportunity, of suggesting to you the expediency of intimating to the President of the United States, the propriety of making an application to the British Government; for the records of the former province of West Florida.[1] They are of little or no consequence to that Government, but may be of importance to ours, and many of our Citizens. In the first place, the Mississippi Territory which is the northermost part of West Florida, is without doubt, among the finest portions of land (if not the first in point of fertility of soil) in the United States; it appears therefore a matter of primary consideration to quiet the inhabitants as much as possible in their titles to their lands; which never can be effectually done, without a reference to those records: for in the course of the War, and the variety of changes which that territory has undergone, since its original settlement, so many grants, conveyances and evidences of property have been lost or mislaid that it will be extremely difficult, if not altogether impracticable, for those really entitled to land to make good their claims without them. It will be important too in another point of view. Among them, will be found the records of the different Commissions under the Great Seal of Great Britain, constituting the Original boundaries of West Florida, and afterwards enlarging them, as far North as the river Yassous, together with the Kings instructions to his different Governors, who presided over that country; which will shew beyond all contradiction, that every act of Government was exercised over the Territory North of the 31st degree of latitude up to the above river Yassous, such as granting land, reserving places for fortifications, building forts, appointing civil magistrates &c &c. in as full and complete a manner as was exercised in any of the other British Colonies, or Plantations in America, from the year 1764 till its final surrender to Spain.

It will also, further appear from those records, that, that country was divided into districts, which sent members to the General assembly at Pensacola; and that the District of the Natchez in particular which extended from Softus' Clifts, up to the Yassous sent 4 Members to the Colonial assembly, who were elected by the freeholders in that District, and who assisted in passing laws at the Seat of Government. My residence in West Florida for several years before it was reduced by Spain, and previous to my settlement in Carolina in 1781, and a thorough acquaintance with the records in question (having acted as Deputy Secretary for several years) gave me an opportunity of knowing correctly, almost every thing relative to that Territory before it fell to Spain; after which event the records were committed to my care to be sent to England; but choosing to remain among my fellow citizens and Countrymen in Carolina, I confided them to the care of Lieutenant Governor Graham of Georgia, who had them deposited in the Plantation Office White Hall, London, where I presume they now are, or in some other of the Offices for Plantation affairs.[2] If this communication will be of any service, or in the least degree worthy the attention of the Executive of the Union, it will afford me pleasure.[3] At any rate, I shall have complied with the promise I made you, and am Sir, With the highest consideration, and Esteem, your most Obt. Sert

(signed)   ELIHU HALL RAY[4]

Copy, CSmH.

1. Bay (ca. 1754–1838) was born in Maryland, moved to West Florida, and then to South Carolina after the Revolution. Elected an associate judge in 1791, he remained on the bench until his death in 1838. Bay was the first reporter of South Carolina cases (John Belton O'Neall, *Biographical Sketches of the Bench and Bar of South Carolina* [2 vols.; 1859; Spartanburg, S.C., 1975 reprint], I, 53–65).

2. Lt. Gov. John Graham (ca. 1718–1795) was Georgia's last royal lieutenant governor. He moved to Florida during the Revolution and later retired to England.

3. James Madison enclosed this copy of Bay's letter in his letter to Rufus King, 28 July 1801 (Rutland, *Papers of Madison: Sec. of State*, I, 485). The *National Intelligencer, and Washington Advertiser* (Washington, D.C.), 2 Apr. 1804, reported the safe arrival of the West Florida records at Baltimore.

4. The copyist misread "Bay" as "Ray."

From John Adams

Dear Sir   Washington February 10th. 1801

Inclosed is a Newbury Port Herald, in which is quoted "a Letter from John Adams, dated Amsterdam 15 of December 1780 to Thomas Cushing, Lieutenant Governor of Massachusetts." This Letter has been for Some years past reprinted and quoted in many American Pamphlets and Newspapers as genuine, and imposes on many People by Supposing and imputing to me sentiments inconsistent with the whole Tenor of my Life and all the feelings of my nature. I remember to have read the Letter in English Newspapers Soon after it was published, at a time when the Same English Papers teamed with forged Letters long tedious flatt and dull in the name of Dr Franklin the most concise, Sprightly and entertaining Writer of his time. The Dr declared them all to be forgeries, which he was not under a necessity of doing because every Reader of common sense and taste knew them to be Such from their Style and Nonsense.

The Letter in my name I also declare to be a forgery. I never wrote any Letter in the least degree resembling it to Lieutenant Governor Cushing nor to any other Person. This declaration I pray you to file in your office and you have my Consent to publish it if you think fit.[1] I am, Sir, with great Esteem, your most obedient and humble servant

JOHN ADAMS

ALS, RG 59, DNA; letterbook copy, Adams Papers, MHi.

1. Although a British forgery, this letter continued to be attributed to Adams during the remainder of his life. One of the earliest publications of the letter was in *The Annual Register . . . for the Year 1781* (London, 1782), 258–61, which stated that it "was found on board the prize Brigantine Cabot, and carried into St. Christopher's." In the reputed letter, Adams reported that European powers considered American independence established, and he reproached Cushing for his "gloomy apprehensions" concerning army recruitment, depreciation of the currency, and complaints of public creditors. He also spoke of the public departments in the U.S. being "filled with men of rapacious principles, who sacrifice the common weal to the private emolument, who encourage gambling, voluptuousness, and every vice." As for the American loyalists, he thought *"their career might have been stopt . . . if the executive officers had not been too timid in a point which I so strenuously recommended at first, namely, to fine, imprison, and hang all inimical to the cause, without favour or affection. I foresaw the evil that would arise from that quarter, and wished to have timely stopt it. I would have hanged my own brother if he had took a part with our enemy in this contest."*

In 1826, the year of Adams's death, the letter was again making the rounds of the newspapers. Hezekiah Niles discovered Adams's letter to JM in "a file of old papers," confirming his "faint recollection" that the letter to Cushing "had been pronounced a forgery many years ago" (*Niles' Weekly Register*, XXX [1826], 436). Nevertheless, in 1889, an editor of diplomatic correspondence published the letter, using the text from the *Annual Register*, though voicing suspicion that this text might have been "tampered with before publication, as was the case with other 'intercepted' letters" (Francis Wharton, *The Revolutionary Diplomatic Correspondence of the American Revolution* [6 vols.; Washington, D.C., 1889], IV, 193–95). The editors are indebted to Celeste Walker of the Adams Family Papers, Massachusetts Historical Society, for information concerning the forged letter.

From Humphrey Marshall

Sir,   [ca. 15 February 1801][1]

The president of the United States will doub[t]less think it proper to nominate and appoint, the Circuit Judges required by Law to organize the new Circuit System. Residing in the sixth circuit where there is one of those Judges to be appointed I shall be excused for placing before you, and through you Sir, before the president, the name of a Gentleman, *Mr. William Mc.Clung*, whom I wish to be appointed, to the office of Circuit Judge: because all circumstances considered, I think him the most fit person in the Circuit, now eligible.[2] Mr. McClung is turned of forty years of age, has been in the practice of the law for twelve, or fifteen years, and is a good lawyer, of fair, and honorable character. Not having Joined the prevailing party in Kentuckey where he resides he has received no State appointments; except that when he chose, he has been elected to either branch of the Legislature, in which he has served.

But before I determined to bring forward Mr. Mc.Clung I thought it necessary to converse with Mr. Mc.Millan the delegate from the North Western Territory, with a veiw to know, if he could fix on a proper person within that Territory for the office.[3] Because if he could, as the Territory is large, and there being already a Judge in both Kentuckey and Tennessee, I should have held it my duty to sacrifice any prepossessions I had formed in favor of Mr. Mc.Clungs appointment, to the Superior consideration of accommodating the people of the Territory by an appointment local to them. But Mr. Mc.Millan admitting that his mind is not satisfied to bring forward any person resident within the Territory, has agreed with me in favor of Mr. Mc.Clung. I am decided, upon proper attention to local and general convenience, that the appoin[t]ment should be of a person within Kentucky, rather than within Tennessee, The former being central in the circuit while the latter, and the Territory ly on opposite extremes. The residence of Mr. Mc.Clung, at Washington, is as convenient to the Territory, as any situation out of it, could be.[4] He lives near the Ohio at a place where the roads through the Territory concentrate more than at any other point; and nearly at equal distances from the extreme, as well as from the most populous Settlements.

To appoint the additional Judge in Kentucky will ensure regular Courts; because if the Judge from *Tennessee* should not attend either at *Bairdstown*, or *Cincinnati*, the Courts can nevertheless be held by the two Judges resident in Kentucky; and one or the other of these can always go into Tennessee to hold the Courts there with the Judge in that State, with abundantly less traveling and more convenience than if two Judges resided in Tennessee.[5] Again, should it be necessary to hold special Courts in criminal cases either in Kentuckey, or the Territory, there is two to one in favor of getting a Court in proper time, should the two Judges reside in Kentuckey, rather than in Tennessee. These observations are made with a view to the possibility of an application for an appointment of a person within Tennessee, tho' I do not know that such an application will be made.[6]

If you can conceive that political Opinions often have an influence in decisions upon private rights, you will readily percieve the importance of placing in the circuit Courts a man well affected to the federal Government, by way of counterpoise. Mr. McClung is a man of good temper great firmness, and a friend to the Government.

I pray you Sir, to make this communication to the president at such time and in such manner as you shall deem proper for attaining its object. I have the honor to be, with consideration, your humble Servt.

H. MARSHALL

ALS, Adams Papers, MHi.

1. Though undated, this letter was written sometime between 13 Feb., when the judiciary act passed, and 21 Feb., when William McClung was nominated to be a judge of the sixth circuit. Humphrey Marshall, JM's cousin and brother-in-law, was then a U.S. senator from Kentucky (*PJM*, I, 132 and n. 6).

2. McClung, also JM's brother-in-law, had been appointed attorney for Kentucky in 1794. He was nominated as a circuit court judge on 21 Feb. and confirmed on 24 Feb. (*PJM*, III, 45 n. 2; *Senate Executive Journal*, I, 160, 383, 385).

3. William McMillan. See his letter to JM, 25 Feb. 1801 (App. I, Cal.).

4. The village of Washington, Ky., was just south of Limestone (later Maysville).

5. The sixth circuit was composed of the districts of East Tennessee, West Tennessee, Kentucky, and Ohio. This court was to meet twice a year in each of the towns of Knoxville (East Tennessee), Nashville (West Tennessee), Bairdstown (Kentucky), and Cincinnati (Ohio). The act of 1801 called for the appointment of only one circuit court judge, who with the already existing district judges of Tennessee and Kentucky was to compose the circuit court (*U.S. Statutes at Large*, II, 90–91).

6. See William Cocke and Others to JM, 17 Feb. 1801 (App. I, Cal.), recommending Archibald Roane of Tennessee.

From John Adams

Dear Sir   Washington Feb. 19. 1801

Inclosed is a Letter to me from the Vice President of the United States with a Resolution of the Senate dated the Eighteenth of this month and a Certificate of the Vice President of the Election of Aaron Burr to be the future Vice President of the United States.[1]

I request you to Select a proper Person according to the usage in Such Cases to proceed to New York and convey this Certificate to Mr Burr. With great Esteem I have the honor to be, sir your most obedient Servant

JOHN ADAMS

ALS, RG 59, DNA; letterbook copy, Adams Papers, MHi.

1. The enclosed letter from Thomas Jefferson to Adams of 18 Feb., with the Senate resolution of the same day requesting the president to transmit to Aaron Burr notification of his election as vice president, is in RG 59, DNA.

From Edward Thornton

Sir,   Washington 20th February 1801.

I have the honour of transmitting to you duplicate copies of the letters which I wrote some time ago to New Providence in behalf of Mr Price, and of returning his letter, in which the request is made.[1]

As the one addressed to Mr. Franks is private, and as neither of them contain any assertions relating to Mr Price's vessel but such as are founded on his own documents, of which you favoured me with the perusal, it is impossible (independently of other considerations) that they can be produced in proof in favour of his suit. I see therefore no reason why the letters should be conveyed to him open, as he requests.

At the same time I will not seal them, till they have been submitted to your confidential perusal: though I am persuaded you want no such proof of the real solicitude I feel, to remove every cause of complaint or discontent, arising within the narrow sphere of my duty, and to cultivate the most cordial understanding between the two countries. I have the honour to be with perfect truth and respect, Sir, Your most obedient humble servant,

EDWD THORNTON.

ALS, RG 59, DNA.

1. The letter from Price to JM, requesting duplicate copies of the letters, has not been found.

To Edward Thornton

Sir,   Dept of State Washington Feb. 24 1801.

I pray your very serious attention to the inclosed extract of a letter received by the Secretary of the Navy.[1]

Our dispatches from our Minister at London give us assurances of the friendly dispositions of the British cabinet towards the United States, and have encouraged the opinion that no orders justify the late conduct of your Courts of Vice-Admiralty and Cruizers in your American Colonies and in the American Seas. We are therefore at a loss to account for the almost indiscriminate captures and condemnations of which our merchants daily and bitterly complain. You will perceive, Sir, the absolute impossibility of maintaining that harmony which at present subsists between the two nations, and which it is the interest of both to preserve, unless these practices be restrained. There can be ⟨no⟩ pretext for preventing in American bottoms ⟨a⟩ commerce with the Spanish Colonies, which ⟨is⟩ carried on in those of Britain.

The good dispositions you ⟨have⟩ ever manifested, and your regard for jus⟨tice⟩ and the honor and interests of your own ⟨nation⟩ assure us of the sincerity, with which you ⟨will⟩ endeavour to restrain proceedings, which f⟨urnish⟩ such deep and serious causes of complaint. With very high and respectful consideration I am &c.

(signed)   J. MARSHALL.

Copy, F.O.5/32, P.R.O. In Thornton's hand. Enclosed in Thornton to Lord Grenville, 28 Feb. 1801. Angle brackets enclose letters obscured in margin.

1. As chairman of the Philadelphia chamber of commerce, Thomas FitzSimons wrote to Benjamin Stoddert on 17 Feb. He complained about British captures of American vessels trading with Spanish ports in Cuba and on the Spanish Main. Thornton copied the extract and forwarded it along with JM's letter in his dispatch to Grenville of 28 Feb. JM also enclosed copies of FitzSimons's letter in his official letter to King of 26 Feb. and in his report to the president of 27 Feb.

To Oliver Wolcott, Jr.

Dear Sir   Washington Feb. 24th. 1801

It is with peculiar pleasure I transmit you the commission which accompanies this letter.[1] Permit me to express my sincere wish that it may be acceptable to you. At the same time I will allow myself to hope that this high & public evidence given by the President of his respect for your services & character will efface every unpleasant sensation respecting the past & smooth the way to a perfect reconciliation. I am dear Sir with much esteem, your Obedt

J MARSHALL

ALS, Oliver Wolcott, Jr., Papers, CtHi.

1. Wolcott had been appointed as a judge of the second circuit.

To Rufus King

Dear Sir,   Department of State Feb. 26th. 1801

The inclosd extract of a letter from Mr. Fitzsimmons to the secretary of the navy is transmitted to you for the purpose of giving you a view of the impression made by the late conduct of the british cruizers & courts of Vice admiralty in America. The endeavors of Mr. Liston to check this piratical system have I believe been uniform & sincere, & Mr. Thornton who in the absence of the minister is chargé d'affaires of his Britannic Majesty, gives me assurances on which I implicitly rely, that any influence which he may possess will be exerted to limit captures & condemnations within those bounds which are prescribd by the laws of nations & the particular subsisting treaty between the United States & Great Britain. I wish his representations may be treated with the respect they deserve. I own that I do not promise much good from them. The British courts of Vice Admiralty appear organizd for the purpose of legalizing plunder & I fear that without decisive measures from the Cabinet of London a system totally incompatible with the preservation of peace will be perseverd in.

It is understood that all cargoes consisting in part of the produce of the Spanish colonies are condemnd. If they are confiscated as being enemy property it is certain that the courts proceed without any respect to testimony & without even the semblance of justice. It cannot be doubted that condemnations very frequently take place when it is entirely certain that the property is really & bona fide american.

This has inducd an opinion that the courts have proceeded on another principle. That other principle is that all trade with the Spanish colonies is unlawful, because it was not allowd in time of peace. Without inquiring into the validity of this principle in cases & situations to which it will apply we deem it totally inapplicable to the existing state of things. The trade with the Spanish colonies being openly carried on by the british themselves the object & effect of excluding American vessels from the same commerce is, not to distress the enemy, but to advantage Britain by a monopoly of this trade. This pretension being entirely & clearly inadmissible the proceedings founded on it cannot be submitted to.

Since however a new administration is about to manage the affairs of the United States the President is not disposd to give instructions which may in any degree embarrass them.

He only wishes you to make amicable & serious remonstrances to the british government on the present state of things, when a proper occasion may present itself, & to prepare for those documents which will be forwarded to you I presume, so soon as they shall be collected.

I have receivd your letters up to No. 93 except 91 which has not yet reachd me.[1]

The inclosd letter from Mrs. Washington to Sir John Sinclair I hope will be forwarded to that gentleman. With very much respect & esteem, I am dear Sir your obedt. Servt.

J MARSHALL

ALS, Collection of Mrs. John Hammond, Washington, D.C. Endorsed by King: "Sec. State No. 12 Feb: 26. 1801/Recd. July 7. At the same time and under cover of Mr. Madisons Dispatch of the 21 May—It is extraordinary that this letter shd. have been so long in coming to hand!"

1. King's No. 91, dated 10 Dec. 1800 (App. I, Cal.), was received on 27 Feb.

To Rufus King

private

Dear Sir   Washington Feb. 26th. 1801

You will undoubtedly receive from your correspondents in this country full & detaild accounts of the present state of our political system.

The strange revolution which has taken place in public opinion has I doubt not been attributed to various causes & it woud afford you no satisfaction that I shoud add my conjectures also to those which have been made by others.

The course to be pursued in future is of more importance & is not easily to be determind by those who have no place in the confidence of the President elect. So far as relates to our domestic situation it is beleivd & feard that the tendency of the administration will be to strengthen the state governments at the expence of that of the Union

& to transfer as much as possible the powers remaining with the general government to the floor of the house of representatives.

The cabinet is supposd not to be perfectly formd. Mr. Madison of Virginia is undoubtedly the Secretary of State. Mr. Dearbourne of Massachussetts it is conjecturd will be the secretary of war. The Treasury has been supposd to be destind for Mr. Galatin, but doubts are now entertaind concerning this office & some beleive that it will be filld by Mr. Baldwin. It is as supposd that Genl. Smith of Baltimore was fixd on as the Secretary of the Navy—but this too is now brought into doubt. Mr. Lincoln of Massachussetts has been spoken of at one time as the Attorney General & at another Mr. Livingstone of New York.

What the conduct of Mr. Jefferson will be with respect to foreign powers is uncertain. Among those who have supported him are men who on this subject differ widely from each other. The most inteligent among them are in my opinion desirous of preserving peace with Britain but there is a mass of violence & passion in the party which seems to me disposd to press on to war. My private conjecture is that the government will use all its means to excite the resentment & hate of the peopl⟨e⟩ against England without designing to proceed to actual hostilities. For this the ill conduct of the british cruizers & still more of their courts of Vice Admiralty furnishes very abundant materials. Our merchants are preparing remonstrances on this subject which will pour in on the new administration & will have a great effect on the public mind.

If you have not yet concluded an agreement with the british minister I submit it privately to your consideration whether it will not be most wise to delay the completion of that business til you hear from the new Administration. Perhaps the agreement proposd wd. not be ratified & it woud certainly be more desirable that it shoud not be made. I am dear Sir with great & sincere respect & esteem, your obedt

J MARSHALL

Mr. Short is spoken of as the minister to France.

ALS, PP. Addressed by JM to King in London and marked "private." Endorsed by King as received 7 July.

To John Adams

Sir   Department of State feby. 27th. 1801

The order of the house of representatives of the 24th. of this month requesting an account of the depredations commited on the commerce of the United States by vessels of Great Britain, of which complaint has been made to the government, having been referd to this department, I have the honor to transmit herewith an abstract of such cases as have been complaind of since the commencement of the year 1800:[1]

The order of the house having fixd no period at which the account it requests is to commence, I have, from a consideration of the short space for which the present session can continue, thought it compatible with their view to limit the abstract to the time above mentiond.

From various reasons it is to be presumd that many captures have been made of which no complaint has been forwarded to the government. Under this impression & for the purpose of giving a comprehensive view of the subject I have thought it not improper to annex to the abstract several extracts of letters from our Consuls & also an extract of a letter from the President of the Chamber of commerce at Philadelphia to the Secretary of the Navy.[2]

I will also take the liberty to observe that neither the communications from our minister at London, nor my conversations with the Chargé d'affaires of his Britannic majesty in the United States woud lead to an opinion that any additional orders have been lately given by the british government authorizing the system of depredation alluded to in the letter from Mr. Fitzsimmons.[3] I am Sir with every sentiment of the most entire respect, your Obedt. Servt

J MARSHALL

ALS, RG 233, DNA.

1. For the resolution of the House, see *Annals of Congress*, X, 1052–53. The abstract lists seventeen captured vessels, including those owned by Chandler Price, Charles DeWolfe, and William Patterson, mentioned in their correspondence with JM. Adams communicated JM's letter and its enclosures to the House on 27 Feb. See *Message from the President of the United States, Transmitting A Report from the Secretary of State . . . [27 Feb. 1801]* (Washington, D.C., 1801; S #1513). The report is also printed in *ASP, Foreign Relations*, II, 345–47.

2. The report includes extracts from the following consular letters to the secretary of state: William Savage, agent at Kingston, 5 June 1800; John Gavino, consul at Gibraltar, 19 Nov., 14 Dec. 1800; Thomas Bulkeley, consul at Lisbon, 27 June 1800; and an extract of Thomas FitzSimon's letter of 17 Feb. 1801 to Benjamin Stoddert.

3. In his dispatch to Lord Grenville on 28 Feb., Edward Thornton reported a conversation with JM on the subject of the captures:

"In a conversation which I had ⟨with⟩ Mr Marshall on this subject, I made no hesita-⟨tion⟩ in expressing to him my perfect conviction, that ⟨no⟩ orders had been given by

His Majesty's Govern⟨ment⟩ to depart from the liberal system, which had been adopted for so long time past towards the United ⟨States⟩, and I find that he made use of my assurances, ⟨in⟩ the communication of the President laid before ⟨the⟩ House, in order, to tranquillize the minds of peo⟨ple⟩ which had been a good deal agitated by the occurrence of these untoward circumstances at ⟨this⟩ particular a crisis. He lamented to me very seriously the effect which they were daily producing on the public opinion, and the triumphant use, which was made of them to prejudice the people as well against Great Britain as against the federal government: and when I mentioned instances of fraudulent transactions that had come within my knowlege, and which possibly the Commanders of privateers in the indiscriminating spirit of plunder had converted into a general accusation, he allowed that he should be rather pleased to see the illegitimate commerce of unprincipled adventurers checked by the vigilant scrutiny of His Majesty's Ships of war, if it were confined to them alone. He adverted also particularly to a principle lately adopted in the Courts of Vice-Admiralty at Jamaica and Providence, that no commerce would be permitted between a belligerent and neutral nation in the vessels of the latter, but such as had been authorized previously to the commencement of hostilities. However regular, he observed, this principle might be, where it was pursued with a view of distressing the enemy, and thereby red⟨ucing⟩ him to terms of peace; yet that motive ceases ⟨to⟩ operate, when a kind of licensed commerce w⟨as⟩ allowed between the subjects of the hostile natio⟨ns⟩ themselves; and there could be no just reason ⟨for⟩ proscribing in American vessels an intercour⟨se⟩ which was permitted in British bottoms" (F.O.5/32, P.R.O.).

To Theodore Sedgwick

Sir   Department of State: 27 Feby. 1801.

In my report of this day to the President, on the subject of British captures, and which he will have transmitted to Congress, it was accidentally omitted to insert the case of the Brigantine Ruby, Capt. Wrigley, belonging to Mr. Ambrose Vasse of Philadelphia. This vessel proceeding for Port au Prince, with a cargo consisting of American produce and some German goods, was lately captured by the British Ship of War Tisiphone and carried to Jamaica, where, the owner informs me, both vessel and cargo were condemned as enemy's property.

I therefore request, that the House will consider this letter, as an appendage to my report above alluded to.[1] I have the honor to be, With great respect, Sir, your most obed. Servt.

J MARSHALL

LS, RG 233, DNA. Addressed, "The Honble/The Speaker of the House of Representatives." Endorsed as received 27 Feb.

1. This letter is also printed in *ASP, Foreign Relations*, II, 345.

From Thomas Jefferson

Sir   Washington Mar. 2. 1801.

I was desired two or three days ago to sign some sea letters to be dated on or after the 4th. of Mar. but in the mean time to be forwarded to the different ports; and I understood you would countersign them as the person appointed to perform the duties of Secretary of state, but that you thought a reappointment to be dated the 4th. of March would be necessary: I shall with pleasure sign such a reappointment nunc pro tunc, if you can direct it to be made out, not being able to do it myself for want of a knowledge of the form.

I propose to take the oath or oaths of office as President of the US on Wednesday the 4th. inst. at 12. oclock in the Senate chamber. May I hope the favor of your attendance to administer the oath? As the two houses have notice of the hour, I presume a precise punctuality to it will be expected from me. I would pray you in the mean time to consider whether the oath prescribed in the constitution be not the only one necessary to take? It seems to comprehend the substance of that prescribed by the act of Congress to all officers, and it may be questionable whether the legislature can require any new oath from the President.[1] I do not know what has been done in this heretofore; but I presume the oaths administered to my predecessors are recorded in the Secretary of state's office.

Not being yet provided with a private Secretary, & needing some person on Wednesday to be the bearer of a message or messages to the Senate, I presume the chief clerk of the department of state[2] might be employed with propriety. Permit me through you to ask the favor of his attendance on me to my lodgings on Wednesday after I shall have been qualified. I have the honor to be with great respect Sir, your most obedt humble sert.

Th: Jefferson

ALS (press copy), Jefferson Papers, DLC.

1. *U.S. Statutes at Large*, I, 23.
2. Jacob Wagner.

To Thomas Jefferson

Sir   Washington March 2d. 1801

I am this instant honord with yours of to day.

Not being the Secretary of State, & only performing the duties of that office at the request of the President, the request becomes indispensably necessary to give validity to any act which purports to be done on the 4th. of March.

In the confidence that it will be receivd I shall immediately proceed to sign the sea letters. No form is prescribd. Any letter desiring me to do the duties of the office generally on the 4th. of March will be sufficient.

I shall with much pleasure attend to administer the oath of Office on the 4th. & shall make a point of being punctual. The records of the office of the department of state furnish no information respecting the oaths which have been heretofore taken. That prescribd in the constitution seems to me to be the only one which is to be administerd. I will however enquire what has been the practice.

The chief clerk of this department will attend you at the time requested. I have the honor to be with great respect Sir, Your most obedt. hble. Servt

J MARSHALL

ALS, Jefferson Papers, DLC. Endorsed by Jefferson.

From Oliver Wolcott, Jr.

Sir   Middletown March 2d. 1801

I have had the honour to receive your favour of Feby. 21st.[1] accompanying a Comn. as Judge of the Circuit Court, for the second Circuit & take the liberty to request you to present my sincere and grateful acknowledgements to the President of the United States, for this distinguished proof of his Confidence and favour.

It is with great diffidence, that I undertake to discharge the duties of this appointment yet if diligence & fidelity can compensate for the qualifications which I may not possess, I indulge a hope, that my services will be approved. I have the honour to be with perfect respect, Sir, your obedt. Sert:

OLIV WOLCOTT

ADfS, Oliver Wolcott, Jr., Papers, CtHi.

1. No letter of 21 Feb. has been found. This is apparently Wolcott's formal reply to JM's letter of 24 Feb. The inside address is to "The Honble John Marshall Esqr. Secy. of State."

From Oliver Wolcott, Jr.

My Dear Sir,   Middletown Mar. 2d. 1801.

I have recd. your favour of the 24th. of February, and cordially thank you for the oblidging expressions of your friendship.[1] The appointment with which I have been honoured, was unexpected and I learn with pleasure that it was unsolicited by my friends.

Being sensible that I owe this distinguished proof of confidence, to the favour of the President, duty and inclination naturally inspire sentiments of gratitude and good will and I assure you that I yield to their influence not only without reluctance or reserve, but with the highest satisfaction.

It is impossible that I should not feel the greatest diffidence of my qualifications for the appointment, yet so far as diligence & fidelity can compensate for the deficiencies of which I am conscious, I may hope to render my services acceptable. I am Dear Sir, with the highest esteem, your obed Sert.

O. W.

ADfS, Oliver Wolcott, Jr., Papers, CtHi.

1. The inside address is to "The Honble John Marshall Esq," indicating that this was a private letter.

From Thomas Jefferson

Sir   Washington Mar. 4. 1801.

In pursuance of the act of Congress providing that in case of vacancy in the office of Secretary of state the President of the US: may authorize a person to perform the duties of the same,[1] I am to ask the favor of you, & hereby authorize you to perform the duties of the Secretary of state until a successor to that office shall be appointed. I have the honor to be Sir, Your most obedt: sert.

TH: JEFFERSON

ALS, RG 59, DNA; ALS (press copy), Jefferson Papers, DLC.

1. *U.S. Statutes at Large*, I, 415.

To Thomas Jefferson

Sir March 4th. 1781 [1801]

I have receivd your letter requesting me to perform the duties of Secretary of State until a successor be appointed. I shall with great pleasure obey this request & beg leave to assure you that I am with high & respectful consideration, Your Obedt. Humble Servt.

J MARSHALL

ALS, Jefferson Papers, DLC. Endorsed by Jefferson.

To Charles Cotesworth Pinckney

Dear Sir Washington March 4th. 1801

I had the pleasure of receiving a few days past your letter of the 11th. Feb.¹ For your friendly expressions on my late appointment I am infinitely obligd to you. Of the importance of the judiciary at all times, but more especially the present I am very fully impressd & I shall endeavor in the new office to which I am calld not to disappoint my friends.

Before I receivd your letter Judge Bay had left us with the intention of visiting the Mississipi territory. It was not in my power to be otherwise useful to him than by giving him letters to the governor & secretary of that country who will I hope facilitate his enquiries concerning his property.

To day the new political year commences—The new order of things begins. Mr. Adams I believe left the city at 4 OClock in the morning & Mr. Jefferson will be inaugurated at 12. There are some appearances which surprize me. I wish however more than I hope that the public prosperity & happiness may sustain no diminution under democratic guidance. The democrats are divided into speculative theorists & absolute terrorists: With the latter I am not disposd to class Mr. Jefferson. If he arranges himself with them it is not difficult to foresee that much calamity is in store for our country—if he does not they will soon become his enemies & calumniators.

4 OClock

I have administerd the oath to the President. You will before this reaches you see his inauguration speech. It is in the general well judgd & conciliatory. It is in direct terms giving the lie to the violent party declamation which has elected him; but it is strongly characteristic of the general cast of his political theory. With great & sincere esteem, I am dear Sir your Obedt

J MARSHALL

ALS, ScC. Addressed by JM to Pinckney in Charleston and franked; postmarked Washington, 4 Mar. Endorsed by Pinckney.

1. Letter not found.

To James M. Marshall

My dear Brother   Richmond March 18th. 1801

I learn with infinite chagrin the "developement of principle" mentiond in yours of the 12th.[1] & I cannot help regreting it the more as I fear some blame may be imputed to me.

I did not examine Mr. Cranch's commission & do not know how the error coud have been commited unless the clerk who filld it up has omited some words intended to have been inserted.[2] If this has happend it is probable that it has been recorded in the office of state with the proper words & if so no inconvenience I presume can occur.

I did not send out the commissions because I apprehended such as were for a fixd time to be completed when signd & seald & such as depended on the will of the President might at any time be revokd. To withhold the commission of the Marshal is equal to displacing him which the President I presume has the power to do, but to withhold the commission of the Justices is an act of which I entertaind no suspicion.[3] I shoud however have sent out the commissions which had been signd & seald but for the extreme hurry of the time & the absence of Mr. Wagner who had been calld on by the President to act as his private Secretary.

I have passd Pennocks two first notes to Brown & Burton for their bills at 25 per cent exchange & shall remit them to Murdock with instructions to receive the money & hold it to be applied as instructed by you.[4]

It will be advisable to bring the deed up to winchester with you where it may be acknowledgd & transmited to Norfolk.

I am excessively mortified at the circumstances relative to the appointment of the Chief Judge of the district. There was a negligence in that business arising from a confidence that Mr. Johnston woud accept, which I lament excessively. When Mr Swan parted with us at your house I thought he went to send an express the next morning.[5] I wish to hear how principles continue to develope & am your affectionate brother

J MARSHALL

Let me know the day of meeting at winchester. Write also to Mr. Colston. I set out the 1st. of Apl or so to Buckingham & thence to winchester.[6]

Pay Stewart six dollars for me which I forgot to do for myself. Ask Major Taylor for the money.

Photostat of ALS, Marshall Papers, DLC.

1. Letter not found.

2. William Cranch, John Adams's nephew, had been appointed a judge of the U.S. Circuit Court for the District of Columbia.

3. JM alluded to the withholding of the commissions of the justices of the peace for the District of Columbia, which precipitated the mandamus action by William Marbury and others against Secretary of State Madison. See James Marshall's affidavit summarized in the report of Marbury v. Madison (1 Cranch 146).

4. William Murdock was a London merchant who acted as agent for the Marshalls in their dealings with Denny Martin Fairfax and Philip Martin concerning the purchase of Leeds Manor. See JM to James Marshall, 13 Feb. 1806.

5. Thomas Johnson formerly served as associate justice of the Supreme Court. President Adams nominated Johnson as chief judge of the circuit court for the District of Columbia, along with James M. Marshall and William Cranch as assistant judges and Thomas Swan of Alexandria as attorney. Johnson declined his appointment, but news of his refusal came too late for the outgoing administration to name a replacement. President Jefferson nominated William Kilty of Maryland as chief judge in Jan. 1802 (*Senate Executive Journal*, I, 387, 389, 401, 405).

6. The Buckingham trip was undoubtedly for the purpose of selling his land in that county (Robert Craig to JM, 22 Dec. 1800; JM to Edward Carrington, 28 Dec. 1800). The Winchester meeting probably related to the taking of depositions in the suit of John and James Marshall against Philip Pendleton and David Hunter, then pending in the High Court of Chancery and later transferred to the Superior Court of Chancery at Staunton. JM and his brother were in the Winchester and Martinsburg region for this purpose during Aug. and Sept. 1801. See Marshall v. Hunter and Pendleton, editorial note (preceding Notice, 15 Sept. 1801).

To [William Croghan?]

Dear Sir[1] Richmond March 31st. 1801

Several years past I was inducd to enter into a bond as security for Daniel Brodhead conditiond that he woud carry out with him to Kentucky certain certificates & warrants belonging to the soldiers I beleive of the Illinois regiment, that he woud publish generally &

especially at the several court houses in the State that he was possessd of those certificates, & that he woud be careful not to deliver them to persons not entitled to receive them. I am told that you are probably acquainted with the fact, especially that you know Brodheads advertizement was set up at the court house of Jefferson county.[2] If you do not know this perhaps Colo. Anderson does & it is very interesting to me who am now sued by the commonwealth, to establish it.[3] I have taken a commission & have given notice to take depositions at your house on the 5th. of May. I have taken the liberty to name your house lest it shoud be inconvenient to you to go elsewhere. You will very greatly oblige me if you will be so good as to give in a deposition if you know any thing of the circumstance or if you do not & Colo. Anderson does that you will ask him or any other person who recollects the advertizement to depose conce[r]ning it on the 5th. of May at your house.

I send out a blank commission which I beg the favor of you to fill up with any names of Magistrates who can attend & request that they will certify the deposition or depositions to have been taken on the 5th. of May at your house in Jefferson County in the state of Kentucky & annex it to the queries I now inclose. Any expence which may attend this business be so good as to draw on me for & I will pay it with much pleasure.

I hope you will excuse this trouble & beleive me to be with very much respect & esteem, your Obedt. Servt

J Marshall

Please to inclose the depositions to Colo. Harvie[4] or myself or the Clerk of the Genl. court. We wish to receive them by the 9th. of June.

ALS, Marshall Papers, ViW.

1. Although the address leaf is missing, the recipient was probably William Croghan (1752–1822), whose home "Locust Grove" was in Jefferson County, near Louisville. (JM speaks of "your house in Jefferson County.") Croghan was married to Lucy Clark, sister of George Rogers Clark, and their son George Croghan won fame during the War of 1812 (Hutchinson, *Papers of Madison*, XI, 365 n. 4; James F. Hopkins and Mary W. M. Hargreaves, eds., *The Papers of Henry Clay, I: The Rising Statesman, 1797–1814* [Lexington, Ky., 1959], 423, 424 n. 4).

As one of the commissioners appointed under a Virginia law for surveying and apportioning lands granted to members of George Rogers Clark's Illinois regiment, William Croghan was in a position to know the facts JM was seeking to establish in defending the suit brought against him by the Commonwealth of Virginia (Hening, *Statutes*, XII, 397). Another circumstance pointing to Croghan as the recipient is that a letter from JM to William Croghan was offered for sale in 1892. The catalog description reads: "ALS, 2pp, 4to, Richmond, 1801. To William Croghan, regarding his appointment as a commissioner to investigate some Illinois troubles" (*The Collector* [Jan. 1892], 81.) This may be the letter eventually purchased by the College of William and

Mary in 1937. (There was no address leaf with the letter at the time of this purchase.)

2. See the Virginia law of 1796 "giving further time to the commissioners appointed for surveying and apportioning the lands granted to the Illinois regiment, to execute deeds for the same." Earlier laws on this subject had been enacted in 1783 and 1786. Daniel Brodhead, Jr. (1755–1831), originally from New York, moved to Kentucky after serving as an officer in the Continental army during the Revolution. He represented Jefferson County in the 1788 session of the Virginia General Assembly. A remark in a letter from George Rogers Clark to Gov. Patrick Henry, dated May 1786, may have some bearing on this matter: "Since my return to this Country, report says that Mr. Daniel Broadhead has got a number of Certificates and other papers from the Soldiery who serv'd in this Country, and that the manner of getting them is not much to his Credit" (Shepherd, *Statutes*, II, 51; Hening, *Statutes*, XI, 335; XII, 397; National Society of the Daughters of the American Revolution, *DAR Patriot Index* [Washington, D.C., 1966], 88; Earl G. Swem and John W. Williams, eds., *A Register of the General Assembly of Virginia, 1776–1918, and of the Constitutional Conventions* [Richmond, Va., 1918], 351; *CVSP*, IV, 122).

3. Richard Anderson had served as principal surveyor on behalf of the Continental Line (*PJM*, I, 166 and n. 7; II, 214, 298). The papers in this suit were presumably lost in the Richmond fire of 1865.

4. Col. John Harvie, formerly register of the Virginia Land Office (*PJM*, I, 92 n. 8; II, 321 n. 5).

Articles of Agreement

[11 September 1801]

Articles of agreement made & enterd into between James M. Marshall of the one part & Rawleigh Colston John Ambler & John Marshall of the other part.[1]

It is agreed that James M. Marshall will sell & he does hereby sell to Rawleigh Colston John Ambler & John Marshall that part of the Manor of Leeds which lies between the Cobler mountains & the rattle snake mountains,[2] which land is now occupied by Benjamin Bradford John Heater John Wolf Thomas Austin Jesse Thompson Eli Thompson Joel Little Nehemiah Dile Angus Cameron Benjamin Shute Hester Oldacre James Smith, Andrew Barbee John Keith George Moorehead Thomas Massie Thomas Swan George Thompson Philip Mallory Senr. William Dearing Richard Rixey Adam Wolf Samuel Taylor James Foley Burkett Jett John Hamrick Joseph Barbees heirs John Moorehead John Dearing Isaac Arnold, Elizabeth Redman William Hemmings Thomas Humstead George Holmes Andrew Francis Henry Shank Priest, Moorehead, Peter Lawrence & William Shoemate together with vacant lands within the said bounds.

For this land Rawleigh Colston John Ambler & John Marshall agree to give twenty shillings per acre.

In the division ultimately to be made of the manor of Leeds the property sold as above mentiond & which is to be in the share of Rawleigh Colston John Ambler & John Marshall is to be rated at the price above mentiond. They are to have immediate possession & entire control of the property but the rents are to be for the common benefit of the proprietors until the purchase money for the manor shall be paid & a division thereof be made.[3] Witness our hands & seals this eleventh day of September one thousand eight hundred & one.

Signd Seald & deliverd   J M Marshall [L.S.]
in presence of: Rawleigh Colston [L.S.]
Ephm. Gaither   John Ambler [L.S.]
P. Nadenbousch   J Marshall [L.S.]

It is agreed that John Marshall is at liberty to sell such part of the lands herein sold to us at the next Fauquier court as he may then agree for to be carried to the general account of all the proprietors of the manor of Leeds.

P. Nadenbousch   Rawleigh Colston [L.S.]
                                   John Ambler

 ADS, NIC. Entirely in JM's hand except for other signatures. Endorsed: "Articles of agreement between J. Marshall. R Colston J. Ambler & John Marshall."

 1. This agreement was probably executed in the town of Martinsburg, Berkeley County (now W.Va.), or its vicinity, where Rawleigh Colston (and the two witnesses) resided. JM and James Marshall were in this region in August and September, taking depositions in their suit against Philip Pendleton and David Hunter.

 2. The area between the Cobler and Rattlesnake mountains is just west of the town of Marshall (then known as Salem), in Fauquier County.

 3. The Marshall syndicate did not acquire title to the manor of Leeds until 18 Oct. 1806, upon paying the final installment of the purchase money of fourteen thousand pounds sterling to Philip Martin. Martin inherited the manor from his older brother Denny Martin Fairfax, who had died in 1801. A partition deed between John and James Marshall on the one part and Rawleigh Colston on the other was executed on 5 Oct. 1808 (*PJM*, II, 149 and n. 7).

Marshall v. Hunter and Pendleton

EDITORIAL NOTE

As purchasers of the Fairfax estate in the Northern Neck of Virginia, the brothers John and James Marshall frequently resorted to the courts to assert their title—first to the manor lands as a whole and then to specific tracts within this larger purchase. The contest between the Marshalls and the commonwealth over the title to the former Northern Neck proprietary was resolved by compromise under an act of the General Assembly adopted in November 1796. By this act, the Marshalls (as purchasers through Denny Fairfax, heir of the last proprietor, Thomas, sixth Lord Fairfax) relinquished all claim to the waste and ungranted lands and were confirmed in their title to the lands specifically reserved by Lord Fairfax to his use—the manor lands.[1]

The compromise, however, proved to be the beginning, not the end, of litigation for the Marshalls. Lands they considered to be part of their purchase, that is, those tracts previously set aside by Lord Fairfax for his personal use, were also claimed by persons holding patents from the commonwealth. They contended that their patents were for tracts formerly designated as waste and ungranted. To settle these disputes, the Marshalls, beginning in the late 1790s, brought suits in the state High Court of Chancery. Although the papers of this court were destroyed in 1865, a few of the Marshall suits survive because they were transferred to the Superior Court of Chancery at Staunton in 1802, when chancery jurisdiction was split among three courts (Richmond and Williamsburg were the others). The original papers in these suits are filed in the clerk's office of the Augusta County Circuit Court, Staunton. The following are the cases in which the Marshalls (or each singly) were parties: *Marshall v. Brewbaker and Blessing*, 1798–1808; *Marshall v. Janney*, 1799–1816; *Marshall v. Hunter and Pendleton*, 1799–1805; *Marshall v. Thompson*, 1799–1802; *Simpson v. Marshall*, 1800–1802.

Among these chancery papers are pleadings and other documents in the hand of John Marshall, which show that he was closely involved in prosecuting the suits. He drafted bills in chancery and took depositions in Winchester, Martinsburg, and other locations in the lower Shenandoah Valley region where the disputed lands lay. Documents from two of the cases at the Staunton Superior Court of Chancery are presented in this volume: *Marshall v. Hunter and Pendleton* (notice and depositions below and at 28 August 1802); and *Marshall v. Janney* (amended bill in chancery, 29 November 1803). Both suits began in the High Court of Chancery in June 1799 with the filing of bills drawn by Marshall on behalf of his brother and himself.[2]

David Hunter and his father-in-law, Philip Pendleton, were familiar opponents of the Marshalls in contesting titles to valuable Northern Neck lands.[3] The dispute in this instance concerned a tract of eight hundred acres near Shepherdstown, in present-day Jefferson County, West Virginia. The Marshalls claimed it on the basis of a survey made for Lord Fairfax, who originally intended to give the land to Robert Beale. After Beale left for England (never to return), Fairfax, according to the bill in chancery, resurveyed the land for himself, which during his life was considered "universally as his property." Hunter and Pendleton contended that "Bealls Land" had become grantable by the commonwealth as unappropriated Northern Neck lands. The parties began to collect the testimony of witnesses late in the summer of 1801.[4]

1. For the Marshalls' purchase of the Fairfax manors and the legal proceedings that produced the compromise of 1796, see *PJM*, II, 140–49; V, 228–51.

2. Bill in chancery, [22 June 1799], Marshall v. Janney; bill in chancery, [22 June

1799], Marshall v. Hunter and Pendleton, Office of the Clerk, Augusta County Circuit Court, Staunton, Va.; JM to James M. Marshall, 3 Apr. 1799 (*PJM*, IV, 10).

3. *PJM*, V, 229–30, 235 n. 9.

4. Bill in chancery, [22 June 1799]; answer of David Hunter and Philip Pendleton, 16 Feb. 1801; notice, Hunter and Pendleton to John and James Marshall, 26 Aug. 1801, Marshall v. Hunter and Pendleton.

Notice

Gentlemen   Sept. 15th. 1801
    Please to take notice that thursday the twenty fourth day of this present month between the hours of six oclock in the morning & six oclock in the evening, at the Clerks office for the County of Frederick in Winchester we shall proceed to take depositions which we shall offer in evidence in the suit depending in the High Court of Chancery in which we are complainants & you are defendants.[1]

J MARSHALL
Js MARSHALL

ADS, Marshall v. Hunter and Pendleton, Office of the Clerk, Augusta County Circuit Court, Staunton, Va. Entirely in hand of James Marshall, including both signatures. On verso: Hunter's acknowledgment (same date) of service.

1. Earlier in the month, Hunter and Pendleton took depositions of witnesses on their behalf in Martinsburg and vicinity in Berkeley County. James Marshall received notice, though it is not clear whether he or JM attended (notice, Hunter and Pendleton to John and James Marshall, 26 Aug. 1801; deposition of Robert Cockburn, 4 Sept. 1801; deposition of Peter Light, 5 Sept. 1801, Marshall v. Hunter and Pendleton).

Deposition

[24 September 1801]
The deposition of Witnesses taken at the clerks office in the county of Frederick in Winchester on thursday the 24th. day of September in the year 1801 about one OClock in the afternoon in pursuance of Notice and by virtue of the commission annexd,[1] in the cas⟨e⟩ depending in the high court of chancery in which John Marshall & James Marshall are plaintiffs & Philip Pendleton & David Hunter defendents.[2]

John Peyton being first sworn on the Holy Evangelists of Almighty Deposeth and saith that the Copy her⟨e⟩to Annexed is a true Transcript taken from a book Containing sundry Surveys made by Richard Rigg formerly a Surveyor employed by Thomas Lord Fai⟨r⟩fax, which book was deposited in the deponents Office by John McCool Exor of the said Richd. Rigg Deceased by Order of the Winchester District Court in a Suit then depending between the Lessee of John James Maund Plt. and Richard Comyne Deft. And further the Deponent saith not.[3]

J PEYTON

John McCool of the society of friends being solemnly affirmd says that the extract mentiond in the foregoing deposition of John Peyton which he has examind & which is annexd is a true copy from the book in which Richard Rigg deceasd of whom he is executor & who was a surveyor employd by the late Thomas Lord Fairfax recorded the notes of surveys made by him: And that the entry from which the extract is taken is entirely in the hand writing of the said Richard Rigg.[4]

JNO. M:COOLE

Taken & sworn to in due form before us magistrates of the　　　this 24th. of Septr. 1801 in the clerks office in the county of Frederick in winchester about one oClock in the afternoon.

W DAVISON
JOSH. GAMBLE

AD, Marshall v. Hunter and Pendleton, Office of the Clerk, Augusta County Circuit Court, Staunton, Va. In JM's hand except for passage in hand of John Peyton and signatures. Copy of survey by Richard Rigg annexed. Clerk's notations on cover indicate that deposition was returned sealed to High Court of Chancery on 12 Oct. 1801. Angle brackets enclose letters obscured in margin.

1. The various commissions to take depositions in this suit are in the case papers (Marshall v. Hunter and Pendleton).

2. The next portion of the document is in the hand of John Peyton, clerk of Frederick County and of the Winchester District Court.

3. The Marshalls submitted the annexed survey, executed by Richard Rigg in Nov. 1773, as evidence that Lord Fairfax resurveyed for his own use the tract formerly intended for Robert Beale.

4. Another deposition in this case is under date of 28 Aug. 1802.

From Edmund Randolph

Richmond Nov. 23. 1801.[1]

Edm: Randolph presents his compliments to Gener⟨al⟩ Marshall, and will thank him, if convenient, to subjoin an answer to the questions underneath. E. R. wishes to establish certain usages in the department of state; which seem to him to be connected with his defence in the suit of the United States against him. E. R. thus troubles Mr. Marshall, on account of the impracticability of obtaining his attendance in person on the 7th. day of the next month, when Mr. M's official duty will call him to Washington.[2]

1. Is it, or is it not a principle in the settlement of the accounts of the department of state, that the secretary shall not obtain a quietus for monies, remitted to Europe, until the receipt of it shall be acknowledged by some responsible agent or banke⟨r⟩ there?

2. Is it or is it not the practice for the accounting officers to examine the accoun⟨ts⟩ of that department once a year; and is the secretary require[d] to settle them oftener than once a year?

E. R. had purposed to trouble General Marshall with some other queries, which will probably be now unnecessary from some information, being attainable from another quarter.

ALS, U.S. v. Randolph, U.S. Circuit Court, Va., Ended Cases (Restored), 1804, Vi. JM's reply on verso. Addressed to JM in unknown hand. Endorsed by Randolph: "No. 12/General Marshall's certificate." Angle brackets enclose letters obscured in margin.

1. This letter and JM's reply were filed in the suit brought by the U.S. against Randolph (JM to Randolph, 12 Nov. 1800 and n. 1).

2. The Supreme Court was to meet the first Monday in December (the seventh). Randolph's case was in the circuit court at Richmond, whose session was to commence on Saturday the fifth (*U.S. Statutes at Large*, II, 89, 91).

To Edmund Randolph

[ca. 23 November 1801]

A. 1st. It is a practice in settling the accounts of the department of State, not to give a quietus to the Secretary, until the receipt of monies remited by him to Europe shall be acknowledgd, but to receive a statement into the treasury department with the vouchers of the remitances which have been made, after which the secretary is considerd as exonerated so far as the vouchers exhibit proper disbursements.

A. 2d. The secretary is not requird to settle oftener than once a year. I beleive it is customary to examine his vouchers annually, tho of this I cannot speak positively as I did not continue one year in office.

J MARSHALL.

J Marshall with his compliments returns to Mr. Randolph his answers to the queries propounded to him. He has been prevented by company from returning the paper earlier.

ALS, U.S. v. Randolph, U.S. Circuit Court, Va., Ended Cases (Restored), Vi. On verso of Randolph to JM, 23 Nov. 1801.

United States v. Schooner Peggy
Opinion
U.S. Supreme Court, 21 December 1801

EDITORIAL NOTE

The French schooner *Peggy*, captured by the American ship *Trumbull* in April 1800 a few miles offshore of Port-au-Prince, was condemned as a lawful prize by the U.S. Circuit Court for Connecticut in September 1800 (reversing an earlier decree by the U.S. district court). The case was removed to the Supreme Court by writ of error dated 2 October 1800. On 21 December 1801, the same day the court gave judgment, President Jefferson promulgated final ratification of the convention between the United States and France (originally signed on 30 September 1800). The fourth article of the convention provided for the mutual restoration of "property captured, and not yet *definitively* condemned." The principal question to be decided was whether the circuit court's decree of September 1800 was a definitive condemnation within the meaning of the fourth article.[1]

The case was argued on 14 and 17 December 1801 by Roger Griswold and James A. Bayard for the captors and by John T. Mason for the claimant. The reporter William Cranch did not have notes for this case and was unable to report the "very ingenious arguments." A brief set of notes on counsel's arguments, taken by Justice Paterson, survives in manuscript.[2]

1. 1 Cranch 103–8; U.S. v. Schooner Peggy, App. Cas. No. 93.
2. U.S. Sup. Ct. Minutes, 14, 17 Dec. 1801; 1 Cranch 108n; U.S. v. Schooner Peggy, Notes [in hand of William Paterson], Dec. 1801, NjMoHP.

OPINION

In this case the court is of opinion that the schooner Peggy is within the provisions of the treaty entered into with France and ought to be restored.[1] This vessel is not considered as being definitively condemned. The argument at the bar which contends that because the sentence of the circuit court is denominated a final sentence, therefore its condemnation is definitive in the sense in which that term is used in the treaty, is not deemed a correct argument.[2] A decree or sentence may be interlocutory or final in the court which pronounces it, and receives its appellation from its determining the power of that particular court over the subject to which it applies, or being only an intermediate order subject to the future control of the same court. The last decree of an inferior court is final in relation to the power of that court, but not in relation to the property itself, unless it be acquiesced under. The terms used in the treaty seem to apply to the actual condition of the property and to direct a restoration of that which is still in controversy between the parties. On any other construction the word *definitive* would be rendered useless and inoperative. Vessels are seldom if ever condemned but by a final sentence. An interlocutory order for a sale is not a condemnation. A stipulation then for the restoration of vessels not yet condemned, would on this construction comprehend as many cases as a stipulation for the restoration of such as are not yet definitively condemned. Every condemnation is final as to the court which pronounces it, and no other difference is perceived between a condemnation and a final condemnation, than that the one terminates definitively the controversy between the parties and the other leaves that controversy still depending. In this case the sentence of condemnation was appealed from, it might have been reversed, and therefore was not such a sentence as in the contemplation of the contracting parties, on a fair and honest construction of the contract, was designated as a definitive condemnation.

It has been urged that the court can take no notice of the stipulation for the restoration of property not yet definitively condemned, that the judges can only enquire whether the sentence was erroneous when delivered, and that if the judgment was correct it cannot be made otherwise by any thing subsequent to its rendition.[3]

The constitution of the United States declares a treaty to be the supreme law of the land. Of consequence its obligation on the courts of the United States must be admitted. It is certainly true that the execution of a contract between nations is to be demanded from, and, in the general, superintended by the executive of each nation, and therefore, whatever the decision of this court may be relative to the rights of parties litigating before it, the claim upon the nation if unsatisfied, may still be asserted. But yet where a treaty is the law of the land, and as such affects the rights of parties litigating in court, that treaty as much binds those rights and is as much to be regarded by the court as an act of congress; and although restoration may be an executive, when viewed as a substantive, act independent of, and unconnected with, other circumstances, yet to condemn a vessel, the restoration of which is directed by a law of the land, would be a direct infraction of that law, and of consequence, improper.

It is in the general true that the province of an appellate court is only to enquire whether a judgment when rendered was erroneous

WILLIAM PATERSON
Pastel on paper attributed to James Sharples, ca. 1800. *Courtesy of the Office of the Curator, Supreme Court of the United States*

or not. But if subsequent to the judgment and before the decision of the appellate court, a law intervenes and positively changes the rule which governs, the law must be obeyed, or its obligation denied. If the law be constitutional, and of that no doubt in the present case has been expressed, I know of no court which can contest its obligation. It is true that in mere private cases between individuals, a court will and ought to struggle hard against a construction which will, by a retrospective operation, affect the rights of parties, but in great national concerns where individual rights, acquired by war, are sacrificed for national purposes, the contract, making the sacrifice, ought always to receive a construction conforming to its manifest import; and if the nation has given up the vested rights of its citizens, it is not for the court, but for the government, to consider whether it be a case proper for compensation. In such a case the court must decide according to existing laws, and if it be necessary to set aside a judgment, rightful when rendered, but which cannot be affirmed but in violation of law, the judgment must be set aside.

Printed, William Cranch, *Reports of Cases Argued and Adjudged in the Supreme Court of the United States* . . . , I (Washington, D.C., 1804), 108–10.

1. The effect of the Convention of 1800 was the main question. Mason, for the claimant, also denied the legality of the capture on the ground that the *Peggy* was not an "armed vessel" within the meaning of the 1798 act "further to protect the Commerce of the United States" and that the capture had not been made on the "high seas" (U.S. v. Schooner Peggy, Notes [Paterson], Dec. 1801, NjMoHP; *U.S. Statutes at Large*, I, 578–80).

2. Bayard contended that "the sentence below was definitive, as contradistinguished from interlocutory" (U.S. v. Schooner Peggy, Notes [Paterson], Dec. 1801, NjMoHP).

3. Bayard maintained that the Supreme Court could enquire only into "the legality of the cond[emnatio]n below" (ibid.).

From Rufus King

Dear Sir,   London January 12. 1802

It was more than six months after you left the Department of State, before I received your last official Letter, which was accompanied by a private one of nearly the same date.[1] I ought sooner to have acknowledged its receipt; but I have been waiting in hopes that I should be enabled to inform you, which I have now the satisfaction of doing, that the difficulties respecting the execution of the 6 & 7. Articles of the Treaty of 1794. had been settled.

I have signed a Convention with Lord Hawkesbury by which England agrees to accept £600,000 payable in three equal instalments of one two and three years next after the date of the Exchange of Ratifications, in satisfaction of her Claims under the 6. article which is abolished; and moreover consents that the Commissioners under the 7. article shall immediately reassemble and proceed in the discharge of their Duties, according to the Provisions of the Article, except only, that instead of their awards being made payable at such times as they might appoint, the same shall be payable in three equal instalments corresponding with those to be paid by the United States.[2] The second article of the Convention is in these words "whereas it is agreed by the 4. article of the definitive Treaty of Peace concluded at Paris on the 3d. day of September 1783. between his Britannic Majesty and the United States That Creditors on either side should meet with no lawful Impediment to the recovery of the full value in sterling money of all bonafide Debts theretofore Contracted, it is hereby declared that the said 4th. article, so far as respect its future operation, is hereby recognized, confirmed, and declared to be binding and obligatory on his Britannic Majesty and the said United States and the same shall be accordingly observed with punctuality and good faith, and so as that the said Creditors shall hereafter meet with no lawful impediment to the Recovery of the full value in sterling money of their bonafide Debts."

This article was inserted for the purpose of enabling the English Minister to meet the Complaints of the Creditors against the sum we are to pay, by referring them to their Judicial remedies; we could have no objection to it, provided it was so drawn up, as not to enlarge the legal operation of the Article it recognizes. Upon this point I have no doubt. It confirms the future operation of the 4th. article, or in other words, limits its operation to what is now a legal subject for it to operate upon: what is now a bona fide Debt, that is what is a legal subject, will not depend upon a Reference to what once might have been so, but is a question of Judicial Competence, and must consequently be decided by those general and acknowledged Principles by which Similar Cases are decided. Here it is understood and expected that the affair of the Debts is finally settled as between the two Governments; and with that share of Prudence which the Tribunals of every Country are disposed to observe in questions affected by national Stipulations, I am persuaded we shall hear no more of them. Being pressed for time to complete my official Dispatches in season for the Packet, I will only add to this hasty communication, the assurance of sincere regard and respect with which I have the honour to be Dear sir, Your obt faithful sr

R. K.

P.S. I have sent to the Secretary of State a full and exact report of every material occurrence which happened in the course of a difficult and tedious discussion respecting this Settlement.[3]

Letterbook copy, King Papers, NHi.

1. See JM's letters to King of 26 Feb. 1801, both of which King received on 7 July. A note in the left margin opposite this sentence reads: "Substance and Construction of the Convention respecting the 6 and 7. articles of the Treaty of amity &c."

2. JM's last instructions on this subject were communicated in his letter to King of 4 Dec. 1800. King and Lord Hawkesbury signed the convention on 8 Jan. 1802. Article 6 of the Jay Treaty of 1794 created a mixed commission to hear claims of British creditors for their prewar debts. Article 7 of that treaty established a similar commission to determine compensation due claimants for losses resulting from unlawful captures and condemnation of vessels and merchandise.

3. All the documents relating to the negotiation of the Convention of 1802 are published in *ASP, Foreign Relations*, II, 382–428.

To Oliver Wolcott, Jr.

Dear Sir   Richmond April 5th. 1802

I thank you very sincerely for the copy of the last judicial bill you were so good as to inclose me.[1] It is a subject on which I felt some sollicitude as I was entirely uncertain what destiny woud be decreed to us. There are some essential defects in the system which will I presume be remedied as they involve no party or political questions, but relate only to the mode of carrying causes from the circuit to the supreme court. They had been attended to in the bill lately repeald & I make no doubt will be again.[2]

The terms of the courts of the 5th circuit are I beleive inconvenient to the bar, but if they are they will I presume request to have them changd.[3]

I regret that the next June term will be put down, but I have no doubt the immediate operation of the bill will be insisted on.[4]

I consider the bill for repealing the internal revenue as passd, as I do every other measure which is reported, & which is favord by those who favor the bill for repealing the late judicial system.[5] The power which coud pass that act can fail in nothing.

I have no doubt of finding the north Western territory added in spite of itself to the number of States if any apprehension can be entertaind that their votes will be necessary at the next election. I had however supposd that Gentlemen in office felt themselves too strong in the favor of the people to suppose that an addition of three votes coud be necessary.[6] I am dear Sir with much esteem & regard, Your Obedt

J MARSHALL

Is not the jury tax most unreasonable & designd to discourage a resort to the federal courts?

ALS, Oliver Wolcott, Jr., Papers, CtHi.

1. Letter not found. Since there is no cover, the only evidence identifying Wolcott as the recipient of this letter is its depository location. Wolcott had been appointed a circuit court judge under the act of 1801 and thus stood to be displaced by the repeal.

2. The repealing act passed 8 Mar. A new judiciary bill was introduced in the Senate on 26 Mar. It passed the Senate on 8 Apr. and became law on 29 Apr. (*Annals of Congress*, XI, 205, 251, 252, 256–57; *U.S. Statutes at Large*, II, 132, 156–67).

3. The new act set the terms of the fifth circuit, comprising Virginia and North Carolina, as follows: in Virginia, the court was to convene on 22 May and 22 Nov.; in North Carolina, 15 June and 29 Dec. The chief justice was assigned to this circuit (*U.S. Statutes at Large*, II, 157–58).

4. Under the act of 1801, which was repealed, the Supreme Court was to meet in June. The act of 1802 provided for an annual sitting of the court commencing the first Monday in February. Thus the Supreme Court, which last met in Dec. 1801, would not sit again until Feb. 1803. Bayard unsuccessfully introduced an amendment to postpone the operation of the act until 1 July. In his speech advocating the amendment, the representative from Delaware remarked: "They are about to pronounce that the Supreme Court, a court formed under the Constitution, shall not sit for fourteen months, instead of sitting in six months. Are gentlemen afraid of the judges? Are they afraid that they will pronounce the repealing law void?" (*Annals of Congress*, XI, 1229).

5. The bill for repealing internal taxes was approved on 6 Apr. (*U.S. Statutes at Large*, II, 149–50).

6. An act to enable the people of the eastern division of the Northwest Territory to form a constitution and state government passed on 30 Apr. 1802 (ibid., 173–75).

To William Paterson

Dear Sir   Richmond April 6th. 1802

Your favor of the 29th. of March reachd me last night.[1] The letter addressd to Judge Washington I shall immediately inclose to him.[2] Unfortunately the mail to Westmoreland is forwarded only once a week & had set out yesterday morning, so that a week will yet elapse before he can receive the letter. I have never seen that, the publication of which is sollicited & am entirely unacquainted with its contents.[3]

I shall feel great pleasure in promoting so far as may be in my power the interests of Princeton College. I regret extremely the misfortune which has befallen it & wish very sincerely that the proper remedy may be applied.[4]

You have I doubt not seen the arrangement of our future duties as markd out in a bill lately reported to the Senate. They are less burthensome than heretofore, or than I expected. I confess I have some strong constitutional scruples. I cannot well perceive how the performance of circuit duty by the Judges of the supreme court can be supported. If the question was new I shoud be unwilling to act in this character without a consultation of the Judges; but I consider it as decided & that whatever my own scruples may be I am bound by the decision. I cannot however but regret the loss of the next June term. I coud have wishd the Judges had convend before they proceeded to execute the new system. With great respect & esteem, I am dear Sir your Obedt.

J MARSHALL

ALS, Paterson Papers, NjR; Tr, NN. Addressed by JM to Paterson at New Brunswick; postmarked Richmond, 6 Apr. Endorsed by Paterson.

1. Letter not found.

2. Paterson wrote to Bushrod Washington on behalf of Egbert Benson, who desired some information from George Washington's papers. See JM to Paterson, 3 May.

3. This is possibly a reference to a note by William A. Rind, editor of the *Washington Federalist* (Georgetown, D.C.), which he inserted in his paper of 27 Mar. It stated that a biography of Washington "is now in the work-shop of an artist eminent for his erudition, and possessed of the materials which were collected by *Washington* himself. The public are therefore requested to defer subscriptions to the daily proposals for lives of this great man, as the editor has authority to state that an accurate and elegant performance on this subject will very shortly be presented to the world." The printers in the different states were requested "to give the above note a corner in their respective papers."

4. Paterson was a trustee of the college, which recently had suffered a disastrous fire. Newspapers reported the calamity, along with an appeal for support (see *Washington Federalist*, 5 Apr. 1802).

To James A. Bayard

Dear Sir   April 12th. 1802

I have the mortification to perceive in a publication of a report made by the secretary of the treasury that my accounts while in the department of state are not yet settled.[1]

It was my wish to settle them quarterly but the officers to whom that business was entrusted coud not easily be prevaild on to deviate so far from antient usage.

On my leaving the office however I understood that no difficulty existed other than a wish to receive the vouchers from europe for monies paid there.

On calling upon the comptroller in December I was not a little astonishd to be told that a sum of about 1000$ paid to Mr. Johnston[2] for money advancd by him while a consul in England for public purposes was supposd to have been improperly paid because there was, as it was said, no appropriation which authorizd it, & that on this account the settlement was not completed.

This money the accounting clerk had paid from a mistake of my instructions. I had told him the money ought to be paid as the claim was just & that I woud apply to the President for a warrant on the contingent fund. On this conversation he paid the money, &, as he was a very correct young man & coud not afford to lose it I sanctiond the payment tho Mr. Adams, contrary to my expectation was unwilling to grant the warrant.

On hearing this I informd the comptroller & auditor that if it was incumbent on them to refuse me a credit for this item I begd they woud say so—that however unworthy it might be of the government to endeavor to obtain from an individual 1000$ by such means I woud much rather pay it than permit the account to remain unclosd; & I therefore desird if this was necessary that they woud tell me so. They both discoverd much unwillingness to settle the business in that way, & I parted with them supposing it woud not be necessary, nor did I expect to change this opinion till I perceivd by the report of the secretary that the account is yet open. To settle this business I think it incumbent on me to repair to the city & I shall wait on the officers who are to decide this business in the course of next week.[3]

Mr. Hill staid a day with us & set out this morning for North Carolina.[4] I had the pleasure of hearing from you by him & am happy to hear that the difficulties & vexations experiencd in a minority still leave you in health & spirits. I am dear Sir with much respect & esteem, Your Obedt Servt

J MARSHALL

ALS, DeHi. Addressed by JM to Bayard at Washington and franked; postmarked Richmond, [?] Apr. Endorsed by Bayard.

1. JM referred to a *Communication from the Secretary of the Treasury, to the Chairman of the Committee, Appointed to Investigate the State of the Treasury* . . . (Washington, D.C., 1802; S #3264). In this report, dated 2 Mar., Secretary Gallatin commented that "the accounts of Mr. Marshall have been rendered, but are not yet settled" (16).

2. Joshua Johnson, formerly consul in London. See Johnson to JM, 3 Nov. 1800 (App. I, Cal.).

3. JM did make a trip to the capital, as shown by his letters written from Alexandria on 19 Apr.

4. William H. Hill, a Federalist congressman from North Carolina.

To William Cushing

Dear Sir   Alexandria April 19th. 1802[1]

A bill is now before Congress which will I am persuaded pass into a law by which the June term of the supreme court will be done away & the Judges directed to ride the circuits before they will again assemble.

For myself I more than doubt the constitutionality of this measure & of performing circuit duty without a commission as a circuit Judge. But I shall hold myself bound by the opinions of my brothers. I am not of opinion that we can under our present appointments hold circuit courts, but I presume a contrary opinion is held by the court & if so I shall conform to it. I am endeavoring to collect the opinion of the Judges & will when I shall have done so communicate the result. I will thank you to give me your opinion & direct your letter to me in Richmond. With very much respect I am dear Sir, Your Obedt. Servt

J MARSHALL

ALS, Robert Treat Paine Papers, MHi. Enclosed in JM to Paterson, 19 Apr.

1. Paterson forwarded this letter to Cushing on 6 May (Paterson to Cushing, 6 May 1802, Paterson Papers, NjR).

To William Paterson

Dear Sir   Alexandria April 19th. 1802

It having now become apparent that there will be no session of the supreme court of the United States holden in June next & that we shall be directed to ride the circuits, before we can consult on the course proper to be taken by us, it appears to me proper that the Judges shoud communicate their sentiments on this subject to each that they may act understandingly & in the same manner.

I hope I need not say that no man in existence respects more than I do, those who passd the original law concerning the courts of the United States, & those who first acted under it. So highly do I respect their opinions that I had not examind them & shoud have p⟨roceed⟩ed without a doubt on the subject, to perform the duties assignd to me if the late discussions had not unavoidably producd an investigation of the subject which from me it woud not otherwise have receivd. The result of this investigation has been an opinion which I cannot conquer that the constitution requires distinct appointments & commissions for the Judges of the inferior courts from those of the supreme court. It is however my duty & my inclination in this as in all other cases to be bound by the opinion of the majority of the Judges & I shoud therefore have proceeded to execute the law so far as that task may be assignd to me; had I not supposd it possible that the Judges might be inclind to distinguish between the original case of being appointed to duties markd out before their appointments & of having the duties of administering justice in new courts imposd after their appointments. I do not myself state this because I am myself satisfied that the distinction ought to have weight, for I am not—but as there may be something in it I am inducd to write to the Judges requesting the favor of them to give me their opinions which opinions I will afterwards communicate to each Judge. My own conduct shall certainly be regulated by them.

This is a subject not to be lightly resolvd on. The consequences of refusing to carry the law into effect may be very serious.[1] For myself personally I disregard them, & so I am persuaded does every other Gentleman on the bench when put in competition with what he thinks his duty, but the conviction of duty ought to be very strong before the measure is resolvd on. The law having been once executed will detract very much in the public estimation from the merit or opinion of the sincerity of a determination, not now to act under it.

Not knowing how to direct to Judge Cushing I inclose my letter to him in this & ask the favor of you to forward it.

I shall be happy to hear from you in Richmond where I shall be in a few days & am dear Sir, With very much respect & esteem, your obedt servt

J Marshall

Will you also write to Mr. Cushing?

ALS, Paterson Papers, NjR; Tr, NN. Addressed to Paterson at New Brunswick; postmarked Alexandria, 19 Apr. Endorsed by Paterson. Edges of MS frayed.

1. JM may have recalled the similar situation faced by the judges of the Virginia Court of Appeals in 1788, which produced their "remonstrance" against an act creating district courts. See "Cases of the Judges of the Court of Appeals" (4 Call 135).

From Samuel Chase

My dear Sir   Baltimore 24th. April 1802

I am honoured with your letter of the 19th. instant, from Alexandria.[1] I have seen the Act repealing the Judiciary Law of the last session, and reviving the former System; and I have also a copy of the Bill dividing thirteen Districts into six Circuits, and assigning one to each of the Judges of the Supreme Court &c, as passed by the Senate. I most anxiously wish that the Judges could meet me, at Washington, on the first Monday of August next, when I must be there to prepare the Cases for trial.[2] I greatly prefer a personal Conference to a Communication by letter; and in that case, I think it would be proper to lay the result before the President; as our predecessors did in a similar case.[3] I feel every desire to yield my opinion to my Brethren; but my Conscience must be satisfied, although my ruin should be the certain consequence. My Office is necessary for the support of a numerous family; but I cannot hesitate one moment between a performance of my duty, and the loss of Office. If my Brethren should differ from me in opinion, and I should only *doubt* what conduct I shall pursue, I will readily submit my Judgement to theirs; which I very highly respect. Without any reserve I will give you my present thoughts; holding myself at perfect liberty to change them, on being convinced that they are erroneous.

I suppose it will not be questioned, that the repealing Act is *Constitutional*, and will reverse every part of the Law repealed, except the Establishment of the Circuit Courts, described in the Law, and the appointments, commissions, and salaries, of the Judges, who qualified, and acted, and are ready to act, under the Law. It is a *great doubt* with me, whether the Circuit Courts, established by the Law, can be *abolished*; but I have *no doubt*, that the Circuit Judges cannot, *directly*, or *indirectly*, be deprived of their *Offices*, or *Commissions*, or *Salaries*, during their *lives*; unless only on impeachment for, and conviction of, high Crimes and Misdemeanours, as prescribed in the Constitution. As the Act of Congress evidently intended to *remove* the Circuit Judges from their Offices, and to take away their Salaries, I am of opinion that it is *void*. The distinction of taking the Office from the Judge, and not the Judge from the Office, I consider as puerile, and nonsensical.

It appears to me that the Constitution of the United states (Art 1st. s 8, and Art 3d s 2d) makes it the *duty* of Congress to constitute, ordain, and *establish* Courts *inferior* to the Supreme Court; for the trial and decision of *all* cases, to which the Judicial power of the United States is extended by the Constitution (Art 3, s 2 & 3); *and of which* the supreme Court by the Constitution, has not *Original* Jurisdiction; for I much doubt, whether the Supreme Court can be vested, by Law, with *Original* Jurisdiction, in any other Cases, than the very few enumerated in the Constitution. In *all other* Cases, to which the Judicial power extends, the Supreme Court is vested with an *appellate* Jurisdiction; and if it can have *Original* Jurisdiction, in *Other* Cases, the Citizen would be deprived of the benefit of a hearing in the inferior Tribunals; and obliged to resort, in the Commencement of his suit, to the Supreme Court. If Congress *neglect* to *establish* inferior Courts to decide *all* the cases, to which the Judicial power of the United States extends, they disobey the plain injunctions of the Constitution; and by such *neglect of duty*, they deprive the *several States*, and our own Citizens, and also Foreigners, of their *Right* of suing in such inferior Courts; but there is no Remedy. In the establishment of Courts inferior to the Supreme Court, the Congress are the *sole* Judges of the *time*, when such Courts shall be established; of the number of such Courts; of the number of Judges to be appointed to hold them; of the portion, or District of the United States over which such Courts shall have *Jurisdiction*; of the time, and place at which such Courts shall hold their sessions; and of the Cases (Civil and Criminal) of which they shall take Cognizance. But whenever Congress constitute Inferior Courts, and Judges are *appointed, commissioned*, and *qualified*, I am of opinion that, immediately thereupon, eo instante, such Judges become *Constitutional* Judges, and hold *their Offices, and Commissions, and Salaries under the Constitution*; and on the *three* terms prescribed therein, to wit; 1°. That they shall hold their *offices* during *their good behaviour*; 2°. That they shall be removed from Office only in *one* way, namely; by impeachment for, and conviction of Treason, bribery, or other high crimes and misdemeanours; 3°. That their salaries shall not be diminished (a fortiori, not taken away) during their continuance in Office.

It appears to me self-evident, that the Office, Commission, and Salary (all three) of a Judge, *under the Constitution* of the United States, are to be of *equal* duration. The tenure of his Office is for *life*, if he does not forfeit it; his Commission is to continue as long as his Office, to wit, for *life*; and his salary is to remain *undiminished*, as long as his *Office* and Commission, that is, for life, unless forfeited. If inferior Courts, once established, can be *abolished* by Congress (which I doubt) it will not necessarily follow, that the Judges of *such* Courts will cease to be Judges. I admit that Congress may, in their discretion, increase the number of Judges in any of the Courts established; they may also lessen the number of Judges in *such* Courts, on the death of any of them; they may diminish, or enlarge the Jurisdiction of any of the Courts; they may enlarge or contract the extent of the Districts, or Circuits; and they may require *additional Judicial* duties of any of the Judges, agreably to the provisions of the Constitution; But still the Judges, and their Offices must remain independent of the Legislature. If Congress should require of the Judges, duties that are *impracticable*; or if Congress should impose duties on them that are *unreasonable*, and for the *manifest* purpose of compelling them to resign their Offices; such cases (if they should ever happen) will suggest their own remedy. It cannot be questioned, that the Judges of the inferior

Courts were intended by the Constitution, to be as independent as the Judges of the Supreme Court. By the Constitution, these Courts were invested with Jurisdiction (Civil & Criminal) of all Cases, in Law and Equity, arising under the Constitution and Laws of the United States, except only in a very few cases, of which the Supreme Court was invested with *Original* Jurisdiction; and therefore the Independence of the Judges of the Inferior Courts is as essentially necessary to guard the Constitution, and the *Rights* of the States, and the *Rights* of *private* Citizens, and also the Rights of *Foreigners*, as the Independence of the Judges of the Supreme Court. The Constitution of the United States is certainly a *limited* Constitution; because (in Art. 1 s. 9.) it *expressly prohibits* Congress from making *certain enumerated Laws*; and also from doing certain specified Acts, in *many* cases; and it is very evident that these restrictions on the *Legislative* power of Congress would be entirely nugatory, and merely waste paper, if there exists no power, under the Constitution, to declare Acts made, *contrary to these express prohibitions*, null and void. It is equally clear that the *limitations* of the power of Congress can only be preserved by the *Judicial* power. There can be no other rational, peaceable and secure barrier against violations of the Constitution by the Legislature, or against encroachments by it on the Executive, or on the *Judiciary* branches of our Government.* It is provided by the Constitution (Art 6. s. 2) that the Constitution of the United States shall be the *supreme* law of the Land; and *by the Oath of Office* prescribed by the statute (24th. September 1789) all Judges engage to discharge and perform all their duties, as Judges, *agreeably to the Constitution*. Further, all Judges, by the Constitution (Art 6 s 6) are required to bind themselves, by Oath, to *support* the Constitution of the United States. This engagement, in my judgement, obliges every Judge (or other taker thereof) not to do any *affirmative* act to contravene, or render ineffectual, any of the provisions in the Constitution. It has been the uniform opinion (until very lately) that the Supreme Court possess the power, and that they are bound in duty, to declare acts of Congress, or of any of the States, contrary to the Constitution, *void*: and the Judges of the Supreme Court have *separately* given such opinion. If the Supreme Court possess this power, the inferior Courts, must also have the same power; and of course ought to be as independent of Congress as the supreme

---

*The House of Representatives, from their wealth, and numbers, have, now, greater influence than the senate; and it will rapidly increase; while the power of the senate must forever remain almost stationary. These two bodies united will always controul the Executive alone; and even if supported by the Judiciary. The Judicial power is most feeble indeed; and if the Legislative, and Executive unite to impair, or to destroy its Constitutional Rights, they must be irresistible, unless the great body of the people take the alarm and give their aid.

Court; but the Judges of *both* Courts will not be independent of but dependent on, the Legislature, if they be not entitled to hold their *Offices* during *good behaviour*; or if they have not a fixed and certain provision for their support, that cannot be *diminished*; or if they can be *removed from* Office, (or which is the same thing) if their Offices can be taken from them by Congress. The Constitution has established *good behaviour* as the *tenure* by which all Federal Judges shall hold their *Offices*; and it has prescribed the mode, by which only, any of them can be removed from Office. By these wise provisions it evidently follows, that they cannot be removed, *directly*, or *indirectly* by Congress; and that they cannot be removed in any *other* way than by Impeachment: Every other mode is a mere subterfuge and evasion of the Constitution. It appears to me, that the repealing Act, *so far*, as it contemplates to affect the appointment, commission, and office, or Salary of any of the Judges of the Circuit Courts, is contrary to the Constitution, and is therefore, *so far*, void. If the Constitutionality of this Act could be brought before the Supreme Court, by action of assize of Office, or by action to recover the Salary, I should decide (as at present advised) that the Act is void; and I would, by the first action restore the Judge to his Office, and, by the latter, adjudge him his Salary: But by neither of these modes, nor by any other (as Mandamus, & Quo Warranto) could remedy be obtained. This *Defect* of *Remedy* to obtain a Right (which Justice abhors) will induce every Judge of the Supreme Court to act with the greatest caution; and he must, in my judgement, decline to execute the office of a Circuit Judge, if he apprehends that he shall, thereby, violate the Constitutional Rights of the Circuit Judges. But are the Judges of the supreme Court bound in duty to hold the Circuit Courts? I sincerely wish it was not our duty (especially at this time) to decide this question; but I am glad that we are not, in any manner, interested in the determination. If the Circuits had been as remote from our several places of residence, and as extensive, as heretofore, our ease and convenience might be said, by ignorant, or bad men, to have some influence; but by the system proposed, of holding only *one* Supreme Court in the year, and all of us (except Judge Washington), having a convenient District, no such suspicion can be entertained.[4]

I have *three* objections to the Judges of the supreme Court holding the Circuit Courts. First. If the repealing Law has not *abolished* the Circuit Courts, which it certainly has not done, but has established Circuit Courts in the repealing Act, and also in the Bill intended to be passed, *substantially the same* with the Circuit Courts in the Law repealed; and if the repealing Act has not destroyed the Office of the Judges appointed, commissioned, and qualified under the Law repealed; it follows that the Offices of these Judges are *now full*; and consequently no Judge of the Supreme Court (nor any Judge of any District Court) holding this opinion can exercise the Office of a Judge of such Courts, without violating the Constitution. Secondly—If the repealing Act be void, *so* far, as it intends to destroy the Office of the Judges under the Law repealed, and a Judge of the Supreme Court (or of a District Court) should hold the Circuit Court, I think he would, thereby, be *instrumental* to carry into effect an *unconstitutional* Law. If he executes the Office of Circuit Judge, I think he thereby decides that the repealing was *constitutional*. I think that he must, before he acts, decide whether the repealing Act be constitutional, or not. If he thinks it unconstitutional he cannot act under it. If one person exercises an office, to which another has *legal* title he is a *wrong doer*, and ought to be removed; and the injured person ought to be restored to his Office. Shall a Judge be a wrong-doer? It has never been controverted that Congress can, by Law, require the Judges of the Supreme Court to perform *additional Judicial* duties in the *supreme Court*. I will admit, for the sake of argument only, that Congress may, by Law, require the Judges of the Supreme Court to hold the Circuit Courts; yet, if Judges have been commissioned, and qualified as Judges of such Courts, and have not been removed according to the Constitution, I cannot agree that, in *such cases*, the Judges of the *supreme* Court can be obliged, by Law, to act as Judges of the Circuit Courts; because, they will thereby *dissieze*, or dispossess the Circuit Judges of their *Offices*. If there were *no* Judges of the Circuit Courts, and if Judges in one Court could be required to be Judges in another *distinct* and *separate Court*, with different Jurisdictions; and if the Supreme Court can take *original* Jurisdiction of such cases, of which the Constitution gives them Appellate *Jurisdiction*; yet, I cannot assent, that the Judges of the Supreme Court shall hold the Circuit Courts; *because I* conceive that they would, thereby, become the *instruments* to execute an *unconstitutional* Law; and would, thereby, assist to deprive the Circuit Judges of their Offices. If other persons had been appointed, and should hold the Circuit Courts, the Judges of the Supreme Court would be bound in duty, to redress this wrong, if the Case could be brought before them. It seems to me, that there is a great, and manifest difference between the Judges of the Supreme Court acting as Judges of the Circuit Courts under the *former*, and under the *present* system.

I am inclined to believe, that a Judge of the Supreme Court cannot act as a Judge of a Circuit Court, *without*, or *with* a commission. No one can deny that a Judge of the Circuit Court is an *Officer* of the United States; and the Constitution (art. 2. s 3) directs the President to commission *all the Officers* of the United States. I apprehend that, no one can hold *any Office* under the United States, without a Commission to hold such office.

But I think (as at present advised), that a Judge of the Supreme Court cannot accept, and act under, a Commission, as *Judge* of a *Circuit Court*. The Constitution (art 3 s 1.) vests the Judicial power of the United States in one *Supreme Court*, and in such Inferior Courts as Congress may, from time to time, ordain, and *establish*; and gives the Supreme Court (art 3 s 2) *original* Jurisdiction in Cases of ambassadors &c. &c.; and *appellate* Jurisdiction of the Cases enumerated. It appears to me, that Congress cannot, by Law, give the Judges of the Supreme Court, *original* Jurisdiction of the *same* Cases of which it *expresly* gives them *appellate* Jurisdiction. If a case originates in the Circuit Court, and is tried there, the Judge of the supreme Court may, alone, (or with the District Judge) hear and decide a case, of which the Constitution expresly gives him *appellate* Jurisdiction. The Constitution intended that the Judges of the Supreme Court should not have *original* Jurisdiction, but only in the few Cases enumerated. The inference is just, that, as the Constitution only gave the supreme Court original Jurisdiction in a few specified cases, it intended to *exclude* them from *original* Jurisdiction in all other cases; and more especially as it gives them *appellate* Jurisdiction in all Cases that should arise under the Constitution or Laws of the United states. But the Judges have held Circuit Courts ever since the formation of the Federal Government, until the late Judiciary Law. The fact is so. I can truly say that I never considered the question. I acted as a Circuit Judge, because my predecessors had done so before me, without any enquiry into the subject. But I now see that my holding the Circuit Court will *certainly* do an injury to the *Rights* of other Judges and will assist to exclude them from their Office. It is under this impression that I feel a very great reluctance to act as a Circuit Judge. By the Constitution (art 2 s 2), all Judges are to be nominated by the President to the senate, and the President, with the advice and consent of the Senate, is to appoint them. If Congress, by Law, requires a Judge of the supreme Court to hold a Circuit Court, does not Congress, thereby, *substantially* nominate and appoint a Judge of the Circuit Court? All Judges are to act under an *Oath of Office*. Does the oath of *Office* of a Judge of the *Supreme* Court extend to his duties as a Judge of a *Circuit Court*? If not, he will act as a Judge of a Circuit Court *without any Oath*.

Unless the sentiments of my Brethren should induce me to change my present opinion, I shall certainly decline to take the Circuit assigned me; which would be very convenient and highly agreable to me, if my objections can be removed.

I think it is in the power of the Judges to meet at Washington in July, or August next; and I wish you would urge it. I am confident their opinions would have great weight with the District Judges. I shall be happy to receive Copies of the opinions of all my brethren.[5] The burthen of deciding so momentous a question, and under the present circumstances of our Country, would be very great on all the Judges assembled; but an individual Judge, declining to take a Circuit, must sink under it. With my best wishes for your health and happiness, and with the highest respect and esteem, I have the honour to be, dear sir, Your affectionate and obedient Servant

Copy, NHi; another copy, Robert Treat Paine Papers, MHi; ADfS (fragment), Etting Collection, PHi; Tr, NN. NHi and MHi copies in unknown hand and unsigned; PHi fragment is last page of Chase's draft; NN transcript made from copy sent to Paterson (includes transcript of Chase's cover letter to Paterson of same date).

1. Letter not found but undoubtedly similar to those sent to Cushing and Paterson on that day.

2. The new act provided for the Supreme Court to hold one session each year, beginning the first Monday in February. There was to be no August term, as under the former system established in 1789, but the associate justice resident in the fourth circuit (Chase) was to be present the first Monday in August "to make all necessary orders touching any suit, action, appeal, writ of error, process, pleadings or proceedings, returned to the said court or depending therein, preparatory to the hearing, trial or decision" (U.S. Statutes at Large, II, 156).

3. Chase alluded to the protest against an act of 1792, which required the justices sitting on circuit to decide the claims of disabled veterans seeking placement on the pension list. JM also mentioned this incident in Marbury v. Madison. See Opinion, 24 Feb. 1803 and n. 12.

4. The act assigned "the senior associate justice . . . residing within the fifth circuit" to the second circuit. This meant that Bushrod Washington, of Virginia, had to hold circuit in Connecticut, New York, and Vermont. A year later the law was amended to assign Justice Washington to the third circuit, which embraced Pennsylvania and New Jersey (U.S. Statutes at Large, II, 157, 244).

5. The following extract of William Cushing's reply to Chase is contained in a letter from Hannah Cushing to Abigail Adams, 25 June 1802 (Adams Papers, MHi):

"I received your favor with a copy of your letter to the Ch Justice on the subject of the Judiciary containing much good sense & argument. But can we, after Eleven years practical exposition of the Laws & Constitution by all federal Judges, now say, that Congress has not power to direct a Judge of the Sup Court to act with a Dt. Judge in an inferiour Court, with or without a Commission, yet making one of the Sup bench to hold appellate Jurisdiction? I think we cannot. As to being instrumental (by taking the Circuits) in violating the rights of the Judges & the Constitution, I do not see that it carries that inference. It is not in our power to restore to them their Salaries or them to the exercise of their Offices. Declining the Circuits will have no tendency to do either. We violate not the Constitution. We only do duties assigned us by Constitutional authority. Suppose we apply or represent or remonstrate to the President; what can he say? 'Gent There is the Law I cannot control Congress.' And you & I know We cannot control the Majority."

To William Paterson

Dear Sir   Richmond May 3d. 1802

I receivd a few days past from Mr. Washington a letter of which the following is an extract.[1]

"I am embarassd by Judge Bensons application because, altho my wishes are to oblige such a respectable number of Gentlemen, my judgement opposes & must prevent me from doing it.[2] I formd a resolution shortly after the papers came to my possession, not to use or permit them to be usd, for party purposes. If I opend them to my political friends, I coud not refuse like access to those from whom I differd in opinion. How coud I, without incurring imputations of unfairness, & subjecting my self to charges which nothing but a resort to the papers coud remove. Suppose for instance I shoud be accusd of publishing partial parts of a correspondence, how coud I defend myself, & why shoud I involve myself in difficulties, from which I shoud never be able to extricate myself without opening the papers to both parties? The unmerited abuse of the democratic party I shoud disregard, but were I to use these papers as weapons against them, I shoud feel myself wrong when they sought aid from them, to refuse their request. I shoud not in short act as I belcive Genl. Washington woud have wishd, coud he have foreseen that I shoud be calld upon to act at all upon the case. From these considerations I declind complying with a request of General Hamiltons to send him copies of some papers,[3] & I must be consistent (tho in error) in the present instance.

["]I must get the favor of you to inform Judge Patteson that a resolution formd at the time I receivd the papers, not to use them for party purposes, to which I have hitherto adherd & upon which I have had occasion to act, will prevent me in the present instance, from complying with the request which has been made. That I have felt much embarassd by the application & feel still greater distress at being compelld to refuse the request of respectable men whose political conduct I admire, & whose wishes I shoud take so much pleasure in gratifying coud it be done with propriety."

Mr.[4] Washington also states it as his opinion that the question respecting the constitutional right of the Judges of the supreme court to sit as circuit Judges ought to be considerd as settled & shoud not again be movd. I have no doubt myself but that policy dictates this decision to us all. Judges however are of all men those who have the least right to obey her dictates. I own I shall be privately gratified if such shoud be the opinion of the majority & I shall with much pleasure acquiesce in it; tho, if the subject has never been discussd, I shoud feel greatly embarassd about it myself.

I have also receivd a letter from Judge Chase whose opinion is directly opposite to that of Judge Washington but he expresses an earnest desire, which he has requested me to communicate to every member of the bench, that we shoud meet in Washington for the purpose of determining on the course of conduct to be pursued, in August next when he is directed to hold a sort of a demi session at that place. I shall communicate this wish to Judge Moore[5] & will thank you to correspond with Judge Cushing on the subject & let me know the result.[6]

If we determine certainly to proceed to do circuit duty it will I presume be entirely unnecessary to meet in August. If we incline to the contrary opinion, or are undecided we ought to meet & communicate verbally our difficulties to each other.[7]

After hearing from Judge Moore I will again write to you. With very much respect & esteem, I am dear Sir your Obedt

J MARSHALL

ALS, Paterson Papers, NjR; Tr, NN. Addressed by JM to Paterson at New Brunswick; postmarked Richmond, 6 May. Endorsed by Paterson.

1. Original letter not found.

2. See JM to Paterson, 6 Apr. Egbert Benson of New York was a judge of the second circuit, appointed under the act of 1801 (Haskins and Johnson, *Foundations of Power*, 133, 178).

3. See Bushrod Washington to Alexander Hamilton, 21 Nov. 1801 (Syrett, *Papers of Hamilton*, XXV, 432–33).

4. JM inadvertently placed open quotation marks at the beginning of this paragraph.

5. Alfred Moore (1755–1810) of North Carolina served on the Supreme Court from 1799 to 1804 (Haskins and Johnson, *Foundations of Power*, 101–2).

6. In a letter to William Cushing of 25 May, Paterson apparently enclosed a copy of his reply to JM, ca. 25 May, in which Paterson responded to the points JM raised here. Paterson's letter to JM has not been found, but Cushing's wife incorporated a passage from the copy sent to her husband in a letter she wrote to Abigail Adams: "On the constitutional right of the Judges of the supreme court to sit as circuit judges, my opin[i]on coincides with Judge Washington's. Practic[e] has fixed construction, which it is too late to disturb. If open for discussion, it would merit serious consideration; but the practical exposition is too old and strong & obstinate to be shaken or controled. The question is at rest. If this should be the prevailing opinion, & their be nothing more in the case, our meeting would be of no use" (Hannah Cushing to Abigail Adams, 25 June 1802, Adams Papers, MHi). Paterson reported Cushing's position to JM in his two letters of 11 and 18 June.

7. JM here inadvertently placed close quotation marks.

To Rufus King

Dear Sir   Richmond May 5th 1802

With very much pleasure, I receivd a few weeks past, your letter of 12th. January, & I cannot omit to thank you for the communication it containd.

This fortunate accomplishment of the long & difficult negotiation with which you were chargd, is peculiarly gratifying to those who unite a knowledge of the embarassing circumstances attending it, to a real wish that your embassy may be as honorable to yourself, as it has been useful to your country.

You have effected what, in America, has been heretofore deemd impracticable. You have made a treaty with one of the great rival nations of europe, which is not only acceptable to all, but the merit of which is claimd by both parties. The advocates of the present administration ascribe to it great praise, for having, with so much dexterity & so little loss, extricated our country from a debt of twenty four milion of dollars¹ in which a former administration had involvd it; while the friends of the antient state of things, are not slow in adding the present happy accomodation to the long list of their merits.

Yet amidst this universal approbation so correctly given to an adjustment of differences which unquestionably deserves it, the mortifying reflection obtrudes itself, that the reputation of the most wise & skilful conduct depends, in this our capricious world, so much on accident. Had Mr. Adams been reelected President of the United States, or had his successor been a gentleman whose political opinions accorded with those held by the preceding executive, a very different reception, I still beleive, woud have been given to the same measure. The payment of a specific sum woud then have been pronouncd, by those who now take merit to themselves for it, a humiliating national degradation, an abandonment of national interest, a free will offering of milions to Britain for her grace & favor, by those who sought to engage in a war with France, rather than repay, in part, by a small loan to that republic, the immense debt of gratitude we owe her.

Such is & such I fear will ever be human justice!

When I recollect the advantage actually gaind by Great Britain, in having attaind the fifth commissioner, I am truely surprizd at the sum agreed on.² I beleive it is as much, & not more, than, in strict justice ought to be paid; but, after the impressions made by the late board of commissioners I really apprehended strict justice to be unattainable; & I think, not only, that great credit is due to the american negotiator for having reducd this enormous claim to a reasonable amount, but that, all circumstances considerd, some sentiment of respect shoud be felt for the moderation & equity of the english minister.

The national tribunals, I hope will continue to manifest, in the exposition of the treaty of peace, "that share of prudence," which is requird by justice, & which can alone preserve the reputation of the nation.

Public opinion in this quarter of the union has sustaind no essential change. That disposition to coalesce with what is, now, the majority in America as well as in this state, which was strongly displayd by the minority twelve months past, exists no longer. It has expird. But the minority is only recovering its strength & firmness. It acquires nothing.

Our political tempests will long, very long, exist, after those who are now tossd about by them shall be at rest. With very much respect & esteem, I am dear Sir, your Obedt. Servt

J MARSHALL

ALS, King Papers, NHi. Endorsed by King as received 20 July and answered 5 Aug.

1. This was the amount in a statement of British claims presented to the former commission under the Jay Treaty. President Jefferson laid this statement before the Senate in Apr. 1802, no doubt as an inducement to accept the convention (*ASP, Foreign Relations*, II, 427).

2. In the mixed commission created under the Jay Treaty, the fifth seat fell by lot to Great Britain, so that the board consisted of three Britons and two Americans. After a number of rulings favoring British creditors, the American commissioners refused to participate further. In the Convention of 1802, the mixed commission was scrapped in favor of a lump sum payment of six hundred thousand pounds by the U.S. For the work of the commission, see Moore, *International Adjudications*, III.

From William Paterson

Dear Sir,   New Brunswick, 11th. June, 1802

In a letter, which I recd. a day or two ago from Judge Cushing, dated at Scituate, May 29th., is the following passage. "I have received yours of the 6th. with the Chief Justice's letter respecting the necessity of commission's as circuit judges; as to which, if the point had been started at first, I believe doubts would have arisen. But as the case is—to be consistent I think we must abide by the old practice."[1]

It appears, that Mr. Cushing had not recd. my second letter of the 25th. of May at the date of his; but I suppose, that his sentiments on the subject may be clearly collected from the above passage. When I receive his answer to mine of the 25th. I will let you know its contents. Your's sincerely,

WM. PATERSON.

ALS (copy), NHi; Tr (typed), NN.

1. The original of Cushing's letter of 29 May to Paterson is at NHi.

From William Paterson

Dear Sir,   New Brunswick, 18th June, 1802.
  I have just rec'd a letter from Judge Cushing dated the 3d instant in answer to my second letter of the 25th of last month. He refers to his former letter, and further is of opinion, that if a majority of the judges be in favor of the old practice, it will not be necessary to meet in August.[1] I am with great respect, Yr. obt. hb. servt.

WM. PATERSON.

Tr (typed), NN.

1. By attending their circuits in the fall of 1802, the justices of the Supreme Court signified their acquiescence in the repeal of the Judiciary Act of 1801 and in the restoration of the former system. They formally ratified their acceptance in the case of Stuart v. Laird (1 Cranch 299), decided at the Feb. 1803 term, a few days after the decision in Marbury v. Madison.

From Rufus King

Dear Sir,   London Augt. 5. 1802
  I have duly received, and beg you to accept my acknowledgments for your obliging Letter of May 4th.[1] Notwithstanding I do think the settlement of the British Claims, circumstanced as they were, both honourable and advantageous to us, as well as the Evidence of a conciliatory disposition on the part of the English administration, I am with you entirely persuaded that it would have met with a different Reception at home had the administration remained in the hands of those from whom it has been lately removed.
  In a private Letter to you, connected and influential as you have been in the promotion of this adjustment, I may without impropriety say that if there be any merit in this Settlement, it is in every respect due to those who projected and approved the plan which led to it: for not only every material part of the negotiation was Completed, but

the precise sum finally accepted had been offered as an ultimatum before I had any knowledge of the opinion of the present administration. I would not insinuate that any sentiments unfavourable to the Settlement which has been made were entertained by the present administration; on the contrary it approved of what had been done here, and I think sincerely desired to see the Business closed upon the Terms which had been offered. I earnestly wish that on other and still more important concerns its sentiments had been equally correct, as they have been in respect to this business; but I must disregard opinions formed with solicitude and after careful reflexion not to hesitate in believing this to have been the case; and it is for this reason among others that upon mature consideration of my duty to the public, as well as of what I owe to myself, I have thought it incumbent upon me to resign my mission, and ask leave to return home.

Although I am quite sensible that this is a measure of no sort of importance in a public view, the interest which you have so kindly taken in what personally concerns me, induces me to make you this Communication, and not without the hope that it will receive your approbation. With sentiments of the highest respect &c.

                                                    R. K.

Letterbook copy, King Papers, NHi.

1. A note in the left margin reads: "Settlement respecting British Debts both honorable and advantageous. Resignation of mission and to return *home* next Spring."

Marshall v. Hunter and Pendleton
Deposition

[28 August 1802]

The deposition of Philip Smith in the suit now depending in the district court of Chancery holden at Stanton, in which John Marshall & James Marshall are plaintiffs & David Hunter & Philip Pendleton defendants, taken in presence of the parties this 28th. day of August 1802 at the house of Edmund Graham in the town of Martinsburg.[1]

Philip Smith being first sworn deposes & says

That some time about the beginning of the revolution war he was placd on the land in controversy by Jacob Morgan now deceasd, as he understood by the directions of Lord Fairfax, & was instructed to prevent the depredations which were committed on it. He always understood in the neighborhood that the land was under the direction of Lord Fairfax, but has heard that after it was surveyd, he made a present of it to one Beall, who left this country many years past. He has understood from the neighbors & from the persons themselves that Lord Fairfax offerd the land to Jacob Morgan, to Colonel Van Swearingan, & to Thomas Cowan for sixteen hundred pounds in specie, but they coud neither of them pay that sum in hard money, they offerd paper which his Lordship refusd.

On being questiond by the defendent he says that he never saw Lord Fairfax, that an instrument of writing which Morgan said was given by Lord Fairfax, authorizing him to take care of the land was read to him by Jacob Morgan but he cannot read himself & does not know whether it was in the handwriting of Lord Fairfax or not.

On questiond by the plaintiffs he further says that one Cooke he beleives John Cooke, during the war had the land surveyd for the purpose of escheating it & selling it as british property under the idea that it belongd to a british subject.[2] The sale was advertizd & numbers assembled for the purpose of purchasing it. The deponent was one of the company. While they were assembled a letter was receivd from Lord Fairfax forbidding the sale & stating the land to be his property. Cook who was the person conducting the sale desisted from selling & the land so far as he understands was never sold. But Cook did not admit the right of Lord Fairfax but said he had not proceeded according to law by advertizing the sale in other states as well as Virginia.[3]

<table>
<tr><td></td><td></td><td>his</td><td></td></tr>
<tr><td>Sworn and Subscribed at the House of Edmund Graham by virtue of the enexed Dedimus in presence of the Parties before us</td><td>PHILIP</td><td>✕</td><td>SMITH</td></tr>
<tr><td></td><td></td><td>mark</td><td></td></tr>
</table>

    WILLIAM RIDDLE
    JAMES ANDERSON

AD, Marshall v. Hunter and Pendleton, Office of the Clerk, Augusta County Circuit Court, Staunton, Va. In JM's hand except for certification of magistrates. Cover addressed by JM to clerk of "court of Chancery holden at Stanton." According to clerk's notations on verso, deposition returned under seal on 21 Nov. 1802.

1. For the background to this case, see Marshall v. Hunter and Pendleton, editorial note (preceding Notice, 15 Sept. 1801).

2. In 1779 the Virginia legislature adopted an act "concerning escheats and forfeitures from British subjects." The courts later recognized Lord Fairfax's status as a loyal citizen of Virginia at the time of his death in 1781 (Hening, Statutes, X, 66; PJM, V, 229, 241–42).

3. A concluding statement was crossed out: "Just before the letter of Lord Fairfax was receivd however Cook had told him that he woud be under the necessity of moving off as the land woud certainly be sold."

Late in September JM and his brother, along with David Hunter, attended the taking of the depositions of William Rush and Richard Morgan (son of the Jacob Morgan mentioned above) in Berkeley County. Further depositions were taken the following year in Martinsburg, Charles Town, and Winchester. Hunter put in an amended answer in 1804, but the Marshalls did not further prosecute the suit and it was dismissed in July 1805 (depositions of William Rush and Richard Morgan, 25 Sept. 1802; Robert Stephen, 3 Sept. 1803; Thomas Rutherford, 5 Sept. 1803; John Peyton, 10 Sept. 1803; amended answer of David Hunter, 21 Apr. 1804; memorandum of proceedings, Marshall v. Hunter and Pendleton).

To Thomas Massie

Dear Sir[1]   Aug. 31st. 1802

I am informd that you are desirous of parting with your fauquier land & woud probably exchange it for some to the southward. If that is your inclination I woud propose to give you for it in exchange a part of my Buckingham tract.[2] If you are dis[posed] to make such a barter I shall be glad to hear from you. I shall be in winchester on saturday after which I am going up to the Allegheny & on my return shall be in Martinsburg till late in September where a letter will reach me.[3] I am dear Sir very respectfully, Your Obedt. Servt

J MARSHALL

ALS, Massie Family Papers, ViHi. Addressed to Major Massie "care of Colo. Meade" in Frederick County. Endorsed by Massie. A note, presumably in hand of bearer (Col. Meade) reads: "If the Majr is at home, the bearer will wait for an/answer; if not an answer is requested by friday/by the middle of the day, or hereafter/Wednesday."

1. On Massie, see *PJM*, II, 113 n. 9; III, 3; Malcolm Hart Harris, *Old New Kent County* . . . (2 vols.; West Point, Va., 1977), I, 223.
2. On JM's Buckingham land, see Robert Craig to JM, 22 Dec. 1800 and n. 2.
3. At the time JM wrote this letter, he was probably at the home of Rawleigh Colston (his brother-in-law) near Martinsburg. On the twenty-eighth he had attended the taking of a deposition in Martinsburg in his suit against Philip Pendleton and David Hunter. Late in September he attended further depositions in this suit (Deposition, 28 Aug. 1802 and n. 3). The journey to the Allegheny probably concerned his South Branch Manor lands in Hampshire and Hardy counties.

To Charles Cotesworth Pinckney

My dear Sir   November 21. 1802—Richmond

In march last Mr. Washington placd the papers of our late respected & belovd General in my hands, & requested me to enter, as soon as possible, on the very difficult task of composing the history of his life. This I do not wish to be known; but I have no difficulty in communicating it to you, & I do so now because there is much information, especially in relation to the war in the southern States, which the papers do not communicate & which I have some hope of being able to receive, at least in part from you.

General Lincoln was persimonious of his communications & of consequence his letters to the Commander in Chief do not contain so much as might have been expected.

In his letter stating the attempt on Savannah in 1779 he refers General Washington to Colonel Laurens for information & gives no other himself than that the attempt faild. Is it asking too much to request from you a statement of the facts respecting that affair within your knowledge? Was the American Column distinct from the french & if so who led it? Who led the different columns of french troops? What was the loss? Was the attempt rash & impracticable, or if not so to what causes is the failure to be attributed? What were the numbers of D Estaings army—what of the continental troops—& of the militia? What the order of attack & the situation of the works? Did the failure produce any animosity between the french & Americans? Anything further which may appear to you interesting I will thank you for. In what situation did Pulaski receive his wound? Where was his corps & how did it behave?[1]

You will also greatly oblige me by any particulars respecting the seige of Charlestown which you may deem important. I have not however yet examind the papers of that transaction & do not know how far they may be defective. There are some enquiries respecting the first attack which I coud wish to make.

Who was the Enginier that directed the artillery from fort Moultrie on Sullivans island? What is the depth of water between Long island & Sullivans island, & what the communication between Long island & the continent? Coud Clinton have crossd over to Sullivans island to have attackd the fort by land & what was the force guarding the passage.[2]

Shall we ever see you again in Richmond? I assure you few things woud give me greater pleasure. I have now scarcely any gratification which can be compard with the occasional conversation I have with the few friends I love & who deserve to be esteemd. There is so much in the political world to wound honest men who have honorable feelings that I am disgusted with it & begin to see things & indeed human nature through a much more gloomy medium than I once thought possible. This new doctrine of the perfectability of man, added to the practice of its votaries begins to exhibit him I think as an animal much less respectable than he has heretofore been thought.

It is whisperd among those who affect to know a great deal that a certain eminent personage is already fatigued almost beyond bearing with a great democratic & religious writer whose *useful* labors were of sufficient magnitude to entitle him to an invitation to cross the Atlantic in a national frigate.³ I cannot help feeling some gratification at this. I wish such deeds woud always bring their own reward. It woud induce infidels to beleive there was a possibility of there being a superintending providence.

Are you growing worse in South Carolina? In Virginia we are I think stationary. If our Legislature shoud not follow the example of Pennsylvania or establish a general ticket the elections for Congress will be very warmly contested in five or six districts, & federalism will I am inclind to think, prevail in three of them.

Mrs. Marshall requests me to present her respects to Mrs. Pinckney. I am dear General with much esteem & affection, Your obedt

J MARSHALL⁴

ALS, Pinckney Papers, DLC. Addressed to Pinckney in South Carolina "by the way of Charles town"; postmarked Richmond, 23 Nov. Endorsed by Pinckney.

1. For JM's account of the unsuccessful siege of Savannah in Sept. and Oct. 1779, see *Life*, IV, 97–104.

2. For the capture of Charleston, see *Life*, IV, 142–52.

3. JM alluded to Thomas Paine's recent arrival in the U.S. from France. In a letter written shortly after he became president, Jefferson had offered passage to Paine at his request. Paine subsequently went public with this offer, and Federalist newspapers made the most of the episode. For an account, see Malone, *Jefferson the President: 1801– 5*, 192–200.

4. Below JM's signature are several lines in an unknown hand (Pinckney's?), which read: "D Estaing landed the 12th. Sep/Savannhah summoned 16th/Broke ground 23d. Batteries opend Oct ⟨8th?⟩/The assault—the 9th."

The United States Circuit Court for Virginia

EDITORIAL NOTE

John Marshall no doubt accepted his appointment as chief justice of the United States under the expectation that Supreme Court justices would not have to hold circuit courts. The Judiciary Act of 1801, which became law soon after Marshall's confirmation, provided for separate appointment of circuit court judges. The repeal of that law one year later, however, restored the circuit-riding system that had been in effect from 1789 to 1801. The act of 1802 established circuit courts composed of one justice of the Supreme Court and the judge of the U.S. district court. It assigned the chief justice to the fifth circuit, comprising the districts of Virginia and North Carolina.¹ Under the circumstances, this was the most convenient assignment Marshall could have had, for it meant that he could hold one of his circuits without leaving home.

The U.S. Circuit Court, District of Virginia, convened in Richmond on 22 May and 22 November each year throughout Marshall's tenure on the bench.² The Virginia court was among the busiest of the circuit courts, sitting on the average between two and three weeks each term. Over the next thirty

CYRUS GRIFFIN

Watercolor (?) on ivory by Lawrence Sully, 1799. *Courtesy of the Historical Society of Pennsylvania*

years, five different district judges served with Marshall on this court; Cyrus Griffin (1802–10), John Tyler (1811–12), St. George Tucker (1813–24), George Hay (1825–29), and Philip P. Barbour (1830–35).

Marshall's surviving judicial papers include a valuable collection of autograph opinions delivered in the circuit court at Richmond. These manuscripts, preserved at the American Philosophical Society in Philadelphia, were presented to the society in 1837 by John W. Brockenbrough. That same year Brockenbrough published his *Reports of Cases Decided by the Honourable John Marshall . . . in the Circuit Court of the United States for the District of Virginia and North Carolina* (2 vols.; Philadelphia, 1837). A Virginia lawyer and later a federal judge and law professor, Brockenbrough apparently came into possession of Marshall's opinions during the lifetime of the chief justice. In his preface he stated that he had "persevered in" the labor of preparing his edition "for years." Presumably, Marshall gave his blessing to this enterprise. Although Brockenbrough printed eighty-eight opinions by Marshall between 1802 and 1833, including three that were given in the circuit court at Raleigh, only sixty-four of the original manuscripts are extant. (The accession records of the American Philosophical Society do not indicate whether the reporter gave the entire set of Marshall's drafts to that institution.)[3] The chief justice's papers supplied the reporter only with the bare opinion, for no notes of arguments were preserved "in a single instance." In the great majority of cases, Marshall did not write out an opinion. Written opinions were resorted to "only in cases of real difficulty," which explains why so large a proportion of the reported cases were suits in equity.[4]

The cases for which there is an opinion by Marshall can be documented in the voluminous records and case papers of the U.S. circuit court deposited at the Virginia State Library in Richmond.[5] The case papers consist mainly of writs, pleadings, depositions, mercantile accounts, and the like, though occasionally a Marshall autograph document turns up. Examples include notes of arguments in a criminal case and a decree in an equity suit, both of which are published below.[6] Newspapers provide important supplementary information on Marshall's cases and sometimes serve as a primary source. The texts of the chief justice's remarks in sentencing Thomas Logwood and of his previously unreported opinion in *Bond* v. *Ross* have been taken from the Richmond *Enquirer*.[7]

The editors have set the context of a given opinion in the first numbered footnote, or, if the contextual information proved too extensive, in an introductory editorial note. Where the text of an opinion is Marshall's manuscript draft, the editors have supplied detailed textual notes following the numbered footnotes. For the method and symbols used in compiling these notes, see Editorial Apparatus (xxxiii–xxxiv).

1. *U.S. Statutes at Large*, II, 157–58.

2. Ibid., 158.

3. Two cases in Brockenbrough were reprinted from the sixth volume of Daniel Call's *Reports of Cases Argued and Decided in the Court of Appeals of Virginia* (Richmond, Va., 1833).

4. 1 Brock. v–vii.

5. For a description of this collection, see *PJM*, V, 164–65.

6. See U.S. v. Johnson, Notes on Arguments, 11 June 1806; Short v. Skipwith, Opinion and Decree, 2 Dec. 1806.

7. See Sentence, 1 June 1804; Opinion, 14 Dec. 1805.

Tabb's Administrators v. Gist
Opinion
U.S. Circuit Court, Virginia, 9 December 1802

This suit is brought to enjoin judgments to a large amount obtained by the defendant *Samuel Gist*, against the intestate of the complainants, as surviving partner of *Moss Armstead & Co.*, *Richard Hill & Co.*, *Richard Booker & Co.*, and *William Watkins & Co.*[1]

The points made by the counsel for the complainants[2] are,

1st. That their intestate was in such a state of mental derangement when the suits were instituted, and the judgments complained of were rendered, that those judgments ought not to bind him; and his representatives ought yet to be permitted to defend his estate against the claims on which they are founded.

2ndly. That he is not liable for the debts of *Moss Armstead & Co.*, and *Richard Hill & Co.*; because he was never a member of either of those firms.

3dly. That *Samuel Gist* is greatly indebted to their intestate on private account; which debt ought to be opposed to the debts due from him as surviving partner of *Richard Booker & Co.*, and *William Watkins & Co.*

Without going into a minute investigation of the testimony respecting Mr. *Tabb's* state of mind for several years before his death; or determining, whether its derangement was so complete, during the whole of that time, as to invalidate any specific contract he might have entered into, it is sufficient to observe, that the condition of his mind was certainly such, as might well account for his having failed to search out, and set up, a real defence, at law; and therefore, if he possessed such real defence, the judgments ought not to preclude his representatives from it now.

The question, whether he was a partner of either or both the concerns of *Richard Hill & Co.*, and *Moss Armstead & Co.*, is therefore considered as now perfectly open, to be decided on such testimony as may be adduced by either party.

It is admitted that Mr. *Tabb* was a partner of *Richard Hill & Co.*,[3] and that *Richard Booker & Co.* held an interest in *Moss Armstead & Co.* and *Richard Hill & Co.*: But it is denied, that Mr. *Tabb* knew of that interest; and it is contended, that he would not be made a partner of those firms by any act of his copartners, or otherwise, than by his own consent.

It is also admitted, that *Gist* was unacquainted with the members of either *Richard Hill & Co.*, or *Moss Armstead & Co.*; that he did not credit them on the confidence, that *Richard Booker & Co.* were of the partnership: and, of consequence, that the accountability of Mr. *Tabb*, for them, cannot be maintained, on the ground of their being led to consider him as a partner.

It was stated by one of the counsel for the defendants,[4] that, being bound by all the acts of the company, Mr. *Tabb* became a member of any copartnery into which *Richard Booker & Co.*, should enter, whether he did, or did not, assent individually to being engaged.

To this opinion, in the latitude in which it was laid down, I cannot subscribe; and, if in the progress of the suit, it should be deemed necessary to insist upon it, and the gentleman who has advanced it, still retains it, I will thank him to furnish me with those authorities, on which, he may rely. The opinion to which I now incline is, that the assent of any member of a particular firm, is necessary to engage him as a member of a new firm; and that the general authority given by all to each, or even to the acting or managing partners, to bind the whole company, does not extend to the erection of new companies, composed of new members.

In order to subject Mr. *Tabb* as a partner of *Richard Hill & Co.*, and *Moss Armstead & Co.*, his consent to become a partner must be shown. But to show this consent, an express declaration from himself cannot be considered as indispensible; other testimony ought to be received, and circumstances must be resorted to in order to ascertain the fact.

It is relied upon, by the counsel for the defendant, as *prima facie* evidence of his assent, that *Booker* and *Field* cannot be presumed to have engaged the firm in a new partnership, without his approbation.

The circumstances of the company strongly support this presumption. The members of it resided at no great distance, and its business was conducted almost under the eye of Mr. *Tabb*. In the ordinary course of human affairs, he must frequently have fallen in with his partners, and have made some enquiries into the affairs of the company. It is presuming too much to suppose he could have remained uninformed of a circumstance so interesting to himself, as that *Richard Booker & Co.*, of whom he was one, had entered into a new partnership; and, if he did know it, and made no objection to it, his consent to the transaction would very certainly be implied. It is not stated that the members composing the firms of *Richard Hill & Co.*, and *Moss Armstead & Co.*, were concealed from the world; or less known than is usual on such occasions. Nor is it stated, not to have been a matter of notoriety, that a share in each was held by *Richard Booker & Co.* I cannot, therefore, presume any extraordinary concealment to have been used, or that Mr. *Tabb* was unacquainted with a circumstance which it so much concerned him to know, and which it was so much in his power to know.

This presumption has been met by the complainants, who state their intestate withdrew himself in 1771 from the copartnery of *Richard Booker & Co.*, and might therefore very well be presumed no longer to enquire concerning their transactions.

The articles of agreement entered into with *Shore*, in 1774, seem to me to be very strong on this point.[5] In that paper, *Tabb* states himself one of the surviving partners of the company: he contracts with an agent for the management of its affairs; binds himself for the salary of that agent, whom he obliges to account to him as well as to *Theophilus Field*, and to pay him as well as *Field*, the money which might be collected. If he had left only his name to the company, and had no real interest in it, this agreement would, most probably, have been expressed in very different terms. Another evidence on this subject is, I think, his opening a letter to *Richard Booker & Co.* It is a liberty which only a member of that company would have taken. The counsel for Mr. *Tabb's* administrators, endeavour to account for it by stating that the London mark was on the letter, and might well be considered by him as containing a dun. That, I believe, does not follow. Letters from London to American merchants are not necessarily written for the purpose of demanding money. But should this even be conceded, the fact would still evidence a solicitude to enquire into the affairs of *Richard Booker & Co.*; and that solicitude would have informed him they had taken an interest in the other firms.

Another circumstance of some weight with me, is furnished by the correspondence with *Gist. Richard Booker & Co.* (which *Gist* considered as *Tabb*), had recommended *Moss Armstead & Co.*, and *Richard Hill & Co.*; and *Gist* complained of their want of punctuality. He enquires who they are, and employs *Tabb* to collect from them. It is scarcely possible, that, under such circumstances, *Tabb* should not learn that *Richard Booker & Co.*, were interested with them.

That an open letter, directed to *Richard Hill & Co.*, should be among *Tabb's* papers, is not a circumstance of entire indifference. It is true, that letter may have been obtained by his administrators since his death, or may have been received by himself, after he was rendered liable as a partner. If so, these, or any other circumstance tending to do away the influence arising from being in possession of such a letter, may, and ought to be shewn.

It does not appear when *Tabb*, if he ever did, withdrew from *Richard Booker & Co.*; or when the two other companies were formed. It is said by the plaintiff's counsel, that he withdrew in 1771; and, in January 1772, *Gist* writes to *Tabb* concerning *Richard Hill & Co.*, as his correspondents, and asks concerning their punctuality.[6] It is probable that the new companies were formed prior to the date of the supposed withdrawing; and if so, then, according to the view I have been taking, he would be responsible, whether he withdrew or not: But, if afterwards, (supposing the withdrawing can be proved,) even then, according to the same view, he may be liable to one not knowing that he had withdrawn, as he suffered his name to be used, without any public declaration of dissent.

It is unnecessary, however, to decide this question absolutely now; other testimony may be obtained, which may change its present appearance. There may, perhaps, be the testimony of merchants of that day to show that it either was, or was not understood that *Richard Booker & Co.* had an interest in the two firms of *Richard Hill & Co.* and *Moss Armstead & Co.*, or other circumstances may be adduced to influence the case. But I have thought it right to signify the impressions received from the testimony now in the cause. If nothing further should appear, the opinion to which I strongly incline is, that Mr. *Tabb* cannot be considered as ignorant of the copartnership formed by *Richard Booker & Co.* with *Moss Armstead & Co.* and *Richard Hill & Co.*; and, if he was not ignorant of those copartnerships, his silent acquiescence, under their use of the firm, to which he was known to belong, is evidence of his consent, that they should use it.

The most material enquiry in the case is, to what commissions was the defendant, *Samuel Gist*, entitled, on the sales of the tobaccos shipped to him by *Tabb*?

The bill charges expressly an agreement, entered into, with *Samuel Gist*, by *John Tabb*, while in England in 1768, that he should sell the tobaccos shipped to him by *Thomas Tabb & Son*, at a commission of ten shillings per hogshead.

The counsel for the complainants suppose this allegation of the bill to have required a much more explicit answer than it has received; and presuming it to have been evaded, infers from thence a consciousness, in the defendant *Gist*, of its truth. If this explicit allegation had not been as explicitly answered, the answer might very properly have been excepted to, as insufficient. But, on examining the answer it does not appear, to me, liable to the objection, which has been made to it.[7]

The defendant, *Gist*, states, that *Thomas Tabb & Son* had, in 1768, shipped, in different vessels, a very large quantity of tobacco to *Debert, Burkett & Sayre*, and had drawn bills, on them, to a great amount. That *John Tabb* preceded both the tobacco and bills, and on his arrival in London, found *Debert, Burkett & Sayre*, unable to pay his bills, and unfit to be trusted with the sale of his tobacco. That, from friendship to *Tabb*, and compassion for his distress, he consented to sell the tobaccos consigned, to *Debert, Burkett & Sayre*, on the same commission, at which the original consignees were to have sold them. That *Tabb* applied to him to sell future consignments on the same terms, but he peremptorily refused to do so. The answer then, without stating any agreement respecting commissions on future consignments of tobacco, proceeds to detail the advantageous terms on which he agreed to transact the other business of *Thomas Tabb & Son* in London. In this answer no agreement whatever, respecting future commissions, on the sales of tobacco, is stated.

In the supplemental answer,[8] this subject is again taken up. The agreement for the ten shillings per hogshead is again declared to have been limited to the sales of the cargoes consigned to *Debert, Burkett & Sayre*; and that whole transaction is stated more in detail. The answer then proceeds to aver, explicitly, that *Gist* refused to extend the agreement to future consignments, and that, with respect to them, it was positively contracted that he should sell on a commission of two and a half per cent, with the addition of half per cent. for guaranteeing the debts.

The answer adds another circumstance of infinite importance, which, if untrue, it is incumbent on the complainants to disprove. It is, that, for seven years, he continued to transmit accounts of sales and accounts current to *Thomas Tabb*, and *Thomas Tabb & Son*, conforming to this idea of the agreement between them, and that they never objected to such accounts. It is, I say, incumbent on the complainants to disprove it, because, if it is untrue, they must be supposed to possess the means of shewing its untruth.

The counsel for Mr. *Gist* have insisted very strongly on the evidence furnished by the answer, which, they say, is explicit, and is responsive to the bill. It is admitted to be so; and unless there be sufficient reason for questioning the verity of these allegations of the answer, they must decide the cause.

Without saying what the opinion of the court may be, when that further information shall be received, which will now be required, I think the different averments of the defendant's answer, and the documents referred to, afford sufficient reason for believing that some agreement, other than that stated by Mr. *Gist*, must have been entered into by the parties; and consequently that a decision ought to be suspended for further enquiry.

I shall not rest, much, on the omission in the first answer to state what was the real contract to govern future sales to be made, by *Gist*, for *Tabb*; because, although such a statement might have been expected, yet the bill does not require it; and the omission to state it was therefore excusable. But I think the motives leading to the contract for ten shillings per hogshead, on the tobaccos consigned to *Debert, Burkett & Sayre*, deserve some notice. Mr. *Gist* was aware that his consenting to sell a considerable quantity of tobacco for a commission of ten shillings per hogshead would lead to the expectation of his continuing to sell on that commission, and might create some presumption that an agreement, to that effect, was actually made. He, therefore, searches for a motive which should discriminate between that particular transaction and the general course of business. The motive which he assigns is friendship and compassion for *Tabb*.

One of the most opulent merchants of Virginia, having near a thousand hogsheads of tobacco at his disposal, is not much an object of compassion. But Mr. *Gist* very soon forgets the motives assigned for his own conduct. He considers himself as absolved from the contract he had made, by the act of Mr. *Tabb* in selling himself the cargo of the Molly, which amounted to about five hundred hogsheads. Now if, from motives of friendship and compassion, he had consented to sell all the tobaccos consigned to *Debert, Burkett & Sayre*, at a commission which did not compensate his trouble, I cannot conceive how a diminution of the quantity to be sold, on such terms, could be considered as injurious to him. But the compassion and friendship of Mr. *Gist*, displays itself in a still more extraordinary manner. He represents himself to have purchased originally the whole cargo of the Molly; but that *Tabb* afterwards sold a part of it, for about £400 more than he was to have given. This is a profit to which he thinks himself, in equity, entitled; and because another person in the market purchased the commodity of his friend at a much higher price than his compassion would allow him to give, he considers it as so much profit withdrawn from himself, for which he is entitled to compensation. In still another view, the statements of Mr. *Gist* on this subject deserve to be noticed.

A comparison between the answers of *Gist* and *Shore*, on the subject of commission, suggests a remark too, not altogether unworthy of attention. Mr. *Gist* says that Mr. *Tabb* objected, since the conclusion of the war, to the charge of commissions in his accounts, and that he had fully explained that subject in his letters to Mr. *Shore*. We should expect then that Mr. *Shore* would, in his answer, altogether omit the subject, or give the explanation he had received from Mr. *Gist*. He does neither. He would appear to have received no information whatever from *Gist* on the subject, and to remark, only, on the statement made by the complainants in their bill. This would certainly indicate that the explanation, given him by Mr. *Gist*, was not such as Mr. *Shore* chose to rely on.

The parties admit some agreement in 1768. *Tabb* says it was for future consignments; *Gist,* that it was for those addressed to *Debert, Burkett & Sayre.*

In examining the testimony in the cause, other than is to be found in the answers themselves, the first document is that of October 10th, 1768, which says, "your son, no doubt, has acquainted you with his selling me the Thomas's cargo, and the price, as also the terms on which I have agreed to sell the Molly's cargo when it arrives, but as these things are out of the common road, I must beg you not to mention it to any person living."

This letter plainly relates to a single cargo. Not to future consignments, nor to the whole tobacco consigned to *Debert, Burkett & Sayre.*

The next letter is December 31, 1768, which says, "your son will inform you the terms we are upon as to the commission, as well as that on which I am to sell your tobacco; which I desire may be an entire secret." At the foot of this letter is a memorandum made by Mr. *Tabb,* at what time is unknown, in these words, "the terms for selling the tobacco was ten shillings per hogshead for commission, and we to have every advantage for king's allowance, &c."9

This letter is averred by the defendant to relate, only, to the cargo of the Molly, and in this he may be correct; but I will state some reasons in support of a supposition that he has, perhaps, confounded dates, and that this observation was rather designed for the letter of October 10th, than that of December 31.

Mr. *Gist* had already mentioned the Molly to Mr. *Tabb,* and had expressed a confidence, that his son had informed him of the terms on which that cargo was to be sold. When speaking of a contract to have related to a single vessel, he uses terms applying, only, to a single vessel; when, then, he changes his language, and uses terms applicable to the business generally, there is reason to suppose he speaks of a contract embracing the business generally. He says too, *"your son will inform you."* A phraseology which contrasted with that of the letter of October 10th, strongly indicates a different contract, of which information had not probably been before given. It is the language which would be used, if the son was then about to sail, or had just sailed, for America; and would give the information verbally. The idea, that the fact is so, receives some support from the circumstance that the letter of December 31st, is addressed to *Thomas Tabb,* and that of March 25th following, is addressed to *Thomas Tabb & Son.*

It is true, that the words "your son will inform you the terms we are upon as to the commission, as well as that on which I am to sell your tobacco," may be limited by other testimony to a single cargo; but it is not less true, that the words naturally import a general contract; and when it is observed that the agreement, respecting the commission, is confessedly a general one, there is the more reason to believe that,

that respecting the tobacco, made between the same persons, probably at the same time, relative to a branch of the same business, and communicated in the same sentence, and with the same mode of expression, was of the same extent. The whole agreement then subsisting, may have respected a single cargo, and the agreement may have been extended. This is said to be explained by the letter of October 10th. I think so.

The next letter, upon this subject, is not to me conclusive; but I think it rather less equivocal than that which has just been noticed.

It is the letter of the 25th of March, 1769, and is addressed to *Thomas Tabb & Son*. In that letter Mr. *Gist* states his conviction that the extravagant charges on goods, together with the large commissions on tobacco, have driven the consignment business from London: He is therefore determined to do business, with punctual people, on the very best terms.

This resolution is, certainly, not limited to a single transaction, but is to govern permanently; for it is to retain the consignment business, which was leaving London in consequence of the "extravagant charges on goods, together with the large commissions on tobacco;" and the business he was determined to do "on the best terms," and clearly on better terms than those which had driven the consignments elsewhere, related to the charges on goods, and the commission on tobacco.

He then proceeds to state to Mr. *Tabb*, the terms on which he shipped his goods, and did his insurance business, which he adds, "with the commission I charge on the sale of your tobacco, will enable you to ship tobacco as well to this port, as to any other place in the kingdom: indeed the prices are always better here, but it is the great charge attending it that destroys the sale."

A criticism on this sentence cannot be necessary to shew that the words, according to their natural import, relate to the general course of doing business; and, if to any specific agreement whatever, to one which extends to the business generally.

Mr. *Gist*, however, in his answer, avers that these expressions allude only to an agreement to sell the cargo of the Nancy, and that no agreement, at the rate that cargo was sold, was ever made for future consignments.

This may be true. Admitting it to be true, the necessary enquiry is, what then is the operation of this letter?

An agreement has been made between *Gist* and the younger *Tabb* for his father, for the sale of a particular cargo of tobacco, at a specified commission. They separate, and the younger *Tabb* returns to America, and reports the contract to his father. *Gist* then writes a letter to *Tabb & Son*, in which he represents the high charges on goods, and on the sales of tobacco, as the causes which had driven the consignment business from London, whither the price of tobacco would allure it, but for these causes. He is determined to do business on better terms. You perceive, he says, what I have charged on the shipment of your goods, and this, with the commission I charge on your tobacco, will enable you to ship to this port. What commission is here alluded to? Mr. *Gist* says the commission on the sales of the cargo of the Nancy. Be it so. But how was that? The letter is clearly designed to affect his future conduct through the medium of his future interest. It must then be understood as a proposition for the transaction of future business. The present commission on the cargo of the Nancy, as well as the present charge on insurance, and shipment of goods, must be understood as constituting the rule for future charge, or the letter is deceptive.

It would seem as if Mr. *Gist* was aware of this, and therefore his answer proceeds to state, that in consequence of the sale, by Mr. *Tabb's* agreement, of the greater part of the tobacco consigned to *Debert, Burkett & Sayre*, he had considered himself as absolved from the contract of selling the cargo of the Nancy at ten shillings per hogshead, and had determined to charge two and a half per cent. on the gross amount of sales, and this was the commission particularly agreed on for the business generally with *Tabb*, and the particular commission alluded to in his letter of the 25th of March.

Let us enquire how far this explanation will answer the purpose.

The letter does not mention the amount of the commission, but plainly alludes to a charge supposed to be known to Mr. *Tabb*. This, he says, was the charge on the sales of the cargo of the Nancy. Mr. *John Tabb* left England in the expectation that this cargo was to be sold according to the original contract, for Mr. *Gist* does not alledge that he ever told Mr. *Tabb* he intended to charge a higher commission than was stipulated. The sales of the cargo did not accompany this letter. They were not sent till June in the following year. How, then, could Mr. *Gist* refer to two and a half per cent. as the commission on the sales of the cargo, when he had stipulated to sell for ten shillings, and had never informed Mr. *Tabb* of his internal resolution to charge a higher commission? Admitting Mr. *Tabb* to understand this as referring to the sales of that cargo, he must understand it as referring to ten shillings per hogshead commission: because that was the agreement, and it was not changed.

But it may be supposed, that this is mere inaccuracy of expression, and that the words refer to the general agreement of two and a half per cent. commission asserted in the answer. Even this will not serve the purpose. The letter apparently alludes to a commission lower than that which it complains of as too high, and the answer expressly states, that the commission alluded to was the customary commission.

The defendant also states, that he determined to charge a commis-sion of two and a half per cent., when the letter of the 25th of March was written, and that this is the commission that letter alludes to. Yet, in his letter of the 9th June, 1770, he says, "I have already wrote you by this opportunity, and sent sales of your 315 hogsheads by the Nancy last year, which you will see are made out in the common way, as I did not care to let even my clerks know it was to be made out different. I will give you credit for the difference in account current."

Even so late as the 24th March, 1771, he says, "You will perceive in your account current, I have not charged you any interest; that shall come in against the commission on your tobacco, which I did not care should be seen in the counting house." Thus two years after the letter was written, which Mr. *Gist* asserts alluded to a different commission from that which had been stipulated, he continues to assure Mr. *Tabb* that the stipulation will be observed.

This is not all. There is no reason to suppose the account current, alluded to, contained only the sales of the cargo of the Nancy. His expression is, "I send all your accounts;" and in a different part of the same letter, he speaks of the sales of a different cargo, as being trans-mitted. There is no reason to suppose that the commission on the tobacco, which is spoken of generally, is not the commission on all the tobaccos of which accounts of sales were rendered by that convey-ance, and the letter makes no discrimination between the commission chargeable on the different cargoes.

I have still another observation to make on this subject. There is much reason to doubt, whether the Nancy was really consigned to *Debert, Burkett & Sayre*. The allegation of the answer is not, in this respect, responsive to the bill, and consequently is not evidence.

It does not appear when Mr. *Tabb* arrived in England. No doubt, on his first arrival, he informed his father of the state of the house of *Debert, Burkett & Sayre*; and, of consequence, no further consignments would be made to them. How soon this information may have been given, does not appear, but, it certainly, very considerably preceded the 10th of October, 1768; because, on that day, *Gist* gives his father notice, that he had before that time agreed to sell the cargo of the Molly, and purchased from *John Tabb*, the cargo of the Thomas, and had loaded her with goods, by *John Tabb's* order, to the amount of £1137.8.0-½. When the Nancy arrived is not stated; but it was cer-tainly some time in the year 1769. The letter of June 1770, speaks of her as a vessel arriving in 1769. These dates make it very probable, though by no means certain, that she was originally consigned to *Gist* himself.

These appearances, from the answer and letters, the counsel for

Mr. *Gist* have endeavoured to account for in different ways, but they have used one argument which would have very great weight if true; and which, if clearly supported by the fact, might perhaps be conclusive. It is that the accounts current, transmitted by Mr. *Gist*, have regularly been received by Mr. *Tabb*, and never complained of. For this assertion they have the evidence of the answer, and from the nature of mercantile transactions, it must be supposed true, if not disproved by the complainants.

The complainants have adduced several letters on which they rely, but there are two which seem to me really to evidence that Mr. *Tabb* always considered himself as entitled to the credit he now claims. They are of March 10th, 1773, and March 6th, 1774.[10]

These letters demonstrate that Mr. *Tabb* claimed a credit for a deduction on account of the commission, and his own secret mode of transacting the business might prevent their complaining in a different manner; but they do not shew what that deduction was. For this, the memorandum at the foot of the letter of the 31st of December, is appealed to. This, the answer, avers Mr. *Gist* to be entirely ignorant of; and from the mode of expression used, there is reason to believe the memorandum was made in Virginia. I will not *now* say, what its influence ought to be. The answer also admits the contract for the sales of the tobaccos consigned to *Debert, Burkett & Sayre*, to have stipulated for a commission of ten shillings per hogshead. These circumstances would certainly favour the opinion, that the difference between the commission charged, and ten shillings per hogshead, is the credit to which Mr. *Tabb* is entitled, if it shall be ultimately determined that he is entitled to any thing. But there are other circumstances of no inconsiderable weight, which would diminish this allowance. The answer, in the most explicit terms, denies an agreement to sell generally at ten shillings; and Mr. *Giles*, in his letter to Mr. *Shore*, of December 12th, 1797, states his information from Mr. *Tabb*, to be, that the business was to be done at half commissions.[11] There is, then, a good deal of difficulty on this point; and if, on the production of the papers which will be directed, the opinion of the court should still be that the complainants are entitled to some deduction, it will then be necessary to determine what that deduction is.

It is very apparent, that many letters and papers must have passed between the parties, which would throw light on this subject. The complainants require that Mr. *Gist* should be directed to produce on oath all the letters he ever received from the intestate of the complainants. I have no objection to making such an order, but I think justice requires, that it should comprehend the complainants likewise. The letter book of Mr. *Tabb*, in such a case as this, ought to be exhibited. That a merchant doing business as extensively as Mr. *Tabb*, should be without a letter book, is a phenomenon in the mercantile world, which requires very clear testimony to be credited.

The shipments made since the war, I consider as very clearly out of the contract. There is not only evidence in the case that *Gist* claimed the customary commission, but I am well satisfied that the war terminated the old contract.

The complainants also require, that *Gist* should be compelled to exhibit accounts of sales of the tobaccos in his hands in 1775 and 1776. If he has not already exhibited such accounts, it surely would be reasonable that he should do so. The bill does not alledge that they have not been received, and the answer states them to have been transmitted. If, therefore, to transmit duplicates would be any inconvenience to Mr. *Gist*, I certainly should not direct it; but as they may be exhibited without inconvenience, I have no objection to ordering them, though if any expense attends the filing them, it ought to be defrayed by the complainants.

There is another part of the case which may be of very considerable magnitude. The answer states that several calculations of interest have been omitted, to which the defendant *Gist* is entitled. The letters leave it not improbable that these omissions were designed to balance the commissions. Should the fact be so, and Mr. *Tabb's* estate should be credited with the difference of commissions, it is reasonable that it should be debited with the omissions of interest. I give no opinion as to the fact; but I shall direct the commissioner to notice it in the account.

On these principles, the following decree is to be entered:

This cause, which abates as to the defendant, *Thomas Shore*, by his death, came on to be heard on the bill, answers (that of *Thomas Shore* being read by consent), the depositions and other exhibits filed in the cause, and was argued by counsel. On consideration whereof, it is the opinion of the court that the complainants ought not to be precluded by the proceedings at law, from setting up in this court a just defence (if any they have,) against the judgments in the bill mentioned. The several claims, therefore, on which the judgments against *John Tabb*, as surviving partner of *Richard Booker & Co., William Watkins & Co., Richard Hill & Co.,* and *Moss Armstead & Co.,* were referred, are referred to one of the commissioners of this court, who is directed to examine, settle and report the same, stating such matters specially, as either party may require, or he may think fit. And the court is further of opinion, that if, as is in the bill alledged, any balance be due from *Samuel Gist* to the estate of *John Tabb*, on the various transactions between them, that balance ought to be set off from the judgments obtained by the said *Samuel Gist*, against the said *John Tabb*, as surviving partner of the several trading companies aforementioned, to ascertain which fact the accounts between the said *Samuel Gist* and the said *John Tabb*, are also referred to one of the commissioners of this court to be examined and settled by him. And he is specially directed to state the accounts between the parties on the following principles:

1st. So as to shew how they will stand, allowing the defendant, *Samuel Gist*, a commission of ten shillings sterling money of Great Britain, on each hogshead of tobacco shipped to him by *Thomas Tabb & Son*, and *John Tabb*, previous to the —— day of ——, 1775, and sold by him on their account, or on the account of either of them subsequent to the 31st of December, in the year 1768.

2dly. So as to shew how the same accounts will stand on an allowance of one and one half per cent. commission on the gross amount of sales of all tobaccos shipped and sold by the same parties respectively, between the same periods.

3dly. In making up these accounts, he is to calculate interest on the sums due either of the parties, according to any special agreement which may be proved to have subsisted between them, or in default of such agreement being shewn, according to the custom of merchants; however, in the accounts rendered, such calculations of interest may have been omitted.

The commissioner is further directed also to state the accounts in such other manner as may be required by either of the parties, stating such matters specially as they or either of them may direct, or he may think fit, and make report to the court in order to a final decree. And the more effectually to enable the commissioner to make up his report, it is further ordered and directed, that the said *Samuel Gist* do, on oath, exhibit and file with the clerk of this court, all the letters he has ever received from *Thomas* or *John Tabb* between the first day of January, 1769, and the —— day of ——, 1775, or if it be not in his power to produce such letters, that he state in like manner the cause of such disability. And he is further directed to file with the clerk of this court, such accounts of sales of all the tobaccos received by him prior to the signing of the preliminary articles of peace between the United States of America, and his Britannic majesty, to be sold on account of the said *John Tabb*, as had not been rendered by him previous to the last mentioned time.

And it is further ordered, that the complainants do file with the clerk of this court the letter book of the said *John Tabb*, or copies of all the letters written by him to the said *Samuel Gist*, previous to the —— day of ——, in the year 1775, verified on oath, or if there be no letter book, that they do, on oath, file all the copies which are, or have been, in their possession.

All which matters and things are decreed and ordered this 9th day of December, 1802; and by consent of parties, general commissions are awarded the parties, to be executed before any notary public, upon giving reasonable notice thereof.[12]

Printed, Daniel Call, *Reports of Cases Argued and Decided in the Court of Appeals of Virginia*, VI (Richmond, Va., 1833), 289–307. Text in 1 Brock. 44–61 taken from Call.

1. Frances Tabb and William B. Giles, administratrix and administrator of John Tabb, filed their bill in the state High Court of Chancery in Sept. 1798. As an alien, the defendant, London merchant Samuel Gist, could petition to remove this suit to the U.S. circuit court, which he did by his counsel in Mar. 1800. In Dec. 1795 Gist had obtained four judgments against Tabb in the federal court amounting to nearly fifty thousand dollars (proceedings in High Court of Chancery [copy], Tabb's Administrators v. Gist, U.S. Cir. Ct., Va., Ended Cases [Unrestored], 1829, Vi; U.S. Cir. Ct., Va., Ord. Bk. II, 55, 58, 70–71).

2. George Hay and John Wickham (6 Call 287–88).

3. This should read "*Richard Booker & Co.*" The bill expressly denied that Tabb had been a partner of Richard Hill & Co.

4. George Keith Taylor and Daniel Call (6 Call 288–89).

5. By this agreement, dated 1 Jan. 1774, Tabb and Theophilus Field, surviving partners of Richard Booker & Co., contracted with Thomas Shore of Petersburg to collect the debts of the company. Shore, who at the time of this suit acted as Gist's agent, filed the original of this agreement with his separate answer to the bill (answer of Thomas Shore, 16 Apr. 1800, Tabb's Administrators v. Gist [Unrestored]).

6. The original of this letter, dated 28 Jan. 1772, was filed as an exhibit (Tabb's Administrators v. Gist, U.S. Cir. Ct., Va., Ended Cases [Restored], 1829, Vi).

7. Gist's answer was sworn in London in Oct. 1799 (ibid. [Unrestored]).

8. Sworn in London in Oct. 1801 (ibid.).

9. A search of the restored and unrestored case papers has failed to turn up the originals of the letters of 10 Oct. and 31 Dec. 1768 and also of those (referred to below) dated 25 Mar. 1769, 9 June 1770, and 24 Mar. 1771. The extant case papers contain two files of letters, 1772–73 and 1774–76.

10. The originals were filed as exhibits (Tabb's Administrators v. Gist [Restored]).

11. A copy of this letter was annexed to Shore's answer (ibid. [Unrestored]).

12. In accordance with this decree, Master Commissioner Hay sent notices to the parties on 22 Dec. 1802 and again on 20 June 1805 appointing a day for settling the accounts. Apparently, no settlement and report were executed and no final decree was issued in this suit, which remained on the docket until 1829 (decree and notice [copies], T.79/31, P.R.O.; U.S. Cir. Ct., Va., Ord. Bk. IX, 442; XII, 296).

The United States Circuit Court
for
North Carolina

EDITORIAL NOTE

Shortly after Christmas of 1802, Marshall set out for Raleigh for his first session of the U.S. Circuit Court, district of North Carolina. During the next three decades he made this trip twice each year, missing only six terms out of more than sixty. From 1802 through 1806, the terms began on 15 June and

29 December; thereafter, on 12 May and 12 November.[1] The term never lasted more than five or six days, and at most terms two or three days were sufficient to get through the docket. Sitting with Marshall on the Raleigh bench throughout the entire period was U.S. District Judge Henry Potter, who survived the chief justice by many years.

Of Marshall's semiannual journeys to North Carolina barely a scrap of documentation survives. For the years covered by this volume, only one letter has a Raleigh dateline. This is an amusing account to his "Dearest Polly" of his inauspicious first visit, in which he not only lost fifteen silver dollars through a worn waistcoat pocket but also had to appear in court dressed as a "sans culotte," his servant having forgotten to pack his breeches.[2]

If the law had provided for reimbursement of justices' expenses, Marshall's expense accounts might have found their way into the public archives and yielded valuable information about his circuit-riding itinerary. The distance between Richmond and Raleigh, taking the main post road, was approximately 165 miles. The post road passed through Petersburg, Harris's, and Gholson's in the counties of Dinwiddie and Brunswick and then to Warrenton, North Carolina. The route from Warrenton to Raleigh was by way of Louisburg. Marshall probably spent at least two nights on the road, more if the weather was inclement, as it was likely to be in December and January.

South of Richmond the road traversed numerous creeks and rivers and skirted the edges of swamps. Jonathan Mason, a former senator from Massachusetts, made the journey from Richmond to Raleigh in January 1805, just after Marshall had returned from the winter term. The New Englander described the roads as "wretched" or "execrable" and the countryside "miserable." From Petersburg, about 140 miles from Raleigh, he and his party took three days to reach the North Carolina capital. Bad weather that year also delayed Marshall's arrival. A British traveler in 1820 covered the distance between Petersburg and Raleigh in thirty-eight hours.[3]

The capital of North Carolina since 1792, Raleigh in 1810 was a small village of a thousand inhabitants and 120 (mostly wooden) dwelling houses. At the town's center was a square of ten acres on which stood the brick State House constructed in 1794. Two blocks south of this square, on Fayetteville Street, was the Wake County Courthouse, completed in 1795, where the federal circuit court held its sessions. Mason dismissed Raleigh as "a miserable place, nothing but a few wooden buildings and a brick Court [i.e., State] House, built for the accommodation of the Government."[4]

While in Raleigh, the chief justice could choose from among several inns and taverns for accommodations. According to family tradition, Marshall patronized the establishment of a Mr. Cooke. This was apparently Henry H. Cooke, whose house, about a quarter mile from the State House, could "accommodate ten or twelve Gentlemen" and "take a few Horses to feed, at two shillings and sixpence a Day." Owing to the landlord's frugality, the boarders at Cooke's had to forgo certain amenities. On one occasion Marshall was observed gathering wood early in the morning outside his boardinghouse. "Yes," he explained, "I suppose it is not convenient for Mr. Cook to keep a servant, so I make up my own fires."[5]

No manuscripts of Marshall's opinions given in the circuit court at Raleigh have been preserved. Nor have any significant Marshall documents been found in the extensive collection of records and case papers of the North Carolina circuit court. The minutes of the court are in the National Archives (Record Group 21, Records of the District Courts of the United States); the case papers are housed at the Federal Records Center, East Point, Georgia. Among printed sources are a small number of reports of cases heard in the federal court, most of them falling into the period of this volume. Eighteen cases in the federal court between 1802 and 1806 are included in the second volume of John Haywood's *Cases Adjudged in the Superior Courts . . . of North Carolina* (Raleigh, N.C., 1806). Brockenbrough also reported three Marshall opinions delivered on the North Carolina circuit in 1815, 1825, and 1833. The newspapers published at Raleigh—the *Register*, the *Minerva*, and the *North Carolina Star*—supply useful information about the proceedings of the federal court and occasionally summarize the opinions of the court in cases not reported in any other source.

Marshall would not permit his grand jury charges to be published, as he explained on the occasion of his first charge given at the Raleigh court. After delivering "an elegant and learned charge to the Grand Jury," reported the *Minerva*, "the Chief Justice declined granting a copy for publication which was requested, saying that he had laid it down as a rule from which he did not intend to depart, not to allow his charges to be published." The *Register* commented more briefly that the chief justice delivered "a concise and appropriate charge, fully explaining their duty, without the least political intermixture."[6] Marshall's refusal to have his charges published and to use them as occasions for political statements reflected a more cautious judicial posture than had been the recent custom among his colleagues. Without a text to publish, the newspapers were reduced to brief descriptions of Marshall's charges as "very learned and pertinent," delivered "in his usual plain and perspicuous manner."[7]

The texts of Marshall's opinions in the North Carolina court are taken from Haywood's reports. Haywood did not report what was probably the most important case heard in that court during these years. This was *Granville* v. *Allen and Collins*, an ejectment that brought into issue the title to an extensive region of the state known as the Granville District. In declining to give an opinion in this case, Marshall stated his reasons for recusing himself. That statement, as reported by the *Register*, is published in this volume.[8]

1. *U.S. Statutes at Large*, II, 158, 413.

2. JM to Mary W. Marshall, 2 Jan. 1803.

3. "Diary of the Honorable Jonathan Mason," *Proceedings of the Massachusetts Historical Society*, 2d ser., II (1885–86), 20–21; *North-Carolina Minerva* (Raleigh), 31 Dec. 1804; Adam Hodgson, *Letters from North-America . . .* (2 vols.; London, 1824), I, 34–35.

4. Jedidiah Morse, *The American Gazetteer* (3d. ed., 1810); "Diary of Mason," *Proceedings of the Massachusetts Historical Society*, 2d ser., II (1885–86), 21.

5. *Raleigh Register, and North-Carolina State Gazette*, 24 Oct. 1803; Sallie Ewing Marshall, "Chief-Justice John Marshall," *Magazine of American History*, XII (1884), 69.

6. Raleigh *Minerva*, 4 Jan. 1803; *Raleigh Register*, 4 Jan. 1803.

7. Raleigh *Minerva*, 20 June 1803; *Raleigh Register*, 18 June 1804, 5 Jan. 1807.

8. See Remarks, 18 June 1805.

Sanders v. Hamilton
Opinion
U.S. Circuit Court, North Carolina, 31 December 1802

MARSHALL, Chief Justice. It is said Hamilton warranted the wench from whom desended the slaves afterwards recovered by Streater from Sanders.[1] The record of that recovery is now offered, to be read to prove Streater's title. I am of opinion, that as Hamilton was not party to that suit, nor privy, it cannot be read to prove Streater's title: it may, however, to shew that Sanders was evicted.[2]

Printed, John Haywood, *Cases Adjudged in the Superior Courts . . . of North Carolina*, II (Raleigh, N.C., 1806), 226–27.

1. John Hamilton sold a female slave to Hardy Sanders, who agreed to defend a suit by one Streeter for the increase. Hamilton in turn agreed to make good the damages recovered by Streeter against Sanders. JM's opinion presumably was given during the course of the trial on 31 Dec. (U.S. Cir. Ct., N.C., Min. Bk., 31 Dec. 1802).

2. After the jury returned a verdict for the plaintiff, the defendant was awarded a new trial (ibid., 31 Dec. 1802, 3, 4 Jan. 1803). See the further opinion in this case at 17 June 1803.

To Mary W. Marshall

My dearest Polly   Rawleigh Jany. 2d. 1803[1]

As I know you will feel the same pleasure in hearing from me that I do in writing to you I set down to tell you that I find everything here as pleasant as I coud expect & that my journey has been not a disagreeable one. The weather was uncommonly mild & tho rain was continually threatend it did not begin to fall till I was safely hous'd. This was extremely fortunate, but with this my good fortune ended. You will laugh at my vexation when you hear the various calamities that have befallen me. In the first place when I came to review my funds, I had the mortification to discover that I had lost 15 silver dollers out of my waist coat pocket. They had worn through the various mendings the pocket had sustaind & sought their liberty in the sands of Carolina. I determind not to vex myself with what coud not be remedied & orderd Peter to take out my cloaths that I might dress for court when to my astonishment & grief after fumbling several minutes in the portmanteau, staring at vacancy, & sweating most profusely he turnd to me with the doleful tidings that I had no pair of breeches. You may be sure this piece of inteligence was not very graciously receivd; however, after a little scolding I determind to make the best of my situation & immediately set out to get a pair made. I thought I shoud be a sans culotte only one day & that for the residue of the term I might be well enough dressd for the appearance on the first day to be forgotten. But, 'the greatest of evils, I found, was followd by still greater!' Not a taylor in town coud be prevaild on to work for me. They were all so busy that it was impossible to attend to my wants however pressing they might be & I have the extreme mortification to pass the whole term without that important article of dress I have mentiond. I have no alleviation for this misfo⟨r⟩tune but the hope that I shall be enabled in four or five days to commence my journey homewards & that I shall have the pleasure of seeing you & our dear children in eight or nine days after this reaches you. In the meantime I flatter myself that you are well & happy. Adieu my dearest Polly, I am your ever affectionate

J MARSHALL

ALS, Marshall Papers, ViW. Addressed to Mrs. Marshall at Richmond. MS torn.

1. JM was then attending his first session of the U.S. Circuit Court for North Carolina. The term began on 30 Dec. and adjourned on 5 Jan.

Ogden v. Blackledge
Opinion
U.S. Circuit Court, North Carolina, 5 January 1803

EDITORIAL NOTE

The full title of this case is *Robert Ogden, Administrator of Samuel Cornell*, v. *Richard Blackledge, Executor of Robert Salter*. The reporter John Haywood mistakenly named the defendant as David Witherspoon, administrator of Abner Nash. Although the plaintiff had indeed also sued Witherspoon in the federal court, there is no mention of that case in the minutes of the December 1802 term. The error is of no consequence, however, for both cases (along with numerous others) had similar factual situations and identical pleadings. The case against Blackledge was chosen to decide the issue raised in the pleadings.

The case began in 1798 as an action of debt on a bond given in March 1775 by Salter, a citizen of North Carolina, to Cornell, a subject of Great Britain. Salter had died in 1780, and his executor Blackledge pleaded a North Carolina act of 1715 that required creditors of deceased persons to "make their claim within seven years after the death of said debtor" or "be forever barred." The plaintiff in reply set up the fourth article of the peace treaty of 1783, which stipulated that creditors should meet with no "lawful impediment" to the recovery of debts contracted before the war. The defendant demurred to this replication and the plaintiff joined in demurrer. The argument turned on the effect of the 1715 act, whether it was a bar to the action or had been repealed by a subsequent act of 1789.[1] Marshall's opinion called forth some brief comments on the nature of judicial power and on the operation of the contract clause of the Constitution.

1. U.S. Cir. Ct., N.C., Min. Bk., 5 Jan. 1803; 2 Haywood 227.

OPINION

Marshall, Chief Justice. In the act of 1789, there is this clause: "That all laws, and parts of laws, that come within the meaning and purview of this act, are hereby declared void, and of no effect." There are two rules for determining what act shall be deemed to be repealed by a latter one. *If the latter be inconsistent with the former, it repeals the former. If it be reconcilable with the former, but legislate upon the same subjects as the former does, and repeals all other laws within its purview, the former is repealed.* Then what is the subject of the ninth section of the act of 1715? The estates of all dead men, and all the creditors upon them, and a limitation of the time for the exhibition of such claims. What is the subject of the latter act? Precisely the same estates and persons, and a limitation of the time for bringing forward their claims.[1] There is a legislation in both acts upon the same cases. The repealing clause then extends to the section in question. The act of 1715 prescribes a limitation, without an exception of persons; the act of 1789 excepts persons under disabilities, such as femes covert and the like. If the act of 1715 be in force, persons under disabilities will be excepted until the expiration of seven years, and not afterwards; for at that period all persons will be barred by the act of 1715, if it stand with the act of 1789. But why should the legislature design a permission for persons under disabilities to sue after the time prescribed in the act of 1789 for other persons, and until the completion of the seven years fixed by the act of 1715, and not afterwards? The same reason which continued the exception till the expiration of seven years, will still operate to continue it longer. If the exceptions are to last as mentioned by the act of 1789, until the disabilities be removed, then the act of 1715 must be repealed.[2] The act of 1799 declares that the act of 1715 hath continued, and shall continue to be in force.[3] I will not say at this time that a retrospective law may not be made; but if its retrospective view be not clearly expressed, construction ought not to aid it: That however is not the objection to this act. The bill of rights of this state, which is declared to be a part of the constitution, says in the fourth section, "That the legislative, executive and supreme judicial powers of government, ought to be forever separate and distinct from each other.["] The separation in these powers has been deemed by the people of almost all the states, as essential to liberty. And the question here is, does it belong to the judiciary to decide upon laws when made, and the extent and operation of them; or to the legislature? If it belongs to the judiciary, then the matter decided by this act, namely, whether the act of 1789 be a repeal of the 9th section of 1715, is a judicial matter, and not a legislative one. The determination is made by a branch of government, not authorised by the constitution to make it; and is therefore in my judgment, void.[4] It seems also to be void for another reason; 10th section of the first article of the federal constitution, prohibits the states to pass any law impairing the obligation of contracts. Now will it not impair this obligation, if a contract, which, at the time of passing the act of 1789, might be recovered on by the creditor, shall by the operation of the act of 1799, be entirely deprived of his remedy?

Upon the point of suspension of the act of 1715, prior to its repeal by the act of 1789, I am of opinion with my brother judge, and for the reasons by him given, that it was suspended and continued so till the act of 1787, declaring the treaty of 1783 to be a part of the law of the land; for it was not settled till the making of the federal constitution, that treaties should *ipso facto* become a part of the laws of every state, without any act of the state legislature to make them so.[5] It has been argued that, by an act passed in 1791, all acts and parts of acts retained in the compilation of Mr. Iredell, and not by him declared to be repealed or obsolete, or not in force, shall be held to be in force; and that 9th section of 1715, being retained therein, and having no such declaration attached to it, is therefore in force. The whole of 1789 is also retained, and the repealing clause, as well as the other parts of the act: and if the repealing clause be in force, as no doubt it is, it had the same effect in 1791 as in 1788 and 1789, and continued to keep 9th section of the act of 1715 repealed, until the passing of the act of 1799.[6]

Printed, John Haywood, *Cases Adjudged in the Superior Courts . . . of North Carolina*, II (Raleigh, N.C., 1806), 227–29.

1. The 1789 law stated that resident creditors must bring their actions within two (and foreign creditors three) years from the qualification of the executors or administrators of the deceased debtor. For the texts of the relevant sections of the 1715 and 1789 acts, see James Iredell's compilation, *Laws of the State of North-Carolina* (Edenton, N.C., 1791), 30, 677–78. Iredell's work has been reprinted in two volumes (continuously paginated) as *The First Laws of the State of North Carolina* (Wilmington, Del., 1984).

2. In a separate opinion, Potter maintained that the 1789 act was consistent with that of 1715. The earlier act was thus a bar to the action, more than seven years having elapsed before the case was brought in the federal court. The effect of the 1789 act was the material point on which the two justices were opposed (2 Haywood 227).

3. In 1799 the North Carolina legislature attempted to remove doubts concerning the 1789 act's effect on the 1715 act by declaring that the latter "shall be deemed, held

and taken to be in full force." This act is reprinted in a note to Ogden v. Blackledge, 2 Cranch 276 (1804).

4. On this point, Potter contended that the North Carolina legislature's action in 1799 merely reenacted the 1715 act from the date of the reenacting act, that is, 1799. It could not have the effect of continuing in force the 1715 act after the passage of the 1789 act. (As noted, he believed that, independently of the legislative declaration of 1799, the 1715 act remained in operation after 1789.) Therefore, since the 1799 act only legislated for the future, in a general way, there was no infringement of the separation of powers doctrine.

5. Potter cited wartime acts disabling British subjects from suing in North Carolina courts. This disability continued until the 1787 act to enforce the treaty of peace (*First Laws of North Carolina*, II, 607).

6. Haywood stated that this case was removed to the Supreme Court by writ of error. In fact, it went up on a certificate of a division of opinion of the two circuit court judges, as provided by the Judiciary Act of 1802. In a brief opinion delivered by Justice Cushing, the Supreme Court in Feb. 1804 affirmed JM's opinion, holding that the 1715 act was repealed by the act of 1789, at which time seven years had not elapsed from the final ratification of the peace treaty (*U.S. Statutes at Large*, II, 159–61; 2 Cranch 272–79).

To Samuel Hunt

My dear Sir   Richmond Jany. 14th. 1803

On my return to this place a few days past from a tour of duty to North Carolina I had the pleasure of receiving your letter of the 26th. of December.[1] I recollect with as much satisfaction as you do our voyage from Bourdeaux, a voyage which was undoubtedly rendered much more pleasant to me than it coud otherwise have been by your being a fellow passenger.

I hope to see you in february when I shall be calld to the city of Washington, but I coud not postpone till then my acknowledgements for your recollection of me. They woud be given with still more pleasure if they coud be accompanied with felicitations on an event which you say has not yet taken place, but which the communications of our friend General Morris[2] had led me to suppose had happend some time since.

I wish you a much more agreeable session than you have in prospect & am dear Sir, with much esteem, your Obedt. Servt

J: MARSHALL

ALS, MH.

1. Letter not found. The depository identifies Samuel Hunt as the recipient, though the address leaf is now missing. Hunt (1765–1807) was then attending the Eighth Congress as a representative from New Hampshire. He later moved to Ohio.

2. Lewis R. Morris had recently served as a Federalist representative from Vermont.

Marshall v. Pendleton and Others
Bill in Chancery

[28 January 1803]

To the Honble. the Judge of the high court of Chancery[1] sitting in Richmond orator John Marshall humbly showeth

That some time in or about the year 1790 your orator purchasd from Charles Minn Thurston[2] a tract of land lying in the county of Buckingham which the said Charles had before that time purchasd from George Webb Senr. & George Webb junr.[3] The said Charles Minn Thurston George Webb senr. & George Webb junr. united in a conveyance of the said land to your orator & the said Charles either jointly with the other vendors or singly warranted the title thereto against all persons whatever; all which will more fully appear by the deed of conveyance now of record in the General court of this Commonwealth.

Your orator further shows that previous to the sale of the said land to the said Charles Minn Thurston the said George Webb Senior had conveyd a part thereof to John Pendleton either singly or jointly with some other person to secure a considerable debt due from the said George Webb Senior to Caron de Beaumarchais,[4] with a power to the trustee or trustees to sell the same in such manner & at such time as is in the said deed specified. Of this incumbrance your orator had notice at the time of the purchase, but he felt no concern at the circumstance because the said Charles faithfully promisd to pay the debt & releive the land from the incumbrance imposd on it, & because the payments from himself became due at distant times, & he relied on being able shoud it be necessary, to appropriate a part of the purchase money to the discharge of the debt due the said Caron de Beaumarchais.

Your orator further states that he has now fully paid up the to last shilling[5] of the money contracted to be paid for the said land. The last payment was made in the year 1798. Soon after this payment was made he was applied to by John A Chevallie the agent of Caron de Beaumarchais & informd that a balance of between six & seven hundred pounds as well as your orator recollects, still remaind due on the debt securd on the land purchasd as aforesaid by your orator. Application on this subject was made to the said Charles Minn Thurston who promisd to adjust the business so as to protect your orators property from the debt. This application was frequently repeated & your orator continually expected, & inducd Mr. Chevallie to expect that the money woud certainly be paid. At length Caron de Beaumarchais having departed this life his representatives who as your orator is informd still continued the said John A Chevallie as their agent, re-

quird as your orator beleives that all their business under his management shoud be closd as speedily as possible. The said John A Chevallie applied to you⟨r⟩ orator representing the absolute necessity of
bringing this transaction to a termination; & he promisd to see the
said Charles Minn Thurston himself & know certain⟨ly⟩ what was to
be depended on. In consequence of this engagement your orator
paid a visit to the said Charles Minn Thurston in the summer of 1802
when he was informed by the said Charles that he contested the claim
set up by the said John A Chevallie on account of the representatives
of Caron de Beaumarchais. On enquiry it appeard that there might
be some trivial difference between them in their accounts but the
material subject of controversy respected a house in the city of Richmond which had been taken on account of the said Caron de Beaumarchais from George Webb at between four & five hundred pounds
& had been credited to the said Webb in account before the sale made
by Webb to Thurston. After the sale made by Thurston to your orator, this house was recoverd as your orator is informd, from the person in possession, in a suit brought in the county court of Henrico;
after which the credit given the said Webb on account of the said
house was disallowd & the sum at which it had been taken rechargd.

The said Thurston alledges that on the faith of an account renderd
by the agent of the said Beaumarchais exhibiting the balance actually
due, he made the purchase, & has retaind in his hands only so much
money as woud satisfy the balance stated to be due, & has paid without suspicion of any further demand, the residue of the purchase
money to the said George Webb Senior who is since dead insolvent &
who was actually insolvent before he had any notice of the defect in
the title to the said house, or any cause to suspect such defect. Un-
de⟨r⟩ these circumstances he alledges that no claim can be made on
him or on the land sold to him, for the amount of the said house,
since shoud he be compeld to pay it, it will be a clear loss to him
occasiond by his confiding implicitly to the account renderd by the
agent of Beaumarchais. He however promisd your orator explicitly to
be in Richmond early in the month of December to adjust this difference with Mr. Chevallie. Your orator stated this promise to Mr. Chevallie who agreed to take no further step till Dec[e]mber. The time
has elaps⟨d⟩ & the said Thurston has not complied with his promise
to see Mr. Chevallie nor has your orator heard from him. The said
John A Chevallie presses for the payment of the money he claims &
your orator does not think it reasonable that further delays shoud be
practisd in bringing the controversy to a close. But he humbly states
that shoud the land be sold under the deed of trust or shoud he pay
the money without a sale & it shoud afterwards appear that objections
made by the said Thurston to the payment of the balance now claimd

are well founded he woud lose so much money & woud be entirely
without remedy which woud be contrary to equity. Your orator is
therefore extremely desirous that the controversy between the said
Charles Minn Thurston & the representatives of Caron de Beaumarchais by John A Chevallie their agent shoud be settled, & that the sum
actually due from the former to the latter securd by the deed of trust
before mentiond shoud be ascertaind.

To the end therefore that the said John Pendleton the trustee
nam⟨d⟩ in the said deed, the representatives of Caron de Beaumarchais by John A Chevallie their agent, & Charles Min Thurston may
be made defendents hereto & may on oath true answer make to the
premisses, & that the said Charles Minn Thurston may be decreed to
account with the said John A Chevallie & to pay him whatever balance may be really due to the representatives of the said Caron de
⟨Beau⟩marchais & chargeable on the land sold to your orator as
aforemention⟨d⟩ or in default thereof that he may be decreed to pay
the same to your orator, & that the said John Pendleton may be
enjoind from selling the said land under the said deed of trust, & may
be decreed to convey the same to your orator on the sum with which
the same shall be actually chargeable being paid & that your orator
may have such releif as is proper. May it please your Honor &c.

J MARSHALL

City of Richmond[6] to wit
John Marshall appeard before me a magistrate for the city[7] aforesaid
this 28th. day of Jany. 1803 & made oath in due form of law to the
foregoing bill.

GEO PICKETT

The injunction is awarded on giving security in the penaltie of two
hundred dollars 28 january 1803.

G. WYTHE.[8]

ADS, Chamberlain MSS, MB. Entirely in JM's hand except for George Pickett's
signature to affidavit and Chancellor George Wythe's endorsement. Angle brackets
enclose letters obscured in margin.

1. The proper address was to the Superior Court of Chancery. The High Court of
Chancery had recently been split into three Superior Courts of Chancery sitting at
Richmond, Williamsburg, and Staunton (Shepherd, *Statutes*, II, 320–23).

2. Charles Mynn Thruston (whose name JM consistently misspelled throughout),
then living in Winchester (*PJM*, II, 39–40 n. 7).

3. On the Webbs, see ibid., 13 and nn. Beginning in July 1791, JM listed expenses for
going to Buckingham and for paying taxes on his land in that county (ibid., 422, 446,
462, 470). He eventually sold his Buckingham land to William Bernard (JM to Bernard, 8 Sept. 1803).

4. The French playwright had furnished supplies to Virginia during the Revolution. After the war, JM served as counsel for Beaumarchais's agent, John Chevallié, in his attempts to recover the Frenchman's claim against the commonwealth (*PJM*, II, 124, 125–26 and n. 8; III, 528–29 and n. 3).

5. JM meant to write "up to the last shilling."

6. "City of Richmond" filled in later.

7. "City" filled in later.

8. The outcome of this suit is unknown, the records and papers of this court having been destroyed by fire in Apr. 1865. JM's surviving correspondence sheds no further light on the controversy.

Fenwick v. Sears's Administrators
Notes on Arguments
U.S. Supreme Court, 18–19 February 1803

EDITORIAL NOTE

Although Marshall must have regularly taken notes during the hearing of arguments, only a handful of his case notes have survived. Those presented below are preserved in the appellate case file in the National Archives (misleadingly docketed as an opinion). A comparison with the very full report of this case in Cranch shows that Marshall's notes are a memorandum of the main lines of arguments and authorities cited. The court gave no opinion in the case, rendering only a brief judgment on a technical point.[1]

This case began in the U.S. Circuit Court for the District of Columbia, sitting at Washington, as an action for the recovery of money on a protested bill of exchange brought by the administrators of George Sears (John Stricker and Henry Payson) against Joseph Fenwick. After the circuit court rendered judgment against him in August 1802, Fenwick sued out a writ of error from the Supreme Court. The case was argued on 18 and 19 February 1803 by John T. Mason for the appellant and by Charles Simms and Charles Lee for the appellees.[2]

1. 1 Cranch 282 and n.

2. Fenwick v. Sears's Administrators, App. Cas. No. 122; U.S. Sup. Ct. Minutes, 18, 19 Feb. 1803; 1 Cranch 264.

Fenwick
v
Stricker & Payson admrs. of Sears

On first point.[1]

A protest on foreign bill of exchange the only evidence which can be receivd in a court of justice of non acceptance or non payment. Kid 136. 142.[2]

Only the notary public, can make the protest, Kid 137

By laws of Maryland Hanson not a notary. 48th. Sec. of Const. authorizes Governor to appoint all civil officers of government. 55 Sec. every person before appointed to an office of profit or trust to take an oath, ⟨see?⟩ act of Feb. 77. Ch. 5. Act of Novr. 79 ch. 25. Sec. 2 gives fees to notary public.

If he had been permitted to show that Hanson had not taken the oaths, coud have shown that the instrument was not protested.[3]

2d.[4] Kid 9. 138. 142. protest for non acceptance will authorize a suit, but judgt. ought not to be renderd without protest for non payment.[5]

will consider the duties & undertakings of Drawer indorser & holder.

Drawer Kid 109–10.11.   Holder Kid 117.18.19.20.   137.8.

3d. Dal. 386. custom of merchants does not require protest for non acceptance on a suit for non payment.[6]

3d.[7] This involves two questions

1st. on the right to recover on the count on the bill—2. on that for money had & receivd.[8]

1. bill of exchange. Kid 117.

want of funds dispenses with notice to drawer but not to indorsers. Kid 129. 131. 1. term 714[9]—As to time of notice. If the bill found its way here in seven months why shoud it be 3 years in getting back.[10]

Non intercourse law passd & took effect in June & July 98. twice a year public vessels went to France to carry frenchmen, & there was the whole time a circuitous passage for letters. Indorser with notice might have indemnified himself: In fact no notice Kidd 126.

That court shoud not decide due notice, 126.7. Metcalf v Hall Doug. 515. 1 term 171.[11]

If the province of the court, it is error not to have given notice.

2. count for money had & receivd.

Where does the idea of money had & receivd come from?[12]

4. In substance same as the foregoing[13]

objects also

Oyer of letters of admn. prayd, & letters granted by orphans court of Baltimore county. contends that those letters did not authorize him to administer in Columbia. Always decided that foreign letters do not authorize a person to sue in Maryland.

The laws of Maryland operate in Columbia as if the laws of Congress. therefore laws of Maryland foreign & grant of administration ought to be by Columbia.

Simms for deft. in error[14]

1st. No authority to support this exception.[15] It woud be extremely inconvenient if a ministerial officers acts shd. be invalidated for having omitted to take an oath. laws of Maryland give penalty for acting before oath. It was an attempt to prove a negative therefore rightly to be objected since it was impossible. No person calld on to show that a notary was duly qualified. Seal is conclusive testimony. Therefore not to be controverted. Evans 94.[16] protest may be made by a creditable person if there be no notary.

2. On usage as to time of protest 4 Ba. 687. N.E.[17] In 4. term 173 difference of opinion between Lord Kenyon & Judge Buller.[18] practice of the U.S. to protest the day after the last day of grace.

---

on protest for non payment Evans 66. Kid 140. Doug. 55. Buller 269 3 Wil. 16.[19]

Reasons of protest that party may send off immediately—In this case no necessity of notice because indorser had notice that there was no effects in the hands of the drawee.

3d. As to count for money had & recd. 1. term. 408. Evans 59.[20]

Indorser having knowledge that drawee has no effects—same as drawer.

4. As to matter of law & fact. Kid 127 Doug. 515. 681. 1. term. 167. partly fact, partly law. 2. H. Black. 569. 2. Wash. 231. 1 Dal. 252[21]

4th. Evans 57.

On demurrer to evidence.[22]

In England profit to Bishops from granting letters of admn.—admr. service of ordinary & can extend no further than the diocese or jurisdiction of the bishop. Gives history of Admn. in Eng.

Act of assumption removes all doubt.[23]

C Lee[24]

on the ability of the admr. to maintain this action

Tho Admn. granted out of Maryland will not authorize suit in that State the principle will not apply to this case.

Admr. had a vested right to sue when the assumption took place.

Laws of Congress relative to the district do not divest this right.

1st. The objection is not that he was not a notary, but that he was not qualified by having taken an oath.

Oaths of office do not constitute the officer but direct his conduct & are prescribd for the purpose of influencing His conduct—Directory not conditional, between officer ⟨&⟩ the public, not to invalidate his acts or affect third persons.

2d. a regular protest & ought to have been admitted—if not it was unnecessary as the suit is brought for non acceptance.

In Lefly v Mills[25] 4. term 173. diffce. between Judges Kenyon &
Buller. custom of banks. But unnecessary. court did not give opinion that the protest was regular—prferrd to say irregular. justifiable because the protest not important.

3d. bill of exceptions does not state that all the circumstances to excuse the want of notice are on the record.

Notice of non payment was unnecessary, therefore court did right
not to direct the jury that it was necessary to support the action.
exception not taken to the failure of the court to give an opinion but
to the opinion actually given.

On the opinion on the count for money had & receivd the law of
france is the law of the contract & ought to govern it by that law
where there are no effects in the hands of the drawees notice to
indorser unnecessary Evans 62. 60.—The principle of fraud is in this
case as applicable to drawer as indorser since indorser knew the bill
was drawn without effects in the hands of drawee. 2d. Esp. rep.
515.[26]

As to laches.[27]

The complaint is not that there was no notice—but that notice was
not given sooner. Question whether under all the circumstances of
this case it was matter of fact or of law. In different States law is
different.

admits general rules on the subject of laches, one of which is that
notice must be given of a protest—but if there are various excuses set
up for not giving notice in time, jury may decide—In our constitution
9th amendment.[28] 2 Dal. 158. 192. 233. 1. Call. 123. 232.[29] In England 1. Term 167. partly law & partly fact. laches may be matter of
fact & law mixd & are in here—Then if court to have cognizance
shoud direct special verdict—court cannot say this fact given in evidence or this witness sworn is to be beleivd that not.

3 Burrow 1516. that indorsement is evidence on a count for money
had & receivd.[30]

4th. If any error in the opinion of the court it is in saying that notice
was necessary to support the action on the first count. It was not
necessary—but this is not complaind of. a french case—according
to the british law correct. notice before october 1800. See testimony
of Simms.[31]

Mason in reply.[32]

testamentary system of Maryland previous to revolution like that
of England. Commissary general coud grant letters throughout the
Colony & had deputies for each county.

On revolution orphans courts were appointed in each county who had power to grant letters for the county. At length by various acts of Assembly letters granted by one court gave powe⟨r⟩ to administer throughout the state. At l⟨e⟩ngth in Nov⟨r⟩. 1798 Ch. 101 sub. ch. 8 general law on the subject. No person can sue as admr. in Maryland unless letters of Admn. be granted in Maryland. This law adopted by Congress.

As to vested rights which are not to be considerd as divested by assumption Grant of letters was in Novr. 1801. What right did these letters vest? Not to sue Fenwick then in France. Examine nature of duty of admr. under the law of Maryland—to distribute all the funds without regard to dignity.

On 2d. bill of exceptions or 1st. point in argument.

admits the sole question is whether he is Notary public before he takes the oath. Act of Assembly prescribes the oath of office which is a different oath than that prescribd by the constitution.

2d. True ground of exception that protest for non payment was necessary, but if unnecessary additional reason for excluding it as irrelevant.

Kidd 120. 137.8. as to its being necessary. If it must be protested for non payment it ought to be a legal protest. Kidd 120.1. promissory notes protested on 4th. day on account of diffce: between Inland & foreign bills by 4th. of Anne.[33]

Whenever bill of exception states testimony & prays the opinion of the court, the legal inference is that all the testimony is stated. 3d. Dal. 19. See page 38.[34]

As to necessity of notice on the ground that there were no effects in the hands of the drawee. Indorser may indorse bill honestly altho he knows there be no funds. Might have supposd they were to bear his expences.

Action for money had & receivd cannot be maintaind on a bill of exchange.

If bard by laches from recovering on count on bill of exchange cannot recover on genl count.

As to law of France—place where the money is to be paid governs the transaction.

Place where suit is brought ought to govern.

As to notice being law or fact—law of Maryland binds—if not is it reasonable that this subject shoud be settled by the court, or left to the uncertain & fluctuating verdicts of various juries.[35]

AD, Fenwick v. Sears's Administrators, Appellate Case No 122, RG 267, DNA.

1. JM here begins his summary of Mason's opening argument on behalf of the appellant Fenwick (fully reported in 1 Cranch 264–68). Mason first contended that the court below should not have admitted in evidence the protests of the bill of exchange because Samuel Hanson, the person making the protests, was not a notary.

2. This and other citations to "Kid" are to Stewart Kyd, *A Treatise on the Law of Bills of Exchange and Promissory Notes* (1st Am. ed.; Boston, 1798, from 3d London ed. [1795]). The treatise was originally published in London, 1790. For a brief introduction to the law of bills of exchange, see *PJM*, V, 215–27.

3. The court below refused to admit evidence proving that Hanson had not taken the required oaths and therefore was not a notary (1 Cranch 261).

4. Mason's second point was that the protest for nonpayment was made too late, one day after the last day of grace. The bill of exchange was payable sixty days after sight, computed from the day of presentment for acceptance and allowing three days of grace (1 Cranch 266).

5. The corresponding passage in the printed report clarifies the meaning: "And although a right of action accrues upon the protest for non-acceptance, yet the holder is held to have discharged the drawer and indorsers, unless he presents it for payment when due, and regularly protests it for non-payment" (1 Cranch 266). In this case, Fenwick was the indorser of the bill of exchange, Sears the holder.

6. The correct citation is 3 Dall. 365, reporting the case of Brown v. Barry, decided by the Supreme Court in 1797. Mason denied the authority of this case (1 Cranch 266).

7. The third point argued by Mason was that Fenwick did not have such notice of the protests as to render him liable.

8. In the court below, the plaintiffs declared on two counts, one in special assumpsit on the bill and protest, the other a common count in general assumpsit for money had and received by the defendant to the plaintiff's use. This was a common form of declaring in such cases. At the trial below, the court refused to instruct the jury that the plaintiffs' neglect in giving reasonable notice of the protests released the defendant (Fenwick) from liability. The court was divided in opinion whether the question of reasonable notice was a matter of law to be determined by the court or a matter of fact to be determined by the jury. Instead, the court instructed the jury that, if in their opinion the indorser (Fenwick) knew at the time of the indorsement that the drawer had no funds in the hands of the drawees, notice was not necessary to support the action on the second count (for money had and received). At the same time the court instructed the jury that such notice was necessary to support the action on the first count (1 Cranch 263–64).

9. Kyd cited Goodall v. Dolley, 1 T.R. 712, 714, 99 Eng. Rep. 1336–37 (K.B., 1787).

10. The bill had been drawn in Paris on 5 Aug. 1797 and presented for acceptance in Georgetown on 30 Mar. 1798. Notice of the protest was not given until early 1801.

11. Medcalf v. Hall, 3 Doug. 113, 99 Eng. Rep. 566 (K.B., 1782); Russel v. Langstaffe, 2 Doug. 514, 515, 99 Eng. Rep. 328 (K.B., 1780); Tindal v. Brown, 1 T.R. 167, 171, 99 Eng. Rep. 1033, 1035 (K.B., 1786). Kyd cited these cases in the margin.

12. Mason objected to the distinction made by the court below on the necessity of notice on the one count but not the other (see n. 8).

13. The fourth and last point urged by Mason was that Sears's administrators had no standing in court because their letters of administration had been granted in Maryland rather than in the District of Columbia.

14. The argument of Charles Simms took up the remainder of this day's session (1 Cranch 268–75).

15. See n. 1.

16. William David Evans, *Essays on the Action for Money Had and Received, on the Law of Insurances, and on the Law of Bills of Exchange and Promissory Notes* (Liverpool, 1802; Newbern, N.C., 1802). These three essays are separately paginated; the page references are to the essay on bills of exchange and promissory notes.

17. Bacon, *Abridgment* (1st Am. ed.). "N.E." stands for the new edition (6th London) in seven volumes, edited by Henry Gwillim, which was used for the 1st Am. ed.

18. Leftley v. Mills, 4 T.R. 170, 173, 174, 100 Eng. Rep. 955, 957 (K.B., 1791).

19. Milford v. Mayor, 1 Doug. 55, 99 Eng. Rep. 39 (K.B., 1779); Sir Francis Buller, *An Introduction to the Law, Relative to Trials at Nisi Prius* (1817; New York, 1979 reprint, from 7th ed.), 269, citing Bright v. Purrier, 3 Burr. 1687, 97 Eng. Rep. 1047 (K.B., 1765); Chilton v. Whiffin and Cromwel, 3 Wils. K.B. 13, 16, 95 Eng. Rep. 906, 908 (K.B., 1768).

20. Bickerdike v. Bollman, 1 T.R. 405, 408, 99 Eng. Rep. 1164, 1166 (K.B., 1786).

21. Russel v. Langstaffe (see n. 11); Rushton v. Aspinall, 2 Doug. 679, 681, 99 Eng. Rep. 430–32 (K.B., 1781); Tindal v. Brown (see n. 11); Muilman v. D'Eguino, 2 Black. H., 565, 569, 126 Eng. Rep. 705, 708 (C.P., 1795); Mackie v. Davis, 2 Wash. 231 (1796); Robertson v. Vogle, 1 Dall. 252 (Pa., Court of Common Pleas, Philadelphia Co., 1788).

22. The citation to Evans belongs under the discussion of the third point. JM evidently referred in the pleadings rather than to a demurrer to evidence. In the court below the defendant pleaded that the plaintiffs had not obtained letters of administration that were valid in the District of Columbia; the plaintiffs replied by reciting the letters granted in Baltimore, to which the defendant demurred (1 Cranch 260–61).

23. The reference is to the act "concerning the District of Columbia" (1801), which provided for the laws of Maryland and of Virginia to continue in force in that part of the federal district ceded by those two states (*U.S. Statutes at Large*, II, 103–5).

24. Charles Lee, also for the appellees, was the first to speak on 19 Feb. (1 Cranch 275–78).

25. Leftley v. Mills. See n. 18.

26. Walwyn v. St. Quintin, 2 Esp. 515, 170 Eng. Rep. 439 (C.P., 1796), cited by Evans (61n).

27. "Laches" refers to the neglect or omission to assert a right or claim—in this instance, the lack of due diligence in giving notice of the protest.

28. That is, the seventh amendment, guaranteeing trial by jury. It was ninth on the list of twelve originally sent to the states for ratification in 1789.

29. Bank of North America v. M'Knight, 2 Dall. 158 (Pa. Supreme Court, 1792); Mallory v. Kirwan, 2 Dall. 192 (Pa. Supreme Court, 1792); Warder v. Carson's Executors, 2 Dall. 233 (Pa. Supreme Court, 1795); M'Williams v. Smith, 1 Call 123 (1797); Wood v. Luttrel, 1 Call 232 (1798).

30. Grant v. Vaughan, 3 Burr. 1516, 97 Eng. Rep. 957 (K.B., 1764).

31. A reference to the testimony of Charles Simms, attorney for the appellees, at the trial below (Fenwick v. Sears's Administrators, Record on Appeal, 28, App. Cas. No. 122).

32. For Mason's rebuttal, see 1 Cranch 279–82.

33. A reference to the English statute of 1705 (3 and 4 Anne, c. 8/9) making promissory notes negotiable and actionable in the same manner as bills of exchange.

34. Bingham v. Cabbot, 3 Dall. 19, 38 (1795).

35. In a brief judgment given on 25 Feb., the court reversed the judgment of the circuit court on the ground that Sears's administrators had not taken out letters of administration in the federal district and were therefore not competent to bring the original action (1 Cranch 282).

Marbury v. Madison
Opinion
U.S. Supreme Court, 24 February 1803

EDITORIAL NOTE

The opinion given by Chief Justice Marshall in *Marbury* v. *Madison* enjoys the status of a landmark, perhaps the most prominent, of American constitutional law. In deciding this case, the Supreme Court for the first time declared an act of Congress void as contrary to the Constitution. *Marbury* hence became the leading precedent for "judicial review," the court's power to pass upon the constitutionality of legislative acts.

Marshall considered this case to be among the most important decided during his tenure as chief justice, though perhaps not for the same reasons that later generations so regarded it. The only part of his opinion that is read and remembered today is the concluding and comparatively brief section setting forth the doctrine of judicial review. To Marshall, the court's power to pronounce a law unconstitutional was not the only point he undertook to decide and probably not the most important. In his mind the preceding discussion of the other points—what critics then and later dismissed as "dicta"—constituted the real heart of the opinion.

The case began at the December 1801 term of the Supreme Court. Charles Lee moved for a rule to Secretary of State James Madison to show cause why a mandamus should not issue commanding him to deliver the commissions of William Marbury, Robert T. Hooe, and Dennis Ramsay as justices of the peace for the District of Columbia. Marbury and his co-complainants were among a total of forty-two persons who had been nominated justices of the peace by departing President Adams on 2 March 1801. After the Senate confirmed these appointments the same day, Adams on 3 March, his last day in office, signed the commissions and transmitted them to Secretary of State Marshall to affix the seal and send out. Neither on that day nor on 4 March, when Marshall (at President Jefferson's request) continued to act as secretary of state, were the commissions dispatched. Assuming that he had discretion to revoke these appointments because the commissions had not been delivered, President Jefferson on 5 March made appointments of his own (later confirmed by the Senate), reducing the number of justices to thirty. Although Jefferson reappointed many who had been nominated by his predecessor, Marbury, Hooe, and Ramsay were not among them.[1]

Lee presented his motion to the Supreme Court on 17 December, supported by the applicants' affidavits setting forth their unsuccessful attempts to obtain their commissions or any information relating to their appointments from the secretary of state's office. The chief justice on 18 December announced the decision of the court to grant the rule, assigning the fourth day of the next term for hearing arguments on the question whether a mandamus should issue for delivery of the commissions.[2] The next term, as provided by the Judiciary Act of 1801, was scheduled for June 1802. In the meantime, however, Congress repealed that act and abolished the June term, which meant that Marbury's case was postponed until February 1803.

The hearing began on 10 February, with Chief Justice Marshall and Associate Justices Paterson, Chase, and Washington in attendance. As counsel for Marbury and others, Lee first tried to show that his clients had been nominated and confirmed as justices of the peace and that their commissions had been signed, sealed, and recorded. Unable to obtain voluntary affidavits and rebuffed in his efforts to obtain from the Senate a certified record of the confirmation of the appointments, Lee summoned Jacob Wagner and Daniel Brent, clerks in the State Department, to give their testimony. Ordered by the court to be sworn, these reluctant witnesses accordingly testified. Another reluctant witness, Attorney General Levi Lincoln (who had served as acting secretary of state until James Madison assumed office in May 1801), was permitted to postpone testifying until the next day. The first part of 11 February was devoted to Lincoln's testimony and to the reading of the affidavit of James M. Marshall, brother of the chief justice and himself an assistant judge of the U.S. Circuit Court for the District of Columbia. Satisfied that this evidence was sufficient to prove the existence of the commissions, Lee then launched a long argument in support of issuing a mandamus. The cause was not argued on the other side, Lincoln stating that he was not instructed. The court asked for the observations of anyone who was disposed to offer any, but there was no reply.[3]

Nearly two weeks elapsed before the court rendered its decision, an indication of the difficulty of the case, though the delay can be attributed in part to Samuel Chase's ill health. To accommodate the indisposed Chase, the court on 16 February adjourned from the Capitol to nearby Stelle's Hotel, where it presumably continued to sit for the remainder of the term. William Cushing, the ailing senior associate justice, did not attend the 1803 term. Alfred Moore arrived on 18 February, after the argument but six days before the opinion. If he abstained from the deliberations, then there was a bare quorum of four justices who sat in the cause: Marshall, Paterson, Chase, and Washington.[4]

A singular circumstance of this case is that the chief justice himself, as President Adams's secretary of state, was the official responsible for sending out the commissions of Marbury and the other appointees. Would the application for a mandamus never have occurred but for Marshall's inattention to this duty? Writing to his brother two weeks after Jefferson's inauguration, Marshall explained his conduct: "I did not send out the commissions because I apprehended such as were for a fixd time to be completed when signd & seald & such as depended on the will of the President might at any time be revokd. To withhold the commission of the Marshal is equal to displacing him which the President I presume has the power to do, but to withhold the commission of the Justices is an act of which I entertaind no suspicion."[5] At the time, then, Marshall believed the process of commissioning justices of the peace was complete without actual delivery, a position he was to maintain two years later in the opinion. Whatever the merits of his position on this technical point, Marshall's not delivering the commissions provided President Jefferson the opportunity to withhold them.

From the beginning, Marbury's application to the Supreme Court for a mandamus was more than a private "legal" dispute. It arose directly from the victorious party's resentment at the outgoing administration's eleventh-hour appointments to a host of new judicial offices created by the Judiciary Act of 1801 and the act concerning the District of Columbia. The lame-duck Federalist Congress had enacted both laws during the waning days of Adams's presidency. The very bringing of the action, which coincided with the meeting of the first session of the new Congress under a Republican majority, hastened the repeal of the judiciary act and prompted the accompanying act by which the Supreme Court lost a term and did not meet again for another fourteen months.

Marbury can scarcely be understood without firmly anchoring it to the political context of Thomas Jefferson's first administration. The opinion delivered by the chief justice, whether denounced by Republicans or hailed by Federalists, was interpreted by contemporaries almost exclusively in partisan terms. Even today, critics find fault with Marshall for using the case to lecture the president, while admirers praise him for striking a blow for judicial independence in the face of a determined assault on the federal judiciary by the Jeffersonian political majority. Yet to read the opinion solely in the light of the raging party battles of the day, or to read it only as a "landmark" that established the doctrine of judicial review, is to miss the full significance of the case.

The only documentary evidence of the justices' motives in deciding the case in the manner they did is the opinion itself. A reading of the whole opinion on its own terms leaves little doubt that the court intended the mandamus case to be the occasion of a major statement of the judiciary's role in the American constitutional system. In this regard, however, the court was less concerned to assert its power to review acts of Congress than to discover and apply a principle for bringing executive acts under judicial scrutiny. The latter constituted the "peculiar delicacy" and "real difficulty" of the case according to Marshall. More than half the opinion is devoted to an inquiry into the nature of executive acts, which were found to fall into two categories: "political," or discretionary, which were not examinable by courts; and "ministerial," where the law imposes a duty on an officer to perform a certain act on which individual rights depend. Acts of this class were properly reviewable by courts in the course of enforcing legal rights.

Marshall anticipated that even this limited claim would be "considered by some, as an attempt to intrude into the cabinet, and to intermeddle with the prerogative of the executive." If the court's disclaiming "all pretensions to such a jurisdiction" failed to mute criticism of the opinion, still there is no reason to doubt the sincerity of the declaration. Given the peculiar circumstances of the case, the unavoidable connection between Marbury's claim to his commission and the political defeat of the Federalists, the court faced a formidable task of writing an opinion that breathed disinterested judicial statesmanship. There was an inherent difficulty in assimilating this highly political case to the realm of legal rights and remedies and in making it the occasion for denying jurisdiction in political questions.

The first part of the opinion affirmed that Marbury had a legal right and remedy. Since it ultimately denied that it had jurisdiction to issue the mandamus, the court was denounced for improperly deciding the merits of the case before taking up the question of jurisdiction. In a broader sense, however, the entire opinion centered on the single issue of jurisdiction. Before deciding whether a mandamus could issue in this particular case, the court logically had to consider the more general question whether there were any cases in which a high officer of the executive department could be made answerable in court for his conduct. Indeed, the chief justice and his associates could hardly avoid the question, for it had been argued at great length by Charles Lee. They might have concluded at once that the secretary of state could not be brought into court under any circumstances, thereby obviating judicial review or statutory construction as a means of deciding upon Marbury's claim.

The ground for denying the mandamus was that section 13 of the Judiciary Act of 1789, which empowered the Supreme Court to issue that writ, was an unconstitutional enlargement of the court's original jurisdiction. No part of the opinion has provoked more commentary by legal scholars than this holding. The chief justice, it is pointed out, could have denied the motion for a mandamus without concluding that section 13 was unconstitutional; alternatively, he could have supported the motion by a less literal reading of the judiciary article of the Constitution.[6] Why did the court resort to judicial review, seemingly going out of its way to contrive a constitutional conflict? And why, after stating in such emphatic language that Marbury had a legal right and that mandamus was the appropriate remedy, did the court then deny itself the authority to issue the writ? Such a narrow construction of the Constitution seemed to be directly at odds with the court's interpretation and practice in earlier mandamus cases.

Scholars attribute the motives behind the decision in *Marbury* largely to the political circumstances attending the case—circumstances that compelled Marshall to eschew sounder legal arguments in favor of judicial finesse. The chief justice, it is explained, wanted to declare the authority of the court to bring certain acts of the executive under judicial cognizance and to draw a line that would separate "political" from "legal" questions. Given the vulnerable situation of the federal judiciary, however, he had to avoid the direct confrontation with the administration that would have occurred if the court granted Marbury's motion. Unable to strike a direct blow against the executive, Marshall recognized an opportunity to stake out the court's jurisdiction over legislative as well as executive acts. By declaring section 13 unconstitutional, he adroitly coupled judicial review of an act of Congress with the denial of the mandamus. In *Marbury* the court thus accomplished what it could not have done in *Stuart* v. *Laird* (also decided at the February 1803 term), a case that brought into issue the constitutionality of the repeal of the Judiciary Act of 1801. For all his doubts about the legitimacy of the repeal, the chief justice understood that the court had no choice but to bow to the will of Congress in that case.[7]

Seen in this light, the *Marbury* opinion has been acclaimed as a brilliant political coup, at once bold and cautious, a masterpiece of judicial statesmanship in which the court yielded the immediate point while gaining its more important long-range aims. The dubious legal and constitutional arguments, the seemingly willful disregard of past practice and precedents, pale into insignificance when viewed against the larger purposes accomplished by the chief justice.

Why the court decided the case as it did and how Marshall was able to secure the apparent unanimity of the justices are questions to which there can be no certain answer, only reasoned conjecture. For all its persuasiveness, the "political" explanation rests on the assumption that the opinion cannot be read at face value. The justices, so it is assumed, did not really believe that section 13 was unconstitutional; nor did they seriously consider awarding the mandamus, knowing they were powerless to compel obedience to the court's command.

In retrospect, *Marbury* does have the appearance of an ingeniously conceived and executed act of judicial politics, the handiwork largely of John Marshall. Yet hindsight may obscure what to the chief justice and his brethren was a tentative, makeshift, and unsatisfactory resolution of the case. Was the author of the opinion as subtle, calculating, and foresighted as has been commonly assumed? Did he have it in mind, as part of a preconcerted agenda, to establish a precedent for judicial review, selecting this case as the opportune moment to strike? The perfunctory, almost matter-of-fact, exposition of judicial review was perhaps a clever tactic to win acceptance of a highly controversial doctrine. On the other hand, this language may have been nothing more than a straightforward expression of Marshall's belief that judicial review was a settled question, that the court was not boldly asserting a claim to a new power but merely restating a power it already possessed. In that case there would be no reason to contrive a case to exercise judicial review.

Perhaps, after all, Marshall genuinely believed that section 13 was unconstitutional—a view that, as indicated by the absence of any criticism of this part of the opinion in the contemporary commentary on the case, was not novel or eccentric. On this supposition, his stated reason for refusing the mandamus was the real one, not just a pretext to disguise his unwillingness to provoke a direct clash with the executive. And if the first part of the opinion was not idle rhetoric, if it is taken to mean what it expressly stated, then the chief justice was prepared to risk the consequences of ordering the secretary of state to deliver Marbury's commission.

No manuscript of the opinion survives. The text below is taken from the *Washington Federalist*, the first newspaper to print the opinion in full, on 14 and 16 March. Although many newspapers printed the opinion, the fullest coverage was provided by the *National Intelligencer*, which published the entire report of the case (including the preliminary proceedings and the argument of Charles Lee) in its issues of 18, 21, and 25 March 1803. The newspapers obtained copies of the report and opinion from the reporter William Cranch, whose first volume of reports (containing the *Marbury* opinion) was published in July 1804. The original case file of *Marbury v. Madison*, partly destroyed by fire, contains the affidavits of Marbury and the other plaintiffs and the testimony of the witnesses.[8]

1. Haskins and Johnson, *Foundations of Power*, 183–84.

2. U.S. Sup. Ct. Minutes, 18 Dec. 1801; *National Intelligencer*, 21 Dec. 1801.

3. Marbury v. Madison, 1 Cranch 137–53; U.S. Sup. Ct. Minutes, 10, 11 Feb. 1803. Newspaper accounts provide additional details. See *National Intelligencer*, 14 Feb. 1803; Philadelphia *Aurora*, 15 Feb., 22 Feb. 1803.

4. U.S. Sup. Ct. Minutes, 15, 16, 18, 24 Feb. 1803.

5. JM to James M. Marshall, 18 Mar. 1801.

6. See, for example, Haskins and Johnson, *Foundations of Power*, 199–201; David P. Currie, *The Constitution in the Supreme Court: The First Hundred Years, 1789–1888* (Chicago, 1985), 67–69.

7. R. Kent Newmyer, *The Supreme Court under Marshall and Taney* (New York, 1968), 29–32; Donald O. Dewey, *Marshall Versus Jefferson: The Political Background of Marbury v. Madison* (New York, 1970), 99–100, 129–33; Haskins and Johnson, *Foundations of Power*, 201–4; Susan Low Bloch and Maeva Marcus, "John Marshall's Selective Use of History in *Marbury v. Madison*," *Wisconsin Law Review* (1986), 333–37.

8. Marbury v. Madison, Orig. Case Files, Feb. 1803 term.

OPINION

At the last term on the affidavits then read and filed with the clerk, a rule was granted in this case, requiring the Secretary of State to shew cause why a Mandamus should not issue, directing him to deliver to William Marbury his commission as a justice of peace for the County of Washington, in the district of Columbia.

No cause has been shewn, and the present motion is for a Mandamus. The peculiar delicacy of this case, the novelty of some of its circumstances, and the real difficulty attending the points which occur in it, require a complete exposition of the principles, on which the opinion to be given by the court, is founded.

These principles have been, on the side of the applicant, very ably argued at the bar. In rendering the opinion of the court, there will be some departure in form, though not in substance, from the points stated in that argument.[1]

In the order in which the court has viewed this subject, the following questions have been considered and decided.

1st. Has the applicant a right to the commission he demands?

2dly. If he has a right, and that right has been violated, do the laws of his country afford him a remedy?

3dly. If they do afford him a remedy, is it a *Mandamus* issuing from this court?

The first object of enquiry is,

1st. Has the applicant a right to the commission he demands?

His right originates in an act of Congress passed in February 1801, concerning the district of Columbia.

After dividing the district into two counties, the 11th section of this law, enacts, "that there shall be appointed in and for each of the said counties, such number of discreet persons to be justices of the peace, as the President of the U. States, shall, from time to time, think expedient, to continue in office for five years.["]²

It appears, from the affidavits, that in compliance with this law, a commission for William Marbury as a justice of peace for the county of Washington, was signed by John Adams, then President of the United States; after which the seal of the United States was affixed to it; but the commission has never reached the person for whom it was made out.

In order to determine whether he is intitled to this commission, it becomes necessary to enquire whether he has been appointed to the office. For if he has been appointed, the law continues him in office for five years; and he is entitled to the possession of those evidences of office, which, being completed, became his property.

The 2d section, of the 2d article of the Constitution, declares, that "the President shall nominate, and, by and with the advice and consent of the Senate, shall appoint ambassadors, other public ministers and consuls, and all other officers of the United States, whose appointments are not otherwise provided for."

The 3d section, declares, that "he shall commission all the officers of the United States."

An Act of Congress, directs the Secretary of State, to keep the seal of the United States, "to make out and record, and affix the said seal to all civil commissions to officers of the United States to be appointed by the President, by and with the consent of the Senate, or by the President alone; provided that the said seal shall not be affixed to any commission before the same shall have been signed by the President of the United States."

These are the clauses of the constitution and laws of the United States, which affect this part of the case. They seem to contemplate three distinct operations—

1st. The nomination. This is the sole act of the President, and is completely voluntary.

2d. The appointment. This is also the act of the President, and is also a voluntary act, though it can only be performed, by and with the advice and consent of the Senate.

3d. The commission. To grant a commission to a person appointed, might perhaps be deemed a duty, enjoined by the constitution. "He shall," says that instrument, "commission all the officers of the United States."

The acts of appointing to office, and commissioning the person appointed, can scarcely be considered as one and the same; since the power to perform them is given in two separate and distinct sections of the constitution. The distinction between the appointment and the commission, will be rendered more apparent, by adverting to that provision in the 2d section, of the 2d article of the constitution, which authorises Congress, "to vest, by law, the appointment of such inferior officers, as they think proper, in the President alone, in the courts of law, or in the heads of departments;" thus contemplating cases where the law may direct the President to commission an officer appointed by the courts, or by the heads of departments. In such a case, to issue a commission would be apparently a duty distinct from the appointment, the performance of which, perhaps, could not legally be refused.

Although that clause of the constitution which requires the President to commission all the officers of the U. States, may never have been applied to officers appointed otherwise than by himself, yet it would be difficult to deny the legislative power to apply it to such cases. Of consequence the constitutional distinction between the appointment to an office and the commission of an officer, who has been appointed, remains the same as if in practice the President had commissioned officers appointed by an authority other than his own.

It follows too, from the existence of this distinction, that, if an appointment was to be evidenced by any public act, other than the commission, the performance of such public act would create the officer; and if he was not removeable at the will of the President, would either give him a right to his commission, or enable him to perform the duties without it.

These observations are premised solely for the purpose of rendering more intelligible those which apply more directly to the particular case under consideration.

This is an appointment made by the President by and with the advice and consent of the Senate, and is evidenced by no act but the commission itself. In such a case therefore the commission and the appointment seem inseparable; it being almost impossible to show an appointment otherwise than by proving the existence of a commission; still the commission is not necessarily the appointment; tho' conclusive evidence of it.

But at what stage does it amount to this conclusive evidence?

The answer to this question seems an obvious one. The appointment, being the sole act of the President, must be completely evidenced, when it is shewn that he has done every thing to be performed by him.

Should the commission, instead of being evidence of an appointment, even be considered as constituting the appointment itself; still it would be made when the last act to be done by the President was performed, or, at furthest, when the commission was complete.

The last act to be done by the President, is the signature of the commission. He has then acted on the advice and consent of the

Senate to his own nomination. The time for deliberation was then passed. He has decided. His judgment, on the advice and consent of the Senate concurring with his nomination, has been made, and the officer is appointed. This appointment is evidenced by an open, unequivocal act; and being the last act required from the person making it, necessarily excludes the idea of its being, so far as respects the appointment, an inchoate and incomplete transaction.

Some point of time must be taken when the power of the executive over an officer, not removeable at his will, must cease. That point of time must be when the constitutional power of appointment has been exercised. And this power has been exercised when the last act, required from the person possessing the power, has been performed— This last act is the signature of the commission.

This idea seems to have prevailed with the legislature, when the act passed converting the department of foreign affairs into the department of State. By that act it is enacted, that the Secretary of State, shall keep the seal of the United States, "and shall make out and record, and shall affix the said seal to all civil commissions, to officers of the United States, to be appointed by the President:" "Provided that the said seal shall not be affixed to any commission, before the same shall have been signed by the President of the United States; nor to any other instrument or act, without the special warrant of the President therefor."[3]

The signature is a warrant for affixing the great seal to the commission; and the great seal is only to be affixed to an instrument which is complete. It attests, by an act supposed to be of public notoriety, the verity of the President's signature.

It is never to be affixed till the commission is signed because the signature, which gives force and effect to the commission, is conclusive evidence that the appointment is made.

The commission being signed, the subsequent duty of the Secretary of State is prescribed by law, and not to be guided by the will of the President. He is to affix the seal of the United States to the commission, and is to record it.

This is not a proceeding which may be varied, if the judgment of the executive shall suggest one more eligible; but is a precise course accurately marked out by law, and is to be strictly pursued. It is the duty of the Secretary of State to conform to the law, and in this he is an officer of the United States, bound to obey the laws. He acts, in this respect, as has been very properly stated at the bar, under the authority of law, & not by the instructions of the President. It is a ministerial act which the law enjoins on a particular officer for a particular purpose.

If it should be supposed, that the solemnity of affixing the seal, is necessary not only to the validity of the commission, but even to the completion of an appointment, still when the seal is affixed the appointment is made, and the commission is valid. No other solemnity is required by law; no other act is to be performed on the part of Government. All that the executive can do to invest the person with his office, is done; and unless the appointment be then made, the executive cannot make one without the co-operation of others.

After searching anxiously for the principles on which a contrary opinion may be supported, none have been found which appear of sufficient force to maintain the opposite doctrine.

Such as the imagination of the Court could suggest, have been very deliberately examined, and after allowing them all the weight which it appears possible to give them, they do not shake the opinion which has been formed.

In considering this question, it has been conjectured that the commission may have been assimilated to a deed, to the validity of which, delivery is essential.

This idea is founded on the supposition that the commission is not merely *evidence* of an appointment, but is itself the actual appointment— a supposition by no means unquestionable. But for the purpose of examining this objection fairly, let it be conceded, that the principle, claimed for its support, is established.

The appointment being, under the constitution, to be made by the President *personally*, the delivery of the deed of appointment, if necessary to its completion, must be made by the President also. It is not necessary that the livery should be made personally to the grantee of the office: It never is so made. The law would seem to contemplate that it should be made to the Secretary of State, since it directs the Secretary to affix the seal to the commission *after* it shall have been signed by the President. If then the act of livery be necessary to give validity to the commission, it has been delivered when executed and given to the Secretary for the purpose of being sealed, recorded and transmitted to the party.

But in all cases of letters patent, certain solemnities are required by law, which solemnities are the evidences of the validity of the instrument. A formal delivery to the person is not among them. In cases of commissions the sign manual of the President, and the seal of the U. States, are those solemnities. This objection therefore does not touch the case.

It has also occurred as possible, and barely possible, that the transmission of the commission, & the acceptance thereof, might be deemed necessary to complete the right of the plaintiff.

The transmission of the commission, is a practice directed by con venience, but not by law. It cannot therefore be necessary to constitute the appointment which must precede it, and which is the mere act of the President. If the executive required that every person appointed to an office, should himself take means to procure his commission, the appointment would not be the less valid on that account. The appointment is the sole act of the President; the transmiss⟨ion of th⟩e commission is the sole act of the officer to whom that duty is assigned, and may be accelerated or retarded by circumstances which can have no influence on the appointment. A commission is transmitted to a person already appointed; not to a person to be appointed or not, as the ⟨lette⟩r inclosing the commission should happen to get into the post office and reach him in ⟨safety, or t⟩o miscarry.

It may have some tendency to elucidate this point, to enquire, whether the possession of the *original* commission be indispensably necessary to authorise a person, appointed to any office, to perform the duties of that office. If it was necessary, then a loss of the commission would lose the office. Not only negligence, but accident or fraud, fire or theft, might deprive an individual of his office. In such a case, I presume it could not be doubted, but that a copy, from the record of the office of the Secretary of State, would be, to every intent and purpose, equal to the original. The act of Congress has expressly made it so. To give that copy validity, it would not be necessary to prove that the original had been transmitted and afterwards lost. The copy would be complete evidence that the original had existed & that the appointment had been made, but, not that the original had been transmitted. If indeed it should appear that the original had been mislaid in the office of State, that circumstance would not affect the operation of the copy. When all the requisites have been performed which authorize a recording officer to record any instrument whatever, and the order for that purpose has been given, the instrument is, in law, considered as recorded, altho' the manual labour of inserting it in a book kept for that purpose may not have been performed.

In the case of Commissions, the law orders the Secretary of State to record them. When therefore they are signed and sealed, the order for their being recorded is given; and whether inserted in the book or not, they are in law recorded.

A copy of this record is declared equal to the original, and the fees, to be paid by a person requiring a copy, are ascertained by law. Can a keeper of a public record, erase therefrom a commission which has been recorded? Or can he refuse a copy thereof to a person demanding it on the terms prescribed by law?

Such a copy would, equally with the original authorize the justice of peace to proceed in the performance of his duty, because it would, equally with the original, attest his appointment.

If the transmission of a commission be not considered as necessary to give validity to an appointment; still less is its acceptance. The appointment is the sole act of the President; the acceptance is the sole act of the officer, and is, in plain common sense, posterior to the appointment. As he may resign, so may he refuse to accept: but neither the one, nor the other, is capable of rendering the appointment a non-entity.

That this is the understanding of the Government, is apparent from the whole tenor of its conduct.

A commission bears date, and the salary of the officer commences from his appointment; not from the transmission, or acceptance of his commission. When a person, appointed to any office, refuses to accept that office, the successor is nominated in the place of the person who has declined to accept, and not in the place of the person who had been previously in office, and had created the original vacancy.

It is therefore decidedly the opinion of the court, that when a commission has been signed by the President, the appointment is made; and that the commission is complete when the seal of the United States has been affixed to it by the Secretary of State.

Where an officer is removeable at the will of the executive, the circumstance which completes his appointment is of no concern; because the act is at any time revocable; and the commission may be arrested, if still in the office. But when the officer is not removable at the will of the executive, the appointment is not revocable, and cannot be annulled. It has conferred legal rights which cannot be resumed.

The discretion of the executive is to be exercised until the appointment has been made. But having once made the appointment, his power over the office is terminated in all cases, where, by law, the officer is not removable by him. The right to the office is *then* in the person appointed, and he has the absolute, unconditional, power of accepting or rejecting it.

Mr. Marbury, then, since his commission was signed by the President, and sealed by the Secretary of State, was appointed; and as the law creating the office, gave the officer a right to hold for five years, independent of the executive, the appointment was not revocable; but vested in the officer legal rights, which are protected by the laws of his country.

To withhold his commission, therefore, is an act deemed by the court not warranted by law, but violative of a vested legal right.

This brings us to the second enquiry; which is,

2dly. If he has a right and that right has been violated, do the laws of his country afford him a remedy?

The very essence of civil liberty certainly consists in the right of every individual to claim the protection of the laws whenever he receives an injury. One of the first duties of government is to afford that protection. In Great Britain the king himself is sued in the respectful form of a petition, and he never fails to comply with the judgment of his court.

In the 3d vol. of his commentaries, p. 23, Blackstone states two cases in which a remedy is afforded by mere operation of law—

"In all other cases," he says, "it is a general & indisputable rule, that where there is a legal right, there is also a legal remedy by suit or action at law, whenever that right is invaded."[4]

And afterwards, p. 109 of the same volume, he says, "I am next to consider such injuries as are cognizable by the courts of the common law. And herein I shall for the present only remark, that all possible injuries whatsoever, that did not fall within [the exclusive cognizance of either][5] the ecclesiastical, military, or maritime tribunals, are for that very reason, within the cognizance of the common law courts of justice; for it is a settled and invariable principle in the laws of England, that every right, when withheld, must have a remedy, and every injury its proper redress."

The government of the United States has been emphatically termed a government of laws, & not of men. It will certainly cease to deserve this high appellation, if the laws furnish no remedy for the violation of a vested legal right.

If this obloquy is to be cast on the jurisprudence of our country, it must arise from the peculiar character of the case.

It behoves us then to enquire whether there be, in its composition any ingredient which shall exempt it from legal investigation, or exclude the injured party from legal redress. In pursuing this enquiry the first question which presents itself, is, whether this can be arranged with that class of cases which come under the description of *damnum absque injuria*—a loss without an injury.

This description of cases never has been considered, and it is believed, never can be considered, as comprehending offices of trust, of honor or of profit. The office of justice of peace in the district of Columbia is such an office; it is therefore worthy of the attention and guardianship of the laws. It has received that attention & guardianship. It has been created by special act of congress, and has been secured, so far as the laws can give security to the person appointed to fill it, for five years. It is not then on account of the worthlessness of the thing pursued, that the injured party can be alleged to be without remedy.

Is it in the nature of the transaction? Is the act of delivering or withholding a commission to be considered as a mere political act, belonging to the executive department alone, for the performance of which, entire confidence is placed by our constitution in the supreme executive; & for any misconduct respecting which, the injured individual has no remedy?

That there may be such cases is not to be questioned; but that *every* act of duty, to be performed in any of the great departments of government, constitutes such a case, is not to be admitted.

By the act concerning invalids, passed in June, 17⟨9⟩4, vol. 3 p. 112, the Secretary at war is ordered to place, on the pension list, all persons whose names are contained in a report previously made by him to congress.[6] If he should refuse to do so, would the wounded veteran be without remedy? Is it to be contended that where the law in precise terms, directs the performance of an act, in which an individual is interested, that the law is incapable of securing obedience to its mandate? Is it on account of the character of the person against whom the complaint is made? Is it to be contended that the heads of departments are not amenable to the laws of their country?

Whatever the practice on particular occasions may be, the theory of this principle will certainly never be maintained. No act of the legislature confers so extraordinary a privilege, nor can it derive countenance from the doctrines of the common law. After stating that personal injury from the king to a subject is presumed to be impossible, Blackstone, vol. 3. page 255 says, "but injuries to the rights of property can scarcely be committed by the crown without the intervention of his[7] officers; for whom, the law, in matters of right, entertains no respect or delicacy; but furnishes various methods of detecting the errors and misconduct of those agents, by whom the king has been deceived and induced to do a temporary injustice."

By the act passed in 1796, authorising the sale of the lands above the mouth of Kentucky river (vol. 3d p. 299)[8] the purchaser, on paying his purchase money, becomes completely entitled to the property purchased; and on producing to the secretary of state, the receipt of the treasurer upon a certificate required by the law, the president of the United States is authorised to grant him a patent. It is further enacted that all patents shall be countersigned by the Secretary of state, and recorded in his office. If the secretary of state should chuse to withhold this patent; or the patent being lost, should refuse a copy of it, can it be imagined that the law furnishes to the injured person no remedy?

It is not believed that any person whatever would attempt to maintain such a proposition.

It follows then that the question whether the legality of an act of the head of a department be examinable in a court of justice or not, must always depend on the nature of that act.

If some acts be examinable, & others not, there must be some rule of law to guide the court in the exercise of its jurisdiction.

In some instances there may be difficulty in applying the rule to particular cases; but there cannot, it is believed be much difficulty in laying down the rule.

By the constitution of the United States, the president is invested with certain important political powers, in the exercise of which he is to use his own discretion, and is accountable only to his country in his political character, and to his own conscience. To aid him in the performance of these duties, he is authorised to appoint certain officers who act by his authority and in conformity with his orders.

In such cases, their acts are his acts; & whatever opinion may be entertained of the manner in which executive discretion may be used; still there exists, and can exist no power to controul that discretion. The subjects are political. They respect the nation, not individual rights, & being entrusted to the executive, the decision of the executive is conclusive. The application of this remark will be perceived, by adverting to the act of congress for establishing the department of foreign affairs. This officer, as his duties were prescribed by that act, is to conform precisely to the will of the president. He is the mere organ by whom that will is communicated. The acts of such an officer, as an officer, can never be examinable by the courts.

But when the legislature proceeds to impose, on that officer, other duties; when he is directed peremptorily to perform certain acts; when the rights of individuals are dependent on the performance of those acts; he is so far the officer of the law; is amenable to the laws for his conduct; and cannot at his discretion, sport away the vested rights of others.

The conclusion from this reasoning is, that where the heads of departments are the political, or confidential, agents of the executive, merely to execute the will of the president, or rather to act in cases, in which the executive possesses a constitutional, or legal discretion, nothing can be more perfectly clear, than that their acts are only politically examinable. But where a specific duty is assigned by law, and individual rights depend upon the performance of that duty, it seems equally clear that the individual who considers himself injured, has a right to resort to the laws of his country for a remedy.

If this be the rule, let us enquire how it applies to the case under the consideration of the court.

The power of nominating to the Senate, and the power of appointing the person nominated, are political powers, to be exercised by the president according to his own discretion. When he has made an appointment, he has exercised his whole power, and his discretion has been completely applied to the case. If, by law, the officer be removeable at the will of the president, then a new appointment may be immediately made, & the rights of the officer are terminated. But, as a fact, which has existed, cannot be made never to have existed, the appointment cannot be annihilated; and consequently, if the officer, is by law, not removeable at the will of the president; the rights he has acquired are protected by the law, and are not resumable by the president. They cannot be extinguished by executive authority, and he has the privilege of asserting them in like manner as if they had been derived from any other source.

The question whether a right has vested or not, is, in its nature, judicial, and must be tried by the judicial authority. If, for example, Mr. Marbury had taken the oaths of a magistrate and proceeded to act as one: in consequence of which a suit had been instituted against him, in which his defence had depended on his being a magistrate; the validity of his appointment must have been determined by judicial authority.

So, if he conceives that, by virtue of his appointment, he has a legal right, either to the commission which has been made out for him, or to a copy of that commission; it is equally a question examinable in a court, and the decision of the court upon it must depend on the opinion entertained of his appointment.

That question has been discussed, and the opinion is, that the latest point of time which can be taken as that at which the appointment was complete, and evidenced, was when after the signature of the president, the seal of the United States was affixed to the commission.

It is then the opinion of the court,

1st. That by signing the commission of Mr. Marbury, the president of the United States appointed him a justice of peace, for the county of Washington in the District of Columbia, & that the seal of the United States, affixed thereto by the Secretary of state, is conclusive testimony of the verity of the signature, and of the completion of the appointment; and that the appointment conferred on him a legal right to the office for the space of five years.

2dly. That, having this legal title to the office he has a consequent right to the commission; a refusal to deliver which is a plain violation of that right, for which the laws of his country afford him a remedy.

It remains to be enquired whether,

3dly. He is entitled to the remedy for which he applies. This depends on

1st The nature of the writ applied for, and

2dly The powers of this court.

1st. The nature of the writ.

Blackstone in the 3d volume of his commentaries, page 110, defines a Mandamus to be, "a command issuing in the king's name, from the court of King's bench, and directed to any person, corporation, or inferior court of judicature within the king's dominions, requiring them to do some particular thing therein specified, which appertains to their office and duty, and which the court of king's bench has previously determined, or at least supposes to be consonant to right and justice."

Lord Mansfield, in 3d Burrows 1266: in the case of the King vs Baker et al:[9] states with much precision and explicitness, the cases in which this writ may be used.

"Whenever," says that very able judge, "there is a right to execute an office, perform a service, or exercise a franchise (more especially if it be in a matter of public concern, or attended with profit) and a person is kept out of possession, or dispossessed of such right, and has no other specific legal remedy, this court ought to assist by Mandamus, upon reasons of justice, as the writ expresses, & upon reasons of public policy to preserve peace, order, and good government." In the same case he says, "this writ ought to be used upon all occasions where the law has established no specific remedy, and where in justice & good government there ought to be one."

In addition to the authorities now particularly cited, many others were relied on at the bar, which show how far the practice has conformed to the general doctrines that have been just quoted.[10]

This writ, if awarded, would be directed to an officer of government, and its mandate to him would be, to use the words of Blackstone, "to do a particular thing therein specified, which appertains to his office and duty, and which the court has previously determined, or at least supposes, to be consonant to right and justice." Or, in the words of Lord Mansfield, the applicant, in this case, has a right to execute an office of public concern, and is kept out of possession of that right.

These circumstances certainly concur in this case.

Still, to render the Mandamus a proper remedy, the officer to whom it is to be directed, must be one to whom, on legal principles, such writ may be directed; and the person applying for it must be without any other specific and legal remedy.

1st. With respect to the officer to whom it would be directed. The intimate political relation, subsisting between the president of the United States and the heads of departments, necessarily renders any legal investigation of the acts of one of those high officers peculiarly irksome, as well as delicate; and excites some hesitation with respect to the propriety of entering into such investigation. Impressions are often received without much reflection or examination, and it is not wonderful that in such a case as this, the assertion, by an individual, of his legal claims, in a court of justice; to which claims it is the duty of that court to attend; should at first view be considered by some, as an attempt to intrude into the cabinet, and to intermeddle with the pre rogatives of the executive.

It is scarcely necessary for the court to disclaim all pretentions to such a jurisdiction. An extravagance, so absurd and excessive, could not have been entertained for a moment. The province of the court, is, solely, to decide on the rights of individuals, not to enquire how the executive, or executive officers, perform duties in which they have a discretion. Questions, in their nature political, or which are, by the constitution and laws, submitted to the executive, can never be made in this court.

But, if this be not such a question; if, so far from being an intrusion into the secrets of the cabinet, it respects a paper, which, according to law is upon record, and to a copy of which, the law gives a right, on the payment of ten cents[11]—if it be no intermeddling with a subject, over which the executive can be considered as having exercised any controul—what is there in the exalted station of the officer, which shall bar a citizen from asserting, in a court of justice, his legal rights, or shall forbid a court to listen to the claim; or to issue a mandamus, directing the performance of a duty, not depending on executive discretion, but on particular acts of congress & the general principles of law?

If one of the heads of departments commits any illegal act, under color of his office, by which an individual sustains an injury, it cannot be pretended that his office alone exempts him from being sued in the ordinary mode of proceeding, and being compelled to obey the judgment of the law. How then can his office exempt him from this particular mode of deciding on the legality of his conduct, if the case be such a case as would, were any other individual the party complained of, authorise the process?

It is not by the office of the person to whom the writ is directed, but the nature of the thing to be done, that the propriety or impropriety of issuing a mandamus, is to be determined. Where the head of a department acts in a case, in which executive discretion is to be exercised; in which he is the mere organ of executive will; it is again repeated, that any application to a court to controul, in any respect, his conduct, would be rejected without hesitation.

But where he is directed by law to do a certain act affecting the absolute rights of individuals in the performance of which he is not placed under the particular direction of the president, and the performance of which the president cannot lawfully forbid, and therefore is never presumed to have forbidden; as for example, to record a commission, or a patent for land, which has received all the legal solemnities; or to give a copy of such record; in such cases, it is not perceived on what ground the courts of the country are further excused from the duty of giving judgment, that right be done to an injured individual, than if the same services were to be performed by a person not the head of a department.

This opinion seems not now, for the first time, to be taken up in this country.

It must be well recollected that in 1792, an act passed, directing the Secretary at war to place on the pension list such disabled officers and soldiers as should be reported to him, by the Circuit courts; which act, so far as the duty was imposed on the courts, was deemed unconstitutional; but some of the judges, thinking that the law might be executed by them in the character of commissioners, proceeded to act and to report in that character.[12]

This law being deemed unconstitutional at the circuits, was repealed, and a different system was established;[13] but the question whether those persons, who had been reported by the judges, as commissioners were entitled, in consequence of that report, to be placed on the pension list, was a legal question, properly determinable in the courts, although the act of placing such persons on the list was to be performed by the head of a department.

That this question might be properly settled, congress passed an act in February, 1793, making it the duty of the Secretary of war, in conjunction with the Attorney General, to take such measures, as might be necessary to obtain an adjudication of the Supreme Court of the United States on the validity of any such rights, claimed under the act aforesaid.

After the passage of this act, a mandamus was moved for, to be directed to the Secretary at war, commanding him to place on the pension list, a person stating himself to be on the report of the judges.

There is therefore, much reason to believe, that this mode of trying the legal right of the complainant, was deemed by the head of a department, & by the highest law officer of the United States, the most proper which could be selected for the purpose.

When the subject was brought before the court the decision was, not that a mandamus would not lie to the head of a department, directing him to perform an act enjoined by law, in the performance of which an individual had a vested interest; but that a mandamus ought not to issue *in that case*; the decision necessarily to be made if the report of the commissioners did not confer, on the applicant a legal right.[14]

The judgment in that case, is understood to have decided the merits of all claims of that description; and the persons on the report of the commissioners found it necessary to pursue the mode prescribed by the law subsequent to that which had been deemed unconstitutional, in order to place themselves on the pension list.[15]

The doctrine, therefore, now advanced is by no means a novel one.

It is true that the mandamus, now moved for, is not for the performance of an act expressly enjoined by statute.

It is to deliver a commission; on which subject the acts of congress are silent. This difference is not considered as affecting the case. It has already been stated that the applicant has to that commission a vested, legal right, of which the executive cannot deprive him. He has been appointed to an office, from which he is not removeable at the will of the executive; and being so appointed, he has a right to the commission which the Secretary has received from the president for his use. The act of congress does not indeed order the secretary of state to send it to him, but it is placed in his hands for the person intitled to it; and cannot be more lawfully withheld by him, than by any other person.

It was at first doubted whether the action of detinue was not a specific legal remedy for the commission which has been withheld from Mr. Marbury; in which case a mandamus would be improper. But this doubt has yielded to the consideration that the judgment in detinue is for the thing itself, or its value. The value of a public office not to be sold, is incapable of being ascertained; and the applicant has a right to the office itself, or to nothing. He will obtain the office by obtaining the commission, or a copy of it from the record.[16]

This then, is a plain case for a mandamus, either to deliver the commission, or a copy of it from the record; and it only remains to be enquired,

Whether it can issue from this court.

The act to establish the judicial courts of the United States authorises the supreme court "to issue writs of mandamus, in cases warranted by the principles and usages of law, to any courts appointed, or persons holding office, under the authority of the U. States."

The secretary of state, being a person holding an office under the authority of the United States, is precisely within the letter of the description; and if this court is not authorised to issue a writ of mandamus to such an officer, it must be, because the law is unconstitutional, and therefore absolutely incapable of conferring the authority, and assigning the duties which its words purport to confer and assign.

The constitution vests the whole judicial power of the United States in one Supreme court, ⟨and in⟩ such inferior courts as congress shall, from ⟨time⟩ to time, ordain and establish. This power is expressly extended to all cases arising under the laws of the United States: and consequently in some form may be exercised over the present case: because the right claimed is given by a law of the United States.

In the distribution of this power it is declared, that "The supreme court shall have original jurisdiction in all cases affecting ambassadors, other public ministers & consuls, and those in which a state shall be a party. In all other cases, the supreme court shall have appellate jurisdiction."

It has been insisted, at the bar, that as the original grant of jurisdiction, to the Supreme and inferior courts, is general, and the clause, assigning original jurisdiction to the supreme court, contains no negative or restrictive words; the power remains to the legislature, to assign original jurisdiction to that court in other cases than those specified in the article which has been recited; provided those cases belong to the judicial power of the United States.[17]

If it had been intended to leave it in the discretion of the legislature to apportion the judicial power between the Supreme and inferior courts, according to the will of that body, it would certainly have been useless to have proceeded further than to have defined the judicial power, and the tribunals in which it should be vested. The subsequent part of the section is mere surplussage, is entirely without meaning, if such is to be the construction. If Congress remains at liberty to give this court appellate jurisdiction where the constitution has declared their jurisdiction shall be original—and original jurisdiction where the constitution has declared it shall be appellate—the distribution of jurisdiction, made in the constitution, is form without substance.

Affirmative words are often, in their operation, negative of other objects than those affirmed; and in this case, a negative or exclusive sense must be given to them or they have no operation at all.

It cannot be presumed that any clause in the constitution is intended to be without effect; and therefore such a construction is inadmissible, unless the words require it.

If the solicitude of the convention, respecting our peace with foreign powers, induced a provision that the Supreme Court should take original jurisdiction in cases which might be supposed to affect them—yet the clause would have proceeded no further than to provide for such cases, if no further restriction on the powers of congress had been intended. That they should have appellate jurisdiction in all other cases, with such exceptions as Congress might make, is no restriction; unless the words be deemed exclusive of original jurisdiction.

When an instrument organizing fundamentally a judicial system, divides it into one Supreme, and so many inferior courts as the legislature may ordain and establish; then enumerates its powers, and proceeds so far to distribute them, as to define the jurisdiction of the Supreme Court by declaring the cases in which it shall take original jurisdiction, and that in others it shall take appellate jurisdiction—the plain import of the words seems to be, that in one class of cases its jurisdiction is original, and not appellate; in the other it is appellate, and not original. If any other construction would render the clause inoperative, that is an additional reason for rejecting such other construction, & for adhering to their obvious meaning.

To enable this court then to issue a mandamus, it must be shewn to be an exercise of appellate jurisdiction, or to be necessary to enable them to exercise appellate jurisdiction.

It has been stated at the bar that the appellate jurisdiction may be exercised in a variety of forms, and that if it be the will of the legislature that a mandamus should be used for that purpose, that will must be obeyed. This is true—yet the jurisdiction must be appellate—not original.

It is the essential criterion of appellate jurisdiction, that it revises and corrects the proceedings in a cause already instituted, and does not create that cause. Although, therefore, a mandamus may be directed to courts, yet to issue such a writ to an officer for the delivery of a paper, is in effect the same as to sustain an original action for that paper, and therefore seems not to belong to appellate, but to original jurisdiction. Neither is it necessary in such a case as this, to enable the court to exercise its appellate jurisdiction.

The authority, therefore, given to the Supreme Court, by the act establishing the judicial courts of the United States, to issue writs of mandamus to public officers appears not to be warranted by the constitution—and it becomes necessary to enquire whether a jurisdiction, so conferred, can be exercised.

The question whether an act, repugnant to the constitution, can become the law of the land, is a question deeply interesting to the United States; but happily not of an intricacy proportioned to its interest. It seems only necessary to recognize certain principles, supposed to have been long and well established, to decide it.

That the people have an original right to establish, for their future government, such principles as, in their opinion, shall most conduce to their own happiness, is the basis, on which the whole American fabric has been erected. The exercise of this original right is a very great exertion; nor can it, nor ought it to be frequently repeated. The principles, therefore, so established, are deemed fundamental. And as the authority, from which they proceed, is supreme, and can seldom act, they are designed to be permanent.

This original and supreme will organizes the government, and assigns, to different departments, their respective powers. It may either stop here; or establish certain limits not to be transcended by those departments.

The government of the United States is of the latter description. The powers of the legislature are defined, and limited; and that those limits may not be mistaken, or forgotten, the constitution is written.

To what purpose are powers limited & to what purpose is that limitation committed to writing, if these limits may, at any time, be passed by those intended to be restrained? The distinction between a government with limited and unlimited powers, is abolished, if those limits do not confine the persons on whom they are imposed, and if acts prohibited and acts allowed, are of equal obligation. It is a proposition too plain to be contested, that the constitution controls any legislative act repugnant to it; or, that the legislature may alter the constitution by an ordinary act.

Between these alternatives there is no middle ground. The constitution is either a superior, paramount law, unchangeable by ordinary means, or it is on a level with ordinary legislative acts, & like other acts, is alterable when the legislature shall please to alter it.

If the former part of the alternative be true, then a legislative act contrary to the constitution is not law—if the latter part be true, then written constitutions are absurd attempts, on the part of the people, to limit a power, in its own nature, illimitable.

Certainly all those who have framed written constitutions, contemplate them as forming the fundamental and paramount law of the nation, and consequently the theory of every such government must be, that an act of the legislature, repugnant to the constitution, is void.

This theory is essentially attached to a written constitution, and is consequently to be considered, by this court, as one of the fundamental principles of our society. It is not therefore to be lost sight of in the further consideration of the subject.

If an act of the legislature repugnant to the constitution, is void, does it not withstanding its invalidity, bind the courts, and oblige them to give it effect? Or, in other words, though it be not law, does it constitute a rule as operative as if it was a law? This would be to overthrow in fact, what was established in theory; and would seem, at first view, an absurdity too gross to be insisted on. It shall, however, receive a more attentive consideration.

It is emphatically the province and duty of the judicial department to say what the law is. Those who apply the rule to particular cases, must of necessity expound, and interpret that rule. If two laws conflict with each other, the courts must decide on the operation of each.

So if a law be in opposition to the constitution; if both the law and the constitution apply to a particular case, so that the court must either decide that case conformably to the law, disregarding the constitution; or conformably to the constitution, disregarding the law; the court must determine which of these conflicting rules, governs the case. This is of the essence of judicial duty.

If then the courts are to regard the constitution; and the constitution is superior to any ordinary act of the legislature—the constitution, and not such ordinary act, must govern the case to which they both apply.

Those then who controvert the principle that the constitution is to be considered in court as a paramount law, are reduced to the necessity of maintaining that courts must close their eyes on the constitution, and see only the law.

This doctrine would subvert the very foundation of all written constitutions. It would declare that an act, which, according to the principles and theory of our government, is entirely void; is yet, in practice, completely obligatory. It would declare that if the legislature shall do what is expressly forbidden, such act, notwithstanding the express prohibition, is in reality effectual. It would be giving to the legislature a practical and real omnipotence, with the same breath which professes to restrict their powers within narrow limits. It is prescribing limits, and declaring that those limits may be passed at pleasure.

That it thus reduces to nothing what we have deemed the greatest improvement on political institutions—a written constitution—would of itself be sufficient, in America, where written constitutions have been viewed with so much reverence, for rejecting the construction. But the peculiar expressions of the constitution of the United States furnish additional arguments in favour of its rejection.

The judicial power of the United States is extended to all cases arising under the constitution.

Could it be the intention of those who gave this power, to say that, in using it, the constitution should not be looked into? That a case arising under the constitution should be decided without examining the instrument under which it arises?

This is too extravagant to be maintained.

In some cases then, the constitution must be looked into by the judges. And if they can open it at all, what part of it are they forbidden to read, or to obey?

There are many other parts of the constitution which serve to illustrate this subject.

It is declared that "no tax or duty shall be laid on articles exported from any state." Suppose a duty on the export of Cotton, of Tobacco, or of Flour; and a suit instituted to recover it. Ought judgment to be rendered in such a case? Ought the judges to close their eyes on the constitution, and only see the law.

The constitution declares, that "no bill of attainder or ex post facto law shall be passed."

If however such a bill should be passed and a person should be prosecuted under it; must the court condemn to death those victims whom the constitution endeavours to preserve?

"No person," says the constitution, shall be convicted of treason, "unless on the testimony of two witnesses to the same overt act, or on confession in open court."

Here the language of the constitution is addressed specially to the courts. It prescribes, directly for them, a rule of evidence not to be departed from. If the legislature should change that rule, and declare *one* witness, or a confession *out* of court, sufficient for conviction, must the constitutional principle yield to the legislative act?

From these, and many other selections which might be made, it is apparent, that the framers of the constitution contemplated that instrument, as a rule for the government of *courts*, as well as of the legislature.

Why otherwise does it direct the judges to take an oath to support it? This oath certainly applies, in an especial manner, to their conduct in their official character. How immoral to impose it on them, if they were to be used as the instruments, and the knowing instruments, for violating what they swear to support!

The oath of office, too, imposed by the legislature is completely demonstrative of the legislative opinion on this subject.

It is in these words, "I do solemnly swear that I will administer justice, without respect to persons, and do equal right to the poor and to the rich; and that I will faithfully and impartially discharge all the duties incumbent on me as according to the best of my abilities and understanding agreeably to *the constitution*, and laws of the United States."

Why does a judge swear to discharge his duties agreeably to the constitution of the United States, if that constitution forms no rule for his government? if it is closed upon him and cannot be inspected by him?

If such be the real state of things, this is worse than solemn mockery. To prescribe, or to take, this oath, becomes equally a crime.

It is also not entirely unworthy of observation, that in declaring what shall be the *Supreme* law of the land, the *constitution* itself is first mentioned; and not the laws of the United States generally, but those only which shall be made in *pursuance* of the constitution, have that rank.

Thus the particular phraseology of the constitution of the United States confirms & strengthens the principle, supposed to be essential to all written constitutions, that a law repugnant to the constitution is void; and that *courts*, as well as other departments, are bound by that instrument.

The rule must be discharged.

Printed, *Washington Federalist* (Georgetown, D.C.), 14 March, 16 March 1803. Text contains slight variations in spelling, punctuation, and capitalization from that in William Cranch, *Reports of Cases Argued and Adjudged in the Supreme Court of the United States* . . . , I (Washington, D.C., 1804), 153–80. Angle brackets enclose words or portions of words illegible in newspaper source.

1. Lee framed his argument around three questions: (1) "Whether the supreme court can award the writ of mandamus in any case." (2) "Whether it will lie to a secretary of state in any case whatever." (3) "Whether in the present case the court may award a mandamus to James Madison, secretary of state" (1 Cranch 146). He discussed the jurisdictional issue in terms of the court's power to issue the writ of mandamus, moving from the general to the particular. Like Lee, JM also set forth three questions and moved from the general to the particular. His "departure in form" was in taking a broader approach to the jurisdictional issue by first considering whether Marbury had a legal claim that could be enforced by courts and then taking up the question of the appropriateness of mandamus as a remedy.

2. *U.S. Statutes at Large*, II, 107.

3. Ibid., I, 68–69.

4. Blackstone, *Commentaries*, III, 23.

5. Words within brackets were omitted by the newspaper and are supplied from 1 Cranch 163.

6. *U.S. Statutes at Large*, I, 392–93. JM cited the edition *The Laws of the United States of America* . . . (4 vols.; Philadelphia, 1799). This was a cumulative series, with new volumes appearing at regular intervals.

7. In Blackstone, "it's"; 1 Cranch 165 corrected to "its."

8. *U.S. Statutes at Large*, I, 467–68.

9. King v. Barker, 3 Burr. 1265, 97 Eng. Rep. 823 (K.B., 1762).

10. Lee cited a number of English cases (1 Cranch 152–53).

11. JM alluded to the act of 1789 "for the safe-keeping of the Acts, Records and Seal of the United States." The secretary of state was to be paid ten cents a sheet (containing one hundred words) for "making out and authenticating copies of records" (*U.S. Statutes at Large*, I, 68–69).

12. The act for regulating claims of invalid pensioners (ibid., I, 244) provoked remonstrances from the judges sitting on circuit in New York, Pennsylvania, and North Carolina. Citing the principle of separation of powers, the judges objected that the duties assigned to them under this act were not properly judicial. They objected fur-

ther that their decisions under the act would be subject to revision by the secretary of war and by Congress, "whereas, by the constitution, neither the Secretary of War, nor any other executive officer, nor even the Legislature, are authorized to sit as a court of errors on the judicial acts or opinions of this court." The judges of the New York circuit agreed to act as commissioners, performing nonjudicial duties; those of North Carolina expressed doubts about acting in that character; and those of Pennsylvania refused to proceed under the act. In consequence of the Pennsylvania judges' refusal to act, Attorney General Randolph in Aug. 1792 moved in the Supreme Court for a mandamus to issue directing the circuit court to proceed on the application of William Hayburn to be put on the pension list. The Supreme Court took the motion under advisement until the next term, but in the meantime Congress repealed the law, and no decision was made (*ASP, Miscellaneous*, I, 49–53; Hayburn's Case, 2 Dall. 409). For accounts of this episode, see Charles Warren, *The Supreme Court in United States History* (2 vols.; Boston, 1926), I, 70–82; Goebel, *Antecedents and Beginnings*, 560–65.

13. A new pension law was enacted in Feb. 1793 (*U.S. Statutes at Large*, I, 325).

14. The first attempt to obtain an adjudication failed. At the Aug. 1793 term, Attorney General Randolph moved for a mandamus commanding the secretary of war to put on the pension list one of those who had been approved by the circuit court judges acting under the act of 1792. Two of the judges, however, were disinclined to hear a motion on behalf of one who had not personally employed counsel for that purpose. The attorney general then suggested to the secretary of war that he communicate these circumstances to those invalids placed on the list in virtue of the 1792 act. At length, at the Feb. 1794 term, John Chandler brought his case to the Supreme Court. His counsel moved for a mandamus to the secretary of war to put Chandler on the pension list "conformably to the Order and Adjudication of the Honorable James Iredell and Richard Law Esquires Judges of the Circuit Court of the United States." The court, on considering the two acts of Congress relating to invalid pensioners, was "of opinion that a Mandamus cannot issue . . . for the purposes expressed in the said motion."

The judgment in the Chandler case disposed of all those cases in the same category, that is, where the invalid had not been placed on the list. At the same term the court heard the case of U.S. v. Yale Todd. Unlike Chandler, Todd had been placed on the list as a result of an adjudication by the circuit court judges and had received payments. His case was not a mandamus action but a friendly suit by the U.S. for the recovery of money paid to Todd. The court ruled for the U.S., thereby holding that adjudications by the judges under the 1792 act were not valid. Accordingly, pensioners who had been put on the list under that act had to apply again under the act of 1793 (*ASP, Miscellaneous*, I, 78; Maeva Marcus and James R. Perry, eds., *The Documentary History of the Supreme Court of the United States, 1789–1800* [New York, 1985—], I, pt. 1, 222, 226, 228; Warren, *Supreme Court*, I, 80–82; Goebel, *Antecedents and Beginnings*, 564 and n.).

JM's account appears to combine the facts of both the Chandler and Todd cases, though only the former was a mandamus action. His treatment of these invalid pension cases as precedents is discussed at length in Bloch and Marcus, "Marshall's Selective Use of History in *Marbury v. Madison*," *Wisconsin Law Review* (1986), 301–37. The authors contend that JM used these cases to support the proposition that a mandamus could issue to an executive officer but then conveniently disregarded them when he sought to deny the Supreme Court's jurisdiction to issue the writ on behalf of Marbury.

15. Unlike the 1792 act, by which circuit court judges were to determine whether the claimant should be put on the pension list, the 1793 act merely directed district court judges to transmit a list of the claims, accompanied by supporting evidence, to the secretary of war.

16. Detinue was not an adequate remedy in this instance, for there was no way to assess damages either for the value of the thing (where it could not be specifically

recovered) or for its detention. Although the court in such an action might award the plaintiff his commission, such judgment would only place him in the same situation as before.

17. JM's summary is more detailed than the actual report of Lee's remarks on this point. "Congress," said Lee, "is not restrained from conferring original jurisdiction in other cases than those mentioned in the constitution" (1 Cranch 148). Lee cited as authority the case of U.S. v. Ravara, decided in the U.S. Circuit Court, Pennsylvania, in 1793. Speaking for the court, Judge Wilson held that although the Constitution vests in the Supreme Court original jurisdiction in cases affecting consuls, it did not preclude Congress from vesting concurrent jurisdiction in inferior courts. Judge Iredell, dissenting, insisted that the Constitution intended to invest exclusive jurisdiction in the Supreme Court in such cases (2 Dall. 297, 298).

To Oliver Wolcott, Jr.

My dear Sir   Washington March 2d. 1803

On my return from a long tour into the country last fall I had the pleasure of finding your treatise on the report of the investigating committee of the last session of Congress.[1]

Receive my thanks for this valuable work which is renderd to me the more valuable by the proof its being transmitted by the author gives of my being yet in his recollection.

I always considerd the report, both for the matter it contains & the manner in which it was usherd to the world as among the most disreputable acts of the present administration. If I had ever entertaind any doubts on this subject your pamphlet woud have removd them.

"We have fallen upon evil times" & I do not clearly perceive a prospect of better.

It will always give me real pleasure to hear of your happiness & I beg you to beleive that with much truth & sincere esteem, I am your

J MARSHALL

ALS, Oliver Wolcott, Jr., Papers, CtHi.

1. The reference is to Wolcott's *An Address to the People of the United States* (Boston, 1802; S #3576). The former secretary of the treasury's pamphlet was a response to the report of *The Committee Appointed to Examine and Report Whether Monies, Drawn from the Treasury, Have Been Faithfully Applied to the Objects for Which They Were Appropriated* . . . ([Washington, D.C.], 1802; S #3397). This report, dated 29 Apr. 1802, was widely published in the newspapers and is reprinted in *ASP, Finance,* I, 752-821.

Rules of Court

[2 March 1803][1]

Rule 1t.[2]

Where the Writ of error issues within the thirty days before the meeting of the Court, the Defendt. in error is at liberty to enter his appearance & proceed to trial, otherwise the cause must be continued.

Rule 2d.[3]

In all cases where a writ of error shall delay the proceedings on the judgement of the circuit court & shall appear to have been sued out meerly for delay damages shall be awarded at the rate of ten per centum per annum on the amount of the Judgement.[4] In such cases where there exists a real controversy the damages shall be only at the rate of 6 per centum per annum. In both cases the interest is to be computed as part of the damages.[5]

ADf, RG 267, DNA. Partly in JM's hand.

1. This is the date the rules were entered in the minute book (U.S. Sup. Ct. Minutes, 2 Mar. 1803).

2. The first rule is not in JM's hand. This is Rule XVI in 1 Cranch xv–xvii, which prints all the rules adopted since 1790.

3. This rule is entirely in JM's hand. The original draft of the second rule is in the same hand as the first rule. It was deleted and replaced by JM's draft.

4. This part of the second rule is Rule XVII in 1 Cranch xvii.

5. The remainder of the second rule is Rule XVIII in 1 Cranch xvii.

To George Simpson

Sir   Richmond March 15th. 1803

I am desirous of drawing my salary as chief Justice in future through the bank of the United States. To enable me to do this I have transmitted to the comptroller to be lodgd in his office a power of attorney authorizing you as the cashier of the bank to receive my salary.[1]

Permit me Sir to request that you will be so good as to inform me whether the steps I have taken will be sufficient, & whether I shall be authorizd to draw on you.

If any particular rules are to be observd you will greatly oblige me by giving the necessary information. With very much respect, I am Sir your obedt. Servt

AL[S], Etting Collection of Jurists, PHi. JM's signature clipped. Addressed to Simpson at Philadelphia; postmarked Richmond, 20 Mar.

1. Simpson was cashier of the Bank of the U.S. from 1795 to 1812 (James O. Wettereau, "New Light on the First Bank of the United States," *PMHB*, LXI [1937], 277).

Teasdale v. Branton's Administrator
Opinion
U.S. Circuit Court, North Carolina, [15–21 June 1803]

And by *Marshall*, Chief Justice, to which *Potter*, Justice, assented; it is in the discretion of the court to permit the addition of a plea at any time before the trial; and the court will admit the plea where the justice of the case requires it.[1] And the plea now offered is such an one as justice requires the admission of. It would be a monstrous proposition that when judgments after plea had taken away all the assets, the executor or administrator should notwithstanding be compelled to answer the debts first pleaded to.[2]

Printed, John Haywood, *Cases Adjudged in the Superior Courts . . . of North Carolina*, II (Raleigh, N.C., 1806), 281.

1. There is no entry for this case in the minute book for this term, which ran from 15 to 21 June. Isaac Teasdale sued the administrator of Thomas Branton, whose attorney now sought to add a plea of no assets beyond the amount of judgments obtained against the administrator since he first pleaded (2 Haywood 281).
2. The reporter noted that the plea was added. The trial took place on 31 Dec. 1804, the jury awarding damages to the plaintiff but finding that the defendant had fully administered the assets (U.S. Cir. Ct., N.C., Min. Bk., 31 Dec. 1804). Further litigation between these parties arose in consequence of this verdict. See Opinion, 4 Jan. 1806.

Gibson v. Williams
Opinion
U.S. Circuit Court, North Carolina, 16 June 1803

Per curiam. So much of the lands as the money secured by the mortgage was worth, shall be deemed to have been purchased by the heir, by payment of the debts of the ancestor; the surplus of the land shall be estimated as worth at the time of sale in 1801.[1] It must not be valued as worth at the time of descent to the defendant, for the intermediate profits are a recompence for the expences incident to holding the land, such as taxes and the like.[2]

Printed, John Haywood, *Cases Adjudged in the Superior Courts . . . of North Carolina*, II (Raleigh, N.C., 1806), 281.

1. James Gibson and others recovered judgment on a bond debt against the executor of William Williams, who successfully pleaded that he had fully administered the assets. The plaintiffs then proceeded by scire facias against Samuel F. Williams, heir and devisee of William Williams, as provided by the 1784 statute "directing the Mode of proceeding against the real Estates of deceased Debtors." The heir pleaded that the lands he had by descent had been mortgaged and sold to pay bond debts of his ancestor. After holding that the heir was not liable for the interest on the surplus beyond the amount paid for the ancestor's debts, the court gave its opinion on estimating the value of the surplus land (*First Laws of North Carolina*, II, 530–31; 2 Haywood 281).

2. A jury accordingly determined that the defendant had real estate valued at seven hundred dollars subject to the plaintiffs' demand (U.S. Cir. Ct., N.C., Min. Bk., 16 June 1803).

Sanders v. Hamilton
Opinion
U.S. Circuit Court, North Carolina, 17 June 1803

Marshall, Chief Justice. The jury should assess damages according to the value at the time of recovery;[1] for supposing he is to have the present value, he should bear the loss in case of the death of the Negroes or other loss since the judgment; and besides, plaintiff's demand arises immediately upon the recovery, and is not to be influenced by after circumstances.[2]

Printed, John Haywood, *Cases Adjudged in the Superior Courts . . . of North Carolina*, II (Raleigh, N.C., 1806), 282.

1. See the first opinion in this case at 31 Dec. 1802 and n. 1. The question was whether the jury should assess the damages according to the value of the slaves at the time Streeter recovered them against Sanders or at their present value.

2. At this point the reporter repeated the substance of the ruling made by JM at the first trial. After further proceedings, Sanders obtained a judgment at the Dec. 1804 term (U.S. Cir. Ct., N.C., Min. Bk., 1 Jan. 1805).

Flemming & Company v. Murfree
Opinion
U.S. Circuit Court, North Carolina, 21 June 1803

Marshall, Chief Justice. I doubt whether an admission of the debt by the administrator will take the case out of the act of limitations; for the admission presupposes a promise made within three years, and how can this be when the intestate has been dead ten years?[1] If it were true that an admission of the debt did take the case out of the act, and it could not be given in evidence at all unless allowed of upon such a replication, I should think that a strong argument for admitting the evidence.[2] But the premises are not correct; it is not true that a count upon the intestates promise, and upon that of the administrator to pay the debt of the intestate may not be joined; the contrary is directly proved by the case cited from H. Bl. Re. 104; where the administrator upon an *insimul computasset* and promise thereon, was held liable *de bonis testatoris*.[3] The other cases cited, which state that he is bound *de bonis propriis*, are where the consideration for the promise arose after the death of the intestate, and in the time of the administrator;[4] here the promise was on a consideration arising in the time of the intestate. The cases are reconcileable.[5]

Printed, John Haywood, *Cases Adjudged in the Superior Courts . . . of North Carolina*, II (Raleigh, N.C., 1806), 283.

1. Haywood mistakenly titled this case "Wilkings v. Murphey, Administrator, etc." The parties to the suit were Henry Flemming & Co., plaintiff, and Hardy Murfree, administrator of Joseph Dickinson, defendant. On 18 June 1803 a jury found for the plaintiffs, subject to the court's opinion on the right of the plaintiff to give in evidence an acknowledgment of the debt by the administrator so as to avoid the statute of limitations. The opinion was given on 21 June (U.S. Cir. Ct., N.C., Min. Bk., 18, 20 June 1803).

2. This was an action of assumpsit, the defendant pleading the act of limitations. The plaintiff replied that the intestate had assumed within the time allowed by the statute (three years). Counsel for the defendant contended that the administrator's acknowledgment of the debt could not be offered in evidence under this replication (2 Haywood 282).

3. Plaintiff's counsel argued that the replication could not depart from the declaration, which stated a promise by the intestate. A declaration could not join counts founded on the promise of the intestate with a count founded on the promise of the administrator because they required different judgments. This was precisely the argument in Segar v. Atkinson (1 Black. H. 102, 104–5, 126 Eng. Rep. 62–63 [C.P., 1789]), where three counts against the intestate were joined with a count founded on a promise arising from an "account stated" (*insimul computasset*) between the plaintiff and the defendant, as administratrix. It was objected that on the first three counts judgment would be levied against the goods of the intestate (*de bonis testatoris*) and on the fourth against the administratrix's own goods (*de bonis propriis*). The court held that judgment on all four counts would be de bonis testatoris, the judge remarking that the fourth count was "the common mode of declaring against executors and administrators, to save the Statute of Limitations."

4. The other cases (identified by Haywood) were Rose v. Bowler and Read, 1 Black. H. 108, 126 Eng. Rep. 65 (C.P., 1789), and Jennings v. Newman, 4 T.R. 347, 100 Eng. Rep. 1056 (K.B., 1791).

5. The verdict was set aside, and the plaintiff given leave to amend the declaration by adding counts and to amend the replication. The case was tried again on 2 Jan. 1805, the jury finding for the plaintiff but that the administrator had fully administered the assets. The plaintiff then sought recovery of the judgment from the heirs and devisees

of the estate (U.S. Cir. Ct., N.C., Min. Bk., 20 June 1803, 2 Jan., 20 June 1805, 14 Nov. 1808; scire facias, 20 June 1806, Flemming & Co. v. Dickinson, GEpFRC).

The Missing George Washington Diary

EDITORIAL NOTE

From the moment of George Washington's death, the disposition of his papers contained political ramifications. Bequeathed to Bushrod Washington, the manuscripts at Mount Vernon did not come into his possession until eight months after his uncle's death; in the interval they were in Tobias Lear's hands.[1] Continuing to function as the late general's secretary, Lear stated at the time that he was the only person with access to the papers and that among them were "many which every public (and) private consideration should withold from further inspection. These I have put by themselves, and on delivering them to Judge Washington shall tell him how sacred their contents are and have no doubt but in his hands they will be a sacred deposit." Alexander Hamilton, to whom Lear wrote this assurance, was himself interested in the disposal of Washington's manuscripts, for "our very confidential situation will not permit this to be a point of indifference to me." A year and a half later, Hamilton pressed Bushrod Washington to send him papers from the period he was secretary of the treasury. Besieged by such requests, Washington declined, lest the papers be appropriated by either party for partisan purposes.[2]

As primary caretaker of Washington's manuscripts for much of the 1790s, Tobias Lear inevitably came under such suspicion. Although loyal to Washington, Lear in his political leanings was Republican rather than Federalist. Jefferson, soon after taking office as president, considered Lear for secretary of the navy but instead appointed him commercial agent at St. Domingo. Lear sailed for that island on 2 June 1801. Events there forced his return to the United States in April 1802. In the following spring, Jefferson named Lear consul general at Algiers, with powers to negotiate a treaty with Tripoli and the Barbary rulers.[3] Lear was on his way to this post when he encountered a rumor circulating in Boston that he had "suppressed certain papers of the late General Washington" to gain "the favor & confidence of Mr. Jefferson." In searching out the source of this accusation, Lear traced it to Marshall, which occasioned an interchange of letters among Lear, Marshall, and Benjamin Lincoln.[4]

According to Marshall, he and Bushrod Washington found a gap in the journals when examining George Washington's papers in the spring of 1802. While denying he had implicated Lear, Marshall admitted he had informed a highly esteemed "gentleman" that a diary was missing for the period 1 June 1791 to 30 September 1794. He claimed that journals existed for the prior and subsequent portions of Washington's life, which made this "chasm" puzzling.[5] The omission covered the years of Jefferson's feud with Hamilton in the cabinet and Jefferson's subsequent withdrawal from the government, which suggested a reason for the disappearance of the journal.

During the first part of 1806, in the controversy surrounding the peace settlement signed by Lear with the pasha of Tripoli, Federalists revived and elaborated upon the charges against Lear and Jefferson. Lear was supposed to have turned over not only a presidential diary but also a later exchange of letters between Washington and Jefferson concerning Jefferson's publicized 1796 letter to Philip Mazzei, criticizing the Washington administration. According to the calumny, in return for receipt of politically damning documents, Jefferson gave Lear political preferment, advancing him in diplomatic posts and defending him against attacks over the terms of the Tripolitan treaty.

Although the identity of the intermediary "gentleman" to whom Marshall communicated his observation of a missing diary is uncertain, several people in Virginia said they knew of the discontinuity in the journals shortly after it was discovered. The source of information was Bushrod Washington, who told his cousin Lawrence Lewis, who passed it on to Dr. David Stuart, who told Col. William Heth. Relating what he knew, Heth in 1806 stated that after his first hearing it from Stuart, "it has *certainly* been confirmed by those, who have the best right to know *what* papers are missing," presumably Bushrod Washington and Marshall. Heth repeated a rumor to Timothy Pickering that Lear, while in the employ of George Washington, privately corresponded with Jefferson and that Lear had access to the missing papers, which had never been found. If this information came down through "the highly *respectible channel*" it was said to have, then it could not be doubted, asserted Heth. Writing to Pickering in 1809 about the disappearance of the documents, Stuart posed the rhetorical question of who could be so "invenomed" against George Washington when living, as "to deprive the natural Guardians of his fame when dead, of these lights and illustrations of character in events, which have not unfrequently been communicated even by a Diary."[6]

Years later, when asked about "the papers, which Lear has been charged with having taken away," Bushrod Washington "said that no such charge had ever been made by him." After taking possession of the papers from Lear, Bushrod "found that the private journal for a certain period was missing; he thought about the year 1793, and that suspicions of having withdrawn it fell upon Mr. Lear, yet there was no other evidence of the circumstance; nor had he reason to suppose that any letters were taken away by Mr. Lear."[7] In fact, the presently located diaries for the presidential years are episodic, with many gaps occurring. A journal fragment for 2 June through 4 July 1791, completing the account of Washington's southern tour, is now a part of the diary series in the Washington Papers at Library of Congress. No journal for the remainder of the supposed gap, 1 June 1791 to 30 September 1794, is known to exist.[8]

1. Herbert B. Adams, *The Life and Writings of Jared Sparks, Comprising Selections from his Journals and Correspondence* (2 vols.; Boston and New York, 1893), II, 46–47; see Tobias Lear to JM, 12 Dec. 1800 and n. 4.

2. Lear to Hamilton, 16 Jan. 1800; Hamilton to Lear, 2 Jan 1800; Bushrod Washington to Hamilton, 21 Nov. 1801 (Syrett, *Papers of Hamilton*, XXIV, 198–99, 155 and n. 2; XXV, 432–33); see also JM to William Paterson, 6 Apr. 1802 and n. 2, 3 May 1802.

3. Jefferson to James Madison, 12 Mar. 1801; Lear to Madison, 29 May 1801 (Rutland, *Papers of Madison: Sec. of State*, I, 12, 13 n. 5, 237); Lear to Benjamin Lincoln, 5 June 1803, Benjamin Lincoln Papers, MHi.

4. See Lear to JM, 13 Aug. 1803; JM to Lincoln, 21 Nov. 1803; Lincoln to JM, 25 Apr. 1804; JM to Lincoln, 6 May 1804.

5. JM to Lincoln, 21 Nov. 1803.

6. Timothy Pickering to Fisher Ames, 21 Mar. 1806; William Heth to Pickering, 6 Apr., 19 Apr. 1806; David Stuart to Pickering, 24 Jan. 1809; Pickering, "Memorandum," 16 May 1822, Timothy Pickering Papers, MHi; Brighton, *Checkered Career of Lear*, 169–75, 268–73. If Jefferson and Washington ever corresponded over the Mazzei affair, the present location of such letters is not known.

7. Jared Sparks, journal entry, 17 Jan. 1828 (Adams, *Life of Sparks*, II, 46–47).

8. Washington Papers, ser. 1B, DLC; Jackson and Twohig, *Diaries of Washington*, I, xlvi; VI, 154–69; see Lear to JM, 12 Dec. 1800 and nn. 10, 11. Except for entries from Dec. 1789 to July 1790, the diaries that do exist do not detail Washington's days as president. Rather, they cover the exceptional or pedestrian: his New England (Oct.–Nov. 1789) and southern (Mar.–July 1791) tours, the Whiskey Rebellion expedition (Sept.–Oct. 1794), or brief weather notations (1795–96). No journal is extant for the period immediately following Washington's departure from western Pennsylvania on 20 Oct. 1794. Although JM's stipulation of specific dates for the missing diary suggests there were prior and subsequent journals, JM may have been misled by the fragmentary nature of Washington's diary-keeping, for, as Lear noted, "the Diaries are broken & interrupted" (Lear to JM, 12 Dec. 1800). Possibly, George Washington himself destroyed the most political of his diaries before his death, or perhaps they never existed. If they did exist, they are either in private hands or lost, or were indeed "suppressed" by Lear.

From Tobias Lear

(Copy)

                                On board the U.S. Frigate Constitution[1]
Sir,   Boston Harbour, Augt. 13th: 1803

It was with the utmost surprize, and with extreme sensibility, that I hea[r]d, a few days ago, of a report having been circulated in Boston, after my arrival there, that I had suppressed certain papers of the late General Washington, which were under my charge for some time after his death; and that those papers were apart of his Diary containing remarks during his administration of the Govt. and while Mr. Jefferson was Secretary of State. To this Report was added a suggestion, that, in consequence of such suppression, I had gained the favor & confidence of Mr. Jefferson. Indignant at the Report and its inference, I felt it my duty to trace it, if possible, to its source, and shew its falsehood. I brought it up to the Revnd. Mr. Kirkland,[2] a Clergyman of Boston, whom I saw only the day before yesterday, and a few hours before I embarked. I visited him, in company with Commodore Preble;[3] and when I told him what I had heard as coming from him, he acknowledged that he had been informed by a Gentleman, *who said he had it from you,* that there was a chasm in the Diaries of the late Genl. Washington, for the period above mentioned, and that, as the papers had been for some time in my care, you inferr'd that they must have been suppressed by me; but that you did not wish the thing to be made publickly known, lest it should injure the work, or the sale of the History of the General's life. As to the inference which was said to have been made, that I had thereby insured the favor &c. of Mr. Jefferson, Mr. Kirkland observed that the Gentleman did not say you had made such; but that it might have been made by others. I requested Mr. Kirkland to give me the name of the Gentleman who had given him this information; which, after some hesitation, he declined doing, saying he could not feel himself a[t] liberty to give his name, as he did not know whether he (Mr. Kirkland) had acted justifiably in mentioning the report, altho' it was not delivered to him under injunctions of secrecy. I told him his profession, as a Clergyman, would prevent my *demanding* the name from him in the same manner I should, most assuredly, demand it from another person; but I called upon him by all the feelings of a man of honor, who had been one mean[s] of circulating a report intended to injure me in the most tender point, to give me the clue by which it might be traced to its source. He acknowledged he had done very wrong in having mentioned it, and that he did not beleive that any suppression of the kind mentioned, had been made by me; and as the Gentln. who gave it to him was not then in Boston, and he could not tell when he would be there, he would consult some of his friends on the occasion, and if they should think he ought to give up the name of his informer, he would divulge it to such friend of mine as I would mention in Boston, and who might, in my behalf, trace the Report and do me justice. Finding I could do nothing more with Mr. Kirkland, I named Genl. Lincoln as my friend, who would take upon himself to see justice done me in this business, and who could not be suspected of being biased by any other motive than a wish to investigate the truth, and place it in its proper light. He then assured me he would see Genl. Lincoln, and as he had been unguardedly the means of doing me an injury he should feel himself bound to do everything he could to correct the evil. Thus I left Mr. Kirkland; and Genl. Lincoln will attend to the business in my behalf. With him (Genl. Lincoln) I have left a copy of my letter to you of the 12h of Decr. 1800, and of the Inventory of papers &c. forwarded to you, with that letter, in the City of Washington.[4]

Now, Sir, I shall not doubt for a moment, but you will communicate
to Genl. Lincoln, whatever you may have said, if anything, on this
subject, and do me that justice which I am convinced your own heart
will tell you I am entitled to. For I am persuaded that if you had
suspected me of being base enough to have done an Act of the kind
reported, you would not have failed, in justice to yourself, and to the
work in which you are engaged, to have had it made known to me in
some way or another before this time; or, if important documents had
been wanting in their regular place, it would have been very easy to
have made an enquiry of me whether I could give any information
respecting them, without conveying an idea that I had suppressed
them. In the Inventory sent you on Decr. 1800, I mentioned that the
Diaries were broken & incomplete; but not a hint or suggestion did I
ever hear, from any source, on this subject, until the report communicated to me a few days ago, as herein stated.[5] And this Report having
been made at the moment of my leaving the U.S. perhaps for some
years, has all the appearance of being intended to answer some unworthy purpose, as it is well known I should not have been able,
before my departure, to trace it, and contradict it in the extent to
which it may have been spread; but this circumstance will also tend to
give it less credit with those who do not know me. With those who do
know me, I have no fears of its gaining beleif.[6] With great Respect, I
have the honor to be, Sir, Your most Obedt Sert

TOBIAS LEAR.

ALS (copy), Madison Papers, DLC. Enclosed in Lear to James Madison, 23 Aug.–5
Sept. 1803. See n. 6 below.

1. Flagship of relief squadron sent to the Mediterranean to replace U.S. naval vessels
engaged in the war with Tripoli. She sailed the next day, 14 Aug. (Ray W. Irwin, *The
Diplomatic Relations of the United States with the Barbary Powers, 1776–1816* [Chapel Hill,
N.C., 1931], 130–31).

2. John Thornton Kirkland (1770–1840), later president of Harvard University.

3. Edward Preble (1761–1807), commander of the squadron departing for the Mediterranean. He sailed on the *Constitution* the next day with Lear.

4. Benjamin Lincoln was Lear's patron, having originally recommended him to
George Washington for his private secretary. The copy of Lear's 12 Dec. 1800 letter,
with the inventory, is in Benjamin Lincoln Papers, MHi.

5. JM asserted near the end of his reply that he had urged Bushrod Washington to
inform Lear of the gap in the diaries and that Washington had done so (JM to Lincoln,
21 Nov. 1803).

6. Lear enclosed this copy of his letter in one to James Madison of 23 Aug.–5 Sept.
1803, in which he said: "I take the liberty to enclose you the Copy of a letter which I
wrote to Judge Marshall, the day before I left Boston. The letter will explain itself. I
think the Party or Parties who foolishly & wickedly propagate falsehoods of this kind
must feel them recoil most severely upon themselves. The Clergymen of Boston, and I
fear of some other places, are deviating very much from their christian Characters in

being the warm & zealous promoters of scandal & falsehoods to answer the ends of a desperate faction" (Madison Papers, DLC).

To Oliver Wolcott, Jr.

⟨De⟩ar Sir   Richmond Aug. 15th. 1803

With much pleasure I made the enquiries suggested in your letter of the 4th. inst.[1]

The expences of Colonel William Davies's ⟨ag⟩ency for stating the claims of this state for expenditures ⟨d⟩uring the revolutionary war before the board of commission⟨e⟩rs of the United States, including his pay, clerk hire, office ⟨r⟩ent, & contingencies was three thousand seven hundred & seventy four pounds ten shillings & two pence—the dollar at six shillings. The compensation to Colonel Davies was six dollars per day.[2]

There were other expenses incurd in preparing the accounts for a settlement which do not come within your enquiry. Considerable sums were paid, before Colonel Davies was engagd, to officers whose duty it was to collect prepare & arrange the papers for a settlement. Their services however were of very little use.

If you wish any further or more satisfactory inteligence which it may be in my power to procure I shall feel a pleasure in obtaining it.

I heard with real gratification, of your translation to New York, & that you were about taking a station to be held really, not nominally, during good behavior.[3]

Present me respectfully to Mrs. Wolcott & beleive me to be dear Sir with real esteem, Your Obedt. Servt

J MARSHALL

ALS, Oliver Wolcott, Jr., Papers, CtHi. Angle brackets enclose letters obscured in margin.

1. Wolcott's letter of 4 Aug. has not been found, but filed with this letter is an extract of his letter to an unknown correspondent requesting information about the agent's expenses for settling Maryland's accounts with the U.S. Wolcott stated that this information would "be useful to me personally and is wanted for that purpose only." This request was probably related to the report of a congressional committee inquiring into the expenditures of the previous administration. See JM to Wolcott, 2 Mar. 1803 and n. 1.

2. On William Davies, see Hutchinson, *Papers of Madison*, III, 32 n. 1; *CVSP*, VII, 43–57.

3. Wolcott had been appointed a judge of the second circuit under the Judiciary Act of 1801. The repeal of that law deprived him of his judgeship. He subsequently

moved to New York and established a commission and agency firm known as Oliver Wolcott & Co.

To William Bernard

Dear Sir   Richmond Septr. 8th. 1803

I receivd through Colo. Carrington your propositions for purchasing my land lying south of Randolphs creek.[1]

You know that I have agreed to let those who at present occupy it sow wheat this fall on rent. This agreement I cannot break. If you can settle with the tenants considering yourself as bound by my agreement I shall have no objection to accepting your proposition.[a] I am to receive the corn rent of this year & you may take immediate possession subject only to the claim of the tenants to gather their corn & to sow wheat if you cannot induce them to give up that privilege. You will be entitled to one fourth of the wheat.

In laying off the lotts north of Randolphs creek I have agreed to except from that adjoining Gay fifty acres to include the mill seat, some meadow or flat land on the creek uncleard & some old field. I think these fifty acres woud be an addition to the land on the south side both on account of the mill seat & of the creek low grounds. The old field is worth very little. If you wish to add this quantity of land you may have it for one hundred pound to be divided between the two last payments. I am dear Sir with very much regard & esteem, Your Obedt Servt

J MARSHALL

[a]The proposition is £800 for the 352 acres as surveyd by Mr. Patteson. Half paid down & the residue in two annual payments.[2]

ALS, Collection of Thomas W. Bullitt, Louisville, Ky. Addressed to Bernard in Buckingham County "by the way of New Canton"; postmarked Richmond; date obscured by address. Endorsed by Bernard. Notations and calculations on cover presumably by Bernard.

1. JM had been trying to sell this land for some time. See his letter to Edward Carrington, 28 Dec. 1800. See also his bill in chancery, 28 Jan. 1803, in the suit of Marshall v. Pendleton, which recites the history of his Buckingham purchase. Bernard had served as a justice of the peace for Buckingham since 1796 (Commission Book No. 1, Vi). See also Whitley, *Genealogical Records of Buckingham County*, 32, 121, 124, 133.

2. JM wrote this note sideways in the left margin.

To Benjamin Lincoln

Sir   Richmond Novr. 21st. 1803

I recievd some time past a letter from Mr. Lear complaining in terms of some bitterness, of a report circulating in Boston which states a chasm in a diary kept by General Washington in his own hand writing, & implicates Mr. Lear, to whose care the papers of the General were confided, as the cause to which is to be attributed the loss of those said to be missing.[1] This report, Mr. Lear informd me, was traced up to the reverend Mr. Kirkland to whom the fact was communicated by a gentleman who receivd it from me: & he wishd me to explain to you, as his friend, how far I may have authorised, what he states to be, a calumny.

With much truth I can assure you that the manner in which this fact has been disclosed has given me real pain, & that I have never been desirous of criminating Mr. Lear on the occasion. His request that I shoud communicate to you all I know of the transaction will certainly be complied with, & woud have been sooner attended to, had I not deemd it proper first to ascertain precisely what I am alleg'd to have said: for so high is my opinion of the gentleman with whom I held the conversation alluded to, that had he asserted me to have said more than I recollected or supposed my self ever to have utterd, I shoud have distrusted my own memory, & admitted him to have been correct.

The fact is this.

In the year 1781 General Washington commenced a regular journal of all his transactions, which he inserted in small pocket volumes containing generally some what less than 150 pages. This journal from the 1st. of June 1791 to the 30th. of Septr. 1794 is missing. Judge Washington has assured me that he has searchd most diligently for them & cannot find them.

Mr. Lear transmitted to me while in Washington, a trunk containing sundry books & papers most of which were of not much importance, but in it were several of the journals which had been preserved. He at the same time sent me a receipt enumerating the papers said to be in the trunk, which I signd without keeping a duplicate, & (such was my confidence in that gentleman as the friend & private secretary of General Washington) without inspecting the books themselves. I will thank you sir for a copy of this receipt.[2] The trunk was brought with my baggage to this place, & in the fall of the year 1781[3] Mr. Washington sent me the other trunks which had been deliverd over by Mr. Lear to him. In the spring of 1802 he came to this place when we examind the trunks together (for I had been unable to open most of them from the peculiar structure of their locks) & he took the journals home with him, in the hope of being able to supply, those which were not to be found. He soon informd me that those which were missing had been searchd for in vain, & that he gave them up as lost.

To me I confess it appeard unaccountable that, of this the most material part of his administration, no account shoud be preservd by himself, while exact memoranda were retaind of the preceding & subsequent parts of his life. The fact made a deep impression on my mind which it was not in my power to resist. This impression was renderd the stronger by certain injurious reports relative to the papers in possession of the person composing the life of General Washington, circulated by a gentleman then filling a high political station.[4] For any expressions I may have used in consequence of this impression I admit myself to be accountable & shall not readily pardon myself if I have been, however unintentionally, the cause of injury to an innocent man.

I have made a point of withholding this unpleasant & extraordinary circumstance from the knowlege of the public, because I did beleive that it woud injure Mr. Lear with many, & because, however strong appearances were, yet the suspicions they woud excite, might be unfounded. My brother & my other very near connections & intimate friends residing in the same town with me, persons with whom I am in habits of strict friendship & confidential intercourse, are to this moment unacquainted with the fact. I mention this sir that you may rightly estimate what course of conduct I have observd.

I did mention the loss of these journals in a very confidential conversation with the gentleman from whom Mr. Kirkland receivd the communication. The conversation in a great measure led to it. I mentiond it, to the best of my recollection, as one among many instances which woud illustrate the extreme tenderness observd by certain gentlemen towards persons from whom no mercy had been experienced: & I beleive I stated the conjectures the world woud form on such a circumstance if disclosed & taken in connection with subsequent events. But I have no recollection of having chargd Mr. Lear with any knowlege[5] respecting the missing papers or of having expressd any suspicion to that effect. It was on this point I wrote to Mr. Kirkland. I was not willing to admit myself to be the author of such a charge, because, so far as I coud trust my own memory I had not made it; & I was also unwilling to deny it because, as I have already stated, so perfect is my confidence in the gentleman who held the conversation with me, that if he had clearly recollected my having declard such suspicions, I shoud have distrusted my own memory too much to have insisted on his being mistaken.

I am releivd from this perplexity by a letter from Mr. Kirkland in which he informs me that it was never alleged that I had chargd a suppression of the papers on Mr. Lear or said more than to mention the fact I have now stated to you.

Mr. Lear complains that I did not mention the chasm in the diary to him as he perhaps might have accounted for it. Had I designd to bring a charge against that gentleman this is the course which I shoud certainly have made a point of pursuing. But I have not intended to bring such a charge, & in addition to this I have never seen him since I have known that the chasm existed. It is however proper for me to declare that I expressd to Judge Washington my opinion that the fact ought to be stated to Mr. Lear, & the Judge has assured me that he did state it. That gentleman did not pretend to account for the circumstance; so far from showing any surprise at it, declard that he had himself observd the chasm when he first opend the trunks & was totally unable to assign the cause of it.

I repeat sir my regret that this fact shoud have been made known in the manner it has: yet I cannot accuse myself with any conduct respecting it which I can look back to & condemn.

It is probable that I shall now think it my duty to mention on a proper occasion this unfortunate chasm in the diary of General Washington, but I have not intended so to mention it as to imply suspicions of Mr. Lear. I have done all in my power to stop the report. It is with that gentleman & his friends to determine whether the fact shall now be proclaimd to the world or not. With great respect & very sincere esteem, I am Sir your Obedt. Servt

J MARSHALL

I shall either send a copy of this letter to Mr. Kirkland or refer him to you for a sight of it.[6] I think it necessary that gentleman shoud see it. Yours very respectfully

J M

ALS, Benjamin Lincoln Papers, MHi. In left-hand margin of last page marked "J. Marshall/1803" in an unknown hand.

1. See The Missing George Washington Diary, editorial note (preceding Tobias Lear to JM, 13 Aug. 1803).

2. When Lear sent JM the trunk of papers in 1800, he made no mention of a "receipt" but enclosed a "list," in which Lear stated that "the Diaries are broken & interrupted (much to be regretted)" (Lear to JM, 12 Dec. 1800). This list, with the letter, is now at the College of William and Mary, deposited there by JM's great-granddaughter, and is presumably the copy received by JM. See also Lear to JM, 13 Aug. 1803 and n. 4, and Lincoln's reply to JM, 25 Apr. 1804.

3. JM should have written "1801."

4. Jefferson suspected that JM was using Washington's papers for political ends. The president believed that JM meant the Life "to come out just in time to influence the

next presidential election. It is written therefore principally with a view to electioneering purposes." Urging Joel Barlow to undertake a history of the U.S. under Madison's and his guidance, Jefferson thought that JM's work would appear in time "to point out the perversions of truth necessary to be rectified" by Barlow. By late 1802 rumors had circulated enough to worry the publisher and his subscription agent, Mason Locke Weems. Bushrod Washington tried to reassure Caleb P. Wayne that "the democrats may say what they please, and I have expected they would say a great deal, but this is at least not intended to be a party work, nor will any candid Man have cause to make this charge." But Weems warned Wayne that "the People are very fearful that it will be prostituted to party purposes. I mean, of course, the Life of Washington. For Heaven's sake drop now and then a cautionary hint to John Marshal Esqr." Weems implied there would be few purchasers of the volumes if the biography proved to be a Federalist tract (Thomas Jefferson to Joel Barlow, 3 May 1802 [Paul Leicester Ford, ed., *The Writings of Thomas Jefferson* (10 vols.; New York and London, 1892–99), VIII, 151]; Bushrod Washington to Caleb P. Wayne, 19 Nov. 1802, Dreer Collection, PHi; Mason Locke Weems to Wayne, 14 Dec. 1802 [Skeel, *Weems*, II, 256]).

5. JM first wrote here "of the hands into which," then struck through that phrase, interlined above it "respecting the," and finally deleted his duplicate "the."

6. No communications between JM and Kirkland have been found, but see Lincoln to JM, 25 Apr. 1804.

Marshall v. Janney
Amended Bill and Answer in Chancery

[29 November 1803]

To the Honble. the Judge of the court of chancery sitting at Staunton, for the district of Staunton your orator John Marshall humbly showeth[1]

That your orator filed his bill of complaint in the court of chancery then sitting in Richmond for the commonwealth of Virginia in which he stated his claim to a certain tract of land on new creek in the county of Hampshire, by regular conveyances from Thomas Lord Fairfax who had appropriated the same to his own use by a survey thereof.[2] The land was stated to be in possession of a certain William Jenny who filed his answer to the said bill after which the said cause was transferred by act of Assembly to the Honble. the court of chancery sitting in Staunton.[3] Your orator now prays leave to change by way of amendment to his said bill.

That Thomas Lord Fairfax in his life time directed Guy Broadwater, one of the surveyors employed by him, to survey & lay off certain lotts on New Creek from No. 1. to No. 8, & extending as low down the creek as to its confluence with the Potowmac, which surveys were made & returned into his office, as will appear by the plott of them now in the land office of this commonwealth a copy of which is hereunto annexed & referred to.[4]

Your orator humbly states that it was usual for Lord Fairfax to lay off certain tracts of land by survey in the northern neck which he afterward disposed of to others or retained for his own particular use as his own inclination might direct, but no lands surveyd by his order were considerd as being afterw⟨ards⟩ liable ⟨to be⟩ taken up by any person who might chuse to locate them. The act of ⟨compromise?⟩ was understood to be a complete separation of the land surveyd, from the mass of property termed waste or vacant which every person was at liberty to acquire by complying with the rules establishd in the office for granting lands lying in the northern neck.[5] Lord Fairfax frequently barterd away, or otherwise disposed of such surveys but did not permit his general warrants to be laid on them, & unless he did dispose of them they remained his property & were considered as reserved to his private use.

Your orator humbly states that Lord Fairfax never did grant the lott no. 5 in the platt of surveys made by Guy Broadwater as already mentiond. A deed for that lott was prepared in 1752 soon after the survey was made, & entered blank in the books of his office, but the contract relative to this property having been by some means unknown to your orator broken off, the deed never was filled up nor executed. This will fully appear by a copy of the deed annexed & referred to, which also serves to show that Lord Fairfax when about to dispose of the property treated for it under his title by the survey made by Broadwater, & described it by its number as a lott already surveyed.[6]

Having never parted with his property in the said lott thus distinctly acquired by the survey already mentioned, he long afterwards entered into a treaty with a certain John Rousseau for leasing to him one of the lotts contained in the said survey made by Guy Brodwater on new creek as will appear by a copy of the said lease filed by your orator in this suit & referred to in his original bill. The said lease contains the description of lott No. 6 which lies below & adjoining to lott No. 5 & is also in possession of the said William Jenny.[7] But your orator beleives that altho it conveys lott No. 6 it was really intended for lott No. 5 & that this error was committed in the office of Lord Fairfax. Be this as it may however it cannot affect the title of your orator who claims not under the lease which is expired; but under Lord Fairfax whose appropriation of the lotts surveyd by Guy Brodwater is as much evidenced by a lease for the one as for the other of them. Your orator is the more inclined to suppose this lease to have been actually designed for lott No. 5 because he has always understood that that lott was held for some time under it by John Rousseau & by others claiming under him. But if it really applies to lott No. 6 & if that lott or any part of it was really ungranted at the time, your orator then requires that the said William Jenny who is required to show by what title he claims the sa⟨me⟩ shoud surrender lott No. 6 to him also.

As a further conclusive evidence that lott No. 5 was appropriated by the survey already mentiond to the particular use of Lord Fairfax your orator humbly states that long after the said appropriation to wit in the year 1773 a certain John Myers obtaind a warrant for 400 acres of vacant land under a general description, 300 acres of which he caused to be surveyd so as to include that quantity of lott No. 5, in the hope that a grant might issue therefor without examination. This survey was assignd to a certain Ignatius Wheeler & was returnd into the office of the late proprietor of the Northern ⟨Neck⟩ where a caveat was enterd against it at the instance of Robert Stephen one of the ⟨agents?⟩ of Lord Fairfax for this cause, that it was within the bounds of his Lordships lott No. 5. In ⟨consequ⟩ence of this discovery the grant was refused; All which will more fully appear by ⟨the⟩ copy of the said warrant & survey with the indorsements thereon which are annexd & referred to.[8] No book was kept by Lord Fairfax in which was enterd his decision in cases of caveat. The issuing of the grant was the only evidence which was deemd necessary to show his determination in such cases, & the refusal of a grant in this instance appears to have been acquiesced under.

Your orator states that long after the death of Lord Fairfax & after the papers of the northern neck had been transferred into the land office of this commonwealth to wit in August 1788 the said Ignatius Wheeler obtaind a patent on these very works which containd evidence of the right of Lord Fairfax & conveyd the land to the defendent William Jenny who has since that time also obtaind a patent under a land office treasury warrant for the remaining hundred acres of the said lott No 5.[9]

Your orator States that the lease to the said John Rousseau has expird as will appear by a copy thereof annexd to the original bill filed in this cause & William Jenny has been for several years in possession thereof. The title to the said lott is in your orator as is stated in his original bill, but the original deed of partition which was executed before the institution of this suit among the purchasers of the estate of Lord Fairfax has been mislaid & was never recorded.[10] This lott however was in the share of your orator & the equitable title is in him tho the legal estate still remains in James M. Marshall to whom the deed of conveyance was made by Denny M. Fairfax the devisee of the late Thomas Lord Fairfax.

Your orator humbly states that this case is within the treaty of peace between the United States & Great Britain and is plainly & expressly within the compromise enterd into between the commonwealth of Virginia & the purchasers of the estate of Denny M. Fairfax, yet the said William Jenny refuses to convey the same to him or to deliver possession thereof. To THE END therefore that the said William Jenny & the said James M. Marshall may be made defendents hereto, & may on oath true answer make to the premises & that the said William Jenny may be decreed to pay the rent which has accrued on the said lott No. 5 leased as aforesaid, during the continuance of the said lease, & the reasonable profits which have accrued since its expiration, & also to convey the same to your orator & that the said James M. Marshall may also be decreed to convey to your orator the title which is in him & that your orator may have all such other releif as is adapted to his ca⟨se.⟩ May it please your Honor &c

[Answer]

The answer in chancery of James M. Marshall to the bill of complaint exhibited against William Jenny & himself in this Honble court by John Marshall.

This respondent admits the partition of property ⟨mentioned in the⟩ bill of the complainant & that land on New Creek was in the portion of the said John Marshall. The deed of partition was never fully recorded & he is entirely willing to convey the land in the bill mentiond to the complainant.[11]

Js. M. MARSHALL

AD, Vi. JM also wrote James M. Marshall's answer below last line of bill and signed his brother's name. Endorsed by JM. Clerk's notations on verso: "spa issued filed 29th Nov. 1803/decree Novr. term/1816." MS torn.

1. For the background to this and similar suits brought by the Marshalls, see Marshall v. Hunter and Pendleton, editorial note (preceding Notice, 15 Sept. 1801). Except for the amended bill, the papers in this suit are filed in the Office of the Clerk, Augusta County Circuit Court, Staunton, Va. The amended bill, which once belonged to this file, was purchased by the Virginia State Library in 1967 from King V. Hostick of Springfield, Ill.

2. JM drew the original bill, which was filed in the High Court of Chancery on 22 June 1799 (Marshall v. Janney).

3. JM consistently misspelled the name of William Janney, a Quaker then residing in Hardy County (now W.Va.). Janney's answer claimed the land under a grant from the commonwealth of Aug. 1788 (answer of William Janney, 22 Aug. 1800, Marshall v. Janney).

4. A copy of the plat of Guy Broadwater's surveys of New Creek lots Nos. 1 through 8 was filed as an exhibit (Marshall v. Janney).

5. By the compromise act of 1796 JM and the other purchasers of the Fairfax estate yielded their claims to the waste and ungranted lands of the former Northern Neck proprietary in return for confirmation of their title to the lands specifically reserved by

Lord Fairfax (Shepherd, *Statutes*, II, 99–73), For the background to this compromise, see *PJM*, II, 140–49; V, 228–33.

6. A copy of the blank deed of 10 Jan. 1752 was filed as an exhibit (Marshall v. Janney).

7. A copy of the lease between Lord Fairfax and John Rousseau of Hampshire County, executed on 31 Aug. 1778, was filed as an exhibit (ibid.). JM's original bill identified Rousseau as one of Lord Fairfax's surveyors.

8. Copies of warrant No. 287, dated 13 Aug. 1773, and the survey returned on this warrant, dated 9 June 1774, were filed as exhibits. The survey is endorsed: "June 14th 1776 Caveat entd. on Information of Jno. Rousseau by Mr. Robt Stephen it being supposed to be within the bounds of his lordships Lot No. 5" (ibid.).

9. The grant from the commonwealth to Ignatius Wheeler was issued on 30 Aug. 1788. Wheeler deeded this land to William Janney on 20 Sept. 1789. Janney obtained a grant from the commonwealth for the remaining hundred acres on 7 Dec. 1789 (ibid.).

10. JM referred to the deed of partition, dated 24 June 1799, between James M. Marshall of the first part, JM of the second part, Rawleigh Colston of the third part, and Charles and William Marshall of the fourth part. Among the lands apportioned to JM by this deed was the New Creek tract of four hundred acres "originally granted by lease to John Rousseau." A copy of this deed, in JM's hand, was filed in the suit papers of Martin v. Moffett, U.S. Cir. Ct., Va., Ended Cases (Restored), 1824, Vi.

11. This suit remained on the docket until 1816. Janney submitted his answer to the amended bill in Sept. 1804. Depositions of witnesses were taken in 1807, 1808, and 1810. In Nov. 1812 the court dismissed the bill as to lot No. 5 and ordered Janney to produce his title papers to lot No. 6. The bill was wholly dismissed in Nov. 1816 on Janney's producing evidence that his title to lot No. 6 derived from Lord Fairfax previous to the Marshalls' purchase (answer of William Janney; depositions of Edward McCarty, John Vandivear and William Vandivear, John Popejoy and Terrance Popejoy, Hannah Baker, John Ravenscroft, and John Sturman, and John Vanmeter and Robert Cockburn; memorandum of proceedings, 9 Nov. 1812; decree, Nov. 1816, Marshall v. Janney).

Owen v. Adams
Opinion
U.S. Circuit Court, Virginia, 7 December 1803

Owen

v

Adams surviving partner
of Hunt & Adams[1]

¶1   In this case the plaintiff who is a London Mercht. offerd in evidence an account taken from his books which commenced in the year 1784 connected with a receipt signd Hunt & Adams for a box deliverd in January 85, & a letter from the same persons dated in June 90 mentioni[n]g a remittance then made in snuff & acknowleging a further balance to remain due in terms which imply that balance to have been by no means inconsiderable.[2] The books from which the account was taken are provd to have been kept by a clerk who is since dead: & the account is provd to be an exact copy from those books. Another witness swears that he has compard the account with the original entries & that it corresponds with them but he does not depose to the handwriting in which those original entries were made.[3]

The plaintiff contends that under these circumstances the account may be submitted to the consideration of the jury. ¶2

This question depends entirely on the law of evidence, &, as no legislative provision has been made for the case, it is supposd to be governd by the rules of the common law. ¶3

The common law on this subject is beleivd to have been laid down with perfect accuracy by Mr. Blackstone in his commentaries vol. 3. p. 368. "So too" says that author, "books of account or shop books are not allowd of themselves to be given in evidence for the owner; but a servant who made the entry may have recourse to them to refresh his memory, & if such servant who was accustomd to make those entries be dead, & his hand be provd the book may be read in evidence."[4] ¶4

This apparently relates to original entries, not only because the principle that the best legal evidence which the nature of the thing affords is directly recognizd by Blackstone while speaking on the same subject, but because the expression that "the servant who made the entries might refer to the book to refresh his memory," plainly designates such a servant, as coud have provd the delivery of the goods. The counsel for the plf.[5] has not controverted this principle of law but has contended that the clerk who is dead in this case was the person by whom the original entries were made. Privately I am inclind to beleive the fact to have been so, but I do not think myself at liberty to deliver that opinion in this place. Exact uniformity of decision ought to be observd & when principles are departed from those which are substituted in their place ought to be so strongly markd as not afterwards to be misunderstood. In this cas⟨e⟩ the term books is usd, & if that term might be understood to mean all the book[s], or the original books of entry in this case, it ought so to be understood in every case, & then the rule woud be completely changd. ¶5

Neither do I think the form of the entries evidence that the original books were kept by the clerk who is dead. ¶6

This essential fact on which the admissibility of the account depends, ought to be plainly stated by the party who woud avail himself of that account. ¶7

Neither do I think the collateral testimony which has been offerd can help the case. That testimony shows the existence of a debt but not its amount. The plaintiff can only be admitted to establish its amount by legal evidence, & to make his books legal evidence he ought to prove that the clerk who made the original entries is dead. It ¶8 woud be as dangerous to admit a plaintiff to establish the amount of a debt by his books as to prove the existence of the debt by the same evidence.

¶9   I therefore felt no doubt when this case was first mentiond, in determining the testimony to be inadmissible, if it was a case of the first impression in this court, & if I coud draw it out of the case of Lewis exr. of Thruston v. Norton.[6]

¶10   A case was referd to as having establishd the admissibility of such testimony but on a reference to the record it appeard that the books from which the copy had been taken were the original books or the books in which the original entries had been made & the clerk who kept them was dead. The terms used were considerd as synonimous with shop or day books, & that decision will be adherd to.

¶11   I had much more difficulty in getting over the case of Lewis v Norton & was at first disposd under the authority of that case to permit the present verdict to stand, altho directly against my own opinion. But upon reflection I think myself obliged to change that opinion & to set aside this verdict. I feel no doubts concerning the law of the case. I have no doubts but that the amount of a debt can only be establishd by testimony which is in itself legal, & that such collateral testimony as will make an account otherwise inadmissible, legal testimony, must apply to the account itself & not merely to general transactions which have no tendency to verify the particular account produced, but woud equally support a claim for 100 or 1000£.

¶12   I think it of the most dangerous tendency to admit such evidence, & as there is a difference between decisions which meerly respect the rules of evidence & those which affect rights; & also between a single decision subject to revision, & a series of decisions which may be considerd as fixing the law of the land; and as it is in my opinion of much importance that exact uniformity shoud be observd in decisions on that testimony which will be requird by the court in order to support a claim on account, which is best to be obtaind by an inflexible observance of the rules establishd by law, & not by deviating occasionally from them on circumstances perpetually varying in slight unimportant degrees; I think it right to adhere to the safe & well understood rules of the common law & shall therefore direct a new trial in this case.[7]

AD, Marshall Judicial Opinions, PPAmP; printed, John W. Brockenbrough, *Reports of Cases Decided by the Honourable John Marshall . . .* , I (Philadelphia, 1837), 72–76. For JM's deletions and interlineations, see Textual Notes below.

1. The parties were Edward Owen, a London merchant, and Ashley Adams, surviving partner of Hunt & Adams. Adams and Charles Hunt, formerly residents of London, had entered into a partnership in 1785 and moved to Williamsburg to set up as

merchants. The principal business of the firm was the manufacture and sale of snuff. The object of this suit, which began in 1802, was to recover an account balance for transactions that took place in the years 1784 and 1785. A jury on 28 Nov. 1803 awarded the plaintiff damages and costs. JM's opinion set aside this verdict and ordered a new trial (advertisement, *Virginia Gazette and Weekly Advertiser* [Richmond], 15 Mar. 1787; agreement of copartnership, 17 Feb. 1785; account current, Edward Owen in account with Hunt & Adams; capias, 2 July 1802; declaration, [Jan. 1803], Owen v. Adams, U.S. Cir. Ct., Va., Ended Cases [Unrestored], 1807, Vi; U.S. Cir. Ct., Va., Ord. Bk. IV, 291, 361, 398).

2. The account filed in the suit states that Hunt & Adams had debits totaling £430 and credits of £97, leaving a balance of £333 as of June 1787. A letter from Hunt & Adams to Owen, dated 28 June 1790, mentions sending a quantity of snuff (655 pounds) and promises to pay the balance of the debt due in a few months (Owen v. Adams).

3. This testimony is in the depositions of Edward Owen, John Stubbs, and James Stead, taken in London in Sept. 1803. Owen stated that the account was a true and correct copy taken from his books of account, which were kept by William Green, since deceased. Stubbs deposed that he knew Green and was acquainted with his handwriting and further that the account of Hunt & Adams entered in Edward Owen's books was in Green's hand. Stead testified that he had carefully examined the account with the original entry in the books and found it to be a true and accurate copy. Attached to these depositions was an affidavit, dated 28 Nov. 1792 and signed by Owen and Green, stating that the account was a true account taken by Green from Edward Owen's books (deposition, 2 Sept. 1803, Owen v. Adams).

4. The quoted passage is from Blackstone's discussion of written evidence (*Commentaries*, III, 367–69).

5. John Wickham represented the plaintiff Owen. Counsel for Adams was George Hay (agreement, 21 Jan. 1804, Owen v. Adams).

6. Lewis, Executor of Thruston, v. Norton, 1 Wash. 76, was decided by the Virginia Court of Appeals in 1792. In that case the claimant's store books, which were proved to be in the handwriting of one of his bookkeepers, then dead, were admitted in evidence at the trial in the lower court. The Court of Appeals affirmed the admission of this evidence, stating that it was settled law "that a book of accounts in the hand writing of, and kept by, a clerk who is since dead, is proper evidence upon those facts being proved."

7. Along with the order for a new trial, general commissions were awarded to take further depositions of witnesses in London. Adams, then living in Petersburg, died in Aug. 1804, and the suit was revived against his executor, William Moore, at the Nov. 1804 term. After the depositions had been taken and returned, the second trial took place at the May 1807 term, the jury returning a verdict awarding the plaintiff damages of $2,880 and costs (death notice, *Virginia Argus* [Richmond], 8 Aug. 1804; U.S. Cir. Ct., Va., Ord. Bk. V, 10; VI, 99, 130).

Textual Notes

Title	ll. 3–4	Adams ↑surviving partner of Hunt & Adams↓
¶ 1	ll. 1–2	plaintiff ↑who is a London Mercht.↓ offerd in evidence ~~his books of account~~ an account
	l. 2	which ~~commences~~ ↑commenced↓ in
	l. 4	January 85, ~~&~~ ↑&↓ a letter
	ll. 4–6	June 90 ~~mentions~~ ↑mentioni[n]g↓ a remittance then made

	in snuff & ~~acknowleges~~ ↑acknowleging↓ a further balance ↑to remain due↓ in terms
l. 7	books ~~on~~ ↑from↓ which
ll. 9–12	dead. ~~Under~~ ↑: & the account is provd to be an exact copy from those books. Another witness swears that he has compard the account with the original entries & that it corresponds with them but he does not depose to the handwriting in which those original entries were made.↓
¶ 3 ll. 1–2	as [*erasure*] ↑no↓ legislative
¶ 5 l. 2	best ↑legal↓ evidence
ll. 3–4	on the ↑same↓ subject
l. 5	to the ~~accoun~~ ↑book to↓ refresh
l. 11	opinion ~~as a Judge~~ ↑in this place.↓ Exact
ll. 16–17	ought ↑so↓ to ~~mean them~~ ↑be understood↓ in every
¶ 6 ll. 1–2	evidence ~~of their being~~ ↑that the↓ original
¶ 8 l. 4	books ↑legal↓ evidence
¶ 9 ll. 1–2	mentiond, ~~on~~ ↑in↓ determining
¶10 l. 2	the ~~ex~~ books
ll. 3–4	taken ~~a~~ ↑were↓ the original books ↑or the books in which the original entries had been made↓ & the
l. 5	dead. ~~The original~~ The terms
¶11 ll. 3–4	stand, ↑altho directly against my own opinion.↓ But
ll. 4–5	to ↑change that opinion & to↓ set
l. 5	doubts ~~about cases~~[?] ↑concerning↓ the
l. 9	testimony, [*erasure*] ↑must↓ apply
¶12 ll. 7–8	court ↑in order to support a claim on account,↓ which
l. 9	law, [*erasure*] ↑& not↓ by

Blane v. Drummond
Opinion
U.S. Circuit Court, Virginia, 9 December 1803

EDITORIAL NOTE

The plaintiff, Thomas Blane, a London merchant, brought an action of debt against William Drummond of Fredericksburg in 1802. His suit was founded on a bond executed in 1793 by John Proudfit to Blane, which Drummond cosigned as surety. Proudfit entered into bond in consequence of an interlocutory decree by the Virginia High Court of Chancery in March 1793 in a suit brought by Proudfit against Blane and two of Blane's debtors in Virginia. The decree ordered Blane's debtors to pay Proudfit, out of Blane's money in their hands, the principal sum of seventeen hundred pounds Virginia currency and interest from August 1790. Proudfit subsequently received payments in August and October 1793. His bond to Blane was in the penal sum of thirty-four hundred pounds, conditioned on Proudfit's abiding by the final decree in his suit against Blane. The High Court of Chancery in June

U.S. CIRCUIT COURT OPINION

The first page of Marshall's autograph opinion in *Blane* v. *Drummond*,
1803. *Courtesy of the American Philosophical Society Library*

1799 confirmed the interlocutory decree of 1793, but Blane appealed to the Court of Appeals and obtained a reversal in May 1802. The Court of Appeals decreed that Proudfit should repay Blane the money received by him under the interlocutory decree of 1793. Blane apparently decided to sue Drummond because Proudfit and his other surety, Fontaine Maury, were insolvent.[1]

The commercial transactions that gave rise to this case are similar to those that produced the case of *Hopkins* v. *Blane*, decided by the Court of Appeals in December 1798, in which Marshall represented Hopkins. At issue was the liability of Blane for certain bills of exchange drawn on him by Alexandria merchant William Hunter, Jr., whom Blane had empowered to purchase cargoes of grain and other articles. The Court of Appeals decreed in both suits that Hunter had drawn the disputed bills in his private capacity rather than as Blane's agent and that the London merchant therefore did not have to pay them.[2]

In the present case Blane was represented by John Wickham, Drummond by George Hay and Daniel Call. At the November 1803 term the defendant entered a special plea that Blane was a bankrupt under Great Britain's statutes and that the assignees appointed in accordance with those laws had the exclusive right to bring suit for the bankrupt's debts. The plaintiff replied specially that the assignees had appointed John Hamilton, the British consul at Norfolk, as their agent to sue in Blane's name for debts owed the plaintiff in America. After the defendant demurred to this special replication, a jury assessed damages for the plaintiff of $9,510.75, but judgment was suspended pending the court's ruling on the demurrer. JM delivered his opinion on 9 December.[3]

1. Capias, 22 Sept. 1802; bond, 15 June 1793; decrees (copies) of the High Court of Chancery, 11 Mar. 1793, and of the Court of Appeals, 3 May 1802; memorandum of Joseph Dykes, 12 May 1803; certificate of Robert Patton, 1 June 1803, Blane v. Drummond, U.S. Cir. Ct., Va., Ended Cases (Unrestored), 1803, Vi; Blane v. Proudfit, 3 Call 207 (1802).

2. *PJM*, V, 534–40; Hopkins v. Blane, 1 Call 361 (1798); Blane v. Proudfit, 3 Call 207 (1802).

3. Plea, replication, and demurrer, Blane v. Drummond; U.S. Cir. Ct., Va., Ord. Bk. IV, 274, 285, 354, 362–63, 406.

Blane
v   } on demurrer
Drummond

¶1   The only question in this case is whether an action at law can be maintaind in this court in the name of a person who has become a bankrupt in a foreign country.

¶2   In support of the action it is contended that bankrupt laws have no positive extra territorial force, & that altho other nations will notice the rights which are vested by them, yet they cannot give a form of action in a foreign country nor entitle a person to maintain an action who by the laws of that country coud not main[tain it?]. From this position it is inferd that altho a foreign court will respect the right of the assignees to money due a bankrupt, yet that money must be sued for according to the forms of the place where the action is brought.

For the defendent it is contended that the right to personal things ¶3 is regulated by the law of the domicil, & not by the law of the place where they happen to be found, & consequently that the right to the effects of a bankrupt wherever they may be, unless the law of the place shall otherwise direct, is vested in those to whom the law of his residence gives it; It is also contended that an action can only be maintaind by him who has the right & that consequently no action can be maintaind in the name of the bankrupt. The law of foreign nations it is said constitutes a part of the law of every nation, so far as to govern foreign contracts & foreign rights.

In examining this proposition that only the person having the right ¶4 can maintain an action it is necessary to be more definite in the terms imployd. If it is intended to say that only the person having the legal right can maintain an action at law the position is perhaps correct, but if it is intended to say that the person not having the equitable right to retain the money sued for cannot maintain an action at law the truth of the proposition cannot be admitted. The common case of a bond not legally assignable, sued for in the name of the obligor[1] for the use of his assignee disproves it[2] (see sep. paper).[3]

The proposition too that the laws of foreign nations become a part ¶5 of the law of every civilizd nation is true to a certain extent. It is true also that generally speaking the rights to personalties are determind by the law of residence & not by the law of the place where the property is found. The right to claim the effects of a deceasd person in foreign countries is generally securd by treaties but the principle woud probably be adopted independent of compact. Whether the same principle extends to rights under bankrupt laws seems not to have been so well settled. But the person having this right according to the laws of a foreign country sues in conformity with the principles of jurisprudence establishd in the country where the suit is brought. If according to those principles any person having the right may maintain an action then it is sufficient to show that the person suing is entitled to the thing claimd by the laws of the domicil. But if those principles oppose any obstacle to the person suing on his original right he must give himself a character which will authorise him to maintain his action.

Thus the hæres factus or natus[4] of a Frenchman claiming personal ¶6 property in England has a complete title & most probably in France where proceedings are according to the forms of the civil law might maintain an action for the property of his testator or intestate: But the forms of jurispi udence established in England require if he woud proceed at common law, that he shoud qualify himself according to the requisites of the common law to maintain his action. He must therefore take out letters of administration. His right to the personal estate gives him a right to administer but does not give him a right of action before administration granted. The right to personal property then may be regulated by the laws of the domicil; but the right of action must be regulated by the law of the court where that action is brought.[5]

¶7   The question then is whether the operation of a bankrupt law can be such as to transfer to the assignees the legal title or the right of action in debts due in a foreign country, or to extinguish the legal title or right of action of the bankrupt. If it effects the one or the other of these objects the present action cannot be maintaind.

¶8   The general proposition that the laws of one nation may give a form of action in the courts of another, or authorise a person to maintain an action who coud not maintain it by the principles of that forum to which he has applied has been already denied. The plainest principles of national law refute such an idea, & it woud be time utterly mispent further to demonstrate its error. A debt therefore which by the laws of Virginia is not assignable cannot be assignd by the laws of any other country so as to enable the assignee to sue in this. The right of property may be changed by those laws but the righ⟨t⟩ of action cannot be given. Debts due by Open account therefore cannot be sued for in the name of the assignees. Yet in the country of the bankrupt the assignees sue in their own name for debts in themselves unassignab⟨le⟩ by any act of the party. This follows from the principle that suits must be prosecuted by virtue of the law of the country where they are instituted & not of that where the claimant resides. This being true the assignment as well as the nature of the debt sued for must conform to that law. Not only must the debt be assignable but it must be assignd according to law.

¶9   Bonds by the laws of Virginia are assignable, but they can only be assignd by the act of the party himself. The declaration must state a legal assignment in order to give the assignee an action. A declaration stating an assignment by virtue of the law of a foreign country woud not be good, for that woud be equally effectual in the case of an unassignable debt. It then only remains to enquire whether if the assignees in this case had declard on an assignment by the bankrupt, they coud have given in evidence the assignment made in conformity with the bankrupt law.

¶10   This woud be by legal inference totally to change the nature of the fact itself, an operation which woud require very plain legal principles for its support. The counsel for the defendent has cited a principle of which I supposd at the time he designd to make this use. It is that every subject is intended to give his assent to an act of Parliament. He did not however so apply it nor coud it be properly so applied for this plain reason that the assent follows the nature of the act & is only an admission that it shall be an act of Parliament not that it is in truth his personal act; nor can such an assent give the act an extraterritorial force, or change the requisites of a law of a foreign country respecting assignments.

The admission then of one of the counsel that an action at law is not maintainable in the name of the assignees was correctly made & it remains to enquire whether such an assignment without transferring a right of action to the assignees has extinguishd that of the bankrupt.   ¶11

Upon principle I cannot percieve any solid ground on which the distinction taken can be maintaind, or on which such extinguishment is to be supported.   ¶12

To deprive a man having a right to sue in a foreign country of that right is giving to the law which woud effect this object an extraterritorial operation which I belcive has never been admitted.   ¶13

In this case it is the less allowable because it woud not be to conform to the intention of the law itself. That intention is one entire thing. The law takes the right out of the bankrupt for the purpose of transferring it to his assignees & unless this transfer can be made the intention of the law cannot be effected.   ¶14

To give a foreign legislative act an extraterritorial operation which woud defeat the intention of the act woud be peculiarly improper.   ¶15

The whole argument in favor of this proposition so far as it is meerly an argument on principle is that only he who has the right to the thing can have the right of action; but this is answerd by saying that the rule is not universally true because nothing is more frequent than suits at law in the name of a person whom equity will compel to deliver over the property to another. The common case of a suit in the name of the assignor of an unassignable paper is sufficient evidence of this position. The right of action distinct in different courts in the same country of course in different countries. The defendent attempts to get over this common case by saying that the common law takes no notice of such assignments, but the council does not recollect that assignments under the bankrupt law must be equally unnoticed by the common law courts of a foreign country, or the assignees woud be permitted to sue in that foreign country.   ¶16

These laws are said to be noticd & the rights they give protected in pursuance of that curtesy which one nation pays to the institutions of   ¶17 another. But this curtesy extends only to the substantial rights of the parties & not to the forms of action; & it woud display itself very ungraciously indeed in denying the foreigner an action in any form.

¶18   The defendent states the bankrupt law to operate by way of contract between the bankrupt & his assees. This is very probably correct, but a contract[6] not being an actual assignment can not divest the contracting party of the legal right of action which was vested in him.

¶19   The situation of a right without a remedy is so unusual that the counsel for the defendent has thought it necessary to state several cases showing that it may exist. The cases put are those of a release of all actions, of an alien, of an outlaw & of a person excommunicated.

¶20   That it is within the compass of the legislative power of any country to deprive a person having a right, of a particular remedy or of any remedy whatever within its own territory is not questiond. But the cases put are understood to apply to that before the court very differently from the manner in which they have been applied.

¶21   In the cases put the law operates according to its intention. In the case at bar the law woud not so operate. But what is of more importance is, that in the cases put so far as they coud occur in a foreign country the party might sue in his own name.

¶22   It is a settled principle that disabilities to sue affect the party only in the courts of the country imposing them. They do not like natural defects adhere to the person & pass with it to distant regions, but fall off when he travels out of the jurisdiction which has imposd them. I beleive no man doubts that a person excommunicated, or outlawd in a foreign country might maintain a personal action in this.

¶23   The argument that the act operates by way of estoppel cannot be admitted without agreeing that a foreign law has a positive operation & at the same time giving it an operation contrary to its intention.

¶24   Upon principle then I shoud feel not much difficulty in saying that the suit is maintainable in the name of the bankrupt. —— Convenience.

¶25   The cases cited do not change this opinion. They only support principles which have been already considerd & which do not defeat the action. The only circumstance which excited doubt in my mind was the practice of suing in chancery in the names of the assignees in cases of foreign bankruptcy. I thought it strange that no case shoud have occurd where a suit was instituted in the name of the bankrupt himself if such a suit was thot maintainable—I still think so—but this accounted for perhaps by a general disinclination to use the name, by the authority of the chancellor over bankrupt cases, by the point never having been doubted.[7]

AD, Marshall Judicial Opinions, PPAmP; printed, John W. Brockenbrough, *Reports of Cases Decided by the Honourable John Marshall . . .* , I (Philadelphia, 1837), 62–71. For JM's deletions and interlineations, see Textual Notes below.

1. JM should have written "obligee."

2. Bonds for the payment of money, as distinct from bonds with a collateral condition, had been legally assignable in Virginia since 1705, that is, the assignee of such a bond was permitted to bring an action for the recovery of the debt in his own name. In 1795 the legislature extended assignability to all bonds, bills, and promissory notes. For a JM case dealing with bonds and their assignability, see *PJM*, V, 201–14.

3. The following two paragraphs are written on a separate sheet, which JM intended to be inserted at this point.

4. *Hæres factus* and *hæres natus* are terms of the civil law, the former meaning the heir made by will, the latter the born heir or heir at law.

5. At the end of this inserted passage, JM repeated the first part of the next sentence ("The question then is whether the operation of the") in order to indicate where he wished it to be inserted.

6. Following this word JM made a deletion but failed to strike through "to."

7. The court overruled the demurrer and entered judgment for the plaintiff according to the jury verdict of the same day. Execution for the damages and costs was levied on 26 Dec. 1803, which Drummond discharged by payment on 4 Jan. 1804 (U.S. Cir. Ct., Va., Ord. Bk. IV, 406; fieri facias, 20 Dec. 1803, Blane v. Drummond).

By paying the debt Drummond, as surety on the bond, could sue for recovery by summary motion against either Proudfit, the principal obligor, or Maury, the other surety (*PJM*, V, 398 n. 5).

Textual Notes

¶ 1 ll. 1-2   whether ↑an action at law can be maintaind in this court in the name of↓ a person

¶ 2 ll. 1-2   no ↑positive↓ extra territorial

ll. 4–5   action ~~not~~ in a foreign country ~~& consequent~~ ↑nor entitle a person to maintain an action who by the laws of that country coud not main[tain it?]. ↓ From

¶ 3 ll. 1–2   that ↑the right to↓ personal things ~~are~~ ↑is↓ regulated

l. 3   the ~~legal~~ right

ll. 8–10   bankrupt. ~~It is not alledgd that a suit is maintainab(le) at law by the assignees, but that such suit is not maintainable by the bankrupt himself.~~ ↑The law of foreign nations it is said constitutes a part of the law of every nation, so far as to govern foreign contracts & foreign rights.↓

¶ 4 l. 1   that [erasure] ↑only↓ the person

l. 2   maintain [erasure] ↑an↓ action

l. 4   the ~~pers~~ ↑position↓ is

ll. 5–6   that the ~~legal right to sue but not~~ ↑person not having↓ the equitable right to retain ↑the money sued for↓ cannot

ll. 6–7   the ~~p~~ ↑truth↓ of

l. 7   admitted. [erasure] ↑The↓ common

¶ 5 l. 1   laws of ~~all~~ ↑foreign↓ nations

ll. 4–5   where the ~~party~~ property is found. ~~This~~ ↑The↓ right

l. 8   to ~~bankrup~~ rights

l. 14   of the ~~country where the person~~ [domicil.↓] But

¶ 6   l. 1 beg.   ~~Thus those who are entitled~~ Thus

l. 2   title ↑& most probably in↓ in France

l. 7   the ~~laws of that country~~ ↑requisites of the common law↓ to maintain [erasure] ↑his↓ action.

l. 10   to ↑personal↓ property

l. 11   be ~~acquird~~ ↑regulated↓ by the laws of ~~foreign nations~~ ↑the domicil; but↓ the right

¶ 7   ll. 2–3   transfer ↑to the assignees↓ the legal title ~~to the assignees, or to~~ ↑or the right of action ~~of~~ in debts↓ due

ll. 3–4   title ↑or right of action↓ of

¶ 8   l. 1 beg.   ~~The counsel for the defendent does not contend for the first, yet it appears to me to be proper to examine the question on principle, as the reasoning which leads to a decision on it, will be found not inapplicable to the point for which he does contend.~~ The general

l. 1   that ↑the laws of↓ one

ll. 3–4   not ~~otherwise~~ maintain it ~~need not be examind.~~ ↑by the principles of that forum to which he has applied has been already denied.↓ The

l. 5   & ~~as~~ ↑it↓ woud

l. 6   mispent ↑further↓ to

ll. 8–9   of ~~England.~~ any other country ↑so as to enable the assignee to sue in this.↓ The ↑right of↓ property

ll. 10–11   given. ↑Debts due by↓ Open ~~accounts~~ ↑account↓ therefore

l. 11   assignees ~~but[?]~~ ↑.↓ ~~This being obvious it follows~~ Yet

ll. 12–14   sue ↑in their own name↓ for debts ~~due by simple contract in their own name.~~ ↑in themselves unassignab⟨le⟩ by any act of the party.↓ This ~~being admitted it~~ follows ↑from the principle↓ that

l. 14   prosecuted ~~was~~ by

ll. 15–16   where the ~~creditor~~ ↑claimant↓ resides. This ~~as~~ ↑being↓ true

¶ 9   l. 6   It ↑then↓ only remains to enquire ~~then~~ whether

¶10   l. 1   change ↑the nature of↓ the

ll. 3–4   cited a ~~case~~ ↑principle↓ of

l. 4   he ~~proposd~~ ↑designd↓ to

l. 5   is ~~supposd~~ ↑intended↓ to

l. 6   be ↑properly↓ so

l. 9   such an ~~act~~ ↑assent↓ give

¶11   l. 1   of ↑one of the↓ counsel

l. 3   whether ↑such↓ an

¶12   ll. 1–2   ground ↑on which the distinction taken can be maintaind, or↓ on

¶13   ll. 2–3   extraterritorial ~~jurisdiction~~ ↑operation↓ which

¶14   ll. 2–3   thing. ~~It~~ ↑The law↓ takes

l. 5   effected. ~~The disability to sue~~

¶15   l. 1   foreign ~~act of Pa~~ ↑legislative act↓ an

¶16 ll. 2–3   right ~~can maintain an action~~ ↑to the thing can have the right of action;↓ but

ll. 8–10   position. ↑The right of action distinct in different courts in the same country of course in different countries.↓ The ~~counsel~~ ↑defendent↓ attempts

l. 10   this ~~poin~~ common

l. 13   by the ↑common law↓ courts

¶17 l. 2   that ~~comité~~ ↑curtesy↓ which

l. 3   But ~~according to the counsels own showing~~ this ~~comité~~ ↑curtesy↓ extends

l. 5   ungraciously ↑indeed↓ in denying ~~to~~ the

¶18 l. 2   assees. ~~If Dfs~~[?] ↑This↓ is

l. 3   contract to ~~pe transfer~~ not

l. 4   legal ↑right of↓ action

¶19 l. 2   has ↑thought it necessary to↓ ~~stated~~ several

¶20 ll. 2–3   any remedy ↑whatever↓ within

ll. 3–4   the ~~application of the~~ [*erasure*] cases put ~~to that~~ are

¶22 l. 3   defects [*erasure*] adhere

l. 4   he ~~passes~~ ↑travels out of↓ the

¶25 l. 10   doubted. ~~& not~~[?]

The Life of George Washington

EDITORIAL NOTE

George Washington bequeathed all his papers, concerning both his civil and military administrations as well as his private affairs, to his nephew Bushrod Washington.[1] Almost immediately following Washington's death in December 1799, Bushrod formed plans for publishing a biography of the general based on his papers. At first Bushrod intended that he and Tobias Lear collaborate in its preparation, but in the winter and spring of 1800, Bushrod looked elsewhere for an author. He informed Lear, "'I cannot help thinking that Genl. Marshall may be induced to undertake the writing of the history, and I write to him by this post. . . . I am extremely anxious to see this work commenced & finished as well upon your account as my own . . . as pecuniary considerations are less operative with me than many others I cannot be otherwise than very nice in selecting a proper person to be the author.'"[2]

Exactly when Marshall agreed to write the *Life* is not clear. Bushrod Washington asserted to one prospective publisher on 11 April 1800 that he had consulted "With Genl Marshall who is to write the history . . . when I saw him in Feby last respecting the proposition which you and others had made to purchase the Copy right." Marshall certainly had consented by the autumn of 1800, at which time Bushrod described him as "the person who I thought could best assist in doing full Justice to the Subject."[3] In the following six years, Marshall wrote a five-volume biography of George Washington, totaling over thirty-two hundred pages in print and encompassing a history of the British colonies ("Introduction" in volume I), the Revolution (volumes II–IV), and the first decade of government under the Constitution (volume V).

Influencing Marshall in his decision to undertake the project were filiopietistic and patriotic sentiments. He revered Washington and believed "the life of the favourite Son of America" held "the deepest interest" for his fellow countrymen. Washington's pivotal role in winning independence and then establishing an effective national government made his history doubly significant. While illuminating his illustrious character, his story also was the story of the nation he was so instrumental in founding. As background to this, Marshall wrote the introductory volume to provide an understanding of "the genius" of the people Washington led to victory. A second reason, intertwined with the first, was Marshall's intention to present the "truth" about Washington's conduct. In making "a faithful representation" of Washington and his era, Marshall may not have meant to produce a partisan history of the period, but his Federalist convictions necessarily imbued the Life.[4]

Another motive for agreeing to do the biography was financial exigencies. Marshall's partnership in a syndicate buying the Fairfax manor lands entailed a continuing commitment of funds. Purchase of Leeds Manor was not finally consummated until October 1806. As completion of that deal approached, his need for returns from sales of the Life increased. Bushrod Washington urged the publisher to make further remittances, which would "be highly acceptable, particularly to Mr Marshall, whose arrangements I know are bottomed upon the expectation of the money he is to receive from you."[5]

The remunerative aspects of publishing figured prominently in both Bushrod's and Marshall's consideration. Rather than attempt to sell the volumes themselves, they determined to sell the copyright, "if it can be done upon proper terms." Of the applications received for printing the work, Washington gave Caleb P. Wayne's "every possible respect." Wayne was the Federalist editor of the Gazette of the United States in Philadelphia, and Bushrod and Marshall probably favored him for his politics. Nevertheless, Bushrod drew out negotiations with Wayne for over two years. In part, the delay owed to Washington and Marshall's initial determination to wait until the work was ready to go to press before concluding a contract. For the rest, they had high expectations of their endeavor's profitability.[6]

Projecting four or five volumes of four to five hundred pages each and thirty thousand subscribers, they wanted a total of $150,000 (at a dollar per volume) and claimed they would not accept less than $100,000 for the U.S. copyright. Wayne found their calculations unreasonable, and he and Washington haggled over terms until they finally reached an agreement on 22 September 1802. Finding a purchaser for the European copyright took longer, and Washington did not conclude arrangements for publication in England until early 1804. He sold a copy of the manuscript for $2,000 to John Morgan in Philadelphia, who conveyed it to the publisher Richard Phillips in London. Phillips published volumes of the Life in England at the same time as they appeared in the United States.[7]

Under his contract with Washington, Wayne received the U.S. copyright and the right to sell the history in the western hemisphere. For this privilege, he was to pay one dollar for every volume subscribed to or sold, for duration of the copyright. Payment was due on the first three volumes upon publication of the third and on the remaining volumes as they appeared. Delivery of manuscript copies was to occur simultaneously to the American and European proprietors of the publication rights. Wayne committed to collecting subscriptions and to promoting sales throughout America. Washington limited the price to no more than three dollars per volume in boards.[8]

Wayne published "Proposals" for the work as soon as he concluded his contract with Washington. To underwrite this publishing venture, Wayne sold the biography by subscription. He required that the price of one volume, three dollars, be paid in advance and that the advance be continued with the appearance of each volume. Subscription publishing had become a common mode of selling books in the eighteenth century, and Wayne took advantage of it not only to raise funds but to attain the widest possible distribution. Originally, Wayne meant to tour major towns in the United States to collect subscriptions himself, but he abandoned this plan and authorized postmasters throughout the country to accept subscribers' names and collect the money. In addition to these twelve hundred agents, Wayne employed two active salesmen to canvass towns and countryside. Beginning at the end of 1802, Mason Locke Weems traveled through the South peddling the *Life*. John Ormrod, a printer from Philadelphia, covered the North. Weems worked on consignment, receiving one volume for every ten he sold and one dollar per diem allowance. Presumably, Ormrod agreed to similar conditions.[9]

A year after advertising, Wayne had about four thousand subscribers. By 1807, when the last volume appeared along with the *Maps*, there were over seven thousand. (These numbers do not include direct sales.) At the back of the atlas was published a list of the subscribers arranged geographically. Many prominent men of the day signed up for a set of the *Life*, both Federalists and Republicans, including John Adams, Thomas Jefferson, James Madison, and Marshall himself. Publishing subscription lists was a way of promoting sales, and Wayne advertised at the outset that purchasers' names would be printed. Although the number of subscriptions fell far short of Marshall and Washington's imagining and did not even match Wayne's goal of fifteen thousand, seven thousand was a respectable number. David Ramsay sold fewer than sixteen hundred copies of his *History of the American Revolution* in ten years. Press runs of various books printed by the successful Philadelphia publisher Mathew Carey in the same period did not equal that of the *Life*, the first printing of which totaled about seventy-three hundred.[10]

Washington and Wayne were both disappointed by the first year's return of subscriptions. Washington blamed it on the use of postal agents. "Being in general (I believe) democrats," he asked Wayne, "Are you sure they will feel a disposition to advance the work?" Washington declared he "would not give one honest *soliciting* agent, for 1250 quiescint postmasters." Wayne attributed the lag in subscriptions to other causes. The price of the volumes was too high; even more, procrastination in their appearance discouraged prospective buyers. Uncertainty had dampened sales. Worse, some were demanding their money back. The public was dissatisfied with the delay.[11]

From the beginning, Washington and Marshall were overly optimistic about the time required to write the biography. Marshall began volume I sometime in the spring or summer of 1801. Near the end of that year, Bushrod complained of "the difficulties which have occurred to embarrass all my efforts to hasten this work. They have been such as I could not remove nor in any manner control." He predicted then that the *Life* would be done at the end of 1802; in his contract with Wayne in September 1802, he supposed it would "be compleated in less than two years." Wayne's 1802 advertisement informed the public that the *Life* was "in considerable forwardness" and would be ready for the press early next year.[12]

By the summer of 1803 Washington had to inform Wayne that only the first volume would be ready at year's end. Apologizing for the delay, Washington insisted it was "unavoidable, and were the subscribers still more clamorous than they are, the work could not go on faster. If they had any conception of the labour & time required to examine many trunks of papers, they might perhaps be more considerate, tho' of this I should doubt." Marshall could not "carry on the work with so much rapidity" as was wished; volumes II and III would not be done until the spring and summer of 1804, respectively. After promising volume IV for September 1804, Marshall did not get it off to Wayne until the end of February 1805. In March he confessed to Wayne that he had not yet begun the fifth and final volume and that it would not be ready for another twelve months. Wayne received it in July 1806 and published it in the spring of 1807.[13]

As Marshall's writing of the work became protracted and Wayne's publication costs rose, Wayne came to rue the contract's terms. Wayne played the traditional role of combined publisher-printer-bookseller in producing the *Life*. In preparation for publishing volume I, he rented a house and hired printers in the early fall of 1803. When in January he was still waiting to proceed, the exasperated man declared, "Happy indeed shall I be when I can announce this work in the Press. Of idleness, & paying men, house rent &c. without doing any thing, I am sick." This delay cost him more than two thousand dollars, but worse was the length of the manuscript. Their agreement was premised on volumes under five hundred pages. Wayne claimed that the first volume would exceed eight hundred. Complaint of each volume's excessive length became a familiar refrain. By the time he received the third, he told Washington that "Mr. Marshall will ruin me by making the Vols. so large." Expenses for the first two exceeded his calculations by fifteen hundred dollars, all because of "the extra matter." To recoup his losses, on more than one occasion he proposed revising the contract. In the end, though, he completed publication without renegotiating.[14]

Bushrod defended Marshall, "for unless he had types & the skill of the printer, it is impossible that he can know when he has written too much or too little for a volume. Afraid of falling short of your engagements to the publick he has generally gone too far beyond it." Composition of the *Life* caused Marshall consternation from beginning to end. The problem of prolixity plagued him. For the first three volumes, he had Wayne juggle chapters and notes, transferring concluding chapters to the beginning of the next volume and consigning extraneous material to appendices. But with volumes IV and V he recognized the necessity of cutting the manuscripts before he even sent them to Wayne, reducing each "to a proper size." On the last he spent time "expunging about one third of it."[15]

He quickly came to regret having devoted volume I to a general history of the North American colonies. The Revolution consumed the next three volumes, so that when he reached Washington's presidency in the fifth, he had run out of space. The public did not receive Marshall's "Introduction" well either, and even Marshall recognized it as a patchwork of passages lifted from published sources. Not a word of General Washington appeared until volume II, which disappointed readers already frustrated by the long delay. Republican reviewers were quick to criticize the author, commenting that "whatever may be the professional talents of Chief-Justice Marshall, it is feared that, as an historian, he will add nothing to our literary reputation as a nation." Although Federalist editors defended volume I, Marshall was "mortified beyond measure to find that it has been so carelessly written. Its inelegancies are more numerous than I had supposed coud have appeared in it."[16]

Chagrined as well by the printed results of his efforts in volume II, Marshall was not pleased until the fourth volume, which he thought "much less inaccurate than those which preceded it, as I have bestowed more attention on the style than was given to them." He had learned by sad experience "that under the pressure of constant application the spring of the mind loses its elasticity." Although all the volumes took him longer to finish than he anticipated, Marshall worked under strict time constraints. Writing under the demands of public expectations and Wayne's deadlines, Marshall also had to fit his composition of the *Life* into his schedule as a justice on the Supreme Court and the Virginia and North Carolina circuit courts. He wrote only while he was in Richmond, and that meant he had at most five or six months out of each year to devote to his researches and writing, except for 1802 and 1803, when he completed volumes I through III. Almost every summer he went on a trip to the mountains of Virginia to escape the hot weather and to attend to his Fairfax land business. During those vacations he corrected proofs of volumes in print but did not proceed on the work.[17]

When Marshall finished writing each volume, his job was not done. He turned over his manuscript to hired copyists in Richmond, who made two fair copies, one for Caleb Wayne and one for the English publisher. Marshall found it necessary to supervise the copyists, who proved to be "very incorrect" and "idle" in his absence. While he was in the mountains in the summer of 1804, they quit, which contributed to the delay in preparing volume IV for the publishers. Marshall reviewed the copyists' work, making corrections and, in the case of the last two volumes, considerable reductions in the text. Bushrod Washington also went over each volume and prepared tables of contents. On the last three, Washington worked in conjunction with Marshall at Richmond or Washington. In spite of their efforts, Marshall enjoined Wayne to "amend any obvious impropriety" and "inaccuracies" in punctuation, paragraphing, and spelling. Provoked by the assumption that he would clean up poorly edited copy, Wayne suggested to Marshall in future "that your orders to me shall be to *'adhere strictly in every particular to the manuscript.'"* This re proof was ineffectual, and Marshall continued to send his copies with instructions to Wayne to put right what was wrong or inconsistent.[18]

Inevitably, Marshall discovered errors in print that he had not noticed in the manuscript. He labored under a misconception that his corrections on proof sheets would be incorporated into the volumes before final publication. Once disabused of that notion, he and Wayne purposed putting out a second edition with Marshall's revisions before the first was fairly under way. Marshall eagerly embraced this proposal, but as the summer progressed, they postponed plans for a second edition and ultimately deferred the idea to an indeterminate future time. By mid-September, though, Wayne discovered he did not have enough copies to supply all subscribers and would have to re-print volumes I and II. Piqued by the negative reception of volume I, Marshall seized the opportunity to get his alterations on the proof sheets into a second impression, and he devoted the fall and winter to making further changes. Wayne published a second, corrected, impression of volumes I through III of the *Life* during the first part of 1805.[19]

So numerous and detailed were Marshall's revisions that pages do not match in the two impressions from beginning to end in the first three volumes. Almost certainly, the second impression was a second edition rather than impression.[20] Wayne must have distributed and reset type for the corrected volumes, and he probably distributed and reused type as he printed off sheets in the first impression, as was normal practice in the hand-press period. Generally, at that time each impression tended to be a new edition, that is, a new printing where over half—or all—of the type has been reset. Indeed, Wayne seems to have used the two terms interchangeably in his correspondence with Marshall.[21]

Marshall in his own mind distinguished between the two. Once Wayne and he had abandoned the idea of a "second edition," he referred to the 1805 impression as "revised" or "corrected" copies of the first edition. In spite of the fact that Marshall had made extensive alterations, he did not consider these to amount to the careful reading and revision that he wished to make for a second edition. He held on to the hope that all the copies of both impressions would sell out and afford him the opportunity to perfect his work. This did not occur until much later, when in 1832 James Crissy of Philadelphia published a two-volume "second edition, revised and corrected by the author."[22] That set omitted volume I, revised by Marshall as *A History of the Colonies Planted by the English on the Continent of North America, from Their Settlement, to the Commencement of That War Which Terminated in Their Independence,* which Abraham Small of Philadelphia published separately in 1824. To simplify matters here, the second edition of 1805 will be called the second impression, which Marshall definitely preferred over the first. He considered it more accurate and stipulated that only sets of the revised volumes be sent to members of his family, the Whig Society, former President John Adams, and himself.[23]

Stung by criticisms of the introductory volume, Marshall recognized that "whatever might have been the execution, the work woud have experienced unmerited censure." Knowing that his authorship would evoke political recrimination, he had been reluctant to allow his name on the title page and had agreed only at the insistence of Wayne and Washington. But word that Marshall was to write the *Life* preceded publication, and many people assumed it would be a Federalist propaganda tract. As early as 1802 Republican rumors, fed by President Jefferson's apprehension, circulated that Marshall meant to publish the *Life* in time to influence the 1804 election. So concerned was Jefferson that he gathered together pertinent documents covering his years as secretary of state in Washington's administration. Jefferson intended to use them to repudiate what he anticipated Marshall's interpretation would be. As only volumes I and II, barely getting into the Revolution, appeared by the fall of 1804, Jefferson's fears were not immediately realized. Upon publication of volume IV in 1805, completing Washington's military career, the Republican press suggested that Marshall stop and allow later, impartial historians to write the events of the 1790s. Ignoring the advice, Marshall persisted with volume V, but when he was done, he confessed, "I have reason to fear that the imprudent task I have just executed will draw upon me a degree of odium & calumny which I might perhaps otherwise have escaped."[24]

Federalist reviewers defended Marshall "as a SCHOLAR, PATRIOT, and STATESMAN. . . . He owed the cause of truth, and the persecuted sages of his country much, in his fifth volume, and he has discharged the obligation." His was "not the pen of a partizen" and his only crime was delineating "that faction which now triumphs, from its birth; and Mr. Jefferson will need no monument to transmit his name, or his *honest patriotism* to posterity." Jefferson did not relinquish his intention of having a Republican history written to counteract Marshall's work. Having proposed such a project to Joel Barlow in 1802, Jefferson promised to send him memoranda, including notes on volume V, in 1809. No such history ever appeared, but in 1818 Jefferson wrote "Explanations" to the three volumes of documents he had collected to rebut Marshall. In this long prefatory note he excoriated the author of the *Life* for culling from George Washington's papers a history "as different from what Genl. Washington would have offered, as was the candor of the two characters." He charged Marshall with "abuse of these materials" to satisfy his "party feelings."[25]

Marshall did make liberal use of Washington's manuscripts for volumes II through V, quoting so extensively from his letters that the *Life* may be considered as a first, selected edition of Washington's papers.[26] Tobias Lear forwarded a trunk containing Washington materials to Marshall in December 1800; in early fall 1801 Bushrod Washington shipped more to Marshall; and at the end of 1804 Marshall received papers relating to the presidential years.[27] For the first volume on the colonies, though, Marshall used the standard printed histories of the day, from which he incorporated whole passages into his book.[28] Not until the spring of 1802 did Marshall begin perusing Washington's papers. To supplement the information contained in them, he and Bushrod Washington sent out inquiries to Revolutionary War veterans for details of various campaigns.[29] The *Life* is contemporary history, based on eyewitness accounts, including Marshall's own. Although much of it is ill digested, volumes II through IV on the Revolution particularly contain vivid descriptions of events and battles.[30] Marshall encountered the greatest difficulty in writing the last volume on Washington's administration and the attendant political divisions. Besides the president's manuscripts, he relied on newspapers for congressional debates, legislation, official communications, and party editorials. To double-check his own impressions of certain incidents he consulted former members of the executive.[31]

Marshall experienced the perils as well as benefits of publishing a history of his own time. As the volumes appeared, he received corrections, additional information, demands for special mention or suppression from actors in the events he narrated. Some suggestions he accepted gratefully and incorporated into the second impression; to others he gave a more guarded response. In errors of omission, Marshall wished not to be "unjust," but where "the incorrectness consists only in the omission of minute circumstances, there is no occasion for being more particular." A complaint from John Dickinson caused Marshall to correct his mistake in wrongly attributing the authorship of a 1774 address to the king by Dickinson to Richard Henry Lee.[32]

On the question of including names in a negative context, he and Bushrod Washington tried to avoid incriminating individuals by directly naming them. In opposition to Wayne's wish to do so, for "the Public expect names," Washington demurred that "this is seldom done in history during the lives of the persons concerned, unless in party works." The cause of their perplexity was the Conway Cabal, in which among others Benjamin Rush was implicated. When Rush heard that a communication of his criticizing General Washington would appear in volume III, he fired off letters to both Marshall and Bushrod, protesting his innocence and asking that relevant portions of the correspondence be deleted. Under pressure, the two men acquiesced in Rush's request. Wayne objected, arguing that they should let the record stand, for "the real enemies & the real friends of Gen. W. ought now to be known."[33]

Marshall's primary goal in writing the *Life* was to portray Washington as a noble character and primary mover in founding the American nation. John Adams assured Marshall that he would achieve in his biography "a more glorious and durable Memorial of your Hero, than a Mausoleum would have been." In elevating Washington so high, Marshall made Washington's accomplishments less accessible than if he had embedded him squarely in the human drama of which he was a part. The *Life* helped set the mold for idealization of George Washington as the great republican leader. But Marshall's five volumes are more than an encomium; he provided readers in the new nation with the first comprehensive history of their origins, Revolution, and political foundations.[34]

1. Last Will and Testament, 9 July 1799 (Fitzpatrick, ed., *Writings of Washington*, XXXVII, 284).

2. See Lear to JM, 12 Dec. 1800 and n. 4; Bushrod Washington to Lear, 13 June 1800 ([extract], Sotheby Parke Bernet Auction Catalog, 28 Apr. 1981, item #179). In Feb. 1800 Washington let it be known that he intended to publish a history of George Washington from his papers and was about to select "a fit character" (Washington to

Jedidiah Morse, 18 Feb. 1800 [Lawrence B. Custer, "Bushrod Washington and John Marshall: A Preliminary Inquiry," *American Journal of Legal History*, IV (1960), 48]; *Columbian Mirror and Alexandria Gazette*, 27 Feb. 1800).

3. Washington to Caleb P. Wayne, 11 Apr., 18 Sept. 1800, Dreer Collection, PHi; Wayne to JM, 3 Oct. 1800 (*PJM*, IV, 314).

4. See Preface, [ante 22 Dec. 1803]; Arthur H. Shaffer, *The Politics of History: Writing the History of the American Revolution, 1783–1815* (Chicago, 1975), 151–59; William Raymond Smith, *History as Argument: Three Patriot Historians of the American Revolution* (The Hague and Paris, 1966), 175, 186–204.

5. Articles of Agreement, 11 Sept. 1801 and n. 3; App. IV, The Sale of South Branch Manor; Washington to Wayne, 25 Dec. 1804; see also Washington to Wayne, 11 Dec. 1804, 15 Jan., 22 Feb., 9 June 1805, 1 Apr., 29 June 1806, Dreer Collection, PHi.

6. Washington to Wayne, 18 Sept. 1800, 10 June 1801; see Washington-Wayne correspondence, 1800–1802, Dreer Collection, PHi. Wayne turned over the *Gazette of the U.S.* to Enos Bronson in Nov. 1801. Wayne had become involved in legal controversy with William Duane, editor of the Republican newspaper, the Philadelphia *Aurora* (Burton Alva Konkle, "Enos Bronson, 1774–1823," *PMHB*, LVII [1933], 356; *Washington Federalist*, 16 Dec. 1801).

7. Washington to Wayne, 11 Dec. 1801, 22 Jan., 2 Apr., 9 May 1802, 11 Feb., 12 Aug., 18 Dec., 22 Dec. 1803, 9 Jan. 1804; Wayne to Washington, 17 Mar. 1802, 17 Feb., 29 Aug., 12 Sept., 2 Dec. 1803, 8 Sept. 1804; articles of agreement between Bushrod Washington and Caleb P. Wayne, 22 Sept. 1802, Dreer Collection, PHi; JM to Wayne, 23 [22] Dec. 1803 and n. 6; see Phillips's advertisement, 3–5 May 1804, *London Chronicle*, German, Dutch, and French translations of the *Life* also were published between 1805 and 1809 (W. S. Baker, *Bibliotheca Washingtoniana: A Descriptive List of the Biographies and Biographical Sketches of George Washington* [Philadelphia, 1889], 20–25, 28–29).

8. Articles of agreement, 22 Sept. 1802, Dreer Collection, PHi.

9. *Philadelphia Gazette & Daily Advertiser*, 22 Sept. 1802; Skeel, *Weems*, I, 316 n. 4; Weems to Wayne, 22 Dec. 1802, 12 Aug. 1803, 15 Feb., 12 Apr. 1804 (Ibid., II, 258, 270, 292, 294–95 and n. 2); Wayne to Washington, 17 Feb. 1803, Dreer Collection, PHi; JM to Henry Potter, [ca. 10 Jan. 1804] and n. 2; Beveridge, *Life of Marshall*, III, 235; see John Tebbel, *A History of Book Publishing in the United States*, I: *The Creation of an Industry, 1620–1865* (New York and London, 1972), 114–15, 158–59; Cathy N. Davidson, *Revolution and the Word: The Rise of the Novel in America* (New York and Oxford, 1986), 15–27; James Gilreath, "American Book Distribution," in *Needs and Opportunities in the History of the Book: America, 1639–1876*, ed. by David D. Hall and John B. Hench (Worcester, Mass., 1987), 137–38.

10. Beveridge, *Life of Marshall*, III, 235; Washington to Wayne, 22 Sept. 1806, Dreer Collection, PHi; *Maps*, 1–22 passim; *Philadelphia Gazette & Daily Advertiser*, 22 Sept. 1802; Rollo G. Silver, *The American Printer, 1787–1825* (Charlottesville, Va., 1967), 98, 173–74; Wayne to JM, 20 Aug. 1804.

11. Washington to Wayne, 1 Mar., 23 Mar., 24 Nov. 1803; Wayne to Washington, 27 Nov. 1803, Dreer Collection, PHi; Beveridge, *Life of Marshall*, III, 235–56. As early as the summer of 1800, the press carried notices that an author was engaged in writing Washington's biography and would complete the work expeditiously (*Va. Argus*, 29 Aug. 1800; Baker, *Bibliotheca Washingtoniana*, 21n; *Washington Federalist*, 27 Mar. 1802).

12. Wayne to Washington, 1 June 1801; Washington to Wayne, 10 June, 21 Nov., 11 Dec. 1801; articles of agreement, 22 Sept. 1802, Dreer Collection, PHi; *Philadelphia Gazette & Daily Advertiser*, 22 Sept. 1802.

13. Washington to Wayne, 12 Aug., 18 Dec. 1803, Dreer Collection, PHi; JM to Wayne, 6 June, 11 June, 3 Sept., 6 Sept. 1804, 19 Feb., 27 Feb., 19 Oct. 1805, 27 June 1806 and n. 2.

14. Tebbel, *History of Book Publishing*, I, 9–1, 110 and II., 148–49; Silver, *American Printer*, 97, 106; Davidson, *Revolution and the Word*, 15, 19; Wayne to Washington, 12 Sept., 27 Nov., 31 Dec. 1803, 16 Jan., 19 Aug. 1804; Washington to Wayne, 24 Nov., 18 Dec. 1803, 18 July 1804, 2 Jan. 1807, Dreer Collection, PHi; Wayne to JM, 20 Aug. 1804; Beveridge, *Life of Marshall*, III, 236. Charging the same price, Wayne did put out a cheaper edition for new subscribers in 1805 (Weems to Wayne, 25 Jan. 1805 [Skeel, *Weems*, II, 311–12]; see App. V; JM to Wayne, 10 Jan. 1805 and n. 2).

15. Washington to Wayne, 26 Aug. 1804, Dreer Collection, PHi; Wayne to JM, 31 Dec. 1803–2 Jan. [1804], 22 Aug., 16 Sept. 1804; JM to Thomas Marshall, Jr., 23 Dec. 1803; JM to Washington, [20] Apr. 1804; JM to Wayne, 23 [22] Dec. 1803, 10 Jan., 3 Sept., 6 Sept. 1804, 19 Feb. 1805, 27 June 1806.

16. See Preface, [ante 22 Dec. 1803]; JM to Wayne, 20 July 1804 and nn. 2, 3, 10 Aug., 3 Sept. 1804, 29 June 1805; Wayne to JM, 25 July 1804 and n. 2, 20 Aug. 1804 and nn. 5, 6; *American Citizen* (New York), 15 Aug. 1804; Weems to Wayne, 28 Jan., 15 Feb., 12 Apr. 1804 (Skeel, *Weems*, II, 290–91, 293, 296).

17. JM to Wayne, 3 Sept., 6 Sept. 1804, 27 Feb. 1805; see Marshall Chronology.

18. JM to Wayne, 10 Jan., 7 Feb., 27 Mar., 17 May, 11 June, 3 Sept. 1804, 27 Feb. 1805, 28 June 1806; JM to Washington, 25 Mar. 1804; Wayne to JM, 20 Mar. 1804; Wayne to Washington, 16 Jan. 1804, Dreer Collection, PHi. See *The Life of George Washington*, Volume IV, Chapter 8, Draft and Published Version, [ca. July 1804], editorial note.

19. JM to Wayne, 1 June, 5 July, 20 July, 6 Sept., 4 Oct., [22 Oct.], 30 Oct. and nn., 21 Dec. 1804, 10 Jan., 1 Mar. and nn., 12 May, 5 Oct. 1805; Wayne to JM, 4 June, 26 June, 20 Aug., 16 Sept. 1804; Weems to Wayne, 25 Jan. 1805 (Skeel, *Weems*, II, 311).

20. For differences between the first and second impressions of the *Life*, see App. V. For purposes of annotation in this volume of *PJM*, all references to the first impression of the *Life* are based on the William Holliday set and to the second impression on the Jno. McClelland set, both at the University of Virginia Library. Detailed notes on changes made in the 1805 impression of vols. I–III can be found in JM to Noah Webster, 4 Oct. 1804; JM to Wayne, [22 Oct.], 30 Oct. 1804, 19 Feb., 1 Mar. 1805.

21. Wayne to JM, 4 June, 26 June 1804. By the end of 1804 even JM and Wayne were confused by each other's terms (see JM to Wayne, 21 Dec. 1804). For bibliographic distinctions of edition and impression, see Philip Gaskell, *A New Introduction to Bibliography* (Oxford, 1972), 313–17; for a listing of editions of the *Life*, see Irwin S. Rhodes, *The Papers of John Marshall: A Descriptive Calendar* (2 vols.; Norman, Okla., 1969), I, 510–11; for detailed bibliographic information on various editions, see Baker, *Bibliotheca Washingtoniana*, 20–25, 28–29, 68, 83, and James A. Servies, *A Bibliography of John Marshall* (Washington, D.C., 1956), 23–24, 42, 54, 60.

22. Although Crissy published this second edition, the publishers Carey & Lea owned the copyright (see copyright page, *Life* [1832 ed.]; JM to Carey & Lea, 19 May 1831, Edward Wanton Smith Collection, PHC; JM to Carey & Lea, 10 Apr. 1832, PP).

23. JM to Wayne, 5 July, 4 Oct., [22 Oct.] 1804, 10 Jan., 1 Mar., 12 May, 5 Oct. 1805, 27 June 1806.

24. JM to Wayne, 3 Sept. 1804, 23 [22] Dec. 1803 and nn. 3, 4, 10 Jan. 1804; JM to Thomas Marshall, Jr., 23 Dec. 1803; Wayne to JM, 31 Dec. 1803–2 Jan. [1804]; JM to Benjamin Lincoln, 21 Nov. 1803 and n. 4; "The 'Anas'" (Boyd, *Papers of Jefferson*, XXII, 33–38, esp. 34); see Jefferson's "Explanations," written in 1818, to "The Anas, 1791–1806" (Ford, *Writings of Jefferson*, I, 154–68); *United States' Gazette, for the Country* (Philadelphia), 21 May 1807; JM to Oliver Wolcott, Jr., 28 June 1806; JM to John Adams, 6 July 1806.

25. *U.S. Gazette, for the Country*, 18 May, 21 May 1807; Ford, *Writings of Jefferson*, I, 155–56; VIII, 151; IX, 262–64 and n.; Boyd, *Papers of Jefferson*, XXII, 34. In other

comments, published after his death by his grandson, Jefferson also impugned JM's use of history. JM retaliated in a detailed note added to the second edition of the *Life* concerning Jefferson's 1796 letter to Mazzei about the monarchical tendencies of Washington's administration (Thomas Jefferson Randolph, ed., *Memoir, Correspondence, and Miscellanies, from the Papers of Thomas Jefferson* [4 vols.; Charlottesville, Va., 1829], IV, 402; *Life* [1832 ed.], II, app., 23–32). James Madison gave a more balanced assessment of the *Life*. He found it "highly respectable, as a specimen of historical composition" except for vol. V, which was "quite inaccurate and ill-digested. . . . The bias of party feeling is obvious," and Madison believed that JM "would write differently at the present day and with his present impressions" (Jared Sparks, journal entry, 25 Apr. 1827 [Adams, *Life of Sparks*, II, 36–37]). In this Madison was wrong, as JM's vituperative note in the second edition bears witness.

26. JM was fairly accurate in his transcriptions by the standards of his day. He changed punctuation, spelling, and abbreviations and substituted words or phrases to clarify matters without altering substantive meaning. For a brief description of some of JM's transcriptions, see JM to Wayne, 27 June 1804 (2d letter), n. 1. JM also sent original letters or letterbooks to Wayne, from which Wayne set type. Four pages of notes in JM's hand give directions for incorporating portions of General Washington's letters in vol. II. He made them in 1804 either for his copyists or for Wayne (MS, Marshall Papers, DLC; see also JM to Wayne, 27 June 1804 [1st letter] and n. 2).

27. See Lear to JM, 12 Dec. 1800 and nn.; Bushrod Washington to Alexander Hamilton, 21 Nov. 1801 (Syrett, *Papers of Hamilton*, XXV, 432); JM to Benjamin Lincoln, 21 Nov. 1803; JM to Wayne, 23 [22] Dec. 1803.

28. See Preface, [ante 22 Dec. 1803] and nn., for JM's sources. Other authors cited at the ends of chapters are Lescarbot, Charlevoix, and Hume. Marc Lescarbot, *Histoire de la Nouvelle France, contenant les navigations, découvertes, & habitations faites par les François és Indes Occidentales & Nouvelle-France* . . . (Paris, 1609); Pierre François de Charlevoix, *Histoire et description générale de la Nouvelle France, avec le journal historique d'un voyage fait par ordre du roi dans l'Amérique Septentrionnale* (6 vols.; Paris, 1744); *Journal of a Voyage to North-America* . . . (2 vols.; London, 1761); David Hume, *The History of England, from the Invasion of Julius Caesar to the Revolution in 1688* (1754–62; new ed.; 8 vols.; London, 1763) (1st Am. ed.; 6 vols.; New York, [1776]). Probably sometime in 1802, JM made eight pages of notes in French on the early explorations and settlements of the North American colonies (MS, Marshall Papers, ViW). The source or sources from which he took them have not been identified; he may have used these notes in writing vol. I, chaps. I–IV, but no particular passage appears to have been directly translated into the text. The closest parallel is between the eighth page of JM's notes and vol. I, chap. 1, 5–6, concerning Lescarbot's observations of early French presence on the Newfoundland coast.

In the second impression of the *Life*, vol. I, JM changed his references from the ends of the chapters to footnotes at the bottom of appropriate pages, with superscript letters. In the other revised volumes, he amplified his footnotes and supplied additional ones, so that the second impression is more fully annotated and gives a better indication of JM's researches and sources.

29. JM to Benjamin Lincoln, 21 Nov. 1803; JM to Charles Cotesworth Pinckney, 21 Nov. 1802; JM to John Eager Howard, 2 Nov. 1804; Howard to JM, 14 Nov. 1804 and n. 2; Washington to Alexander Hamilton, 15 Apr. 1802 (Syrett, *Papers of Hamilton*, XXV, 602–4); Washington to Col. Robert McGaw, 15 Apr. 1802; Washington to Wayne, 18 Apr., 9 May 1802, Dreer Collection, PHi. JM wrote to Col. William Heth in the fall of 1803, inquiring about the assault on Quebec at the end of 1775. Heth sent him extracts from a journal he kept during the campaign, which JM used in his account (Heth to John Heth, 9–20 Nov. 1803, Heth Papers, ViU; vol. II, chap. 5, 322–43 and

n.; *Life* [1832 ed.], I, 53n, 57n). The first twenty-five sheets of Heth's diary are missing, which would have covered the march of Morgan's Rifle Company and unsuccessful attempt on Quebec (MS, DLC; B. Floyd Flickinger, ed., "The Diary of Lieutenant William Heth while a Prisoner in Quebec, 1776," *Annual Papers of Winchester Virginia Historical Society*, I [1931], 37 n. 1, 27–118).

30. For a reference to assessments of the *Life*, see Servies, *Bibliography of Marshall*, 23– 24, 100–101, 106, 124–25, 136, 145 passim.

31. See two pages of notes in JM's hand made in 1805 from *Aurora, Gazette of U.S.*, and congressional journals for subjects covered in vol. V, chaps. 7, 8 (on one side of sheet is invitation for dinner from John Brockenbrough to JM and Thomas Marshall) (MS, Marshall Papers, DLC); *Life*, V, app., Note VI, 14–17; JM to Wayne, 8 June, 29 June, 5 Oct., 19 Oct. 1805; JM to Oliver Wolcott, Jr., 21 Apr., 28 June 1806; JM to John Adams, 6 July 1806; Adams to JM, 17 July 1806.

32. See JM to Wayne, 30 Oct. 1804 and nn.; JM to Noah Webster, 4 Oct. 1804 and nn.; JM to Wayne, 10 Jan., 19 Feb., 27 Feb., 1 Mar., [18 May] 1805; JM to George Logan, 28 Jan. 1805, 19 Jan. 1805 [1806].

33. Wayne to JM, 2⟨6?⟩ July 1804; JM to Wayne, 27 June 1804 (1st letter) and n. 2, 27 June 1804 (2d letter) and nn. 2–5, 10 Aug., 24 Sept. 1804 and n. 2; Washington to Wayne, 26 Aug., 6 Sept. 1804; Wayne to Washington, 8 Sept. 1804, Dreer Collection, PHi; Rush to JM, 5 Sept. 1804.

34. Adams to JM, 4 Feb. 1806; Shaffer, *Politics of History*, 139–40.

Preface

In December 1803 Marshall prepared a "Preface" to appear at the beginning of volume I. In it he stated his premises in writing a history of the British colonies and of America's first citizen, George Washington. He also revealed an awareness of the shortcomings of his work—hurried composition, overwhelming detail, and reliance on published sources bordering on plagiarism. In his comments he anticipated the criticism he would receive and tried to deflect it. Because the preface is a clear, and the only, statement of Marshall's apprehensions and reasons for presenting the *Life* to the public, it is printed here, preceding Marshall's correspondence with his publisher, Caleb P. Wayne.

[ante 22 December 1803][1]

A DESIRE to know intimately those illustrious personages, who have performed a conspicuous part on the great theatre of the world, is, perhaps, implanted in every human bosom. We delight to follow them through the various critical and perilous situations in which they have been placed, to view them in the extremes of adverse and prosperous fortune, to trace their progress through all the difficulties they have surmounted, and to contemplate their whole conduct at a time when, the power and the pomp of office having disappeared, it may be presented to us in the simple garb of truth.

If among those exalted characters which are produced in every age, none can have a fairer claim to the attention and recollection of mankind than those under whose auspices great empires have been founded, or political institutions deserving to be permanent, established; a faithful representation of the various important events connected with the life of the favourite Son of America, cannot be unworthy of the general regard. Among his own countrymen it will unquestionably excite the deepest interest.

As if the chosen instrument of Heaven, selected for the purpose of effecting the great designs of Providence respecting this our western hemisphere, it was the peculiar lot of this distinguished man, at every epoch when the destinies of his country seemed dependent on the measures adopted, to be called by the united voice of his fellow citizens to those high stations on which the success of those measures principally depended. It was his peculiar lot to be equally useful in obtaining the independence, and consolidating the civil institutions, of his country. We perceive him at the head of her armies, during a most arduous and perilous war on the events of which her national existence was staked, supporting with invincible fortitude the unequal conflict. That war being happily terminated, and the political revolutions of America requiring that he should once more relinquish his beloved retirement, we find him guiding her councils with the same firmness, wisdom, and virtue, which had, long and successfully, been displayed in the field. We behold him her chief magistrate at a time when her happiness, her liberty, perhaps her preservation depended on so administering the affairs of the Union, that a government standing entirely on the public favour, which had with infinite difficulty been adopted, and against which the most inveterate prejudices had been excited, should conciliate public opinion, and acquire a firmness and stability that would enable it to resist the rude shocks it was destined to sustain. It was too his peculiar fortune to afford the brightest examples of moderation and patriotism, by voluntarily divesting himself of the highest military and civil honours when the public interests no longer demanded that he should retain them. We find him retiring from the head of a victorious and discontented army which adored him, so soon as the object for which arms had been taken up was accomplished; and withdrawing from the highest office an American citizen can hold, as soon as his influence, his character, and his talents, ceased to be necessary to the maintenance of that government which had been established under his auspices.

He was indeed "first in war,* first in peace, and first in the hearts of his fellow citizens."[2]

A faithful detail of the transactions of a person so pre-eminently distinguished will be looked for with avidity, and the author laments his inability to present to the public a work which may gratify the expectations that have been raised. In addition to that just diffidence of himself which he very sincerely feels, two causes beyond his control combine to excite this apprehension.

Accustomed to look in the page of history for incidents in themselves of great magnitude, to find immense exertions attended with inconsiderable effects, and vast means employed in producing unimportant ends, we are in the habit of bestowing on the recital of military actions, a degree of consideration proportioned to the numbers engaged in them. When the struggle has terminated, and the agitations felt during its suspense have subsided, it is difficult to attach to enterprises, in which small numbers have been concerned, that admiration which is often merited by the talents displayed in their execution, or that interest which belongs to the consequences that have arisen from them.

The long and distressing contest between Great Britain and these States did not abound in those great battles which are so frequent in the wars of Europe. Those who expect a continued succession of victories and defeats; who can only feel engaged in the movements of vast armies, and who believe that a Hero must be perpetually in action, will be disappointed in almost every page of the following history. Seldom was the American chief in a condition to indulge his native courage in those brilliant achievements to which he was stimulated by his own feelings, and a detail of which interests, enraptures, and astonishes the reader. Had he not often checked his natural disposition, had he not tempered his ardour with caution, the war he conducted would probably have been of short duration, and the United States would still have been colonies. At the head of troops most of whom were perpetually raw because they were perpetually changing; who were neither well fed, paid, clothed, nor armed; and who were generally inferior, even in numbers, to the enemy; he derives no small title to glory from the consideration, that he never despaired of the public safety; that he was able at all times to preserve the appearance of an army, and that, in the most desperate situation of American affairs, he did not, for an instant, cease to be formidable. To estimate rightly his worth we must contemplate his difficulties. We must examine the means placed in his hands, and the use he

---

*The expressions of a resolution prepared by general Lee and passed in the house of representatives of the United States, on their being informed of the death of general Washington.

made of those means. To preserve an army when conquest was impossible, to avoid defeat and ruin when victory was unattainable, to keep his forces embodied and suppress the discontents of his soldiers, exasperated by a long course of the most cruel privations, to seize with unerring discrimination the critical moment when vigorous offensive operations might be advantageously carried on, are actions not less valuable in themselves, nor do they require less capacity in the chief who performs them, than a continued succession of battles. But they spread less splendour over the page which recounts them, and excite weaker emotions in the bosom of the reader.

There is also another source from which some degree of disappointment has been anticipated. It is the impossibility of giving to the public in the first part of this work many facts not already in their possession.

The American war was a subject of too much importance to have remained thus long unnoticed by the literary world. Almost every event worthy of attention, which occurred during its progress, has been gleaned up and detailed. Not only the public, but much of the private correspondence of the commander in chief has been inspected, and permission given to extract from it whatever might properly be communicated. In the military part of this history, therefore, the author can promise not much that is new. He can only engage for the correctness with which facts are stated, and for the diligence with which his researches have been made.

The letters to and from the commander in chief during the war, were very numerous and have been carefully preserved. The whole of this immensely voluminous correspondence has, with infinite labour, been examined; and the work now offered to the public is, principally, compiled from it.[3] The facts which occurred on the continent are, generally, supported by these letters, and it has therefore been deemed unnecessary to multiply references to them. But there are many facts so connected with those events, in which the general performed a principal part, that they ought not to be omitted, and respecting which his correspondence cannot be expected to furnish satisfactory information. Such facts have been taken from the histories of the day, and the authority relied on for the establishment of their verity has been cited. Doddesly's Annual Register,[4] Belsham,[5] Gordon,[6] Ramsay,[7] and Stedman[8] have, for this purpose, been occasionally resorted to, and are quoted for all those facts which are detailed in part on their authority. Their very language has sometimes been employed without distinguishing the passages, especially when intermingled with others, by marks of quotation, and the author persuades himself that this public declaration will rescue him from the imputation of receiving aids he is unwilling to acknowledge, or of wishing, by a concealed plagiarism, to usher to the world, as his own, the labours of others.

In selecting the materials for the succeeding volumes, it was deemed proper to present to the public as much as possible of general Washington himself. Prominent as he must be in any history of the American war, there appeared to be a peculiar fitness in rendering him still more so in one which professes to give a particular account of his own life. His private opinions therefore; his various plans, even those which were never carried into execution; his individual exertions to prevent and correct the multiplied errors committed by inexperience, are given in more minute detail; and more copious extracts from his letters are taken, than would comport with the plan of a more general work. Many events too are unnoticed, which in such a composition would be worthy of being introduced, and much useful information has not been sought for, which a professed history of America ought to comprise. Yet the history of general Washington, during his military command and civil administration, is so much that of his country, that the work appeared to the author to be most sensibly incomplete and unsatisfactory, while unaccompanied by such a narrative of the principal events preceding our revolutionary war, as would make the reader acquainted with the genius, character, and resources of the people about to engage in that memorable contest. This appeared the more necessary as that period of our history is but little known to ourselves. Several writers have detailed very minutely the affairs of a particular colony, but the *desideratum* is a composition which shall present in one connected view, the transactions of all those colonies which now form the United States.

The materials for the complete execution of such a work are perhaps not to be found in America; and, if they do exist, their collection would require a length of time, and a labour of research, which neither the impatience of the public, nor the situation of the author would enable him to bestow on the subject. Yet he thought it more eligible to digest into one volume the most material of those facts which are now scattered through several books, than to commence his history abruptly with the war between Great Britain and her colonies.

The difficulties attending even such an undertaking as this, were soon perceived to be greater than had been expected. In several of the English colonies, either no accounts whatever, or such vague accounts of their transactions have been given, that long intervals of time pass away without furnishing a single document relative to their affairs. In others very circumstantial details of their original settlements have been published, but the relation stops at an early period. In New England alone has the history of any colony been continued to the war of our independence; mr. Belknap,[9] mr. Hutchinson[10] and mr. Minot[11] have faithfully transmitted to those who succeed them, the events which occurred in New Hampshire and Massachussetts. Mr. Trumbull is engaged in a similar undertaking for Connecticut, but has not yet progressed far in its execution.[12] In New York, mr. Smith has made a valuable commencement;[13] and in Virginia mr. Stith,[14] and mr. Beverly,[15] have detailed at great length the hardships of the original settlers; but in the other colonies, until we reach South Carolina and Georgia,[16] scarcely an attempt has been made at a history of any sort. To the reign of William and Mary, mr. Chalmer has furnished almost all the facts which the historian of the United States would require. It is much to be regretted that he has not prosecuted his very valuable work according to his original design. So far as it has been executed, it contains internal evidence of the means he possesses for its completion: means unattainable by any inhabitant of the United States.[17] The author has made free use of the materials he has furnished, as well as of those collected by mr. Belknap, mr. Hutchinson, mr. Minot, mr. Smith, and the historian of South Carolina and Georgia. He has also made large extracts from the two chapters written by mr. Robertson and published since his decease.[18] Had that gentleman lived to finish the work he began, an elegant and valuable history of our country would have been in possession of the public, and the author of the following sheets would have deemed it unnecessary to have introduced the Life of General Washington with any narrative of events preceding the time when that great man appeared on the theatre of action. But we have received from mr. Robertson only an account of the settlements of the two eldest colonies, and therefore the necessity of prefixing to this work some essay, though a crude one, towards a general history of the English settlements on this continent, still remained.

If mr. Chalmer, or any other person, shall complete the publication of that collection of facts which he has so successfully commenced, and intelligent individuals of other states could be induced to follow the example set them by mr. Belknap, mr. Hutchinson, mr. Minot, and mr. Trumbull, a fund of information would then be collected from which a correct and valuable history of the now United States might readily be compiled. Until one or both of these events occur, such a history is not to be expected. The author is by no means insensible of the insufficiency of that which is now presented to the public, but the Life of General Washington required some previous general knowledge of American affairs, and he thought it more advisable to accompany that work with even the imperfect sketch of our history which he has been enabled to draw, than to give it publicity unconnected with any narrative whatever of preceding events.

In executing the determination produced by this opinion, he soon perceived that though human nature is always the same, and consequently man will in every situation furnish useful lessons to the discerning politician; yet few would be willing to employ much time in searching for them through the minute details of the sufferings of an infant people, spreading themselves through a wilderness preoccupied only by savages and wild beasts. These details can interest themselves alone, and only the desire of knowing the situation of our own country in every stage of its existence, can stamp a value on the page which contains them. He has, therefore, omitted entirely many transactions deemed of great moment while passing, and yet he is more apprehensive of having overcharged his narrative with facts not of sufficient importance to be preserved, than of having contracted it too much.

For any inattention to composition an apology ought never to be necessary. A work of any importance ought never to be submitted to the public until it has been sufficiently revised and corrected. Yet the first part of the Life of General Washington goes into the world under circumstances, which might bespeak from candour less severity of criticism, than it will probably experience. The papers from which it has been compiled have been already stated to be immensely voluminous, and the public was already looking for the work, before the writer was fixed on and the documents from which it was to be composed placed in his hands. The impatience since discovered by many of the subscribers has carried the following sheets to the press much more precipitately than the judgment of the author would have permitted him to part with them, and he cannot flatter himself that they are free from many defects which on a re-perusal will attract even his own observation.

Printed, John Marshall, *The Life of George Washington . . . to Which Is Prefixed, an Introduction . . .* , I (Philadelphia, 1804), iii–xvi.

1. JM must have finished the preface sometime before 22 Dec., when Bushrod received it from him, but after the beginning of the month, when JM's son Thomas left Richmond with two copies of vol. I (minus the preface) to be delivered in Philadelphia (see JM to Caleb P. Wayne, 23 [22] Dec. 1803 and nn. 2, 3).

2. JM presented a series of resolutions, drafted by Henry Lee, to Congress on 19 Dec. 1799. As reported at the time, this resolution ended not with "fellow citizens," but "country." *Annals of Congress* has "countrymen" (*PJM*, IV, 48 and nn. 4, 5; see also *Life*, V, 765n, 766, where JM quoted the resolution as above).

3. For a description of Washington's papers used by JM, see Tobias Lear to JM, 12 Dec. 1800 and nn. 6–16.

4. *The Annual Register, or, A View of the History, Politics, and Literature, for the Year . . .* (London), first published for the year 1758 by Robert Dodsley (1703–1764), author and bookseller. Edmund Burke served as initial editor and principal contributor for a number of years. Dodsley's brother James (1724–1797) continued to publish it until the

1790s when a group of booksellers took it over. It became known as "Dodsley's Annual Register," although appearing under its original title into the mid-nineteenth century.

5. William Belsham, *Memoirs of the Kings of Great Britain of the House of Brunswic-Lunenburg* (2 vols.; London, 1793); *Memoirs of the Reign of George III. to the Session of Parliament Ending A.D. 1793* (4 vols.; London, 1795); *History of Great Britain, from the Revolution to the Accession of the House of Hanover* (2 vols.; London, 1798); *Memoirs of the Reign of George III. to the Commencement of the Year 1799* (2 vols.; London, 1801). Once the last two volumes were published in 1804, the entire series was issued as *History of Great Britain, from the Revolution, 1688, to the Conclusion of the Treaty of Amiens, 1802* (12 vols.; London, 1805).

6. Gordon, *History of the Independence of the U.S.*

7. Ramsay, *History of the American Revolution.*

8. Stedman, *History of the American War.*

9. Jeremy Belknap, *The History of New-Hampshire* (3 vols.; Philadelphia and Boston, 1784–92).

10. Thomas Hutchinson, *The History of the Colony of Massachusetts-Bay* . . . (2d ed.; 2 vols.; London, 1760–68). The first American edition appeared under the title, *History of Massachusetts from the First Settlement Thereof in 1628, until the Year 1750* (3d ed.; 2 vols.; Boston, 1791) and in 1795, "*With Additional Notes and Corrections.*"

11. George Richards Minot, *Continuation of the History of the Province of Massachusetts Bay, from the Year 1748 [to 1765]* . . . (2 vols.; Boston, 1798–1803). This was a continuation of Hutchinson's work.

12. Benjamin Trumbull, *A Complete History of Connecticut, Civil and Ecclesiastical, from the Emigration of Its First Planters from England in MDCXXX, to MDCCXIII,* 1 (Hartford, Conn., 1797). Volume II did not appear until 1818, published in New Haven, Conn.

13. William Smith, *The History of the Province of New-York, from the First Discovery to the Year M.DCC.XXXII.* . . . (London, 1757). A second edition was published in Philadelphia in 1792.

14. William Stith, *The History of the First Discovery and Settlement of Virginia: Being an Essay towards a General History of this Colony* (Williamsburg, Va., 1747).

15. Robert Beverley, *The History and Present State of Virginia, in Four Parts* . . . (London, 1705).

16. Alexander Hewatt, *An Historical Account of the Rise and Progress of the Colonies of South Carolina and Georgia* . . . (2 vols.; London, 1779).

17. George Chalmers, *Political Annals of the Present United Colonies, from Their Settlement to the Peace of 1763: Compiled Chiefly from Records, and Authorised Often by the Insertion of State-Papers,* I (London, 1780). Book I covered "From their Settlement to 1688." The New-York Historical Society in 1868 published book II, which goes to the end of the seventeenth century. In gathering materials for the *Political Annals,* Chalmers had access to the records of the plantation office, where the Board of Trade's secretary aided him in his research ("Preface," n.p.).

18. Robertson, *History of America, Bks. IX. and X.* Robertson died in 1793.

To Caleb P. Wayne

Sir   Richmond Decr. 23d. [22][1] 1803

Letters lately receivd from my son in Philadelphia contain several enquiries to which he says you wish to receive answers from me.[2]

The title page & preface have been forwarded to Mr. Washington with a request that he woud peruse them, &, if they receive his approbation transmit them to you. You will please to give the title page such form as your judgement & taste may direct.[3]

My son informs me that you think the name of some author must necessarily be given with the title page to the clerk of the district court to be recorded, & that the requisites of the law cannot otherwise be complied with.

I have read the act of Congress with attention & do not so understand it. The name of the book, as it appears to me, may be given in by the proprietor without mentioning the author. There is no expression in the act which has an aspect towards requiring the name of the writer in order to secure the copyright to a person who has purchased it, & I percieve nothing in the nature of the thing which shoud render necessary a construction varying from the words of the law. If this construction has been established I am unacquainted with it & in that case must submit to it, but I confess I am unwilling to be named in the book or in the clerks office as the author if it be avoidable.[4]

Neither does the law appear to me to require that the number of volumes shoud be mentiond, & it is out of my power to speak with certainty on this point. The trunks containing the papers relative to the civil administration have reachd me only this week & have not yet been opend. I shall not be releivd from my circuits & from the session of the supreme court till the spring after which I must attend to the copy making out of the 2d. vol. & to the completion of the 3d. It will of consequence be some time in May before I can examine those papers & form a tolerably correct opinion of the extent of detail they will require. I can percieve no objection to omitting the number of volumes altogether; but I do not know what might be the consequence of specifying a number which might not be the true one.

I had supposed that the preliminary part & the actual history of General Washington woud form one work but that the preliminary part shoud be denominated an introduction. I learn from my son that it will contain a much greater number of pages than I had conjectured & of course to print it all in one volume woud very unreasonably increase your expences.[5] This produces a difficulty I had not foreseen & which it is not now easy to remedy. I coud make considerable deductions from its bulk myself but another might not willingly undertake the task. On reflection I have thought that the first volume might close with the peace of 1763 & that the contests preceding the actual commencement of hostilities may very well be placed in the 2d. volume. If you think so I wish to know how many pages will by this operation be in your hands for the 2d. volume that I may make the proper arrangements in copying the residue which is yet to be transmitted to you. Even after this deduction the first volume will probably remain too large. There are some not very interesting notes in it which may without much injury be dispensd with. The proclamation issued at the conclusion of the war in 1763 is probably one & you may in reading over the book select others which may be parted with. Shoud this be done I wish you to mention to me the particular parts you are inclind to dispense with, but to leave at least 500 pages in the book. Other volumes may possibly be rather smaller than is expected.

I do not think the copies of the 2d. & 3d. can be made out till May & perhaps July or August next. This however will in some measure depend on the contract with Mr. Morgan.[6]

I mention that if you think proper you may delay putting the first volume to the press so long that the 2d will be ready by the time you have finishd it. This delay is produced by the necessity of the copying being superintended by myself which my other indispensable avocations render for the present impossible

If my son is with you tell him I do not write to him because I suppose him to be in Princeton. I am Sir very respectfully, your obedt Servt

J MARSHALL

ALS, Dreer Collection, PHi; Tr, Marshall Papers, DLC. Addressed to Wayne at Philadelphia; postmarked Richmond, 22 Dec. Endorsed by Wayne.

1. The correct date is 22 Dec., as indicated by the postmark and by JM's remark to his son on 23 Dec. that he had written "yesterday to Mr. Wayne."

2. Letters not found. JM's son Thomas delivered two copies of the manuscript for vol. I to Wayne in Philadelphia by the second week of December (Bushrod Washington to Wayne, 18 Dec. 1803, Dreer Collection, PHi). Thomas Marshall was on his way back to Princeton, where he was a student at the College of New Jersey.

3. Bushrod Washington wrote to Wayne on 22 Dec. that he had received that day a letter from JM containing the title page and preface. In a letter of the same date, Washington communicated to JM Wayne's wishes on shortening vol. I and on inserting JM's name in the title page. On both points Washington "entirely" concurred with Wayne. Washington intended to send the title page and preface on to the publisher in eight or ten days, once he had received a reply from JM (Dreer Collection, PHi; see n. 4 below).

4. See 1790 copyright act, sec. 3 (*U.S. Statutes at Large*, I, 125); also supplementary act of 1802 (ibid., II, 171–72). Wayne told Washington on 16 Dec. that he was "'astonished'" with the information conveyed by JM's son "'that his father's name was not to appear in the Title'" (Beveridge, *Life of Marshall*, III, 236 and n. 3). Washington agreed with Wayne that JM's name should be included as author of the work and urged JM of its "necessity" (Washington to Wayne, 22 Dec. 1803, Dreer Collection, PHi).

5. Upon receiving the manuscript, Wayne estimated it would make at least eight hundred pages in print (Beveridge, *Life of Marshall*, III, 236).

6. John Morgan was a bookseller, publisher, and stationer in Philadelphia at 26 S. Third (H. Glenn Brown and Maude O. Brown, "A Directory of the Book-Arts and Book Trade in Philadelphia to 1820 . . . ," *Bulletin of the New York Public Library*, LIII

[1949], 619). He negotiated with Bushrod Washington during the fall of 1803 to purchase the manuscript for an English edition. In the meantime, Washington prohibited Wayne from typesetting vol. I, so as to preclude his publishing the American edition first and sending it to the Continent ahead of Morgan. Not until early Jan. 1804 did Washington conclude a contract with Morgan, who bought the British rights for two thousand dollars (Wayne to Washington, 29 Aug., 12 Sept., 2 Dec. 1803; Washington to Wayne, 10 Nov., 18 Dec., 22 Dec. 1803, 9 Jan. 1804, Dreer Collection, PHi).

To Caleb P. Wayne

Sir   [23 December 1803]
    If my son shoud have left Philadelphia you will please to open &
read the inclosed. I am very respectfully, Your obedt. Servt
                                                         J MARSHALL

ALS, Dreer Collection, PHi. Addressed to Wayne at Philadelphia; postmarked Richmond, 23 Dec. Endorsed by Wayne, "J. Marshall/& copy of my answer." Enclosure was JM to Thomas Marshall, Jr., 23 Dec. 1803. Wayne drafted his reply of 31 Dec.–2 Jan. [1804] on this letter and enclosure.

To Thomas Marshall, Jr.

My dear Son   Richmond Decr. 23d. 1803
    I have this instant received your letter of the 15th.[1] Yours to Jack
Nicholson had stated the extent of the first volume in consequence of
hearing which I wrote yesterday to Mr Wayne expressing my opinion
that it might terminate with the war which ended in 1763 & that
other retrenchments might be made from its bulk. I mentiond particularly the proclamation issued by the crown on the conclusion of
peace & I am perfectly disposed to add to it those you have mentiond.
They are the notes respecting the witches & the dispute between the
house of representatives of Massachussetts & Governor Burnett.[2] If
these shoud not sufficiently diminish the volume I shall not object to
making others; but from your letter I presume they will reduce it
sufficiently—perhaps too much. If the contract with Mr. Morgan remains, correspondent alterations must be made in the copy designd
for him, & I hope you have gone on to compare them tho it may be
uncertain whether that to Morgan will be deliverd or not.
    The charter of Massachussetts is certainly not to be inserted, nor is
that to Virginia.[3] I thought the note to that purpose had been expunged & it is entirely to be attributed to inattention that it remains.

LIFE
OF
GENERAL WASHINGTON.

The Subscriber having purchased of the Hon. Bushrod Washington, the copy-right of the History of the
LATE
GEN. GEORGE WASHINGTON,
COMMANDER IN CHIEF
OF THE
Armies of North America,
DURING THE WAR WHICH EFFECTED
THE INDEPENDENCE OF OUR COUNTRY,
AND
FIRST PRESIDENT OF THE U. STATES,
Has it now in his power to offer to the public the following

PROPOSALS
FOR PUBLISHING IT BY SUBSCRIPTION.

The Work will be faithfully composed under the inspection of JUDGE WASHINGTON himself, principally from the *original papers* bequeathed to him by the deceased General. On its correctness the most entire confidence may be placed.

The Life of this illustrious Citizen necessarily comprises so large and interesting a portion of the History of this Country, that the work, it was conceived, would be rendered much more complete, as well as much more gratifying to the reader, by connecting with it some general account of the origin and progress of the People, who were conducted, under his auspices, from dependent colonies to self-government.

A compendious view, therefore, will be taken, by way of introduction to the *Life of General Washington*, of the settlements of the Europeans in North America, and of the advance of the British Colonies from their feeble and infantine condition, until they attained that state of manhood, when, with arms in their hands, they asserted and established their Independence.

Various circumstances have delayed the execution of the work; but it is now in considerable forwardness, and will soon be ready for the press.—Bond with security has been given that it shall be published.

CONDITIONS.

The work will be handsomely printed with a new type, on vellum paper, HOT PRESSED, to be comprised in four or five octavo volumes, of from 450 to 500 pages each, and embellished with an elegant portrait of the General, engraved by the best artist in the country from an original painting by the celebrated STUART. The price to subscribers will be Three Dollars each volume, in boards; and the price of one volume to be paid in advance, on subscribing; this advance to be continued with each volume, until the work is completed. To non-subscribers it will be enhanced.

It is intended to furnish plans and charts of those parts of the country which were the scenes of the most important events during the War; these to be published in a volume by themselves, & charged as such. It is contemplated to put the work to press early next year. The intermediate time will be occupied in obtaining subscribers, and making arrangements for printing.

☞ The names of subscribers to be published.

Those who wish to be possessed of this invaluable history, will do well to transmit their names early.— In the country, and in small villages, an union can take place among all who mean to subscribe, and in one letter several names may be forwarded, specifying the number of copies, and enclosing the requisite advance money.

The Publisher intending to visit many of the large towns in the United States, for the purpose of obtaining subscribers, declines, at present, employing agents for that purpose. Subscriptions will be received by himself alone, at *No.* 36, *Market street, Philadelphia.*

Orders from Canada, Nova-Scotia, and the West-Indies, will be received, and punctually executed.

☞ All letters must have the postage paid.

C. P. WAYNE.

September 22.   d3t.

ADVERTISEMENT FOR THE LIFE OF GEORGE WASHINGTON

Caleb P. Wayne's proposals for publishing the biography and selling the volumes by subscription. Printed in the *Gazette of the United States,* 22 September 1802. *Courtesy of the Historical Society of Pennsylvania*

I think it proper that the contents of the chapters shoud be run down on the sides, & designd to have done this myself; but you recollect our hurry & my being under the necessity of attending to the business of the court.

With the change now made in the quantity of matter to be inserted in a volume, & the deductions which may be made from the 2d. in consequence of what will be carried into it from the first, I think there will be five volumes, tho of this I cannot be certain, as I am not yet acquainted with the papers relative to the civil administration. If however it be absolutely necessary to mention the number of volumes I think it woud be most advisable to mention five. They will conform in bulk to the advertizement.[4]

Unless there be some law which I have not seen, the clerk of the district court in my opinion transcends his duty, & requires more than the act of Congress requires when he demands the name of the author. If he persists in this demand I wish Mr. Wayne to inform me of it & I will then consult with Mr. Washington on the course to be pursued. But I wish Mr. Wayne when he receives the title page which was sent some time since with the preface to Mr. Washington, to present it to the clerk, & to call his attention to the law. I do not wish to give in my name as the author, & will only do so if it be unavoidable. The book is expressed to be written under the inspection of Judge Washington & that in my opinion is more than sufficient.

I wish Mr. Wayne to write freely to me on this subject & to suggest without difficulty anything which occurs to him. I am not among those who feel wounded at a criticism on my writings, & in the present instance at least, woud much rather it shoud be directly made than felt & suppressed. I am much inclined to beleive that the first part of the work is too minute in its details & have often regretted that I did not abridge it.

Before this reaches Philadelphia you will undou⟨bt⟩edly have receivd letters from Judge Washington by which you will be able to regulate your conduct. On first hearing from him that his contract with Morgan was incomplete I wrote a letter advising him to direct the volumes to be deposited with some friend in Philadelphia till some thing conclusive shoud be done.[5] I have no doubt of his having given these instructions but I hope that before they are obeyed the corrections of the second copy so as to make it completely conform to the first will be made.

The business of transposing & expunging paragraphs is a delicate one & must be executed with care. If this shoud be necessary further than entirely to leave out the notes we have mentiond I shoud wish to receive a memorandum of the alterations designd that I might myself pay some attention to them. I am my dear Son your affectionate Father

J MARSHALL

ALS, Dreer Collection, PHi. Addressed to "Thomas Marshall jr. esquire." MS torn. Enclosed with JM's letter to Wayne of this date. Since JM's son had already left Philadelphia, Wayne, as directed by JM, opened and read the letter, which he retained. Wayne began a draft of his 31 Dec.–2 Jan. [1804] reply on JM's cover letter and continued it below JM's signature on this letter to his son.

1. Letter not found.
2. Utilizing smaller point type, Wayne placed JM's notes in an appendix at the end of vol. I. The 1763 royal proclamation became Note X, 39–45, keyed to the end of chap. 13, 488; the Salem witch trials are described in Note V, 9–19, referenced at chap. 7, 241; and the 1728 dispute over salary between Gov. William Burnet and the Massachusetts assembly is in Note VI, 19–28, indicated at chap. 8, 293.
3. These were omitted.
4. Wayne advertised proposals for publication of the *Life* by subscription in Sept. 1802. He promised the biography would be four or five octavo volumes of between 450 and 500 pages each (*Philadelphia Gazette & Daily Advertiser*, 22 Sept. 1802; *Gazette of U.S.*, 22 Sept. 1802). And on the next two days, he advertised in the Philadelphia *Aurora General Advertiser*, requesting printers throughout the U.S., Canada, Nova Scotia, and the West Indies to publish his proposals in their newspapers.
5. Letters not found.

From William Paterson

Dear Sir,   New Brunswick, 31st. Decemr. 1803.

On the 26th. of octbr. the coachee, in which I was returning home, overset down a precipice of ten feet. In consequence of which, I was so much injured, particularly in my right side and left shoulder, that I am not yet able to dress, undress, &c without assi[s]tance. In my situation, it is probable, that I will be unable to meet you at Washington in feby, although I will certainly go on if I can with safety: but my physicians inform me, that it will be very imprudent for me to venture on such a journey; and, indeed, that I must give it up. Permit me to suggest the propriety of your writing to Judge Moore, and urging the necessity of his attendance at the next term. It would be an unpleasant circumstance, if a number of judges, sufficient to constitute a quorum, should not attend. Your's respectfully,

Copy.   W. P.

ALS (copy), Paterson Papers, NjR. Inside address to "C.J. Marshall."

From Caleb P. Wayne

Sir   Philad Dec 31. 1803 Jan 2 [1804][1]

I have the satisfaction to acknowledge the rect of your two letters under the dates of Dec. 23, & 24, the latter under cover for your son, who had, *4 hours* previous to its receipt, left this city for Princeton.[2] I am much gratified that we coincide respecting the termination of the 1st vol at the conclusion of the 13th Chapter; bringing up the history to the peace of '63. The only note I propose leaving out is that respecting witches. This alteration will leave upwards of 500 pages!!— say 550 but I would rather print a little extra than omit any other note unless it is your [or]der. Notes exc[e]edin[g] half a page I purpose to publish in form of an Appendix. Your opinion perfectly satisfies me in respect to the law of Copy rights; but I still could wish to have your name in the Title, as I feel a confidence that it would enhance the value of the work in the Public estimation. I shall make the European Copy strictly conform, to mine. Your son & myself had completed the examination before he went to Princeton. Do you wish me strictly to adhere to the manuscript in Spelling, punctuation, & the placing of Capital letters? or must I follow Johnson? The two Chapters carried from the first to the 2d vol. consisting of 160 pages manuscript will furnish from about 200 to 210 pages of type for the 2d. vol. Your son deposited in my hands at Judge Ws request, the two Manuscript[s] subject to his Judge Ws[3] order, with liberty to put some of mine in *type* but not to *print* any part of it—I pledged my word not to print it.[4] With respect to the entitling of the preliman[ar]y part of the history, I submit to your superior judgment, but were I to give an opinion on the subject I would propose to have the whole denominated the 'Life &c['] as I presume the Preface & Title will inform the reader that [the] first part is introductory. When the 1st vol. is finished shall I commence the 2d vol. with the 14th & 15 Chapter now in my hands? The writing of the first vol. will make in type about one third more than the manuscript: thus 100 pages Manuscript will make 133 print —this is an average. Be pleased to answer this letter as early as convenient.

ADf, Dreer Collection, PHi. Written on JM's letters of 23 Dec. to Wayne and to Thomas Marshall, Jr. (See n. to latter letter.)

1. Wayne dated draft 31 Dec. but wrote "Jan 2" above it. The recipient's copy of the letter was dated 2 Jan., as acknowledged by JM in his reply of 10 Jan. 1804.

2. JM's letters were dated 23 Dec., although the first was actually written on 22 Dec. Thomas Marshall left Philadelphia on the morning of 30 Dec. (Wayne to Bushrod Washington, 31 Dec. 1803, Dreer Collection, PHi).

3. Wayne wrote "Judge Ws" above the line.

4. Bushrod Washington asserted that he had specifically forbidden Thomas Marshall

from delivering the two copies of vol. I to Wayne without Morgan's permission and that Wayne's setting his copy in type was a violation of Washington's contract with Morgan. Wayne exonerated young Marshall, saying that he had requested him "to permit me to employ men *then in pay* to put it in Type & pledged my honor it should not be printed, not a line has been touched" (Washington to Wayne, 9 Jan. 1804; Wayne to Washington, 16 Jan. 1804, Dreer Collection, PHi).

Hamilton v. Jones
Opinion
U.S. Circuit Court, North Carolina, 31 December 1803

Marshall, Chief Justice.[1] The seller impliedly gave power to the vendee to plead such pleas in his name as were necessary for the defence of the land; and should a plea be now put in by Arrington in the name of the vendor, I would not consent to strike it out.[2]

Printed, John Haywood, *Cases Adjudged in the Superior Courts . . . of North Carolina*, II (Raleigh, N.C., 1806), 291.

1. John Hamilton & Co. had recovered judgment against the estate of John Jones of Halifax County, the executors and executrix pleading that they had fully administered the assets. As provided by law (see Gibson v. Williams, Opinion, 16 June 1803 and n. 1), the plaintiff then proceeded by scire facias against the heirs—John Jones, Robert Jones, and Judith Jones—who were alleged to have real estate by descent or devise from the testator sufficient to satisfy the judgment. Peter Arrington had purchased a portion of the land from one of the heirs, apparently Judith Jones. Judith Jones pleaded that the executors had sufficient assets, that they had wasted and concealed assets, and that they had not fully administered the estate. Previous to the trial, however, she withdrew these pleas and confessed judgment (scire facias, 15 June 1803; confession of judgment, 23 Dec. 1803, Hamilton v. Jones, GEpFRC; U.S. Cir. Ct., N.C., Min. Bk., 31 Dec. 1803).

2. Arrington pleaded assets in the hands of the executor sufficient to satisfy the judgment. The issue was tried at the next term, the jury finding this plea to be good (U.S. Cir. Ct., N.C., Min. Bk., 18 June 1804).

Murray & Munford v. Marsh & Marsh
Opinion
U.S. Circuit Court, North Carolina, 2 January 1804

PER CURIAM.
MARSHALL, Chief Justice, and POTTER, Judges.
Loomis and Tillinghast assigned to the plaintiffs the note sued on, which was made by the defendants, and afterwards became bank-

rupts, and obtained a certificate.[1] And now Loomis is offered as a witness for the plaintiffs. He is a competent witness; for he is by the certificate discharged of all debts proveable under the commission, and his endorsement to the plaintiffs rendered him liable to them, so as to make their demand against him. Secondly; the record of the proceedings against them, attested by the clerk of the district court, without any certificate of the presiding Judge, is good evidence; for the act of Congress relates to certificates in case of officers of the several states, not to those of the United States.[2] Thirdly; if the objection to a witness arises from proof made by the objector, the witness cannot discharge himself of the objection, by any matter sworn by himself; it must be removed by proof drawn from some other source. Fourthly; depositions taken,[3] not specifying the parties between whom they are taken in the caption, nor naming them as parties in the body of the deposition, cannot be received. Fifthly; if a plaintiff supposing himself ready, press for trial, and it is found on trial that the testimony he relied on cannot be given in evidence as he expected and he be nonsuited, the allegation of surprize shall not prevail to set aside the nonsuit.[4]

Printed, John Haywood, *Cases Adjudged in the Superior Courts . . . of North Carolina*, II (Raleigh, N.C., 1806), 290.

1. Haywood mistakenly named the plaintiffs as "Murray & Murray." This suit was an action of special assumpsit to recover money on a promissory note given by Jonathan Marsh and Daniel Marsh, merchants of Washington, N.C., to John Corlis & Co. of Providence, R.I., in 1795. Corlis & Co. assigned the note to Libbius Loomis & Stephen Tillinghast, merchants, who in turn endorsed it to John P. Murray & John B. Munford, merchants of New York City (declaration [filed June 1800 by Blake Baker, attorney for plaintiff], Murray & Munford v. Marsh & Marsh, GEpFRC).

2. The reference is to the 1790 act prescribing the mode of authenticating public acts, records, and judicial proceedings of each state. To have effect in other courts, records and judicial proceedings of a state court had to be attested by the clerk and certified by the chief judge or presiding magistrate. Since bankruptcy proceedings under the federal bankruptcy law took place in federal district courts, no such certificate of a judge was required (*U.S. Statutes at Large*, I, 122).

3. The original edition of Haywood has "to him," doubtless a printer's error. This error was corrected in later editions.

4. The court declared a nonsuit and awarded a new trial on a motion by the plaintiff's attorney. The plaintiff eventually obtained a verdict at the June 1805 term (U.S. Cir. Ct., N.C., Min. Bk., 18 June 1805).

Hamilton v. Simms
Opinion
U.S. Circuit Court, North Carolina, 3 January 1804

PER CURIAM. This is a debt upon bond, against the heir of the obligor;[1] and if the plea of nothing by descent or devise, be falsified by verdict, the judgment will be *de bonis propriis* of the heir or devisee.[2] And it will not help the defendant if the jury should find the value of the land on such issue, for still the court would give the judgment against the defendant *in jure proprio* for the whole debt.[3]

Printed, John Haywood, *Cases Adjudged in the Superior Courts . . . of North Carolina*, II (Raleigh, N.C., 1806), 291.

1. This suit was for the recovery of a debt on a bond given in 1776 by Isham Simms of Wake County to John Hamilton & Co. The plaintiff had obtained a default judgment against Mary Simms, his widow and executrix, at the Nov. 1797 term of the circuit court. Execution against the testator's estate failed to produce enough money to satisfy the judgment, and the plaintiff then proceeded by scire facias against Isham and Adam Simms, sons and heirs of the testator (bond, 20 Jan. 1776; scire facias, 1 Dec. 1800, Hamilton v. Simms, GEpFRC). On proceedings by scire facias in cases of this kind, see Gibson v. Williams, Opinion, 16 June 1803 and n. 1.

2. Isham Simms pleaded, among other things, that he had nothing by descent or devise except for a remainder of two hundred acres of land, in which a life estate had been devised to the testator's widow (U.S. Cir. Ct., N.C., Min. Bk., 3 Jan. 1804).

3. A jury was unable to agree on a verdict either at this term or the ensuing one in June 1804. On 3 Jan. 1805 the defendants Isham and Adam Simms confessed judgment separately (ibid., 3 Jan., 19 June 1804, 3 Jan. 1805).

McAlester v. Berry
Opinion
U.S. Circuit Court, North Carolina, 3 January 1804

PER curiam.[1] Misrepresentations, and obtaining a bargain in consequence thereof, disadvantageous to the party deceived by them, is a ground in equity for setting aside the conveyance, although the party imposed on were of sound understanding, and had time enough to detect the falsehood before he made the contract. In this case the debts due from the testator were represented to his legatees to be very large, and likely to fall upon the estate in remainder devised to them; and it was concealed from them, that a fund was provided by the testator for payment of his debts. The conveyance must be set aside but the grantee shall be allowed for the improvements made on the estate.[2]

Printed, John Haywood, *Cases Adjudged in the Superior Courts* *of North Carolina*, II (Raleigh, N.C., 1806), 290.

1. The parties to this equity suit were John McAlester (also spelled "McAllister" or "McAlister"), surviving acting executor of Archibald McAlester, plaintiff, and William Graves Berry and others, defendants. John McAlester was a brother of Archibald McAlester, the testator; Berry's wife Sarah Elizabeth had been married to James McAlester, now deceased, another brother. The defendants were devisees and legatees of Archibald McAlester, and the dispute concerned the disposition of an estate called Bellville in Brunswick County (McAlester v. Berry and others, GEpFRC; U.S. Cir. Ct., N.C., Min. Bk., 3 Jan. 1804).

2. John McAlester, who held Bellville by devise from Archibald McAlester, deeded the estate to James McAlester in 1793. The formal decree of the court, entered on the minutes of this day, set aside this deed and ordered the estate to be divided up between the plaintiff and defendants according to their respective rights. The court also ordered an accounting to ascertain the payment of the testator's debts, the value of the permanent improvements to Bellville, and the profits of the estate. This interlocutory decree was the first of many decrees issued in this suit during the next several years (U.S. Cir. Ct., N.C., Min. Bk., 3 Jan. 1804, 4 Jan. 1805, 2 Jan., 21, 24 June 1806, 2 Jan., 14 May, 16 Nov. 1807).

Young v. Walker
Opinion
U.S. Circuit Court, North Carolina, 3 January 1804

PER CURIAM. An appeal from an inferior court of admiralty, takes the cause from that court, and such court can no longer act in it: But it still retains power to take care of the goods seized, which are the subject of the suit; and to that end it may order a sale of such goods as are likely to perish.[1] What raised the greatest doubt with us was the uncertainty whether the goods in question were sold by order of the court. The proceedings shew that after the appeal, the now plaintiff was ordered to pay for salvage, one third in value of the property by a certain day, or otherwise an order of sale should issue. Then it appears that the counsel for the claimant procured a postponement of the sale till the 4th of February. It appears also, by a deposition of the Marshal, that he sold by order of the court. And it appears by other depositions that the papers of this court were kept very loosely, on slips of paper, which were often removed from the office, as applied for by individuals.[2] From all these circumstances we have concluded that the evidence is in favor of the order of sale. Then if the court ordered a sale, those who purchased under it should be protected; and the defendants are those persons. It was argued that all the world are parties to a prize cause in the admiralty; and are affected by a decree in the appellate court. This should be understood with some restriction. Upon the publication made of the suit depending, in order that all persons interested may come in and defend, all persons are bound by the decree pronounced upon the point then in controversy. But there is no controversy between the libelants or claimants and those who afterwards became interested by a purchase, under orders and proceedings of the court in the cause between the libelant and claimants. Such intervening persons are not bound by a decree made between the libelants and claimants in the appellate[3] court. The defendants are entitled to retain the property they have purchased, although the decree of the appellate court declared it to belong to the claimant.[4]

Printed, John Haywood, *Cases Adjudged in the Superior Courts . . . of North Carolina*, II (Raleigh, N.C., 1806), 291–92.

1. Haywood mistakenly named the plaintiffs "Jones and Wife." The minute book and other records confirm that this opinion was given in the case of Thomas Young and Wife v. John Walker and Others. Young, of Georgia, claimed the value of certain slaves, which had been on board a vessel captured by an American privateer in 1780 and libeled as British property. The North Carolina Court of Admiralty in Dec. 1780 decreed a restoration of this property to Young on his paying one-third of the value to the captors in lieu of salvage. On Young's failure to pay this amount, a portion of the slaves was sold for this purpose by order of the state admiralty court early in 1781. In the meantime, the captors carried an appeal to the Court of Appeal in Cases of Capture, which in Aug. 1781 reversed the decree of the state admiralty court and condemned the slave property as lawful prize. That court also decreed that two-thirds of the appraised value of the slaves should be restored to Mrs. Thomas Young if within two years she proved that the slaves were her property. This proof was made to the satisfaction of the court, which in its final decree of May 1784 ordered the delivery of two-thirds of the slaves or of their appraised value to Mrs. Young. Young subsequently brought his case in the federal district court of North Carolina for the purpose of carrying into effect the 1784 decree. The defendants were the purchasers of the slaves sold in early 1781 pursuant to the decree of the state admiralty court. The district court in June 1801 ruled in favor of Young and ordered the defendants to pay the difference between the appraised value of the slaves and the sum for which they were actually sold, plus interest from 1784 to 1801 (Young v. Walker, App. Cas. No. 178).

2. See answers of Roger Cuttar and John Walker, 5 Feb. 1801; deposition of Thomas Davis, 26 May 1794; deposition of James Walker, 2 Jan. 1804, ibid.

3. "Appellant" in the original, a printer's error.

4. The circuit court reversed the decree of the district court, dismissing Young's claim. Young then appealed to the Supreme Court, which on 6 Feb. 1808 affirmed the decree of the circuit court (U.S. Cir. Ct., N.C., Min. Bk., 3 Jan. 1804; U.S. Sup. Ct. Minutes, 6 Feb., 16 Mar. 1808; Young v. Walker, App. Cas. No. 178).

To Caleb P. Wayne

Sir   Richmond Jany. 10th: 1804

Your letter of the 2d. inst. has just reachd me.

I think the note respecting the controversy between the house of representatives & Governor of Massachussetts on the subject of a fixd salary may well be omitted: & it is probable there are other notes which escape my memory & which may also be passed over without injury to the work. Shoud such occur I wish you to mention them, & I make no doubt of my perfect concurrence with you on such subjects. I have no objection to your plan of placing the long notes at the end of the volume in the form of an appendix: indeed I think it the more eligible mode of printing the work.

My repugnance to permitting my nam⟨e⟩ to appear in the title still continues, but it shall yield to your right to make the best use you can of the copy. I do not myself imagine that the name of the author being given or withheld can produce any difference in the number of subscribers or of purchasers; but if you think differently, I shoud be very unwilling by a pertinacious adherence to what may be deemd a meer prejudice, to leave you in the opinion that a real injury has been sustaind. I have written to Mr. Washington on this subject[1] & shall submit my scruples to you & him, only requesting that my name may not be given but on mature consideration & conviction of its propriety. If this shall be ultimately resolvd on I wish not my title in the judiciary of the United States to be annexd to it.[2] Mr. Washington will probably write to you but I have requested that no decision be made, unless it shall be necessary, till I see him which will be at Washington early in february.

With respect to punctuation I shall thank you to make such corrections as may be judgd proper. I have no doubt of there being frequent inaccuracies of this sort in the manuscript which I shall regret my inability to correct when I see them in print. I conjecture too that the same observation will apply with equal justice to the paragraphs, & I request that you will amend any obvious impropriety in this or any other respect which you may discover. I am also willing to conform to Johnsons mode of spelling except where a well settled modern practice has so departed from his authority as to give an observance of it the appearance of affectation. I consider as of this description many words terminating in "our"—as Governour, in which the present establishd usage drops the "u." It is not however a subject on which I am solicitous, & in any doubtful case I woud decidedly prefer to follow Johnson. With respect to Capitals I wish common usage to be observd with this only regulation—that where it is

THE

LIFE

OF

GEORGE WASHINGTON,

COMMANDER IN CHIEF

OF THE

AMERICAN FORCES,

DURING THE WAR WHICH ESTABLISHED THE INDEPENDENCE
OF HIS COUNTRY,

AND

FIRST PRESIDENT

OF THE

UNITED STATES.

COMPILED
UNDER THE INSPECTION OF
THE HONOURABLE BUSHROD WASHINGTON,

FROM

ORIGINAL PAPERS

BEQUEATHED TO HIM BY HIS DECEASED RELATIVE, AND NOW IN POSSESSION
OF THE AUTHOR.

TO WHICH IS PREFIXED,

AN INTRODUCTION,

CONTAINING

A COMPENDIOUS VIEW OF THE COLONIES PLANTED BY THE ENGLISH

ON THE

CONTINENT OF NORTH AMERICA,

FROM THEIR SETTLEMENT
TO THE COMMENCEMENT OF THAT WAR WHICH TERMINATED IN THEIR

INDEPENDENCE.

BY JOHN MARSHALL.

VOL. I.

PHILADELPHIA:
PRINTED AND PUBLISHED BY C. F. WAYNE.

1804.

TITLE PAGE TO THE LIFE OF GEORGE WASHINGTON

Title page to volume I of the first edition of Marshall's biography of
George Washington, published in 1804. From the set in the Adams
family library. *Courtesy of U.S. Department of the Interior, National Park
Service, Adams National Historic Site, Quincy, Massachusetts*

matter of doubt or absolute indifference I woud rather the word shoud commence with a common than with a capital letter.

The two chapters taken from the first volume will not commence the second. The second volume will commence with a chapter beginning with the birth & ending with the marriage of General Washington. After which there will be one, perhaps two pages introductory to the 14th. whic⟨h⟩ will form the 2d. chapter of the 2d. volume & I am not sure that it may not be necessary to make some slight alterations in the concluding part of the 15th. or 3d. chapter. Shoud Mr. Washington have contracted with Mr. Morgan these observations must be communicated to that Gentleman & only the 13 first chapters ought now to be deliverd to him.

The preliminary part of the history will properly have the same title with the residue of the work as there will be a continuation of the volumes, but I think it will be more correct to place on the top of each page the word "Introduction." I am not however anxious about it.[3]

If you will let me know by what time you will be ready to commence the 2d. volume I will endeavor to transmit to Mr. Washington, certainly the first chapter, & probably the residue in time to prevent your being delayd. This however cannot be done further than respects the first chapter previous to my return from the february term of the supreme court. I am Sir very respectfully, Your obedt. Servt

J MARSHALL

ALS, Dreer Collection, PHi; Tr, Marshall Papers, DLC. Addressed to Wayne in Philadelphia; postmarked Richmond, 11 Jan. Endorsed by Wayne. MS torn.

1. Letter not found.
2. JM's name did appear on the title page as author without any indication of his judicial office.
3. All five volumes carry the same title page. Included on it is the information that to the *Life* "is prefixed, An Introduction, containing a compendious view of the colonies planted by the English on the Continent of North America, from their settlement to the commencement of that war which terminated in their Independence." As suggested by JM, Wayne printed vol. I with "Introduction" as the running heads.

To Henry Potter

Dear Sir   [ca. 10 January 1804][1]

I take the liberty to introduce to you Mr. Weims a gentleman from Maryland who has engaged in the business of obtaining subscriptions to the life of General Washington now about to be publishd.[2] Being entirely unacquainted in North Carolina he has askd me to give him a letter to some gentleman of my acquaintance & I beg leave to mention him to you as a person who will be disposed to further his undertaking. You will much oblige me by naming to him such persons, as he may probably apply to with success & by giving him your countenance.

With a little breaking down, walking, & traveling in a waggon I reachd virginia agreeably enough without any accident to procrastinate the journey.

I hope Mrs. Potter & the young gentleman are by this time in perfect health, & am dear Sir with respectful esteem, your Obedt.

J MARSHALL

ALS, Gratz Collection, PHi. Addressed to Potter in Raleigh. Endorsed by Potter.

1. JM wrote this undated letter soon after his return to Richmond from attending the term of the federal circuit court in Raleigh, which ended on 5 Jan. Henry Potter (1766–1857) had been appointed judge of the U.S. District Court of North Carolina in Apr. 1802 and served with JM on the bench of the circuit court for more than thirty years (*Senate Executive Journal*, I, 418, 419; Crockette W. Hewlett, *The United States Judges of North Carolina* [3d. ed.; New Bern, N.C., 1978], 29–33).

2. Mason Locke Weems (1759–1825), Episcopal minister, writer, musician, and itinerant book agent. Engaged by Wayne in late 1802 to procure subscriptions to the *Life*, Weems did not devote full attention to peddling the biography until 1804 because of prior commitments to publisher Mathew Carey. At Bushrod Washington's urging, Weems set out on a southern tour with letters of recommendation from Washington and JM. He spent the next several years traveling through the South, soliciting subscriptions and distributing volumes of the *Life* (see *The Life of George Washington*, editorial note [preceding Preface, (ante 22 Dec. 1803)]; Weems to Wayne, 14 Dec., 17 Dec., 22 Dec. 1802, 12 Aug. 1803, 23 Jan., 28 Jan., 12 Apr. 1804 [Skeel, *Weems*, 256–58, 270, 290–91, 294–96, 297–380 passim]; Wayne to Washington, 17 Feb., 29 Aug. 1803; Washington to Wayne, 1 Mar., 27 Dec. 1803; Washington to Weems, 18 Dec. 1803, Dreer Collection, PHi). See also Lawrence C. Wroth, *Parson Weems: A Biographical and Critical Study* (Baltimore, 1911); Beveridge, *Life of Marshall*, III, 230–34 and nn., 252–53 and nn.; Skeel, *Weems*, I, 316–20nn.

To William Bernard

Dear Sir   Richmond Jany. 17th. 1804

I receivd yours of the 8th. inst.[1] & am very sorry that the corn rent fell so far short both of your expectation & mine. I shoud with much pleasure close with your proposition for receiving the whole sixty barrels but I really do not know how I coud purchase the 13½ barrels which woud in that case be due to you. If Mr. Tally can spare it I will very cheerfully take yours, but I am sure he has not a barrel for sale & that it is all he can do to make both ends meet. My distance is such as to put it out of my power to purchase the corn. If you can do it in your neighborhood at a price not exceeding 14 I will very readily pay the money & take the whole 60 barrels.

I do not know how to account for it but I have somehow mislaid both the plats of the land & cannot lay my hands on either of them. If you can obtain another copy from Mr. Patteson I will readily pay for it, & if you will send it to me or will send me the courses of your land I will immediately execute the deed for it.

I really have not enquired how much you have overrun the first payment but whatever it is will of course be credited with interest from the time it was placed to my credit with Mr. Fisher. I am dear Sir with much regard, Your Obedt. Servt

J MARSHALL

ALS, Collection of Henry N. Ess III, New York, N.Y. Addressed to Bernard in Buckingham County "by the way of New Canton." Postmarked Richmond, 1⟨7?⟩ Jan. Endorsed by Bernard. Noted on cover: "Barrel . . . 80/Box . . . 35."

1. Letter not found. Bernard was the purchaser of JM's Buckingham land. See JM to Bernard, 8 Sept. 1803.

To Caleb P. Wayne

Sir   Richmond Jany. 22d. 1804

Previous to the receipt of your letter of the 10th.[1] I had answerd all the enquiries which had before been made respecting the work in which we are engaged. I am a good deal puzzled to decide what is to be done respecting the authorities quoted. There was some difficulty in fixing the references because several pages successively are substantially taken from the same books & it was my idea that the whole shoud be considerd as referd to by placing the names of the authors at the foot of the pages. I cannot now correct it as I have not the manuscript, & can only advise that the mark of reference be placed at the end of some paragraph, as your judgement shall direct, on each page at the foot of which you find the names of the authors written. It will probably be generally right to place the letter of reference at the close of the last paragraph.[2]

As the volume still continues too large, it is most advisable to reduce it by omitting such notes as your own judgement & that of any friend you may consult, shall dictate. I have mentiond that respecting the controversy in Massachussetts concerning a fixd salary & the ro[y]al proclamation issued after the conclusion of the war. I am desirous that you shoud select such others as you think may be parted with, so as to bring the book within a reasonable compass.

There is one subject of some importance to which I wish to draw your attention. In a history of military transactions, plans or cutts are of vast importance. Those preservd by General Washington are not all that shoud be inserted in the work. There are several in Gordons history of the war which appear to me to be minute & accurate, & which of course woud contribute much to the satisfaction of the reader. I woud mention as examples the plan of Boston & its environs; & of the camp at Brooklyn on Long-island with the different posts occupied by the enemy previous to the action of the 27th. of August.[3]

I beleive there is no obstacle to your using these cutts, & I do not think there woud be any thing unhandsome in it, if in a preface of your own you shoud state the fact. I only suggest it however to be reflected on by you. I am Sir respectfully, Your Obedt

J MARSHALL

ALS, Dreer Collection, PHi; Tr, Marshall Papers, DLC. Addressed to Wayne in Philadelphia; postmarked Richmond, 29 Jan. Endorsed by Wayne.

1. Letter not found, but see n. 2.

2. In a letter of 16 Jan. to Bushrod Washington, Wayne noted that "in the manuscript copy there is in various place[s] at the bottom of the pages, the names of authors such as *Stith*, *Chalmer*, *Robinson*, &c &c. & there is no reference made from the text. I know not how to place them. If intended as notes there ought to be referrences: if not, I conceive they ought not to be placed in print, but if in at all, I would suggest their being placed at the end of each Chapter. I hope the preface will explain & do away the necessity of inserting them. I have written to the Chief Justice respecting them, the punctuation, spelling, Title at the head of each page, of the Introductory part, &c &c. &c.—on this points I wish explicit & full instructions" (Dreer Collection, PHi). In his preface to vol. I, JM did not give a comprehensive list of his historical sources, although he did discuss historians of the various colonies on whom he had relied (see Preface, [ante 22 Dec. 1803] and nn.). For vol. I Wayne did not use any footnotes or letters of reference but simply placed at the end of each chapter the last names of authors of works cited by JM. Beginning with vol. II, sources appear in footnotes at the bottom of appropriate pages. The second impression of vol. I conforms to this system of annotation.

3. Gordon, *History of the Independence of the U.S.* In vol. II, a fold-out map of "Boston, with its Environs" (Plate II) faces the title page, and a map of "New York Island, & parts adjacent" faces p. 310, in the text describing the Battle of Long Island, 27 Aug. 1776. T. Conder of London engraved the maps.

To James M. Marshall

My dear brother   Richmond Feby. 2d. 1804

I have receivd a letter from Mr. Morris[1] stating the testimony taken at the Indian Queen which is entirely unimportant. I have written to our lawyers to press the trial of the issue.[2]

Mr. Hopkins paid you on my account in March 1802 five hundred dollars. I do not recollect on what account it was paid & will thank you to inform me. Was it on the account of Alexanders money, or on any other company account, or was it a personal affair between ourselves & if so what was the nature of the arrangement? I have forgotten everything about it & am now settling my accounts.

I wish very much that you coud be in Richmond in the spring. Woud it be worth your while to attend the court of appeals in April.[3]

A bill has passed for establishing a bank to be considerd & denominated a state bank. The monied here have many objections to it the most essential of which is that it is entirely under the control of the state & will of course as they think be rather a political than a money institution.[4]

There have been many caucusses lately among the democrats about which some curious stories are told. Burr is not only to be dropped but he has very narrowly as it is said escaped being denounced as a traitor. Some prudential considerations have induced the resolution to make the blow less open but not less deadly than was at first designd.

It was proposed to nominate John Breckenridge as the Vice President, but on more mature reflection it was determind to wait for further orders. Your

J MARSHALL

I set out tomorrow for Washington.

ALS, Collection of Ellen Morris Manganaro, Westtown, Pa. Addressed to James Marshall at Front Royal, Frederick County; postmarked Richmond, 2 Feb.

1. This letter, written either by Robert Morris or his son Robert Morris, Jr., has not been found.

2. The reference is to the suit of Morris v. Alexander. See JM to James M. Marshall, 1 Apr. 1804.

3. James Marshall was the appellant in the case of Marshall v. Conrad, which was to be argued at the spring term of the Court of Appeals. See JM to James M. Marshall, 1 Apr. 1804.

4. For the act "incorporating the Bank of Virginia," enacted on 30 Jan. 1804, see Shepherd, *Statutes*, III, 100–108. On the political significance of the bank, see Kathryn R. Malone, "The Fate of Revolutionary Republicanism in Early National Virginia," *Journal of the Early Republic*, VII (1987), 34–43.

To Caleb P. Wayne

Sir   Washington feb. 7th. 1804

I transmit you the assignment of the copy right corrected as you wishd.

I have no objection to the mode you propose respecting the title to the introduction. On subjects of this sort I shall be pleasd with whatever you may on reflection deem most proper. You will recollect that in spelling, capitals &c. I wish to avoid whatever may have the appearance of affectation or singularity.

I am perfectly willing that the work shoud be publishd without running the contents down the margin, but I think the dates must be inserted. The mind is not satisfied without an exact knowlege of dates, & it not unfrequently happens that their insertion in the text will have an aukward appearance & an ill effect.

I have not retaind an exact copy of that part of the chapter originally designd to conclude the first volume, which respects the appointment of General Washington to the command of the American army. It is probable that it may require some alteration in order to avoid a repetition of the same statements in the same volume.[1] According to the original arrangement it was perhaps unavoidable to mention the same fact twice but the change which has taken place may probably require some alteration in that passage. I will therefore thank you to transcribe so much as respects this subject & immediately transmit it to me at this place. It is very short & I coud wish to receive it immediately. You will also oblige me by informing me at what time you will be prepared for the second volume. I will endeavor to furnish it in time, but I wish to retain it as long as your convenience will admit for the purpose of a more satisfactory examination. It is now transcribing & unless my copyer disappoints me will be finishd early in march when I shall return to Richmond & commence the examination & correction of the copy.

Judge Washington is now here & requests me to say that if Mr. Morgan has paid the money into[2] bank which he askd the favor of you to attend to for him, & a credit with the branch bank at this place can be obtaind, he wishes it done immediately. If such a credit is unattainable then he desires the money to be immediately inclosd to him at this place in post notes.[3] The session of the court is uncertain as to duration & therefore he will be much obligd to you to write immediately. I am Sir very respectfully, Your Obedt. Servt

J MARSHALL

ALS, Dreer Collection, PHi; Tr, Marshall Papers, IHC. Addressed to Wayne at Philadelphia; postmarked "Washn. City," 8 Feb. Endorsed by Wayne. Draft of Wayne's reply of 11 Feb. written on verso of cover and across page beneath JM's signature.

1. See JM to Bushrod Washington, 25 Mar. 1804 and n. 2.
2. JM omitted "the."
3. These bank notes, intended for transmission by post, were payable at a future specified date rather than on demand.

From Caleb P. Wayne

Dr. Sir   Philada. Feby. 11. 1804

Above you will read the only paragraph in which Genl. W. is mentioned. It is copied from the 8th page of the 15th. Chapter Folio 72, & I presume it is the part you requested me to Copy. I have also copied above, the concluding paragraph of Page 8, Folio 73. Chap 15—being the end of the vol. as at first intended.[1] I believe you are already acquainted that the two Chapters 14 & 15 which are to be carried to the 2d vol. occupy 20 Folios, or 160 pages of Manuscript; you may say 200 pages of Type for the 2d vol. I shall be ready to go on with the 2d vol. early in April if I could have a part the beginning or about the middle of that month & the whole by the 1st. of May it would suit me very well. It would injure me very much to be delayed after the 1st. May. Not willing to omit any thing that I could insert without great expense, I have so enlarged my pages as to be able to compass the whole of the Notes; this will make the vol contain from 500 to 530 or 40 pages. I hope the increase of expence in printing this vol will be balanced by the future vols. which I could wish might not exceed 470 Pages at most. That number would form a vol. larger than most of the Octavos now published & would give the subscribers as much as they were promised, from 450 to 500. I shall place the dates & contents down the sides; the omission of one without the other would not answer the end I had in view. I thank you for the assignment.

Tuesday Afternoon—Feb 14

I have delivered Mr. Morgan his Copy & recd payment, which I forward by this Mail to Mr. Washington.

I have deposited the Title, taken out a Certificate & publish "In the Press" this Afternoon.[2]

ADf, Dreer Collection, PHi. Written on verso of JM to Wayne, 7 Feb. 1804 (see n.).

1. Wayne did not include in his draft the paragraphs mentioned as "copied above."

2. Under section 3 of the 1790 copyright law, Wayne was required to deposit a printed copy of the title page in the clerk's office of the district court where he resided. He did this on 13 Feb. 1804 in the district court of Pennsylvania, where the clerk entered the copyright to the *Life* under Wayne's name as proprietor (record book, Pennsylvania Copyright Records, DLC). A copy of the record appears on the verso of the title page of the published biography, as stipulated in section 1 of the 1802 supplementary act. Within two months of his entering the copyright, Wayne also had to publish in one or more U.S. newspapers a copy of the record for a period of four weeks (*U.S. Statutes at Large*, I, 125; II, 171). This notice appeared in the *Gazette of the U.S.*, beginning on 14 Feb. and running until 19 Mar. Immediately beneath it, Wayne published an announcement that the first volume of the *Life* was "Now in the Press," after "occurrences unforeseen and uncontrollable have tended to procrastinate its appearance."

Murray v. Schooner Charming Betsey
Opinion and Decree
U.S. Supreme Court, 22 February 1804

EDITORIAL NOTE

In its early years the Marshall court decided a series of cases arising from the naval war with France of 1797 to 1800. These cases originated in actions taken by American naval commanders to enforce the several acts of Congress suspending American trade with France. Two involved vessels owned by Jared Shattuck, a native of Connecticut who had resided for some years at St. Thomas in the Virgin Islands and who claimed to be a Danish subject. Shattuck's schooners, the *Charming Betsey* and the *Mercator*, had been seized for violating the nonintercourse laws in 1800, both captures coming to Marshall's attention while he was secretary of state.[1]

The facts of *Murray v. Charming Betsey* are sufficiently stated in the opinion below. Captain Alexander Murray, commander of the U.S. frigate *Constellation*, exhibited his libel against the *Charming Betsey* in the U.S. District Court of Pennsylvania in February 1801. District Judge Richard Peters on 28 April decreed the restoration of the vessel and payment by the libellant of the amount of the cargo's sale along with damages and costs. This decree was affirmed in part by the U.S. Circuit Court for Pennsylvania in May 1802. Both parties then appealed to the Supreme Court, where the case was extensively argued for six days extending over the 1803 and 1804 terms. Luther Martin, Philip Barton Key, and Jeremiah Mason represented the claimant (Richard Söderström, the Swedish consul general who exercised the consular functions of the Danish government). Alexander Dallas was counsel for the libellant Murray.[2]

1. Haskins and Johnson, *Foundations of Power*, 407–15; JM to Lendemenn, 20 Nov. 1800 and n. 1. The case of the *Mercator* was Maley v. Shattuck, 3 Cranch 458 (1806).

2. Murray v. Charming Betsey, App. Cas. No. 115; 2 Cranch 64–115.

OPINION

The *Charming Betsy* was an *American* built vessel, belonging to citizens of the *United States*, and sailed from *Baltimore*, under the name of the *Jane*, on the 10th of *April*, 1800, with a cargo of flour for *St. Bartholomew's*; she was sent out for the purpose of being sold. The cargo was disposed of at *St. Bartholomew's*; but finding it impossible to sell the vessel at that place, the captain proceeded with her to the island of *St. Thomas*, where she was disposed of to *Jared Shattuck*, who changed her name to that of the *Charming Betsy*, and having put on board her a cargo consisting of *American* produce, cleared her out as a *Danish* vessel for the island of *Guadaloupe*.

On her voyage she was captured by a *French* privateer, and eight hands were put on board her for the purpose of taking her into *Guadaloupe* as a prize. She was afterwards recaptured by captain *Murray*, commander of the *Constellation* frigate, and carried into *Martinique*. It appears that the captain of the *Charming Betsy* was not willing to be taken into that island; but when there, he claimed to have his vessel and cargo restored, as being the property of *Jared Shattuck*, a *Danish* burgher.

Jared Shattuck was born in the *United States*, but had removed to the island of *St. Thomas* while an infant, and was proved to have resided there ever since the year 1789 or 1790. He had been accustomed to carry on trade as a *Danish* subject, had married a wife and acquired real property in the island, and also taken the oath of allegiance to the crown of *Denmark* in 1797.

Considering him as an *American* citizen who was violating the law prohibiting all intercourse between the *United States* and *France* or its dependencies, or the sale of the vessel as a mere cover to evade that law, captain *Murray* sold the cargo of the *Charming Betsy*, which consisted of *American* produce, in *Martinique*, and brought the vessel into the port of *Philadelphia*, where she was libelled under what is termed the non-intercourse law. The vessel and cargo were claimed by the consul of *Denmark* as being the *bona fide* property of a *Danish* subject.

This cause came on to be heard before the judge for the district of *Pennsylvania*, who declared the seizure to be illegal, and that the vessel ought to be restored and the proceeds of the cargo paid to the claimant or his lawful agent, together with costs and such damages as should be assessed by the clerk of the court, who was directed to inquire into and report the amount thereof;[1] for which purpose he was also directed to associate with himself two intelligent merchants of the district, and duly inquire what damage *Jared Shattuck* has sustained by reason of the premises. If they should be of opinion that the officers of the *Constellation* had conferred any benefit on the owner of the *Charming Betsy* by rescuing her out of the hands of the *French* captors, they were in the adjustment to allow reasonable compensation for the service.

In pursuance of this order the clerk associated with himself two merchants, and reported, that having examined the proofs and vouchers exhibited in the cause, they were of opinion that the owner of the vessel and cargo had sustained damage to the amount of 20,594 dollars and 16 cents, from which is to be deducted the sum of 4,363 dollars and 86 cents, the amount of monies paid into court arising from the sales of the cargo, and the further sum of 1,300 dollars, being the residue of the proceeds of the said sales remaining to be brought into court, 5,663 dollars and 86 cents. This estimate is exclusive of the value of the vessel, which was fixed at 3,000 dollars.

To this report an account is annexed, in which the damages, without particularizing the items on which the estimate was formed, were stated at 14,930 dollars and 30 cents.[2]

No exceptions having been taken to this report, it was confirmed, and by the final sentence of the court captain *Murray* was ordered to pay the amount thereof.

From this decree an appeal was prayed to the circuit court, where the decree was affirmed so far as it directed restitution of the vessel and payment to the claimant of the net proceeds of the sale of the cargo in *Martinique*, and reversed for the residue.

From this decree each party has appealed to this court.

It is contended on the part of the captors in substance,

1st. That the vessel *Charming Betsy* and cargo are confiscable under the laws of the *United States*. If not so,

2d. That the captors are entitled to salvage. If this is against them,

3d. That they ought to be excused from damages, because there was probable cause for seizing the vessel and bringing her into port.

1st. Is the *Charming Betsy* subject to seizure and condemnation for having violated a law of the *United States*?

The libel claims this forfeiture under the act passed in *February*, 1800, further to suspend the commercial intercourse between the *United States* and *France* and the dependencies thereof.[3]

That act declares "that all commercial intercourse," &c. It has been very properly observed, in argument, that the building of vessels in the *United States* for sale to neutrals, in the islands, is, during war, a profitable business, which Congress cannot be intended to have prohibited, unless that intent be manifested by express words or a very plain and necessary implication.

It has also been observed that an act of Congress ought never to be construed to violate the law of nations if any other possible construction remains, and consequently can never be construed to violate neutral rights, or to affect neutral commerce, further than is warranted by the law of nations as understood in this country.

These principles are believed to be correct, and they ought to be kept in view in construing the act now under consideration.

The first sentence of the act which describes the persons whose commercial intercourse with *France* or her dependencies is to be prohibited, names any person or persons, resident within the *United States* or under their protection. Commerce carried on by persons within this description is declared to be illicit.

From persons the act proceeds to things, and declares explicitly the cases in which the vessels employed in this illicit commerce shall be forfeited. Any vessel owned, hired or employed wholly or in part by any person residing within the *United States*, or by any citizen thereof residing elsewhere, which shall perform certain acts recited in the law, becomes liable to forfeiture. It seems to the court to be a correct construction of these words to say, that the vessel must be of this description, not at the time of the passage of the law, but at the time when the act of forfeiture shall be committed. The cases of forfeiture are, 1st. A vessel of the description mentioned, which shall be voluntarily carried, or shall be destined, or permitted to proceed to any port within the *French* Republic. She must, when carried, or destined, or permitted to proceed to such port, be a vessel within the description of the act.

The second class of cases are those where vessels shall be sold, bartered, entrusted, or transferred, for the purpose that they may proceed to such port or place. This part of the section makes the crime of the sale dependent on the purpose for which it was made. If it was intended that any American vessel sold to a neutral should, in the possession of that neutral, be liable to the commercial disabilities imposed on her while she belonged to citizens of the *United States*, such extraordinary intent ought to have been plainly expressed; and if it was designed to prohibit the sale of *American* vessels to neutrals, the words placing the forfeiture on the intent with which the sale was made ought not to have been inserted.

The third class of cases are those vessels which shall be employed in any traffic by or for any person resident within the territories of the *French* Republic, or any of its dependencies.

In these cases too the vessels must be within the description of the act at the time the fact producing the forfeiture was committed.

The *Jane* having been completely transferred in the island of *St. Thomas*, by a *bona fide* sale to *Jared Shattuck*, and the forfeiture alleged to have accrued on a fact subsequent to that transfer, the liability of the vessel to forfeiture must depend on the inquiry whether the purchase was within the description of the act.

Jared Shattuck having been born within the *United States*, and not being proved to have expatriated himself according to any form prescribed by law, is said to remain a citizen, entitled to the benefit and subject to the disabilities imposed upon *American* citizens; and, therefore, to come expressly within the description of the act which comprehends *American* citizens residing elsewhere.

Whether a person born within the *United States*, or becoming a citizen according to the established laws of the country; can divest himself absolutely of that character otherwise than in such manner as may be prescribed by law, is a question which it is not necessary at present to decide. The cases cited at bar and the arguments drawn from the general conduct of the *United States* on this interesting subject, seem completely to establish the principle that an *American* citizen may acquire in a foreign country, the commercial privileges attached to his domicil, and be exempted from the operation of an act expressed in such general terms as that now under consideration. Indeed the very expressions of the act would seem to exclude a person under the circumstances of *Jared Shattuck*. He is not a person under the protection of the *United States*. The *American* citizen who goes into a foreign country, although he owes local and temporary allegiance to that country, is yet, if he performs no other act changing his condition, entitled to the protection of our government; and if, without the violation of any municipal law, he should be oppressed unjustly, he would have a right to claim that protection, and the interposition of the *American* government in his favour, would be considered a justifiable interposition. But his situation is completely changed, where by his own act he has made himself the subject of a foreign power. Although this act may not be sufficient to rescue him from punishment for any crime committed against the *United States*, a point not intended to be decided, yet it certainly places him out of the protection of the *United States* while within the territory of the sovereign to whom he has sworn allegiance, and consequently takes him out of the description of the act.

It is therefore the opinion of the court, that the *Charming Betsy*, with her cargo, being at the time of her recapture the *bona fide* property of a *Danish* burgher, is not forfeitable, in consequence of her being employed in carrying on trade and commerce with a *French* island.

The vessel not being liable to confiscation, the court is brought to the second question, which is:

2d. Are the recaptors entitled to salvage?

In the case of the *Amelia**[4] it was decided, on mature consideration, that a neutral armed vessel in possession of the *French* might, in the then existing state of hostilities between the two nations, be lawfully captured; and if there were well founded reasons for the opinion that she was in imminent hazard of being condemned as a prize, the recaptors would be entitled to salvage. The court is well satisfied with the decision given in that case, and considers it as a precedent not to be departed from in other cases attended with circumstances substantially similar to those of the *Amelia*. One of these circumstances is, that the vessel should be in a condition to annoy *American* commerce.[5]

The degree of arming which should bring a vessel within this description has not been ascertained, and perhaps it would be difficult precisely to mark the limits, the passing of which would bring a captured vessel within the description of the acts of Congress on this subject. But although there may be difficulty in some cases, there appears to be none in this. According to the testimony of the case, there was on board but one musket, a few ounces of powder, and a few balls. The testimony respecting the cutlasses is not considered as shewing that they were in the vessel at the time of her recapture. The capacity of this vessel for offence appears not sufficient to warrant the capture of her as an armed vessel. Neither is it proved to the satisfaction of the court, that the *Charming Betsey* was in such imminent hazard of being condemned as to entitle the recaptors to salvage.

It remains to inquire whether there was in this case such probable cause for sending in the *Charming Betsey* for adjudication as will justify captain *Murray* for having broken up her voyage, and excuse him from the damages sustained thereby.

To effect this there must have been substantial reason for believing her to have been at the time wholly or in part an *American* vessel, within the description of the act, or hired, or employed by *Americans*, or sold, bartered, or trusted for the purpose of carrying on trade to some port or place belonging to the *French* Republic.

The circumstances relied upon are principally,

1st. The *proces verbal* of the *French* captors.

2d. That she was an *American* built vessel.

3d. That the sale was recent.

4th. That the captain was a *Scotchman*, and the muster roll shewed that the crew were not *Danes*.

5th. The general practice in the *Danish* islands of covering neutral property.

1st. The *proces verbal* contains an assertion that the mate declared

**Ante vol.* I. *p.* 1.

that he was an *American*, and that their flag had been *American*, and had been changed during the cruise to *Danish*, which declaration was confirmed by several of the crew.

If the mate had really been an *American*, the vessel would not on that account have been liable to forfeiture, nor should that fact have furnished any conclusive testimony of the character of the vessel. The *proces verbal* however ought for several reasons to have been suspected. The general conduct of the *French West-India* cruisers and the very circumstance of declaring that the *Danish* colors were made during the chase, were sufficient to destroy the credibility of the *proces verbal*. Captain *Murray* ought not have believed that an *American* vessel trading to a *French* port in the assumed character of a *Danish* bottom, would have been without *Danish* colors.

That she was an *American* vessel, and that the sale was recent, cannot be admitted to furnish just cause of suspicion, unless the sale of *American* built vessels had been an illegal or an unusual act.

That the captain was a *Scotchman* and that the names of the crew were not generally *Danish*, are circumstances of small import, when it is recollected that a very great proportion of the inhabitants of *St. Thomas's* are *British* and *Americans*.

The practice of covering *American* property in the islands might and would justify captain *Murray* in giving to other causes of suspicion more weight than they would otherwise be entitled to, but cannot be itself a motive for seizure. If it was, no neutral vessel could escape, for this ground of suspicion would be applicable to them all.

These causes of suspicion taken together ought not to have been deemed sufficient to counterbalance the evidence of fairness with which they were opposed. The ship's papers appear to have been perfectly correct, and the information of the captain uncontradicted by those belonging to the vessel who were taken with him, corroborated their verity. No circumstance existed, which ought to have discredited them. That a certified copy of *Shattuck's* oath, as a *Danish* subject, was not on board, is immaterial, because, being apparently on all the papers a burgher and it being unknown that he was born in the *United States*, the question, whether he had ceased to be a citizen of the *United States* could not present itself.

Nor was it material that the power given by the owners of the vessel, to their captain to sell her in the *West-Indies*, was not exhibited. It certainly was not necessary to exhibit the instructions under which the vessel was acquired, when the fact of acquisition was fully proved by the documents on board and by other testimony.

Although there does not appear to have been such cause to suspect the *Charming Betsy* and her cargo to have been *American*, as would justify captain *Murray* in bringing her in for adjudication, yet many other circumstances combine with the fairness of his character to produce a conviction that he acted upon correct motives, from a sense of duty; for which reason this hard case ought not be rendered still more so by a decision in any respect oppressive.

His orders were such as might well have induced him to consider this as an armed vessel within the law, sailing under authority from the *French* republic; and such too as might well have induced him to trust to very light suspicions respecting the real character of a vessel appearing to belong to one of the neutral islands. A public officer entrusted on the high seas to perform a duty deemed necessary by his country, and executing according to the best of his judgment the orders he has received, if he is a victim of any mistake he commits, ought certainly never to be assessed with vindictive or speculative damages. It is not only the duty of the court to relieve him from such when they plainly appear to have been imposed on him, but no sentence against him ought to be affirmed where, from the nature of the proceedings, the whole case appears upon the record, unless those proceedings are such as to shew on what the decree has been founded, and to support that decree.

In the case at bar damages are assessed as they would be by the verdict of the jury, without any specifications of items which can shew how the account was made up, or on what principles the sum given as damages was assessed. This mode of proceeding would not be approved of if it was even probable from the testimony contained in the record that the sum reported by the commissioners of the district court was really the sum due. The district court ought not to have been satisfied with a report giving a gross sum in damages unaccompanied by any explanation, of the principles on which that sum was given. It is true captain *Murray* ought to have excepted to this report. His not having done so however does not cure an error apparent upon it, and the omission to shew how the damages which were given had accrued, so as to enable the judge to decide on the propriety of the assessment of his commissioners, is such an error.

Although the court would in any case disapprove of this mode of proceeding, yet in order to save the parties the costs of further prosecuting this business in the circuit court, the error which has been stated might have been passed over, had it not appeared probable that the sum, for which the decree of the district court was rendered, is really greater than it ought to have been according to the principles by which the claim should be adjusted.

This court is not therefore satisfied with either the decree of the district or circuit court, and has directed me to report the following decree:

[Decree][6]

This cause came on to be heard on the transcript of the record of the circuit court & was argued by counsel on consideration whereof it is adjudged orderd & decreed as follows to wit, That the decree of the circuit court, so far as it affirms the decree of the district court which directed restitution of the vessel & payment to the claimant of the nett proceeds of the sale of the cargo in Martinique deducting the costs & charges there according to the account exhibited by Capt. Murrays agent, being one of the exhibits in the cause & so far as it directs the parties to bear their own costs be affirmd, and that the residue of the said decree whereby the claim of the owner to damages for the seizure & detention of his vessel was rejected be reversed.

And this court proceeding to give such further decree as the circuit court ought to have given doth further adjudge order & decree, that so much of the decree of the district court as adjudges the libellant to pay costs & damages be affirmd but that the residue thereof by which the said damages are estimated at $20594.16 & by which the libellant was directed to pay that sum be reversed & annulled.

And this court doth further order & decree that the cause be remanded to the circuit court with directions to refer it to commissioners to ascertain the damages sustaind by the claimant in consequence of the refusal of the libellant to restore the vessel & cargo at Martinique, & in consequence of his sending her into a port of the United States for adjudication; and that the said commissioners be instructed to take the actual prime cost of the cargo & vessel with interest thereon, including the insurance actually paid & such expences as were necessarily sustaind in consequence of bringing the vessel into the United States as the standard by which th⟨e⟩ damage⟨s⟩ ought to ⟨be⟩ measured.

Each party to pay his own costs in this court & in the circuit court. All which is orderd & decreed accordingly.[7]

Printed, William Cranch, *Reports of Cases Argued and Adjudged in the Supreme Court of the United States . . .* , II (New York, 1806), 115–25. Decree, AD, Murray v. Charming Betsey, Appellate Case No. 115, RG 267, DNA.

1. For the decree of District Judge Peters, see 2 Cranch 64–70.

2. This report is embodied in the record certified from the U.S. Circuit Court, Pennsylvania (Murray v. Charming Betsey, Record on Appeal, 57–58, App. Cas. No. 115). The record contains pleadings, testimony, and exhibits presented at the district court, the decree of the district court, and the decree of the circuit court.

3. *U.S. Statutes at Large*, II, 7–11.

4. Talbot v. Seeman, 1 Cranch 1 (1801), the first case in which JM delivered the opinion of the Supreme Court.

5. Key, for the claimant, denied the applicability of Talbot v. Seeman, pointing to the great difference in arming between the *Amelia* and the *Charming Betsey* (2 Cranch 94–95).

6. The text of the device (printed, 2 Cranch 195–26) is from the original manuscript in JM's hand filed with the case papers (see n. above).

7. Five days later, on 27 Feb., JM delivered the opinion in Little v. Barreme, in which the court held another American naval commander, George Little, liable for damages for the seizure of the *Flying Fish,* also a Danish vessel. At issue was whether Little should be answerable for obeying instructions from the secretary of the navy, although those instructions exceeded the strict letter of the law suspending commercial intercourse with France. The chief justice confessed that "the first bias of my mind was very strong in favour of the opinion that though the instructions of the executive could not give a right, they might yet excuse from damages. . . . But I have been convinced that I was mistaken, and . . . acquiesce in that of my brethren, which is, that the instructions cannot change the nature of the transaction, or legalize an act which without those instructions would have been a plain trespass" (2 Cranch 179).

Unsuccessful in the Supreme Court, Captains Murray and Little sought relief from Congress, which approved special acts for this purpose (*Annals of Congress,* XIV, 985, 994, 1005; XVI, 230–31, 260–61). The court's opinions in these two cases were printed together in a report on Little's claim by the House Committee of Claims. See *Report from the Committee of Claims, to Whom Were Referred . . . the Memorial of George Little, . . . December 10, 1805* (Washington, D.C., 1805; S #9599).

Contract With Joseph Thompson

[Washington, ca. February 1804][1]

It is agreed between John Marshall & Joseph Thompson that John Marshall will sell at ten shillings per acre his survey adjoining the tract sold by John Marshall to Joseph Thompson & his brothers & that Joseph Thompson will pay on the first day of September after the last payment of the land already sold shall become due which is in September 1804, the said sum of ten shillings per acre for the whole of the said land.[2] And that the land shall remain as security for the purchase money. The money is to be paid in September 1805. The parties bind themselves & their heirs to perform this agreement.

J MARSHALL [L.S.]

Sealed & delivered in   JOSEPH THOMPSON [L.S.]
presence of
CHARLES LEE

ADS, ViU. In JM's hand except for Thompson's signature and attestation of Charles Lee. Undated (see n. 1).

1. This document was annexed to Thompson's bill in chancery against JM, which was filed in the Superior Court of Chancery at Winchester in 1816. Although the bill has not been found, JM's answer is extant (answer, 9 Dec. 1816, Thompson v. Marshall, ViU). The answer does not state the date of the contract but says that it was reduced to writing and executed "at Washington." Since the text of the contract indicates that it was drawn sometime before Sept. 1804, the editors have conjectured that the meeting

between JM and Thompson took place during the Feb. 1804 term of the Supreme Court.

2. JM on 31 Aug. 1802 sold a tract of land containing nearly seven hundred acres on the "North River of Cacapon" in Hampshire County (now W.Va.) to John, Joseph, and James Thompson. The present contract was for an adjoining tract of two hundred acres. Final payment for these lands did not occur until 1819 and 1822, when JM executed deeds to James Thompson, John Thompson, and Joseph Thompson (deeds, JM to James Thompson, 5 Nov. 1819; JM to John Thompson, 5 Nov. 1819; JM to Joseph Thompson, 5 Nov. 1819, 18 June 1822, Hampshire County Deed Book XXII [1820–22], 57–58, 58–59, 243–44; XXIII [1822–24], 73, Wv-Ar).

Deposition

[Washington, 2 March 1804][1]

John Marshall deposes that when he first heard the fact which Jonathan Snowden is stated by the chairman of this committee to have sworn to, relative to a conversation between judge Chase and judge Washington in his presence, relative to the trial of James Thompson Callender, he had not the slightest recollection of any conversation resembling that reported by the said Snowden.[2] On endeavoring since to retrace in his mind impressions formerly received, he has a vague and indistinct recollection of some conversation resembling that said to be stated by the said Snowden, but cannot pretend to particularise the words, or even the precise sentiment which was uttered. He does, however, positively assert his perfect conviction, that no such conversation was ever understood by him to be serious. He should certainly have entertained opinions of both those gentlemen very different from those he really entertains, if he had supposed such motives for judicial conduct to have been acknowledged by the one, or attributed to him by the other, without even the semblance of reproach.[3]

J. MARSHALL.

Sworn to before me this 2d day of March, 1804.

JOHN RANDOLPH,

Chairman of the Committee
of Inquiry into the official
conduct of Samuel Chase and
Richard Peters, Esquires,
or either of them.

Printed, *National Intelligencer and Washington Advertiser* (Washington, D.C.), 16 March 1804.

1. This deposition was embodied in the report of a committee "to enquire into the official conduct of Samuel Chase and Richard Peters." The committee, appointed on 7 Jan. and chaired by John Randolph, submitted its report on 6 Mar. (*Report of the Committee . . . "To Enquire into the Official Conduct of Samuel Chase . . ."* [Washington, D.C., 1804; S #7593]). Soon after, the *National Intelligencer* began to publish the report in installments.

2. Jonathan Snowden deposed to the committee on 3 Feb. that he had "accidentally" been in the company of JM and Justices Washington and Chase in the public room of a hotel during the meeting of the Supreme Court. The conversation, said Snowden, turned on Callender's publications against President Jefferson, Justice Washington remarking to Chase that had he known about this he "would scarcely have fined Callender so high at Richmond." According to Snowden, Chase replied in a serious tone that "to tell you the truth if I had known then, as much as I do now, I should not have fined him so high" (*National Intelligencer*, 14 Mar. 1804).

3. Washington deposed to the same effect as JM, stating that he had often been in the habit of conversing "jocosely" with Chase and that the alleged conversation, "if it ever took place, was altogether of this cast" (ibid., 16 Mar. 1804). On 12 Mar. the House approved the committee's recommendation that Chase be impeached. For an account of the preliminaries leading up to the impeachment, see Haskins and Johnson, *Foundations of Power*, 223–34.

From Caleb P. Wayne

Sir,   Philada. March 20. 1804

I have now completed *one half* the first vol. & expect to finish it in *four weeks* from this date; at which time I shall wish to have the 2d vol. or at least a part. I shall be glad to hear from you on this subject; & would be gratified to know by whom & how I am to receive it. Such difficulty have I had in arranging dates, at the sides of the pages (which I fear I have not done correctly) that I must express a hope that you will have the goodness to arrange them accurately in the manuscript of the 2d vol. & that your orders to me shall be to "*adhere strictly in every particular to the manuscript.*" I shall deem it a favour if the 2d vol. is not delayed many days beyond the time I mention. I am, very respectfully, Your Most Obe

                                                              CPW

ADfS, Dreer Collection, PHi; Tr, Marshall Papers, DLC. Endorsed on verso: "Copy to the Chief Justice/C P. Wayne."

CALEB P. WAYNE

Oil on canvas attributed to Bass Otis, ca. 1840. *Courtesy of Thomas C. Roberts, Princeton, New Jersey (Photographed by T. Wayne Roberts)*

To Bushrod Washington

My dear Sir   March 25th. 1804

So idle were the gentlemen I had employed in my copying business during my absence, that with my utmost exertions I coud not get the books in readiness in time to send them to you before your departure from Alexandria. Every thing is now prepared, & I watch the stage continually for some person who will take them to Philadelphia. I am extremely anxious that you shoud give the volume an attentive reading & make all those corrections which I am sure will suggest themselves to you.

I have not been able to compare the second copy with the first & I am sure it is very incorrect in many respects. A part of it has been made by a person who will insert very different words from those intended by the author & who is also extremely inattentive to pointing. When the book is read by yourself it may perhaps be compared, or if not Morgan must attend to comparing it immediately before Wayne puts it to the press. In going over the first copy I have been struck with the propriety of making paragraphs where none are at present made & have marked such places thus # or thus ¶. Mention this both to Wayne & Morgan.

I hope you will come on to Philadelphia as soon as your business in Jersey is over as I cannot say how soon an opportunity of sending on the box may present itself.[1]

I repeat my a[n]xious wish that you will read the book with attention enough to make corrections. I wish too that you woud note them & inform me of them.

The papers originally designed to close the first volume mention the appointment of General Washington. The alterations of the arrangement of volumes require an alteration in this respect also as the appointment is mentioned more at large & more properly in the beginning of the chapter which will now follow that in which it is first stated. This repetition woud now be improper. It will therefore be necessary to make some alterations. The sentence may stop with saying that Congress proceeded "to organize the ⟨higher⟩ departments of the army" without ⟨na⟩ming the persons appointed, & afterwards when in the succeeding chapter the appointment of the commander in chief is mentioned the other appointments may be stated in a note.[2] Your

J MARSHALL

ALS, Dreer Collection, PHi; Tr, Marshall Papers, DLC. Addressed to Washington at Trenton, N.J.; postmarked 2⟨7?⟩ Mar., Richmond. Washington noted on cover, "Paragraph marks/mode—." MS torn where seal was broken.

1. Washington would be in Trenton to attend the federal circuit court term beginning on 1 Apr.

2. Quoted passage at vol. II, chap. 3, 222. George Washington's appointment as commander-in-chief is at the beginning of chap. 4, 235–37, with a note on other appointments at the bottom of p. 237.

To Caleb P. Wayne

Sir   Richmond March 27th. 1804

Mr. Davison of Richmond set out this morning for Philadelphia in the stage & has done me the favor to take with him a box addressd to Judge Washington containing two copies of the second volume of the work you are publishing. My sollicitude to get on the second volume was such that I have not compared the copies a precaution of absolute necessity as I know the copyist to be very incorrect. I feared that if I missed the present opportunity another might not present itself in time.

Mr. Washington ought to receive the box, but if he shoud be still at Trenton I fear Mr. Davison will not have an opportunity of delivering it to him as his stay in Philadelphia will be only three or at most four days. I must therefore request you, as he will reach the city a day before this letter, to inquire for him at Hardys tavern[1] where I am informed he proposes lodging, & take the box into your possession. If you will be so good as to show him this letter he will be obliging enough to deliver it to you. I wish it not to be opened till Mr. Washington receives it.

It will be necessary to strike out that part of the concluding chapter now in your possession which relates to the appointment of a commander in chief & other General officers to the army. The change in the arrangement by which the two chapters designed for the first are transfered to the second volume will render this alteration proper. Those appointments are mentiond in what will now be the 4th. chapter of the second volume, & the immediate repetition coud not be tolerated. The appointments made by Congress of other General officers shoud be inserted in a note in the 4th. chapter where the appointment of the commander in chief is mentiond. In the third chapter the sentence may stop with stating that "Congress proceeded to organize the higher departments of the army." I have unfortunately mislaid your letter received while at Washington so that I cannot direct the alteration precisely but must request Mr. Washington & yourself to take this trouble.

On reading over one of the copies of the volume now sent I was a good deal dissatisfied with the general dissertation which concludes one of the chapters—I think the 9th.[2] I[t] contains I think several repetitions which ought to be avoided & I designed materially to have altered it, but the importance of availing myself of the present opportunity to send it, has obliged me to assign that task to Mr. Washington. I wish you woud call his attention particularly to it.

I have sent several maps which may perhaps require some alteration & amendment. By comparing them with similar maps in Gordon this may readily be done. It is probable that in several instances what is in one map may be divided to advantage, & that parts of one may be transfered to another. I am Sir very respectfully, Your Obedt. Servt

J MARSHALL

ALS, Dreer Collection, PHi; Tr (typed), Marshall Papers, DLC. Addressed to Wayne at Philadelphia; postmarked Richmond, 27 Mar. "Washington" written, inverted, at top of cover. Along edge of cover, Bushrod Washington summarized JM's directions concerning MS of *Life*: "To strike out that part of the Concluding chapter on Mr Wayne's Copy, relating to the appointment of Command. in chief & new officers/9th. Chapt. repetitious—see."

1. Joseph Hardy kept an inn at 98 High St. (James Robinson, *The Philadelphia Directory for 1804, Containing the Names, Trades and Residence of the Inhabitants of the City, Southwark, Northern Liberties, and Kensington* [Philadelphia, (1804)], 102).

2. In published form, vol. II concludes with chap. 8. JM was probably referring to what became either chap. 1 or chap. 5 of vol. III. At the end of chap. 1 are "Observations on militia and other defects in the structure of the American army" (54–63). In JM's letter of the next day (28 Mar.), he asked Washington to correct the repetitions in the chapter covering "the loss of Ticonderoga," which is found in vol. III, chap. 5. This chapter continues the account begun in chap. 1 of the northern campaign around Lakes Champlain and George in 1776–77. As it now reads, most of chap. 5 narrates military actions. Possibly, Washington eliminated the "series of observations on miscellaneous subjects" that JM thought repetitious.

To Bushrod Washington

My dear Sir   Richmond March 28th. [1804]

The day after I wrote to you I was informed that a Mr. Davidson of this place was setting out for Philadelphia & woud take charge of a box to you. I thought it most advisable to send it tho' I had not had it in my power to examine the second copy, or to correct the first. There is a part about which I wish you to be particularly attentive, as, on reading it over I had designed to change it, but the opportunity of sending it was so sudden that I have omitted to make the corrections I intended. It is in that chapter which states the loss of Ticonderoga,[1] after which there are a series of observations on miscellaneous subjects some of which appeard to me when reading them to be improper repetitions of what had before been said in other places. I had intended to compare that chapter with the prior passages on the same subjects & to make the necessary corrections but have not been able to do so without foregoing an opportunity of sending you the books which perhaps might not offer again in a short time.

The maps constitute a subject of great interest to which I also request your particular attention. I have sent several but they are not perhaps exactly as they ought to be engraved, & may I presume very easily receive some valuable alterations. I have sent a map of Boston & its environs to be inserted in the first volume where the siege of that town is stated. Gordons history of the war contains also a very excellent plan of the town & of the position of the armies. It will be well to compare them & make any improvements in that sent which the other may suggest.[2]

I have also sent a plan of the country about Brooklyn, which shoud be inserted a little before the battle of Long island. Of this too there is a very excellent engraving in Gordon & it will be well to compare them.[3]

It will be proper to have a map of the island of New York representing forts Washington & Lee, & the adjacent country on the east side of the Hudson up to Croton river representing the positions taken by the two armies till fort Washington was stormed.[4] I have sent such charts in two or three parts. Perhaps two maps shoud be made of the whole, the one laying down York island at large with a glance of the adjoining country & the other describing the adjoining country & showing its connection with New York.

There shoud also be a plan of that part of New Jersey adjoining the Hudson laying down the country & rivers as far as Brunswick,[5] and another plan laying down the Delaware from Philadelphia for a considerable distance above Trenton with all the towns upon it & the positions of the armies.[6] This plan shoud also comprehend Allenstown & Princeton, & I think Morristown.

I have sent plans such as those described & they may very probably be improved by maps of the country. I shoud also think it worth while to lay down the country occupied by both armies in January & february 1777 including Morris town, Middlebrook, bound brook, Bonhamtown quibble town &c, & Brunswic & Amboy.[7]

If I coud see Mr. Wayne & converse with him on this subject it woud be gratifying to me, but this is certainly impossible. I hope, & have no doubt of it, that he will be extremely attentive to the correctness of the work, & that he will advert to any apparent inaccuracies which may escape you as well as me in the hurried examination we are both obliged to be content with. I flatter myself we shall see you in May & that you will then give a very deliberate reading to so much of the 3d. vol. as shall be finished by that time.

I beleive I mentiond to you that Mr. Morgans copy has not yet been examined & compared with the other.

Mr. Davidson who puts up at Hardy's will leave town probably about the time this reaches Philadelphia. I therefore wrote to Mr. Wayne yesterday requesting him, if you shoud not be in town to call on Mr. Davidson & receive the box, to be kept unopened till your arrival. Your

J MARSHALL

ALS, Dreer Collection, PHi; Tr (typed), Marshall Papers, DLC. Addressed to Washington at Philadelphia; postmarked Richmond, 28 Mar. Endorsed by Washington, who summarized JM's directions below his endorsement: "attend to the observations following & preceding the taking of Tyconderoga & correct repetitions if they occur."

1. The evacuation of Ticonderoga is covered in vol. III, chap. 5. See JM to Wayne, 27 Mar. 1804 and n. 2.

2. Wayne published a set of ten maps in a separate atlas, *The Life of George Washington. Maps and Subscribers' Names* (Philadelphia, 1807), as promised in the "Proposals" for publishing the *Life* (*Philadelphia Gazette & Daily Advertiser*, 22 Sept. 1802). Plate I shows "Boston with its Environs," engraved by John Vallance. JM's account of the siege of Boston, 1775–76, is in vol. II, chap. 4. This map is nearly identical to the one in Gordon, *History of the Independence of the U.S.*, II, facing the title page. All observations concerning the *Maps* are based on copy 2 (bookplate, Westmoreland Club) at the Virginia State Library. (See Wayne to JM, 20 Aug. 1804, n. 9, for full information on the draftsman and engravers of all the plates).

3. Plate II, "A Plan of New York Island, part of Long Island &c. shewing the Position of the American and British Armies, before, at, and after the Engagement on the Heights, August 27th. 1776." This map was drawn by Samuel Lewis and engraved by Joseph H. Seymour. The Battle of Long Island occurs in vol. II, chap. 7, beginning at p. 440. (Marginal dates here are incorrect; rather than "July," the month should read August.) The cartographic features of this plan of New York do not match those of the map in Gordon, *History of the Independence of the U.S.*, II, facing p. 310.

4. Plate III, "A Plan of the Country from Frog's Point to Croton River shewing the Positions of the American and British Armies from the 12th. of October 1776 untill the Engagement on the White Plains on the 28th.," engraved by Marshall. This and the plans mentioned below were "Drawn by S. Lewis from the Original Surveys made by order of Gen Washington." In vol. II, chap. 8, 514–17, JM described the storming of Fort Washington, which occurred on 16 Nov. 1776.

5. Plate IV, "A Plan of the Northern Part of New Jersey, shewing the Positions of the American and British Armies after crossing the North River in 1776," engraved by Francis Shallus.

6. Plate V, "A Map of the Country from Rariton River in East Jersey to Elk Head in Maryland Shewing the several Operations of the American and British Armies, in 1776 & 1777," engraved by Seymour.

7. These towns appear on the map in Plate IV.

To James M. Marshall

My dear brother   Richmond April 1st. 1804

I have just receivd your letter of the 15th. of March.[1] The proposition you made respecting the money from Seymour was not at first accurately understood by me.[2] I supposed you to wish to pay Mr. Colston not the whole sum, but only that part of it to which he was entitled so that the residue woud be a remittance from you & myself in proportion to our interests. It was in consequence of this that I have remitted all the money in my hands. I am however entirely willing to pay the whole sum to Mr. Colston, & to consider that part of it which I have received as being remitted either on our joint account or for myself separately. If the latter shoud be your choice I wish to know it that I may prepare your part of the money to be disposed of as you may chuse.

I am desirous of settling all our accounts with Mr. Colston as soon as possible, & am very sensible of the necessity of doing so, but I cannot go up the country before my return from North Carolina which will be early in July. I hope the whole of our pecuniary affairs may be then arranged.

No other indication was given by the court of an opinion in the winchester case than is implied in the continuances on an argument turning almost entirely on the old question of the escheatability of the property. Had it been supposed that the act of Assembly had clearly settled that point, the cause woud not have lain over for another argument.[3] The election of Judge Tucker has bettered your prospects so far as respects that part of your case, but I am a little afraid of him on some others.[4]

The Clarksons, I beleive I mentiond to you, have not yet filed their bill. I begin to fear the event of every suit however clear th⟨e⟩ merits may be in my estimation & am consequently afrai⟨d⟩ that even this suit & that of Beverly may go against us.

I have just receivd to my inexpressible astonishment, a letter from our lawyers in Staunton infor⟨m⟩ing me that the issue has been tried & that the jury have found that Alexander purchased 60,000$ of the note⟨s⟩ at par & the residue at 4/6 for the dollar.[5] Prepared as I wa⟨s⟩ to count on anything which I deemd within the compass of human depravity, I did not look for such a verdict as this. I ⟨do⟩ not know what may be the consequence of it. It is very probabl⟨e⟩ we may be ordered to convey the stock we have receivd, &, in that event we may possibly be compelld to pay a larger sum th⟨an⟩ it has netted us. I presume he will now listen to no proposit⟨ion⟩ for settling this affair on the principle of the uti possidetis.[6]

I shall direct a motion for a retrial of the⟨e⟩ issue & shall appeal if that motion be rejected.[7] But if there shoud be a decree against Mr. Morris & not against us for mon⟨ey⟩ it will require deliberation before we give security.

I have not seen young Alexander:[8]

The novel principle introduced into the law establ⟨ish⟩ing the virginia bank of giving the direction of it entirely to the legislature is so very exceptionable that very few of the monied men of this place appear disposed to subscrib⟨e⟩ to it. I woud not trust a single dollar to it. I have not heretofore mentioned my opinion to you because I thought you woud read the law & decide for yourself. Some of the most judic⟨ious⟩ here think that, shoud the bank fill, which is very doubtful, the shares will not long remain at par.

The last accounts from England render an invasion more probable than ever. The King is understood not to be dead bu⟨t⟩ mad.

I have just received the articles of impeachment against Judge Chase.[9] They are sufficient to alarm the friends of a pure & of course an independent judiciary, if among those who rule our land there be any of that description. I am my dear brother, your affectionate

J MARSHALL

Photostat of ALS, Marshall Papers, DLC. Angle brackets enclose letters obscured in margin.

1. Letter not found.

2. By a deed of 13 Dec. 1802, the Marshalls sold the remainder of the South Branch Manor (comprising eleven thousand acres) along with arrears of rent to Abel Seymour of Hardy County for the sum of £2,284 Virginia currency. Seymour was to pay the purchase price in four annual installments, beginning on 1 Mar. 1804 (Hardy County Deed Book V, 187–90, Wv-Ar).

3. The case of James Marshall v. Daniel Conrad was then being argued in the Virginia Court of Appeals. It had begun as an ejectment for certain lots in the town of Winchester, brought by Marshall in the Winchester District Court in 1799. Marshall claimed the lots for nonpayment of rents—rents that he contended had passed to him in the 1797 deed from Denny Fairfax conveying the Fairfax manor lands. The case reopened the question of Fairfax's title, which had been at issue in earlier litigation between Fairfax and David Hunter. The Conrad ejectment also involved the effect of the compromise act of 1796. Under this measure the commonwealth gained title to the unappropriated lands of the Northern Neck, and the Marshall syndicate was confirmed in its title to the manor lands. Marshall lost in the district court but won on appeal at the Oct. 1805 term (5 Call 264). On the Marshalls' purchase of the Fairfax lands and the legal controversy over the title, see *PJM*, II, 140–49; V, 228–56.

4. St. George Tucker had been elevated to the Court of Appeals in Jan. 1804. JM alluded to Tucker's opinion in the case of Hunter v. Fairfax, given in the Winchester District Court in Apr. 1794. Ruling in favor of Fairfax, Tucker maintained that an alien's property could escheat to the commonwealth only by a solemn inquest of office, which had not taken place in this case (*PJM*, V, 248–49nn). As it happened, Judge Tucker did not sit in Marshall v. Conrad because his son, Henry St. George Tucker, was

a resident of Winchester and interested in the outcome. See Henry St. George Tucker to St. George Tucker, 3 Dec. 1805 (Tucker-Coleman Papers, ViW).

5. The trial mentioned by JM grew out of a complex series of suits between Robert Morris and William Alexander arising from Morris's tobacco contract with the Farmers-General of France in the 1780s. The litigation began in the High Court of Chancery in 1788, with JM serving as one of Morris's lawyers. That court issued a decree in 1798, which was appealed to the Court of Appeals. The Court of Appeals in 1801 sustained the decree in part and remanded the suits to the High Court of Chancery for further proceedings. In 1802 the suits were transferred to the newly created Superior Court of Chancery at Staunton. For the earlier proceedings, see *PJM*, V, 93–116.

Morris by this time had endured debtor's prison and bankruptcy proceedings. JM and his brother James (Morris's son-in-law) apparently had a power of attorney to continue this litigation in the chancery court at Staunton. One of the pending issues involved Alexander's claim for a full discount for his company's purchase of promissory notes drawn and endorsed by Morris and by John Nicholson. The nominal value of these notes was $110,500. The notes had been purchased in 1798, when speculators were buying them up at ten cents on the dollar. The High Court of Chancery, sustained by the Court of Appeals, had decreed that Alexander be allowed to discount only the price he paid for the notes. This price was to be settled by a jury, and it was this verdict that JM was reporting to his brother (report of Commissioner William Hay, 12 May 1798, Morris v. Alexander, Arents Tobacco Collection, NN; Morris v. Alexander, 3 Call 102–5 [1801]; Chernow, *Robert Morris*, 211, 228).

6. "Uti possidetis"—a phrase in international law signifying that parties to a treaty are to retain possession of what they have acquired by force during the war.

7. A motion for a retrial was unnecessary, for the court on 2 Apr. had already set aside the verdict on the ground that improper evidence had been admitted. After a new trial at the Charlottesville District Court, final decrees in these suits were issued on 3 Dec. 1804 and 6 Apr. 1805 (Superior Court of Chancery, Augusta County, Order Book, 1802–5, 221, 253, 340–41, 402–4 [microfilm], Vi).

8. Probably Robert Alexander, son of William Alexander. See JM to Robert Alexander, 16 Mar. 1807.

9. Impeachment articles against Associate Justice Samuel Chase were reported to the House of Representatives on 26 Mar. (*Trial of Samuel Chase* . . . [2 vols.; 1805; New York, 1970 reprint], I, 1–4).

To Bushrod Washington

My dear Sir   Richmond April [20][1] 1804

I have just received your letter inclosing your notes on the parts of the life which you have read.[2] I am sorry they are not more ample— but I hasten to advert to the circumstance mentiond by Mr. Wayne which is of real importance. I had designed barely to hint at Braddocks defeat in the first volume & to detail the circumstances minutely in the second & thought I had done so, but on looking into what I beleive is the 12th. chapter I find I have been much more particular than I thought myself or woud wish to be. There is certainly a repetition which is improper & ought to be avoided. It appears to me extremely difficult to part with what is inserted in the 2d. volume as it belongs to the life of General Washington & there will be a chasm shoud it be omitted.[3] I do not know whether it is possible to leave out what is inserted in the first. If it is possible I very much wish it to be done. There woud be no difficulty in it if the work shoud be in a situation which admits the alteration. I woud propose after stating the arrival of Braddock at fort Cumberland "from whence the army destined against fort Du Quesne was to commence its march," to proceed with a new paragraph—thus.[4]

["]The difficulties of opening a new road through a very rough country having been at length surmounted, Braddock left his heavy baggage with the rear division of his army under Colonel Dunbar, & pressing forward himself at the head of about twelve hundred men, proceeded against the enemy, as if entirely unapprehensive of danger. Within about seven miles of the fort he fell into an ambuscade laid for him by a party of French & Indians & was defeated with immense slaughter. The General himself & several officers of rank were killed; & the remnant of the detachment fled in confusion & dismay to the camp of Dunbar. The terror excited by this unexpected calamity &c." Then to proceed as in the copy originally sent. If this alteration can take place it must also be made with Mr. Morgan. If it cannot be so good as to give me immediate information that I may change those parts of the first chapter of the second volume which relate to the same transaction in such a manner as to diminish if it shoud be impossible to remove the palpable & almost verbal repetition which at present appears. If the copy is deliverd to Mr. Morgan before this correction is made you will of course inform him of it & request him to retain the copy for the correction. It shall be forwarded the second post after I know its necessity. Indeed I will forward it in a few days to be used eventually.

Your conjecture respecting the Chapters is right. The 1st. chap. in the sheets sent you is to be designd to be the first of the 2d. vol. & the 14th. & 15th. Chapters formerly sent Mr. Wayne to be the 2d. & 3d. of the 2d. vol. On this account the 2d. chap. of the sheets sent you is marked as the 4th. of the vol. & those which succeed it are markd the 5th—6th. &c. I have mentiond to Mr. Wayne a change in what will be the 3d. chapter of the 2d. volume. The appointment of General officers must be omitted & the sentence must stop I think with the statement that Congress proceeded to organize the higher departments of the army. The appointments of the other officers may be mentioned in a note to that part of the 4th. chapter which states the appointment of General Washington. This change you will please to superintend & you will of course communicate it to Mr. Morgan. The last sentence in the chapter was forwarded to me by Mr. Wayne. It is that which states the determination of each party to appeal to the sword. That sentence will remain as it is & will conclude what will be the third chapter of the 2d. volume.[5]

I very much regret that the manuscript is so voluminous. Had I suspected this circumstance at first I coud have diminishd it to advantage, but it is now impossible without recomposing the whole. The history of the war cannot be completed in the 3d. volume. The 4th. must comprehend a part of it but it may also embrace all those circumstances which relate to the organization of the present government so that the civil administration may be comprized in one volume. It is however necessary for me to know precisely where the 2d. volume will end & the sooner I know the better, as it will have an effect on what I am now engaged in copying & what I have yet to write. I woud propose that it shoud terminate with that Chapter which details the battles of Trenton & Princeton. The only objection to it is that there may be more than 500 pages in the volume shoud it extend to the close of that chapter. Shoud this be the fact, let me know how many pages will be comprized in the volume including that chapter & also let me know with what that chapter begins. This is necessary because I am not sure that the copies conform in this particular to the original manuscript in my possession. In the manuscript that chapter is a very long one. It commences with the first operations in New York & probably the 2d. volume woud be too much abridged by giving the whole of it to the third.[6] Let me have immediate & precise information on this subject.

If Mr. Short[7] is still in Philadelphia present [him] with my compliments & my thanks for the aid he has been so good as to give you & tell him the obligation woud have been much greater if he woud more freely have corrected the inaccuracies which must have presented themselves to him as well as you. Indeed my dear Sir I am persuaded that I have reason to complain of you. I feard that you woud not censure & alter freely & therefore particularly requested that you woud do so. I do not think you can have complied with my wishes. You mistake me very much if you think I rank the corrections of a friend with the bitter sarcasms of a foe, or that I shoud feel either wounded or chagrined at my inattentions & inaccuracies being pointed out by another. I know there are many & great defects in the composition—defects which I shall lament sincerely & feel sensibly when I shall see the work in print. The hurried manner in which it is pressed forward renders this inevitable.

Of the two copies which you have one is copied by a single person, the other by several. That copied by a single person you will readily distinguish by the sameness of the hand & the continuity of the copy. It is the most correct & where the two copies differ that is to be your guide.

There is a note in one of the chapters which will probably be thought to convey a malignant & unnecessary aspersion on the author of the farmers letters. I am myself disposed to think so, & unless you are desirous of retaining it I wish it to be expunged.[8] I hesitated when I inserted it & my subsequent reflections lead me to disapprove it.

I must see you at our circuit court in may.[9]

I woud make a slight alteration in the sentence which mentions the circumstance of Colo. Washingtons joining Braddock. Instead of saying "Colonel Washington joind Braddock immediately after his setting out from Alexandria," I woud say "Colo. Washington joind Braddock immediately after his departure from Alexandria."[10]

After this let the text remain unalterd till that part is reachd where after his sickness he rejoind the army. Then say

He rejoined the General in a covered waggon the day before the action on the Monongahela, an account of which has been given in the preceding volume.

Tho very weak he immediately enterd on the duties of his station. In a very short time after the action had commenced he was the only aid remaining alive & unwounded. On him alone devolved, in an engagement with marksmen &c[11] continue the text till Dunbar retired to Philadelphia—then strike out the state of the loss & the reflections on the conduct of General Braddock[12] & resume the text with the words

"Colo. Washington was greatly disappointed & disgusted" &c & make no other alteration except in that part of his letter to Governor Dinwiddie which states that near sixty of the officers were killed & wounded. The fact is that above sixty were killed & wounded & I think we may take the liberty to strike out the word "near" & insert either, "above" or "upwards of."[13] This however I leave entirely to you. It is probable the name of the river may be often improperly spelled. It shoud be Monongahela.

Dear Sir

In the expectation that no change can with convenience be made in the first volume I send you the alterations in the second which will avoid improper repetition as far as possible & will retain what immediately respects General Washington. It woud probably be not less difficult to correct the copy of the first volume actually sent to England, than to correct that which remains. I therefore think on reflec-

tion we had better not attempt it, but content ourselves with reform-
ing the secon⟨d⟩.

I enclose you a copy of General Lees letter for the note & am
astonishd at its having been omitted. Perhaps I had designd not to
insert it, but I think it was copied & transmitted with the papers. I
may however be mistaken. Perhaps it is in one copy & not in the
other. You will please to have it inserted in both copies.¹⁴

I am very anxious to know where the 2d. volume may stop. I woud
prefer its ending with the chapter containing the battle of Princeton.
If it cannot let me know whether it must end with the preceding
chapter & let me know in either case how many pages will remain for
the 3d. Volume.

What number of copies will Wayne strike off for his first edition &
what is the intelligence respecting subscribers? Your,

J MARSHALL

ALS, Dreer Collection, PHi; Tr (partial), Marshall Papers, DLC. Addressed to Washington at Philadelphia; postmarked Richmond, 20 Apr. "Philadelphia" and "Thos."
inscribed several times on cover, probably by JM's son Thomas, who was due in Philadelphia in April to assist on vol. II of *Life* (see JM to Bushrod Washington, 29 Apr.
1804).

1. Day supplied from postmark (see n.).
2. Letter not found.
3. JM described the 1755 campaign of Gen. Edward Braddock against Fort Duquesne and the defeat of his British and colonial forces on the Monongahela in vol. I,
chap. 12, 389–93 and again in vol. II, chap. 1, 14–19. JM gave greater detail concerning George Washington's role in the second account.
4. At vol. I, 390. This alteration was not incorporated in either the first or second
impression.
5. "But Britain had determined to maintain, by force, the legislative supremacy of
parliament; and America had determined, by force, to repel the claim" (vol. II, chap.
3, 234).
6. The last chapter in vol. II is chap. 8, which includes near the end the battles of
Trenton, 26 Dec. 1776 (543), and of Princeton, 3 Jan. 1777 (551–53). In print vol. II
came to 560 pages, excluding the appendix of notes, which was another 72 pages.
Although chap. 8 is long (86 pages), the original chapter apparently was divided into
two, as chap. 7 in the published volume contains the initial movements of troops in
New York, including the Battle of Long Island and subsequent evacuation. Chap. 8
begins with the skirmish on Harlem Heights in Sept. 1776.
7. Most probably William Short, who was in Philadelphia in the winter and spring of
1804. He and JM were old acquaintances from their days together at George Wythe's
law lectures at the College of William and Mary and on the Virginia Council of State.
Both were in France at the same time in 1797–98 (William Short Papers, DLC; *PJM*, I,
40 n. 5, 117 and n. 6, 142).
8. JM referred to John Dickinson, *Letters from a Farmer in Pennsylvania* (1767–68).
The note was deleted, for JM simply comments that "many very able political essays
appeared in the papers" refuting the premises of the Townshend Acts (vol. II, 103).
9. The U.S. Circuit Court for Virginia was to meet in Richmond from 22 May until 8
June. The first part of JM's letter ends here, near the bottom of the fourth page. At the

top of the next page he added a set of alterations for vol. II, which he followed with a letter of explanation to Washington.

10. At vol. II, 14. Alteration incorporated.

11. At vol. II, 18. Alteration incorporated, though with minor changes in placement of phrase and indentation.

12. At vol. II, 20. Deletion made.

13. At vol. II, 20. Quotation from Washington's letter changed to read: "'there being upwards of sixty killed and wounded.'" Original letterbook copy of Washington to Governor Dinwiddie, 18 July 1755, reads: "there being near 60 killd and woundd" (Abbot, *Papers of Washington: Col. Ser.*, I, 339). JM took more than one "liberty" with the text of this and other Washington letters. While placing extracts within quotation marks, JM freely deleted or substituted words, changed spelling, abbreviations, and punctuation.

14. Gen. Charles Lee to John Hancock, president of the Continental Congress, 22 Jan. 1779 [1776]. Printed as Note XVII in vol. II, app., 64–68, with incorrect year of 1779 in dateline; mentioned in text at vol. II, 290.

From Benjamin Lincoln

Sir   Boston April 25 1804

Your favour of the 21 Novr Last came safely to hand and has been, until a few days since, in the possession of Mr Kerkland.

While I lament the loss of any of Genl Washingtons papers & that any circumstance should exist which may be construed by any one so as to involve my friend Mr Lear in any degree[1] of responsibility for the unfortunate event I am consoled by having had the most positive assurance from him, "that the loss of them happened without his privity or knowledge."

Mr Lear did not leave with me any receipt for papers delivered over to you he left in my hand a memorandum of sundry packages said to contain papers delivered to you to which your signature has not been affixed. If you wish that memorandum I will send a Copy of it with pleasure.

ADf, Benjamin Lincoln Papers, MHi. With many deletions and insertions, only the most substantive of which has been noted. Marked in top left-hand corner "Judge Marshall" in an unknown hand.

1. "Of guilt" deleted here.

To Bushrod Washington

My dear sir   Richmond april 29th. 1804

In the letters lately addressed to you I have forgotten to mention a circumstance which deserves some attention. In the old books from which I extracted the facts composing the first volume I found our bay spelt thus—*Chessapeake*. Without any examination of the orthography I beleive I have gone on to spell it in the same manner. My attention was not attracted to the word till I began to compare some sheets which have been copied for the 3d. volume with the original when I noticed it & on looking into some modern books find it spelt with a single s & without the e final; thus—*Chesapeak*. The latter is I beleive the approved orthography & of consequence I coud wish to have the correction made.[1]

I have also observed that I have in the word enterpri⟨z⟩e, used the letter z. instead of s. It shoud be written *enterprise*. This I hope has been corrected. If not I wish it to be done.[2]

I hope my son is in Philadelphia assisting to compare the 2d. volumes with each other.[3] If he is not & you wish his aid I will thank you to drop him a line requesting him to see you.

I am very desirous of hearing how many printed pages the written manuscript for the 2d. vol. will overrun the printed copy & at what place the 2d. vol. will terminate. I also wish to know whether you correct the 2d. volume respecting Braddocks defeat in conformity with my letter & how many copies Mr. Wayne proposes to strike off for the first edition. The prospects of subscribers too will not be unacceptable information. I shall expect you in may & am, dear Sir your

J MARSHALL

ALS, Dreer Collection, PHi; Tr, Marshall Papers, DLC. Addressed to Washington at Philadelphia; postmarked Richmond, 30 Apr. MS marred by ink blots.

1. Wayne apparently was able to change the spelling to "Chesapeak" at the front of vol. I in the table of contents but not in the text where it appears as "Chessapeake" (e.g., 28, 30, 39). It was not too late to change it in vol. II, however, where it is spelled according to JM's direction (e.g., 382). The second impression of vol. I has the revised spelling of "Chesapeak" (e.g., 29, 31, 41).

2. The word occurs spelled correctly in vol. I.

3. See JM to Bushrod Washington, 20 Apr. 1804, n.

To Benjamin Lincoln

Sir   Richmond May 6th. 1804

I have to acknowlege the receipt of your letter of the 25th. of April. It was never my wish to excite an opinion in you or any other person that Mr. Lear had secreted the journal kept by General Washington. My letter to you evidences my dispositions on this subject & even that letter was written because Mr. Lear had rendered it unavoidable.

I understood Mr. Lear as stating that I had given a receipt for the papers containd in the trunk he had deposited with me. If this had been the fact I shoud have wishd to have seen a copy of it. As it is not I woud not give you the trouble of transmitting me the list you possess. With very great respect, I remain Sir your Obedt. Servt

J MARSHALL

ALS, Norcross Collection, MHi.

To Caleb P. Wayne

Sir   Richmond May 17th. 1804

In what will constitute the 3d. chapter of the 2d. vol. & which was originally designd for the last of the first, is a quotation from a speech of Mr. Burke relative to the Earl of Chattham. It is in that part of the chapter which treats of the measures of the british Parliament late in 1774 & early in 1775. The sentence now reads thus. "This splendid orb," to use the bold metaphor of Mr. Burke, "had not yet set for ever. The western horizon yet blazed with his descending glory" & he determined to employ the few remaining moments of his life in the service of his country.

The quotation from Mr. Burke was made from memory, &, happening to look the other day at the speech I percieved it was not perfectly accurate. As a very slight alteration will make it so, & that alteration may take place without inconvenience I coud wish it to be made.

The sentence may stand thus. "This splendid orb," to use the bold metaphor of Mr. Burke, "was not *yet* entirely set. The western horizon was *still* in a blaze with his descending glory"; and the evening of a life which had exhibited one bright unchequered course of elevated patriotism, was devoted to the service of that country whose aggrandizement had swallowed up every other passion of his soul.[1]

You will please to communicate this alteration to Mr. Morgan.

In copying the work words will often be mispelt. I repeat my request that you will correct these mistakes when you fall in with them. It is my wish that the word which is frequently spelt *shew* shoud be uniformly spelt *show*. In several instances a z is used where according to correct orthography an s ought to be employd, & through my own inattention, the word Chesapeak is frequently, perhaps uniformly mispelt.

Be so obliging as to inform by what time you wish to receive the 3d. volume. I am Sir very respectfully, Your obedt. Servt

J Marshall

ALS, Dreer Collection, PHi; Tr, Marshall Papers, DLC. Addressed to Wayne at Philadelphia; postmarked Richmond, 19 May.

1. At vol. II, chap. 3, 191. Correction made. The quotation is from Edmund Burke's Speech on American Taxation, 19 Apr. 1774: "For even then, Sir, even before this splendid orb was entirely set, and while the Western horizon was in a blaze with his descending glory, on the opposite quarter of the heavens arose another luminary," Charles Townshend (Edmund Burke, *The Writings and Speeches of Edmund Burke*, II: *Party, Parliament, and the American Crisis, 1766–1774*, ed. by Paul Langford [Oxford, 1981], 452). In his review of British colonial policy, Burke here was speaking of Chatham's ministry of 1766–67. This speech was published as a pamphlet, *Speech of Edmund Burke, Esq., on American Taxation, April 19, 1774* (London: J. Dodsley, 1775), which went through numerous editions. Source text in the *Writings* was the third edition. JM may also have had access to *The Beauties of the Late Right Hon. Edmund Burke, Selected from the Writings, &c. of that Extraordinary Man, Alphabetically Arranged* (2 vols.; London: J. W. Myers, 1798), II, 456. The quotation is identical there to that printed in Burke, *Writings*.

From John Page

Sir, Richmond Sunday ½ past 6 P.M. May 27th. 1804.

Having, in consequence of information just received, called on the Mayor of the City and the Captain of the publick guard to co-operate with him, as far as his present important charges will permit, in the measures which may be necessary to prevent the apprehended rescue of Thomas Logwood, I have to request that you will be pleased to-morrow to give such orders for his safe Custody as you may deem proper.[1] I am with great respect &c.

John Page

Copy, Executive Letterbook, Vi.

1. Logwood, a Buckingham County planter, had been indicted by a federal grand jury for counterfeiting notes of the Bank of the U.S. He was tried and found guilty on four separate indictments on 24, 25, and 26 May (U.S. Cir. Ct., Va., Ord. Bk. IV, 421, 427–28, 428–29, 432). See also Page to JM, 30 May; JM to Page, 31 May; Sentence, 1 June 1804.

Logwood was part of a larger counterfeiting ring operating in Virginia and North Carolina during the winter and spring of 1804. When captured, he was in possession of more than twenty thousand dollars in counterfeit notes of the bank. His case was the subject of frequent communication between Governor Page and President Jefferson (Jefferson to Page, 15 Apr., 8 June 1804; Page to Jefferson, 18 June, 3 Nov. 1804, Jefferson Papers, DLC; Page to Jefferson, 1 June 1804, Executive Letterbook, Vi).

On receiving this letter, JM called on Governor Page and received an account of the information concerning an attempt by Logwood to escape. "He approved of the cautionary measures pursued by the Executive—but said he did not recollect that the Court had any power to direct guards but that he would examine the laws and inform me how far he could act in this business. On the day following (Monday 28th May) he sent the Marshall with a verbal Message on the subject, which I communicated to the Council at their first meeting which was on the 30th" (Page to Jefferson, 1 June 1804, Executive Letterbook, Vi). Page subsequently asked JM to state his opinion in writing (Page to JM, 30 May; JM to Page, 31 May 1804).

From John Page

Dear Sir,   Richmond May 30th. 1804

As I have been advised by the Council to keep a constant guard of six men at the prison in which Thomas Logwood is confined till the government or authority of the United States shall determine and direct in what manner the execution of the sentence of the Circuit Court on him shall be duly enforced, I have to request, that you will state to me in writing what you verbally stated by Major Scott the Marshal the other day,[1] respecting the doubts you entertained of the extent of your powers with respect to directing the Guards which might be necessary for the safe custody of this prisoner of the General government.[2] I am Sir with great respect &c.

                                                    JOHN PAGE

Copy, Executive Letterbook, Vi.

1. Joseph Scott had replaced David M. Randolph as U.S. marshal in Jan. 1802 (*Senate Executive Journal*, I, 403).

2. In addition to the immediate steps to be taken to prevent Logwood's escape, a question arose concerning the prisoner's ultimate place of confinement. JM and District Attorney George Hay asked Governor Page if Logwood would be admitted to the state penitentiary. A majority of the executive council advised the governor that Logwood could properly be so admitted, though one councillor, Alexander McRae, vigorously dissented from this advice. McRae contended that a state law enacted in 1789 giving the U.S. use of the state's jails applied only to the jails of the counties, corporations, and districts of the state. The penitentiary, on which construction did not begin until 1797, could not in his opinion be considered as a jail within the meaning of that law. Reinforcing McRae's strict interpretation of the law was a fear that the dangerous Logwood would probably effect his escape and that of many other convicts if he were to be housed in the penitentiary (Page to Council of State, 28 May 1804 [containing

council's written opinions]; advice of Council of State, 30 May 1804 [accompanied by McRae's protest], Executive Papers, Vi; Hening, *Statutes*, XIII, 3).

To John Page

Sir   Richmond May 31st. 1804

The intelligence you gave me respecting an intention to rescue Logwood who is convicted of felony in the court of the United States woud certainly have induced me to order a guard for his security if the laws had entrusted the Judge with that power. But I find no act of Congress to that effect & am therefore not satisfied that I ought to exercise it. I think it most advisable that an application shoud be made to the executive of the United States on this subject where alone the requisite authority exists.[1] With very much respect, I am Sir, your obedt. Servt

J MARSHALL

ALS, Executive Papers, Vi. Addressed by JM to Page. Endorsed by Page: "Judge Marshall's Opinion on his power to appoint a guard for the security of Logwood convicted in U.S. Court."

1. The Council of State also advised the governor to write the president of the U.S., which he accordingly did on 1 June, enclosing a copy of JM's letter. In his letter to President Jefferson, Page set forth the circumstances of the Logwood case and requested that the state "be relieved from the farther Care of Logwood and reimbursed the expences which may be incurred until the General Government shall take charge of their Prisoner." Jefferson replied on 8 June that Secretary of the Treasury Gallatin had instructed the U.S. marshal to reimburse the state for its expenses. He also noted that it was the practice of all the states to permit the general government the use of their jails and penitentiaries (Page to Jefferson, 1 June 1804, Executive Letterbook, Vi; Jefferson to Page, 8 June 1804, Jefferson Papers, DLC).

To Caleb P. Wayne

Sir   Richmond June 1st. 1804

During the pressure of my official business I have been able to give the sheets composing the first volume only a hasty reading. I inclose you a paper containing corrections—principally of errors in pointing.[1] I wish it may be possible to make them before the first volume shall be published—but I fear this cannot be done. I have not had time to read the notes. Before any second edition I shall be glad to have the enclosed returned to me that I may at more leisure make more alterations.

I shall be very glad to receive the proof sheets of the 2d. vol. I leave this place on the 12th. & shall return late in the month.

The errors in pointing very probably most of them, existed in the manuscript copy & therefore I fear will be found in the whole printed work. I congratulate you on the neatness & general correctness with which your part of the work has been executed. I am Sir very respectfully, Your Obedt.

J MARSHALL

ALS, Dreer Collection, PHi; Tr, Marshall Papers, DLC. Addressed to Wayne at Philadelphia; postmarked Richmond, 1 June. Draft of Wayne's reply of 4 June written on verso of cover and across page beneath JM's signature.

1. Enclosure not found.

United States v. Logwood
Sentence
U.S. Circuit Court, Virginia, 1 June 1804

Judge Marshall after having made his remarks on the formality of the Indictments, proceeded to pronounce the sentence.[1] He observed, that the punishment was left by the law to the discretion of the court; but that it could not exceed 10 years imprisonment, and a fine of 5000 dols.[2] that the present case, seemed as atrocious, as any case could possibly be, and that it therefore merited the very highest punishment which the law had permitted the court to inflict: that he was not one of those, who thought that a separate punishment could be inflicted for every separate charge; because according to this principle, the punishment might be so multiplied on the head of a criminal, as to exceed the very greatest limit which the *letter* of the law had assigned; and because from the very nature of the crime he did not believe the legislature had ever intended that this limit should be exceeded, as they would readily have considered that any one who would have undertaken to counterfeit one note, would have extended their ingenuity to notes of a different value: that the court would therefore sentence the criminal to the highest term of imprisonment which the law mentioned without pretending to multiply those terms for each separate charge: that as to the fine of 5000 dollars, which would fall most heavily, not upon the criminal, but upon his family, & which might perhaps absorb those resources which ought to reimburse his defrauded creditors, the Court was not so anxious to approach the greatest possible limit: they should condemn him to pay a fine of only 500 dollars. The Court therefore decided, that Thomas

Logwood should be imprisoned 9 years and 8 months, on the First indictment, and fined 490 dollars.[3]—On the Third indictment, he should be imprisoned 2 months, and fined 5 dollars;[4] And, on the Fifth, 2 months longer and 5 dollars more.[5]—it is presumed that the executive council will grant him a lodging in the State Penitentiary.[6]

Printed, *Enquirer* (Richmond, Va.), 2 June 1804.

1. Instead of one indictment reciting several charges, Thomas Logwood was prosecuted under five separate indictments for forging bank notes of various denominations payable at the Savannah and Charleston branches of the Bank of the U.S. and at the main bank in Philadelphia. The reason for the multiple indictments was that if one or more were dismissed for being defectively drawn, the accused might still be convicted under the others (Richmond *Enquirer*, 2 June 1804).

2. Logwood was prosecuted under a 1798 act "to punish frauds committed on the Bank of the United States" (*U.S. Statutes at Large*, I, 573–74).

3. The first indictment was for counterfeiting two notes of twenty dollars payable at the Savannah branch. Edmund Randolph, Logwood's attorney, moved to arrest judgment on the grounds that the first count of this indictment did not "charge the President, Directors & company of the Bank of the U.S, as being a corporation, nor conclude against the form of any act of congress, or against the form and dignity of the U.S." The second count likewise failed to describe the bank as a corporation and was also defective "because the intention to defraud is not charged to be to defraud a corporation, a body politic, or any persons by name." The court denied this motion (first indictment, 22 May 1804; motion in arrest of judgment, 1 June 1804, U.S. v. Logwood, Ended Cases [Unrestored], 1804, Vi; U.S. Cir. Ct., Va., Ord. Bk. IV, 464).

The second indictment was for forgery of a fifty-dollar note payable at the Savannah branch. It stated that Logwood "did forge on paper, a note . . . in form and to the likeness and Similitude, of a lawful and genuine note issued by order of the said president directors and Company of the said bank of the said United States." Randolph also sought to throw out this indictment on the ground that no law existed "whereby it is made criminal to forge any note issued by the President, Directors, and company of a bank of the United States of America." For reasons not clear from the record, the court upheld this objection and quashed the indictment (second indictment, 23 May 1804, U.S. v. Logwood; U.S. Cir. Ct., Va., Ord. Bk. IV, 428–29, 464; *U.S. Statutes at Large*, I, 574).

4. The third indictment stated that Logwood "did willingly assist persons unknown" in counterfeiting a twenty-dollar note payable at the Charleston branch (third indictment, 23 May 1804, U.S. v. Logwood).

5. The fifth indictment is not among the case papers. The trial on the fourth indictment was postponed pending the arrival of George Simpson, cashier of the Bank of the U.S. It stated that Logwood "did utter as true, three false forged and Counterfeited notes" of the bank. District Attorney Hay dropped further prosecution of this charge on 4 June (fourth indictment, 22 May 1804, U.S. v. Logwood; U.S. Cir. Ct., Va., Ord. Bk. IV, 470; Richmond *Enquirer*, 2 June 1804).

6. Whether Logwood served his full term in the penitentiary is not known. He was still there in Oct. 1808, when his wife attempted for a second time to procure a pardon from President Jefferson (Polly Logwood to Jefferson, 28 Aug. 1805, 29 Oct. 1808, Jefferson Papers, DLC).

To Caleb P. Wayne

Sir   Richmond June 2d. 1804

Mr. Washington is now here & some conversation with him has satisfied me that my opinion respecting the manner of placing the maps &c was ill founded.[1] I beleive it to be most proper that they shoud constitute a separate & additional volume as promised in the prospectus. In this arrangement it woud be proper that the plan of Boston shoud be placed in the same volume with the others. It woud be improper to make it an exception from the general rule.

If there is to be a separate book of plates it will not I think be necessary to divide the maps sent you as mentiond in my last. You may consult your own convenience on this point. Your Judgement will direct you what will be most satisfactory.

If I can have any proofsheets of the 2d. vol. by the 25th. of the month it will be as early as I can read them. I am respectfully, your obedt

J MARSHALL

ALS, Dreer Collectión, PHi. Addressed to Wayne at Philadelphia; postmarked Richmond, 4 June.

1. See JM to Wayne, 27 Mar. 1804; JM to Washington, 28 Mar. 1804 and n. 2.

From Caleb P. Wayne

Sir,   Philada. June. 4. 1804

Yesterday I recd. your letter of the 1st. with its enclosure. I am sorry it is not possible to make the corrections you have marked, in the first vol. in this edition. The whole volume is done & in the Bookbinders hands.[1] On comparing the corrections with the manuscript I find that most of them are *alterations* from it; with the exception of some of the punctuation in the 1st. 16 or 20 pages.

I feel much gratified with the opinion you are pleased to express of the exeaction of the printing.

It was my wish that you should prepare the book for a second edition as it was impossible to make corrections in the first & therefore agreeable to your request I return you the sheets, with those of the 2d vol. as far as we have progressed.[2] Beside the corrections you may think proper to make in phraseolegey for a second edition, I will consider it as a particular favour, if you will arrange all the dates accurately in the text; as in that form I contemplate a second impression it being the most modern & approved style, & I have marked one or two to show how I wish them. If you could make the Chapters of contents nearly of a size it would also add to it's beauty when printed. In one of the chapters I think Chap 6. The contents at the head of the text contain these words "*schenectady destroyed*" & not one word is mentioned of it until you come to Chap 7.[3] I did not discover this till it was too late. With respect to the maps you sent; I find it morally impossible to get them drafted or engraved in any reasonable time; so that their insertion in the body of the work will be out of the question unless it is very much delayed for the purpose; however, their omission, needed not be regretted, as their publication as an Atlas will be much more comfortable to the modern London style of publishing; in fact all their best works are now published in that way and are approved of. I could urge a variety of reasons for publishing them seperate could I see you, which under existing circumstances I cannot. If you can revise the first volume & send it back about the beginning of July, I should like it. The 3d. volume ought to be in Philada. about the same time so that if I do not reprint the first & 2d. I may go on with that; but I now think it very probable that I must reprint. If the 3d vol. could be placed in somebody's possession here, to be given me the moment I want it & not before, it would be very satisfactory; as in that case I should not fear it's appearance in Europe earlier than here.

ADf, Dreer Collection, PHi. Written on verso of JM to Wayne, 1 June (see n.). MS mutilated.

1. Wayne advertised that vol. I of the *Life* was "This Day Published" on 11 June 1804 (*United States' Gazette* [Philadelphia]).

2. As sales lagged, by the end of the summer JM and Wayne gave up on an immediate second edition. See *The Life of George Washington*, editorial note (preceding Preface, [ante 22 Dec. 1803]) and n. 21, and App. V for an account of impressions and editions of the *Life*.

3. Mentioned in contents at beginning of chap. 6 (vol. I, 204), but not discussed in text until early in chap. 7 (vol. I, 237–38). In *Life* (1805 ed.) the discrepancy between contents and text in the two chapters was rectified (vol. I, 212, 239, 245).

To Caleb P. Wayne

Sir   Richmond June 6th. 1804
    Your letter of the 27th. of May has just reachd me.[1] Before receiving it I had written to you expressing my change of opinion respecting the maps. The prospectus having stated that a volume of maps woud be given, a circumstance which had escaped my recollection, is conclusive on this subject. There are too some reasons of convenience

in favor of it. Between the publication of that part of the work which respects the war & that which relates the civil transactions a considerable interval must elapse. This will afford a very convenient time for attending to the plates.

I think all the maps you mention will be important additions & ought to be copied & inserted in the volume of maps. That Stedman was a british officer or that any other drafts man may be of that country constitutes no objection if he possessd the means of information.[2] I will send you on some other maps with the 3d. vol. which will be in readiness by the time you mention. The fourth will be necessary to complete the time preceding the civil administration & will be forwarded in the fall. I can send Braddocks plan of march but no other of the plans for which you enquire. I had not time to read the notes at the end of the 1st. vol. but am much pleasd with the general execution of the work. I am Sir very respectfully, your obedt. servt

J MARSHALL

ALS, Dreer Collection, PHi; Tr, Marshall Papers, DLC. Addressed to Wayne at Philadelphia; postmarked Richmond, 6 June.

1. Letter not found.
2. Stedman's *History of the American War* contained folding maps and plans. See Philo-Historia to JM, 1 Feb. 1801, n. 6.

To Caleb P. Wayne

Sir   June 11th. 1804

I am just setting out to North Carolina & shall take with me the sheets of the 2d. vol. which are just receivd. I shall return about the 25th. by which time I hope to find the sheets for great part of the 2d. vol. I have deliverd the 3d. vol. to Mr. Washington with several maps which belong to it. I showd him your letter & he will take care to have the two copies in Philadelphia to be deliverd when you are ready for them.[1] I am Sir your Obedt

J MARSHALL

ALS, Dreer Collection, PHi; Tr, Marshall Papers, DLC. Addressed to Wayne at Philadelphia; postmarked Richmond, 13 June. Transcript misdated 10 June.

1. In Wayne's 4 June letter to JM, he requested that vol. III be delivered to him at the beginning of July. Washington had been in Richmond with JM in late May and early June going "through the reading & correcting of the 3d Vol." Washington then returned to Mt. Vernon with the manuscript, where he read it a second time in order to make the table of contents. In the last week of June he sent it under the care of a resident of Philadelphia returning to that city. Wayne received it on 2 July (Washington

to Wayne, 22 June 1804, ViU; Washington to Wayne, 2 July 1804, Dreer Collection, PHi; Wayne to JM, 3 July 1804).

From Caleb P. Wayne

Sir,   Philada. June 26 1804

In the hurry of publishing I neglected to forward an additional number of sheets of the 2d. vol. but by this mail I have sent you as many as are complete. They are not proof sheets. The work is complete of those that are sent & no alteration of them can be made in this impression. I send them that you may have time to revise for a *second edition*. You will oblige me much by sending as quick as possible the sheets of the first vol. corrected, as you wish them to appear in a *second impression*. I wish the dates to be placed in text &c &c. as mentioned in former letters. Immediately on finishing the Second Vol. I wish to reprint the first & the sooner you can give it me the better, as the 2d. vol will be finished in a few days. I am, very respectfully, your

CPW

ADfS, Dreer Collection, PHi.

To Caleb P. Wayne

Sir   Richmond June 27th. 1804

I have just returned from North Carolina & shall return you by this or the next mail the printed sheets you enclosed me belonging to the 2d. vol. I am a little disappointed in not receiving others which I may run over & correct. I am persuaded that a slight reading of the printed sheets will suggest defects much more readily than they are discernd in the manuscript. I coud wish Mr. Morgan to be furnishd with the alterations except those of meer punctuation. I will thank you to tell him that the punctuation of the manuscript copy is very defective & that I wish the english editor to correct it according to his own judgement.

Mr. Washington has requested me to forward to you the enclosed papers to be added to the note respecting the combination against General Washington in the last of 1777 & beginning of 1778. I shoud myself have inserted them but from some unaccountable inattention totally forgot that they were in my possession. I am not certain whether any part of that transaction is detaild in a note or whether the whole forms a part of the text If the latter the present papers must be introduced in a note.[1] In the one case or the other some introductory sentences must be prepared. Not having the work before me I cannot ⟨p⟩repare them. They will be very short. Mr. Morgan will ⟨of⟩ course be permitted to take a copy of the note.

Mr. Henry was at the time Governor of Virginia & had been a very conspicuous member of the Congress of 1774.

I am unwilling that any allusion shoud be made to the author, & if the second letter of Mr. Henry shoud be inserted I wish a blank substituted for "General Mifflin." Only so much of that letter, if any, need be copied, as relates to this affair. Let the papers be kept together & preserved.[2]

There is a blank in fol. 5. p. 7. of one copy, & in fol. 5 p. 3 of the other copy of the 3d. vol. transmitted by Mr. Washington for a brigade part of which was captured in Germantown. That blank is to [be] filld up with "Scott's."[3] I am Sir very respectfully, Your Obedt. Servt

J MARSHALL

ALS, Dreer Collection, PHi; Tr (typed), Marshall Papers, DLC. Addressed to Wayne at Philadelphia; postmarked Richmond, 28 June. MS torn. Wayne made notes on the cover pertaining to that portion of text and appendix of vol. III to which JM wished alterations made: "The combination is detailed in the text. & a reference to a note which contains only a letter of G. to W. & Ws. answer—a remonstrance of the pennsylvanian is struck out—Defects i⟨n?⟩ Commissary Department—distress of A. Arm at valley forge—represen. of W. to Congress & the subsisting of the army by impressments[.] The combination is commenced with the 'About this time a combination was formed against the commander in C. in.'" These notes were apparently the basis for Wayne's reply of 2⟨6?⟩ July 1804.

1. As originally sent to Wayne, the manuscript of vol. III treated the Conway Cabal in the main text (chap. 6, 336–41), accompanied by a reference (on p. 337) to Note V in the appendix, which contained only the correspondence between Gen. Horatio Gates and George Washington of 18 [8] Dec. 1777 and 4 Jan. 1778 (app., 8–11) (see Wayne to JM, 2⟨6?⟩ July 1804 and n. 2). With this 27 June letter to Wayne, JM sent three additional letters, which Wayne subsequently placed in Note V (app., 12–16): Patrick Henry to George Washington, 20 Feb. 1778; unsigned [Benjamin Rush] to Henry, 12 Jan. 1778; and Patrick Henry to Washington, 5 Mar. 1778. For a discussion of the Conway Cabal, see Don Higginbotham, *The War of American Independence: Military Attitudes, Policies, and Practice, 1763–1789* (New York, 1971), 216–22.

2. Wayne did not delete Gen. Thomas Mifflin's name from Henry's letter of 5 Mar. 1778 to George Washington, which Wayne printed in full (app., 15–16) (see Wayne to JM, 2⟨6?⟩ July 1804). JM sent the originals of the two Henry letters and unsigned Rush letter to Wayne, who apparently retained them. They are now in the Dreer Collection, PHi.

3. Brig. Gen. Charles Scott. "Scott's" filled in at vol. III, chap. 4, 181.

To Caleb P. Wayne

Sir   Richmond June 27th. 1804

In my letter of [to]day transmitting for a note to that part of the 3d. volume which states the letter of General Conway & the faction in Congress against General Washington some letters of Governor Henry of Virginia & an anonymous letter to that gentleman I omitted to send you also the letters of General Washington which ou[gh]t to form a part of the note.[1] They follow.

No. 3

Dear Sir   Valley Forge March 27th. 1778

About eight days past I was honord with your favor of the 20th. ultimo.

Your friendship, Sir, in transmitting me the anonymous letter you had received lays me under the most grateful obligations; &, if anything coud give a still further claim to my acknowlegements, it is the very polite & delicate terms with which you have been pleased to make the communication.

I have ever been happy in supposing that I held a place in your esteem, & the proof of it you have afforded on this occasion makes me peculiarly so. The favorable light in which you hold me is truely flattering, but I shoud feel much regret if I thought the happiness of America so intimately connected with my personal welfare, as you so obligingly seem to consider it. All I can say, is, that she has ever had, &, I trust, she ever will have, my honest exertions to promote her interest. I cannot hope that my services have been the best; but my heart tells me they have been the best that I could render.

That I may have erred in using the means in my power for accomplishing the objects of the arduous, exalted station with which I am honored, I cannot doubt; Nor do I wish my conduct to be exempted from the reprehension it may deserve. Error is the portion of humanity, & to censure it, whether committed by this or that public character, is the prerogative of free men. However, being intimately acquainted with the man I beleive to be the author of the letter transmitted, & having always received from him the strongest professions of attachment & regard, I am constraind to consider him as not possessing a great degree of candour & honest sincerity, though his views in addressing you shoud have been the result of conviction, & founded in motives of public good.[2] This is not the only secret insidious attempt that has been made to wound my reputation. There have been others equally base, cruel, & ungenerous; because conducted with as little frankness & proceeding from views perhaps as personally interested. I am, dear Sir, &c.

To His Excellency Patrick Henry, esquire,

    Governor of Virginia.

       No. 5

Dear Sir,   Camp, March 28th. 1778.

Just as I was about to close my letter of yesterday, your favour of the 5th. instant came to hand.

I can only thank you again, in the language of the most undissembled gratitude, for your friendship; & assure you, the indulgent disposition which Virginia in particular & the States in general entertain towards me, gives me the most sensible pleasure. The approbation of my country is what I wish; and, as far as my abilities & opportunity will permit, I hope I shall endeavour to deserve it. It is the highest reward to a feeling mind; & happy are they who so conduct themselves as to merit it.

The anonymous letter with which you were pleased to favor me, was written by ———,[3] so far as I can judge from a similitude of hands. This man has been elaborate & studied in his professions of regard for me; & that long since the letter to you.[4]

My caution to avoid anything that coud injure the service, prevented me from communicating, except to a very few of my friends, the intrigues of a faction which I know was formd against me, since it might serve to publish our internal dissensions, but their own restless zeal to advance their views has too clearly betrayed them, & made concealment on my part fruitless. I cannot precisely mark the extent of their views, but it appeared in general that General Gates was to be exalted on the ruin of my reputation & influence. This I am authorised to say from undeniable facts in my own possession, from publications the evident scope of which coud not be mistaken, & from private detractions industriously circulated. ———,[5] it is commonly supposed bore the second part in the cabal; and General Conway, I know, was a very active & malignant partisan; but I have good reason to beleive that their machinations have recoiled most sensibly upon themselves.

I hope you will find no difficulty in either adding these papers to the note already prepared on this subject or inserting them in a note for the particular purpose. If you do I will thank you to give me the information & also to state what letters are at present in a note on this subject, & I will immediately transmit a few lines to precede this correspondence. I am Sir very respectfully, Your Obedt

            J Marshall

ALS, Dreer Collection, PHi. Addressed to Wayne at Philadelphia; postmark obscured by tear in MS but appears to have been stamped 28 June. Cover filed separately, as Wayne wrote draft of his reply of 3 July 1804 on verso. Cover contains docket in unknown hand pertaining to Wayne's reply.

1. JM most likely copied the Varick transcripts of these Washington letters to Patrick Henry, but there are also file copies in a secretary's hand (Washington Papers, ser. 3H; ser. 4, DLC). There are only minor differences in spelling and abbreviation between the two copies of each letter. In either case, JM made stylistic changes in words and phrases, departing from the text he was transcribing but not altering the meaning. Wayne published JM's transcriptions in vol. III, app., Note V, 16–18, with slight variations in punctuation, spelling, and wording.

2. Wayne omitted this sentence, reflecting on Benjamin Rush's character, under instruction from JM, who received a complaint from Rush about the publication of these letters (see vol. III, app., 17; Rush to JM, 5 Sept. 1804; JM to Wayne, 24 Sept., 4 Oct. 1804).

3. JM omitted "Doctor Rush" here and in published vol. III (app., 17).

4. Wayne omitted this sentence (vol. III, app., 17), which Rush particularly wished deleted. See n. 2 above.

5. JM omitted "General Mifflin" here and in published vol. III (app., 18).

From Caleb P. Wayne

Sir,   Philada. July 3. 1804

The printed sheets of vol 2. with the corrections; the letters of gov. Henry; & the answers of general Washington have all come to hand; as well as the 3d vol. which reached me yesterday. I would instantly comply with the request made in your letters of the 27th. relative to the conspiracy against General Washington, & the manner it has been introduced in the work &c. were it in my power: but it is the express desire of judge Washington that the seals be not broken, nor even the box opened which contains the 3d. vol. until I am completely prepared to deliver the copy to Mr. Morgan—so that some time must necessarily elapse before I can give you the desired information.[1] In the mean time, however I shall write Mr. W. on the subject & perhaps he will grant me permission to examine the manuscript.

A few days ago I sent you an additional number of sheets of the 2d. vol. & expressed my anxious desire to have the first vol. completely revised for a 2d. edition. Permit me to renew the request to have the 1st. vol. with the dates all arranged in the text, authorities ⟨a⟩ll referred to in each page, & the whole completely revised & corrected as speedily as your convenience will permit, & transmit it to me by post. If I had the 1st. vol. it should be begun immediately, as the 2d. will be done in a few days. I am, very respectfully, Your ⟨obed⟩

ADf, Dreer Collection, PHi. Written on verso of cover of JM to Wayne, 27 June 1804 (2d letter). MS torn.

1. In a letter of 22 June 1804 Bushrod Washington instructed Wayne, "You will deliver Mr Morgan his Copy whenever you are ready to begin the printing of it, but before you have set the types or done any thing towards it. Indeed I do not wish the seals of the papers to be broken until you are prepared to deliver Morgan his Copy, that there may not be even the appearance of unfairness" (ViU).

To Caleb P. Wayne

Sir   Richmond July 5th. 1804

I return you the sheets last sent me with some few corrections which occurred on a very hasty reading given them this morning.

Altho I ought to have known that I was too far from Philadelphia to inspect the proof sheets I had still unaccountably considered the corrections I had made as to find a place in the first impression & am not a little mortified to discover my mistake. There are however some very few inaccuracies which you will readily percieve ought to be mentiond in the errata. These are where some word is obviously omitted or has been mistaken for another as "there" for "these"—an error which very probably has crept into the manuscript copy.

I percieve that the authorities of the 3d. chapter are entirely omitted.[1] If this circumstance is occasiond by their having been omitted in the manuscript copy you have retained it is attributable to the excessive hurry in which they were sent. The other copy I am persuaded containd them.

I regret your determination to print a second edition immediately. I have not time to correct the first at present, nor can I have time till the work shall be completed. The employment of finishing the 4th. vol. & of superintending the copying, added to my various other avocations absolutely disables me from giving the sheets you send me such a reading as I can be satisfied with. The 3d. vol. has been for some time in Mr. Washingtons hands & I shoud hope has been forwarded to you before this time. If it has not you will certainly receive it in a few days so it will furnish you with employment. If you make an additional impression I hope it will be a very small one & I cannot consent to its being stated to be revised & corrected by the author. It woud perhaps be as well to make the amendments which I have suggested & to add to the number of the first edition so much as there may be an absolute demand for. I am anxious before the books shall be very much multiplied to give them a very serious reading at perfect leisure & prepare them for a second edition. There are really errors in the present publication which manifest a greater degree of carelessness than I had suspected when I had only seen the manuscript.

My state of health requires that I shoud pass the residue of the summer in the mountain country. As I cannot take the papers with me to prosecute the work I had proposed to retain the first volume & to read it while in the country. Perhaps the transmission of the 3d. to you will enable you to leave the first with me. I wish to know your situation in this respect. If the first volume continues to be required I will send it by the return of mail after recciving your letter. I have not however been able to look into it, nor can till I go up the country. I shall set out after the 20th. of the month.

July 8th.

I happened to omit sending this letter, & since writing the above I have thought it most advisable, if it will in any degree comport with your convenience, that I shoud take both the first & 2d. volume with me up the country. I can read them with attention & return them to you in the month of august. I write to Mr. Washington to day & shall urge to lose no more time in forwarding the 3d. to you.[2] If, as I hope, this proposition shoud be such as you can comply with the sheets I returnd to you shoud be again sent & the residue forwarded to me as early as possible. I shall then be able to revise the work so as to correct its most obvious inaccuracies without arresting its progress further than it must be arrested by my going up the country. In the expectation of having the residue of the 2d. volume I do not send on that which is in my hands. I am Sir respectfully, your obedt

J MARSHALL

ALS, Dreer Collection, PHi; Tr, Marshall Papers, DLC. Addressed to Wayne at Philadelphia; postmarked Richmond, 9 July. MS torn where seal was broken.

1. Beginning in vol. II, source notes appeared at the bottom of the appropriate pages within chapters. As published, vol. II, chap. 3, contains such footnotes.
2. Letter not found.

To Caleb P. Wayne

Sir   Richmond July 20th. 1804

I have received your letter with part of the sheets of the 2d. vol. & your resolution to postpone the 2d. edition of the first.[1] I am just setting out for the upper country where I shall give the 1st. vol one considerate reading & then forward it to you by the post. You will please to direct to me at Front Royal, Frederick county Virginia. I will thank you to transmit me immediately at that place a copy of the corrections before made to the first volume, unless you shoud already have addressed the paper to me in Richmond in which case it will follow me.

I have no doubt that the errors noticed are principally if not entirely in the manuscript. Some very few I beleive are not but they are very few. I am confident of the care you have bestowd on the subject & wish every other person coud have performd his part with as much attention & exactness as you have done. I thank you for the two papers you sent me. I take the gazette of the United States & shall of course see anything which may appear in that paper.[2] The very handsome critique in the political & commercial register was new to me. I coud only regret that there was in it more of pannegyric than was merited. The editor of that paper, if the author of the critique, manifests himself to be master of a style of a very superior order & to be of course a very correct Judge of the compositions of others.[3]

Having, Heaven knows how reluctantly, consented against my judgement, to be known as the author of the work in question I cannot be insensible to the opinions entertaind of it, but I am much more sollicitous to hear the strictures upon it than to know what parts may be thought exempt from censure. As I am about to give a reading to the first volume & as not much time can be employed upon it the strictures of those who are either friendly or hostile to the work may be useful if communicated to me because they may direct my attention to defects which might other wise escape a single reading however careful that reading may be. I will therefore thank you to convey to me at Front Royal every condemnatory criticism which may reach you. It woud be impossible & I shall not attempt to polish every sentence. That woud require repeated readings & a long course of time; but I wish to correct obvious imperfections & the animadversions of others woud aid me very much in doing so.

I shall probably return about the beginning of october, but you will hear from me long before that time & will know when I shall leave the upper country. I am Sir very respectfully your Obedt

J MARSHALL

ALS, Dreer Collection, PHi; Tr, Marshall Papers, DLC. Addressed to Wayne at Philadelphia; postmarked Richmond, 21 July. Endorsed by Wayne, who wrote draft of his reply of 25 July on verso of cover.

1. Letter not found.

2. Wayne probably sent JM the review of vol. I in the Federalist newspaper, the *U.S. Gazette*, 6 July 1804. The editors, Wayne's former colleagues and then successors on the paper, commended his and JM's efforts and upheld JM's justifications, contained in his preface, of publishing a general history of the North American colonies as an introductory volume to the *Life*.

3. Review of vol. I in *Political and Commercial Register* (Philadelphia), 9 July 1804, written by the editor, Maj. William Jackson (see Wayne to JM, 25 July 1804 and n. 2). In his review Jackson countered JM's reasons given in his preface for why the *Life* might not satisfy the public. Jackson took into consideration the constraints of time and official duties under which JM wrote the first volume. Under these circumstances, Jackson allowed that "whoever expects to see in a work thus rapidly written every sentence highly polished, who looks, in every page, for the splendid ornament of Gibbon, or the continued elegance of Hume, may not have their expectations answered, but it has, nevertheless, conspicuous merit. The style is chaste, energetic and elevated. A narrative interesting, because it is our own history, but deficient in striking incident, is conducted with ease and perspicuity, & every proof afforded of a mind vigorous, comprehensive, and discriminating. . . . [A history of the colonies] is a proper introduction to his work, and forms a valuable accession to American literature. In the latter part of the volume, where events of higher interest are described than those on which the earlier pages of it are occupied, we mark in Mr. Marshall's style a corresponding elevation" (reprinted in *Va. Argus*, 4 Aug. 1804).

To John Baylor

Dr. Sir   Richmond July 23d. 1804
I have just receivd your letter of the 20th.[1] Mr. Call finishd all the business in which I was employd, but if you have any application to make respecting the suit you mention it must be to Colo. Pendleton who is the attorney in fact & is the only person authorised to give any directions to the Marshal. I presume however there will be no occasion for any application to him as Mr. Rootes has returnd. I have some idea that Genl. Minor obtaind the judgement.[2] I am Sir very respectfully, your Obedt. ⟨Serv⟩t

J MARSHALL

ALS, ViU. Addressed to Baylor at "New Market/Near the Bowling green"; Richmond postmark (date illegible). Endorsed by Baylor.

1. Letter not found. John Baylor (1750–1808) of Newmarket, Caroline County (Frances Norton Mason, ed., *John Norton & Sons: Merchants of London and Virginia* [Richmond, Va., 1937], 509, 515).

2. The suit has not been identified but may be connected with two judgments obtained by the General Court judges (St. George Tucker and others) on behalf of British plaintiffs Rebecca Backhouse and Murdocks, Donald & Co. against John Baylor at the May 1803 term of the U.S. circuit court. These cases were motions for judgments on a forthcoming bond given by Baylor, with Thomas R. Rootes as security. John Minor was the attorney for the plaintiff in these suits. See U.S. Cir. Ct., Va., Ord. Bk. IV, 278; Tucker for use of Backhouse v. Baylor and Tucker for use of Murdocks, Donald & Co. v. Baylor, App. Cas. Nos. 150, 151.

Thomas Reade Rootes (1763–1824) of Federal Hill, near Fredericksburg, had represented Caroline County in the House of Delegates, 1793–95 (*VMHB*, IV [1896–97], 208–9; Swem and Williams, *Register*, 424).

From Caleb P. Wayne

Dr Sir, Philada. July 25. 1804

Enclosed I send you the original paper containing the corrections for the first vol.[1] Every review of the work which I can lay my hand shall be forwarded to you. The Editor of the commercial & Political Register is Wm. Jackson, Esq. formerly I believd an aid to Gen Washington, & recently dismissed from a situation in the Custom house. He bears the title of Major.[2] You will pardon me for mentioning what I have heard spoken of as a fault in the work;—it is where the *enemy* is spoken of. It has been suggested than[3] an author ought not to write as an American, but assume an independent ground. I understand the vol. will be reviewed in a magazine published here. I shall send it.[4]

ADf, Dreer Collection, PHi. Written on verso of cover of JM to Wayne, 20 July 1804. MS torn where seal was broken.

1. Corrections presumably sent with recipient's copy, not found.
2. Maj. William Jackson (1759–1828) had served in the Southern Department as an aide-de-camp to Maj. Gen. Benjamin Lincoln during the Revolution. He was secretary to the Federal Convention and was one of George Washington's private secretaries between 1789 and 1791. In 1796 Washington appointed him surveyor of customs for the port of Philadelphia, in which office he continued until 1804 when Jefferson replaced him with a Republican appointment. Jackson then began publishing the *Political and Commercial Register*, the first issue of which appeared on 2 July 1804.
3. Wayne meant to write "that."
4. *The Literary Magazine, and American Register*. See Wayne to JM, 20 Aug. 1804 and n. 5.

From Caleb P. Wayne

Sir, Philada. July 2⟨6?⟩. 1804

Judge Washington permitted me to place the two copies of the 3d. vol., in the hands of Charles Chauncy Esq. in order to get the information you desired & to fill up the blanks.[1] In the 6th Chapter you mention the conspiracy in the *text*, commencing with these words *"About this time a combination was formed against the Commander in Chief, &c &c &c.'['] A reference to a note is then made, which note contains only the letter of Gen Gates to Gen W. with the answer of the latter.[2] There was also a reference to another note, which consisted of the remonstrance of the Pennsylvania assembly,[3] but the note & reference are both erased. Just preceding the paragraph in the text mentioning the combination, The Defects in commissary's department, the distress of the American army at valley forge, & the represen[ta]-

tions of Gen W. to congress in subsisting the army by impressments, are detailed.[4] You will please to forward the paragraph which is to precede, the letters of Gov. Hen[r]y to Gen. W. & the answers, as soon as possible, & to inform whether they must make part of the note above mentioned or be inserted in the text. I am, With the highest respect, Your Most Obed. Ser

C: P: WAYNE

P. S. I am shipping the books for subs in your city. A fellow by the name of *Poe*, Post Master in Md. has swindled me out of 500. Dolls. He obtained a great many Subs for the book, got the advance & has decamped.[5]

Gen. M. is dead[6]—may not his name be inserted—indeed the Public expect names—I have heard many express themselves so.

ADfS, Dreer Collection, PHi. Endorsed on verso, "Copy/to/Gen. Marshall/July 21. 1804." Wayne apparently was uncertain of date of his own letter; second digit appears to be either "o" or "6." See n. 1 for date of 26 July assigned. MS mutilated.

1. Bushrod Washington wrote to Wayne on 18 July, giving him this permission (Dreer Collection, PHi). Letters between Virginia and Philadelphia normally took about five days in transit. JM acknowledged on 10 Aug. receipt from Wayne of two letters (this and 25 July) addressed to Front Royal, which Wayne only could have known to do after receiving JM's letter of 20 July. Charles Chauncey (1777–1849) was a Federalist attorney in Philadelphia, at 46 Walnut St., and a political associate of Enos Bronson's, Wayne's partner and then successor as editor of the *Gazette of the U.S.* (Robinson, *Philadelphia Directory for 1804*, 48; Charles Henry Hart, "Thomas Sully's Register of Portraits, 1801–1871," *PMHB*, XXXII [1908], 420; Konkle, "Enos Bronson," *PMHB*, LVII [1933], 356–57).

2. Gates's letter of 8 Dec. 1777 (incorrectly dated 18 Dec. in vol. III, app., 8; date in Washington's acknowledgment also was changed to the eighteenth, ibid., 10) and a draft copy of Washington's reply of 4 Jan. 1778, in his own hand, are in Washington Papers, ser. 4, DLC; a second copy of Washington's letter is in the Varick transcripts, ibid., ser. 3B, DLC. There are other contemporaneous copies of these letters in other depositories, but JM would have been making transcriptions from the copies available to him in the Washington Papers.

3. In Dec. 1777 the Pennsylvania council and assembly protested locating the army's winter quarters on the west side of the Schuylkill River. The remonstrance was laid before Congress on 17 Dec., and on 19 Dec. Congress passed a resolution referring the complaint to General Washington and requesting information on the cantonment of the army and his plans for defending the east side of the Schuylkill and New Jersey. Washington's letter of 23 Dec. to Congress, which JM quoted at length, was in part a response to the issues raised by the remonstrance and resolution of Congress (*Journals of the Continental Congress, 1774–1789*, IX: *1777. October 3–December 31* [Washington, D.C., 1907], 1033 and n. 1, 1035, 1036; *Life*, III, chap. 6, 341–46, esp. 345; Freeman, *Washington*, IV, 563 and n. 107).

4. Vol. III, chap. 6, 327–36.

5. David Poe, Jr., postmaster at Upper Marlboro, Md. Poe had signed up many subscribers and taken their deposits without remitting any money to Wayne. Bushrod Washington had warned Wayne previously of Poe from whom Wayne "never recd. a

cent" (Washington to Wayne, 23 Mar. 1803; Wayne to Washington, 12 Sept., 2 Dec. 1803, Dreer Collection, PHi).

6. General Mifflin died in 1800. In Patrick Henry's 5 Mar. 1778 letter to Washington, Mifflin's name is printed, but it is omitted in Washington's 28 Mar. 1778 letter to Henry (see JM to Wayne, 27 June 1804 [1st letter] and n. 2; [2d letter] and n. 5).

The Life of George Washington
Volume IV, Chapter 8
Draft and Published Version

EDITORIAL NOTE

Only two fragments of Marshall's manuscript for the *Life* are extant. One, owned by the Maryland Historical Society, consists of two sheets, closely written on both sides in Marshall's hand, with intervening pages missing. These sheets contain his original draft of a portion of volume IV, chapter 8, pages 401–5 and 411–15. The first sheet concerns the mutiny of the Pennsylvania line at the beginning of January 1781, and the second sheet covers actions of the Continental Congress taken during February 1781 with regard to the crisis in foreign and financial affairs.[1] This fragment is presented below in the left-hand column. The other known draft belongs to volume V and is presented later in this volume.[2]

After Marshall completed a manuscript for a volume of the *Life*, he employed copyists in Richmond to make two fair copies of his text. One was for Caleb Wayne and the other for the English publisher. Both Marshall and Bushrod Washington went over the copies, entering corrections on them. Beginning with volume IV, Marshall made major revisions on the fair copy, deleting paragraphs and entire pages in order to cut it to an acceptable length for Wayne. Wayne's copies for volumes I through III no longer exist. According to a note inside the cover of the copy for volume IV, they were destroyed by a fire in Wayne's office at the end of 1804. The Philadelphia publisher's copies of volumes IV and V are in the Dreer Collection at the Historical Society of Pennsylvania and contain Marshall's alterations, as well as occasional insertions by Bushrod Washington and Wayne. The copyists also sometimes corrected their own mistakes, so that interlineations in the copies appear in a number of different hands. In shortening his manuscript, Marshall in places rewrote one or more paragraphs, inserting them in the text. In total for the two volumes, he made about a dozen such rewritten entries, only two of which amounted to more than a page.[3]

Marshall and Bushrod Washington gave Wayne preference of the two fair copies, usually indicating which of the two was the more accurate. When sending volume V to Wayne, Washington wrote him, "You had best retain for yourself the 1st. Copy of *the volume*, as it is probably the most correct, tho the greatest care has been taken to make both equally so."[4] This was not true for every volume, particularly volume II. Marshall warned that part of the En-

DRAFT OF THE LIFE OF GEORGE WASHINGTON

The first page of a fragment of Marshall's manuscript for volume IV, chapter 8. *Courtesy of the Maryland Historical Society, Baltimore*

glish copy was very inaccurate and that he had not time to examine or correct it.[5] The copies designated for Wayne can be assumed to contain the text most nearly as Marshall intended it for publication. Wayne's copies of volumes IV and V clearly show signs of the author's having read and corrected them. Comparison with the autograph fragment of volume IV, chapter 8, suggests that the fair copy was made directly from Marshall's rough manuscript, for it accurately duplicates his original draft, observing his deletions and insertions. Any variations in the English edition from the American may have arisen from discrepancies between the sets of publisher's copies as well as changes introduced by the printers. The location of the English copies has not been ascertained, if they still exist.

Composition of the *Life*, then, had four distinct stages: Marshall wrote the manuscript; amanuenses made fair copies; Marshall and Washington revised the copies; Wayne's printers set it into type. The fair copy represents a composite text of Marshall's manuscript and of all the corrections made to the copy by Marshall, Washington, Wayne, and the copyist. Incorporating these alterations, the printed volumes reproduce fairly accurately the composite text of the copies. By disregarding the revisions on Wayne's fair copies, recension of Marshall's lost original manuscripts for volumes IV and V is nearly possible.

The fragment for volume IV, chapter 8, is part of Marshall's initial manuscript, heavily emended by him. It is printed here along with the final published version. Textual notes to the draft indicate Marshall's revisions within it.[6] The intermediate document, the fair copy used by Wayne's typesetter, is not included because it is no more than a composite of Marshall's manuscript draft and the published text. Anything in the first version but not in the final was deleted by Marshall on the printer's copy, and any words or phrases in the published text not found in the manuscript were added by Marshall to the copy. In the minor instances where a copyist or printer did introduce a word different from Marshall's, it is noted in a footnote. The two texts are placed in parallel columns to allow comparison of the two versions. When Marshall's draft begins or ends in mid-sentence, the text from the published version includes the complete sentence.

1. For details of these crises, see Higginbotham, *War of American Independence*, 236, 298, 403–5; Hutchinson, *Papers of Madison*, II, 302–4 and nn.

2. See *The Life of George Washington*, Volume V, Chapter 3, Draft and Revised Version, [ca. May 1806].

3. One is a passage for vol. V, chap. 3. JM drafted his revision before he rewrote it on the fair copy. This draft is the other extant fragment for the *Life*, mentioned above. Both draft and interlined version are published in this volume (see n. 2). The second extensive addition to the fair copy in JM's hand consists of two and a half pages in vol. V that follow after the end of chap. 5. The insertion is Note VI to that chapter, footnoted at p. 387 and appearing in app., 14–17, of the published volume. The note concerns the political war in the press in 1793. There is a transcript of the note in Marshall Papers, DLC.

4. 20 July 1806, Dreer Collection, PHi.

5. JM to Washington, 25 Mar., 28 Mar., [20] Apr. 1804; JM to Wayne, 27 Mar. 1804.

6. The textual notes follow the numbered footnotes. For the method and symbols used in compiling these notes, see Editorial Apparatus (xxxiii–xxxiv).

Draft   [ca. July 1804][1]

Published version

¶1 utter detestation in which every idea of going over to the common enemy was held. This favorable symptom however was not unattended by circumstances of suspicion. Refusing to give up the british emissaries, they retaind them in their own possession, nor could they be prevaild on to cross the Delaware, or to march from Princeton—a position convenient for a revival of the intercourse with New York. They woud not permit any of their former officers other than those already mentiond to enter their camp, & General St. Clair the Marquis de la Fayette & Lt. Colonel Laurens were orderd immediately to leave Princeton.

His emissaries were immediately seized by the revolters, and their proposals communicated to general Wayne, with assurances of their being rejected, and of the utter detestation in which every idea of going over to the common enemy, was held.

This favourable symptom, however, was not unattended by circumstances of suspicion. They retained the British emissaries in their own possession; and could not be prevailed on to cross the Delaware, or to march from Princeton, a position convenient for a revival of the intercourse with New York. They would not permit any of their former officers, other than those already mentioned, to enter their camp; and general St. Clair, the marquis de La Fayette, and lieutenant colonel Laurens, were ordered immediately to leave Princeton.

¶2 Such was the state of things when the Committee of Congress &[2] Governor Reid with a part of his executive council arrivd[3] in ⟨the⟩ neighborhood of the camp of the revolters. The former having delegated their powers to the latter a conference was held with the Serjeants who now commanded, after which proposals were immediately made which were printed & distributed among the troops for consideration. In these proposals the Government offerd; 1st. To discharge all those who had enlisted indifinitely for three years or during the war, the fact to be examind into by three commission-

Such was the state of things, when the committee of congress, and president Reed, with a part of his executive council, arrived in the neighbourhood of the revolters. The former having delegated their powers to the latter, a conference was held with the serjeants who now commanded. Immediately afterwards, proposals were made, and distributed among the troops for consideration.

In these proposals the government offered . . .
1st. To discharge all those who had enlisted indefinitely for three years or during the war; the fact to be examined into by three commis-

ers to be appointed by the executive and to be ascertained, where the original inlistment coud not be producd, by the oath of the soldier.[4]

¶3 2dly. To give immediate certificates for the depreciation on their pay & to settle their arrearages as soon as circumstances woud admit.

3d. To furnish them immediately with certain specified articles of cloathing which were greatly wanted.

¶4 On receiving these propositions the troops agre⟨e⟩d to march to Trenton. At that place the terms offered by the civil authority were accepted, with the addition that three commissioners shoud also be deputed by the line, who, conjointly with those of the executive, shoud constitute the board authorizd to determine what soldiers shoud be dischargd; & thereupon the british emissaries were given up, who were tried, condemnd, & immediately executed as spies.

¶5 Until the investigation shoud be made & discharges given to those found to be intitled to them, the Serjeants retaind their command. In consequence of the irksomeness of this state of things the business was enterd upon with so much precipitation, that, before the inlistments themselves coud be brought from the hutts, almost the whole of the artillery, & of the five first regiments of infantry were liberated on the testimony of their own oaths. The inlistments being producd before a further progress was made, it was found that not many of the remaining regiments had inlisted on the terms which under the compact woud intitle them to leave the service; & that, of those actually dismissed, far the greater number were[5] inlisted abso-

sioners, to be appointed by the executive; and to be ascertained, where the original enlistment could not be produced, by the oath of the soldier.

2d. To give immediate certificates for the depreciation on their pay, and to settle the arrearages as soon as circumstances would admit.

3d. To furnish them immediately with certain specified articles of clothing which were greatly wanted.

On receiving these propositions, the troops agreed to march to Trenton. At that place the terms offered by the civil authority were accepted, with the addition that three commissioners should also be deputed by the line, who conjointly with those of the executive, should constitute the board authorized to determine what soldiers should be discharged; and thereupon, the British emissaries were surrendered; who were tried, condemned, and immediately executed as spies.

Until the investigation should be made, and discharges given to those who should be found entitled to them, the serjeants retained their command. In consequence of the irksomeness of this state of things, the business progressed with so much precipitation, that before the enlistments themselves could be brought from the huts, almost the whole of the artillery, and of the five first regiments of infantry, were liberated on the testimony of their own oaths. The enlistments being then produced, it was found that not many of the remaining regiments had engaged on the terms which, under the compact, would entitle them to leave the service; and that of those actually dismissed, far the greater number was enlisted absolutely for lutely for the war. The discharges given however were not canceld; & the few who were to be retaind in service receivd furlows for forty days with directions, on the expiration of that time to assemple at convenient specified places in Pennsylvania, where officers were to meet & take[6] command of them.

¶6 Thus ended in a temporary dissolution of the whole line of Pennsylvania, a mutiny which a voluntary performance of much less than was now extorted woud have prevented & which, when the condition of the army is considerd, was of a nature & extent to inspire the most serious alarm. Apprehensions that the insurgents might go over to the enemy were the greater, because few of them were native Americans; &, on that account, their attachments to the country were the less relied on. The private letters of General Wayne stated that about three hundred of them actually manifested a disposition to accede to the propositions made them by Sir Henry Clinton & to join the british standard: but they were overruld by a decided majority, among whom were many who reluctantly united with the revolters, but who were advisd by the General & field officers who followd them, to continue with them for the purpose of moderating their violence & using their best endeavors to bring about an accomodation.[7] Many censurd severely the concessions made by the executive of Pennsylvania, but in a letter addressd to Mr. Reid acknowledging a receipt of his report of his proceedings, a report which exhibits in strong colors the critical & hazardous situation of affairs, on his arrival in the neighborhood of Princeton; General Washington declared his persuasion, that in the actual st⟨ate⟩

the war. The discharges given, however, were not cancelled, and the few who were to be retained in service, received furloughs for forty days, with directions on the expiration of that time, to assemble at convenient specified places in Pennsylvania, where officers were to meet and take the command of them.

Thus ended, in a temporary dissolution of the whole line of Pennsylvania, a mutiny which a voluntary performance of much less than was now extorted, would have prevented; and which, in the actual condition of the army, was of a nature and extent to inspire the most serious alarm.

⟨o⟩t things, what had been done was for the best; & that nothing now remaind, but to ⟨use every⟩ exertion to repla⟨ce the⟩ men who were dischargd & to complete the regiments as soon as possible.

¶7   The dangerous policy of yielding even to the just demands of soldiers made with arms in their hands, a policy resulting perhaps inevitably from an original denial of justice was soon illustrated. The success of the Pennsylvania line inspird a part of that of Jersey many of whom were also foreigners with the hope of obtaining similar advantages, & stimulated them to the attempt. On the night of the 20th. a part of the Jersey brigade which had been stationd at Pompton, rose in arms; &, making precisely the same claims which had been yielded to the Pennsylvanians, marchd to Chatham where a part of the same brigade had been stationd, in the hope of exciting them also to join in the revolt.

¶8   General Washington who altho satisfied with the conduct both of the civil & military officers had been yet extremely chagrind at the issue of the mutiny in the Pennsylvania line, & who was now confident of the reliance to be placd at least for the present in the fidelity of the eastern troops, who were composd of natives, determind at once to stop the further progress of a spirit which threatend the total destruction of the army. In pursuance of this determination he immediately orderd a detachment from the troops of New Hampshire Massachusetts & Connecticut under General Howe, to proceed as rapidly as possible against the mutiniers, & to bring them to unconditional submission. Howe was instructed to make no terms whatever

The dangerous policy of yielding even to the just demands of soldiers, made with arms in their hands; a policy resulting perhaps inevitably from an original denial of justice, was soon illustrated. The success of the Pennsylvania line inspired a part of that of Jersey, many of whom were also foreigners, with the hope of obtaining similar advantages, and stimulated them to the attempt. On the night of the 20th, a part of the Jersey brigade which had been stationed at Pompton rose in arms, and making precisely the same claims which had been yielded to the Pennsylvanians, marched to Chatham, where a part of the same brigade had been stationed, in the hope of exciting them also to join in the revolt.

General Washington, who, though satisfied with the conduct both of the civil and military officers, had been extremely chagrined at the issue of the mutiny in the Pennsylvania line, and who was now confident of the reliance to be placed in the fidelity of the eastern troops who were composed of natives; determined, by strong measures, to stop the further progress of a spirit which threatened the destruction of the army. In pursuance of this determination, he immediately ordered a detachment to march against the mutineers, and to bring them to unconditional submission. General Howe, who commanded this detachment, was instructed to make no terms with the insurgents, while they had arms in their hands, or were in a state of re-with the insurgents while they had arms in their hands, or were in a state of resistance; &, so soon as they shoud surrender, to seize a few of the most active incendiary leaders, & execute them on the spot.[8]

[separate sheet]

¶9 enemy. The british government estimated them even above their real value, & counted with confidence on the speedy conquest of the whole country west & south of the Hudson. Intercepted letters of this date from the minister express the most sanguine hopes that the very great superiority of force at the disposal of Sir Henry Clinton woud compel Washington with his feeble army to take refuge on the eastern side of that river.

10 Even Congress, for an instant, relaxd from the firmness which had uniformly distinguishd that body, & from the decisive manner in which they had insisted on the rights appertaining to the territory of their country.

11 It will be recollected that tho France & Spain were truely desirous of disjoining America from Great Britain, they contemplated her western claims with much sollicitude, & had manisfested no inconsiderable degree of earnestness in their endeavors to restrict the United States on that frontier within very narrow limits, & to exclude them entirely from the Missi(s)sipi. The representations of the french Minister however had not been able to draw from America the surrender of so valuable a territory, or the abandonment of her pretensions to follow the waters which passd through it, into the great high way of nations.

12 From her jealousy on this & other

sistance; and as soon as they should surrender, to seize a few of the most active leaders, and to execute them on the spot.

The perplexities and difficulties in which the affairs of America were involved, could not be concealed from the enemy. The British government estimated them even above their real value, and counted with confidence on the speedy conquest of the whole country west and south of the Hudson. Intercepted letters of this date from the minister, expressed the most sanguine hopes that the great superiority of force at the disposal of sir Henry Clinton, would compel Washington with his feeble army, to take refuge on the eastern side of that river.

Even congress relaxed, for an instant, the firmness which had uniformly distinguished that body, and receded from the decisive manner in which they had insisted on the rights appertaining to the territory of their country.

It will be recollected that France and Spain, contemplated the western claims of the United States with much solicitude, and had manifested no inconsiderable degree of earnestness to restrict them on that frontier within narrow limits; and to exclude them entirely from the Mississippi.

From her jealousy on this and

subjects, Spain, tho engagd in the war, had held herself aloof from the United States; & had refusd to contract any alliance with them, or intimately to blend their interests with hers.

¶13   In the present inauspicious state of public affairs, Congress, for the first time, manifested a disposition to sacrifice remote interests, tho of great future magnitude, for immediate advantages; & directed their minister at Madrid to relinquish, if it shoud be absolutely necessary, the claims of the United States to navigate the Mississipi below the 31st. degree of north latitude, & to a free port on the banks of that river, with in the Spanish territory. It is remarkable that only Massachusetts, connecticut, & North Carolina, dissented from this resolution. New York was divided. On a subsequent day, when the impression producd by the present unpromising appearances had in some degree worn off, the subject was again brought forward and a proposition made for still further concessions, to Spain in that quarter; but on discussion this proposition was unanimously negativd.

¶14   Happily for the United States Mr. Jay, the Minister then representing them at the court of Madrid, requird, in the treaty he was laboring to negotiate advantages at that time unattainable without which he woud surrender no privileges claimd ⟨by⟩ the United St⟨ates⟩, & his conduct receivd the entire approbation of his government:* (see in a note the resolution of Congress from my minutes)/ on Sep. paper[9]

¶15   Inseparably connected with the restoration of credit was the estab-

other subjects, Spain, though engaged in the war, had held herself aloof from the United States; and had refused to contract any alliance with them, or intimately to blend their interests with hers.

In the present inauspicious state of public affairs, congress, for the first time, manifested a disposition to sacrifice remote interests, though of great future magnitude, for immediate advantages; and directed their minister at Madrid to relinquish, if it should be absolutely necessary, the claims of the United States to navigate the Mississippi below the 31st degree of north latitude, and to a free port on the banks of that river, within the Spanish territory. It is remarkable that only Massachusetts, Connecticut, and North Carolina, dissented from this resolution; New York was divided. On a subsequent day, when the impression produced by the present unpromising appearances had in some degree worn off, the subject was again brought forward, and a proposition was made for still further concessions to Spain in that quarter; but on discussion, this proposition was unanimously negatived.

Happily for the United States, Mr. Jay, their minister at the court of Madrid, required as the price of the concessions which he was instructed to make, that the treaty he was labouring to negotiate should be immediately concluded between the two nations. Without obtaining this object, he declared that he would surrender no privileges claimed by America; nor should his government be bound in future by the offers now made. His conduct received the entire approbation of congress.

Inseparably connected with the restoration of credit, was the establishment of a revenue subject only to the control of the Continental government. The efforts therefore which were made to retrieve their affairs by the negotiation of a foreign loan, were accompanied by resolutions calling on the respective states to vest in Congress a fund which woud be both permanent & productive. As duties[10] on imports & on prize goods woud obviously constitute the most eligible & certain fund, a resolution passd recommending it[11] to the respective states to vest a power in Congress to levy for the use of the United States a duty of five percent ad valorem[12] on all goods wares & merchandizes of foreign growth or[13] manufacture imported into any of them; & also on all prizes & prize goods condemnd as lawful prize in any of the American courts of admiralty. This fund was to be appropriated to the payment of both the principal & interest of all debts contracted in the prosecution of the war, & was to continue till[14] those debts shoud be completely dischargd.

¶16 There were not at that time wanting in Congress, men who percievd the advantages which woud result from bestowing on the federal head, the full power of regulating commerce, & consequently of increasing the impost as circumstances might render adviseable; but state influence predominated, & they were overruld by great majorities.

¶17 Even the inadequate plan now recommended was never adopted; &, notwithstanding the greatness of the exigency, the pressure of the national wants, & the influence which strengthening the hands of government woud obviously have on the war; so reluctantly do men possessd of power place it in the hands of oth-

lishment of a revenue subject to the exclusive direction of the continental government. The efforts, therefore, which were made to retrieve their affairs by the negotiation of a foreign loan, were accompanied by resolutions calling on the respective states to vest in congress a fund which should be both permanent, and productive. A duty on imports, and on prize goods, would obviously constitute the most eligible and certain fund. A resolution therefore, passed, recommending to the respective states, to vest a power in congress, to levy for the use of the United States, a duty of five *per centum ad valorem* on all goods, wares, and merchandises, of foreign growth and manufacture, imported into any of them; and also on all prizes, and prize goods, condemned in any of the American courts of admiralty.

This fund was to be appropriated to the payment of both the principal and interest of all debts contracted in the prosecution of the war, and was to continue until those debts should be completely discharged.

There were several persons at that time in congress, who perceived the advantages which would result from bestowing on the federal head the full power of regulating commerce, and consequently of increasing the impost as circumstances might render advisable; but state influence predominated, and they were overruled by great majorities. Even the inadequate plan which they did recommend, was never adopted. Notwithstanding the greatness of the exigency, the pressure of the national wants, and the beneficial influence which a certain revenue in the hands of government would obviously have upon the war, yet never during the existence of the confederation, did

ers, altho it may be there usd more to their own advantage, &

all the states unite to vest in congress the powers now required: so unwilling are men possessed of power to place it in the hands of others, and so difficult is it to effect any objects however important, which are dependent on the concurrent assent of many distinct sovereignties.

ADf, Kennedy Papers, MdHi; printed, John Marshall, *The Life of George Washington* . . . , IV (Philadelphia, 1805), 401–5, 411–15. MS is two loose sheets written on both sides; edges frayed. On separate, third sheet noted in an unknown hand, "Fragment of the original MS. of Marshall's Life of Washington/JBC." On the last page noted sideways along the right margin in a different hand, "(Leaf from M.S. of C.J. Marshall's Life of Washington)." For explanation of two versions, see editorial note. JM's deletions and interlineations are recorded in Draft Textual Notes below.

1. JM began writing vol. IV sometime in the spring of 1804. He sent off the publishers' copies of vol. II in March; in late April he was still working on vol. III (JM to Wayne, 27 Mar.; JM to Bushrod Washington, [20] Apr. 1804). In between supervising the copying of vol. III, reading and correcting it with Bushrod Washington in June, and reading proofs of vols. I and II, he must have begun work on the succeeding volume (Wayne to JM, 4 June; JM to Wayne, 11 June 1804; Washington to Wayne, 22 June 1804, ViU). He also attended the U.S. circuit courts at Richmond and Raleigh in May and June. At the beginning of July he was employed in "finishing the 4th. vol. & of superintending the copying." He left for the mountains toward the end of that month and did not take the manuscript of vol. IV with him (JM to Wayne, 5 July, 20 July 1804). In September from Front Royal he informed Wayne that he would not be able to send him vol. IV by the end of that month as Wayne wished. JM had lost his copyists and would not be able to replace them until he returned to Richmond in October (JM to Wayne, 3 Sept., 6 Sept. 1804). JM did not finally send the volume to Wayne until Feb. 1805 (JM to Wayne, 27 Feb.). In the interval he may have revised his manuscript, although he also was correcting vols. I–III for the second impression and attending court in Richmond and Raleigh. In Nov. 1804 he sent queries to John Eager Howard pertaining to matter in chaps. 7 and 10 (JM to Howard, 2 Nov.), which suggests that JM was still working on vol. IV. Given the numerous alterations on the pages printed here, JM may well have reworked his manuscript in the autumn of 1804, as the copyists proceeded in making fair copies from it.

2. JM wrote "Jany. 6" out in left margin across from lines in MS beginning "& Governor Reid" and "powers to the latter." Copyist did not place this and following marginal dates in publisher's copy. Wayne apparently wrote marginal content notes that appear in the published version. They have not been included on published version here.

3. JM placed a superscript "a" here, marking an insertion, which he wrote sideways at the top of the first page in the left margin. It begins with "⟨the⟩ neighborhood" and ends with "delegated." The last three words are a repetition of what follows in the main text. JM added "&c" at the end of his insertion, indicating a return to the original line. The editors placed the insertion after "in."

4. JM wrote "8th." out in left margin across from line in MS reading "the soldier."

5. Copyist transcribed this as "was."

6. On fair copy, JM inserted "to" before "take"; printer omitted "to" and inserted "the" after "take."

7. The paragraph originally ended at this point. JM placed a superscript "a" here and wrote the following sentence, footnoted with another "a," along the length of the right margin of the second page.

8. End of JM's text on verso of first sheet. There were probably two intervening sheets of paper in the MS, containing the text for 405–11, which follows this first passage found on 401–5. The second sheet contains the text for 411–15. Two pages of JM's writing made up between three and four printed pages.

9. JM's parenthetical note omitted from copyist's version.

10. Copyist substituted "A duty" for the first two words of this sentence, transforming this introductory clause into a run-on sentence. The printer remedied the fault by placing a period after "fund" and creating a new sentence beginning with "A resolution."

11. JM wrote "Feb. 3" out in the right margin across from the first two lines of this sentence in MS.

12. Preceding three words underscored on copyist's version.

13. Copyist substituted "and."

14. Printer rendered this "until."

Draft Textual Notes

¶ 1	l. 1 beg.	↑utter↓ detestation in which ~~they held~~ every
	ll. 2–3	enemy. ↑was held.↓ This
	l. 4	not ~~entirely~~ unattended
	ll. 5–6	suspicion. ~~They refusd~~ ↑Refusing↓ to give
	ll. 6–7	emissaries, ~~but~~ ↑they↓ retaind
	ll. 7–11	possession, ~~& coud not~~ ↑nor could they↓ be prevaild on to ↑cross the Delaware, or to↓ march from Princeton—[erasure] ↑a↓ position ~~favorable to~~ ↑convenient for↓ a
	ll. 12–18	York. ↑They woud not permit any of their former officers other than those already mentiond to enter their camp, & General St. Clair & the Marquis de la Fayette & Lt. Colonel Laurens were orderd immediately to leave Princeton.↓
¶ 2	ll. 1–2 beg.	~~In this~~ ↑Such was the↓ state of things ↑when↓ the
	l. 2 mar.	Jany. ~~7~~ ↑6↓ [see n. 2]
	ll. 3–6	Reid ↑with a part of his executive council↓ arrivd in ~~camp after~~ ↑the night? of the Revolters.↓ ↑⟨the⟩ neighborhood of the camp of the revolters. The former having delegated &c↓ former having delegated ~~to be~~ ↑such[?]↓ their
	ll. 7–9	latter ↑a conference was held with the Serjeants who now commanded, after which↓ proposals
	ll. 12–14	consideration. ~~The offers on the part of~~ ↑In these proposals↓ the Government ~~were a d~~ ↑offerd; lst. To↓ discharge ~~to~~ all
	ll. 16–20	fact ~~where the~~ ↑to be examind into by three commissioners to be appointed by the executive and to be ascertained, where the↓ original
	ll. 20–21	producd, ~~to be ascertained~~ by the
	l. 21 mar.	~~9~~ ↑8↓ th. [see n. 4]

¶ 3 ll. 1–2   To [*erasure*] ↑give↓ immediate certificates ~~for~~ ~~their~~ ‖ the↓ depreciation

¶ 4 ll. 3–5   Trenton ~~, where they were acceded to,~~↑. At that place the terms offered by the civil authority were accepted,↓ with

       ll. 5–6   that ~~their~~ ↑three↓ commissioners [*erasure*] ↑shoud↓ also

¶ 5 l. 1 beg.   ~~While the~~ Until

       l. 2   made ~~the Serjeant~~ ↑&↓ discharges

       ll. 2–3   those ~~determind~~ ↑found↓ to be

       ll. 5–6   of ~~which~~ ↑this↓ the irksomeness of this state of things↓ the

       ll. 11–12   & of ↑the↓ five first regiments ~~were dischargd~~ ↑of infantry were liberated↓ on

       l. 15   made, ~~in the business,~~ it

       ll. 16–22   regiments ~~were enlisted for~~↑had inlisted on↓ the terms which ↑under the compact↓ woud ↑~~under the compact~~↓ intitle them to ~~a discharge~~ ↑leave the service;↓ & that, of those actually ~~dischargd, by~~ ↑dismissed,↓ far the greater number ~~had~~ ↑were↓ inlisted absolutely ~~in~~ ↑for↓ the war.

       ll. 23–24   & ~~all those~~ ↑the few↓ who

       ll. 26–27   on ~~their~~ ↑the↓ expiration ↑of that time↓ to

¶ 6 ll. 1–2   a ~~total~~ ↑temporary↓ dissolution

       ll. 3–6   mutiny ↑which a voluntary performance of much less than was now extorted woud have prevented &↓ which,

       ll. 9–10   that ~~they~~ ↑the insurgents↓ might ~~join~~ ↑go over to↓ the

       ll. 13–14   to ~~this~~ ↑the↓ country were the less ~~strongly to be counted~~ ↑relied↓ on.

       ll. 15–16   Wayne ~~state~~ ↑stated↓ that

       ll. 17–20   disposition ↑to accede to the propositions made them by Sir Henry Clinton↓ ↑&↓ to ~~join~~ ↑go over↓ to join

       ll. 22–23   reluctantly ~~joind~~ ↑united with↓ the

       ll. 24–25   the ↑General & field↓ officers ~~to~~ who

       ll. 27–28   & ~~rendering~~ ↑using their↓ best

       ll. 29–30   censurd ~~very~~ severely

       ll. 32–33   acknowledging a ~~report~~ ↑receipt↓ of

       l. 34   proceedings, th[?] a

       ll. 35–37   in ~~very~~ strong colors the critical & ~~truely~~ hazardous ~~state~~ ↑situation↓ of ~~things~~ ↑affairs↓, on his arrival at the ~~Camp~~ in the neighborhood

       ll. 39–40   the ~~situation~~ ↑actual st⟨ate⟩↓ ⟨o⟩f

       l. 45   possible. [*erasure*]

¶ 7 ll. 1–2   The ~~danger in an army~~ ↑dangerous policy↓ of ~~conceding~~ ↑yielding↓ even ↑to the↓ ~~justice to force, was soon percievd~~ ↑just demands↓ of

       ll. 3–6   hands, ↑a policy resulting perhaps inevitably from an original denial of justice↓ was soon ~~percievd~~ illustrated.

       ll. 8–9   Jersey ↑~~a majority~~ very many of whom were also foreigners↓ with

       l. 12   20th. ~~that~~ a part

       l. 13   been ~~also~~ stationd,

¶ 8 ll. 1–4   who ↑altho satisfied with the conduct both of the civil & military officers↓ had been ↑yet↓ extremely

    ll. 7–8   placd ↑at least for ~~that~~ the present↓ in

    ll. 9–10   troops, ↑who were composd of natives,↓ determind

    ll. 11–13   of ~~this alarming spirit~~ ↑a spirit which threatend the destruction of the army.↓ In

    l. 20   submission. ~~He~~ ↑Howe↓ was

    l. 22   with ~~them~~ ↑the insurgents↓ while

    l. 26   active ~~&~~ incendiary

                 [separate sheet]

¶ 9 ll. 6–7   date ↑from the minister↓ express

¶10 ll. 2–3   had ~~at~~[?] ↑uniformly↓ distinguishd

    l. 4   the ~~high terms & from~~ the decisive

    ll. 5–6   rights ~~appending~~ ↑appertaining↓ to

¶11 ll. 2–5   truely ~~sollicitous~~ to ~~sep disjoin~~ ↑truely desirous of disjoining↓ America from Great Britain, ~~yet they~~ ~~viewd~~ ↑contemplated↓ ↑her western claims↓ with much sollicitude, ~~the western claims of the United States,~~ &

    ll. 8–9   restrict ~~them~~ ↑the United States↓ on that

    ll. 12–13   however ~~of the french Minister~~ had

    ll. 15–16   or ~~of their natural privileges~~ ↑the abandonment of ~~their~~ her pretensions↓ to

¶13 ll. 1–2   present ~~moment~~ ↑inauspicious state ~~of their affairs~~↓ of ~~their~~ ↑public↓ affairs,

    ll. 3–4   to ~~sacrafice~~ ↑sacrifice↓ remote ~~& future~~ interests,

    ll. 4–5   great ~~importance~~ ↑future magnitude,↓ for

    ll. 11–12   port ↑on the banks of that river, with↓ in

    ll. 19–20   had ↑in some degree↓ worn

¶14 l. 1 beg.   [*erasure*] Happily ↑for the United States↓ Mr.

    ll. 2–3   Minister ↑~~at that time~~ then↓ representing ~~the United States~~ ↑them↓ ~~at~~

    ll. 3–5   Madrid, ~~connected the surrender he~~ ↑required, in the treaty he↓ was ~~instructed to make with~~ ↑laboring to negotiate↓ advantages

    ll. 6–8   unattainable ↑without which he woud surrender no privileges claimd ⟨by⟩ the United St⟨ates⟩,↓ & his

    ll. 10–12   government. ↑:* (see in ~~the~~ a note the resolution of Congress from my minutes) on sep. paper↓

¶15 ll. 3–5   revenue ~~to be dis~~ ↑under↓ ↑subject only to↓ the control of ~~Congress~~ ↑the Continental government.↓ The

    ll. 11–15   productive. ~~Duties~~ ↑As duties↓ on imports ~~presented themselves as the most eligible subjects to~~ ↑& on prize goods woud obviously↓ constitute ~~this fund &~~ ↑the most eligible & certain fund,↓ a resolution

    ll. 17–18   levy ~~for the use of the United States~~ ↑for the use of the United States↓ a duty

    ll. 19–22   all ↑goods wares &↓ merchandizes ↑of foreign growth or manufacture↓ imported into ~~the United States~~ any

ll. 23–24   condemnd ↑as lawful prize↓ in any

ll. 26–27   both the ↑principal &↓ interest & principal of all

¶16   l. 5   the [*erasure*] ↑full↓ power

ll. 8–9   but ↑state influence predominated, &↓ they

¶17   ll. 5–7   the apparent necessity of ↑influence which↓ strengthening the hands of government to enable it ↑woud obviously↓ have

ll. 9–10   others, where ↑altho↓ it may be even[?] ↑there↓ usd

l. 11   advantage, that, ↑&↓

To Caleb P. Wayne

Sir   Front Royal aug. 10th. 1804

I have had the pleasure of receiving your two letters addressed to me at this place. As I am not now at home & have not with me any copy of the letters to & from Governor Henry nor of those between General Washington & General Gates I am at some loss respecting the manner of introducing those now to be inserted. I think however unless some other very proper place shoud suggest itself to you they shoud be added to the note which contains the correspondence between Generals Washington & Gates. They may [be] introduced in the following manner modified as a view of the papers themselves may suggest.

"During the existence of this faction an attempt appears to have been made to alienate the affections of the leading political characters in the states from the commander in chief. The following letters exhibit a very unsuccessful effort of this sort which was made on Governor Henry of Virginia by a gentleman not supposed to be a member[1] from that state.["] (insert the letter from Governor Henry to Genl. Washington—then its enclosure &c.[)]

Judge Washington will look at the note & fashion it according to his judgement.

With respect to names I wish you to be guided by Mr. Washington.

I have the pleasure of being acquainted with Major Jackson & have a high opinion of his taste & judgement. I heard him deliver a very excellent oration on the death of General Washington—one of the best which that melancholy occasion produced.[2]

You need make no apology for mentioning to me the criticism on the word "enemy." I am glad you have done so. I will endeavor to avoid it where it can be avoided. It has probably been used improperly & unnecessarily but may I think be occasionally employed without censure. A historian, it is true, is of no nation, but the person whose history he writes is & the word is used to denote, not the enemy of the author, but of the person or army whose actions the historian is relating. I wish however if it can be done that the 3d. volume may be corrected in this respect, where without repetition the term may be changed. For the first & 2d. the correction can only be made for the 2d. edition.[3]

I am just finishing a review of the first vol. & am mortified beyond measure to find that it has been so carelessly written. Its inelegancies are more numerous than I had supposed coud have appeared in it. I have thought it necessary to reconstruct very many of the sentences, & am sorry to impose on you the task of changing your types so materially. I hope you have not printed a greater number of the 2d. vol. than you have of the first, & that y⟨ou⟩ will not print a greater number of the third. I lament that the first edition is so large as you have made it.

In five or six days I shall set out for the Allegheny from whence I shall return towards the last of the month. I will then review the corrections I have made in the first volume & immediately forward them to you. I regret that I shall not have time to reperuse the whole volume. It woud require several readings at distant periods of time to fit it for the public eye.

Continue to write to me at this place till I notify you of my return to Richmond. I am Sir very respectfully, Your Obedt. servt

J MARSHALL

My brother Mr. James Marshall who subscribed for a copy to be bound in Russia leather, supposes it probable that you have not sent with those in blue boards for Alexandria as further time might be necessary to procure the binding. Shoud this be the fact he wishes you if it is not already done to suspend the binding as I have informed him that the first edition will be very imperfect. I[f] his books are not sent let them be addressed to the care of Mr. Kennedy merchant in Alexandria.[4] I have directed my son to make a present to the whig society in Princeton of a copy of the work.[5] I coud wish it to be of the 2d. edition.

ALS, Dreer Collection, PHi; Tr (partial), Marshall Papers, DLC. Addressed to Wayne at Philadelphia; postmarked by hand, "Front Royal Va/11th August." Endorsed by Wayne. Tear in MS.

1. As published, "of congress" inserted here. Otherwise, the paragraph appears verbatim as JM wrote it (vol. III, app., Note V, 12). The letters from Henry, with Rush's unsigned epistle, and Washington's replies follow JM's introductory note.

2. As secretary-general of the Society of Cincinnati, Jackson gave a eulogy to the Pennsylvania chapter in Philadelphia on 22 Feb. 1800, subsequently published as *Eulogium, On the Character of General Washington* ... (Philadelphia, 1800; Evans #37694).

3. In the second impression, other words or phrases were frequently substituted for "enemy." For instance, compare *Life*, II, chap. 4, 249, lines 8, 13, 17, 22, with *Life* (1805 ed.), II, chap. 4, 251, lines 6, 11, 14, 20–21.

4. James Kennedy, Sr., had a store on King St., where he sold subscriptions to the *Life* and delivered copies of vol. I to subscribers (Wayne to Washington, 19 Aug. 1804, Dreer Collection, PHi; *Alexandria Daily Advertiser* [Alexandria, Va.], 23 Aug. 1804; see also Weems to Wayne, 21 Sept. 1804 [Skeel, *Weems*, II, 302 and n. 1]).

5. American Whig Society, formed at the College of New Jersey in 1769. JM's son Thomas was a member (Jacob N. Beam, *The American Whig Society of Princeton University* [Princeton, N.J., 1933], 3, 13).

From Caleb P. Wayne

Sir,   Philada. Aug 20. 1804

Your letter containing the paragraph to precede the note is jus[t] recd. I shall not have time, I fear without delaying the press, to send the note to judge W. to be arranged, however, I shall instan[t]ly write to him on the subject as well as respecting the insertion of names, which I think of importance.[1] I have been enabled, with considerabl[e] difficul[t]y—to fill all the blanks in Vol. III.[2] Capta[i]n Read, commanding Fort Mifflin, very politely measured the Island for me.[3] The road down which Sullivan & Wayne marched to the attack at Germantown, I filled up with *main* by the advice of Col. Clement Biddle.[4] As it meets your approbation I will strike out *"the enemy"* where it can be done with propriety—I mentioned this word to you because it was particularly pointed out to me. I send you with this letter, a Magazine & Newspaper; the former published here, containing a piece condemnatory of the work. The latter is published in N.Y. quotes the piece from the magazine, with an introductory paragraph, joining in the condemnation.[5] I have written to the Editor of the Magazine requesting him, in his next number, to correct two errors in the piece; one, stating the work to be comprized in *three* vols. & the other asserting it to be a general history of the U.S. from Washington's Papers: on this subject I referred him to your preface.[6] I must entreat you not to mention publickly that you intend a revision of the work, as all the subscribers will decline the present copy. The Whig Society are supplied & your brothers book is in Alexandria.[7] It is very fortunate for me you did not comply with my wishes to revise & send in the first vol. for a 2d. edition, as I have all those on hand which I printed over the number for subscribers. I should be glad you would consult your convenience & revise & correct the work at your leisure as present prospects would not induce me to republish, but let the idea of a 2d edit revised & corrected remain a secret. I shall want the *fourth* vol. by the last of September at furthest—Can I have it?—or must I dismiss my people? I print the same number of every vol. perhaps the total quantity of perfect, complete copies, may be 7200 or 7,300 including all for Subscribers & 1000 for Sale. The first Vol. was published in London last May!—I saw the advertisement.[8] I regret exceedingly that the vols have been made so large:—the first & second have cost me (1500) fifteen hundred dollars more than calculated! owing to extra matter beyond the quantity contemplated when Mr. W. authorized me to say in the Proposals from 450 to 500 pages, & I very much fear the 3d. will approach to 600 pages! I am Sir, very respecty, Yours

C. P. W.

The drafting & engraving of the maps &c. prove a laborious, expensive business, I wish they had never been promised.[9]

P.S. I will thank you to prepare a few lines on the subject of the 2d. edition to be inserted when my proposals for it are published.

ADfS, Dreer Collection, PHi; Tr, Marshall Papers, DLC. Endorsed "Copy/to/Hon J. Marshall/Aug 20 1804."

1. Wayne wrote to Bushrod Washington the next day, 21 Aug., about the note and inclusion of names. Lacking the letters and JM's prefatory paragraph for Note V, Washington deferred to Wayne's judgment on the arrangement of the material. He concurred with JM in omitting references to Mifflin and Rush, for mentioning names "is seldom done in history during the lives of the persons concerned, unless in party works" (Washington to Wayne, 26 Aug. 1804, Dreer Collection, PHi).

2. Bushrod Washington had asked Wayne to fill in blank spaces at specified points in the manuscript of vol. III with factual information concerning distances, routes, and place names. Wayne complied, after protesting to Washington the difficulty of obtaining the measured distances required and after Washington persisted in the request (Washington to Wayne, 22 June, ViU; Washington to Wayne, 2 July 1804, Dreer Collection, PHi).

3. Capt. James Read (d. 1813) from Pennsylvania, of the Regiment of Artillerists (Francis B. Heitman, *Historical Register and Dictionary of the United States Army, from its Organization, September 29, 1789, to March 2, 1903* [2 vols.; Washington, D.C., 1903], I, 819). Fort Mifflin was on Mud Island, in the Delaware River near the mouth of the Schuylkill and opposite Fort Mercer at Red Bank on the New Jersey shore. In the fall of 1777 the Americans held both forts, against which the British laid siege in order to open communications up the Delaware to their army encamped at Philadelphia. The Americans evacuated Fort Mifflin on 16 Nov. The island was a half mile in length (*Life*, III, chap. 4, 203, 187–222 passim).

4. In the Battle of Germantown on 4 Oct. 1777, Maj. Gen. John Sullivan (1740–1795) and Brig. Gen. Anthony Wayne led the main attacking force down the Skippack

Road (*Life*, III, chap. 4, 177; Robert Middlekauff, *The Glorious Cause: The American Revolution, 1763–1789* [New York and Oxford, 1982], 393). Col. Clement Biddle (1740–1814), who also was present at Germantown, resumed his mercantile activities in Philadelphia after the war. He remained friends with Washington and held a number of state and federal offices in Pennsylvania during the 1790s.

5. The critique of vol. I was "On the Life of Washington, Now Publishing," signed "Curioso," *The Literary Magazine, and American Register*, II, No. 10 (July 1804), 243–46. The Republican *American Citizen* (New York) reprinted "Curioso's" review on 15 Aug., saying "the delicate censure it conveys is more than justified by the plan and execution of the life of Washington, so far as we are able to judge of the latter by the first volume, which is now before us. Whatever may be the professional talents of Chief-Justice Marshall, it is feared that, as an historian, he will add nothing to our literary reputation as a nation" (see n. 6 below for "Curioso's" comments).

6. The editor of the *Literary Magazine*, and probable author of the review, was Charles Brockden Brown (1771–1810). Brown's sympathies lay with the Republicans. "Curioso" asserted that since there were to be only three volumes and the first was devoted to a history of the colonies, it was evident that the entire work would be a general history of the U.S. drawn from Washington's papers. This might satisfy readers who expected nothing more "and all, whose notions of pleasure or instruction to be reaped from it were connected with the reputation for skill, diligence, and impartiality of Mr. Marshall. . . . But those, whose chief curiosity related to the individual Washington, and who were anxious to see him as pourtrayed by his own pen" will feel "impatience and vexation at their disappointment." Brown in the next issue acknowledged receipt of "the letter, in answer to some remarks on the first volume of Washington," which Brown promised would "receive early insertion" but apparently never printed (*Literary Magazine, and American Register*, II, No. 11 [Aug. 1804], 410; Nos. 12–15; III, Nos. 16–21 passim).

Wayne, in his initial advertisement for the *Life*, promised four or five volumes (*Philadelphia Gazette & Daily Advertiser*, 22 Sept. 1802). In the preface, JM specifically referred to writing "the history of general Washington" and said he would include "copious extracts from his letters" in succeeding volumes so as "to present to the public as much as possible of general Washington himself" (Preface, [ante 22 Dec. 1803]).

7. Wayne had sent a box of vol. I care of James Kennedy for distribution to subscribers in the area (Washington to Wayne, 15 Aug. 1804; Wayne to Washington, 19 Aug. 1804, Dreer Collection, PHi).

8. The English publisher, Richard Phillips, advertised on 2 May that he had received the manuscript of vol. I and would be publishing "a very elegant Edition in Quarto" on 15 May. To follow within two weeks would be an octavo edition (*London Chronicle*, 3–5 May 1804). Wayne also complained to Bushrod Washington. Misreading the advertisement, he claimed that Phillips had published vol. I on 2 May (19 Aug. 1804, Dreer Collection, PHi).

9. Samuel Lewis drew Plates II–V, VII, and X of the *Maps*; he compiled Plate VIII. The engravers were John Vallance for Plate I; Joseph H. Seymour for Plates II and V; Marshall for Plate III; Francis Shallus for Plates IV, VI, VIII, and IX; Benjamin Jones, Philadelphia, for Plate VII; and probably Benjamin Tanner for Plate X. Samuel Lewis (ca. 1757–1822) was a draftsman, geographer, and mapmaker in Philadelphia and worked as proofreader for Mathew Carey between 1794 and 1816 (Tebbel, *History of Book Publishing in the U.S.*, I, 112, 573 n. 92; George C. Groce and David H. Wallace, *The New-York Historical Society's Dictionary of Artists in America, 1564–1860* [New Haven, Conn., 1957], 398). John Vallance (ca. 1770–1823) is known to have been an engraver in Philadelphia, 1791–99 and 1811–23, but apparently was there sometime around 1804–7 to do Plate I for Wayne. Vallance made engravings for Thomas Dobson's

edition of the *Encyclopaedia* (Philadelphia, 1790–97), was a founder of the Association of Artists in America, and treasurer of the Society of Artists in Philadelphia. From 1816 to his death, he was a member of the engraving firm of Tanner, Vallance, Kearny & Co. (*Mantle Fielding's Dictionary of American Painters, Sculptors & Engravers*, ed. by Glenn B. Opitz [2d ed.; Poughkeepsie, N.Y., 1986], 965; Silver, *American Printer*, 153). Employed as an engraver by Isaiah Thomas in Worcester, Mass., between 1791 and 1795, Joseph H. Seymour worked in Philadelphia between 1796 and 1822. He was probably related to the engraver and landscape painter Samuel Seymour (Groce and Wallace, *Dictionary of Artists*, 570; *Mantle Fielding's Dictionary*, 840). Marshall has not been further identified than as the engraver of Plate III for the *Maps*. Groce and Wallace suggest that possibly the author of the *Life* (JM) drew the map and someone else engraved it, but Lewis's name is on the plate as draftsman (Groce and Wallace, *Dictionary of Artists*, 424; *Mantle Fielding's Dictionary*, 585). Francis Shallus (1773–1821), an engraver in Philadelphia from the 1790s to his death, worked on Dobson's *Encyclopaedia* (*Mantle Fielding's Dictionary*, 841; Silver, *American Printer*, 153). Benjamin Jones worked as an engraver in Philadelphia between 1798 and 1815 (Groce and Wallace, *Dictionary of Artists*, 357; *Mantle Fielding's Dictionary*, 462). Benjamin Tanner (1775–1848), an engraver in New York, moved to Philadelphia in 1805 where he continued his profession. His brother, Henry S. Tanner, and he were in business together as engravers and map publishers in Philadelphia in 1811. Benjamin was a member of the firm Tanner, Vallance, Kearny & Co., 1816–24. Plate X carries only the last name, Tanner, but Benjamin was probably the engraver, as he was in Philadelphia at that time and his brother was not (*Mantle Fielding's Dictionary*, 921; James Robinson, *The Philadelphia Directory for 1806, Containing the Names, Trades, and Residence of the Inhabitants of the City, Southwark, and Northern Liberties* [Philadelphia, 1806]). The draftsman and all the other engravers except for Vallance and Marshall appear in the Philadelphia directories of 1806 or 1807.

From Caleb P. Wayne

Dr. Sir,   Philada. Aug 22. 1804

I find myself under the absolute necessity of omitting the last Chap. of Vol. 3 & carrying it to Vol. 4 this can be done in both copies, as the other has not left this for Europe; were I to publish the whole it would make considerably beyond 600 pages & without Chap 10. it will make 550 pages. My purse has already suffered so severely by the extra quantities in Vol. I & 2. that I cannot, think of publishing the whole of this. Please to write to me immediately on this subject. Chap 9. will terminate the Vol. very well it concludes stating the retirement of the troops in winter quarters after the campaign of 1778.

ADf, Dreer Collection, PHi. Bottom half of page contains draft of letter to Bushrod Washington, 23 Aug. 1804. Wayne endorsed verso, "Copy to B. Washington & J. Marshall." An unknown hand noted the date 20 Aug. 1804 and C. P. Wayne.

Webb v. Colston
Deposition

[August–September 1804][1]
In reference to this subject the honourable John Marshall was examined before the subscriber in the year 1804 as a Witness he testified "that he was counsel for Rawleigh Colston in the suit . . . against Morris and Braxton in which a Judgment was rendered in his favour as admr. of Thomas Webb decd. in the district Court holden at Richmond[2] during the trial exceptions were moved by the counsel of Mr. Morris to an Opinion given by the Court, and after the renditure of the Verdict, much time was consumed in giving the exceptions the shape in which they were to be assigned. Pending those contests a resolution was declared by the Agent and Counsel of Mr. Morris to Appeal, and this deponent held a conversation with Mr. Colston respecting the security to be given by the appellant. It was understood that Mr. Benjamin Harrison Junr. who he perceives was also special bail[3] in the suit was to be offered as security. Mr. Colston insisted on his being objected to as being absolutely insufficient to pay the debt. This deponent was on intimate terms with Mr. Harrison and therefore disinclined to make the objection in consequence of which it was agreed that Mr. Colston should attend and make it in person. The bill of exceptions did not take the shape wished for by the counsel of Mr. Morris; and from this OR some other cause the appeal was dropped. This deponent was long intimately acquainted with Mr. Harrison and was regularly his counsel in all the suits depending in the Courts which he attended. He was not however nor is he particularly acquainted with the circumstances of that Gentleman, as he never enquired into them; and has no Other knowledge of them than friends and neighbours will acquire with respect to the affairs of each Other, without searching for the information. As far as his general knowledge will warrant an Opinion he does believe that Mr. Harrison could not have been made to pay the debt for which the Judgment was rendered against Morris and Braxton. He knows the proper debts of Mr. Harrison were considerable, and believes that his personal estate was not large. This deponent further states that at the time the Judgment was obtained the Credit of Mr. Morris was so high that he should himself have relied much more confidently on the Word of that gentleman, for the payment of so large a sum of money as the amount of the Judgment spoken of, than on any means given by the law of forcing it from Harrison. Mr. Colston frequently consulted him while his counsel on the measures to be taken for the payment of the Judgment. He does[4] recollect particularly but knows generally the course which Mr. Colston himself seemed to have taken, or to be

about to take, was that which bid fairest to Obtain the most money in the shortest time."

Copy, Webb v. Colston, Record, 85–86, Superior Court of Chancery, Frederick County, Records, 1784–1820 (microfilm), Vi.

1. This deposition was taken in the course of a suit between the heirs and legatees of Thomas Webb and Rawleigh Colston. Webb and Colston had formed a mercantile partnership for several years in the early 1780s. Webb's heirs filed their bill in the High Court of Chancery in 1794 for the purpose of obtaining settlement of accounts with Colston both as partner of the firm and as Webb's administrator. The suit was still pending in the High Court of Chancery in Feb. 1802, when it was transferred to the Superior Court of Chancery at Staunton. There the suit languished until Mar. 1812, when it was removed to the Superior Court of Chancery at Winchester. A final decree did not issue until Apr. 1820, the court finding a large balance against Colston. JM's deposition is embodied in the report of Master Commissioner Lemuel Bent, dated Winchester, 15 Dec. 1815. The full record of the suit covers 226 pages. The commissioner's report begins at p. 81 of the record. JM was one of several witnesses examined by Commissioner Bent in Winchester in 1804. He presumably testified some time during August or September, when he was in the Winchester region.

2. The judgment obtained in Apr. 1793 by Colston as Webb's administrator against Robert Morris and Carter Braxton, partners in the firm of Morris & Braxton, was for nearly ten thousand pounds Virginia currency (Webb v. Colston, Record, 37). The purpose of JM's testimony was to show that Colston took every precaution to collect this judgment. Braxton was then insolvent, and Morris, who later declared bankruptcy, was reluctant to pay, claiming that Braxton was indebted to him to a great amount. Benjamin Harrison, Jr., who served as special bail for Morris and Braxton, was also on the verge of insolvency. On Morris's unhappy experience as a litigant in the Virginia courts, see *PJM*, V, 93–96.

3. Harrison had been a close business associate of Morris's. As special bail, he was liable for the judgment in case of the defendant's default (*PJM*, V, 105 n. 14, 271 and n. 1).

4. The copyist apparently here omitted "not."

To Caleb P. Wayne

Sir   Front Royal Septr. 3d. 1804

On my return from the Allegheny I received your letter of the 20th. of August with the magazine & paper which accompanied it.

I wish very sincerely that some of those objections which are now made to the plan of the work had been heard when the proposals for subscription were first published. I shoud very readily have relinquished my opinion respecting it if I had percieved that the public taste required a different course. I ought indeed to have foreseen that the same impatience which precipitated the publication woud require that the life & transactions of Mr. Washington shoud be immediately entered upon, &, if my original ideas of the subject had been preserved in the main, yet I ought to have departed from them so far as to have composed the introductory volume at leisure after the principal work was finished.

I have also to sustain increased mortification on account of the careless manner in which the work has been executed. I had to learn that under the pressure of constant application the spring of the mind loses its elasticity & that the style will be insensibly influenced by that of the authors we have been perusing. That compositions thus formed require attentive revisals when the impression under which they were written has worn off. But regrets for the past are unavailing. It is of more service to do what is best under existing circumstances. There will be great difficulty in retrieving the reputation of the first volume because there is a minuteness & a want of interest in details of the transactions of infant settlements which will always affect the book containing them however it may be executed. I have therefore some doubts whether it may not be as well to drop the first volume for the present—that is not to speak of a republication of it, & to proceed with the others. I shall at all events conform to your request & be silent respecting the corrections I have prepared.

I wish the third coud be reduced to the compass you mention. If it is not already in the press that might perhaps be done. I coud effect it if the copy was again in my possession. But I had no idea that the pages of the manuscript woud exceed those of the printed volume. Perhaps you might stop short of the chapter where the volume is now finishd.[1]

I am very sorry that I cannot send on the 4th. Vol. by the time you request. Those whom I applied to as copyers have deserted the business in my absence, & I cannot return to Richmond to engage others till early in october. It will of consequence be perhaps the month of february before you can receive it. Independent of this untoward circumstance, experience has sufficiently admonished me of the ⟨indis⟩cretion of sending another almost unexamined volume to the press.

Whatever might have been the execution, the work woud have experienced unmerited censure. We must endeavor to rescue what remains to be done from such as is deserved. I wish you to consult Mr. Washington. I am very respectfully, your obedt

J MARSHALL

I shall give a very attentive perusal to the printed copy & render it much more fit for the public eye in case of another edition. But this must be postponed.

ALS, Dreer Collection, PHi; Tr, Marshall Papers, DLC. Addressed to Wayne at Philadelphia. MS torn where seal was broken.

1. Bushrod Washington exonerated JM from blame for the volume's length, saying that he had no way of knowing whether his manuscript would exceed or fall short of the five hundred pages promised subscribers. Washington suggested too that a chapter be taken off the present volume and added to the next (Washington to Wayne, 26 Aug. 1804, Dreer Collection, PHi).

From Benjamin Rush

Sir,   Philada Sepr 5. 1804

I wrote to you a few days ago, upon an interesting subject, but as the letter was addressed to you at Washington (supposing you were now there) I fear it will not reach you in time to produce the effect intended by it.[1] I shall therefore briefly mention its Object.

On the 27th of august last I heard, that a letter written by me On the 12 of Jany 1778 to Govr Henry which was sent by him to Genl Washington, was to be printed in the 3rd Vol of his life, with a letter to the Govr: from the Genl:[2] in which he says April 27. 1778[3] *long since* the writing of the letter to Mr Henry, I had "used the most elaborate & studious professions of regard for him." This Sir is certainly a mistake. I wrote two letters to Genl Washington from Princeton in Decemr 1777[4] the One stating the Abuses & Distresses wch prevailed in the mily: hospitals under my care—the Other containing Complaints against the Conduct of the Director ⟨Genera⟩l of the hospitals.[5] Nor did I even see GW Until 14 months afterwards,[6] at Morristown where before I had waited upon him he asked me to dine With him, & treated me with a degree of attention wch led me to beleive he had magnanimously forgotten my letter to Govr Henry. In Consequence of this friendly conduct I visited him every time he came to Philada & was uniformly treated by him as I had been at morristown.

I declare I neither conversed with nor corresponded with the Gentlemen who were publickly said to be hostile to Genl: W: The fears & apprehensions, I expressed in my letter to Govr Henry, were founded upon the fatal tendency of the disorders I saw in the department of the Army in which I acted, & upon some private Anecdotes that had been communicated directly, or indirectly to me by Officers, & citizens of high rank & respectability.[7] Some of them died in friendship with Genl Washington. The Survivors venerate his memory. They all I beleive Altered their Opinions immedy after the sudden & happy

Change wch took place in the affairs of the Army & our Country in the summer of 1778. The private Anecdotes alluded to, with the names of the persons who related them, I have always intended should descend to the grave with me. They were not suspected of entertaining them. You will be surprized when I add that *Governor Henry was one of them.*[8]

I assure you Sir, no expressions or Conduct of mine, between the 12th of Jany & the 27th of April 1778 (the day on wch Genl Washington's letter is dated) could warrant the injurious reflections upon me that are contained in it.

After this statements of facts, permit me to request as an Act of justice as well as of favor to me, that you would eraze the passages objected to from the Genl['s] letter. I repeat again—They are certainly founded in a mistake.

Your speedy Attention to my request will much Oblige Sir (with great respect), your most Obedt Servant[9]

BENJN RUSH

ADfS, Rush Papers, Library Company of Philadelphia MSS at PHi. Endorsed by Rush, "Copy of a letter to/J Marshall Esqr/Sepr 5. 1804/Front Royal/Fredk: County/ Virginia." MS torn. Contains many deletions and interlineations. Printed in L. H. Butterfield, ed., *Letters of Benjamin Rush*, II (Princeton, N.J., 1951), II, 887–89.

1. Letter not found. Rush's son Richard had obtained JM's correct address from Wayne for his father (Wayne to Bushrod Washington, 8 Sept. 1804, Dreer Collection, PHi).

2. Wayne explained to Bushrod Washington how Rush found out about the intended publication of these letters. Rush's friend Samuel Bradford, a publisher in Philadelphia, was one of the holders of the English rights to the *Life*. Bradford had picked up from Wayne the letters of Henry, Rush, and Washington that were meant for the appendix, and Wayne had injudiciously mentioned to Bradford that the anonymous author of the 12 Jan. 1778 letter was Benjamin Rush. Bradford in turn informed Rush, who proceeded to write Bushrod Washington and JM in protest (ibid.; see also Washington to Wayne, 6 Sept. 1804, Dreer Collection, PHi; Rush to Bushrod Washington, 29 Aug., 13 Sept., 21 Sept., 24 Sept. 1804 [Harry G. Good, *Benjamin Rush and His Services to American Education* (Berne, Ind., 1918), 62–69]).

3. Rush erred in this date; he meant George Washington's letter of 28 Mar. 1778 to Patrick Henry (see JM to Wayne, 27 June 1804 [2d letter]). In his letter to Bushrod Washington of 29 Aug., Rush had the correct month but the earlier day of 27 Mar., when Washington also had written Henry a letter on the same subject (Good, *Rush*, 63).

4. Again, Rush misremembered the date of his second letter. In writing to Bushrod Washington, Rush commented that he had mislaid his copy of this letter but pointed out that the original ought to be available in the files of the Continental Congress, where it had been forwarded by George Washington (29 Aug. 1804 [Good, *Rush*, 64]; Butterfield, *Letters of Rush*, I, 208 n. 10). In fact, the second letter was dated 25 Feb. 1778 and was the one to which George Washington referred, when he accused Rush of having "been elaborate & studied in his professions of regard for me; & that long since the letter to" Patrick Henry of 12 Jan. 1778. Rush had closed his 25 Feb. letter to Washington "with the warmest sentiments of regard and attachment your excellency's

most affectionate, humble servant." Following his signature, Rush had added a post-script in which he thanked Washington in flattering terms for instructions he had issued concerning the hospitals. In his earlier letter to General Washington of 26 Dec. 1777, Rush had ended more formally "with the most perfect esteem, I have the honor to be your excellency's most obedient and devoted servant" (Butterfield, *Letters of Rush*, I, 182, 200, 203).

5. At this point in the printed version in Butterfield, *Letters of Rush*, II, 888, four sentences follow that do not appear in the manuscript. In substance, they parallel the content of a deleted paragraph at the bottom of the first page and top of the second in Rush's draft, but they are not a verbatim reconstruction of the fragmentary phrases contained in that passage. In it Rush declared that his two letters ended "with the common expressions of respect to persons in high (stati)ons." He went on to explain about the congressional inquiry into the state of the military hospitals in Jan. 1778 and his subsequent resignation.

6. Another error: twenty-six months later, when Rush was attending the court-martial of Dr. William Shippen, Jr., at Morristown (Butterfield, *Letters of Rush*, II, 890 n. 5, 1205 and nn. 23, 24).

7. In his letter to Henry, Rush had reviewed the dismal circumstances at the end of 1777 and suggested that placing a new general, such as Gates, Lee, or Conway, at the head of Washington's army would make it "irresistible." For an assessment of Rush's intentions in writing his unsigned letter to Henry and its aftereffects on Rush, see Rush to Patrick Henry, 12 Jan. 1778, and appendix I: "Rush and Washington," ibid., I, 182–84 and nn.; II, 1197–1208.

8. Years later in a letter to John Adams, Rush detailed the "Anecdotes" and his informants, who principally were: Maj. Gen. Adam Stephen, Adj. Gen. Joseph Reed, Gen. Horatio Gates, Gen. Thomas Mifflin, Maj. Gen. John Sullivan. Gates was the one who told Rush that Henry had said General Washington was not fit to be commander-in-chief (12 Feb. 1812 [ibid., II, 1119–24, esp. 1120–23, 1126 n. 16]).

9. JM honored Rush's request (see JM to Wayne, 24 Sept. 1804). For the sentences deleted, see JM to Wayne, 27 June 1804 (2d letter) and nn. 2, 4.

To Caleb P. Wayne

Sir   Front Royal Septr. 6th. [1804]
    From some irregularity in the post office your letter of the 22d. of August did not reach me till last evening.

    I am perfectly content with the diminution of the 3d. vol. which you find it necessary to make, & wish you to send me both copies of the 10th. chapter by Judge Washington whom you will see in Philadelphia on his circuit. It is probable that their situation, commencing instead of terminating a volume may require that they shoud be altered.

    If your opinion of the extent of this part of the work is formed on counting the pages & not on examining it more particularly I am persuaded that the reduction you propose making will bring it within less than 500 pages. At least I hope so. A portion of that volume is copied in a hand which is more loose than that you have been accustomed to, & if you have not adverted to that circumstance in your calculation you will be agreeably disappointed by it.

I have been critically examining the 2d. vol. since my return & am sorry to find that especially in the 1st. chapter, there is much to correct. The 3d. I hope will not be so defective & ⟨it⟩ shall be my care to render the 4th. more fit for the public eye. I wish it was possible for me to revise the proof sheets. But I suppose it is not. The words "very" "excessive" & "extremely" frequently burthen the sentence & might be struck out without altering the sense. Perhaps you coud do it. This did not strike my eye in the manuscript but does in the printed copy.[1] Shoud there be a 2d. edition the volumes will all be reduced within the compass you propose; & will of course receive very material corrections. On this subject however I remain silent. Perhaps a free expression of my thoughts respecting the inac[c]uracies of the present edition may add to the current which seems to set against it & may therefore be for the present indiscreet.

It is unnecessary to make any present preparations for republishing the work. That will depend on the reception of the subsequent volumes. The first edition shoud be completely in possession of the public before a second is spoken of. I wish very sincerely that the number of copies had not exceeded the number of subscribers. I am Sir very respectfully, Your obedt. ⟨Serv⟩t

J MARSHALL

Do not fail to return me both copies of the 10th. Chap. by Mr. Washington. They will be sent to you with the residue of the 4th. Vol. which I shoud choose to revise altho the disappointment in procuring the copies had not put it out of my power to forward them immediately.

By[2] some means the packet containing the sheets between page 296 & 425. of the 2d. vol. has miscarried. I wish they coud be forwarded to me in Richmond because I am examining & correcting them to be returned to you for the future & as I score the lines it will be more useful than a paper stating the alterations.

ALS, Dreer Collection, PHi; Tr, Marshall Papers, DLC. Transcript dated 8 Sept. Addressed to Wayne at Philadelphia. MS torn where seal was broken.

1. While JM was reading proof sheets, Wayne had published vol. II on 3 Sept. 1804 (*U.S. Gazette*). In the second impression JM cut down on the use of such adverbs. Compare, for example, *Life*, I, chap. 3, 105, line 12; II, chap. 1, 18, line 4, with *Life* (1805 ed.), I, chap. 3, 109, line 8; II, chap. 1, 19, line 8.

2. JM wrote this paragraph sideways along the left margin of the first page of his letter.

From Caleb P. Wayne

Sir,   Philada. Sep. 16. 1804

Your two favou[r]s from Front Royal are recd. & with this letter I send the sheets of vol. 2. that were lost. I have determined to print the 10th Chap. in vol.[1] rather than to derange your plans in the smallest degree. I am unhappy to learn you have discovered errors that give you pain—and almost regret having sent the severe & unjust criticism in the magazine. The public ought to recollect the short period you have had to prepare for the press. The length of time which you say must elapse before I can have the 4th volume will subject me to great inconvenience, unless you can, by correcting such errors as you think too glaring in the first & 2d. vols, send one or both of them to me to reprint, by the last of Sep. or early in October as from the total returns made by Mr. Weems, & others, lately, I find there will not be enough of books for subscribers & I wish very much to print enough for that purpose & a few more, least they be introduced from England. I hope you can meet my wishes.

I suspect you will be troubled with letters from Dr. Rush or some of his family, as they have learnt, thro the purchaser of the copy for England, that the *anonymous* letter to P. Henry Es. is to be published, & it appears they feel sore on the occasion. When I publish a *revised & corrected 2d edition*, I shall omit the side notes & by that means enlarge the pages, & by so doing bring the matter contained in the present volumes into 500 pages—so that you need [not] diminish the quantity. By reprinting the 1st & 2d. vol. I mean merely to complete the present edition to the amot. for actual subscribers. It will be impossible to send the proof sheets ⟨to⟩ Richmond or indeed any where else, unless they could be always returned, read, in 24 hour[s] at furth[est].

ADf, Dreer Collection, PHi; Tr, Marshall Papers, DLC. Endorsed by Wayne, "Copy/ to/J. Marshall/Sept. 16. 1804."

1. Wayne omitted to insert "3" here. He had intended to transfer chap. 10 to the beginning of vol. IV (see Wayne to JM, 22 Aug. 1804). As printed, chap. 10 appears in vol. III, 534–80, making nearly the six hundred pages predicted by Wayne, exclusive of the additional twenty-eight pages of notes.

To Caleb P. Wayne

Sir   Front Royal Septr. 24th. 1804

I receivd last night a letter from Doctor Rush in which he says that injustice is done him in the letter from General Washington to Governor Henry of the 27th. of april 1778[1] in which the General states that "long since the writing of the letter to Mr. Henry he (Doctor Rush) had used the most elaborate & studious expressions of regard" for him. The Doctor requests that these words may be erased.

As the name of that gentleman was not mentioned in the correspondence, & no allusion was made to him in the note in which it was published, I had not supposed that he woud have been understood to be the person designated in the letter of the General. The fact I now imagine will be different from my expectation respecting it. Be this as it may, I perceive no objection to the omission of those words which might implicate the sincerity of Doctor Rush. The object of publishing those letters is to exhibit truely the difficulties with which the commander in chief was under the necessity of struggling. That object does not require that the candor of any gentleman shoud be rendered questionable. It is therefore my wish that the words of the Generals letter which relate to the professions of Doctor Rush shoud not be published. At the same time it will be necessary either by leaving a space with the usual marks, or by placing inverted commas, or in some other way to denote that some words are omitted. This is not to be disregarded.[2]

I wish this letter to be shown to Mr. Washington who I am persuaded will concur with me on this subject. I am very respectfully, Your Obedt. Servt.

J MARSHALL

The alteration requested will of course be made in Mr. Morgans copy also. Lest this letter shoud by any accident miscarry I have enclosed a copy of it to Doctor Rush.[3]

ALS, Dreer Collection, PHi. Addressed to Wayne at Philadelphia.

1. That is, 28 Mar. 1778. See Rush to JM, 5 Sept. 1805 and n. 3.

2. Wayne had already struck off the page containing General Washington's 27 and 28 Mar. 1778 letters complete with the sentences referring to Rush. Wayne initially had objected to omitting Rush's and Mifflin's names, and he now opposed complying with Rush's request to alter the letters further. The publisher observed that "if it were done in this instance every man who in any way may be implicated in the course of the work, would expect his name & certain parts, perhaps the most material, of his letters to be omitted. . . . It is often asked, '*will it be a party work*' my uniform [answer] has been *no*— but that every thing would be fairly stated; let it operate against or in favour of any man, or party. I hope such answer meets your approbation; as I understood you to say such will be the case. The real enemies & the real friends of Gen. W. ought now to be known." In the end, Wayne deferred to JM and Bushrod Washington, who agreed to accommodate Rush, although Bushrod had "unbounded confidence in the General's correctness." Rush's wish that the erasure "be done so as not to leave a suspicion of a chasm in the letter in the public mind," however, was not honored (Wayne to Bushrod Washington, 8 Sept. 1804; Washington to Wayne, 18 Sept. 1804, Dreer Collection, PHi; Rush to Bushrod Washington, 24 Sept. 1804 [Good, *Rush*, 68]). Following JM's instruc-

tions, Wayne reset the page, deleting the sentences and inserting asterisks to indicate the omissions (vol. III, app., 17).

3. Letter not found.

To Caleb P. Wayne

Sir   Richmond October 4th. 1804

I have just reachd this place where I found your letter of the 16th. of September with the sheets of the 2d. volume which had miscarried. I shall forward to you daily some sheets of the 1st. & second volume with the corrections made at a single reading which I will copy & transmit with the sheets. I do not send them all together because I wish to revise the alterations I have made, especially those respecting punctuation, as I beleive that the pointing woud be too frequent & I shall diminish it. You will consequently see some marks in the margin of which no notice is to be taken. One thing I will observe generally which will require your regular attention. Several Sentences are broken down & in some cases two sentences are united. I have not noted that a consequent change becomes necessary in the letter which begins the sentence according to the new arrangement. When a period is struck out the capital letter following it is of course to be changed to a common letter, & when a new period is formed the sentence will of course begin with a capital. This will require your attention.

I hope the surplus copies will be few in number. Some few I coud wish to be printed with the corrections I shall forward to you, but I trust they will not be numerous. I am anxious that there shoud be a second edition corrected at leisure after the work shall be finished.

I regret that you shoud have the trouble of altering your types so much as the many corrections I have made will require, but I am persuaded it will be permanently advantageous to you to submit to the present inconvenience.

I woud recommend that you shoud not print in the first instance a greater number of the 3d. vol. than were printed of the first & second unless you deem it absolutely necessary—because I coud wish to revise that also after it is in print. It is not so incorrect as the first & second but I am confident that inelegances & even inaccuracies are not so quickly percieved in manuscript as in print.

Mr. Webster has been so obliging as to correct some minute facts which have been mistated for which I am much indebted to him & to which I shall attend.[1]

I have written to you on the subject of Doctor Rush's application &

hope you have received the letter. In the confidence that there is no impropriety in omitting those words which relate to Doctor Rush as a person professing sentiments he did not feel, provided it shoud be apparent that certain words were omitted I have requested that he shoud be gratified. I have no doubt that Mr. Washington will be pleased with this omission & I am persuaded it is in itself at least unobjectionable.

Immediately on my leaving Richmond I lost my copyers. They are both taken into public employment—the one into the bank & the other into the penetentiary as a clerk. I shall go to day in quest of others & will use my best endeavor to repair as far as possible by the utmost expedition the injury sustained by the delays thus occasiond. I am Sir very respectfully, Your obedt. Servt.

J MARSHALL

ALS, Dreer Collection, PHi; Tr (typed), Marshall Papers, DLC. Addressed to Wayne at Philadelphia; postmarked Richmond, 5 Oct.

1. See JM to Noah Webster, 4 Oct. 1804.

To Noah Webster

Sir   Richmond October 4th. 1804

A tour into our mountain country in quest of health for my family prevented my receiving till yesterday your favor of the 21st. of August.[1] Receive Sir my sincere thanks for the real obligation you have conferred on me by enabling me to correct any error into which I may have permitted myself to be betrayed. Be assured that I shall avail myself as far as is now in my power of the information you have been so good as to give, & that I am truely grateful for that information.

I fear it will not be in my power immediately to obtain your book which contains the account of the introduction of representation in Massachussetts. I apprehend that no copy of it has reached Virginia, & as I reside in Richmond, not in Washington, I have no access to the office of the Secretary of State.[2] I shall however make a point of procuring the work. Your remark respecting fort Good Hope[3] will also be attended to.

The tree in which the charter of Connecticut was concealed was taken from Mr. Chalmer to whose statements, in consequence of his situation at the board of commissioners for plantation affairs, were received with great respect. The oak however shall as soon as possible be restored to his rights.[4]

The other corrections you suggest shall also receive my attention.[5] The error respecting the situation of New Haven can only be attributed to a carelessness for which there is no apology.[6] With high respect I am Sir, Your Obedt. Servt

J MARSHALL

ALS, NNPM. Addressed to Webster at New Haven, Conn.; postmarked Richmond, 5 Oct. Endorsed by Webster, "Judge Marshal/Richmond Oct 4th/1804."

1. Noah Webster (1758–1843), American lexicographer. Letter not found; but in a letter to James Madison, 20 Aug. 1804, Webster wrote, "I am reading, and am much pleased with, the first volume of the life of General Washington. One or two errors have escaped the respectable author," which Webster went on to detail (Harry R. Warfel, ed., Letters of Noah Webster [New York, 1953], 256–57). See nn. below.

2. Webster referred JM to his Elements of Useful Knowledge . . . , I (Hartford, Conn., 1802; S #3519), 158, for "a brief but correct statement" of the change in the legislature of colonial Massachusetts. JM's "account from Hutchinson of the origin of representation in the General Court of Massachusetts" was "not perfectly correct." Webster apparently objected to JM's conclusion that the delegation of legislative authority to representatives was "rendered familiar and probably suggested by the practice in the mother country" (Life, I, chap. 3, 105). Webster told Madison that "I am the more anxious to have the causes of that event fully stated, as the facts repel a suggestion often made by French writers, that in the division of houses in our legislatures we have been led by a disposition to imitate the parliament of Great Britain. It appears, however, that the first instance of it arose out of a state of things in Massachusetts altogether extraneous to any such principle" (Webster to Madison, 20 Aug. 1804 [Warfel, Letters of Webster, 256–57]). According to Webster, the immediate circumstances of the colony, where the number of freemen had exceeded a convenient number for participating in law-making, led to the alteration. Webster drew his own conclusions from John Winthrop, A Journal of the Transactions and Occurrences in the Settlement of Massachusetts and the Other New-England Colonies, from the Year 1630 to 1644: Written by John Winthrop, Esq., First Governor of Massachusetts: And Now First Published from a Correct Copy of the Original Manuscript (Hartford, Conn., 1790; Evans #23086), 63–64, 65. Webster, acting as editor, had seen Winthrop's manuscript into print. A copy of Webster's book was deposited in the secretary of state's office for copyright purposes. JM did not revise his interpretation in the second impression (Life [1805 ed.], I, chap. 3, 109).

3. A Dutch post, later Hartford, Conn.

4. In describing Sir Edmund Andros's assertion of royal authority in Connecticut in 1687, JM wrote that "the colony submitted, but the charter itself was secreted and concealed in a venerable elm, long afterwards deemed sacred by the people" (vol. I, chap. 6, 216). Webster apparently informed him this allusion should have been to the Charter Oak. JM took his information from Chalmers, Political Annals, I, 298. See Preface, [ante 22 Dec. 1803], and n. 17. In his revisions, JM changed this reference to "a venerable tree which is still in existence" (Life [1805 ed.], I, chap. 6, 225). In his footnote to that page he did not acknowledge Webster.

5. At the end of chap. 7, JM added a note in the second impression concerning the contested boundary line between Massachusetts and Connecticut. The two colonies came to a compromise in 1713, according to Hutchinson, "but the author is informed by Mr. Webster that the controversy was only finally adjusted in the year 1804" (Life [1805 ed.], I, 277n).

6. JM had located New Haven on the Connecticut River (vol. I, chap. 3, 125), "although thirty-five or forty miles west of it" (Webster to Madison, 20 Aug. 1804 [Warfel,

Letters of Webster, 256]). JM rephrased his statement, locating the town west of the river (*Life* [1805 ed.], I, chap. 3, 130).

To Caleb P. Wayne

[22 October 1804]

In page 8. l. 30.[1] After the sentence which concludes with the word "influence," strike out to the end of the paragraph & read "To select a man qualified for the arduous task of planting a colony in a new world, & disposed to engage in it, was among the first objects to which their attention was directed. Sir Humphry Gilbert of Compton in Devonshire had rendered himself conspicuous for his military services both in France & Ireland, & by a treatise concerning the north west passage, in which great ingenuity & learning are stated by Doctor Robertson, to have been mingled with the enthusiasm the credulity & sanguine expectation which incite men to new & hazardous undertakings. On this gentleman the adventurers turned their eyes, & he was placed at the head of the enterprise which was contemplated. On the 11th. of June 1578 he obtained letters patent from the Queen vesting in him the powers that were required."

Sir

I have just received your letter of the 15.[2] & transmit you (above) a modification of the paragraph you had pointed out to my attention. I thank you for having done so & wish you would continue to mark any passages which appear to require alteration. That I should have perused the work without adverting to the confusion of the sentence as it stands is sufficient evidence that the book must be read at intervals while the attention is alive, or egregious inelegances will escape the reader.

It appears to me that a slight alteration should be made in page 11. line 17. The word private man would indicate that all the expenses of the settlement had been charged on the purse of Gilbert. I took this expression from Doctor Robertson[3] without adverting to circumstances which would seem to imply the fact to have been otherwise. In the page to which the above correction applies, it is stated that the plan was projected & patronised by persons of rank & distinction, & in page 12 it is also stated that Sir Walter Rawleigh was interested in it. I therefore presume that Gilbert alone did not support the expedition & consequently that the expression ought to be changed. I therefore request your attention to the following alteration also.

p 11. l 17. for private man read "few private individuals."[4]

I think also that some additional correction is necessary in page 27. line 11. Instead of the words "and unaffected by the laws they make, while commerce remains unconfined:" I could wish the expression to be varied thus "nor affected by the laws they make, and yet leave commerce entirely unrestrained, the patentees["] &c.[5]

I have not yet received the sheets of the 3d. volume. I will write to Mr. Washington. In the mean time if any palpable errors present themselves to you which may have escaped my attention, fatigued as it is—& which it would be inconvenient to suggest to me, or to wait till my correction could be received, I wish Mr. Washington to make the alteration. I am Sir very respectfully, Your Obedt. Servt.

                                                     J MARSHALL

I had not supposed that you designed to introduce the dates into the body of the work until a 2d. edition & therefore had not adverted to that arrangement. I had however corrected the marginal misplacement of date which I now send you. It will enable you to make the arrangement you wish. I cannot make it myself without reading again the whole book. At the top of p. 3. place 1495. p. 9. strike out 1498 in the margin at the top & insert 1578 which need not stand below. page 12. strike out in the margin 1578 & place 1584. line[6] 23 place 1606 opposite the paragraph above that where it now is. page 30. In the margin place 1607. page 49. at the beginning of the last paragraph place in the margin 1610—p 63 strike out last 1621. page 72 & 73. for 1624 place in the margin 1625. (Charles 1 ascended the throne in march 1625.) p. 83. about six lines from the bottom insert in the margin 1650. page 114 nearly opposite the 10th. line place 1637. page 115. place 1638 about five lines higher than it is. page 123. place 1637 rather higher up, opposite the 7th. line. p 149. place 1650 about 12 lines higher. pages 153. & 154 instead of 1651 read 1653. page 163. place 1663 two lines lower. page 176 for 1661. insert 1664. page 193 instead of 1670 read 1676. pages 198. 199. 200 for 1688 read 1676. p 201. read 1677. p 202 for 1688 read 1680. page 205. for 1666. read 1675. page 209 for 1676 read 1679. p 212. for 1681 read 1684. beginning of the paragraph containing death of Ch. 2 place in margin 1685. p 232. 3d. line from the bottom place in the margin 1691. p 233. strike out 1689. page 248 for 1697 read 1698. page 255. for 1708 read 1709. page 260. for 1713 read 1702—do. in pages 261. & 262. page 263. read 1703. pages 264 265. 266. 267. 268. read 1704. page 269. for 1713 read 1708 & at the beginning of the paragraph in the middle of the page read 1712. p 270 read 1712. p. 272. read 1703. pages 273. 274. read 1706. page 275 read 1709. page 278. read 1714. page 279 read 1714. pages 288 & 289 read 1726. page 316 read 1718. page 315. read 1718. p 345 for 1719. read 1742. page 378 at the ⟨begin⟩ning of the last paragraph read 1754. same in 379. 380. 381. 382. & 383. page 384 read 1755. p 487. read 1762 instead of 1761. ⟨ . . . ⟩ 1762 where it is placed lower down.

The above were designed for the margin. If the date is not to be continued in the margin many of them will be useless but they will enable you to place the date in the body of the work.[7] If the marginal note of date is to be preserved I think it is usual (but of this I am not certain & I have not referred to any book to correct myself if wrong) to place on the top of the page the date of the last occurrence on that page.

ALS, Dreer Collection, PHi. Addressed to Wayne at Philadelphia; letter dated by postmark, Richmond, 22 Oct. Endorsed by Wayne. MS torn where seal was broken. Wayne made check and cross marks throughout letter to indicate he had entered JM's corrections for vol. I.

1. Correction for second printing of vol. I, as are all of the subsequent alterations mentioned in this letter. In chap. 1, 8–9, appears a fifteen-line sentence, in which subject and verb are separated by a subordinate clause eight lines long. JM's revision broke the sentence into four. It appears in *Life* (1805 ed.), I, 9, as it is here, with minor variations in punctuation and spelling.

2. Letter not found.

3. Robertson, *History of America, Bks. IX. and X.*, 43.

4. Correction made in *Life* (1805 ed.), I, 12, line 2.

5. Correction made ibid., 28, lines 15–16.

6. JM meant to write "page."

7. Wayne retained marginal dates in the second impression and altered them in accordance with JM's corrections, although all page and line numbers differ in the second impression.

To Caleb P. Wayne

Sir   Richmond october 30th. 1804

Your letter of the 9th. with the printed sheets of the 3d. vol. only reached me the day before yesterday. Had I received it sooner my corrections of the 1st. vol. should have been forwarded to you more expeditiously. I am truely sorry for the loss you have sustained.[1]

I am greatly obliged to the author of the anonymous letter you transmitted to me & wish very sincerely to know to whom I am indebted that I might make him the proper acknowledgements.[2] I shall certainly avail myself as far as is in my power of the information he has given. There were some facts of which I could not obtain a distinct view from the papers in my possession & the sollicitude I felt while composing the work to remain unknown as the author, a wish I have ever retaind, prevented my making enquiries. I felt some difficulty in ascertaining the cantonment of the British troops before the battle of Trenton & supposed the British statements on that point were to be relied on. The representation made on this subject by your anonymous correspondent is I am persuaded from other circumstances for which I could not account, perfectly correct.[3] With respect to the battle of Long Island there is no doubt respecting its date. It was unquestionably in August. If it appears from the note in the margin to have been in July that note is incorrect. It is either a typographical error or one made in copying the work as there is no such mistake in the original work.[4]

If this Gentleman should become known to you I shall be much obliged by your making my acknowlegements to him & letting me know who he is. I am Sir respectfully your Obedt

J MARSHALL

ALS, Dreer Collection, PHi; Tr (typed), Marshall Papers, DLC. Addressed to Wayne at Philadelphia; postmarked, Richmond, 30 Oct.

1. Letter not found. Wayne was about to publish vol. III, which he advertised in the *U.S. Gazette* on 26 Nov. 1804, and he was anxious for his printers to finish setting the second impression of vol. I. JM had sent corrections for the last pages (465–88) of the first volume and for the notes in the appendix under separate cover from Richmond on 24 Oct. (Dreer Collection, PHi). Wayne incorporated all of JM's alterations in *Life* (1805 ed.), I, 477–500, and app.

2. An anonymous correspondent in Philadelphia wrote to Wayne on 3 Oct. 1804, enclosing a paper with a series of detailed corrections for events in 1776 and 1777 covered in vol. II. Letter and enclosure not found, but printed in *Historical Magazine*, 2d ser., I (May 1867), 286–88. At that time, the original manuscript was in the collection of Francis S. Hoffman, New York, N.Y. (ibid., 286n). Wayne passed the critique along to JM.

3. JM stated that General Cadwallader was to cross the Delaware at Bristol to take the British troops at Burlington; the writer said they were posted not at Burlington but at Mount Holly and Cadwallader crossed at Dunk's Ferry. JM changed his statement accordingly in the second impression (vol. II, chap. 8, 542; *Historical Magazine*, 2d ser., I [May 1867], 287; *Life* [1805 ed.], II, chap. 8, 544). The informant also provided other factual details and corrections surrounding the Battles of Trenton and Princeton covered in vol. II, chap. 8, 541–42, 544–45, 549, 551–54 (*Historical Magazine*, 2d ser., I [May 1867], 287–88). JM revised chap. 8, utilizing the information provided by this correspondent (compare *Life* [1805 ed.], II, 544, 546–47, 554–59 and nn.). In the second impression, JM noted that his account of the battle of Princeton differed from his original version and that "he is indebted for that information to a very intelligent friend to whom he feels great obligation which it gives him much gratification to acknowledge" (ibid., 556n).

4. The correspondent pointed out that the Battle of Long Island and subsequent retreat took place in Aug. 1776, not July, which appears erroneously in the margins in vol. II, chap. 7, 430–48. He also observed that the withdrawal of American troops was viewed "as a masterly stroke of Generalship," which deserved "more notice in history than a mere narrative as of a common transaction" (*Historical Magazine*, 2d ser., I [May 1867], 287). In the second impression, the month appears correctly as August (*Life* [1805 ed.], II, 431–49). JM added a new paragraph concerning General Washington's

abilities, concluding that "the retreat from Long island may justly be ranked among those skilful manœuvres which distinguish a master in the art of war" (ibid., 449).

To John Eager Howard

Dear Sir　　　　　　　　　　　　　　　　　Richmond Novr. 2d. 1804

I persuade myself I need make no apology for the trouble I give in asking the favor of you to answer the following queries.[1]

1st. When your regiment fell back at the battle of the Cowpens was it by your order for the purpose of extricating your flanks, or was it occasioned by the fire of the enemy?[2]

2d. Was the fire which you gave after this circumstance & before you charged bayonets before or after the charge made by Colonel Washington, & was his charge meerly on the british cavalry or had he reached the infantry before they were thrown into disorder?[3]

3d. At Guilford did Colonel Gunby command the same regiment which was at the Cowpens, & was you with him or on the flanks with Washington or Lee?[4]

4th. Did the regiment charge the guards before or after they were charged by Washington?[5]

5th. Were the corps detached or the flanks broken as the first & second line gave way or did they fall back in consequence of that circumstance?[6]

6th. What occasioned the disorder of the two companies on the right of Gunbys regiment at Hobkirks hill or Camden? Were they unofficered—had their officers been killed or wounded—were there an unusual proportion of new levies in them?[7]

7. At what time in the action was Colonel Ford wounded?[8]

I take the liberty to make these enquiries of you because the letters of General Greene do not account for these circumstances fully,[9] & because I am persuaded that you will feel no unwillingness to give me the information I ask if your memory will enable you to do so. With great respect & esteem, I am dear Sir your Obedt.

J MARSHALL

ALS, Dreer Collection, PHi. Addressed to General Howard at Baltimore; postmarked Richmond, 7 Nov. Endorsed by Howard. Noted in an unknown hand, "This letter from Judge Marshall (written previously to his life of Washington) to *Coll.* Howard, was given to R Gilm⟨or?⟩ by B. C. Howard the Colonel's third son, in 1829." See n. 1.

1. John Eager Howard (1752–1827), born near Baltimore, Md., governor of Maryland and U.S. senator, 1796 to 1803. Colonel Howard served with distinction in the

Battle of Cowpens and also participated in the Battles of Guilford Court House, Hobkirk's Hill, and Eutaw Springs. His son Benjamin Chew Howard married Jane Grant Gilmor in 1818.

2. For Howard's action in the Battle of Cowpens, 17 Jan. 1781, see *Life*, IV, chap. 7, 345–46.

3. See ibid., 346–47. Col. William Augustine Washington (1757–1810), George Washington's nephew, served with distinction at Cowpens; later fought in the Battle of Eutaw Springs, where he was taken prisoner (F. B. Heitman, *Historical Register of Officers of the Continental Army during the War of the Revolution, April, 1775, to December, 1783* [Washington, D.C., 1893], 422).

4. For action of Col. John Gunby and the 1st Maryland Regiment, and Howard's and Washington's positions, in Battle of Guilford Court House, 15 Mar. 1781, see vol. IV, 374–76; for Col. Henry Lee's action, ibid., 377.

5. See ibid., 374.

6. See ibid., 369–72.

7. For action of Gunby's regiment in Battle of Hobkirk's Hill, 25 Apr. 1781, see ibid., chap. 10, 512–13.

8. Lt. Col. Benjamin Ford of Maryland died two days after the battle, on 27 Apr. 1781 (Heitman, *Historical Register of the Revolution*, 178); see vol. IV, 519.

9. As commanding general of the southern army, Nathanael Greene reported these battles to the Continental Congress and enclosed copies of the reports to General Washington. JM would have had access to the following in Washington's papers. On Cowpens, Daniel Morgan to Greene, 19 Jan. 1781; Greene to Samuel Huntington, president of Congress, 24 Jan. 1781; Greene to Washington, 24 Jan. 1781; on Guilford Court House, Greene to Huntington, 16 Mar. 1781; Greene to Washington, 17 Mar., 18 Mar. 1781; on Hobkirk's Hill, Greene to Huntington, 27 Apr. 1781; Greene to Washington, 27 Apr. 1781 (Washington Papers, ser. 4, DLC).

To John M. Mason

SIR: RICHMOND, Nov. 4, 1804.

Accept my acknowledgments for the gratification derived from reading the oration you have been so obliging as to enclose me.[1] I lament sincerely the loss of the great man whose character you have drawn so well. While I truly deplore his fate, I may be permitted to indulge a hope that it may have some tendency to cast odium on a practice which deserves every censure you have bestowed upon it.

You have mentioned two facts of which I had never heard. The one is the part he took in producing the commercial meeting at Baltimore[2] which preceded the convention at Philadelphia. The other, which is, indeed, characteristic of General Hamilton, is his resignation of the emoluments his military services gave him a right to claim. With great respect, I am, Sir, your obedient servant,

J. MARSHALL.

Printed, Jacob Van Vechten, *Memoirs of John M. Mason* (New York, 1856), 188.

1. Mason (1770–1829), a clergyman and educator, served as trustee and provost of Columbia College and later as president of Dickinson College He had sent JM *An Oration, Commemorative of the late Major-General Alexander Hamilton* (New York, 1804; S #6731).

2. The "commercial meeting" took place at Annapolis.

From John Eager Howard

Dr. Sir,   Baltimore Novr. 14th. 1804—

I have to acknowledge the receipt of your letter of the 2d. inst. Immediately after the receipt thereof I commenced the answering your questions, but find it will take more time than I at first apprehended, especially as it is to be a groundwork for your history. I have a perfect recollection of many transactions; of some my recollection is more imperfect, however I shall be carefull to be as accurate as possible. My answers will be lengthy and will state many circumstances which are not to be found in the printed accounts.[1] As I shall have occasion frequently to mention Colo. Washington, I wish you to write to him, for no doubt his recollection of transactions in which he was active will be more correct than mine.[2]

I have a book, the campaigns of 1780 & 1781, which is said to have been written with the assistance of Tarleton.[3] It contains more official documents than I have seen in any other work, and also contains some correct plans of some of the actions. If it will be of any use to you and an opportunity offers I will send it to you. With great respect & regard, I am yr. Obedt. Servt.

JOHN EAGER HOWARD—

ALS, Marshall Papers, ViW. Addressed to "The Honble./John Marshall/Chief Justice U.S./Richmond"; postmarked Baltimore, 13 Nov. Either Howard or the postmaster was mistaken about the date.

1. No such account from Howard to JM has been found. The descriptions of the battles about which JM inquired are substantially the same in the second impression as in the first.

2. JM did write to William Washington in the winter and received a reply, neither of which has been found. In a letter of 13 June 1805, Col. William Washington told Howard that he had "received a Letter, last Winter, from Judge Marshall containing a number of Queries relative to the actions at the Cowpens, Guilford & Hobkirk's hill, which I answered in as circumstantial a manner as my memory would allow me after such a lapse of time" (ICHi).

3. Lt. Col. Banastre Tarleton, *A History of the Campaigns of 1780 and 1781, in the Southern Provinces of North America* (London, 1787).

To Caleb P. Wayne

Sir   Richmond Decr. 21st. 1804

I am at some loss how to understand what you say in your letter of the 3d. inst.[1] respecting the corrected copies you are about to print.

I take it for granted that the number of the first impression will not be increased; or if increased that the additional books of the 2d. 3d. & 4th. volumes as well as of the 1st. will be from the corrected copies I have sent & shall send you. When you speak of printing the corrected copies, & of the time between that & the real 2d. edition, I am not sure whether the additional printing alluded to is only of the 1st. volume, to make up for those which have been lost at sea, or is of the whole work. Upon this subject I could wish to be precisely informed, & could also wish to know, if you mean to enlarge the number of the 1st. impression, what will be the amount of the enlargement. I repeat my hope that not one copy uncorrected will be added to the number already printed. I am also anxious that as few even of the corrected copies may be published, as is compatible with your interest, because I am persuaded that I have been too much hurried to make them what I shall be satisfied with. I wish to give them a reading at perfect leisure after the civil administration shall be finished. I am Sir very respectfully, Your Obedt. Servt

J MARSHALL

It is very desirable that I should prepare the 2d. edition from a printed corrected copy of the work.

ALS, Dreer Collection, PHi; Tr (typed), Marshall Papers, DLC. Addressed to Wayne at Philadelphia; postmarked Richmond, 21 Dec. Endorsed by Wayne, "J. Marshall/ Ansd./Dec. 26."

1. Letter not found.

To Caleb P. Wayne

Sir   Richmond Jany. 10th. 1805

I have just returned from North Carolina & have received your letter of the 26th. of Decr.[1]

I was not induced to enquire respecting the plan of publication you had adopted by the statements made me by Mr. Weims.[2] Having never designed to interfere with that part of the business I was always disposed to beleive that your arrangements required no interposition from me. About the mode of publishing the corrected copies I was very solicitous & the plan you have adopted is such as I could have wished. I comprehend it clearly & am pleased with it. I shall have an opportunity which I greatly desired of revising the corrected copies before the 2d. edition goes to the press. I must repeat my request that you will be attentive to the proof sheets for I assure you that errors similar to that which I pointed out frequently occur.

It is impossible for me to give any opinion respecting the notes concerning Colonel McClean unless I could see them.[3] I am well disposed to mention that gentleman favorably on any occasion which will justify it. I think highly of his merit & know that General Washington thought highly of it. But I know not what the purport of the notes may be. If you can be perfectly satisfied of their propriety I shall have no objection to them.

I must beg the favor of you to let me know by return of post or as soon as is in your power, on which side of Schuylkill is French creek & what were called warwick iron works. The papers in my possession do not inform nor have I been able to see any person who can. In consequence of this a part of the 3d. volume riquires correction & I retain some sheets I have looked over for the purpose of making the correction after I shall have ascertained the fact.[4] I am Sir very respectfully, Your Obedt. Servt

J MARSHALL

ALS, Dreer Collection, PHi. Addressed to Wayne at Philadelphia; postmarked Richmond, 10 Jan.

1. Letter not found.

2. Weems saw JM and Bushrod Washington in Richmond on 15 Dec. At that time, he complained to them of the quality of a new printing of vols. I and II, numbering about five hundred copies. Weems objected to the use of "paper so thin" that the volumes looked half as thick as the first impression. Weems did not want to undertake the assignment of distributing the inferior edition to subscribers and asked the two men to intercede with Wayne. Washington wrote Wayne that "it is our decided opinion that if an attempt is made to deliver those books to subscribers, it will do you an irreparable injury, which in some measure we must participate." Wayne shot off angry replies to both Washington and JM, apparently assuming that JM's queries concerning the second impression in his letter of 21 Dec. were meant as part of this criticism. Believing Weems had misrepresented his intentions, the publisher declared he meant this cheaper press run only for new subscribers and purchasers. But as Washington pointed out, the concern was "that subscribers, as well new, as old, would be dissatisfied with the edition termed coarse." Weems finally wrote Wayne himself, telling him that "subs will all think themselves entitled to books of the same excellent quality, and will, as Genl. M. well observed, think themselves *cheated* if worse books be put upon them" (Washington to Wayne, 16 Dec., 25 Dec., 30 Dec. 1804, Dreer Collection, PHi; Weems to Wayne, 25 Jan. 1805 [Skeel, *Weems*, II, 311]). This inexpensive issue included JM's revisions for vols. I–III but omitted the contents notes run down the margins. Whereas in the good-quality second impression the number of pages in vols. I and II actually

increased over the first impression, in this economy edition Wayne was able to reduce substantially the pages of text by extending the length and number of lines on a page. Not only was the paper thinner, but there were fewer pages, with denser print (see App. V).

3. Capt. Allan McLane (1746–1829), born in Philadelphia, settled in Kent County, Del. During the Revolution, he made a name for himself reconnoitering enemy movements around Philadelphia in 1777–78 and gained General Washington's praises for his abilities. From 1797 to his death, McLane served as collector for the port of Wilmington. Wayne apparently had also written Bushrod Washington about McLane and sent him the proposed notes to be added to vol. III. Washington kept them until he saw JM at the Supreme Court in February (Washington to Wayne, 15 Jan. 1805, Dreer Collection, PHi). See JM to Wayne, 19 Feb. 1805 and nn. 3, 4.

4. French Creek and Warwick Furnace were on the west side of the Schuylkill. JM described skirmishes in the vicinity between Washington's and Howe's armies during Sept. 1777 in vol. III, chap. 3, 158–62.

To Samuel Chase

My dear Sir   Richmond Jany. 23d. 1804 [1805][1]

On receiving your letter of the 13th.[2] I instantly applied to my brother & to Mr. Wickham requesting them to state their recollection of the circumstances under which Colo. Taylors testimony was rejected.[3] They both declared that they rememberd them very imperfectly but that they woud endeavor to recollect what passd & commit it to writing. I shall bring it with me to Washington in february. At the same time I shall take with me a list of the grand & petit jury, & a copy of the order of writ directing Callenders arrest.

The foreman of the Jury was Colo. Gamble & the juror who spoke to you was Mr. John Bassett.[4] They are both men of character & intelligence.

Admitting it to be true that on legal principles Colo. Taylors testimony was admissible, it certainly constitutes a very extraordinary ground for an impeachment. According to the antient doctrine a jury finding a verdict against the law of the case was liable to an attaint; & the amount of the present doctrine seems to be that a Judge giving a legal opinion contrary to the opinion of the legislature is liable to impeachment. As, for convenience & humanity the old doctrine of attaint has yielded to the silent, moderate but not less operative influence of new trials, I think the modern doctrine of impeachment shoud yield to an appellate jurisdiction in the legislature. A reversal of those legal opinions deemd unsound by the legislature woud certainly better comport with the mildness of our character than a removal of the Judge who has renderd them unknowing of his fault. The other charges except the 1st. & 4th. which I suppose to be altogether untounded, seem still less to furnish cause for impeachment. But the little finger of ———— is heavier than the loins of ————.[5]

I have not written to Mr. Moore because I count on his setting out for Washington before my letter coud reach him. Farewell—With much respect & esteem, I am dear Sir your Obedt

J MARSHALL

Mr. Nelson is unfortunately dead.[6]

ALS, Etting Collection, PHi. Addressed by JM to Chase in Baltimore; postmarked Richmond, 23 Jan. Endorsed by Chase.

1. Misdated by JM but the context clearly establishes 1805 as the year. Chase was then in the midst of preparing his answer to the eight articles of impeachment adopted by the House on 3 Dec. 1804. The impeachment trial was scheduled to begin on 4 Feb. 1805 (*Trial of Samuel Chase*, I, 5–22).

2. Letter not found.

3. Five of the articles of impeachment concerned Chase's conduct of the trial of James Thompson Callender for seditious libel, which took place at the U.S. circuit court in Richmond in May and June of 1800. The third article read: "That, with intent to oppress and procure the conviction of the prisoner, the evidence of John Taylor, a material witness on behalf of the aforesaid Callender, was not permitted by the said Samuel Chase to be given in, on pretence that the said witness could not prove the truth of the whole of one of the charges, contained in the indictment, although the said charge embraced more than one fact" (ibid., 6).

4. For Robert Gamble's testimony, see ibid., 263–65. The second article of impeachment stated that Chase overruled the objection of John Bassett, who wished to be excused from serving on the jury on the ground that he had already made up his mind. Bassett also testified at Chase's trial (ibid., 5–6, 199–205).

5. "One's little finger is thicker than another's loins" (2 Chron. 10.10). JM originally wrote a word ("democracy"?) in the first blank space but then deleted it.

6. Thomas Nelson was the U.S. attorney who prosecuted Callender.

To George Logan

Sir   Richmond Jany. 28th. 1805

Your letter of the 17th. inst. inclosing an extract of one from Mr. Dickenson reached me only to day.[1] This delay is in some measure attributable to my inattention to the post office, & in some measure to the impediments to the mail occasioned by the bad weather.

I lament sincerely that any mistake should have arisen respecting the author of the petition to the King.[2] I did most certainly beleive that it came from the pen of Mr. Lee. I had heard so at the time; and this report appeared to me to derive much probability from his being the person first named on the committee. It may have originated in his having drawn that which was not approved. The subsequent appointment of Mr. Dickenson on the committee escaped my attention. It being my object to state the address itself without adverting to the changes it experienced in passing through Congress, I did not attend to the recommitment of it. The book mentioned in the extract, I never saw.[3] Had it been in my possession I certainly should not have been unmindful of the considerations which finding this paper among the political tracts of that gentleman would have suggested.

The willingness manifested by Mr. Dickenson to attribute this accident to improper motives, I can readily excuse; nor will it in any degree diminish the alacrity with which I shall render him the justice to which he is entitled.[4] With great respect, I am Sir your Obedt. Servt

J MARSHALL

ALS, Logan Collection, PHi. Addressed by JM to Logan at Washington and franked; postmarked Richmond, 30 Jan.

1. Letter and enclosure (see n. 3) not found. Logan was then a member of the U.S. Senate from Pennsylvania.

2. In a footnote to vol. II (180n), JM stated that the authorship of the Oct. 1774 address to the king "has been generally attributed to mr. Lee." Richard Henry Lee was chairman of the committee to prepare the address. Lee and Patrick Henry, another member of the committee, both composed drafts, but these were rejected in favor of one drawn by John Dickinson. Dickinson was not a member of the original committee but was appointed later. See Edwin Wolf 2nd, "The Authorship of the 1774 Address to the King Restudied," WMQ, 3d ser., XXII (1965), 189–224.

3. The Political Writings of John Dickinson . . . (2 vols.; Wilmington, Del., 1801). Vol. II of this edition contained the address to the king (19–29). The extract undoubtedly was from Dickinson's letter to Logan, 15 Sept. 1804, in which Dickinson expressed his mortification at JM's attribution of Lee as the author. "In the year 1800," wrote Dickinson, "two young printers applied to me for my consent to publish my political writings. . . . I gave my consent, and in the following year they published in this place two octavo volumes, *as my political writings.* . . . Of course I must be guilty of the greatest baseness, if, for my credit, I knowingly permitted writings which I had not composed to be publicly imputed to me, without a positive and public contradiction of the imputation." Dickinson added that he would write JM if he knew him and requested Logan to do so on his behalf (Charles J. Stillé, *The Life and Times of John Dickinson, 1732–1808* [Philadelphia, 1891], 143–46n).

4. JM rectified his error with a statement in vol. IV, which appeared on the page (opposite p. 626) separating the text from the notes. This statement, set off by italic type and a fistnote, reads: "In detailing the early proceedings of the American congress, the opinion was given that the petition to the king was written by Mr. Lee. Justice requires the declaration that this eloquent composition was the work of Mr. Dickenson. The original petition reported by Mr. Lee did not manifest sufficiently that spirit of conciliation which then animated congress, and was therefore disapproved. Mr. Dickenson was added to the committee, and drew the petition which was adopted."

Testimony in the Trial of Samuel Chase

SATURDAY, FEBRUARY 16, 1805.[1]
JOHN MARSHALL *Sworn.*[2]

Mr. *Harper.* Please to inform this honorable court whether you did, or did not, on the part of Col. Harvie[3] make an application for his discharge from the jury; and on what ground that application was made?

Mr. *Marshall.* I was at the bar, when Col. Harvie, with whom I was intimately acquainted, informed me that he was summoned on the jury. Some conversation passed, in which he expressed his unwillingness to serve, and stated that he was an unfit person; for that his mind was completely made up, that he thought the (sedition) law unconstitutional, and that whatever the evidence might be, he should find the traverser not guilty; and requested me on that ground to apply to the Marshal for his discharge. I told the marshal that Col. Harvie was extremely desirous of being discharged, and on his discovering great repugnance to his discharge, I informed him that he was predetermined, and that no testimony could alter his opinion. The marshal said that Col. Harvie might make his excuse to the court; he observed that he was watched, and to prevent any charge of improper conduct from being brought against him, he should not interfere in discharging any of the jurors who had been summoned. I informed Col. Harvie of this conversation, and it was then agreed that I should apply to the court for his discharge upon the ground of his being sheriff of Henrico county, that his attendance was necessary as that court was then in session; I moved the discharge of the juror on that ground, and he was discharged by court.

Mr. *Harper.* Did you communicate to judge Chase, or to the court the reasons which first induced Col. Harvie to make this application.

Mr. *Marshall.* I only stated that he was sheriff of Henrico county, and that it was unusual to require the attendance of sheriffs on juries. I believe the marshal was at that time obtaining jurymen, he had at that time a paper in his hand, and appeared to be setting down the names of persons within his view.

Mr. *Randolph.* Were you in court during a part of the trial, or during the whole of the trial?

Mr. *Marshall.* I think I was there only during a part of the time.[4]

Mr. *Randolph.* Did you observe any thing unusual in the mode of conduct on the part of the counsel towards the court, or the court towards the counsel, and what?

Mr. *Marshall.* There were several circumstances that took place on that trial, on the part both of the bar and the bench, which do not

SAMUEL CHASE

Oil on panel by John Wesley Jarvis, 1811. *Courtesy of the National Portrait Gallery, Smithsonian Institution*

always occur in trials. I would probably be better able to answer the question, if it were made more determinate.

Mr. *Randolph*. Then I will make the question more particular by asking whether the interruptions of counsel were much more frequent than usual?[5]

Mr. *Marshall*. The counsel appeared to me to wish to bring before the jury arguments to prove that the sedition law was unconstitutional, and Mr. Chase said that that was not a proper question to go to the jury; and whenever any attempt was made to bring that point before the jury, the counsel for the traverser were stopped. After that there was an argument commenced (I think) by Mr. Hay, but I do not recollect positively, to prove to the Judge that the opinion which he had given was not correct in point of law, and that the constitutionality of the law ought to go before the jury; whatever the argument was which Mr. Hay advanced, there was something in it which Judge Chase did not believe to be law, and he stopped him on that point. Mr. Hay still went on, and made some political observations, Judge Chase stopped him again, and the collision ended, by Mr. Hay sitting down, and folding up his papers as if he intended to retire.

Mr. *Randolph*. There were many preliminary questions, such as, with respect to the continuance of the cause, the admissibility of testimony, &c. Did the interruptions take place on the part of the court only when the counsel pressed the point of the unconstitutionality of the sedition law?

Mr. *Marshall*. I believe that it was only at those times, but I do not recollect precisely. I do not remember correctly what passed between the bench and bar; but it appeared to me that whenever Judge Chase thought the counsel incorrect in their points, he immediately told them so, and stopped them short; but what were the particular expressions that he used, my recollection is too indistinct to enable me to state precisely; what I do state is merely from a general impression which remains on my mind.

Mr. *Randolph*. Was there any misunderstanding between the counsel and the court, and what was the cause of that misunderstanding, or what was your opinion as to the cause, or did you form one?

Mr. *Marshall*. It is impossible for me to assign the particular cause. It began early in the proceeding and increased as the trial progressed. On the part of the Judge it seemed to be a disgust with regard to the mode adopted by the traverser's counsel, at least I speak as to the part which Mr. Hay took on the trial, and it seemed to increase also with him as he went on.

Mr. *Randolph*. When the court decided the point that the jury had not a right to decide upon the constitutionality of a law, did the counsel for the traverser begin an argument to convince Judge Chase that the opinion which he had delivered on that point was not well founded. Is it the practise in courts when counsel object to the legality of an opinion given by the court to hear the arguments of counsel against such opinion?

Mr. *Marshall*. If the counsel have not been already heard, it is usual to hear them, in order that they may change or confirm the opinion of the court, when there is any doubt entertained. There is however no positive rule on this subject, and the course pursued by the court will depend upon circumstances; where a Judge believes that the point is perfectly clear and settled, he will scarcely permit the question to be agitated. However it is considered as decorous on the part of the Judge to listen while the counsel abstain from urging unimportant arguments.

Mr. *Randolph*. In the circuit courts of the United States, after a circuit is opened for any district, is it the practise of such courts to adjourn over from time to time, in order to hold a court in another district in the intermediate time, and then to return back; or is not the uniform practise to postpone causes when they cannot be conveniently tried, to the next term?

Mr. *Marshall*. I can only speak of courts where I have attended, in which the practise is, that the business of one term shall be gone through as far as possible, before any other court is held.

Mr. *Randolph*. Was it ever the practise of any court, in which you have practised or presided, to compel counsel to reduce to writing the questions which they meant to propound to their witnesses?[6]

Mr. *Marshall*. It has not been usual; but in cases of the kind, the conduct of the court will depend upon circumstances. If a question relates to a point of law, and is understood to be an important question, it might be proper to require that it be reduced to writing. Unless there is some special reason which appears to the court, or on the request of the adverse counsel, questions are not commonly reduced to writing, but when there is a special reason in the mind of the court, or it is required by the opposite counsel, questions may be directed to be committed to writing.

Mr. *Randolph*. When these questions are reduced to writing, it is for a special reason, it is after the court have heard the question, and not before the question has been propounded?

Mr. *Marshall*. I never knew it requested that a question should be reduced to writing in the first instance in the whole course of my practice.

Mr. *Randolph*. I am aware of the delicacy of the question I am about to put, and nothing but duty would induce me to propound it. Did it appear to you, Sir, that during the course of the trial, the conduct of Judge Chase was mild and conciliatory?

Mr. *Marshall.* Perhaps the question you propound to me would be more correct, if I were asked what his conduct was during the course of the trial; for I feel some difficulty in stating in a manner satisfactory to my own mind, any opinion which I might have formed; but the fact was, that in the progress of the trial, there appeared some—

Mr. *Cocke,* (a Senator)[7] here interrupted Mr. Marshall, by observing that he thought the question an improper one.

Mr. *Randolph* said he would not press it, if there were any objection to it.

Mr. *Harper.* We, sir, have no objection; we are willing to abide in this trial by the opinion of the chief justice.

Mr. *Randolph.* Did you ever, sir, in a criminal prosecution, know a witness deemed inadmissible, because he could not go a particular length in his testimony, because he could not narrate all the circumstances of the crime charged in an indictment, or in the case of a libel; and could only prove a part of a particular charge, and not the whole of it?

Mr. *Marshall.* I never did hear that objection made by the court except in this particular case.

(Some enquiry was here made relative to the above question put by Mr. Randolph, and objected to by Mr. Cocke, which Mr. R. answered, by observing that he withdrew it.)

Mr. *Harper.* Please to inform this honorable court, sir, whether you recollect that judge Chase during any part of the proceedings made an offer to postpone the trial of Callender, and if you do, to what time?[8]

Mr. *Marshall.* I recollect at the time a motion was made for the continuance till the next term; that judge Chase declared, as his opinion, that it ought to be tried at the present term. A good deal of conversation took place on the subject. The counsel for the traverser stated several circumstances in favor of their client, particularly relative to the absence of his witnesses; but the whole terminated at that time by a postponement for a few days; so many days, as I thought at the time, were sufficient for obtaining the witnesses residing in Virginia. I do not now recollect what the time was nor do I say it was sufficient. I simply recollect that I thought it was. When the cause came on again, there was no proposition that I recollect on the part of the traverser's counsel for a continuance, but a desire was expressed of a postponement for a few hours in order to give their witnesses time to arrive at Richmond, as it was possible they had been impeded by the badness of the roads; a considerable quantity of rain having fallen the preceding day. There was a declaration on the part of the court that they might take until the next day, and they went on to say that they might have a longer time, if they thought it was necessary, but the precise length of time offered I do not recollect; but I do remember that they said the trial must come on before the present term closed.

Mr. *Harper.* Is it the practice of the circuit courts to hold an adjourned court, and is it not in the power of the circuit court to adjourn the jury, and direct them to meet again at some subsequent time?

Mr. *Marshall.* That is a question of law I have never turned my mind to.

Mr. *Harper.* Do you know an instance in which it has been done?

Mr. *Marshall.* I do not know any instance in which it has ever been done.

The President. Do you recollect whether the conduct of the judge on this trial was tyrannical, overbearing, and oppressive?

Mr. *Marshall.* I will state the facts. The counsel for the traverser persisted in arguing the question of the constitutionality of the sedition law, in which they were constantly repressed by Judge Chase. Judge C. checked Mr. Hay whenever he came to that point, and after having resisted repeated checks, Mr. Hay appeared to be determined to abandon the cause, when he was desired by the judge to proceed with his argument, and informed that he should not be interrupted thereafter. If this is not considered tyrannical, oppressive, and overbearing, I know nothing else that was so.

Mr. *Randolph.* Was the check given to the traverser's counsel more than once.

Mr. *Marshall.* There were several interruptions, as I have stated, for whenever the counsel attempted to shew the unconstitutionality of the sedition law, Judge Chase observed that it was a point which should not go before the jury, and he would not permit a discussion upon it.

Mr. *Randolph.* Then it was these checks that induced the counsel to abandon the cause of the traverser. I understood that the counsel were endeavoring to shew, without any regard to the jury, that the opinion of the court was incorrect.

Mr. *Marshall.* That was my impression.

Mr. *Randolph.* It is not usual when the opinion of the court is not solemnly pronounced, to hear counsel?

Mr. *Marshall.* Yes, sir.

President. Is it usual for a trial to take place on the same term that the presentment is made?[9]

Mr. *Marshall.* My practice while I was at the bar, was very limited in criminal cases, but I believe it is by no means usual in Virginia to try a man for an offence at the same term at which he is presented.

Mr. *Randolph.* Did you hear judge Chase apply any unusual epithets; such as young men, or young gentlemen, to the counsel?[10]

Mr. *Marshall.* I have heard it so frequently spoken of since the trial, that I cannot possibly tell whether my recollection of the terms is derived from the expressions used in court or from the frequent mention since made of them; but I am rather inclined to think that I did hear them from the judge.

Mr. *Randolph.* Are you acquainted with Mr. Wirt; was he a young man at that time; was he single, married or a widower?

Mr. *Marshall.* I am pretty well acquainted with him; he is about 30 years of age, and a widower.

Mr. *Randolph.* Do you know Mr. Norborne Nicholas and Mr. Hay;— they practiced with you at the bar; did you observe any thing in their conduct that required the interposition of the court to check or prevent its consequences?

Mr. *Lee*, objecting to this question—

Mr. *Randolph* said he would decline putting it.

Mr. *Marshall* then withdrew.

Mr. *Randolph.* The managers think themselves entitled to put to any witness, however respectable his standing in life, any questions which they deem necessary to bring out the whole facts.

The *President.* If it is not objected to by the counsel for the respondent, nor decided by the court to be irrelevant or improper, the managers will be gratified by having their questions answered.

At the instance of Mr. Randolph, Chief Justice *Marshall* was again called.

Mr. *Randolph.* Is it the practise of the courts in Virginia to proceed against a person when indicted for an offence less than felony, say for a misdemeanor, by issuing a capias in the first instance?[11]

Mr. *Marshall.* My practice, I before stated, had not taken this course; I therefore cannot well say what the usual practise is.

Mr. *Harper.* I will ask you a question, Sir. When Mr. Hay was interrupted by the court at the commencement of his argument to shew to the jury that they were the judges of the constitutionality of the law, was the interruption that took place, one which went to the argument, or barely reminding them of some erroneous opinion delivered?

Mr. *Marshall.* I believe it was the latter; though I am not certain.

Mr. *Randolph.* Do you recollect, Sir, whether it was as to the matter, or whether the impression has not been made on your mind by some conversations which you have heard since?

Mr. *Marshall.* My impressions are, Sir, that Mr. Hay pressed the matter of the constitutionality of the law in the manner I have heretofore stated.[12]

Printed, *National Intelligencer, and Washington Advertiser* (Washington, D.C.), 5 April 1805.

1. The Chase impeachment trial had begun in the Senate on 4 Feb., with Vice President Aaron Burr presiding. Representative John Randolph led the managers of the prosecution; Robert Goodloe Harper led a team of five eminent lawyers on behalf of Chase. The proceedings were taken down in shorthand by Samuel H. Smith and Thomas Lloyd and published in Smith's paper, the *National Intelligencer*. Their report was later published as *Trial of Samuel Chase* . . . (2 vols.; Washington, D.C., 1805). Another shorthand report, by Charles Evans, was published as *Report of the Trial of the Hon. Samuel Chase* . . . (Baltimore, 1805).

2. JM was one of a number of witnesses giving evidence on behalf of Chase. His testimony concerned his knowledge of Chase's conduct of Callender's sedition trial at Richmond in May and June of 1800. Evans's report of JM's testimony is briefer than that of Smith and Lloyd but does not differ in substance (*Report of the Trial of the Hon. Samuel Chase*, 69–71).

3. John Harvie, formerly register of the state land office. His son, Jacquelin B. Harvie, married JM's daughter Mary, in 1813.

4. JM was in Richmond throughout the period of Callender's trial. He left town on 5 June (the day after the U.S. circuit court adjourned) for Washington to take up his duties as secretary of state. His companion on this trip was Justice Chase (*PJM*, IV, 158).

5. Counsel for Callender were George Hay, William Wirt, and Philip Norborne Nicholas. This question arose from the fourth article of impeachment, charging that Chase's conduct of the trial was marked "by manifest injustice, partiality, and intemperance." One example of this behavior was his "repeated and vexatious interruptions" of Callender's counsel, "which, at length, induced them to abandon their cause and their client" (*Trial of Samuel Chase*, I, 6).

6. The fourth article also charged that Chase required Callender's counsel to submit in writing the questions to be propounded to John Taylor, a witness for the defendant (ibid.).

7. Sen. William Cocke of Tennessee.

8. Another charge recited in the fourth article was that Chase refused to postpone Callender's trial despite an affidavit stating the absence of a material witness (ibid.).

9. According to Evans, this question was asked by Sen. Thomas Worthington of Ohio (*Report of the Trial of the Hon. Samuel Chase*, 71).

10. The fourth article also spoke of Chase's "unusual, rude, and contemptuous expressions towards the prisoner's counsel" (*Trial of Samuel Chase*, I, 6).

11. The fifth article stated that Chase's award of a capias—a writ of arrest—was contrary to Virginia law, which provided that a summons should be issued in cases of non-capital offenses (ibid., 6–7).

12. Sen. William Plumer had this reaction to JM's testimony: "I was much better pleased with the manner in which his brother [William] testified than with him. The Chief Justice really discovered too much caution—too much fear—too much cunning—He ought to have been more bold—frank & explicit than he was. There was in his manner an evident disposition to accomodate the Managers. That dignified frankness which his high office required did not appear. A cunning man ought never to discover the arts of the *trimmer* in his testimony" (Everett Somerville Brown, ed., *William Plumer's Memorandum of Proceedings in the United States Senate, 1803–1807* [New York, 1923], 291).

To Caleb P. Wayne

Sir   Washington Feby. 19th. 1805

Your letter of the 15th. has this instant reached me.¹ I hope the sheets of the 3d. vol. which I had corrected & transmitted have not miscarried. By your not inquiring respecting them I take it for granted you have received them altho I had felt some fears on this subject in consequence of the deranged state of the post office about this time.²

With respect to the passages concerning Capt. McClane I feel much difficulty. I have not the 3d. vol. & fear I can not get it. I do not know therefore in what manner to adapt the passages to the context. To the first which is proposed as a note to page 190. I presume there is no objection. It being a note, the text will not I presume be affected by it, but where it is proposed to introduce any thing into the body of the work the passages must be modified so as to comport with the passages with which it is connected. If I can obtain the 3d. vol. I will attend to the request; &, as it is truely my wish to do any justice to Capt. McClane which may be compatible with the general view of the work I shall regret it if I shall be unable to gratify his friends in this respect. I think on reviewing the notes sent to Mr Washington that the amendment proposed in page 324 & 5. 368 & 372 may be made provided there be no incongruity in it. Of this you may judge. If there is any doubt the alteration cannot be made.³

If there is any incorrectness in the account of the evacuation of Philadelphia I could wish it to be changed. If the incorrectness consists only in the omission of minute circumstances, there is no occasion for being more particular.⁴

The 4th. vol. has been finished for some time; but on getting in the sheets from all the copyists it was found that there would be between 7 & 800 pages. This has produced the necessity of going over the whole vol. again in order to expunge what can best be parted with so as to reduce the volume to a proper size. It will be sent to you as soon as this is finished which I hope will be in tens days.⁵

There are some additional plans which will be sent with the 4th. vol.

I hope your books sent round to Charleston at this rough boisterous season have been ensured.⁶ I am Sir Your Obedt. Servt

                                                    J MARSHALL

ALS, Dreer Collection, PHi; Tr (typed), Marshall Papers, DLC. Addressed to Wayne at Philadelphia; postmarked "Washn. City," 19 Feb.

1. Letter not found. Wayne's letter apparently was sent to both JM and Bushrod Washington, who answered parts of it on 22 Feb. and concluded, "Mr Marshall will answer the other parts of yr letter" (Dreer Collection, PHi).

2. Bad weather had disrupted postal communications, including remunerations to Wayne for subscriptions to the *Life*. Wayne informed JM and Bushrod Washington that he was unable to send them remittances. Washington replied that he and JM, expecting one thousand dollars a week, had "made arrangements from which we know not how to extricate ourselves. I hope however that the opening of the weather will make a favorable change in your operations, so as to enable you to send us on money in a short time" (ibid.).

3. During the British occupation of Philadelphia in the fall and winter of 1777–78, McLane commanded a body of light troops on the lines in Col. John Patton's Additional Continental Regiment. McLane and his troops were employed in reconnoitering, primarily to interdict supplies to the British. Passages in vol. III, chap. 4, 190; chap. 6, 324, 325, generally pertain to these efforts but do not mention McLane. The note sent to JM concerned McLane's reconnaissance activities and appears in *Life* (1805 ed.), III, 189–90n; McLane's name is also inserted at p. 323. In vol. III, chap. 6, 368, 372, JM describes General Washington's attempts to supply his own army at Valley Forge by sending out foraging parties under General Greene, Capt. Henry Lee, and Lt. Col. Tench Tilghman. In the second impression McLane is mentioned along with the others (*Life* [1805 ed.], III, 366, 370).

4. Vol. III, chap. 8, 459. With special permission from Washington, McLane was the first to enter Philadelphia after the British evacuated the city on 18 June 1778. A footnote about his advance entry into the city as well as a second note about his scouting the British encampment at Haddonfield, N.J., are in *Life* (1805 ed.), III, 457nn. Another addition to vol. III, chap. 6, 317, attributes to McLane the discovery of General Howe's attempt to surprise the American camp at Whitemarsh in Dec. 1777 (*Life* [1805 ed.], III, 316). And in *Life* (1832 ed.), I, 246–47, McLane gets credit for warning Lafayette of the British plan to surround him in May 1778 (compare *Life*, III, chap. 8, 447–48; *Life* [1805 ed.], III, 445–46, where McLane is not mentioned).

5. In his letter to JM and Bushrod Washington, Wayne apparently pressed them about sending the manuscript for vol. IV. Washington replied that "we supposed that you did not *wish* it sent on before March. We hope to get it ready to go by some one of the Phila. bar who will leave this next week" (Washington to Wayne, 22 Feb. 1805, Dreer Collection, PHi). See JM to Wayne, 27 Feb. 1805 and n. 2.

6. Wayne apparently lost a shipment of books to Charleston. Washington reiterated the injunction to insure against risk (see JM to Wayne, 21 Dec. 1804; Washington to Wayne, 22 Feb. 1805, Dreer Collection, PHi).

United States v. Fisher

Opinion
U.S. Supreme Court, 21 February 1805

EDITORIAL NOTE

This case came up by writ of error to the U.S. Circuit Court for Pennsylvania. The defendants, James Fisher and others, were assignees of Peter Blight, a Philadelphia merchant, who had become a bankrupt under the federal bankruptcy statute of 1800. Blight was the indorser of a bill of exchange drawn in October 1799 on an Amsterdam firm. This bill was purchased by the United States and was later returned protested. After the commission of bankruptcy had issued against Blight, the United States sued out an attachment against Blight's ship *China* and cargo at Newport, Rhode Island. Blight's assignees in bankruptcy also laid claim to this property. The upshot was an agreement between the U.S. attorney and the attorney for the assignees to bring a case in the U.S. circuit court at Philadelphia for the purpose of deciding the question whether the United States was entitled to priority of payment out of the bankrupt's effects. Justice Bushrod Washington ruled in favor of the defendants on circuit in the spring of 1803.[1]

Arguments in the Supreme Court were heard on 7–9 and 11–12 February 1805. Counsel for the defendants were Robert Goodloe Harper, Jared Ingersoll, William Lewis, and Charles Lee. Alexander J. Dallas, U.S. attorney for Pennsylvania, argued the case for the United States. Notes of the arguments, taken by Justice William Johnson, survive in the case papers of *Hepburn and Dundas* v. *Ellzey*.[2]

Marshall devoted the burden of his opinion to interpreting a statute enacted by Congress in 1797. A subsidiary argument on the defendants' part called into question the constitutionality of this act, which in turn brought forth from the chief justice a brief statement of the doctrine of implied powers.

1. U.S. v. Fisher, App. Cas. No. 148; U.S. v. Fisher, 25 Fed. Cas. 1087 (U.S.C.C., Pa., 1803).

2. See Opinion, 25 Feb. 1805, n. 1.

OPINION

The question in this case is, whether the United States, as holders of a protested bill of exchange, which has been negotiated in the ordinary course of trade, are entitled to be preferred to the general creditors, where the debtor becomes bankrupt?

The claim to this preference is founded on the 5th section of the act, entitled "an act to provide more effectually for the settlement of accounts between the United States, and receivers of public money," *vol.* 3, *p.* 423.[1] The section is in these words, "and be it further enacted that where any revenue officer, or other person, hereafter becoming indebted to the United States, by bond or otherwise, shall become insolvent, or where the estate of any deceased debtor, in the hands of executors or administrators, shall be insufficient to pay all the debts due from the deceased, the debt due to the United States shall be first satisfied; and the priority hereby established, shall be deemed to extend, as well to cases in which a debtor, not having sufficient property to pay all his debts, shall make a voluntary assignment thereof, or in which the estate and effects of an absconding, concealed, or absent debtor, shall be attached by process of law, as to cases in which an act of legal bankruptcy shall be committed."

That these words, taken in their natural and usual sense, would embrace the case before the court, seems not to be controverted. "Any revenue officer, or other person, hereafter becoming indebted to the United States by bond or otherwise," is a description of persons, which, if neither explained nor restricted by other words or circumstances, would comprehend every debtor of the public, however his debt might have been contracted.

But other parts of the act involve this question in much embarrassment.

It is undoubtedly a well established principle in the exposition of statutes, that every part is to be considered, and the intention of the legislature to be extracted from the whole. It is also true, that where great inconvenience will result from a particular construction, that construction is to be avoided, unless the meaning of the legislature be plain; in which case it must be obeyed.

On the abstract principles which govern courts in construing legislative acts, no difference of opinion can exist. It is only in the application of those principles that the difference discovers itself.

As the enacting clause in this case, would plainly give the United States the preference they claim, it is incumbent on those who oppose that preference, to shew an intent varying from that which the words import. In doing this, the whole act has been critically examined; and it has been contended with great ingenuity, that every part of it demonstrates the legislative mind to have been directed towards a class of debtors, entirely different from those who become so by drawing or indorsing bills, in the ordinary course of business.

The first part which has been resorted to is the title. On the influence which the title ought to have in construing the enacting clauses, much has been said; and yet it is not easy to discern the point of difference between the opposing counsel in this respect. Neither party contends that the title of an act can controul plain words in the body of the statute; and neither denies that, taken with other parts, it may assist in removing ambiguities. Where the intent is plain, nothing is left to construction. Where the mind labours to discover the design of the legislature, it seizes every thing from which aid can be derived; and in such case the title claims a degree of notice, and will have its due share of consideration.

The title of the act is unquestionably limited to "receivers of public money;" a term which undoubtedly excludes the defendants in the present case.

The counsel for the defendants have also completely succeeded in demonstrating that the four first sections of this act, relate only to particular classes of debtors, among whom the drawer and indorser of a protested bill of exchange, would not be comprehended. Wherever general words have been used in these sections, they are restrained by the subject to which they relate, and by other words frequently in the same sentence, to particular objects, so as to make it apparent that they were employed by the legislature in a limited sense. Hence it has been argued with great strength of reasoning, that the same restricted interpretation ought to be given to the fifth section likewise.

If the same reason for that interpretation exists; if the words of the act generally, or the particular provisions of this section, afford the same reason for limiting its operation which is afforded with respect to those which precede it, then its operation must be limited to the same objects.

The 5th section relates entirely to the priority claimed by the United States, in the payment of debts.

On the phraseology of this act it has been observed, that there is a circuity of expression, which would not have been used if the intention of the legislature had been to establish its priority in all cases whatever. Instead of saying "any revenue officer or other person hereafter becoming indebted to the United States," the natural mode of expressing such an intent would have been "any person indebted to the United States;" and hence it has been inferred that debtors of a particular description only were in the mind of the legislature.

It is true the mode of expression which has been suggested, is at least as appropriate as that which has been used; but between the two there is no difference of meaning; and it cannot be pretended that the natural sense of words is to be disregarded, because that which they import might have been better, or more directly expressed.

As a branch of this argument, it has also been said that the description commences with the very words which are used in the beginning of the first section; and from that circumstance it has been inferred, that the same class of cases was still in view. The commencing words of each section are "Any revenue officer or other person." But the argument drawn from this source, if the subject be pursued further, seems to operate against the defendants. In the first section the words are, "Any revenue officer or other person *accountable for public money*." With this expression completely in view, and having used it in part, the description would probably have been adopted throughout, had it been the intention of the legislature to describe the same class of debtors. But it is immediately dropped, and more comprehensive words are employed. For persons "accountable for public money," persons "hereafter becoming indebted to the United States, by bond or otherwise" are substituted. This change of language strongly implies an intent to change the object of legislation.

But the great effort on the part of the defendants is to connect the fifth with the four preceding sections; and to prove that as the general words in those sections are restricted to debtors of a particular description, the general words of the 5th section ought also to be restricted to debtors of the same description. On this point lies the stress of the cause.

In the analysis of the foregoing parts of the act, the counsel for the defendants have shewn that the general terms which have been used are uniformly connected with other words in the same section, and frequently in the same sentence, which necessarily restrict them. They have also shewn that the provisions of those parts of the act are of such a nature that the words, taking the natural import of the whole sentence together, plainly form provisions only adapted to a class of cases which those words describe if used in a limited sense.

It may be added that the four first sections of the act are connected with each other, and plainly contain provisions on the same subject. They all relate to the mode of proceeding on suits instituted in courts, and each section regulates a particular branch of that proceeding. Where the class of suits is described in the first section, it is natural to suppose that the subsequent regulations respecting suits apply to those which have been described.

The first section directs that suits shall be instituted against revenue officers and other persons accountable for public money, and imposes a penalty on delinquents, where a suit shall be commenced and prosecuted to judgment.

The second section directs that certain testimony shall be admitted at the trial of the cause.

The third section prescribes the condition under which a continuance may be granted:—and

The fourth section respects the testimony which may be produced by the defendant. These are all parts of the same subject; and there is strong reason, independent of the language of the act, to suppose that the provisions respecting them were designed to be co-extensive with each other.

But the fifth section is totally unconnected with those which precede it. Regulations of a suit in court no longer employ the mind of the legislature. The preference of the United States to other creditors, becomes the subject of legislation; and as this subject is unconnected with that which had been disposed of in the foregoing sections, so is the language employed upon it without reference to that which had been previously used. If this language was ambiguous, all the means recommended by the counsel for the defendants would be resorted to in order to remove the ambiguity. But it appears, to the majority of the court, to be too explicit to require the application of those principles which are useful in doubtful cases.

The mischiefs to result from the construction on which the United States insist, have been stated as strong motives for overruling that construction.[2] That the consequences are to be considered in expounding laws, where the intent is doubtful, is a principle not to be controverted; but it is also true that it is a principle which must be applied with caution, and which has a degree of influence dependent on the nature of the case to which it is applied. Where rights are infringed, where fundamental principles are overthrown, where the general system of the laws is departed from, the legislative intention must be expressed with irresistible clearness to induce a court of justice to suppose a design to effect such objects. But where only a political regulation is made, which is inconvenient, if the intention of the legislature be expressed in terms which are sufficiently intelligible to leave no doubt in the mind when the words are taken in their ordinary sense, it would be going a great way to say that a constrained interpretation must be put upon them, to avoid an inconvenience which ought to have been contemplated in the legislature when the act was passed, and which, in their opinion, was probably overbalanced by the particular advantages it was calculated to produce.

Of the latter description of inconveniences, are those occasioned by the act in question. It is for the legislature to appreciate them. They are not of such magnitude as to induce an opinion that the legislature could not intend to expose the citizens of the United States to them, when words are used which manifest that intent.

On this subject it is to be remarked, that no *lien* is created by this law. No *bona fide* transfer of property in the ordinary course of business is overreached. It is only a priority in payment, which, under different modifications, is a regulation in common use; and this priority is limited to a particular state of things, when the debtor is living; though it takes effect generally if he be dead.[3]

Passing from a consideration of the act itself, and the consequences which flow from it, the counsel on each side have sought to strengthen their construction by other acts in *pari materia*.

The act of the 3d *of March*, 1797, has been supposed to be a continuation of legislative proceeding on the subject which was commenced on the *third of March*, 1795, (*vol. 3, p.* 225.) by the act, "for the more effectual recovery of debts due from individuals to the United States," which relates exclusively to the receivers of public money.[4]

Admitting the opinion, that the act of 1797 was particularly designed to supply the defects of that of 1795, to be correct, it does not seem to follow, that a substantive and independent section, having no connection with the provisions made in 1795, should be restricted by it.

The act of 1795 contains nothing relative to the priority of the United States, and therefore will not explain the 5th section of the act of 1797, which relates exclusively to that subject. But the act of 1797, neither in its title nor its enacting clauses, contains any words of reference to the act of 1795. The words which are supposed to imply this reference are, "to provide *more effectually.*" But these words have relation to the existing state of the law, on all the subjects to which the act of 1797 relates, not to those alone which are comprehended in the act of 1795. The title of the act of 1795 is also, "for the *more effectual* recovery of debts," and consequently refers to certain pre-existing laws. The act of 1797, therefore, may be supposed to have in view the act of 1795, when providing for the objects contemplated in that act; but must be supposed to have other acts in view, when providing for objects not contemplated in that act.

As, therefore, the act of 1795 contains nothing respecting the priority of the United States, but is limited to provisions respecting suits in court, the act of 1797 may be considered in connection with that act while on the subject of suits in court; but when on the subject of preference, must be considered in connection with acts which relate to the preference of the United States.

The first act on this subject passed on the 31*st of July*, 1789, § 21, and gave the United States a preference only in the case of bonds for duties.[5]

On the 4*th of August*, 1790, *vol.* 1, *p.* 221, an act was passed on the same subject with that of 1789, which repeals all former acts, and re-enacts, in substance, the 21st section, relative to the priority of the United States.[6]

On the 2*d of May*, 1792, *vol.* 2, *p.* 78, the priority previously given to the United States is transferred to the sureties on duty bonds who shall themselves pay the debt; and the cases of insolvency, in which this priority is to take place, are explained to comprehend the case of a voluntary assignment, and the attached effects of an absconding, concealed, or absent debtor.[7]

Such was the title of the United States, to a preference in the payment of debts previous to the passage of the act of 1797. It was limited to bonds for the payment of duties on imported goods, and on the tonnage of vessels. An internal revenue had been established, and extensive transactions had taken place; in the course of which, many persons had necessarily become indebted to the United States. But no attempt to give them a preference in the collection of such debts had been made.

This subject is taken up in the 5th section of the act of 1797. The term "revenue officer," which is used in that act, would certainly comprehend any persons employed in the collection of the internal revenue; yet it may be well doubted whether those persons are contemplated in the foregoing sections of the act. They relate to a suit in court, and are perhaps restricted to those receivers of public money who have accounts on the books of the treasury. The head of the department in each state most probably accounts with the treasury, and the sub-collectors account with him.

If this be correct, a class of debtors would be introduced into the 5th section by the term "revenue officer," who are indeed within the title but not within the preceding enacting clauses of the law.

But passing over this term, the succeeding words seem, to the majority of the court, certainly to produce this effect. They are "or other person hereafter becoming indebted to the United States, by bond or otherwise." If this section was designed to place the collection of the internal revenue on the same footing of security with the external revenue, as has been argued by one of the counsel for the defendants, a design so reasonable that it would naturally be attributed to the legislature, then the debtors for excise duties would be comprehended within it; yet those debtors cannot be brought within the title, or the previous enacting clauses of the bill.

The 5th sec. then would introduce a new class of debtors, and if it does so in any case, the act furnishes no principle which shall restrain the words of that section to every case to which they apply.

Three acts of congress have passed, subsequent to that under particular consideration, which have been supposed to bear upon the case.

The first passed on the 11th of July 1798, and is entitled "an act to regulate and fix the compensation of the officers employed in collecting the internal revenues of the United States, and to insure more effectually the settlement of their accounts."[8] The 13th section of this act (vol. 4, p. 196) refers expressly to the provisions of the act of March 1797, on the subject of suits to be instituted on the bonds given by the officers collecting the internal revenue, and shows conclusively that in the opinion of the legislature the four first sections of that act did not extend to the case of those officers; consequently, if the 5th section extends to them, it introduces a class of debtors distinct from those contemplated in the clauses which respect suits in court. The 15th section of this act takes up the subject which is supposed to be contemplated by the 5th section of the act of 1797, and declares the debt due from these revenue officers to the United States to be a *lien* on their real estates, and on the real estates of their sureties from the institution of suit thereon. It can scarcely be supposed that the legislature would have given a *lien* on the real estate without providing for a preference out of the personal estate, especially where there was no real estate, unless that preference was understood to be secured by a previous law.

The same observation applies to a subsequent act of the same session for laying a direct tax. A *lien* is reserved on the real estate of the collector, without mentioning any claim to preference out of his personal estate.[9]

The last law which contains any provision on the subject of preference passed on the *2d of March* 1799. The 65th section of that act has been considered as repealing the 5th section of the act of 1797, or of manifesting the limited sense in which it is to be understood.[10]

It must be admitted that this section involves the subject in additional perplexity; but it is the opinion of the court, that on fair construction, it can apply only to bonds taken for those duties on imports and tonnage, which are the subject of the act.

From the first law passed on this subject, every act respecting the collection of those duties, had contained a section giving a preference to the United States, in case of the insolvency of the collectors of them.

The act of 1797, if construed as the United States would construe it, would extend to those collectors if there was no other provision in any other act giving a priority to the United States in these cases. As there was such a previous act, it might be supposed that its repeal by a subsequent law, would create a doubt whether the act of 1797 would comprehend the case, and therefore from abundant caution it might be deemed necessary still to retain the section in the new act respecting those duties. The general repealing clause of the act of 1799 cannot be construed to repeal the act of 1797, unless it provides for the cases to which that act extends.

It has also been argued that the bankrupt law itself affords ground for the opinion that the United States do not claim a general preference. (*vol.* 5, *p.* 82.) The words of the 62d section of that law apply to debts generally as secured by prior acts.[11] But as that section was not upon the subject of preference, but was merely designed to retain the right of the United States in their existing situation, whatever that situation might be, the question may well be supposed not to have been investigated at that time, and the expressions of the section were probably not considered with a view to any influence they might have on those rights.

After maturely considering this doubtful statute, and comparing it with other acts in *pari materia*, it is the opinion of the majority of the court, that the preference given to the United States by the 5th section is not confined to revenue officers and persons accountable for public money, *but extends to debtors generally.*

Supposing this distinction not to exist, it is contended that this priority of the United States cannot take effect in any case where suit has not been instituted; and in support of this opinion several decisions of the English judges with respect to the prerogative of the crown have been quoted.

To this argument the express words of the act of congress seem to be opposed. The legislature has declared the time when this priority shall have its commencement; and the court think those words conclusive on the point. The cases certainly shew that a *bona fide* alienation of property before the right of priority attaches will be good, but that does not affect the present case. From the decisions on this subject a very ingenious argument was drawn by the counsel who made this point.[12] The bankrupt law, he says, does not bind the king because he is not named in it; yet it has been adjudged that the effects of a bankrupt are placed beyond the reach of the king by the assignment made under that law, unless they shall have been previously bound. He argues, that according to the understanding of the legislature, as proved by their acts relative to insolvent debtors, and according to the decisions in some of the inferior courts, the bankrupt law would not bind the United States although the 62d section had not been inserted. That section therefore is only an expression of what would be law without it, and consequently is an immaterial section: as the king, though not bound by the bankrupt law, is bound by the assignment made under it; so, he contended, that the United States, though not bound by the law, are bound by the assignment.

But the assignment is made under, and by the direction of the law; and a proviso that nothing contained in the law shall affect the right of preference claimed by the United States is equivalent to a proviso that the assignment shall not affect the right of preference claimed by the United States.

If the act has attempted to give the United States a preference in the case before the court, it remains to inquire whether the constitution obstructs its operation.[13]

To the general observations made on this subject, it will only be observed, that as the court can never be unmindful of the solemn duty imposed on the judicial department when a claim is supported by an act which conflicts with the constitution, so the court can never be unmindful of its duty to obey laws which are authorised by that instrument.

In the case at bar, the preference claimed by the United States is not prohibited; but it has been truly said that under a constitution conferring specific powers, the power contended for must be granted, or it cannot be exercised.

It is claimed under the authority to make all laws which shall be necessary and proper to carry into execution the powers vested by the constitution in the government of the United States, or in any department or officer thereof.

In construing this clause it would be incorrect and would produce endless difficulties, if the opinion should be maintained that no law was authorised which was not indispensably necessary to give effect to a specified power.

Where various systems might be adopted for that purpose, it might be said with respect to each, that it was not necessary because the end might be obtained by other means. Congress must possess the choice of means, and must be empowered to use any means which are in fact conducive to the exercise of a power granted by the constitution.

The government is to pay the debt of the union, and must be authorised to use the means which appear to itself most eligible to effect that object. It has consequently a right to make remittances by bills or otherwise, and to take those precautions which will render the transaction safe.

This claim of priority on the part of the United States will, it has been said, interfere with the right of the state sovereignties respecting the dignity of debts, and will defeat the measures they have a right to adopt to secure themselves against delinquencies on the part of their own revenue officers.

But this is an objection to the constitution itself. The mischief suggested, so far as it can really happen, is the necessary consequence of the supremacy of the laws of the United States on all subjects to which the legislative power of congress extends.

As the opinion given in the court below was that the plaintiffs did not maintain their action on the whole testimony exhibited, it is necessary to examine that testimony.

It appears that the plaintiffs have proceeded on the transcripts from the books of the treasury, under the idea that this suit is maintainable under the act of 1797.[14] The court does not mean to sanction that opinion; but, as no objection was taken to the testimony, it is understood to have been admitted. It is also understood that there is no question to be made respecting notice; but that the existence of the debt is admitted, and the right of the United States to priority of payment is the only real point in the cause.

The majority of this court is of opinion that the United States are entitled to that priority, and therefore the judgment of the circuit court is to be reversed, and the cause to be remanded for further proceedings.[15]

Printed, William Cranch, *Reports of Cases Argued and Adjudged in the Supreme Court of the United States . . .* , II (New York, 1806), 385–97.

1. *U.S. Statutes at Large*, I, 519–41. Here and elsewhere in the opinion, JM cited the contemporary edition, *Laws of the U.S.*

2. Harper and Ingersoll stressed the lack of notice in the case of a private individual indorsing a bill to the U.S. "Particular and secret *liens*," observed the latter, "indiscreetly multiplied, . . . destroy *credit*, the life of commerce" (2 Cranch 368–69, 371).

3. Cranch here subjoined a footnote: "The Ch. J. in delivering the opinion, observed as follows: 'I only say for myself, as the point has not been submitted to the court, that it does not appear to me to create a *devastavit* in the administration of effects, and would require notice in order to bind the executor, or administrator, or assignee'" (2 Cranch 390).

4. *U.S. Statutes at Large*, I, 441–42.

5. The reference is to sec. 21 of "An Act to regulate the Collection of the Duties imposed by law on the tonnage of ships or vessels, and on goods, wares and merchandises imported into the United States" (ibid., 29, 42).

6. Ibid., 145, 169.

7. "An Act for raising a farther sum of money for the protection of the frontiers, and for other purposes therein mentioned," sec. 18 (ibid., 259, 263).

8. Ibid., 591.

9. The reference is to sec. 16 of "An Act to lay and collect a direct tax" (ibid., 597, 602–3).

10. "An Act to regulate the collection of duties on imports and tonnage" (ibid., 627, 676–77). This point was urged by Lewis (2 Cranch 380).

11. *U.S. Statutes at Large*, II, 19–36. Sec. 62 reads: "That nothing contained in this law shall, in any manner, affect the right of preference to prior satisfaction of debts due to the United States as secured or provided by any law heretofore passed, nor shall be construed to lessen or impair any right to, or security for, money due to the United States or to any of them" (36).

12. JM referred to the argument of Charles Lee (2 Cranch 380). Cranch's summary of this argument is less detailed than the notes taken by Justice Johnson. In the margin, Johnson noted the following English cases: Phillips v. Hunter, 2 Black. H. 402, 126 Eng. Rep. 618 (Ex., 1795); A.G. v. Capell, 2 Shower K.B. 480, 89 Eng. Rep. 1053 (K.B., 1686); Awdley v. Halsey, Jones, W. 202, 82 Eng. Rep. 107 (K.B., 1629); Stringefellow v. Brownesoppe, 1 Dy. 67b, 73 Eng. Rep. 142 (K.B., 1549); King v. Cotton, Park. 112, 145 Eng. Rep. 729 (Ex., 1751). Johnson's notes are in the file of Hepburn and Dundas v. Ellzey, App. Cas. No. 149.

13. Ingersoll contended that the act of 1797, if construed to include every debtor to the U.S., was "unconstitutional and void," for its operation would "be to impair the obligation of contracts by an *ex post facto* law." If the power under the act was derived from the "necessary and proper" clause, "where is the necessity or where the propriety of such a provision, and to the exercise of what other power is it necessary?" Dallas replied that Congress has "a power to borrow money, and it is their duty to provide for its payment. For this purpose they must raise a revenue, and, to protect that revenue from frauds, a power is necessary to claim a priority of payment" (2 Cranch 379, 384).

14. The evidence submitted on behalf of the U.S. in the court below consisted of transcripts from the books of the treasury, as provided by section 2 of the 1797 act. That section, however, presumably was confined to suits brought against collectors of public money (*U.S. Statutes at Large*, I, 512–13).

15. Though not participating in the appeal, Justice Washington gave a lengthy explanation of the reasons for his opinion given in the U.S. Circuit Court, Pennsylvania (2 Cranch 397–405).

Hepburn and Dundas v. Ellzey
Opinion
U.S. Supreme Court, 25 February 1805

EDITORIAL NOTE

This case came to the Supreme Court on a certificate of division from the U.S. Circuit Court for Virginia, dated 3 June 1803. In the circuit court the opinions of Chief Justice Marshall and District Judge Cyrus Griffin were opposed on the question whether the plaintiffs, citizens of the District of Columbia, could maintain an action in that court against a citizen of Virginia. This question provoked an inquiry into the meaning of "state" as used in the diversity jurisdiction clause of Article III, section 2, of the Constitution, by which federal jurisdiction extended to controversies "between citizens of different States."

Marshall sat in this case and delivered the opinion, even though he had earlier heard the cause on circuit. In all other cases coming up from his circuit through the 1807 term, whether by certificate of division, writ of error, or appeal, the chief justice declined to sit or did not give an opinion if he had participated in the case either as judge or as counsel.[1] Although there was no fixed rule, justices customarily abstained from cases they had heard below. In 1808, however, the situation arose that strict adherence to custom would prevent a quorum from hearing a case. After some discussion, in which three of the six justices present strongly opposed "the practice of a judge's leaving the bench because he had decided the case in the court below," all six justices sat in the case—"so that," reporter Cranch noted, "the practice of retiring seems to be abandoned."[2]

1. Stuart v. Laird, 1 Cranch 299, 308 (1803); Ogden v. Blackledge, 2 Cranch 272 (1804); Winchester v. Hackley, 2 Cranch 342 (1805); Lambert's Lessee v. Paine, 3 Cranch 97, 117 (1805); U.S. v. Heth, 3 Cranch 399, 414 (1806); Randolph v. Ware, 3 Cranch 503, 513n (1806); Hopkirk v. Bell, 3 Cranch 454 (1806), 4 Cranch 164 (1807).
2. Rose v. Himely, 4 Cranch 243n.

OPINION

The question in this case is whether the plaintiffs, as residents of the district of Columbia, can maintain an action in the circuit court of the United States for the district of Virginia.[1]

This depends on the act of congress describing the jurisdiction of that court. That act gives jurisdiction to the circuit courts in cases between a citizen of the state in which the suit is brought, and a citizen of another state. To support the jurisdiction in this case therefore it must appear that Columbia is a state.

On the part of the plaintiffs it has been urged that Columbia is a distinct political society; and is therefore "a state" according to the definitions of writers on general law.

This is true. But as the act of congress obviously uses the word "state" in reference to that term as used in the constitution, it becomes necessary to inquire whether Columbia is a state in the sense of that instrument. The result of that examination is a conviction that the members of the American confederacy only are the states contemplated in the constitution.

The house of representatives is to be composed of members chosen by the people of the several states; and each state shall have at least one representative.

The senate of the United States shall be composed of two senators *from* each state.

Each state shall appoint, for the election of the executive, a number of electors equal to its whole number of senators and representatives.

These clauses show that the word state is used in the constitution as designating a member of the union, and excludes from the term the signification attached to it by writers on the law of nations. When the same term which has been used plainly in this limited sense in the articles respecting the legislative and executive departments, is also employed in that which respects the judicial department, it must be understood as retaining the sense originally given to it.

Other passages from the constitution have been cited by the plaintiffs to show that the term state is sometimes used in its more enlarged sense.[2] But on examining the passages quoted, they do not prove what was to be shown by them.

It is true that as citizens of the United states, and of that particular district which is subject to the jurisdiction of congress, it is extraordinary that the courts of the United States, which are open to aliens, and to the citizens of every state in the union, should be closed upon *them*. But this is a subject for legislative not for judicial consideration.[3]

The opinion to be certified to the circuit court is that that court has no jurisdiction in the case.

Printed, William Cranch, *Reports of Cases Argued and Adjudged in the Supreme Court of the United States . . .* , II (New York, 1806), 452–53.

1. The case was argued on 5 and 13 Feb. by Edmund J. Lee for the plaintiffs and Charles Lee for the defendant. The appellate case file contains a forty-four-page manuscript of notes of arguments, in the hand of Justice William Johnson, in this and five other cases argued at the 1805 term: Reily v. Lamar, U.S. v. More, U.S. v. Fisher, Wilson v. Codman's Executors, and Cooke v. Graham's Administrator (Hepburn and Dundas v. Ellzey, App. Cas. No. 149).

2. See E. J. Lee's argument, 2 Cranch 450–51.

3. Congress remedied this situation in 1940 (Edward S. Corwin, *The Constitution and What It Means Today* [rev. ed.; Princeton, N.J., 1973], 188).

To Caleb P. Wayne

Sir   Washington Feby. 27th. 1805

To the care of Mr. Hopkinson[1] we have entrusted a box containing two copies of the 4th. volume. They are both in a rough state, too rough to be sent if it was avoidable: but it is impossible to have them recopied. They have been detained in order to expunge so much from them as to reduce the volume to a reasonable bulk & this operation has renderd the copies unfit to go into the hands of any other person, and will I fear produce considerable difficulty in uniting parts originally distant from each other but which are now brought together by striking out intermediate passages. On this point I must request you to be particularly attentive.[2]

There is also another subject on which it will be necessary for you to be very watchful. The copies were made by young men who have been altogether unmindful of capital letters, of punctuation, & some times of spelling. It has been absolutely impossible to make corrections in these respects, & with regard to capitals it has not been attempted. You will find them through the whole work where they ought not to be. In reading with one view defects of a different nature often escape us unperceived & this is the case with respect to punctuation. Where ever therefore the punctuation is manifestly improper you will alter it. The capitals you will find perpetual occasion to change. The spelling is I doubt not in some instances erroneous. You will please to communicate these observations to Mr. Morgan.

The Maps are sent. They need not all be inserted I presume as some of them are probably duplicates of those before sent. It appears to me that there should be in the book of maps a deliniation of those parts of New York, New Jersey & Pennsylvania which were the seat of war, in distinct charts—one for each state. It is probable that more full plans of those parts may be taken from the best state maps than from thos(e) which were in possession of General Washington. On them should be marked the particular places noticed in the history. These with the particular plans of actions—and of places will give a good idea of the military transactions of those states. I send you a map of the lower parts of Virginia which was transmitted to me by the Marquis together with a plan of the siege of York town. I think it would be also useful to insert a map of those parts of North & South Carolina on which the most active operations were conducted.[3]

I shall be glad to hear by what time you think the 4th. vol. will be in readiness to be delivered. I shall send you the last sheets of the 3d. corrected as soon as possible: & hope they will reach you in time.

I beleive the 4th. vol. to be much less inaccurate than those which preceded it, as I have bestowed more attention on the style than was given to them. Yet I cannot flatter myself that it will not need a considerable reform. I am confident that I shall perceive when I read it in print many defects that escape me in manuscript. I should therefore wish it were possible to see the proof sheets, or to correct a copy as I have done the three first before the additional number of copies shall be printed. But if this would occasion you additional expence I would not wish it. If any incongruity appears in bringing together parts originally remote I could wish it to be suggested to me that I may remove it. If this cannot be done you may probably find some assistance on the spot which you may depend upon in cases not very essential.

I send two copies of a correction of the mistake respecting the author of the petition to the King to be inserted in the Appendix to the 4th. volume.[4] I am Sir respectfully, your obedt. ⟨Servt.⟩

J MARSHALL

ALS, Dreer Collection, PHi; Tr, Marshall Papers, DLC. Addressed to Wayne at Philadelphia. MS torn. Part of closing obscured by seal. Wayne noted at bottom of last page of letter, "Maps/Letters."

1. Joseph Hopkinson (1770–1842), prominent Philadelphia attorney, then acting as one of Chase's counsel in his impeachment trial. Hopkinson later served as a Federalist congressman, 1815–19, and a federal district court judge for eastern Pennsylvania from 1828 until his death.

2. Publisher's manuscript copy of vol. IV retained by Wayne is in Dreer Collection, PHi, in several copyists' hands, with multiple deletions and corrections in JM's, Bushrod Washington's, and Wayne's hands. For an explanation of the fair copies sent to the publishers, see The Life of George Washington, Volume IV, Chapter 8, Draft and Published Version, [ca. July 1804], editorial note.

3. For Plates II–V of the Maps, which show the various sites of action in New York, New Jersey, and Pennsylvania, see JM to Bushrod Washington, 28 Mar. 1804 and nn. 3–7. Plates III–V were drawn from the original surveys ordered by General Washington. In addition, northern New York is detailed on Plate VI, "A Map of the Country which was the scene of operations of the Northern Army; including the Wilderness through which General Arnold marched to attack Quebec." Plate VII is "A Map of part of Rhode Island Shewing the Positions of the American and British Armies at the Siege of Newport, and the subsequent Action on the 29th of August 1778." Plate VIII is "A Map of those parts of Virginia, North Carolina, South Carolina, & Georgia, which were the scenes of the most important Operations of the Southern Armies." Plate IX has the "Plan of the Investment and Attack of York in Virginia." Plate X contains a "Plan of the Siege of Charleston in S. Carolina." None of the plates after V gives a source for the plan. For the draftsman and engravers, see Wayne to JM, 20 Aug. 1804, n. 9.

4. See JM to George Logan, 28 Jan. 1805 and n. 4.

To Caleb P. Wayne

March 1st. 1805[1]

p 505 l 10. for "called" read "consulted." l 11 exp. "to consult them." l 15. for "to consist of about" read "at." l 16 semicolon after "file." exp. "including artillerists" l 20 exp. "according to the best estimation[2] he could make" & commas. l 27 for "had" read "procured."

p 506. l 5 for "for which." read "of." l 6. exp. "had been undertaken." l 8 for "set out for" read "repaired to." l 13 after "night" read ["]of the 28th." comma. l 19.[3] for "Very early in the" read ["]Early the next." l 22 exp "about seven oClock in the morning" & commas. l 28. for "enemy" read "English."

p 507. l 11. for "oClock" read "in the afternoon." l 24. exp. "very." l 26 for "enemy" read "British."

p 508. l 3 exp. "Very." l 7 exp "in an eminent degree" & commas. l 24 for "were waiting for a strong reenforcement which they expected." read "waited for a reenforcement."

p 509. l 11. No new paragraph. & for "Very fortunately the," read "This." l 18 exp. "with considerable address" & commas l 20 exp. "by strengthening his works & posting his troops" & commas. l 25 exp. "measures were so judiciously taken that his." l 28 exp. "oClock."

p 510. l 1. exp. "The delay of one day must have ruined him." l 3 after "arrived." exp. the rest of the sentence & read "and the return of the american army to the continent would have become impracticable." l 15 for "du" read "de." l 18 exp. "having repaired to Boston for the purposes of conciliation with the French admiral and of endeavoring to secure his return as soon as his fleet should be repaired was absent during the engagement but by great personal exertions, he."

p 511. l 9. exp "in a few days." & commas. l 16 exp. "for the purpose" &c to reenforced inclusive in l 21. l 22 read "manifest"

p 514 exp "Where the independent companies & militia returned in excessive ill humour." & commas[4]

p 515. l. 9 exp. "very." l 19 exp. "independent of the meer loss of the advantages to have been derived from succeeding in the expedition" & commas.

p 519. l 26. exp. "which was afforded him by the arrival of reenforcements to the British fleet.["]

p 521. l 5 exp. "himself extremely." l 7 after "and" read "therefore." exp "very." l 13 exp. "very" l 18 exp. "much." l 27 exp. ["]by the arrangement[5] of the ships, and by batteries on shore & on Hull & Long island" p 522 l 9. exp. "Sir Henry Clinton." l 10 before "returned" read "Sir Henry Clinton." l 15 for ["]left the fleet & proceeded." read "repaired in person."

p 523. l. 1 exp. "which proved a very seasonable supply to the army in New York." l 5 for "there were in New York many indications of an intention" read ["]preparations were making in New York." l 10 exp. "who were now decidedly superior at sea" & commas. l 13 exp. comma after "land." l 14 after "exposing." read "the posts[6] on." l 15 exp. "while the main body of the enemy remained in New York." l 22 exp. "very." l 27 exp. "very." [l] 28 for ["]In order at the same time to approach somewhat nearer both to the important." read "with a view both to the." l 30 exp. "so as to be ready to move with the greater celerity towards either of the two objects now supposed of greatest magnitude."

p 524 l 31.[7] exp. "very"

p 525. l 3. exp. "very rightly." l 7 exp. "by a rapid march." l 16 after "27th." read "of September" l 29 exp. comma after "Campbell."

p 526 l 6 exp. comma after "guard" and read "which had been." l 25[8] exp "which was beleived to have been unnecessary" & commas. l 28 exp. ["]Depositions to establish the facts were." l 30 before "taken." read "depositions to establish the facts were."

p 529. l. 1. exp "In these expeditions["] &c & the whole paragraph. l. 14 exp "As soon as." exp. comma after "who."[9] l 16 period after "September." for "had made the repairs to" read "After repairing." l 17 exp. ["]which were necessary to enable him again to put to sea." l 18 after "sailed" read "in October" l 30 for "set sail" read "sailed"

p 530. l 1. for "rendered" read "required." exp. "of essential importance." l 5 exp "not without reason" & commas. l ⟨9⟩ exp. "to the attainment of which it was entirely competent." l 14 exp. "on which it was impossible to have calculated" & commas. l 28.[10] for "in singly" read "singly into the harbor of New York." period and exp. the rest of the sentence

p 531. l 27. exp "General Washington" l 28 before "was" read "General Washington." l 29 for "his" read "the" after "connexion" read "of this officer."

p 532. l. 16 for "As there was very little" read "There being no." l 18 for "admitted" read "admitting."

p 533. l 1 after "remained" read "in New York." for "to secure New York." read ["]for its defence." l 2 after "retired" read "in December." l 5 period at "Middlebrook." l 6 exp. "while." l 12 exp. as "much as possible." exp. "The great body of the army" &c to the end of the paragraph.

p 534. l 4 exp. "which had been proposed by Lord North." l 8 for "now" read "they."

p 535. l. 1. exp. "they required." l 2 after "sovereign" read "was still required" l 3 for "These were terms to which" read "To this." l 19 exp. comma after "bills." l. 25. exp "however, especially Governor Johnson" & commas.

p 537 l 24 for "On reading" read "In." l 25 before "some" read "were." exp. "were found to be mingled with them" & comma.

p 538. l 8. period after "read." exp "and."

p 539. l 17 after "of" read ["]respect for."

p 542. l 8 exp "at least" & commas.

p 551. l 3 put inverted commas after ["]determination."

p 552. l 20. for "home" read "house."

p 553. l 31. for "the ports" read "from the posts"

p 554. l 11 exp. "to be proved." l 13 for "very much" read "in a great measure." l 15 exp. "very." l 17 after "Congress" read "so early as the 20th. of June."

p 555 l 2. for "another was resolved on from the Mohawk river into." read "it was also determined to enter." l 4 after "Senecas" read "by the way of the Mohawk." l 20 comma after "matured." l 30 exp. "which had flourished in a remarkable degree." & commas.

p 556 l 1. exp. "it is said" & commas.

p 557. l. 8. for "successfully resorted to" read "resorted to with success." l 24 exp. "about three hundred." exp comma after "Indians." l 25 exp. "a number."

p 561. l 14 for "perpetual calls into the field" read ["]repeated tours of duty." l 21 for "The sufferings of the western frontier however were now such and." read "But." l 23 for "it" read "the western frontier." l 27 before "Colonel" read "On the first intelligence of the destruction of the settlement at Wyoming." l 29 exp "on the first intelligence of the destruction of Wyoming" & commas. l 31 after "and" read "to."

p 562 l 1. for "set out on" read "immediately planned" l 3 exp "and made some prisoners." l 4 for "they" read "savages" l 5 exp. "very." l 19 after "country" read "in October."

p 563.[11] exp. "the."

p 564. l. 5 semicolon after "practicable."

p 565 l 11 after "cavalry" read "were voted for its protection" period. for "to be commanded by" read "The command of these troops was given to." l 16 exp. "were ordered to be recruited for its protection." l 21[12] comma after "Hamilton." l 22 exp. "who was understood to have been extremely active in fomenting Indian hostility." l 28 period after "Virginia." exp "When."

p 566. l 20 exp. "mounted." p 567. l. 11 for "little" read "small." l 27 exp. "very."

p 568. l 22 exp. "savage"

p 570. l 12 after "vessels" read "which would be." l 13 exp. first "the" l 23 period after "secret." l 24 exp. "and." l 26 for "and from thence," read "after which."

p 571. l. 19 for "To carry this on the army must be wintered." read "This circumstance would require that the army should pass the winter."

p 574. l 17 exp. "from." l 26 semicolon after "water."

⟨p 575. l 1⟩ ⟨e⟩xp. "very" do. do. l 4 comma after "and." l 25 exp. "in some degree" & commas.

⟨p 576. l 24⟩ inverted commas after "admit."

⟨p 580. l 3⟩ ⟨ex⟩p. "very." semicolon after "up."

By the time this reaches you I expect to be on my way to Virginia. I regret very much the size of the volumes. It is to be attributed to the hurry in which they have been written & revised whereby trivial events are crouded into the work. If a second edition should ever be required they will be greatly reduced. I fear however that the copies of the first will be so multiplied as to satisfy the demand. I did not receive your letter of the 24th. till yesterday afternoon.[13] I send you the memoranda relative to Capt. McClean.[14] That which is to be a note in the first instance & those which only require the insertion of his name will I presume not affect the context. I shall wish to know when the 4th. vol will be out.[15]

I feel truly obliged to Colonel Pettit for the information he has given & will thank him for any further communication on the facts of the war which it may be in his power to make.[16]

AD, Dreer Collection, PHi. Addressed to Wayne at Philadelphia; postmarked "Washn. City," 1 Mar. MS torn where seal was broken.

1. JM transmitted corrections to the *Life* for the end of vol. III, part of chap. 9 and all of chap. 10, 505–80, covering military events from the last days of Aug. 1778 to Feb. 1779. With the exceptions noted below and an occasional date placed in the margin rather than in the text as directed by JM, all of the alterations appear in *Life* (1805 ed.), III, chaps. 9–10, 504–76. Immediately following his list of corrections, JM wrote Wayne a note, dated 1 Mar., which he concluded along the edge of the cover. The date as it appears above JM's note has been moved to the beginning of the document.

2. Reads "computation" in vol. III.

3. JM's line count differs by one from vol. III: l. 19 is 20, l. 22 is 23, l. 28 is 29.

4. This clause appears on lines 30–31 at the bottom of 514 and line 1 on 515.

5. Reads "arrangements" in vol. III.

6. Rendered "forts" in *Life* (1805 ed.), III, 521, line 13.

7. JM's line count differs by one from vol. III: l. 31 is 32.

8. JM's line count differs by one from vol. III: l. 25 is 26, l. 28 is 29, l. 30 is 31.

9. Comma precedes "who" in vol. III. Wayne deleted ", who" and turned a subordinate clause into a declarative sentence, as JM apparently intended to be done.

10. JM's line count differs by one from vol. III: l. 28 is 29.

11. JM left out the line number. Wayne deleted "the" before "roads" on line 30 (in *Life* [1805 ed.], III, 560, line 16).

12. JM's line count differs by one from vol. III: l. 21 is 20, l. 22 is 21.

13. Letter not found.

14. Memoranda not found.

15. Wayne published vol. IV on 12 Aug. 1805 (*U.S. Gazette*).

16. Charles Pettit (1736–1806) served as assistant adjutant general on the staff of General Greene from 1778 until 1781, when he resigned. Originally from New Jersey, Pettit became an import merchant in Philadelphia and served as a Pennsylvania delegate in the Continental Congress, 1785–87.

From Thomas Jefferson

Mar. 1. 1805.

Th: Jefferson presents his respects to the Chief justice of the U S. and asks the favor of him to administer to him the oath which the constitution prescribes to the President of the U S. before he enters on the execution of his office, on Monday the 4th. instant at twelve aclock in the Senate chamber.[1]

AL (press copy), Jefferson Papers, DLC.

1. The Washington correspondent for the Philadelphia *Aurora* made this comment on the inaugural oath ceremony of 4 Mar.: "I observe that the judge did not turn his back upon the president, whilst administering the oath, as he did this day four years" (*Aurora*, 8 Mar. 1805).

To Caleb P. Wayne

Sir   Richmond March 16th. 1805

On looking over the 4th. vol. I had designed to examine a word which I beleive is improperly used in the plural where it ought only to be employed in the singular but the pressure of other business prevented it & I forgot to mention it to you.

The word "quarter" when denoting mercy from an enemy ought I think to be only used in the singular number. I had written it in the plural "quarters" & beleive I did not alter it. Will you please to advert to this error & correct it.

I beleive too that in observing on the reluctance with which General Washington assented to the execution of Major André I have stated him to have obeyed "the stern *dictates* of duty." I think "mandate" would be a better word & will thank you to make the change.[1]

I do not think the 5th vol. will be ready for the press in twelve months. For the ensuing twelve months I shall scarcely have It in my power to be five in Richmond. The volume is not yet commenced. I shall however set about it in a few days. I am Sir your Obedt

J MARSHALL.

Mr. Weims I imagine informed you that I received one hundred & fifty dollars from him, after Mr. Washington left this place.

ALS, Dreer Collection, PHi; Tr (partial), Marshall Papers, DLC. Addressed to Wayne at Philadelphia; postmarked Richmond, 16 Mar.

1. Wayne changed it to read, "stern mandates of duty" (vol. IV, chap. 6, 284).

To Caleb P. Wayne

Sir   Richmond May 12th 1805

I received your letter enclosing a certificate of a credit of 500$ with the branch bank at Washington.[1] The communication between Richmond & Philadelphia is such that I can with much more facility draw money from that place than from Washington & would therefore always prefer a credit with the bank at Philadelphia.

The maps & plans designed to be inserted in the life of Washington have been all transmitted.

On my subscription I have only paid the original sum of three dollars.[2] I have not taken the volumes because I understood that of those copies which were bound in calf not a sufficient number had arrived at this place. If two revised sets of the three first volumes neatly bound in octavo, but not of the hot press letter,[3] could be sent to me in the course of the month of June I should be much pleased with receiving them. If any difficulty occurs in complying with this request I do not wish you to attempt it.

How many copies of the[4] work in its original state have you yet on hand? I had hoped that you were long since through them. Be pleased to let me know whether it is probable that I may expect the copies I have mentioned. I had it also in contemplation to present a copy of the four first volumes to the late Preside⟨nt⟩ Mr. Adams & perhaps to Mr. Smith the president of Princ⟨eton⟩ Colledge[5] but I wish not to direct this immediately as only revised copies could be sent, & I am not sure that I might n⟨ot⟩ interfere with your arrangements. If it was probable that a second edition would be called for I should incline to postpone any thing of that sort until that edition should be struck off.

The copies I speak of must be distinct from the sheets on which are to be made corrections for a second edition. Such sheets will receive many marks & must I preseme be returned to you. I am Sir very respectfully, Your Obedt

J MARSHALL

ALS, Dreer Collection, PHi. Addressed to Wayne at Philadelphia; postmarked Richmond, 14 May. Endorsed by Wayne, "Recd. May 18/Ansd. May 20"; Wayne's reply not found. MS torn.

1. Letter not found.

2. JM was a subscriber to his own work ("Subscribers to the Life of Washington," in *Maps*, 16).

3. A reference to the process of "hot-pressing," in which finest quality paper was glazed by heated metal plates to produce a smooth and glossy finish. This practice was in vogue among book publishers at the end of the eighteenth and beginning of the nineteenth centuries. Wayne in his "Proposals" for the *Life* advertised that "the work will be handsomely printed, with a new type, on vellum paper, *hot-pressed*" (*Philadelphia Gazette & Daily Advertiser*, 22 Sept. 1802). Although considered fancier, hot-pressed editions in fact were not satisfactory. The paper turned beige and the ink smeared (Silver, *American Printer*, 94–95)

4. JM originally wrote "imperfect" here, then deleted it, and inserted "in its original state" after "work."

5. Samuel Stanhope Smith (1750–1819), Presbyterian clergyman, professor of moral philosophy at Princeton beginning in 1779. He was president from 1795 to 1812.

To Caleb P. Wayne

Sir   [18 May 1805]

In the account given by General Greene of the battle of the Eutaws he mentions Captain Lieutenant Gaines with approbation.[1] I have omitted to name him. This I think is unjust & therefore I am desirous of correcting the omission. I will thank you to subjoin to that part which states that the American six pounders were taken and that a three pounder was brought off which had been taken from the enemy the following note.

[The American field pieces which were saved were commanded by captain lieutenant Gaines. The conduct of this officer in the action was mentioned with distinction by general Greene.][2]

The note may be marked at the words "brought off" which close a sentence in the text. I am Sir respectfully, Your Obedt

J MARSHALL

ALS, Dreer Collection, PHi. Addressed to Wayne at Philadelphia; postmarked Richmond, 18 May. Letter dated from postmark. Endorsed by Wayne. MS mutilated (see n. 2).

1. Greene reported on the Battle of Eutaw Springs, S.C., fought on 8 Sept. 1781, to the president of Congress on 11 Sept. 1781. He sent a copy of this letter, in which he mentioned Gaines's effective command of the three-pound artillery pieces, to George Washington on 17 Sept. (Washington Papers, ser. 4, DLC). Capt. Lt. William Fleming Gaines of Virginia served with the 1st Continental Artillery to Jan. 1783 (Heitman, *Historical Register of the Revolution*, 185).

2. Wayne cut JM's note out of the letter. Words supplied from vol. IV, chap. 10, 552, where Wayne set these lines in a note at the foot of the page with an asterisk keying it to the end of the sentence indicated by JM.

To Caleb P. Wayne

Sir   Richmond June 8th[1] 1805

I have just received the package you sent me. On opening the 2d. Vol. I perceive in page 10. l. 8. the word "not" omitted between "as" & "to." so as totally to change the sense. Is it too late to alter this or to mention it as an error?[2]—I have only read the first ten pages but I flatter myself there are not many inaccuracies in the book. I have perceived no other & I have no doubt of the attention you have paid to it.

I will thank you to take some opportunity of sending three volumes to Mr. Adams with the following words written on a blank leaf in each[3]

> Mr. Adams is requested to accept a copy of the[4] life of Washington as a small mark of the respect and attachment of his obliged and obedt. servt.
>
>   THE AUTHOR

I shall not send a copy to Mr. Smith.

I wish very much that I could receive the papers of Freneau.[5] They were forwarded to Mr. Bronson[6] by Mr. Hopkins[7] with a declaration as I am told that they would probably be wanted by me. The Aurora would also be a great acquisition.[8]

The want of these papers & the miscarriage of a box sent by Mr. Washington will I fear delay the work longer than I had expected.

I received your letter and have drawn on you in favor of Messrs. McMurdo & Fisher for £500 as you requested.[9]

In future it is equal to me either to draw on you or the bank, so that you may choose yourself & give me notice of the plan you adopt. I am Sir respectfully Your Obedt. Servt

                                                          J MARSHALL

ALS, Dreer Collection, PHi. Addressed to Wayne at Philadelphia; postmarked Richmond, 8 June. Endorsed by Wayne, "J. Marshall/June 8/Answd. June 13—1805"; Wayne's reply not found.

1. JM first wrote "7th" and then changed it to "8th."

2. The clause in the second impression to which JM referred reads: "the face of the country was such as to permit an enemy to pass unperceived" (*Life* [1805 ed.], II, chap. 1, 10, lines 7–8). JM had rephrased a passage concerning the expedition led by Washington against the French at Fort Duquesne in 1754. In the first impression JM had stated that officers of the British-American force had recommended retirement to Fort Necessity, where "the country would not easily admit the passage of an enemy without being perceived" (*Life*, II, chap. 1, 8–9). No erratum appears with vol. II (1805 ed.).

3. John Adams's set of the *Life* (1805 ed.) is in the Department of Rare Books and Manuscripts, Boston Public Library. Each volume contains the inscription as directed by JM.

4. JM appears to have first written "this" and then erased it to read "the." Wayne transcribed it as "the Life of Washington."

5. Philip Freneau's *National Gazette*, the Republican newspaper published in Philadelphia between 1791 and 1793.

6. Enos Bronson (1774–1823), who succeeded Wayne in Nov. 1801 as publisher of the *U.S. Gazette* (Konkle, "Enos Bronson," *PMHB*, LVII [1933], 355–58; see Wayne to JM, 2(6?) July 1804, n. 1).

7. Probably John Hopkins, of Richmond.

8. Originally published in 1790 as the *General Advertiser* by Benjamin Franklin Bache in Philadelphia. The name changed to the *Aurora, General Advertiser* in 1794, then *Philadelphia Aurora* in 1797. After Bache's death in 1798, the family continued to publish it until William H. Duane took over as publisher in 1800.

9. JM drew his bill of exchange on 27 May 1805, payable thirty days after sight. Wayne accepted it on 3 June. The verso of the bill carries several endorsements (Dreer Collection, PHi).

Corbet v. Johnson
Opinion
U.S. Circuit Court, Virginia, 8 June 1805

EDITORIAL NOTE

This was an equity suit brought by the assignees of Ninian Minzies (Cunningham Corbet, John Laurie, Gilbert Hamilton, John Sterling, and George Lothain). Before the Revolution, Minzies and James Todd were partners in the British merchant firm of Todd & Minzies. The complainants, who were subjects of Great Britain, sought to recover a debt on two bonds given by Edward Johnson of Chesterfield County to Todd & Minzies in 1774. Johnson died in 1780, his will providing that his whole estate should be subjected to the payment of his debts and appointing William Ronald and Andrew Ronald his executors. Both executors died before the commencement of this suit.

The defendants were heirs and devisees of Johnson (Edward Johnson,

Samuel Hobson and Elizabeth his wife, and Henrietta Johnson) and the executor (William Wiseham) of Andrew Ronald, who had been surviving executor of Edward Johnson. The heirs and devisees in their answers contended that the balance owed by William Ronald on his account as executor of Edward Johnson was more than sufficient to discharge the debt and that Ronald's representatives and the sureties on his bond as executor should be made defendants. Although liable for the debt out of the real estate descended or devised to them, the heirs and devisees claimed that the plaintiffs should resort first to the personal estate for payment. Marshall's opinion and decree were delivered on 8 June.[1]

1. Bill and answer, Corbet v. Johnson, U.S. Cir. Ct., Va., Ended Cases (Unrestored), 1827, Vi; U.S. Cir. Ct., Va., Ord. Bk. IV, 397, 486–87; V, 61, 120–21, 147–48.

OPINION

¶1   The material question in this case is how far a bond credito⟨r⟩ coming into a court of equity to subject lands to his debt will be compelled to pursue the personal estate before the lands shall be applied to the satisfaction of his claim.

¶2   At law he has his option to resort to either fund. Originally it appears to have been deemed necessary first to exhaust the personal estate but from the time of Edward the 4th. it has been held that the creditor may elect to sue either the Heir or the Executor. The cases on this subject are reviewed by Powell; & since that period it has been uniformly decided that "assets in the hands of the executor at the time the writ was sued out" is no plea in bar to an action of debt against the heir.[1]

¶3   But although the creditor has this election if he chuses to proceed at law, yet if he comes into a court of equity he must conform to its rules. One of these is that the executor shall be joined in the suit. For this rule two reasons are assigned.

1st.   That he may contest the claim.

2dly.   That the personal fund out of which a reembursement would be decreed to the heir may be applied in the first instance to the payment of the debt.

That the legal personal representative of the first testator must therefore be joined in a suit brought in this court by a creditor against the heirs, seems to be universally acknowleged.

¶4   So far as the question whether the personal estate must be pursued into other hands than the legal representative depends upon principle, it is urged that one of the reasons on which the rule was adopted applies with equal force to its extension so far as to require that the personal fund should be exhausted before recourse is had to the real.

¶5   In a court of equity the effects of the testator may be pursued into the hands of every person whatever; and all those who hold any portion of his estate may be brought before the court in the same suit. If the executor must be brought into court because among other reasons he would be responsible to the heir so any person possessing the personal fund, who would be responsible to the heir, and who can be brought into court ought for the same reason to be associated with him in the suit. It is equitable & convenient that the person who must ultimately pay the debt should be decreed to pay it in the first instance.

For the plaintiff it is contended that the creditor having a legal ¶6 right to pursue the heir equity will respect that right, and will only impose upon him when he comes into this court such conditions as are reasonable, and as will not injure his rights.

The legal representative may be brought before the court without ¶7 much delay or inconvenience, but if he is compelled to go beyond the legal representative, if the various intricate & multiplied questions which must be settled in determining on whom and in what proportions the debt is ultimately to be paid, are all to be discussed before he receives a debt acknowledged to be due, and to pay which adequate funds are acknowleged to be in the hands of the debtors, he will experience delays which are incalculable and thus the rule of equity will work a real wrong to a person possessing a plain title both in law and equity.

These arguments on both sides are entitled to great respect, and a ¶8 course of decisions the one way or the other might be defended by reasons perfectly satisfactory. In which ever way the principle may have been settled there are no inducements for shaking the decisions which have been made.

The case from 3d. Adkyns lays down the general rule as it has been ¶9 stated.[2] But that case contemplates the general rule under its usual circumstances only; not when it comes in conflict with other principles which are also regarded. Lord Hardwicke contemplated meerly the legal personal representative of the deceased, and the case put is the case of both an heir and executor legally accountable to the creditor. The personal fund under such circumstances must be first exhausted. But what the opinion of Lord Hardwicke would have been where the personal fund was not in the hands of the legal representative cannot be asserted from the case in Atkyns.

The case cited from 3d. P. W. is of the same character with that ¶10 from 3d. Atk.[3] It lays down the general principle so far as respects the heir and executor. The reason given for the principle would certainly favor strongly the argument on the part of the heirs. A court of equity said the Chancellor delights to do complete justice, and not by halves: As first to decree against the heir, and then to put the heir upon another bill against the executor to reimburse himself out of the personal assets. Where the executor and heir are both brought before the court complete justice may be done by decreeing against the executor so far as the personal assets extend; the rest to be made good by the heir out of the real assets.[4]

¶11 These expressions are it is true precisely applicable to the case at bar. But the counsel who produced this case has very correctly observed that general principles declared in a particular case must be taken with some reference to the case in which they are declared. The mind of the Judge is fixed upon the circumstances of the case before him, and the abstract principles he lays down must receive some limitation from these circumstances. The words of the Chancellor which follow those that have been quoted seem to give this argument a peculiar application to the case from P. Williams. "And here says Lord Talbot appears no difficulty or inconvenience in bringing the executor before the court."[5] This observation seems to warrant the opinion that Lord Talbot would have allowed weight to arguments drawn from the difficulty or inconvenience of pursuing the personal fund.

¶12 The principles laid down in the books of practice respecting the necessary parties to a bill are drawn from particular decisions which are referred to. It is laid down in those books that all persons materially interested in the subject of a suit ought to be parties to it, and an instance put in illustration of this rule is that of a bill against the heir alone where the personal estate is first liable for the demand. The case from 3d. P. W. is referred to as authority for this rule, and that case relates to the legal representative.

¶13 But how are the representatives of the real or personal estate of W. Ronald interested in the subject of this suit. They are neither concerned in the demand nor interested in the releif prayed. Their responsability can neither be increased nor diminished by any decree which is rendered in it. In the common case of the heir & executor the claim of the heir on the personal estate may depend on the establishment of the debt against the real estate. In such a case as this the representatives of William Ronald owe a certain sum for which they are liable whether this claim be established or not. Upon the ground of interest then there can be no necessity for making them parties—it is only on the principle that they must ultimately account to the heir and therefore ought to be brought in the first instance before the court. This restores the original question how far and into what hands the creditor is obliged to pursue the personal estate.

¶14 It appears to have been frequently decided that he must exhaust it in the hands of the legal personal representative, but never that he is compellable to pursue it into the hands of others. Yet in the infinite variety of situations into which personal assets are thrown it is scarcely conceivable that cases have not occurred where the heir was sued and the personal estate was not exhausted in a legal course of administration though nothing should remain in the hands of its legal representative. The reasoning however for extending the principles laid down respecting the personal fund to the case of its being found in the hands of a person who may be considered as the equitable though not the legal representative, is very strong and the court would have been relieved by finding that authorities relied on against so extending it were decisive.

The case from equity cases abridged which is reported in Viner is an express case of a decree against lands in the first instance, leaving the heir to pursue the personal estate.[6] ¶15

It is said that the decree being given without its circumstances, it must be supposed that the personal estate was absolutely exhausted. This may have been the fact but certainly it cannot be assumed as a fact. If the presumption was absolutely necessary to account for the decree it would be made, but to pronounce it absolutely necessary presupposes what is to be proved—that the law is with the defendants. ¶16

But this case was decided twenty years before that reported by P. W. & 4 years before that reported by Atkyns.[7] The probability therefore is that it was decided before the principle that the personal estate should be first applied in case of the real, and that the creditor should not be at liberty to resort directly to the heir leaving him to take his remedy against the executor was firmly established. This consideration certainly deducts from the authority of that case. ¶17

The case from 3d. Vesey jr. is a question respecting the order in which the real fund shall be applied by a court of equity without containing any instructions as to the necessity of pursuing the personal estate into other hands than those of the legal representative before the creditor can resort to the real.[8] The sentiment with which the case closes relates to the absolute final rights of parties, not to the necessity of proceding against all persons who may be made liable or to the right of electing to confine the suit to those who are immediately liable without joining those who may be afterwards accountable. ¶18

The case from 2d. Vesey jr. is a meer question of intention in the construction of a will. In deciding that question the chancellor says "the court affords an equity to a person entitled to a real estate by devise to have the incumbrances upon it discharged as a debt out of the personal.[9] That can go no farther than this; as between the heir or devisee of the estate and the residuary legatee. It cannot interfere with the disposition of other parts as specific or general legacies, much less with the interests of creditors."[10] ¶19

The counsel for the plf. understands this declaration as relating to the right of the creditor to pursue one fund or the other singly at his election. The court does not so understand it. The question there was ¶20 whether the devisee of a mortgaged estate might resort to the personal estate for its exoneration. The court declares this right to be limited to the case of a residuary legatee and not to extend to the cases of specific or general legacies, much less to the case of a creditor—That is where the personal fund is necessary for the payment of debts.

¶21   No case then has been cited from the english books which is an express authority for this case.

¶22   It has already been suggested that the very circumstance of there being no case in which it has been decided that the personal fund must be pursued into other hands than those of the legal representative is a strong argument against its being necessary. The court of equity has introduced a principle which limits the legal right of the creditor to elect the fund to which he will resort. That principle has only been carried to a certain extent and if extending it farther would impair complete & perfect rights there is reason to suppose those courts will not extend it farther. With respect to the creditor, unless it be for his advantage, the personal estate may be said to be exhausted when there are no longer assets in the hands of the executor.

¶23   Altho the english authorities do not reach the case the decision of this court in the case of Main & Murray is supposed to comprehend it. On inspecting the demurrer in that case it appears not perfectly clear whether this question was fully before the court or not. The devisees alledge themselves not to be responsible for the malversation of the executors of James Murray the devisor. And this would seem to involve the point. Gentlemen who were concerned in it can best say how far this question was brought before the court.[11]

¶24   This court at present inclines to consider it as an authority, but if on a more minute investigation it should not be so, still the court is not inclined in a case where the controversy between those into whose hands the personal estate has passed, is so intricate, diversified and complicated, to extend the principle further than it ever has been extended & postpone the creditor till their disputes shall be settled.

¶25   In the case of W Ronalds admr. question should be settled in appeals.[12]

AD, Marshall Judicial Opinions, PPAmP; printed, John W. Brockenbrough, *Reports of Cases Decided by the Honourable John Marshall . . .* , I (Philadelphia, 1837), 79–85. For JM's deletions and interlineations, see Textual Notes below.

1. Brockenbrough cited "2 Powell on Mortgages, 777–78," a reference to the fourth edition of John Joseph Powell's *A Treatise on the Law of Mortgages* (2 vols.; London, 1797). The passage referred to by JM can be found in the first American edition (2 vols. in 1; New Haven, Conn., 1807), 808–10. Powell noted that down to the time of Henry IV an heir sued on the bond of his ancestor might plead "assets in the hands of

the executor the day of the writ purchased." Since the time of Edward IV, however, this plea was no longer considered good.

2. Brockenbrough inserted a note in the manuscript and in the printed report citing this case: Madox v. Jackson, 3 Atk. 406, 26 Eng. Rep. 1034 (Ch., 1746). A bond creditor sued the principal debtor and the representative of one of the two sureties, his bill stating that the second surety died insolvent. It was objected that the representative of the second surety should have been made a party. Lord Chancellor Hardwicke overruled the objection, declaring that this was a "special excepted case" not falling within the general rule that required the plaintiff to bring all the debtors before the court.

3. Knight v. Knight, 3 P. Wms. 331, 24 Eng. Rep. 1088 (Ch., 1734), cited by Brockenbrough in the printed report. This was a suit for the performance of a covenant brought against the heir, who demurred on the ground that no executor or administrator of the debtor had been made a party. Lord Chancellor Talbot allowed the demurrer.

4. JM here paraphrased Talbot's opinion (3 P. Wms. 334, 24 Eng. Rep. 1089).

5. Ibid.

6. Duncombe v. Hansley, 2 Eq. Ca. Abr. 169, 22 Eng. Rep. 145 (Ch., 1720), cited by Brockenbrough in the printed report. A mortgagee brought a bill against the heir of a mortgagor to foreclose. The court overruled an objection that the executor of the mortgagor ought to be made a party. As JM noted, this case was also abstracted in Charles Viner's *A General Abridgment of Law and Equity* . . . (22 vols.; [n.p.], 1742–53).

7. JM was mistaken as to the dates of the cases. Duncombe v. Hansley was decided in 1720; Knight v. Knight in 1734; and Madox v. Jackson in 1746.

8. Manning v. Spooner, 3 Ves. 114, 30 Eng. Rep. 923 (Ch., 1796), cited by Brockenbrough in the printed report. This was a suit between the devisees and heir over whether the devised or descended estate was first liable for payment of the debt. The court declared that the testator might "arrange between his heir and devisee; but not so as to take away from the creditor a fund, he has a right come upon" (3 Ves. 118–19, 30 Eng. Rep. 925).

9. JM mistakenly placed close quotation marks here as well as at the end of the paragraph where they belong.

10. Hamilton v. Worley, 2 Ves. jun. 62, 30 Eng. Rep. 523 (Ch., 1793), cited by Brockenbrough in the printed report. The quotation is from Lord Chancellor Loughborough's opinion (2 Ves. jun. 65, 30 Eng. Rep. 525).

11. Brockenbrough inserted this note in the manuscript: "Demurrer *overruled* at Nov: Term 1799, by Judge Washington." This unreported case was Thomas Main, executor of John Hyndman, surviving partner of James Buchanan & Co. v. William Murray, executor of John Murray and administrator of James Murray, Edmund Harrison and Mary his Wife, and William Davies and Mary his Wife. Judge Bushrod Washington on 4 Dec. 1799 overruled the demurrer of defendants Davies and his wife, declaring that the assets of James Murray in the hands of the devisees were subject in equity to the plaintiff's demand. This was an interlocutory decree in a suit that was finally concluded in Dec. 1802 (bill, answer, and demurrer, Hyndman's Executor v. Murray, U.S. Cir. Ct., Va., Ended Cases [Unrestored], 1802, Vi; U.S. Cir. Ct., Va., Ord. Bk. III, 191, 322–23; IV, 257–58).

12. The decree accompanying this opinion ordered the defendants to convey a tract of land in Chesterfield County along with lots and warehouses in the town of Manchester in trust for the purpose of receiving and paying over the rents and ultimately to sell those properties for cash to discharge the debt. The court also gave leave to the plaintiff to amend his bill by adding other defendants, including the heirs of Andrew Ronald and heirs and administrators of William Ronald.

After the filing of an amended bill, a further decree on 14 June 1806 ordered the heirs of William Ronald to pay over a large sum of money by 1 Jan, 1807; otherwise, the land descended to them would be sold for the purpose. The records show that the plaintiffs also instituted a separate suit against the securities of William Bentley as administrator of William Ronald and against one of the securities of William Ronald as executor of Edward Johnson. The debt still had not been fully paid in 1825, when a bill of revivor was filed naming a large number of additional parties defendant. The suit was apparently dismissed at the June 1827 term, the complainants failing to give security for costs (amended bill, bill of revivor, Corbet v. Johnson; U.S. Cir. Ct., Va., Ord. Bk. V, 147–48, 231–32, 336, 360–62; XII, 194–95).

Textual Notes

¶ 1   ll. 3–4   before ↑the↓ lands shall be ~~subjected to~~ ↑applied to the satisfaction of↓ his

¶ 2   l. 1   law [*erasure*] ↑he↓ has

      l. 7   plea ↑in bar↓ to an

¶ 3   l. 3   that the ~~personal estate is the first and proper~~ executor

      l. 4   rule ~~three~~ ↑two↓ reasons

      l. 6   reembursement ~~may~~ would

      l. 10   by ~~the~~ a creditor

¶ 4   l. 3   that ↑one of↓ the reasons

¶ 5   l. 4   executor ~~will be decreed~~ must

¶ 6   l. 3   him ↑when he comes into this court↓ such

      l. 4   and ↑as↓ will not

¶ 7   ll. 1–2   without ↑much↓ delay

      l. 3   various ↑intricate & multiplied↓ questions

      l. 5   paid, ~~must~~ ↑are↓ all ↑to↓ be

¶ 8   ll. 1–2   and ~~the~~ a course

¶ 9   l. 2   stated. [*erasure*] ↑But↓ that

      l. 10   case [*erasure*] ↑in↓ ~~Adkyns.~~ ↑Atkyns.↓

¶10   ll. 2–3   principle ~~in~~ ↑so far as respects↓ the

      l. 10   so far as ~~he has~~ ↑the personal↓ assets

¶11   l. 1   are ↑it is true↓ precisely

      l. 6   and the ↑abstract↓ principles

¶12   ll. 1–2   the ↑necessary↓ parties

      l. 8   case ~~refers~~ ↑relates↓ to the legal representative ~~only.~~

¶13   l. 1   how ~~is~~ ↑are↓ the

      ll. 5–6   executor the ~~right~~ ↑claim↓ of the heir ~~to~~ ↑on↓ the

      l. 10   then ~~they have~~ ↑there can be↓ no

      l. 13   far ~~the~~ and

¶14   l. 4   situations in ↑to↓ which

      l. 6   not ~~so~~ exhausted

      l. 7   of ~~the~~ ↑its↓ legal

      l. 8   reasoning ~~founded on analogy is certainly~~ ↑however for extending↓ the

      l. 9   personal ~~estate~~ fund

      ll. 9–10   being ↑found↓ [*erasure*] ↑in↓ the hands of a person who ~~is~~ ↑may be considered as↓ the ll. 11–12   the ↑court would have been [*erasure*] releived by finding that↓ authorities

ll. 12–13   against [*erasure*] ↑so↓ extending it ~~must be examined.~~ were decisive.

¶15   l. 3   heir to ~~his recourse~~ ↑pursue the↓ personal

¶17   l. 1 beg.   ~~This~~ ↑But this↓ case was decided ↑twenty years↓ before ~~those~~ ↑that↓ reported

l. 2   Atkyns. ~~It~~ [*erasure*] ↑The↓ probability

¶18   l. 1   case ~~of~~ ↑from↓ 3d. Vesey

ll. 2–3   equity [*erasure*] ↑without↓ containing

l. 4   than ↑those of↓ the

¶19   l. 1   intention ~~on~~ ↑in↓ the

¶20   l. 4   the [*erasure*] ↑devisee↓ of

¶21   l. 1   been ~~deci~~ cited ↑from the english books↓ which

¶22   l. 2   which [*erasure*] ↑it↓ has

l. 3   must be ~~ex~~ pursued

l. 6   which [*erasure*] ↑he↓ will

ll. 7–8   it ~~further~~ ↑farther↓ would ~~enforce~~ ↑impair↓ complete

ll. 8–9   suppose ~~the~~ ↑those↓ courts will not extend it ~~to further~~ farther.↓ With

¶23   l. 1 beg.   [*erasure*] Altho

l. 6   Murray ~~their testator~~ ↑the devisor.↓ And

l. 7   who [*erasure*] ↑were↓ concerned

¶24   l. 1 beg.   ~~The~~ ↑This↓ court ↑at present↓ inclines

l. 3   inclined ~~to carry~~[?] in a case

l. 4   has [*erasure*] passed,

ll. 5–6   to ↑extend the principle further than it ever has been extended &↓ postpone

¶25   l. 1   Ronalds ~~exrs.~~ admr.

Dunbar v. Miller, Hart & Company
Opinion
U.S. Circuit Court, Virginia, 11 June 1805

EDITORIAL NOTE

This case arose from the business dealings between Robert Dunbar, a merchant residing in Falmouth, and the London firm of Miller, Hart & Company, whose partners were James R. Miller, Patrick Hart, and William McClure. The London merchants obtained a judgment against Dunbar at the November 1800 term of this court for seventy-eight hundred dollars, the balance due on a promissory note, dated 28 June 1796, which Dunbar had executed in settlement of his account. Annexed to this note was Dunbar's memorandum stating that he should be credited for fifty-eight hogsheads of tobacco consigned to Miller, Hart & Company in September 1793, for which he had not received an account of sales. The account ultimately rendered showed that the tobacco was sold at a great loss. At the law trial, the court ruled that Dunbar could not at common law maintain that Miller, Hart & Company, by shipping the tobacco to France in a time of war, had violated Dunbar's instructions. Unable to offset the claim for tobacco against the promissory note, Dunbar in March 1801 applied to the chancery side of the court and obtained an injunction to stay execution of judgment. After depositions and a report from the chancery commissioner were returned, Marshall on 11 June 1805 delivered his opinion and decree on a motion to dissolve the injunction.[1]

1. U.S. Cir. Ct., Va., Ord. Bk. III, 343, 458, 471–72; IV, 267, 388; V, 158; Dunbar v. Miller, Hart & Co., U.S. Cir. Ct., Va., Ended Cases (Unrestored), 1806, Vi.

Dunbar
 v   } injn.
Miller Hart & Co

¶1 The principal question in this case is, What credit is the compt. entitled to for the tobacco consigned by him to M. H & Co. in Septr. 93. In discussing this question he has made two points

1st.   That in shipping the tobo. to France his orders were violated in consequence of which the consignees are responsible for its value.

2dly.   That the account of sales they now render ought not to bind him.

The nature of the trade between the Consignor & Consignee of tobo. requires that a great degree of confidence should be placed by the former in the intelligence and integrity of the latter. He is frequently empowered to choose the market in which the commodoty is to be disposed of. This arises from the circumstance that his situation enables him to decide on the interests of the consignor, with better information than the consignor can decide for himself. A great latitude is therefore allowed for the exercise of his judgement, but it must be exercised within the limits prescribed by the consignor, or where he is silent, within those prescribed by custom.

¶2   In the case at bar the limits prescribed by the consignor are to be looked for in the two letters of the 5th. & 19th. of September. The letter of the 5th. contains the proposition of the consignee.[1] He offers to receive consignments to M. H. & Co in the Molly. This vessel he says "goes to Cork for orders and from thence to any one port of europe out of the streights."

¶3   This is a plain intelligible proposition which authorised the consignee to order the vessel to France or elsewhere in europe provided it was not into the Mediterranean. It is observable that Mr. Hart then proceeds to state the advantage which Mr. Dunbar might derive from accepting it before he advances any opinion respecting the probably particular destination of the vessel. This is a circumstance which may not be entirely immaterial. It may serve to show that in the opinion of the writer the principal proposition was stated. After recommending a shipment in the vessel whose orders were to be received at Cork, and whose destination from thence was to depend on the discretion of the partners in Europe Mr. Hart proceeds to say something respecting the manner in which this discretion would probably be exercised. "If, says he, peace is not established in France by the time the Molly arrives at Cork, it is most probable she will be sent to Rotterdam or some port in Holland.["] It is contended on one side that this amounts to a declaration that the tobo. will not be sent to France if the war should continue. On the other side that this is meerly a conjecture respecting the manner in which the discretion of the consignee would be exercised with out forming a limitation of that discretion.

With the proposition is to be taken into view the declaration of the sense in which it was accepted. For this purpose the court is referred to the letter of the 19th. of September.[2] This was after the tobo. had been put on board the craft; but as no intermediate letter is produced on either side it is presumed that none passed which would affect the case. In the letter of the 19th. of Septr. Mr. Dunbar says "I hope the tobo. will get to a saving market, as the quality is well suited to the Dutch where I expect it will ultimately go as appearances I conceive strongly indicate a continuance of the war." ¶4

That both parties beleived the Molly would not be ordered to France should the war c⟨on⟩tinue is apparent, but whether either of them designed to prohibit the members of M. H & Co from giving such orders if in their judgement it should be for the benefit of the cargo to give them is not so clear. ¶5

Throwing the two letters into the form of an agreement & construing that agreement literally, the express power given to order the Molly to any port in Europe out of the streights would not be restricted by any express declaration that the right to send her to France depended on the restoration of peace. ¶6

But there is great weight in the argument that in mercantile transactions of this sort the impressions made by the communications between the parties ought to be considered, and if a meaning is fairly and justly to be implied from them which the words themselves if digested into a formal agreement would not completely bear, that meaning ought not to be disregarded by the court. ¶7

Altho the letter written by Mr. Hart reserves to his partners the ¶8 power of ordering the Molly to any port in europe, and does not positively restrict their exercise of this power with regard to France to the contingency of peace, yet its terms are such as clearly to convey the opinion that the tobacco would not be sent to France but on that contingency. "If says he peace is not established in France by the time the Molly arrives at Cork it is most probable she will be sent to Rotterdam or some port in Holland.["] This reference with respect to France to the single contingency of peace, unconnected with the state of the market, shows that in the mind of the writer her being ordered to France would depend on that contingency only. It might certainly be fairly so understood by Mr. Dunbar. In strict prudence the complainant ought to have observed the equivocal expressions of the proposition and ought to have objected to the sending of his tobacco to France unless peace should be reestablished; but if he understood that the general power was reserved solely for the purpose of being exercised in its extent, in the event of peace; and he might so understand the letter, he may be excused for not directing that which M. H & Co. had declared themselves previously to have resolved on.

¶9   It is beleived that no person can read that letter without a conviction that at the time of writing it Mr. Hart considered it as perfectly certain that the Molly would not be ordered to France if the war should continue. The letter would not be a fair one if such had not been his opinion. That Mr. Dunbar did beleive the possibility of the power he gave being so exercised as to occasion the tobo. to be shipped to a port in France depended on peace is strongly to be inferred from his letter of the 19th. of September. The whole context of that letter shows it.

¶10   These communications then are to be viewed as an agreement by which the tobacco is consigned to M. H. & Co. with a general power to ship it from Cork to any port of Europe out of the streights. But the application for that general power is accompanied with a representation of the manner in which it is to be exercised, which might well be understood, and which most probably was understood as a declaration that the vessel would only be sent to France on the contingency of peace. Whether this representation is so strong as to charge the consignee with the loss occasioned by sending the vessel to Havre pending the war is a point not absolutely decided by the court because there is another part of the case which renders its decision unnecessary.

¶11   The agreement under which the tobo. was shipped might be understood in the one way or the other. If in the opinion of Mr. Dunbar the consignees had transcended their powers, and he did not mean to abide by their conduct it is perfectly clear that on mercantile principles he should on notice of what they had done, have declared to them that the responsibility of their conduct rested on themselves, that the tobacco was theirs and that he claimed a credit for its reasonable value at those ports to which in conformity with the contract they might have shipped it. He was certainly not at liberty to reserve to himself the power of taking or rejecting the sales at Havre at his discretion; but his silence on the subject, if not an approbation of their conduct, is an acquiescence under it.

It has been contended that this transaction was not communicated to Mr. Dunbar; but the fact will not support his counsel in this respect. His bill admits a knowlege of it when his note was given. (see middle of 2d. page)[3]   ¶12

Had the pressure of Mr. Dunbars circumstances been such as to leave him not a free agent in this respect the court would not have considered his silence as a waiver of his right to object to the shipment of his tobacco to Havre. But this is not pretended. His silence therefore can only be attributed to one of two motives. Either he chose to take the chance of a favorable account of sales, or which is more probable, he expected that the loss would not be considerable & preferred a submission to it to a rupture with his friends & Creditors. Let this be his motive & it will not support him in the attempt now made. If then silence had been observed on the part of Mr. Dunbar he would have been precluded from objecting to the act of sending the Molly to Havre. But he has not been silent. The memorandum at the foot of his note, is a complete relinquishment of all objection to that transaction so far as a relinquishment can be implied.[4]   ¶13

This memorandum is said to have been made for his advantage: and this is true. But what was the advantage he expected to derive from it? Clearly only this. It proves that from the note was to be deducted the tobacco when the account of sales should be received. Why refer to the account of sales if he did not mean to admit that he was to be bound by them? Why not claim an immediate instead of a future credit if the invoice price or any other known standard ascertained the credit to which he was entitled?   ¶14

The subsequent correspondence on which the plfs[5] rely is certainly equivocal in its expression. But when the fact that Mr. Dunbar had full knowlege of the Molly having been ordered to France is ascertained, that correspondence ceases to be equivocal. It relates exclusively to the circumstance that the sum for which Mr. Dunbar ought to be credited on account of this tobo. is uncertain.   ¶15

The court then is perfectly satisfied that the orders given the Molly to sail for Havre are sanctioned by the subsequent conduct of Mr. Dunbar, after having full notice of the fact.   ¶16

To the account of sales which has been returned the objections are to the commissions and to the compromise. With respect to the com-   ¶17 missions, the court has required information respecting the custom & has stated an opinion that only half commissions is chargeable in such cases. If there be no custom, the court will direct that only half commissions be allowed in this case.[6]

¶18 With respect to the compromise, the circumstances under which it was made and the deposition of Mr. Colquhon satisfy the court that it was prudent to compromise the claim.[7] The power of the consignees probably extended to a compromise unless it was the will of the consignor to take the transaction into his own hands. The court perceive no such disposition in him.

¶19 Yet under the circumstances of this case it is the opinion of the court that M. H. & Co ought to explain to the plf. the terms & principles of the compromise. There is so little probability that the transaction has been unfair that the court will not continue the injunction on that account but will retain the suit on the docket if it be requested.

¶20 The accounts between the parties constitute the next subject of consideration.

¶21 The court is of opinion that any errors which may have existed in dealings carried on under the circumstances in which these parties were placed ought to be corrected. It does not appear clearly that a formal & complete settlement has ever taken place. The accounts were conducted under so many different forms as to contribute something to the opinion that they have never been completely adjusted; and the early application of Mr. Dunbar on the subject weakens the argument drawn from the time which has elapsed since accounts have been rendered.[8]

¶22 With respect to the credit claimed for difference in exchange, the arguments of the defendents themselves if rightly understood are in favor of it to a certain extent.[9] The payments made before the judgement ought certainly to be credited according to agreement at the current rate of exchange. The balance for which judgement was rendered ought not to be affected by the exchange.

¶23 Credit the plf for the account of sales
adding half commissions to the amount— } —

¶24 for the difference of exchange on
payments before judgement

¶25 For the balance appearing on
the commrs. report—

¶26   dissolve as to the residue[10]

AD, Marshall Judicial Opinions, PPAmP; printed, John W. Brockenbrough, *Reports of Cases Decided by the Honourable John Marshall . . .* , I (Philadelphia, 1837), 90–96. For JM's deletions and interlineations, see Textual Notes below.

1. The original letter of Patrick Hart, one of the partners of Miller, Hart & Co., to Dunbar, dated 5 Sept. 1793, is in the case papers and is reproduced in Brockenbrough's report (Dunbar v. Miller, Hart & Co.; 1 Brock. 87–88).

2. Dunbar's reply, dated 19 Sept. 1793, is in the case papers; the report includes the quoted passage (Dunbar v. Miller, Hart & Co.; 1 Brock. 88).

3. JM referred to a passage on the second page of Dunbar's bill in chancery, which reads: "Your Orator was dissatisfied with the application for a note without credit for the Tobacco, and considers that in consequence of its being sent to France without his consent or knowledge & contrary to the understanding aforesaid, that he had a right to charge Miller Hart & Co. with it, & to refuse a note 'till credit either by the Invoice price, or sale, was given" (bill in chancery, 11 Mar. 1801, Dunbar v. Miller, Hart & Co.). This passage, as JM observed, showed that Dunbar knew the tobacco had been shipped to France at the time he gave his note in June 1796.

4. Dunbar's memorandum (reproduced in the report along with the promissory note of 28 June 1796) reads: "N. B. 58 hogsheads tobacco, weighing 66,503 lbs., shipped Miller, Hart & Co., in Sept. '93, per the Molly, Capt. Sanford, for which sales are not received, to be accounted for, and to be deducted from the above note when received account of sales appear" (Dunbar v. Miller, Hart & Co.; 1 Brock. 87).

5. Brockenbrough changed this to "defendants," correcting what he believed to be JM's error. It appears, however, that JM was referring to Dunbar and should have used the singular "plaintiff." Some ambiguity remains nonetheless.

6. The account of sales, dated London, 31 Jan. 1803, left a balance in favor of Dunbar of £142.4 after deducting freight, interest, and commission. The commission charged was 21s. per hogshead, amounting to £60.18 (Dunbar v. Miller, Hart & Co.).

7. The deposition of James Colquhoun, of the London firm of James & Robert Colquhoun, was taken on 24 July 1804 and is summarized in the report. Colquhoun testified that his firm agreed with Miller, Hart & Co. to send the *Molly* to Havre, as being the best market in Europe. The tobacco was consigned to Teray & Co. of Havre. After much delay, Colquhoun late in 1802 consented to compromise on behalf of his firm with Teray & Co. (Dunbar v. Miller, Hart & Co.; 1 Brock. 89).

8. Dunbar asserted that Patrick Hart owed him more than a thousand dollars on an old private account, which should be credited against the law judgment. This private account was referred to a commissioner, who reported a balance in Dunbar's favor of £287 Virginia currency (bill in chancery, 11 Mar. 1801, commissioner's report, 3 June 1805, Dunbar v. Miller, Hart & Co.).

9. Dunbar claimed a credit of $383 for the difference on the rate of exchange between Virginia currency and sterling (bill in chancery, 11 Mar. 1801, Dunbar v. Miller, Hart & Co.).

10. The extended decree was entered in the order book on this day. It made the injunction perpetual as to $1,498, the sum of the credits arising from the account of sales, adding the half commissions, the difference in the rate of exchange, and the balance in Dunbar's favor in the report of the commissioner.

On the same day the court granted Dunbar's motion to appeal. At the May 1806 term, the court ordered the bill to be dismissed except that part embraced in the decree of 11 June 1805 (U.S. Cir. Ct., Va., Ord. Bk. V, 158, 160, 272).

Textual Notes

¶ 1	l. 1	is, [*erasure*] ↑What↓ credit
	ll. 5–6	for ~~the~~ ↑its↓ value.
	ll. 7–8	to ~~be regarded.~~ bind him.
	l. 9 beg.	~~The~~ [*erasure*] ~~in~~ The
	l. 9	between the ~~American & British Merchs~~ Consignor
	ll. 11–13	latter. ~~This is peculiarly the case where the consignee is~~ ↑He is frequently empowered↓ to choose the market ~~at~~ ↑in↓ which the commodoty is [*erasure*] ↑to be↓ disposed of.
	ll. 13–14	situation ~~& information~~ enables
¶ 3	l. 4	advantage which ~~M~~ ↑which↓ Mr.
	l. 7	It ↑may↓ serve~~s~~ to show
	ll. 8–9	recommending ~~the~~ a shipment
	l. 10	thence ↑was to↓ depend~~s~~ on
	l. 13	in ~~Europe~~ France
	l. 16	be ~~sold~~ ↑sent↓ to France
¶ 4	l. 4	craft; ~~for~~ but
	l. 5	presumed ↑that↓ none
	l. 6	says "~~he~~[?] ↑I↓ hope
¶ 5	l. 2	France ↑should the war c⟨on⟩tinue↓ is
¶ 6	l. 1 beg.	~~Placing~~ ↑Throwing↓ the
	l. 3	Europe ↑out of the streights↓ would
	l. 4	that the [*erasure*] ↑right↓ to
¶ 7	ll. 2–3	communications ↑between the parties↓ ought
	l. 4	from ~~the letters of the parties~~ ↑communications↓ ↑them↓ which
	l. 5	not ↑completely↓ bear,
¶ 8	l. 1 beg.	~~The~~ ↑Altho the↓ letter written by Mr. Hart ~~might be understood as reserving~~ ↑reserves↓ to
	l. 8	Holland.["] [*erasure*] ↑This↓ reference
	l. 9	to the ↑single↓ contingency
	l. 12	Dunbar. [*erasure*] ↑In↓ strict
	l. 13	observed the ~~enti~~[?] equivocal
	l. 14	to the ~~vesse~~ sending
	ll. 16–17	reserved ~~, to be~~ ↑solely for the purpose of being↓ exercised
	l. 18	letter ~~it would be unnecess~~, he
	ll. 18–19	which ~~was~~ M. H & Co.
¶10	l. 1	to be ~~received~~[?] ↑viewed↓ as an
¶11	l. 3	powers, ~~it is perfectly that on~~ and he
¶13	ll. 5–6	he ~~hoped to have~~ ↑chose to take the chance of↓ a favorable account of sales, ~~& chose~~ or which
	l. 9	not ~~justify~~ ↑support↓ him
¶17	l. 1	returned the ~~court see no other~~ objections
¶18	ll. 3–4	consignees ↑probably↓ extended
	ll. 4–5	consignor ~~that he should~~ to take
¶21	l. 3	appear ↑clearly↓ that
¶22	l. 1	to the ~~exe~~ credit
¶23	l. 2	adding ↑half↓ commissions

———— v. Lewis's Executors
Opinion
U.S. Circuit Court, North Carolina, [15–21 June 1805]

PER Curiam.[1] The act of 1715, whilst it was unrepealed, was suspended from its usual operation by the acts disqualifying British adherents to sue in our courts. It did not begin to operate as to such persons till the end of the war, and then if the seven years were not completed before it was repealed by the act of 1789, no bar could ever be operated under it.[2] Lewis, the testator, died in 1780; between the end of the war and 1789, were not seven years. The demurrer to the plea, stating these facts, and relying upon the act of 1715, must be allowed.

Printed, John Haywood, *Cases Adjudged in the Superior Courts . . . of North Carolina*, II (Raleigh, N.C., 1806), 347.

1. No case brought against Lewis's executors appears in the minutes of this term, which ran from 15 to 21 June.

2. In Ogden v. Blackledge, JM held that the 1715 act of limitations was repealed by that enacted in 1789, an opinion that was confirmed by the Supreme Court. During the war, the state legislature passed a law disabling British sympathizers from suing in the state courts. In the earlier opinion, JM said the disabling act suspended the operation of the statute of limitations until 1787, when the legislature declared the treaty of peace to be part of the law of the land (Opinion, 5 Jan. 1803; 2 Cranch 272 [1804]; *First Laws of North Carolina*, I, 325; II, 607).

Buchanan, Dunlop & Company v. West
Opinion
U.S. Circuit Court, North Carolina, 17 June 1805

PER Curiam. If the Sheriff or Marshal[1] seizes property in execution, and neglects to sell it, and is sued for his neglect, the plaintiff shall recover damages, to the amount of what the property would have produced, had he sold it.[2]

Printed, John Haywood, *Cases Adjudged in the Superior Courts . . . of North Carolina*, II (Raleigh, N.C., 1806), 346.

1. The defendant, John West, was U.S. marshal for the district of North Carolina.

2. The jury on this day found for the plaintiff and assessed damages. A motion for a new trial was overruled (U.S. Cir. Ct., N.C., Min. Bk., 17, 20 June 1805).

Granville's Devisee v. Allen
Remarks
U.S. Circuit Court, North Carolina, 18 June 1805

The Chief Justice[1] gave no opinion upon the motion,[2] nor does he intend to deliver one on the main question. He stated from the bench his reasons for thus declining: saying, that at a former term he enquired of the counsel if this case depended upon a construction of the treaty of peace; that if it did, he should give no opinion, because he had formed an opinion upon that subject so firmly, that he did not believe he could change it; and as that opinion was formed when he was very deeply interested (alluding to the cause of Lord Fairfax in Virginia) he should feel much delicacy in deciding the present question:[3] but upon being informed that the treaty of peace would make no part of the case, he felt himself freed from that delicacy and intended to deliver his opinion. It seemed, however, that upon the argument, the defence assumed the principle of alienage, thereby involving the case with the treaty of peace, and made that question an important point.[4] The only part of the case on which he entertained any doubt was the confiscation laws;[5] and as he could not satisfy himself that the plaintiff was included in those laws, he could not consistently with his duty and the delicacy he felt, give an opinion in the cause.[6]

Printed, *Raleigh Register, and North-Carolina State Gazette,* 24 June 1805.

1. This was an ejectment brought by George William, earl of Coventry, devisee of the earl of Granville, against Nathaniel Allen and Josiah Collins, to try title to the Granville District, an area extending southward approximately sixty miles from the Virginia border and running westward from the coast. This region represented one-eighth of the territory of the Carolinas originally granted by Charles II in 1663 to eight lords proprietors. All but one of the proprietors, John Carteret, relinquished their rights to the Crown in 1729. The one-eighth part retained by Carteret, later Earl Granville, was confirmed by a grant from George II in 1744. Granville, like Lord Fairfax in the Northern Neck of Virginia, appointed agents and opened an office to grant lands within the district to individuals. The ejectment against Allen and Collins, who held tracts within the district by grant from the state of North Carolina, aroused much public excitement. The suit was similar to those between Denny Fairfax and David Hunter brought in the state and federal courts of Virginia. See Henry G. Connor, "The Granville Estate and North Carolina," *University of Pennsylvania Law Review,* LXII (1914), 671–97; A. Roger Ekirch, *"Poor Carolina": Politics and Society in Colonial North Carolina, 1729–1776* (Chapel Hill, N.C., 1981), 127–47. On the Fairfax cases, see *PJM,* V, 228–56.

2. The motion was to discharge a demurrer to the defendants' evidence, which had been filed by counsel for Granville's devisee.

3. As a purchaser of the Fairfax estate, JM had been "deeply interested" in the dispute between Denny Fairfax and David Hunter. His opinion was that the Fairfax

title remained good during the Revolution and was protected by the sixth article of the treaty of peace, which stipulated that there should be no future confiscation of estates belonging to British subjects or sympathizers.

4. At common law an alien was incapable of purchasing or holding lands. If Granville's devisee was considered an alien—a disputed point—then his lands were liable to be escheated to the state of North Carolina. As JM suggested, this raised the question whether the treaty of peace protected the titles of British subjects born before the Revolution. See St. George Tucker's discussion of this point in his *Blackstone's Commentaries*, II, app., 53–65.

5. North Carolina enacted a number of confiscation laws during the war, some of which named the persons whose lands were to be confiscated. Granville's devisee was not mentioned in any of these acts; nor was there any record of escheat proceedings against his estate. Counsel for the defendants relied chiefly on the argument that Granville's title was not that of a private individual but of a public personage clothed with royalty. His title, like that of the crown, was therefore extinguished by the Revolution and vested in the collective body of the people of North Carolina (Connor, "Granville Estate," *University of Pennsylvania Law Review*, LXII [1914], 675–88).

6. Judge Potter overruled the demurrer and ordered the case to be tried at the next term. At the trial Potter delivered a lengthy charge instructing the jury to return a verdict for the defendants. The case was subsequently taken by writ of error to the Supreme Court, remaining on the docket until 1817, when it was dismissed for want of appearance by the plaintiff. The only judicial opinion rendered in this case was Judge Potter's charge to the jury, which was published in the Raleigh newspapers (U.S. Cir. Ct., N.C., Min. Bk., 3 Jan. 1806; Lessee of George William, Earl of Coventry, v. Josiah Collins, U.S. Sup. Ct. Dockets, App. Cas. No. 288; Raleigh *Minerva*, 13 Jan., 20 Jan. 1806; *Raleigh Register*, 20 Jan., 27 Jan. 1806).

Mutter's Executors v. Hamilton
Opinion
U.S. Circuit Court, North Carolina, 19 June 1805

Per Curiam. We will not grant an injunction so as to stay trial,[1] or entering up judgment; therefore this cause now ready for trial shall not be postponed, although the bill in equity which has been read, for obtaining an injunction, may contain matter enough to warrant the granting it.[2]

Printed, John Haywood, *Cases Adjudged in the Superior Courts . . . of North Carolina*, II (Raleigh, N.C., 1806), 346.

1. This was an action of covenant founded on articles of dissolution of the mercantile partnership between Thomas Mutter of Granville County and John Hamilton of Norfolk. Hamilton's lawyer had drawn up a bill in equity for an injunction before the law trial took place (bill in equity, ca. June 1805, Hamilton v. Mutter's Executors, GEpFRC).

2. After a jury found a verdict of covenants broken and not performed, Hamilton's counsel moved for and obtained an injunction to stay further proceedings. The injunc-

tion was dissolved at the Dec. 1805 term, but the equity action remained on the docket for some years (U.S. Cir. Ct., N.C., Min. Bk., 19, 20 June 1805, 2 Jan. 1806; Hamilton v. Mutter's Executors).

To Caleb P. Wayne

Sir   Richmond June 29th. 1805
I have just returned from North Carolina & have found your letter of the 13th. inst.[1]

I wish the books for Mr. Adams to be bound in the same manner with the two copies you sent to me, & I should also be obliged by your interlining with a pen the word "not," in the 8th. line of the 10th. page between the words "as" & "to."

I have not yet seen Freneaus papers, but hope they will soon reach this place.

I wish it could be practicable for you to alter the time for the return of the Aurora. I am now for my own health & that of my family about to make a tour to the mountains, whence I shall not return till October. If therefore the Aurora could reach this place by the middle of October it would be in time; & if the six months could be calculated from that time it would be a most desirable change.

As I cannot take the books & papers with me the work must be suspended till my return and it will be absolutely impossible to complete it by the time I mentioned to you. I regret this very seriously but it is a calamity for which there is no remedy.

I lament sincerely that an introductory volume was written because I find it almost impossible to compress the civil administration into a single volume. In doing it I shall be compelled to omit several interesting transactions & to mutilate others.

I shall leave directions for letters coming to this place to be sent after me, so that you may address to me in Richmond. I am Sir very respectfully, Your obedt. Servt

J MARSHALL

I open this letter to tell you that Freneaus papers have not reached Mr. Hopkins & that he wishes you to say in what manner & by whom they have been sent that enquiries may be made respecting them. Write to him on this subject.

A chest with many books which were necessary for me and with Fennos papers[2] sent from Mount Vernon has miscarried altogether & I can get no intelligence respecting it.

ALS, Dreer Collection, PHi; Tr, Marshall Papers, DLC. Addressed to Wayne at Philadelphia; postmarked Richmond, 3 July. Endorsed by Wayne.

1. Letter not found.
2. John Fenno's *Gazette of the U.S.*, a Federalist newspaper published in New York, 1789–90, and then in Philadelphia. After Fenno's death in 1798, his son continued publishing it until Wayne took it over in 1800.

To Mary W. Marshall

My dearest Polly   Richmond Septr. 27th 1805
    I reached this place yesterday & dined at your Mama's. I found her not so well as I had hoped. ⟨ . . . ⟩[1] She continues to ride out, & is I beleive recovered from a bilious attack. Your sister Carrington[2] is better & your other sisters are well. In your own family I beleive there is nothing amiss.
    At the oaks you will have received fifty dollars which Mr. Morgan promised to deliver you. I totally forgot to pay my brother Charles for Johns expences.[3] His schooling I beleive is five dollars: I do not know what else may be due for him.
    At my plantation I was very much vexed. Things are there very badly conducted. I am my dearest Polly, your ever affectionate
                                                        J MARSHALL

ALS, Collection of the Association for the Preservation of Virginia Antiquities, ViHi. Addressed to "Mrs. Mary W. Marshall/Fauquier Court house/care of Mr. Charles Marshall." Postmark illegible. MS mutilated (see n. 1).

1. Approximately one and a half lines have been clipped.
2. Elizabeth Ambler Carrington, older sister of Mary Marshall and wife of Edward Carrington.
3. JM's son John was then seven. Among a collection of miscellaneous memoranda and accounts kept by JM is a receipt from Robert Laughlin, dated 25 Dec. 1805, for the payment of the tuition of John and James Marshall (Collection of Mrs. James R. Green, Markham, Va.).

To Caleb P. Wayne

Sir   Richmond October 5th. 1805
    I have just recovered from a bilious intermittent which attacked me the day I reached this place, and am anxious to recommence my labors. In the intermission of the fever I wrote to Mr. Washington[1] &

requested him to make some communications to you, but as the fever of Philadelphia has, I learn, occasioned the adjournment of his court, I think it most probable that he will not see you.

In stating the foundation of those divisions which have taken place in the United States, & the first public symptoms of them Freneaus gazette will be indispensable. I do not know where a copy can be obtained unless that furnished you by Mr. Hopkins could be returned. I wrote to you on this subject last spring & did hope from the information you gave me that those papers would have been in possession of Mr. Hopkins in the course of the summer. I beleive they have not yet been received. Mr. Hopkins is not in town but I am persuaded he would have left them where I could have had access to them if they had been in his possession. I must beg you to forward them to me if possible, or if you have already sent them to let me know to whom they were confided & what intelligence you have respecting them.

The first files of the Aurora have not yet arrived. During my absence a box of papers sent from you was brought to my house, but the Captain took them away & I presume returned them to you.[2] I was pleased at this because I presumed it was for the purpose of saving the time of my absence from being a part of the time during which you might be allowed to keep them. I begin now to fear that they will not reach this place again till my official duties recommence which will be on the 22d. of November from which time they continue till the middle of Marc⟨h.⟩

I am desirous of knowing what was the military establishment under the act of April 1790. It is published in the gazette of the United States of the 8th. 9th. or 10th. of May 1790. Unfortunately in the file to which I can obtain access that particular paper is missi⟨n⟩g & in the gazette of Virginia in which the laws of Congress were then published this particular act was not inserted. It is omitted in the volumes of the acts of Congress as one which has expired. You will oblige me by sending me the clause stating the force⟨s?⟩ to be kept up or, if it be a long one, by stating what the force was. If it was not published by Mr. Fenno you will find it in any volume of laws published at the day.[3] I have not those original volumes.

The unavoidable delays which have been experienced, The immense researches among volumes of manuscripts, & chests of letters & gazettes which I am compelled to make will impede my progress so much that it is absolutely impossible to get the residue of the work completed in the short time which remains this fa⟨ll⟩ to be devoted to it. I regret this at least as much as you do but cannot prevent it. I hope you will be able to employ yourself profitably on some other work until the succeeding volume shall be ready for you which will be

I hope next spring, as I shall apply to it again the instant I return from the supreme court. I flatter myself the numbers of the first edition will not be multiplied. I would not be understood to think humbly of it as revised. I have not read more than one hundred pages of the revised copy, but I am persuaded that had the whole work come out originally in that form it would have been better received. Yet the revisal given to the first impression was not only hasty but pursued so unremittingly that many inaccuracies & still more inelegancies must have escaped me. For the sake of giving to the world a more careful correction of the work, & for the sake of some essential alterations which I contemplate I wish a second edition & I am confident that every volume added to the first must tend to prevent any demand for a second edition.

I shall be glad to hear what number of copies you have on hand, what is your prospect of getting clear of them, what number of the revised copies have gone forth, & whether the difference has been discerned between one part of the impression & the other. On this subject I have always be⟨en ap⟩prehensive. Let me know any thing on the subject which you may think worthy of communication. I am Sir very respectfully, your Obedt. Servt

J MARSHALL

Has Mr. Morgan seen the corrections or taken a copy of the corrected work? I had some conversation with Mr. Washington on this subject & think the result was that some communication ought to be made to him respecting it, but I have forgotten what was agreed on, & I know that everything was to be left to Mr. Washington.

ALS, Dreer Collection, PHi; Tr, Marshall Papers, DLC. Addressed to Wayne at Philadelphia; postmarked Richmond, 8 Oct. Endorsed by Wayne. MS torn, and mutilated where seal was broken.

1. Letter not found.

2. Wayne had apparently sent a box of *Aurora* issues by sea. But after the ship's captain had taken the box on board, Wayne told him that a mistake had been made and he should carry the box back to Philadelphia (Bushrod Washington to Wayne, 13 Oct. 1805, Dreer Collection, PHi).

3. "An Act for regulating the Military Establishment of the United States," approved 30 Apr. 1790; published in *Gazette of the U.S.*, 8 May 1790. Sections 1 and 3 stated the size and arrangements of the force (*U.S. Statutes at Large*, I, 119–20). JM wanted the information for a passage on George Washington's opinion of the act. Although the president signed the bill, he did not think 1,216 troops sufficient for the country's needs (vol. V, chap. 4, 274–75 and n.).

To Caleb P. Wayne

Sir   Richmond October 19th. 1805

I received your letter from Philadelphia a few days past.¹ Mr. Hopkins having gone to Kentucky without leaving behind him any clue which could guide me to the papers, I had taken it for granted that he had not received them. On finding by your letter that they had been sent to Mr. Pritchard² I immediately enquired for them & soon learned that they had been loaned to Mr. Prentis³ from whom I have received them. Immediately after writing to you my fever returned & I am not yet recovered. My ill health is not more unwelcome on its own account than on account of the additional delays it will create in the business in whic⟨h⟩ I am engaged. That these delays should affect you in any degree I sincerely lament: they are occasioned by several accidents which concur with the nature of the work (which requires researches beyond measure laborious), to protract the time of its completion. But you may be assured that your interest is still more concerned in having time taken to digest the materials properly, than in the celerity with which they are throne together. Be this as it may my health has compelled me to take refuge in the mountains from th⟨e⟩ sultry heats of our climate; & the continuing fever under which I have labored since my return, & which is only stopped to day, & still threatens me with a visit, admonishes me that my return was premature, & has prevented my deriving from the time I counted on employing in this important business the benefits I expected.

You say that you have seen a letter from an intelligent gentleman in England but you have not suggested the purport of that letter. I am Sir very respectfully, Your Obedt. Servt

J Marshall

You will oblige me by giving me as soon as is in your power the information I requested respecting the military force established by Congress in 1790. While the fever rages in the city I despair of your being able to do this as it is probable that no file of Mr. Fenno will be within your reach. When it ceases I hope there will be no difficulty in the research. I beleive it will be useless to send the Aurora till the session of the supreme court in february shall have terminated. It is probable that you can send the first volume to Judge Washington at that place by some gentleman from Philadelphia.

ALS, Dreer Collection, PHi. Addressed to Wayne at Philadelphia; postmarked Richmond, 21 Oct. Endorsed by Wayne.

1. Letter not found.

2. William Prichard (1760–1815), bookseller in Richmond (Richmond *Enquirer*, 4 Mar. 1815).

3. Probably William Prentis (ca. 1740-ca. 1824), formerly publisher of the *Virginia Gazette* and then of the *Petersburg Intelligencer* until 1804. After his retirement, he continued to offer publications for sale. He resided in Petersburg, where he served several terms as mayor (Hutchinson, *Papers of Madison*, IV, 48 n. 5; Richmond *Enquirer*, 28 Mar. 1805).

Waddington v. Banks
Opinion
U.S. Circuit Court, Virginia, 13 December 1805

Waddington[1]
v
Banks & al

This is an application to this court to direct a trustee to execute a ¶1 trust by selling property on which several different claims are asserted. Before such an order can be made the court ought certainly to be satisfied of the title of the trustee.

The lands conveyed in trust were originally part of a larger lott the ¶2 property of James Currie by whom it was sold & conveyed to Hunter Banks & Co. By Henry Banks the agent & now the surviving partner of Hunter Banks & Co. this lott was divided into small parcels one of which was sold to Nelson Heron & Co. & another to Fulwar Skipwith, who sold a part to F. Graves, who sold to John Stockdell.[2] To Fulwar Skipwith no conveyance was made nor is there any other evidence of the sale to him than a bond executed by the said Skipwith with H. Banks as security, which recites the sale made by Banks to Skipwith & undertakes that Skipwith shall make a good title to Graves. This bond acknowleges the receipt of the purchase money from Graves & is dated on the 29th. of July 1784.

As it is not alleged that Banks had not received the purchase ¶3 money from Skipwith, & as Banks has bound himself that a good title should be made to Graves, who is admitted to have paid a full consideration for the property it will not be questioned that the whole equitable estate was in Graves & that on application a court of chancery would have decreed H. B & Co to convey the legal estate to him also. This bond was afterwards assigned to John Stockdell in whom the equitable estate was thereby completely vested.

In feby. 1788 Stockdell conveyed this lott with other property to ¶4 James Brown in trust to secure a debt to Alexander Donald,[3] he had previously on the 15th, mortgaged it to Young & others. On the 3d. of Decr. 1789. Stockdell & Young & al the previous mortgagees unite in a conveyance to Alexander Donald: This deed purports to be an absolute conveyance.

¶5   Thus was the interest of Stockdell completely vested in Donald & if there were no other circumstances in the case it would be unquestionable that the legal title which still remained in Hunter Banks & Co. was without a single equitable circumstance which could restrain a court of chancery from decreeing a conveyance from him to Donald.

¶6   Against this equitable title the defendent Banks relies upon a counter equity which is produced by a debt due to him from Stockdell to secure which this bond was indorsed in blank by Stockdell, but they had been previously pledged to John Young to whom H. Banks says he paid £800. to for the possession of this pledge & of the deed for another parcel of the same lott which had been also purchased by Stockdell. Having thus united an equity to his legal title, he relies upon that legal title to secure the debt due to him from Stockdell & also to secure the money paid to Young.

¶7   In examining this claim a difficulty presents itself in the very threshhold. To give it efficacy there must be a union of the equitable & legal title. But in this case the equitable claim is in H. B. & the legal title in H. B. & Co. I have not enquired whether H. B. being the surviving partner of H. B. & Co. will have any influence on the case, because that fact does not appear & because, for any thing which is yet shown in the papers I should not deem the enquiry essential.

¶8   But it is material to enquire what was the relation between H. B. & Stockdell when the rights of Donald & of Banks accrued.

¶9   The vendor of an estate who has received the purchase money but retains the legal title is certainly a meer trustee for his vendee, & can avail himself of no act prejudicial to the trust. I beleive this position is correct. If gentlemen think it is not I will with much pleasure hear them upon it. Presuming it for the present to be correct I shall proceed to conside⟨r⟩ the case as if Mr. Banks was a trustee holding the legal estate in trus[t] for the purchaser of the equitable title.

¶10   I will not determine what the law in such a case would be if Mr. Banks had advanced money to Mr. Stockdell under a stipulation that he might retain the lien upon the estate to secure the repayment of that money. Perhaps the agreement would be carried into effect. But I have no hesitation in saying that the situation of a person so circumstanced is delicate, the fairness of his transactions must be completely made out, and he will not be permitted as against the purchaser of the equitable title to derive any advantage from speculation, or from money actually advanced with notice of the equity of the purchaser.

Mr. Banks then would be required to show at what time he ac- ¶11
quired the bonds he holds, what were the circumstances under which
they were acquired, & what sum of actual money was advanced for
them. The whole proof would lie upon him.

When I look for the proof on these points I find none which favor ¶12
the claim of Mr. Banks. His own answer, if it were evidence, does not
furnish them. He does not state these particulars, and it would be
necessary that he should state them in order to make out a case which
the court might enquire into. The proofs in the cause lead to an
opinion destructive of his equity. The most material paper is the
original bond to Skipwith in possession of Mr. Banks with a blank
indorsement.

On the 22d. of fby. 1788 this bond was assigned to Young & others ¶13
to whom a mortgage of the premises was executed on the same day.⁴
This assignment was afterwards erased. It cannot be presumed that
this erasure was made or the bond delivered up until the mortgage
was satisfied. In June 1790 proceedings were instituted on this mortgage in the high Court of Chancery & a decree of foreclosure & sale
of part of the property was obtained. The sale was made in Novr.
1790 & the debt of Young was satisfied. The report however was not
made to the court. Of these proceedings again[s]t the property Mr.
Banks was bound to take notice. He was therefore bound to know
that the claim of Young was satisfied, & that he had no power over the
bond.

The bill filed in June 1790 states a sale it is presumed of this prop- ¶14
erty, to Alexander Donald with the consent of the mortgagees & on
the 3d. of Decr. 1790 a conveyance was made in pursuance of that
sale. Of this sale Mr. Banks cannot be presumed to have been ignorant. He does not state himself to have been ignorant of it. Without
enquiring into other circumstances the possession of Mr. Donald
bound him to take notice of it.

If Young after joining in the conveyance to Donald has given up ¶15
the bond to Banks he has been guilty of a gross fraud which would
merit the severest animadversion of the laws. But be this as it may I
must consider Mr. Banks as a trustee who after notice of the equitable
transfer of the estate endeavors to defeat the rights of the purchaser.
I can therefore perceive no ground on which to sustain his claim.

Respecting the Lott sold to N. H. & Co there can be still less ques- ¶16
tion, because the legal estate is not in H. B. & Co. & the prior equity is
in Donald.

The rights of Doctor Currie cannot be decided on he not being a ¶17
party to this suit. I can only enquire whether Mr. Banks can retain for
him.

There can be I think no case or principle stated which would en- ¶18 able him to pursue a purchaser who has paid the purchase money for his land, altho at the time of[5] the purchase money he had notice that[6] Currie was unpaid.

¶19   His claim rests upon the ground of contract.

¶20   I am inclined to think from the bill in Youngs suit that a part of the purchase money is not credited. Currie may claim for that after the whole debt from Stockdell to Donald is satisfied.[7]

AD, Marshall Judicial Opinions, PPAmP; printed, John W. Brockenbrough, *Reports of Cases Decided by the Honourable John Marshall . . .* , I (Philadelphia, 1837), 98–101. For JM's deletions and interlineations, see Textual Notes below.

1. The plaintiff, Joshua Waddington, was a New York City merchant. He was the same Waddington who had been a loyalist during the Revolution and party to the celebrated 1784 case, Rutgers v. Waddington (Julius Goebel, Jr., et al., eds., *The Law Practice of Alexander Hamilton*, I [New York, 1964], 291 and n.).

Waddington filed two bills in chancery at the June 1805 term. The defendants in the first suit were James Brown, Henry Banks, and Daniel Call. The second bill named Banks and James Taylor, executor of James Heron and guardian of Heron's children, as defendants. The object of both bills was to decree the sale of lots in the city of Richmond and the purchase money to be paid to Waddington. JM's opinion and decree of 13 Dec. 1805 embraced both suits (bills in chancery, [June 1805], Waddington v. Banks, Ended Cases [Unrestored], 1807, Vi; U.S. Cir. Ct., Va., Ord. Bk. V, 122, 208, 249–50).

2. Henry Banks, Fulwar Skipwith, Francis Graves, and John Stockdell were Richmond merchants (*PJM*, V, 166–68, 521; Hutchinson, *Papers of Madison*, IX, 29 n. 6; *CVSP*, IV, 251). The deeds and other documents mentioned in the opinion can be found in the voluminous case file.

3. On Brown and Donald, see *PJM*, II, 86 n. 7; V, 379–83.

4. Stockdell's assignment, which is on the verso of the bond of 29 July 1784, is dated 15 Feb. 1788. This date is consistent with JM's statement above that Stockdell mortgaged the property "on the 15th."

5. Brockenbrough here inserted "paying," which JM omitted.

6. Brockenbrough and the editors here have dropped JM's inadvertent "the."

7. For the complicated decree in this suit, see U.S. Cir. Ct., Va., Ord. Bk. V, 249–50 (also summarized in 1 Brock. 102). See also the further decrees of Dec. 1807 in the suits of Currie v. Waddington, Banks v. Waddington, and Stockdell's Administrator v. Waddington (U.S. Cir. Ct., Va., Ord. Bk. VI, 320, 322–23).

Textual Notes

¶ 1 l. 1   to a ↑this↓ court of chancery to
¶ 2 l. 1   originally ↑part of a larger lott↓ the
l. 2   by whom they were ↑it was↓ sold
l. 5   Co. & the ↑an↓ other
l. 6   sold ↑a part↓ to
¶ 3 l. 3   Graves, I must ↑who is admitted↓ to
l. 5   estate [*erasure*] ↑was↓ in
ll. 6–7   also. The ↑This↓ bond
¶ 4 l. 1   this ↑lott with other↓ property

ll. 2–3   Donald, & afterwards ↑he had previously on the 15th.↓ mort-
           gaged it to Young ↑Prosser↓ ↑Young↓ & others.
l. 4   Stockdell & the Prosser ↑Young & al↓ & al the subsequent
           ↑previous↓ mortgagees
¶ 6 l. 4 Young & ↑to↓ whom
     l. 5 £800. to receive it with for
¶ 7 l. 3 claim in ↑is↓ in
¶ 8 l. 1 to enquiry ↑enquire↓ what
¶10 l. 3 he should might
     l. 10 purchaser. Mr
¶12 l. 7 bond ↑to Skipwith↓ in
¶13 l. 1 assigned by ↑to↓ Young
     l. 8 1790 & ↑the debt of↓ Young
     l. 12 bond. In Decr On the While they were depending the bond
           cannot be presumed to have been surrendered or the
           indorsement to have been erased. Mr. Banks as a trustee
           could not take & avail himself of this satisfied incum-
           brance.
¶14 l. 1 beg. On the 3d. of Decr. 1790 Mr. Stockdell conveyed the land
           to Donald & Young & others joined in the conveyance. If Mr.
           Banks The
¶15 l. 1 beg. I must If
¶17 l. 1 be con decided
¶18 ll. 1–2 enable ↑him↓ to
¶20 l. 1   I do am

Bond v. Ross
Opinion
U.S. Circuit Court, Virginia, 14 December 1805

EDITORIAL NOTE

The text of this opinion is taken from the *Enquirer*, a Richmond newspaper. No manuscript has been found, and the opinion is not among those published by John W. Brockenbrough. "Few legal cases have excited greater curiosity in this city, than the one which called forth the following Opinion of the Chief Justice of the United States," wrote Thomas Ritchie, editor of the *Enquirer*. As Ritchie explained in his prefatory remarks, the parties compromised before Marshall issued his ruling, and the opinion therefore had no official authority. Nevertheless, "the principle, which it supports, may hereafter become a precedent for all future decisions in similar cases."[1]

Phineas Bond, the British consul at Philadelphia, was the nominal plaintiff in this equity suit, acting on behalf of the creditors of Ezekiel Edwards, a subject of Great Britain. David Ross, a prominent merchant and possessor of vast holdings of lands and slaves, was at this time party to numerous suits

brought by his American and British creditors. At the June 1804 term, the
circuit court ordered Ross to pay $181,000 in installments—$10,000 payable
1 Oct. 1804 and 1 Jan. 1805 and $16,667 payable every six months beginning
1 July 1805 until the whole principal sum and interest were paid. In default
of these payments, the marshal was directed to sell Ross's lands, slaves, and
personal property mentioned in two deeds of trust executed in 1795 and
1799. The opinion in this case arose from the execution of the 1804 decree.[2]

1. Richmond *Enquirer*, 19 Dec. 1805.
2. U.S. Cir. Ct., Va., Ord. Bk. IV, 478–81.

OPINION

The motions now made in this cause, respect the execution of a
decree made in this court by consent, in June 1804.

By that decree, the defendant, Ross, was directed to pay to the
plaintiff, the sum of 184,884[1] dols. 70 cents, by certain instalments in
the decree specified: And in default of payment, it was ordered, that
the marshal do, from time to time, make sale of the lands, tenements,
slaves and other personal property mentioned in certain indentures
which are filed in the cause, or such part thereof as shall appear
sufficient to raise the sum of money that shall then be due or payable.
The sales were to be for ready money, and the times and places to be
advertised six weeks in one or more of the Richmond newspapers.
The marshal was to pay to the plaintiff the money so raised, or so
much thereof as would discharge the sums then due, and to bring the
surplus, if any, into court.

Default of payment having been made by the plaintiff, a large tract
of land, consisting of 18,000 acres, called the Oxford iron works,
being one of the tracts comprehended in the decree, was advertised
and sold;[2] and Thomas Taylor became the purchaser, at the price of
13050 dols. The officer has reported his proceedings to the court,
and a motion has been made to confirm the report, and to direct the
marshal to put the purchaser in possession of the premises.[3] A cross
motion has been made on the part of the defendant, to set aside the
sale, as having been irregularly conducted, or to open the bidding in
consequence of an offer now made to purchase the land, at double
the price given for it by Mr. Taylor.

As the success of the first motion depends entirely on the validity
of the objections made to the sale, the court will now review those
objections:

On the first part of this motion—that the sale should be set aside
for irregularity—the defendant urges three points:

1st. That so large and valuable an estate should have been sold in
parcels and not entire.

2dly. That the advertisement did not give sufficient time, did not sufficiently diffuse the information, and was not sufficiently descriptive of the property.

3dly. That the sale was a mere mockery, there being only one person present to bid, except the officer, and therefore the property was sacrificed, not sold.

Whatever weight the court might have been disposed to allow to the objection which respects the conduct of the marshal in offering the entire tract of land for sale, had that officer regulated himself in that particular, by his own judgment or the instructions of the plaintiff, none can be given to it under the actual circumstances of the case. It was referred to Mr. Ross himself to decide whether the land should be sold in parcels or in one entire tract, and he insisted strenuously on the latter mode of sale, giving it as his opinion, through his agents, that the estate could not be divided without material injury.[4] If, after this, the marshal had proceeded to set it up in parcels, and the sales had been low, every person must perceive with what additional plausibility the objections to the mode of sale adopted by the officer might have been urged.

It is suggested that this declaration on the part of Mr. Ross applied to the first and not the second sale.[5] Were this suggestion supported by the fact, the court does not perceive its influence. The circumstances of the estate remained the same, and the officer could not suppose Mr. Ross to have changed his opinion unless he had communicated that change. But the fact is, that Mr. Ross expressed the same sentiment with respect to the 2d sale. In his report, after mentioning the necessity of selling for the instalment which became due in July 1805, Mr. Mosby says, "the sale of the Oxford iron works and lands adjoining, not being completed, the said Ross and Wickham[6] agreed that they should again be exposed to sale in preference to any other part of the trust property; the said Ross then requested that the said iron works and lands might be sold together."

The particular motives of Mr. Ross for making this request have perhaps been truly stated by his counsel; be whatever they might be, it is not for him to object to an act performed at his instance.

The court has felt as little difficulty in deciding on the sufficiency of the advertisement. The sale has been published for a greater length of time, and in a greater number of papers than is required by a decree framed by the parties themselves, but had he not exceeded these limits, it would I think outrage the clearest principles to say, that an officer had executed a decree irregularly, because his advertisement had strictly conformed to that decree. To the objection which respects the description of the property, it has very properly been answered that this notice was in part prepared by Mr. Ross himself, and must therefore be considered as having received his approbation.[7] But in any event, he might have added such a description of the property as his knowledge of it enabled him to give. A minute description from the marshal was not to be expected. An important reason against it is that an error in the description might have affected the sale.

But it is suggested, that the provisions in the decree, which relate to the advertisement,[8] were not made under the contemplation that the whole property contained in the deed of trust, or a very great part of it, would be brought at once into the market. It was conceived by the parties, that only so much would be sold at a time as might be necessary to raise a particular instalment, and therefore a notice less diffusive and for a shorter time was stipulated, than would have been insisted on, had it been supposed that one third of the whole trust property would be sold at the same time. But it appears to the court that the very case, which has happened, must have been contemplated by the parties. After selling the other property contained in the deed, an event, which must have been considered as probable if not certain, the Oxford iron works would of course be sold, on the failure of Mr. Ross to pay the instalments which would afterwards become due.[9] The court must suppose, that the judgment of Mr. Ross always was in favor of selling the estate entire. Of consequence, a sale of the whole property must have taken place, and the parties to the decree must have had in contemplation such a sale, when the decree was formed.

I come now to the third objection to the sale, on which the counsel have, I think with reason, placed their greatest reliance. Their arguments, I own, have excited great doubt in my mind respecting the propriety of the proceeding, nor can I yet feel absolutely and completely satisfied with that decision which, after viewing the subject in all its aspects, I think it my duty to make.

The objection is, that only one bidder being present except himself, and being himself authorised to bid for Mr. Wickham only a small sum compared with the value of the lands, the marshal ought not to have set them up. That it was inconsistent with his duty to sacrifice an estate to be sold under the order of a court of chancery—an event which might with certainty be predicted from the circumstance which has been stated. A public sale it has been said implies the attendance of several purchasers: and the want of such attendance is the want of a circumstance which is essential to the thing itself.

On the other hand it is contended, that the officer was bound by the terms of the decree to sell at all events if he could raise the money, and that he would have become responsible to the creditor had he failed to do so.

Perhaps on neither side has the principle been exactly laid down, and perhaps no precise line for the conduct of any officer under such circumstances can be marked out. In executing a decree, the part of the officer is ministerial so far as the provisions of the decree extend, but on points not expressed he may exercise some discretion. That discretion however, must be limited—for if he should so exercise it as to defeat the decree, or unreasonably to delay its execution, his conduct will be culpable. On the time of sale the decree certainly leaves something to the judgment of the Marshal. In this case the time and place may be fixed by him. After having fixed them he ought not lightly to change them; but certainly circumstances may exist which would justify his doing so. If by extreme bad weather or by any other casualty, it should become apparent that the sale could not be made without great and real injury, and there was ground for the opinion that a postponement of the sale would enable the officer to make it within reasonable time at a fair price, I should be surprised to find the officer arraigned for assenting to such a postponement. Upon this subject then the Marshal may exercise some discretion, but it is a discretion controulable by the court. If in the exercise of it he determines to sell, although the determination may be a hard one, the purchaser acquires rights which ought not lightly to be taken away. He ought also to recollect that when an opinion prevails that a sale will not be made, every postponement not produced by causes which are obvious, will probably strengthen that opinion, and diminish the number of bidders who will afterwards appear. The situation of an officer would not be free from hazard if, without good reason, he should decline selling at the time originally appointed, and should afterwards find himself unable to make the sale.

In the case before the court, the property for sale may be considered as certainly worth 26,000 dols. although it had sold at 20,000 and the officer had reason to be assured that it would sell at not much more than 13,000. This was certainly a great sacrifice, and it ought not to have been made if the state of things was produced clearly by a casualty, the recurrence of which there was no strong reason to expect.

The plaintiffs counsel assign a cause for this state of things which, if true, ought certainly to have had considerable influence on the conduct of the Marshal. They say that it is to be ascribed to Mr. Ross himself, and that there was no ground for the hope of its removal. Some testimony has been produced to prove a common opinion that Mr. Ross possessed inclination and address to prevent the sales entirely, or to annul them if made. So far as this opinion was founded on the defendents controverting the sales made at the Eagle,[10] which were formerly discussed in this court, I do not think it ought to injure him; because, whether those sales would have been set aside or affirmed, there was certainly reasonable ground for contesting them, and no man ought to suffer for appealing to the laws of his country where he has sustained an injury which he believes they will redress.[11]

But this being represented to be the general opinion entertained of the defendent, it was probably not unknown to him; and if known, he must have foreseen the consequences of such an opinion, and ought, in common procedure, and would if he had really designed to carry the decree into full and fair effect, have taken the proper measures to prevent those consequences. He would have given assurances that these apprehensions were ill founded, and would have taken some pains to induce the attendance of bidders. Not only has this been omitted, but every step taken by Mr. Ross, has at least the appearance of an intention to prevent such a competition for this property as it was the interest of the creditor to obtain. The circumstances which produce this opinion shall be briefly stated. Mr. Ross has omitted the use of all those means to draw purchasers to the sale which were not prescribed in the decree, but which were in his power, and which a man of common prudence being about to dispose of property, the sale of which he knew would be difficult, would unquestionably employ.

He has chosen a place of sale which was particularly well calculated to favor the purchase of the property at a low rate. I say he has chosen the place, because when the same property was offered for sale at the Eagle tavern, the place constituted one of his objections. He insisted then that the sale ought to have been made on the premises; and having never expressed a contrary opinion, and having concurred in the advertisement which changed the place to that he had declared to be the proper one, the place must be considered as chosen by him.

At his instance, the land was on both occasions sold entire and not in parcels. It will be readily admitted that in cases of real competition among bidders, desirous of purchasing the property for use, and not for speculation, the iron works, with the lands appertaining to them, would be a more desirable acquisition than the works without the lands. But such a competition was not to be expected. The means to obtain it, if indeed it was attainable by any means, had not been taken: and the sale of so great a property in a single lot, was precisely calculated to promote a scheme for purchasing it in at a low rate. If the reflection of Mr. Ross had not conducted him to this result, he ought to have been led to it by actual experience. The sale at which he was himself the purchaser, must have admonished him of the price at which the Oxford iron works at the same place, and under similar circumstances would sell. Yet he persisted to require that the whole should be sold together.

There remains yet another circumstance which is perhaps more conclusive than any which has been mentioned. It is his insisting that the land should be sold not for the whole amount of the instalment which was due, but only to raise 13000 dolls. the balance remaining unpaid, of the first sale.[12] For this request, what could be the motive of Mr. Ross? This was a declaration, that the whole tract should be sold to raise 13000 dolls. rather than to raise 16000. For this what inducement could he have but to become himself the purchaser?

I conclude from these circumstances, and the marshal to whom they were all known, must also have concluded from them, that Mr. Ross was uniform and systematic in his endeavors to defeat the trust, and the decree rendered with the consent of parties, by becoming himself the purchaser of the trust property at a great under value. That this would materially affect the vested rights of the creditor is not to be doubted.

I do not recite these particulars for the purpose of reproaching Mr. Ross. I can readily conceive that a man pressed as he is, may beguile himself into the opinion that by extricating his property from liens, and recovering his power to dispose of it, he may ultimately do justice to all; and that time will do for him more than time can perform. But I state them to show the real case; and I add to the statement, that if in making such an attempt, the debtor fails, he must not expect the aid of a court to enable him to carry it into effect. He plays a game of great hazard, and he risks his whole stake upon his skill and good fortune.

In enquiring into the duty of the officer, these circumstances are all to be taken into view, and the effect which they would have and ought to have had in regulating his conduct. There was no reason for supposing that the causes which had kept away bidders would cease to operate. There was no ground for the opinion, that if another sale should be advertised, the same motives for a still further postponement would not recur. No point of time could be taken when the force of these motives would be diminished. It would be in fact to countenance the opinion, that the creditor must be kept out of his money until the debtor should pay it without coertion. He could not forget that Mr. Ross had already been indulged from the time of the preceding sale, and he could not be sure that an extension of the indulgence, would change the state of things for the better. Under these circumstances, I cannot say that the officer acted irregularly in selling the property for the sum, to raise which Mr. Ross insisted it should be sold, and at which he expected to have become himself the purchaser.

It has been said that there were other irregularities which will assist in vitiating the transaction. Mr. Mosby's bid has been represented as a nullity; and cases have been cited to prove that he could not have been a purchaser. Those cases certainly go a great way in establishing the position that, had he purchased, Mr. Ross would have been let in to redeem on equitable terms; but they do not prove his bid a nullity. So far as respected the debtor, his bid had the same effect as if he had not been disabled from becoming a purchaser for himself. It affected the bidding of Mr. Taylor in precisely the same manner as if it had been made by a tender unconnected with the sale.

Neither was his declaration that he would bid to a certain price an impropriety which this court can regard. Independent of the consideration that this declaration was drawn from him by Mr. Ross, and was not prohibited by any known rule or usage, I cannot perceive how it affected the case.

It only hastened a discovery which Mr. Taylor must soon have made. When Mr. Mosby ceased to bid, the secret would have been divulged; and that Mr. Taylor would afterwards have bid upon himself, was not to be expected.

It has been also contended that the court will not assist in giving effect to a contract made by its officer, of which it would not decree a specific performance if made by the party himself. But the cases are not the same in principle. The court will not assist a person who has gained an unreasonable legal advantage, because his remedy is at law, and the court is not entangled in the proceeding. But the cases say that for meer inadequacy of price, the court will not take away his legal remedy. In this case, the aid of the court is not required. The decree already rendered makes it the duty of the marshal to complete the transaction unless the court will set aside the sale. A case therefore where the court will not interfere, is no precedent for this. For in this case the court must interfere and set aside the contract of its officer, or the sale stands.

In support of the second part of the motion, that the biddings should be opened in consequence of the offer made by Mr. Giles, many authorities have been cited which prove beyond a question that in England, in a case far short of this, the biddings would be opened.[13]

Those authorities, at first, made a strong impression on the court. These decisions undoubtedly proceeded on the principle, that where sales are made under the authority of a court of chancery, the justice of the court is concerned in having them made to the best advantage.[14] That principle exists, whereon a court of chancery exists, and I was much inclined to pursue it through the same consequences which it had introduced in England. But on further reflection I do not think myself at liberty to do so. The doctrine of opening the biddings is not in itself a principle of equity, but a practice established by particular courts, in consequence of a principle, which practice enters into the contract and forms its character. In consequence of that practice, the contract is in fact, on both sides conditional, until the report of the master is affirmed. But in Virginia, in pursuing the same principle, the courts have established a different practice. In Virginia the contract is absolute. The purchaser is entitled to his purchase, and cannot recede from it. The benefit or the loss is legally his, and it requires some impropriety which vitiates the transaction to set it aside. I will not deny that in my opinion the usage of the English courts is to be preferred; but if I could introduce it, the rule should be prospective, not to affect past transactions.

There is certainly much weight due to the authority of those cases where, after the affirmance of a report, the biddings have been opened; but after mature consideration, I cannot admit their influence in this case. In all of them, it is expressly stated that something more than inadequacy of price is required to set aside a sale after the affirmance of a report, and such is certainly the real principle.[15] It is true that where the under value is gross, the court will strain hard to find the circumstances which will enable it to relieve the injured party: and I believe that in this case an English court would manage to find them: but I think it safer to adhere to the principle itself, and I am much inclined to think that in this country, general principles of policy would not justify such frequent interference in public sales as may be practised in England. It is not, however, on this idea of general policy that my opinion is founded. It depends on the principle itself as stated in the English books.

Nothing can be more irksome to a court than to perceive that principles, with an adherence to which it cannot permit it self to dispense, will produce great individual loss. But these feelings cannot controul the course of justice. I think myself obliged to overrule the motion for setting aside the sale, and of consequence, the report is affirmed.[16]

Printed, *Enquirer* (Richmond, Va.), 19 December 1805.

1. This should be 180,884.

2. Ross had acquired the Oxford Iron Works, situated in Campbell County near Lynchburg, during the Revolution. See Charles B. Dew, "David Ross and the Oxford Iron Works: A Study of Industrial Slavery in the Early Nineteenth-Century South," *WMQ*, 3d ser., XXXI (1974), 189–224.

3. The report of Deputy Marshal Benjamin Mosby on his sales of Ross's property, dated 1 Nov. 1805, is in the case papers (Bond v. Ross, U.S. Cir. Ct., Va., Ended Cases [Unrestored], 1834, Vi).

4. Ross (according to the deputy marshal) objected to dividing the tract, alleging that it could not be done "without great inconvenience and probable loss" (ibid.)

5. The first sale took place on 11 May 1805, the highest bid of $20,000 coming from Ross's agent. Ross paid $7,200 of this amount but did not complete the purchase. The iron works were again sold, on 17 Sept. 1805, to Thomas Taylor for $13,000 (ibid.).

6. John Wickham was attorney for the plaintiff.

7. The advertisement for the first sale, dated 25 Feb. 1805, offered "A NUMBER OF SLAVES And "so much of that Valuable Estate . . . known by the name of the OXFORD IRON-WORKS, as shall appear sufficient to raise" $7,000. The second notice, dated 5 July 1805, announced the sale of the "OXFORD IRON WORKS," containing eighteen thousand acres, together with "STOCK OF EVERY KIND . . . WAGGONS, TEAMS, &C.," to raise $16,666. Both sales took place on the premises in Campbell County (Va. Argus, 17 Apr., 7 Aug. 1805).

8. The decree of June 1804 stipulated that the sales should be advertised for six weeks in one of the Richmond newspapers (U.S. Cir. Ct., Va., Ord. Bk. IV, 478–81).

9. Previous to the sale of the Oxford Iron Works, the deputy marshal sold Ross's tract known as Goochland Courthouse, the Norwich Mills, and his lands in Henrico County (report of Benjamin Mosby, 1 Nov. 1805, Bond v. Ross).

10. A well-known Richmond tavern.

11. JM presumably referred to previous sales of Ross's lands, including the Oxford Iron Works tracts, which were set aside in conjunction with the June 1804 decree (U.S. Cir. Ct., Va., Ord. Bk. IV, 481).

12. The installment due on 1 July 1805 was $16,667. Ross, according to Mosby's report, "insisted that the Ironworks and lands . . . should only be sold to raise the sum of $13,001 and charges that sum being equal to the deficiency in the former sale which had not been compleated." Wickham agreed, provided "Ross would point out other property which would be sufficient to raise the balance due on the instalment." Ross then proposed to offer for sale "the implements and stock" on the land to raise an additional $3,666 (report of Benjamin Mosby, 1 Nov. 1805, Bond v. Ross).

13. The law of sales under the authority of courts of equity was summarized by Edward Burtenshaw Sugden, A Practical Treatise of the Law of Vendors and Purchasers of Estates (2d. Am. ed.; Philadelphia, 1820), 37–50. In arguing this case, counsel may have had access to the first London edition, published in 1805.

14. "But where estates are sold before a master under the decree of a court of equity, the court considers itself to have a greater power over the contract than it would have were the contract made between party and party; and as the chief aim of the court is to obtain as great a price for the estate as can possibly be got, it is in the habit of opening the biddings after the estate is sold" (ibid., 45).

15. "The determinations on this subject assume a very different aspect when the report is absolutely confirmed. Biddings are in general not to be opened after confirmation of the report: increase of price alone is not sufficient, however large, although it is a strong auxiliary argument where there are other grounds" (ibid., 46).

16. By the compromise between Ross and Taylor, which superseded this opinion, Ross was to withdraw his objections to the marshal's report and sale, and it was agreed that Ross should regain possession of the land upon condition that he pay Taylor $13,050 within ten days of the rising of the court and a further sum of $3,100 to Wickham by 22 Jan. 1806. In default of these payments, Taylor was to retain title to the land; if punctually paid, then Taylor was to convey the Oxford Iron Works in fee to Ross (U.S. Cir. Ct., Va., Ord. Bk. V, 261–63).

JM had occasion to deliver further opinion in this case in 1815. Litigation arising from the decree of June 1804 continued until 1834 (Bond v. Ross, Mewburn et al., 1 Brock 316; U.S. Cir. Ct., Va., Ord. Bk. XII, 48–50; U.S. Cir. Ct., Va., Index to Ended Cases, Vi).

Anonymous
Opinion
U.S. Circuit Court, North Carolina
[30 December 1805–4 January 1806]

PER CURIAM.[1] This is a *sci. fa.* against bail; and the plaintiff's counsel urges that he is entitled, against the bail, to *interest* upon the judgment against the principal. We are of opinion that he is not so entitled; for the judgment upon the *sci. fa.* is that the plaintiff have execution against the bail, of the judgment against the principal. The very same execution therefore issues against the bail as issues against the principal; and consequently damages arising after the judgment cannot be included.[2]

Printed, John Haywood, *Cases Adjudged in the Superior Courts . . . of North Carolina*, II (Raleigh, N.C., 1806), 378.

1. The term began on 30 Dec. and concluded on 4 Jan. The minute book records one case at this term in which the defendant was sued as bail: Wills & Morris v. Thomas Ferrebee and Others as bail of John and William Shaw (U.S. Cir. Ct., N.C., Min. Bk., 30, 31 Dec. 1805).

2. The reporter noted that the following cases were cited: Fanshaw v. Morrison, 1 Salk. 208, 91 Eng. Rep. 187 (K.B., 1704); Henriques v. Dutch West-India Company, 2 Str. 807, 93 Eng. Rep. 862 (K.B., 1728), reported more fully in 2 Raym. Ld. 1532, 92 Eng. Rep. 494.

Grubb's Administrator v. Clayton's Executor
Opinion
U.S. Circuit Court, North Carolina
[30 December 1805–4 January 1806]

PER CURIAM.[1] This cause was instituted formerly in Wilmington Superior Court.[2] The act of 1715 was pleaded, and thereupon a case was made and stated for the Court of Conference, who decided that the said act of 1715, ch. 48, sec. 9, was in force. The plaintiff's counsel then replied to the plea; and after the replication, the whole bill was dismissed on their motion, that is to say, on the motion of the plaintiff's counsel. The suit was then instituted in this court, and the defendants counsel have pleaded the former dismission in bar. We are of opinion that was not a dismission *upon the merits*, considered of and decided by the court, and therefore that the plea in bar is not good. There is also another plea in bar; namely, the act of 1789, ch. 23, sec. 4; by which it appears that this suit was not commenced within three years from the qualification of the executors, though there was an administrator of Grubb in England. Now as there was no administrator in this country, there was no person in being who could demand the debt, of course no creditor to be barred. The words of the act are, "the creditors of any person deceased, if they reside without the limits of this state, shall within three years from the qualification of the executor or administrator, exhibit and make demand, &c.—and if any creditor shall hereafter fail to demand and bring suit for recovery, &c. he shall forever be debarred," &c. The plaintiff, therefore, is not within the body of the act. We need not consider whether an exception shall be allowed of, which is not expressly mentioned in the act.[3]

Printed, John Haywood, *Cases Adjudged in the Superior Courts . . . of North Carolina*, II (Raleigh, N.C., 1806), 378–79.

1. There is no entry for this case in the minutes of the Dec. 1805 term, which began on 30 Dec. and ended on 4 Jan.

2. This was an equity suit brought in the state court in 1802 to recover a pre-Revolutionary debt owed by Francis Clayton to Richard Grubb, a British subject. The defendant pleaded the 1715 act of limitations, which barred recovery if no demand was made within seven years after the death of the debtor (Clayton died in 1790). He also pleaded the 1789 act, which required creditors to bring suit within three years after the executor qualified. After argument at the May 1803 term, a case was stated for the Court of Conference, which declared the 1715 act to be in full force and not repealed by that of 1789. Plaintiff's counsel, after replying, moved to have the bill dismissed. He then brought suit in the federal court (proceedings in Wilmington Superior Court [copy], May 1804 term; bill in chancery, ca. June 1804, Grubb's Administrator v. Clayton's Executor, GEpFRC; *First Laws of North Carolina*, I, 30; II, 677–78).

3. With the 1789 act held not to apply, the way was clear for the plaintiff to recover. The Supreme Court in 1804 held, in the case of Ogden v. Blackledge (2 Cranch 272), that the 1715 law had been repealed by the 1789 act, contrary to the opinion of the North Carolina Court of Conference. The federal circuit court, of course, had to follow the Supreme Court's holding in such cases. The court made a final decree in this case in May 1807 (U.S. Cir. Ct., N.C., Min. Bk., 14 May 1807).

United States v. Holtsclaw

Opinion
U.S. Circuit Court, North Carolina, 2 January 1806

PER Curiam.[1] The objection made by Mr. *Seawell*,[2] that no one shall speak as to the hand writing of the president and cashier of the bank, but one who has seen them write, or has been in the habit of receiving letters from them in a course of correspondence, is not a sound one. These signatures are known to the public, and persons who have been in the habit of distinguishing the genuine from the counterfeit

signature, and conversant in dealings for bank bills, are as well qualified to determine of their genuineness, as persons who in private
correspondence have received letters from the person whose hand
writing is in question. Moreover, it is determined by the skilful
whether a bill be genuine, not only by the signature, but also by the
face of the bill, and by the exact conformity of the devices which are
used for the detection of counterfeits, to those in true bills. We are of
opinion that the judgment of persons well acquainted with bank paper, is sufficient evidence to determine whether the one in question
be genuine or otherwise.[3]

Printed, John Haywood, *Cases Adjudged in the Superior Courts . . . of North Carolina*, II
(Raleigh, N.C., 1806), 379.

1. Nathan Holtsclaw had been indicted for uttering counterfeit bank bills at the
preceding term, pleading not guilty.

2. Henry Seawell was attorney general of North Carolina.

3. Holtsclaw was found guilty, fined ten dollars, and sentenced to three years imprisonment (U.S. Cir. Ct., N.C., Min. Bk., 19 June 1805, 2 Jan. 1806). The *Raleigh Register*,
6 Jan. 1806, reported the following account of the trial: "On Thursday morning came
on the trial of Nathan Holtsclaw, for passing counterfeit Bank Notes of the United
States Savannah Branch Bank. It was proved in evidence that he passed two notes of
the above description, for $100 each in purchase of a horse in Montgomery county,
some time last spring; and from the varying stories which he told as to the manner in
which he obtained the notes, and from other circumstances, it appeared that he knew
these notes were counterfeit. The notes were in Court, and were declared to be base by
three several witnesses. The prosecution was sustained by Mr. Woods, and the prisoner
was defended by the Attorney-General. After the arguments of the counsel were
closed, and the Chief justice had addressed a few words only to the Jury, they retired,
and in less than ten minutes returned with a verdict of *Guilty*."

Teasdale v. Branton's Administrators
Opinion
U.S. Circuit Court, North Carolina, 4 January 1806

Per curiam.[1] We must presume according to the loose practice of
this state, that there was a judgment entered pursuant to the verdict,
and therefore we must say there is such a record.[2] As to the demurrer, for that no *devastavit* is returned or found:[3] to be sure by the
English practice, no *sci. fa.* lies against the executor, to subject him *de
bonis propriis*, till a *devastavit* is found upon a *scire fieri* enquiry, and
returned. An action of debt, however, will lie upon suggestion of a
devastavit, and the practice in this state has been to issue a *sci. fa.* upon
such suggestion.[4] And as every defence can be made to the *sci. fa.*
which could be made to the action, there can be no good reason for

adjudging the *sci. fa.* improper. If the *sci. fa.* here be considered in lieu of *scire fieri* enquiry in England, it possesses advantages far above the English mode; for here it is to be executed in court, and under the direction of the court; whereas the other is in the county before a jury. With respect to the demurrer to the plea of judgments and no assets *ultra*, that was pleaded in the original suit;[5] but the defendants counsel say a replication thereto, denying the judgments, is *nul tiel* record; and the record shews that the jury said there were no such judgments: therefore the plea has not been tried, and if so, no judgment can be presumed; for the court ought not to enter judgment when any one plea remains untried. The answer is, the replication may be either *nul tiel* record, or assets *ultra*, or *per fraudom*, or other matter of fact; and such replications was properly triable by jury: and an irregularity committed by the clerk in entering the verdict, will not raise a presumption that the judgment was not given upon the verdict. If there was such a judgment, that estops the defendant from using any plea which he did or might have pleaded prior to that judgment. The demurrer therefore must be allowed.

Printed, John Haywood, *Cases Adjudged in the Superior Courts . . . of North Carolina*, II (Raleigh, N.C., 1806), 377–78.

1. This case grew out of an earlier one between the same parties. See Opinion, [15–21 June 1803], and n. 2. JM was not present in court the day this second opinion was given (U.S. Cir. Ct., N.C., Min. Bk., 4 Jan. 1806).

2. The jury verdict of 31 Dec. 1804 awarded damages to the plaintiff but found that the defendant had fully administered the assets. A scire facias then issued against the administrator to show cause why execution should not be levied de bonis propriis, that is, against the administrator's own goods. One of the defendant's pleas to this action was *nul tiel* ("no such") record. The record produced showed the jury verdict of Dec. 1804 but no judgment having been entered up pursuant to the verdict.

3. The defendant also pleaded that no *devastavit* had been found, showing that he had wasted the assets of his intestate, to which the plaintiff demurred.

4. For the action of debt suggesting a devastavit, see *PJM*, V, 46 n. 8.

5. In the earlier case the defendant had pleaded that he had no assets beyond the amount of the judgments previously obtained against him.

To George Logan

Dear Sir   Richmond Jany. 19th. 1805 [1806][1]
On my return to this place from North Carolina I had the pleasure of finding your favor of the 5th. inst.[2]

As the error committed respecting the writer of the petition to the King had given me considerable chagrin I beg leave to assure you that I am highly gratified at knowing that its correction is satisfactory to Mr. Dickinson.³ With Sentiments of great respect, I am Sir your Obedt

J MARSHALL

ALS, Logan Collection, PHi. Addressed by JM to Logan at Washington and franked; postmarked Richmond, 21 Jan. Endorsement on cover in unknown hand summarizes letter.

1. JM made the common mistake of dating a January letter with the year just ended. The context clearly establishes 1806 as the correct year (see n. 3).

2. Letter not found.

3. JM had corrected this mistake in response to a letter from Logan the preceding January. See JM to Logan, 28 Jan. 1805 and nn.

From John Adams

Dear Sir   Quincy February 4th. 1806

I have received from you, three Volumes of the Life of our late General and President Washington in a condition of convenience and ornament, which has not yet been exceeded by any of the Arts or Artists of our Country, nor indeed much inferiour to any in the most refined Countries of Europe.

I pray you, Sir to accept my best Thanks for this elegant present.

Exegisti monumentum aere perennius.¹ As it is certainly a more rational, I hope and believe it will be a more glorious and durable Memorial of your Hero, than a Mausoleum would have been, of dimensions Superiour to the proudest pyramid of Egypt.²

I wish you, Sir, Health and long Life: and less rancorous Enemies and less treacherous Friends than have fallen to the lott of your Sincere Fri[e]nd and most obedient Servant

J. ADAMS

ALS (letterbook copy), Adams Papers, MHi.

1. "You have erected a monument more durable than bronze." Adams adapted a line from Horace, *Odes*, iii. 30. 1.

2. Writing to Jefferson in 1813, Adams commented: "Marshall's is a Mausolaeum, 100 feet square at the base, and 200 feet high. It will be as durable, as the monuments of the Washington benevolent Societies" (Adams to Jefferson, 3 July 1813 [Lester J. Cappon, ed., *The Adams-Jefferson Letters* (2 vols.; Chapel Hill, N.C., 1959), II, 349]).

To James M. Marshall

My dear brother   Washington Feby 13th. 1806

I have received your letter of the first instant[1] inclosing part of a letter from Mr. Tucker which tried my patience more than any argument I have heard during the term.[2] It would be however to no purpose to exclaim against the state of morals or any other non existing thing: it is more to the purpose to enquire what is best to be done.

I do not know what is proposed by the people of Winchester. If they are willing to pay all the rents not barred by the act of limitations your case is attended with so much difficulty, the prejudices you have to encounter are so great, the delays you must experience are so considerable that I think it more advisable to make the sacrifice great as it is than to commence a new course of litigation for rights so oppressively withheld. You must either sue all, which would be an enormous expense at a great risk, or lose by the statute of limitations your claims against those who are not brought into court. You observe that regardless of the circumstances which have suspended your proceeding individually against them they are now just as ready to avail themselves of that act as if no understanding had existed between you; or as if it was a fair defence.

When I suggested the action of covenant it did not occur to me that it was a deed poll,[3] & if any other action was even maintainable, the act of limitations might certainly be pleaded to it.

I am so excessively pressed with the business of the court that it is not in my power to give your case that degree of consideration which would render my opinion of any value: but it appears monstrous to suppose that a plain legal right can exist without a remedy.

If no remedy at law exists, it follows of necessity that a suit in chancery would be maintainable. It is impossible to fail in such a suit on any other ground than the existence of a remedy at law.

With respect to the rents due to Denny Fairfax before the conveyance to you, I should suppose a recovery could only be defeated by the circumstance that they passed to you by the deed conveying the land. If so, the act of limitations will now bar them. I am not sure that they did pass but I beleive in ordinary leases the back rents pass by a conveyance of the land.

If you get once more into the court of appeals your case will I fear be desperate.

I spoke to Mr. Ambler & wrote to you that he will endeavor to make a payment, by May or June.[4] Edmonds must exert himself to get as much money as possible by that time.[5] I have always considered him as under your particular controul & so he considers himself. Consequently you should write to him on this subject. I will endeavor to raise a considerable part of the money required & have made some applications in Richmond respecting the success of which I cannot yet speak confidently. When I can I will again write to you.

I suppose we ought to give a mortgage on the property for the residue & it would be desirable that the mortgage deed should express the sum for which it is given. Should the conveyances be drawn here & sent over to Murdock or will they be drawn in England, or is a conveyance already prepared.[6]

The powers of attorney must certainly be executed. Could you & Mr: Colston visit Richmond about the last of may? I shall get away from this place early in March & shall know immediately on my return what is the success of my plans for borrowing. I am my dear brother, Your Affectionate

J MARSHALL

ALS, William Keeney Bixby Collection, MoSW. Addressed to James M. Marshall "near Front Royal/Frederick County/Virginia"; postmarked Georgetown, 20 Feb.

1. Letter not found.

2. The letter enclosed by James Marshall may have been from Henry St. George Tucker, son of St. George Tucker. The younger Tucker was a resident of Winchester and thus directly affected by the recent decision of the Court of Appeals in Marshall v. Conrad, which upheld James Marshall's claim to rents on lots in that town. The case had been decided the preceding November and was reported in the newspapers (5 Call 364; Richmond Enquirer, 12, 15, 19, 22, 26 Nov. 1805).

On reading the report, Henry St. George Tucker commented on the decision in a letter to his father: "To my own mind the argument of Judge Roane [in dissent] is inevitably conclusive; tho I will candidly acknowledge, that it is not impossible my feelings may be enlisted on the part of the defendants. I shall nevertheless obey your injunction of paying to Mr. Marshall all arrears and have already requested him to call tomorrow to receive what is due." In the same letter Tucker spoke of James Marshall as "overbearing, haughty & imperious" (3 Dec. 1805, Tucker-Coleman Papers, ViW).

3. A deed poll is a deed made by one party only.

4. John Ambler was part of the syndicate—the others were JM, James Markham Marshall, and Rawleigh Colston—that had contracted to purchase Leeds Manor. See Articles of Agreement, 11 Sept. 1801.

5. Edmonds probably belonged to the prominent Fauquier family of that name. Col. William Edmonds (1734–1817) had been sheriff and county lieutenant (Fauquier Historical Society Bulletin, 1st ser., no. 2 [1922], 147–49).

6. The deed for Leeds Manor was executed on 18 Oct. 1806, after Gen. Philip Martin, brother and heir at law of Denny Martin Fairfax, received payment in full (fourteen thousand pounds sterling) from the Marshall syndicate. William Murdock, a London merchant, acted as the Marshalls' agent in this purchase. A copy of this deed was entered on the record of Marshall's Lessee v. Foley, Fauquier County Land Causes, III, 1833–50, 40–44 (microfilm), Vi.

To Caleb P. Wayne

Sir   Washington March 3d. 1806

I will thank you to send to Mr. Adams the late President the 4th. & 5th. volumes of the life of Washington bound in the same manner with the three first.[1] I am respectfully, Your Obedt

J MARSHALL

ALS, Dreer Collection, PHi. Addressed to Wayne at Philadelphia and "Hond by/ Judge Washington." Bushrod Washington carried this note with him to Philadelphia on his circuit court duties (Washington to Wayne, 1 Apr. 1806, Dreer Collection, PHi).

1. Vol. V was not published until the spring of 1807 (see JM to Wayne, 27 June 1806, n. 2).

Rules Of Court

[5 March 1806][1]

All causes, the records in which shall be delivered to the clerk on or before the 6th. day of a term, shall be considered as for trial in the course of that term. Where the record shall be delivered after the 6th. day of a term, either party will be entitled to a continuance.

In all cases where a writ of error shall be a supersedeas to a judgement rendered in any circuit court of the United States, except that for the district of Columbia, at least thirty days prior to the commencement of any term of this court, it shall be the duty of the plaintiff in error to lodge a copy of the record with the clerk of this court within the first six days of the term, and if he shall fail so to do, the defendent in error shall be permitted afterwards to lodge a copy of the record with the clerk & the cause shall stand for trial in like manner as if the record had come up within the first six days. Or he may on producing a certificate from the clerk stating the cause & that a writ of error has been sued out which operates as a supersedeas to the judgement have the said writ of error docketed & dismissed.[2] This rule shall apply to all judgements rendered by the court for the district of Columbia at any time prior to a session of this court.

In cases not put to issue at the August term It shall be the duty of the plaintiff in error, if errors shall not have been assigned in the court below, to assign them in this court at the commencement of the term, or so soon thereafter as the record shall be filed with the clerk, & the cause placed on the docket; and if he shall fail to do so, & shall also fail to assign them when the cause shall be called for trial, the writ of error may be dismissed at his costs. And if the defendent shall refuse to plead to issue, and the cause shall be called for trial, the court may proceed to hear an argument on the part of the plaintiff & to give judgement according to the right of the cause.

AD, RG 267, DNA.

1. This rule was entered on the last page of the minutes for this term, which ended on 5 Mar. (U.S. Sup. Ct. Minutes, Feb. 1806). It is printed in 3 Cranch 239–40.

2. The preceding sentence was written on the verso, with a direction to be inserted at this point.

To Jonathan Williams

Dear Sir   Richmond March 30th. 1806

I must pray you to pardon the long delay of my answer to your letter enclosing the constitution of your society for the improvement of military knowlege in the United States.[1] Altho I cannot furnish a sufficient apology for not having sooner acknowleged its receipt, yet as in such cases the truth is always best, I will give you the naked fact.

About the middle of January I returned from the circuit court in North Carolina, & found your letter in the post office. As a considerable time had elapsed between its date & receipt, I determined to postpone an answer until february when my duty would call me to Washington to attend the supreme court. While there I was so occupied with official duties, my mind took so entirely a different direction, that I really forgot it. The subject occurred to me repeatedly, but never while in my chamber with pen ink & paper at hand.

I pray you sir to receive, & to present for me to the members of the society my acknowlegements for the honor of being elected an honorary member, & to express at the same time the real regret which is inspired by a consciousness of inability to become useful to them. No man is more strongly impressed than myself with the value of preserving & enlarging the remnant of military skill which is to be found in our country but I feel that it is not in my power to prevent in any degree its extinguishment. My mind has so long taken a totally different direction that the few acquisitions I may have made in early life in the great science of national defence, are lost. With great respect & esteem, I remain Sir your obedt

J MARSHALL

ALS, U.S. Military Philosophical Society Papers, NHi. Addressed by JM to Williams at West Point, N.Y.; postmarked Richmond, 31 Mar. Endorsed (by Williams?).

1. Letter not found. Williams (1750–1819) was the first superintendent of the U.S. Military Academy at West Point.

To Oliver Wolcott, Jr.

Dear Sir   Richmond April 21. 1806

Permit me to trespass on your friendship with a request, a compliance with which will not I trust give you much trouble.

You recollect that it has been asserted that General Washington was disposed to withhold his ratification of the treaty negotiated by Mr. Jay, until the intercepted letter of Mr. Fauchet was placed in his hands.[1] I can perceive nothing decisive upon this subject among his papers. I observe that his original determination was to ratify, but I am not sure that the expression of the public sentiment, or the provision order issued by the British cabinet might have some influence on him; nor am I sure that it had. Will your recollection enable you to give me the details of that transaction? Especially of so much as passed after his return from Mount Vernon? If it will you will greatly oblige me by doing so.

I fancy the democrats begin to discover that a republican government may have secrets. With great respect & esteem, I am dear Sir your

J MARSHALL

ALS, Oliver Wolcott, Jr., Papers, CtHi.

1. See Wolcott to JM, 9 June 1806 and n. 1.

The Life of George Washington
Volume V, Chapter 3
Draft and Revised Version

EDITORIAL NOTE

As Marshall reviewed the fair copy of volume V, he realized he needed to reduce its length considerably.[1] Deciding to make radical cuts in parts of chapter 3, he drafted a briefer passage that condensed more than sixteen pages recounting congressional debates. The manuscript fragment containing this draft is now at Harvard University and is the basis for the text on pages 193–99 in the published version.[2] It deals with debates in the First Congress in April through June 1789 over the impost and tonnage bills and

REVISED VERSION OF THE LIFE OF GEORGE WASHINGTON

A page from the publisher's copy of volume V, containing Marshall's interlined revision for a portion of chapter 3. *Courtesy of the Historical Society of Pennsylvania*

the president's power of removing officers from executive departments.[3] The draft is the second of two surviving autograph fragments of Marshall's manuscript for the *Life*. Unlike the first, which formed part of the original manuscript for volume IV, the Harvard fragment represents a later phase in Marshall's composition, his revision of the fair copy for Wayne.[4]

After Marshall drafted his condensation of chapter 3, he transferred it to the publisher's copy. He first crossed through lines of the original text on the copy and then wrote his new version in between; the interlineation adds up to about four pages. It appears forty-eight pages into the chapter, beginning three-quarters down on the page and covering the next two and a quarter pages. After canceling in toto the next thirteen pages, Marshall retained four paragraphs in the fair copy. Over the following one and a half pages, he interlined parts of two sentences, let stand part of a paragraph, inserted a new paragraph, kept an old one, and added two final paragraphs.

In transcribing his draft onto the fair copy, Marshall made some changes as he wrote; his draft and his initial interlined text are not identical. He then further revised what he had copied. Taking into account these cancellations and insertions, the interlined text, along with the intermittent original six paragraphs, became the published version in volume V, 193–99.

The revised text, interlined on the publisher's copy, constitutes a separate Marshall document. It includes a final paragraph that is not on the draft fragment. The draft is printed here in the left-hand column along with the revised version on the right. The first is the author's revision of the original fair copy; the second represents his rewriting of that revision. Footnotes are numbered consecutively in each column; the set for the right-hand column has the letter "a" affixed. The six paragraphs retained from the original text of the fair copy have not been included in order to facilitate comparison of Marshall's draft and revised text. Where Marshall interlined only a portion of a sentence, the complete sentence from the fair copy is provided and words in the copyist's hand noted. Textual notes accompany both documents.[5] Omitted is the final text published in volume V. Except for punctuation, capitalization, replacement of ampersands with "and," and two noted changes of a word, the published rendition of Marshall's text is the same as his interlined version on the publisher's copy.

1. JM to Wayne, 27 June 1806.

2. For description of manuscript, see provenance to documents below.

3. For a summary of these debates, see Hutchinson, *Papers of Madison*, XII, 53–57.

4. For the earlier fragment and explanation of the phases through which volumes of the *Life* passed on the way to publication, see *The Life of George Washington*, Volume IV, Chapter 8, Draft and Published Version, [ca. July 1804], editorial note.

5. The textual notes follow the numbered footnotes. For the method and symbols used in compiling these notes, see Editorial Apparatus (xxxiii–xxxiv).

Draft   [ca. May 1806][1]

¶1 Fitzsimmons M⟨r⟩. Clymer Mr. Page, & Mr. Jackson

¶2 They relied much upon the public sentiment which had been expressed unequivocally, through the several state legislatures & otherwise against placing foreign nations generally on a footing with the allies of the United States. So strong was this sentiment, that to its operation the existing constitution was principally to be ascribed.

¶3 It was thought important to the interests of the United States to prove to those nations who had declined forming commercial treaties with them, that they possessed & would exercise the power of retaliating any regulations unfavorable to their trade. On the advantages possessed by America in a war of commercial regulation they strongly insisted.

¶4 The disposition France had lately shown to relax with regard to the U:S. the rigid policy by which her counsels had generally been guided, ought to be cultivated. The evidence of this disposition was that American built ships might be sold to French citizens, subject to a duty of five per centum on the price, after which they became naturalized. There was reason to believe that the person charged with the Affairs of the United States at that court had ⟨made⟩ some favorable impressions which the conduct of the american government ought not to efface.

¶5 It was earnestly urged that from artificial or adventitious causes the commerce between the United States & Great Britain had exceeded its natural boundary. It was desirable to

Revised version

¶1 The resolutions as reported, were supported by Mr. Madison, Mr. Baldwin, [+] Mr. Fitzsimmons[‡] Mr. Clymer[‡] Mr. Page,[§] and Mr. Jackson.[*1a]

¶2 They relied much upon the public sentiment which had, they said, been unequivocally expressed through the several state legislatures and otherwise, against placing foreign nations generally, on a footing with the allies of the United States. So strong was this sentiment, that to its operation the existing constitution was principally to be ascribed. They thought it important to prove to those nations who had declined forming commercial treaties with them, that the United States possessed and would exercise the power of retaliating any regulations unfavorable to their trade, and they insisted strongly On the advantages of America in a war of commercial regulation, should this measure produce one.

¶3 The disposition France had lately shown to relax with regard to the United States, the rigid policy by which her counsels had generally been guided, ought to be cultivated. The evidence of this disposition was an edict by which American built ships purchased by French subjects became naturalized. There was reason to believe that the person charged with the affairs of the United States at that court, had made some favorable impressions which the conduct of the American government ought not to efface.

¶4 With great earnestness, it was urged that from artificial or adventitious causes, the commerce between the United States and Great Britain had exceeded its natural boundary.

give such political advantages to other nations as would enable them to acquire their due share of the direct trade. It was also desirable to impart some benefit to nations who had formed commercial treaties with the United States, & thereby to impress on those powers which had hitherto neglected to treat with them the idea that some advantages were to be gained by a reciprocity of friendship.

¶6   That France had claims on the gratitude of the American people which ought not to be overlooked, was an additional argument in favor of the principle for which they contended.

¶7   The discrimination was opposed by Mr. Benson Mr. Lawrence Mr. Wadsworth & Mr. Shermer.[2]

¶8   They did not admit that the public sentimint had been unequivocally expressed; nor did they admit that such benefits had flowed from commercial treaties as to justify a sacrifice of interest in order to obtain them. There was a commercial[3]

[separate sheet]

¶9   to sell ships could not be of this descrip⟨tion . . . ⟩ known that the merchants of the United States did not own vessels enough for the transportation of the produce of the country, & only two, as was beleived, had been sold since the license had been granted. The trade with Great Britain viewed throughout, was upon a footing as beneficial to the United States as that wi⟨th⟩ France.

¶10   That France had claims upon the gratitude of Americ⟨a⟩ was admitted; but that these claims ought to be satisf⟨ied⟩ by premiums on French com-

It was wise to give such political advantages to other nations as would enable them to acquire their due share of the direct trade. It was also wise to impart some benefits to nations that had formed commercial treaties with the United States, & thereby to impress on those powers which had hitherto neglected to form such treaties, the idea that some advantages were to be gained by a reciprocity of friendship.

That France had claims on the   ¶5 gratitude of the American people which ought not to be overlooked, was an additional argument in favor of the principle for which they contended.

The discrimination was opposed   ¶6 by Mr. Benson* Mr. Lawrence Mr. Wadsworth + & Mr. Shermer. + [2a]

They did not admit that the public   ¶7 sentiment had been unequivocally expressed; nor did they admit that such benefits had flowed from commercial treaties as to justify a sacrifice of interest to obtain them. There was a commercial treaty with France; but neither that treaty, nor the favors shown to that nation, had produced any correspondent advantages. The license to sell ships could not be of this description, since it was well known that the merchants of the United States did not own vessels enough for the transportation of the produce of the country, and only two, as was beleived, had been sold since the license had been granted. The trade with Great Britain, viewed in all its parts, was upon a footing as beneficial to the United States as that with France.

That the latter power had claims   ¶8 upon the gratitude of America was admitted, but that these claims would justify premiums for the encourage-

merce drawn from the pockets of the American people was not conceded.

¶11 To the observation founded on the extensivenes⟨s⟩ of the commerce between the United States & Great Britain, it w⟨as⟩ answered that this was not a subject for the interposition of th⟨e⟩ legislature. It was one on which the merchants were the best Ju⟨dges⟩. They would consult their interest as individuals, & this was a cas⟨e⟩ in which the interest of the nation & of the individual was the sam⟨e⟩.

Fitzsimmons[4]

¶12 Mr. White was supported by Mr. Smith Mr. Page, Mr. St⟨one⟩ & Mr. Jackson.

13 In the power over all the executive officers which the bill would confer on the President the most alarming danger to liberty was perceived. It was in the nature of a monarchical prerogative, & would convert them in⟨to⟩ the meer tools & creatures of his will. A dependence so servile on

ment of French commerce and navigation, to be drawn from the pockets of the american people, was not conceded. The state of the revenue, it was said, would not admit of these experiments.

¶9 The observation founded on the extensiveness of the trade between the United States and Great Britain was answered by saying that this was not a subject proper for legislative interposition. It was one of which the merchants were the best judges. They would consult their interest as individuals; and this was a case in which the interest of the nation and of individuals was the same.

¶10 In explanation of this fact, Mr. Fitzsimmons stated that the war of the revolution had deprived the American merchants of their ships, and of the means of acquiring others. On the return of peace the British reestablished their commercial houses; and it was by these men, and by their capital in many of the states, that vessels were furnished for the transportation of their produce, & that the greater part of their trade was carried on.[3a]

¶11 Mr. White was supported by[4a] Mr. Smith of South Carolina,[5a] Mr. Page* Mr. Stone,**[6a] and Mr. Jackson.

¶12 Those gentlemen contended that the clause was either unnecessary or improper.[7a]

¶13 In the power over all the executive officers which the bill proposed to confer upon the President, the most alarming dangers to liberty were percieved. It was in the nature of monarchical prerogative, and would convert them into the meere tools and creatures of his will. A depen-

one Individ⟨ual⟩ would deter men of high & honorable minds from accepting offices; a⟨nd⟩ if, contrary to expectation, such men should be brought into office they would be reduced to the necessity of sacrificing every principle of independence to the will of the chief magistrate, or of exposing themselves to the disgrace & injury of bein⟨g⟩ removed from office at a time when it might be no long⟨er⟩ in their power to engage in other pursuits.

¶14   The amendment was opposed by Mr. Madison ⟨&?⟩ Mr. Sedgewick.

¶15   By the friends of the original bill the amendment was opposed, with arguments of great force, drawn from the constitution and from general convenience. On several parts of the constitution &, especially, on that which vests the executive power in the President, they relied confidently to support the position, that in conformity with that instrument the power in question could reside only with the ⟨c⟩hief magistrate.

¶16   But, if it was a case on which the constitution was silent, the clearest principles of political expediency required that

dence so servile on one individual, would deter men of high & honorable minds from engaging in the public service; and if, contrary to expectation such men should be brought into office, they would be reduced to the necessity of sacrificing every principle of independence to the will of the Chief Magistrate, or of exposing themselves to the disgrace of being removed from office & that too at a time when it might be no longer in their power to engage in other pursuits.[8a]

By the friends of the original bill, ¶14 the amendment was opposed with arguments of great force drawn from the constitution and from general convenience. On several parts of the constitution, and especially on that which vests the executive power in the President, they relied confidently to support the position, that in conformity with that instrument, the power in question could reside only with the Chief Magistrate. No power, it was said, could[9a] be more completely executive in its nature than that of removal from office.

But, if it was a case on which the ¶15 constitution was silent, the clearest principles of political expediency required that neither branch of the legislature should participate in it.

The danger that a President could ¶16 ever be found who would remove good men from office, was treated as imaginary. It was not by the[10a] splendor attached to the character of the present Chief Magistrate alone that this opinion was to be defended. It was founded on the structure of the office. The man in whose favor a majority of the people of this continent could[11a] unite, had probability at least in favor of his principles; in ad-

dition to which, the public odium
that would inevitably attach to such
conduct, would be an effectual security against it.

ADf, Jared Sparks MSS, MH; AD, Dreer Collection, PHi. On draft in Sparks MSS, Sparks noted at top of last page, second line, "(Judge Marshall's hand writing)" This MS originally consisted of one sheet written on both sides but was subsequently torn in two, as well as torn off across the top. Angle brackets enclose words or letters obscured by tears, frayed edges, or in margins by binding. Document at PHi interlined by JM in publisher's copy of vol. V, chap. 3. For discussion of these two versions of passage in vol. V, chap. 3, 193–95, 197–99, see editorial note. JM's deletions and interlineations in both documents are recorded in Draft and Revised Version Textual Notes below.

1. Unable to finish vol. V upon his return to Richmond in the fall of 1805, JM promised Wayne that it would be completed in the spring of 1806 after he got home from the Supreme Court in March. Bushrod Washington joined JM in Richmond from approximately the beginning of May through the third week in June, when the two of them went over all but the last chapter of the manuscript, "expunging about one third of it." During this revisal, in May or possibly the first part of June, JM must have written the draft for condensing chap. 3 (JM to Wayne, 5 Oct., 19 Oct. 1805, 27 June 1806; Bushrod Washington to Wayne, 1 Apr., 22 June 1806, Dreer Collection, PHi).
2. JM meant Roger Sherman of Connecticut.
3. End of the first page. Because the top of the sheet is torn off, the next several lines are missing.
4. Sheet torn in half below here, but JM does not appear to have written any of the intervening sentences between "Fitzsimmons" and "Mr. White . . ." on this draft.

1a. In footnotes at the bottom of the page JM identified the states from which these men came but then deleted the notes. As published, the names appear without these symbols (vol. V, chap. 3, 193).
2a. In footnotes at the bottom of the page JM identified the states from which these men came but then deleted the notes. As published, the names appear without these symbols. Again, JM meant Sherman. The name is printed as "Shermen" in *Life*, V, 194.
3a. JM crossed out about thirteen pages of his original text following this paragraph. He then allowed to stand four paragraphs in the original fair copy, which appear in published form at the top of p. 196 through the first paragraph on p. 197. JM then resumed his interlineation. In the four retained paragraphs, JM concluded discussion of the debate over the impost and tonnage bills and introduced the question of the president's power to remove executive officers.
4a. JM deleted "Mr." here, which printer reinserted (197).
5a. Preceding four words in copyist's hand.
6a. In footnotes at the bottom of the page JM identified the states from which these men came but then deleted the notes. As published, the names appear without these symbols (197).
7a. Preceding two and a half words in copyist's hand. JM let stand three succeeding sentences of his original text, which appear in published form in the last paragraph on p. 197. JM then continued his interlineation.
8a. A paragraph succeeds this from the original text and appears as the second

paragraph on p. 198. JM deleted the second half of it and interlined the following paragraph.

9a. Printer set this as "would" (199).

10a. To clarify a revision of his interlineation here, JM wrote the following note sideways in the left margin: "In the third line after 'by the' insert instead of 'worth' the words 'splendor attached to the character.'"

11a. Printer set this as "would" (199).

Draft Textual Notes

¶ 2	ll. 2–3	had ↑been↓ expressed ~~itself~~ unequivocally, ~~in the~~ through
	l. 4	legislatures ↑& otherwise↓ against
¶ 3	ll. 6–8	any ~~restrictive~~ regulations ~~on~~ ↑unfavorable to↓ their trade. ~~The~~ ↑On the↓ advantages
¶ 4	ll. 2–3	relax ↑with regard to the U:S.↓ the rigid
	ll. 3–4	her ~~cousels~~ ↑counsels↓ had
	ll. 4–5	guided ~~, which was exhibited in her permission to natu-ralize American built ships when purchased by her subjects,~~ ought to be cultivated. ~~A manifestation~~ The evidence
	ll. 7–8	sold ~~in France~~ ↑to French citizens,↓ subject
	l. 10	became ~~naturalized. entitled to all~~ naturalized. ~~The p~~ There was
¶ 5	ll. 1–3	It was ↑earnestly↓ urged that from ~~adventitious &~~ artificial ↑or adventitious↓ causes ~~Great Britain had obtained an undue & unnatural portion of the commerce of the Uni~~ the commerce
	l. 7	as would ~~as would~~ enable
	ll. 9–10	desirable ~~to furnish some advantages~~ ↑that some benefit should be received accrue↓ ↑to impart some benefit↓ to nations
	ll. 12–13	States, ↑& thereby to impress on↓ ~~that~~ those
	ll. 15–16	to be ~~derived from~~ ↑gained by↓ a ~~receprocity~~ ↑reciprocity↓ of friendship.
¶ 6	ll. 1–2 beg.	~~The~~ [erasure] That France ~~was entitled to~~ ↑had claims on↓ the gratitude
	ll. 5–6	the ~~discrimination which was proposed.~~ ↑ principle for which they contended.↓
¶ 8	l. 1	They ~~denied that the~~ did not
	l. 7	them. ~~No advantages had yet been derived from the treaty with France.~~ There was
		[separate sheet]
¶ 9	l. 1	ships ~~was~~ could
	l. 4	own ~~ships~~ ↑vessels↓ enough
	ll. 8–9	Britain ~~taken~~ [erasure] viewed
¶10	l. 2	of ~~the America⟨n⟩ people~~ ↑America↓ was
¶11	ll. 2–3	between [erasure] the
	l. 4	Britain, [erasure] ↑it↓ w⟨as⟩
¶12	l. 2	Smith ~~of South Caro~~ Mr. Page

¶13 ll. 1–2 beg. ~~Upon t~~ ~~From~~ ↑In↓ the power ↑[*erasure*] over all the executive officers↓ which the

l. 9 one ~~man[?]~~ ↑individ⟨ual⟩↓ would

ll. 11–12 to ~~this~~ expectation,

ll. 16–17 of ~~being disgracef⟨ully⟩ removed from office~~ exposing

ll. 19–20 be ~~too late for~~ no long⟨er⟩ in their ~~en~~ power

¶16 l. 1 case ~~of~~ ↑on↓ which

l. 2 silent, ~~&~~ ↑the↓ clearest

Revised Version Textual Notes

¶ 1 footnote ~~⁺from Georgia, ‡from Pennsylvania §Virginia~~

¶ 2 ll. 10–12 ascribed. ~~They thought It was~~ ↑They↓ thought ↑it↓ important ~~to the interests of the United States,~~ to prove to those nations ~~that~~ ↑who↓ had

ll. 13–14 that ~~they~~ ↑the United States↓ possessed

ll. 17–18 trade, ↑and they insisted strongly↓ On the advantages ~~possessed by~~ ↑of↓ America

l. 19 regulation, ~~they strongly insisted~~ should

¶ 3 l. 2 relax ~~the~~ with

¶ 4 l. 6 was ~~desirable~~ wise

¶ 5 ll. 2–3 people [*erasure*] ↑which↓ ought

¶ 6 footnote ~~*From New York ⁺from Connecticut~~

¶ 8 ll. 4–5 premiums ~~on French comm~~ for the encouragement of ~~the~~ French

¶ 9 l. 1 beg. ~~To the~~ ↑The↓ observation

¶11 footnote ~~*from Virginia **Maryland~~

¶13 ll. 1–2 power ~~over all the executive officers~~ ↑over all the executive officers↓ which

ll. 18–20 disgrace ~~and injury~~ of being removed from office ↑& that too↓ at

¶16 ll. 4–5 the ~~worth~~ ↑splendor attached to the character↓ of

From Oliver Wolcott, Jr.

Dear Sir New York June 9th 1806

I recd in due season, your highly esteemed favour of April 21st. in which you refer to an assertion, which has been frequently made "that General Washington was disposed to withhold his ratification of the Treaty negotiated by Mr Jay untill the intercepted Letter of Mr Fauchet was placed in his hands" and in which you request me to give you the details of that transaction.[1]

I consider it my duty to comply with your request, & take the liberty to assure you, that a variety of very pressing avocations and the necessity I have been under of consulting my papers have been the only causes which have delayed my reply till this period.

It is well known to you that the policy of instituting any negociation with Great Britain was severely censured from the time this measure was first resolved on and that unusual exertions were made to prejudice the public mind against any result which could be reasonably expected. You are also fully apprized, that when the Treaty was laid before the Senate, the President although he was not well satisfied with several of its provisions, determined that he would ratify it if so advised by that body. As the advisory act of the Senate was passed on the 24th. of June & the ratification did not take place till about the middle of August, the object of this letter is to assign the causes which in my opinion occasioned the delay.

The first measure of the President in relation to the Treaty, after the close of the Session of the Senate of which I have any knowledge, was a direction to Mr Randolph to communicate it to the French Minister.

Soon after, the following questions were agitated, upon which, the President required the opinions of the heads of Departments in *writing* "1st. Is or is not, the resolution of the Senate of the 24th of June intended to be the final act of that Body, or do they expect that the new article which is proposed shall be submitted to them before the Treaty takes effect? 2d Does or does not the Constitution permit the President to ratify the Treaty without submitting the new Articles after it shall have been agreed to by the British King to the Senate, for their further advice and consent." The report which I delivered, was dated the 30th of June, but the discussions occasioned by these questions & by the consideration of the reply which was directed to be given to the objections of the French Minister, against the Treaty, were not terminated before the 5th. of July.

By this time, artful and well digested publications appeared in the Newspapers; the public passions were considerably excited against the Treaty & it was easy to perceive, that an extensive and concerted opposition was formed.

In this state of things inofficial information was recd that an order had been issued by the British Government authorizing the Capture of American Vessells laden with provisions and bound to France.

It was contended, that this information ought to induce the President to suspend the act of ratification.

Three opinions were communicated to the Pres⟨ident⟩ 1st That he

should *suspend*, the ratification unti⟨ll⟩ he was informed of the existance of the order, & in case it was found to exist, that he should
refuse a ratification, untill the order was revoke⟨d.⟩ Second, to ratify
the Treaty in the mode advise⟨d⟩ by the Senate but at the same time to
prepar⟨e⟩ a note to accompany the exchange of ratification⟨s⟩ declaring that nothing in the Treaty, could in the opinion of the President,
justify such an Order for detaining provision Vessells, as was reported to be in existance: The principles of the advocates of this
opinion, will be found in a Letter from Colo. Pickering to Mr Monroe
date⟨d⟩ the 12 of Sepr. 1795.[2] Third. The other opinion wa⟨s⟩ that the
President ought to ratify the Treaty as advised by the Senate and
transmit it to ou⟨r⟩ American Minister in London with an instruction,
not to exchange the ratifications, till the provision order was re-
scinded; or if the order had existed, but was revoked at the time, then
to accompany the ratification, with a remonstrance against the principle on which the order was supposed to be founded. The first opinion was supported by Mr Randolph the Second by the other Secretaries & Attorney General. The third was suggested by Mr. Hamilton.

When the President discovered that a diversity of opinion existed
as to the course which he ought to pursue, he directed Mr Randolph
to prepare draughts of instructions for the Minister or agent who
might be designated for London and a Memorial or Note for the
British Minister, which after being presented to the other Secretaries
& Attorney General were to be transmitted accompanied with their
observations thereon, to Mount-Vernon.

After the Presidents departure from Philadelphia, the public fer-
ment increased: In one instance at least, as I was informed by the
Author himself, a series of publications in opposition to the Treaty
and addressed directly to the President, were instigated by Mr Randolph: Owing to indisposition or some other cause, but little progress
was made in preparing the Instructions & Memorial and intimations
were circulated that the President was disposed to withhold his ratification.

The first intimation I recd of the existance of Fauchets Letter was
from Mr Hammond[3] on the 26th. of July but it was not till the 28th.
that I could persuade him, to deliver me the original Letter, without
possessing which, I did not consider it prudent, to speak on the subject to any person whatever. On the Evening of the 28th I communicated Fauchets Letter to Col Pickering and it was concluded between
us to shew it to Mr Bradford the Att: General, who was then at his
Seat in the Country: We consulted with Mr Bradford on the 29th.
and it was agreed to request the President to return to Philadelphia;

The Letter expressing this Wish, was written the 31st. The President arrived the 11th of August, when I immediately placed Fauchets Letter in his hands, mentioning at the same time, the circumstances under which I recd. it.

The consideration of all questions of a general nature was necessarily suspended, untill that which affected Mr Randolph could be disposed of: That you may judge for yourself of the Presiden⟨ts⟩ impressions, I shall transcribe a Note in his hand writing which he delivered to me and which has constantly remained in my possession.

"At what time should Mr F——ts Letter be made known to Mr R . . . ?"

"What will be the best mode of doing it?"

"In the presence of the Secretaries & Att: General."

"If the explanations given by the latter are not satisfactory, whether besides removal, are any other measures proper to be taken? and What?"

"Would an application to Mr A.[4] to see the paragraphs in No. 3 & 6 alluded to in Fauchets Letter be proper? These might condemn or acquit unequivocally—and if innocent whether R. will not apply for them, if I do not."

"If upon the investigation of this subject, it should appear less dark than at present, but not so clear as to restore confidence, in wh⟨a⟩t light and on what ground, is the removal to appear before the public?"

"What immediate steps are necessary to be tak⟨en⟩ so soon as the removal of R is resolved on, if that should be the case, with respect to the Archives in that office?"

"If the Letter of F——t is the only evidence and that thought sufficient to the removal, what would be the consequence, of giving the Letter to the public, without any comments, as the grou⟨nd⟩ on which the measure of the Executive respectin⟨g⟩ the removal is founded? It would speak for itself, A part without the whole, might be charged with unfairness. The public would expect reasons for the sudden removal of so high an officer and it will be found not easy to avoid saying too little or too much upon such an occasion, as it is not to be expected that the removed Officer will acquiese, withou⟨t⟩ attempting a justification, or at least to do away by explanation the sting of the Letter of accusation, unless he was let down easily, to do which I see no way: for if he is guilty of what is charged he merits no favour, and if he is not he will accept of none and it is not difficult to perceive what turn *he* and his friends will give to the Act, namely, that his Friendship for the French Nation & his opposition to a compleat ratification, have been the Causes."

The two first of these questions were decided by the President uninfluenced as far as my knowledge and beleif extends, by any suggestions from the Officers of Government: He was greatly dissatisfied that the Instructions and Memorial had not been prepared and submitted to the consideration of the Secretaries & Att: General, that their Reports might be formed, & he peremptorily resolved, that whether Mr Randolph was innocent or culpable, he would require of him the performance of a service which was his official duty & which ought to have been long before compleated.

It was my earnest wish to be excused from being present at the interview, when Fauchets Letter was delivered to Mr Randolph: The President however determined otherwise & inserted his decision on the Note I have transcribed. He observed that Fauchets Letter had necessarily excited *suspicions*: that it was proper that the officers of Government, equally with himself, should possess the same opportunities of having those suspicions removed or established and that notwithstanding the long connexion which had subsisted between Mr Randolph & himself, he was persuaded, that any explanations which would satisfy his own mind, would also be satisfactory to the Officers of Government: After mature consideration, it was considered to be improper to make any application to Mr. Adet, that it was improbable that Mr Adet would permit his *records to be inspected*: that neither Fauchets dispatch nor any Certificate of the French Minister could be regarded as conclusive evidence in favour of or against Mr Randolph—That Mr Randolphs conduct at the time an explanation was required, would probably furnish the best means of discovering his true situation and of duly estimating the defence he might make.

When the Letter was delivered to Mr Randolph the President requested him to read it and to make such observations thereon as he thought proper. He silently perused it with composure, till he arrived at the passage which refers to his "precious confessions" when his embarressment was manifest: After a short hesitation, he proceeded to look over the Letter with great attention: When the perusal was compleated he said with a smile, which I thought forced; *yes Sir I will explain what I know.* He then commenced reading the Letter by paragraphs and though a great part of it contained nothing interesting to himself, yet he commented on every part: His remarks were very desultory & it was evident, that he was considering what explanation he should give of the most material passages. As he was not interrupted, it was however impossible, to speak with precision on one subject, while his reflections were employed on other subjects. When he arrived at the passage in which Fauchet refers to the overtures mentioned in No 6 and the "tarif" which regulated the Consciences of certain "pretended Patriots" his conduct was very remarkable: He expressed no strong emotion; no resentment against Fauchet. he declared that he could not certainly tell what was intended by such remarks: He said that he indeed recollected, having been informed, that Mr Hammond and other persons in New York, were contriving measures, to destroy Govenor Clinton, the French Minister and himself, & that he had enquired of Mr Fauchet, whether he could not by his flouer Contracters provide the means of defeating their Machinations; he asserted however that he had never recd or proposed to receive money for his own use, or that of any other person and had never made any improper communications of the measures of Government.

One question only was put to Mr Randolph, namely, how he intended to be understood when he represented Mr Hammond as contriving to *Destroy, Governor Clinton, Mr Fauchet & himself*: His answer was *that their influence* and popularity *were to be destroyed.*

Mr Randolph retired for a short time but he must have felt, that neither the manner nor the matter of his explanations could afford any degree of satisfaction: the result was a proposal by Mr Randolph of an immediate resignation which he promised to communicate in writing—Mr Randolph has represented that his proposal to resign was accompanied with expressions of resentment at the treatment he had received—Although his Letter of resignation places the affair on this ground yet my impressions of what happened during the personal interview, are very different.

The circumstances which I have narrated will shew how the President was employed from the close of the Session of the Senate in June, till he ratified the Treaty, in August: That his first determination was to ratify is certain & that he ever changed this determination has never been proved. The provision order of the British Government, certainly presented a question of some difficulty and different opinions were entertained of the manner in which it ought to influence the Presidents measures; this question was under consideration when the President left Philadelphia: It was his established & well known practice, to reserve his sentiments on questions of importance, till as late a period as was convenient, before his formal decisions were to be made. It was Mr Randolphs duty to prepare the Papers which were to bring the questions relating to the Treaty, to a final issue and this duty was delayed by him longer than was expected. A Letter from the Prest. to Mr Randolph dated July 22d may be understood to convey an idea that the Treaty would not be ratified while the provision order was supposed to be in existance: but this is not a necessary, or perhaps even the most natural interpretation of that

Letter. The President knew that this would be Mr Randolphs advice & he might not think it proper to controul that opinion at that time: The object of the Letter was to prevent the increase of popular passion, by causing it to be Known, that so far as respected the *merits of the Treaty* he had determined to pursue the advice of the Senate; and from respect to Mr Randolph, he might feel inclined to leave every collateral question, open to discussion: Such certainly was the manner in which the subject was treated by him, after his return to Philadelphia. I have no knowledge what verbal communications were authorized by the President, or were actually made by Mr Randolph, to Mr Hammond.

I regret that I have not been able to write this Letter sooner & I assure you that I will ever execute your commands in the best manner in my power. With high Esteem & respect, I remain Dr Sir your Obedt Sert.

Copy[5]   OLIV: WOLCOTT.

LS (copy), Oliver Wolcott, Jr., Papers, CtHi. Angle brackets enclose letters obscured in margin.

1. The incident JM asked Wolcott to recollect occurred during the summer of 1795. On 24 June the Senate narrowly ratified the Jay Treaty, but President Washington withheld his signature until August. During the interval, news was received of a British order in council instructing naval commanders to seize all ships carrying grain to France or to French possessions. Secretary of State Edmund Randolph advised the president not to give effect to the treaty during the existence of the provision order. In the end, Washington decided to sign the treaty and to send an accompanying memorial protesting against the order. Soon thereafter Randolph resigned his office following disclosures that raised suspicion of improper or criminal conduct. These disclosures were contained in a dispatch from French minister Joseph Fauchet, which had been captured by the British and ultimately placed in the hands of Wolcott, then secretary of the treasury. The ambiguous language of the dispatch, which was hastily and faultily translated, made it appear that Randolph had solicited a bribe from the French minister. Although this charge was completely unfounded, and historians have subsequently exonerated Randolph of wrongdoing, the secretary of state was unable at the time to dispel the cloud of suspicion. See Irving Brant, "Edmund Randolph, Not Guilty!," *WMQ*, 3d ser., VII (1950), 179–98; W. Allan Wilbur, "Oliver Wolcott, Jr., and Edmund Randolph's Resignation, 1795 . . . ," *Connecticut Historical Society Bulletin*, XXXVIII (1973), 12–16. For a detailed narrative of this episode, see Carroll and Ashworth, *Washington*, VII, 265–98.

2. See *ASP, Foreign Relations*, I, 596–98.

3. George Hammond, then British minister to the U.S.

4. Pierre-Auguste Adet, Fauchet's successor as French minister to the U.S.

5. In Wolcott's hand.

United States v. Johnson
Notes on Arguments
U.S. Circuit Court, Virginia, 11 June 1806

United States }
                    errors[1]
Johnson   }

1st. Court has no cognizance[2] v.1. p 55.[3]—last section—
practice whenever new offence, to give the jurisdiction
4 v. 146. 537. 2 v. of 6 Sess. 169.[4] 2 v. of 6 Ses. 537.[5]

———

Bankrupt law no neg. words yet this ct. has not concurrent jurisdiction

———

   1. Ba 592.[6]

———

2. That the route on which the robbery was committed was not established by the act recited in the indictment.[7]

———

3d. The indictment does not show that the letter was put in by
   another
   3d. Bacon 101. 4. 13[8]
4th. Omits to charge embezzlement of the letter.—14th. & 15th. Sec.[9]
Mr. Hay 1st. 33d. Sec. of judicial act.[10]

———

2d Founded on a misapprehension of the words in the indictment.[11]
3d. Unnecessary to guard the entendment—because if Johnson had
      placed the letter there himself, the offence is the same.[12]

———

4th. Not necessary to charge the embezzlement
On the new trial—a mail carrier not employed in the genl. post of
fice—"intended to be conveyed &c."[13]
Botts 1st. The jurisdiction in state courts ousts this
2. The act recited has nothing to do with the mail on this cross route,
   mail must be established according to the act establishing the cross
   route.
3d. Would it be a misdemesnor to give back the letter to him who put
   it in.

———

4th. The act requires embezzlement. The copulative and connects the
   whole—[14]

New trial—The word steal not used when speaking of mail carrier.[15]

AD, United States v. Johnson, U.S. Circuit Court, Virginia, Ended Cases (Unrestored), 1806, Vi.

1. JM made these notes during argument on a motion to arrest judgment against John Johnson, who had been tried and convicted earlier this term for robbing the mail. A laborer from Greensville County on the Southside, Johnson had been hired as a post rider for the mail route from Harris's in Brunswick County to Halifax, N.C. He was charged with taking a twenty-dollar bank note from a letter addressed to Thomas Blount, a member of Congress from North Carolina. After a preliminary hearing in the Greensville County Court in April, Johnson was bound over for trial at the Brunswick District Court in May. The district court then sent him to the federal circuit court in Richmond as the proper tribunal for trial. The federal grand jury returned an indictment on 23 May, and at the trial on the same day a jury found Johnson guilty (proceedings in Greensville County Court [copy], Apr. 1806; order, Brunswick District Court, May 1806, U.S. v. Johnson; U.S. Cir. Ct., Va., Ord. Bk. V, 269–70, 344).

2. Johnson's attorney, Benjamin Botts, assigned four errors in moving for arrest of judgment. The first was that the U.S. court had no cognizance of this offence (motion in arrest of judgment, U.S. v. Johnson).

3. JM's citations are to the contemporary edition of Laws of the U.S. The first reference is to sec. 11 of the Judiciary Act of 1789, which sets forth the jurisdiction of the circuit courts (U.S. Statutes at Large, I, 78–79).

4. The laws cited are the Alien Act (1798), sec. 4; an act "to regulate trade and intercourse with the Indian tribes" (1799), sec. 15; and an act prohibiting the slave trade (1800), sec. 5 (ibid., 572, 747; II, 71). These sections explicitly gave the federal courts cognizance of crimes against the respective acts.

5. The page reference is apparently a mistake; none of the volumes in Laws of the U.S. goes as high as 537.

6. Matthew Bacon, A New Abridgment of the Law (5th. ed.; 5 vols.; Dublin, 1786), I, 592, s.v. "Court of King's Bench." This court, said Bacon, has "so Sovereign a Jurisdiction in all Criminal Matters, that an Act of Parliament, appointing that all Crimes of a certain Denomination shall be tried before certain Judges, doth not exclude the Jurisdiction of this Court, without express negative Words. . . . But where a Statute creates a new Offence, which was not taken Notice of by the Common Law, and erects a new Jurisdiction for the Punishment of it, and prescribes a certain Method of Proceeding, it seems questionable how far this Court has an implied Jurisdiction in such a Case." Under the bankruptcy law of 1800, proceedings in bankruptcy were to take place in the federal district courts (U.S. Statutes at Large, II, 19–36).

7. The second error stated that the mail route between Harris's and Halifax was not established by the act recited in the indictment: "An Act to establish the Post-Office of the United States" (motion in arrest of judgment; indictment, U.S. v. Johnson; U.S. Statutes at Large, I, 733).

8. The third error faulted the indictment for not charging "that the letter or note was of the property of any person other than the said Johnston so as to show otherwise than by intendment that the said Johnston did not himself put the letter & note in P. Office." An indictment in general terms that omitted particular facts was insufficient. It was also a general rule that an indictment must "bring the Offence within all the material Words of the Statute" (motion in arrest of judgment, U.S. v. Johnson; Bacon, Abridgment [5th. ed.], III, 101, 104, 113, s.v. "Indictment").

9. The fourth error set forth a discrepancy between the statute and the indictment The act of 1799 establishing a post office defined the crime as stealing a letter and embezzling the same, the letter containing an article of value. The indictment, however, charged Johnson with embezzling the bank note only, omitting to charge the embezzlement of the letter (motion in arrest of judgment; indictment, U.S. v. Johnson; *U.S. Statutes at Large*, I, 736–37).

10. George Hay was U.S. attorney for the district of Virginia. By sec. 33 of the Judiciary Act of 1789, a person charged with a federal crime could be brought before a state justice or magistrate and be arrested, imprisoned, or bailed for trial before a U.S. court (*U.S. Statutes at Large*, I, 91). Hay, replying to the first error, was attempting to establish that the federal court had cognizance of this crime.

11. The reference is to the second error.

12. A note, apparently in Hay's hand, throws additional light on the U.S. attorney's argument on the third error. He admitted that a common law indictment for stealing should state whose property was stolen but denied that this was an indictment for stealing a letter. "Stealing a letter is no offence under the laws of the U:S. Stealing or taking a letter *from the mail* of the U:S is the gist of the offence. In this case therefore not necessary to aver who was the owner of the letter. When the charge vs. the Prisoner is taking another man's goods, you must aver them to be another man's goods: but when the charge is taking a letter *from the mail*, it does not follow that you must alledge to whom the letter belongs. This is supposed to be clear, if it be true, that a man, might be indicted, for taking a letter from the mail put in by or addressed to himself" (note, U.S. v. Johnson).

13. Hay was apparently arguing that, by sec. 14 of the 1799 act, embezzlement did not have to be charged to a mail carrier, who was not a "person employed in any of the departments of the general post-office" (*U.S. Statutes at Large*, I, 736).

14. Botts apparently referred to this passage in the 1799 act: "And if any person shall steal the mail, or shall steal or take from or out of any mail . . . any letter or packet therefrom . . . and shall open, embezzle, or destroy any such mail, letter or packet, the same containing any article of value . . . " (ibid., 736–37).

15. This is a reference to the concluding clauses of sec. 14, prescribing penalties for mail carriers (ibid., 736).

The court denied the motion in arrest of judgment and sentenced Johnson to one year at hard labor (U.S. Cir. Ct., Va., Ord. Bk. V, 344).

To Caleb P. Wayne

Sir   Richmond June 27th. 1806

I have received your letters of the 27th. of May & of the 6th. & 11th. of this month[1] enclosing me five hundred dollars, two hundred dollars, & fifty dollars: and also informing me that seven hundred & fifty dollars were deposited for me in the bank of the United States. I have given a check for four hundred & fifty & shall to day give two chec⟨ks⟩ for the balance. I have also received from Mr. Washington one hundred & forty one dollars three cents which were paid to him by one of your collectors in Baltimore.

The last chapter will be copied this week & I am now watching for an opportunity to transmit it to Mount Vernon where the preceding chapters are, & whence it will be forwarded to you. The delay which is greater than I expected has been occasioned in part by my personal indisposition & in part by the necessity of going over the work & expunging about one third of it.[2]

I have always felt anxiety respecting a second edition & on that account have wished the copies of the first not to be multiplied. This will be to your advantage because the size of the volume may be reduced or the price augmented. Whether a second edition may ever be required or not I propose after returning from the springs to go over the first at my leisure & make many of those corrections which in the hurry of composition & even of that reading which I afterwards gave to the three first volumes, have certainly escaped my observation. I had proposed a short preface to this volume, but its size notwithstanding the diminutions it has sustained is still too large & I do not wish to stop it one day after an opportunity shall offer to send it forward. I am Sir respectfully, Your Obedt

J MARSHALL

ALS, formerly in collection of Joseph M. Roebling, Trenton, N.J.; offered for sale by Sotheby Parke Bernet in 1981. Addressed to Wayne at Philadelphia; postmarked Richmond, 28 June. Endorsed by Wayne.

1. Letters not found.

2. Owing to "a severe sickness," JM was unable to attend the June session of the U.S. circuit court at Raleigh (*Register*, 23 June 1806). Bushrod Washington did not send the manuscript on to Wayne until July 1806 (Bushrod Washington to Wayne, 14 July, 20 July 1806, Dreer Collection, PHi). Wayne's manuscript copy of vol. V is in Dreer Collection, PHi, in copyist's hand, with deletions and corrections in JM's, Bushrod Washington's and Wayne's hands (see *The Life of George Washington*, Volume V, Chapter 3, Draft and Revised Version, [ca. May 1806], editorial note; and also *The Life of George Washington*, Volume IV, Chapter 8, [ca. May 1804], editorial note). Vol. V, along with the *Maps*, appeared in print in Apr. 1807 (Skeel, *Weems*, I, 318 n. 4; *Va. Gazette, and General Advertiser*, 2 May 1807).

To Caleb P. Wayne

Sir   Richmond June 28th. 1806

I forgot to transmit you the enclosed receipt for three boxes containing the Aurora & Mr. Dunlaps papers.[1]

In the copies which will be transmitted to you of the 5th. volume, there is a total inattention to capitals & small letters. The copier had a system of his own & entirely disregarded the original in this respect. I began with making corrections but soon found that I must relinquish this design unless I could devote one reading to the single object. This being out of my power I leave this task entirely to the editor. There are also many words which are mispelled. This I have corrected in a great many instances, but there are others to which in a single reading I could not advert as my mind was more directed to the language than to the orthography. The same remark applies to punctuation.

I will thank you to communicate these observations to the gentleman who will receive the copy for England. I am Sir respectfully, Your Obedt. Servt

J MARSHALL

I shall set out about the 10th. of July to the sweet springs[2] & shall not return till october.

ALS, Gratz Collection, PHi. Addressed to Wayne at Philadelphia; postmarked Richmond, 30 June.

1. *Dunlap's American Daily Advertiser*, published by John Dunlap in Philadelphia between 1790 and 1793, when it became *Dunlap and Claypoole's American Daily Advertiser*. After Dunlap retired at the end of 1795, David Claypoole continued publishing under the title of *Claypoole's American Daily Advertiser* to 1800.

2. In Monroe County (now W.Va.), Sweet Springs was one of the earlier and more renowned springs to be developed in western Virginia. At the time of JM's visit, there were accommodations for two hundred people (John Edwards Caldwell, *A Tour through Part of Virginia, in the Summer of 1808* . . . [1809; Richmond, Va., 1951 reprint], 25–27; Peregrine Prolix [Philip Holbrook Nicklin], *Letters Descriptive of the Virginia Springs: The Roads Leading Thereto, and the Doings Thereat, 1834 & 1836* [1837; Austin, Tex., 1978 reprint], 35–38, 134–35 n. 4).

To Oliver Wolcott, Jr.

My dear Sir   Richmond June 28th. 1806

I thank you very sincerely for the full & comprehens⟨ive⟩ statement you have made of the circumstances at⟨tend⟩ing Fauchets intercepted letter & the ratification of ⟨the⟩ British treaty. I fear you have given yourself considerable trouble in this business—certainly more than I intended to have imposed on you. I was particularly anxious to know whether the allegation that the ratification was occasioned by a view of the intercepted letter was true. I had disbeleived it, but could discover nothing which could satisfy me absolutely either way. I had though⟨t⟩ that the President reserved his final judgement untill he should have a full view of the whole subject, but of this I could not be certain. Your letter assures me that my impressions were not erroneous.[1] The work is now completed & I prepare myself for charges which are untrue & abuse which is unmerited. Adieu my dear Sir— with real esteem, I remain your Obedt Servt

                                                            J MARSHALL

ALS, Oliver Wolcott, Jr., Papers, CtHi. Margin frayed.

1. JM received Wolcott's account too late to incorporate it into vol. V, though he briefly mentioned the intercepted Fauchet dispatch in a note in the appendix (vol. V, Note XVII, 30–31).

To John Adams

Dear Sir   Richmond July 6th. 1806

I have taken a liberty which may require an apology. Thinking it necessary, I have, without your permission, inserted in the life of General Washington parts of letters written by you to him at the time of his appointment to the command of the army which was to be raised in 1798.[1] I have ventured ⟨to⟩ do this because I thought it impossible that the act could be offensive to you, & because I had not time to obtain your previou⟨s⟩ consent to it. The letters of distinct periods having been read at distinct times, Those subsequent to the Generals retireme⟨nt⟩ to private life were inspected when the work was too nea⟨r⟩ its close to hope for an answer to any application to you until it would be put out of my hands, unless it should be retained for that special purpose.

Since I have given you the trouble of a letter permit me to thank you for the flattering because friendly expressions of yours of the 4th. of Feby. last. Beleive me, sir, no man has felt more sincerely than myself the malignant, unjust, & intolerant spirit which has been exhibited with respect to you. I trust its bitterness is diminishing. With respect to myself, I have reason to fear that the imprudent task I have just executed will draw upon me a degree of odium & calumny which I might perhaps otherwise have escaped. I should never have undertaken it but in the hope, certainly a very fallacious one, that the author would forever remain totally unknown. But having undertaken it I have endeavoured to detail the events of a most turbulent & factious period without unnecessarily wounding the dominant party, but without a cowardly abandonment or concealment of truth. What may be the consequences of having ventured to offend those whom truth however moderately related must offend, it is not difficult to divine.

Mrs. Marshall requests me to unite with mine her respectful compliments, & good wishes for the health & happiness of Mrs. Adams. Beleive me to be dear Sir with sincere esteem & grateful attachment, Your Obedt. Servt.

J MARSHALL

ALS, Adams Papers, MHi. Margin frayed.

1. See vol. V, 753–54.

To Caleb P. Wayne

My dear Sir   July 14th. 1806
The sickness of my son John has thus long detained me in Richmond, but I set out tomorrow morning. To day I have glanced my eyes over the character which I was prevented from doing sooner by my numerous avocations & by a slight indisposition. It appears to me & I submit it entirely to you that it would perhaps be right to enlarge rather more on General Washingtons private qualities. Under this impression I ⟨h⟩ave sketched a paragraph to follow that which sp⟨e⟩aks of his humanity & benevolence. It is

"In the management of his private affairs he exhibited an exact yet liberal economy. His funds were not prodigally wasted on capricious & ill examined schemes, nor refused to beneficial though costly improvements. They remained therefore competent[1] to that expensive establishment which his reputation added to a hospitable temper had in some measure imposed upon him; and to those donations which real distress has a right to claim from opulence."[2]

In the last line of the character I think "untainted" would be a better word than "unstained." Perhaps I altered it, but in the original it is "untainted."[3]

If you write on the receipt of this it is probable that your letter may find me at my brothers. Direct to Port[4] Royal Frederick county Virga.

If you do not write immediately I shall be at the sulphur springs till from the first to the 5th. of august & afterwards at the sweet springs.[5] Your

JM

ALS, Dreer Collection, PHi. Bound in publisher's copy of vol. V, seven pages from the end of chap. 9 at text where JM intended insertion to be made; first and last two paragraphs and first line of third paragraph of letter crossed out, presumably by Wayne.

1. JM first wrote "equal" and then changed it.
2. Wayne marked the place of insertion between two paragraphs in JM's description of Washington's character. The new paragraph was typeset verbatim, except for modifications in punctuation, at vol. V, chap. 9, 773–74.
3. In the printer's copy, "unstained" appears on the last line of the last page. Wayne deleted it and wrote "untainted" below, which is how it reads in vol. V at chap. 9, 779.
4. JM meant Front Royal.
5. Probably White Sulphur Springs in Greenbrier County (now W.Va.), earlier known as Bowyer's Sulphur Springs. Close by, to the south and east, was Sweet Springs, about sixteen miles by road. White Sulphur Springs became a very fashionable watering place in the nineteenth century (Caldwell, *Tour of Virginia*, 30–31 and n. 25; [Nicklin], *Virginia Springs*, x, 14, 19, 81–83, 130 n. 7). For JM's possible route from Front Royal, see ibid., 38–39, 43–45. Jefferson mentioned these springs in his *Notes on the State of Virginia* (ed. by William Peden [Chapel Hill, N.C., 1954], 34–36).

From John Adams

My very dear Sir   Quincy July 17. 1806
Yesterday I received from the Post Office your obliging Letter of the Sixth of this month. It is not necessary for me to r[e]curr to my Letter Books, and examine the few Letters I wrote to General Washington, before I assure you, that I shall take no offence at your inserting in your History, parts or the whole of them. They were written under great Agitation of Mind, at a time when a cruel necessity compelled me to take measures which I was very apprehensive would produce the Evils which have followed from them.

If you have detailed the Events, of the last years of General Washingtons Life, you must have run the Gauntlet; between two infuriated factions, armed with scorpions.

Incedis per ignes Suppositos cineri doloso.[1]
It is a Period, which must however be investigated, but I am very confident will never be well understood. A first Magistrate of a great Republick with a General Offi[c]er under him, a Commander in

Chicf of the Army, who had ten thousand times as much Influence Popularity and Power, as himself, and that Commander in Chief So much under the influence of his second in command, the most treacherous malicious, insolent and revengeful Ennemy of the first Magistrate is a Picture which may be very delicate and dangerous to draw. But it must be drawn.

I Shall be very impatient to see the last Volumes of your History, which are not yet Arrived. There is one fact, perfectly clear and certain in my mind, which it will be difficult for posterity to beleive, and that is that the measures taken by Senators, Members of the House, Some of the heads of departments, and Some Officers of the Army to force me to appoint General Washington, and induce him to accept the Appointment, proceeded not from any regard to him, or any confidence in his Character, but merely from an intention to employ him as an Engine to elevate Hamilton to the head of Affairs civil as well as military. But I am not about to write an History to you, instead of a Letter. I had much rather, at the time have resigned my Office to the General, if I could, than have appointed him in the Army.

Mrs Adams joins in the most friendly Salutations to you and to Mrs Marshall, with your Sincere friend

J. ADAMS

ALS, Feinstone Collection, PPAmP; letterbook copy, Adams Papers, MHi.

1. "You are treading upon fires lying beneath a treacherous ash" (Horace, *Odes*, ii. 1. 7–8).

To Jonathan Williams

Dear Sir   Richmond Novr. 9th 1806

The serious indisposition under which I labored when your letter reached me & the long tour to our mountains which I commenced immediately after receiving it & where I have passed the summer & great part of the autumn must apologize for my neglecting to attend to it. I now enclose you a note for five dollars which I beleive is the sum required from each member. If any additional requisition has been made you will be so obliging as to give me notice of it.

Permit me to repeat my sincere wish that the institution may be productive of the advantages which have been the motives & are the objects of its establishment & to assure you that I am with much respect, Your Obedt. Servt

J MARSHALL

ALS, U.S. Military Philosophical Society Papers, NHi. Addressed by JM to Williams at West Point, N.Y.; postmarked Richmond, 12 Nov. Endorsed (by Williams?).

Short v. Skipwith
Opinion and Decree
U.S. Circuit Court, Virginia, 2 December 1806

Short[1]

v

Skipwith

¶1   In arguing this cause the counsel for both plf. & defendent rely upon the situation of the parties as furnishing strong reasons in favor of that result for which they severally contend.

¶2   The plf., in a distant country, commits his most important interests to his friend in Virginia; places in the hands of that friend large sums of money which are to be employed for the advantage of the owner, manifests a strong preference for their being invested in the public funds & after some time expressly orders that investment. The agency is entered into with alacrity, but the agent was a private gentleman, not in habits of dealing in public paper, & residing at some distance from the great market to which the commodity was most usually brought.[2]

¶3   It certainly was not to be expected that a person under the circumstances of the defendent could execute the orders of the plf. with the celerity & adroitness of a professed dealer in certificates; but it was to be expected that the orders of the plf. would not be disobeyed, & his remote situation increased the obligation not altogether to neglect any part of his business.

¶4   In its origin, the duty of the agent, except as it regarded the collection of a few debts, which will form an object of particular consideration was limited to the safe custody of the certificates of his principal, & to a remittance of the interest. The circumstances of the plf. probably changing so as no longer to require remittances from virga. he formed the resolution of converting the profits of his estate into additional capital which resolution was communicated to the defendent in a letter of the 4th of May 1787. This letter manifests a preference for certificates over other property, but unquestionably submits it to the discretion of the agent who was on the spot, to act according to the opinion he should form on circumstances which were often changing.[3] Nothing can be more obvious than that the judgement of the agent was in direct opposition to that of his principal; & that he was radically opposed to those hazardous investments to which his principal was strongly inclined. Under these impressions he earnestly dissuades the plf. from the measure to which he seemed most inclined, but accompanies his request for positive orders with explicit assurances that those orders whatever they may be, shall be obeyed. This request produced the letter of the 20th. of Decr. which could not be well misunderstood. Only strong circumstances, unknown to the plf. when that letter was written, and rendering it almost certain that the public debt would not be placed on solid funds, could have justified a departure from the instructions contained in the postscript of that letter. Seldom is less latitude given to an intelligent, an upright, & a distant agent. The letters of the 31st. of the same month, & of the 1st. of Feby 1788 are still more positive. The suspicion that any state of things could exist which might render the observance of these orders imprudent seems to have passed away, & they are absolute. The defendent could not misunderstand them.

¶5   In the spring of 1789 the defendent became disposed to relinquish the active part of his agency, & thereupon he placed the fund in the hands of Mr. James Brown.[4] The whole interest which had accrued on the certificates was not at this time accounted for. It appears from the report that £51.16.10 were neither invested in certificates nor delivered to Mr. Brown nor accounted for in any manner.[5] The court know not what disposition was made of this money, & must consider it as having been appropriated by the deft to his own use. If any other application was made of it, it is incumbent on the defendent to show such application.

¶6   Whether this residuum was in specie or in warrants is not expressly stated; but a view of the report would induce the opinion that it was a balance of interest money accruing before the 1st. of Jany. 1789 & consequently must be considered as specie.[6] If the fact be otherwise the defendent ought to show it. Had this money been placed in the hands of Mr. Brown it might have been & would have been, so far as any facts can authorize such a conclusion, converted into certificates.

¶7   The question then arising upon this part of the case is whether an agent who voluntarily disobeys the orders of his principal, & converts to his own use a sum of money belonging to his principal, & distinctly appropriated to a definite object, shall be accountable for the money & interest or for the article into which it ought to have been converted.

The situation of the defendent has no bearing upon this case; be-   ¶8
cause if he found a difficulty in making personally the necessary investment of money in certificates, he could have found no difficulty in delivering the money with the certificates & interest warrants to Mr. Brown. The case appears to be stripped of every circumstance which can give to it any other character than a diversion of funds by a trustee from their proper object to his own use.

That the principal has been essentially injured in the events which   ¶9
have happened by this breach [of] trust, that the restoration of his money with interest will be no compensation for this injury, is too obvious to be controverted; that the agent will sustain great real loss if decreed to compensate the principal is perhaps equally true.

On the part of the defendent it is urged with great force that the   ¶10
condition of him who seeks to avoid a loss is viewed with more favor than that of a person who seeks a gain. The influence of this argument will always be felt by those whose duty it becomes to decide questions of this description, & if other considerations be nearly balanced its influence must be decisive. But there may exist considerations which ought to overcome the mild policy of the rule which has been stated. It is also a maxim which on every principle of morals is intitled to great regard that between contending parties the wrong doer is the person who ought to suffer. In the present controversy no blame can attach to the plf. His instructions are distinct; the means of observing them are placed in the hands of Mr. Skipwith; and it cannot be alleged that the failure to observe them is in the most remote degree to be ascribed to Mr. Short. That the blame whatever it may be, rests entirely with Mr. Skipwith seems incontestible. If, because the loss of Mr. Short is meerly the loss of gain, his compensation should be restricted to the restoration of his money with interest, the encouragement which such a decision would give to dangerous & corrupt practices in the intercourse between a principal & his agent, must be apparent. It would hold forth an inducement in every instance where extraordinary profit might be made, to divert trust money into other channels than those for which it was designed to the great injury of a large portion of society.

It is said & truely said that extravagant calculations of conjectural   ¶11
profits are not to be indulged, & will never be regarded in courts of justice as th⟨e⟩ standard by which damages are to be ascertained. The example given is that the plf. might have subscribed his stock to the

bank might have sold out at a high price & have employed the produce of the sales advantageously. Certainly such possibilities are to be totally disregarded. But certainly where a single investment of money is ordered in a specific article, which article of itself, without any new operation depending on the judgemen⟨t⟩ acquires great additional value, this additional value cannot fairly be denominated the result of an extravagant calculation of imaginary profits. Suppose a contract for the purchase of an increasing property of any description, which contract depended on payment of money on a given day. If th⟨e⟩ agent in whose hands the purchase money was placed, should, instead of executing his trust, convert a part of the money to his own use & thereby defeat the contract, it would seem unjust that the remedy of his principal should be limitted to the money & interest. That this would not necessarily be th⟨e⟩ measure of damages, is to be inferred from the circumstan⟨ce⟩ that the injured person is not confined to an action for money had & received to his use, but may maintain a special action on the case for the damages actually sustained.[7] Between the case supposed & that at bar there seems to be no solid distinction. The difference between a contract actually made, & one which the agent had engaged to make & possessed the absolute power of making seems not sufficient to warrant a different decision in the case of a misappropriation of the fund.

¶12   In reasoning by analogy there are many principles settled by decisions which justify the position that in general cases the agent who voluntarily commits a breach of trust by applying the trust money to his own use must account for the loss which his principal has sustained: But by each party an authority has been cited which is considered as applying directly to the case before the court.

¶13   On the part of the defendents the case of Groves & Graves has been relied on as a direct authority for limiting the recovery of the plf. in this case to his principal money & interest.[8]

¶14   In the case of Groves & Graves the principle that the value of the article when the contract ought to be performed is the proper standard of damages, was not laid down as a general rule to govern in ordinary cases, but is stated to be the proper rule under the peculiar circumstances of that case.[9] What those peculiar circumstances were must be searched for in the record as the opinion of the court makes no allusion to them. That there were circumstances to which the court allowed weight ought to be inferred from their resting the decision not on general principles but on those peculiar circumstances. If we examine the case as reported in 1st. Washington we find no other testimony than the contract & a deed of trust as a collateral security for the performance of that contract. The decree of the Chancellor is founded on the contract being designed to secure an unconscionable advantage, & on its being obtained from a person whom Groves had reason to beleive a needy man. But the opinion of the court of appeals disclaims this ground as the lowest price of certificates mentioned in the contract was meerly a penalty & as the price actually agreed on was only the lowest market price. The contract therefore did not exhibit those peculiar circumstances on which the opinion of the court was founded, & certainly the collateral security could not change the nature of the rights which the contract gave. In fact that case has since been generally considered notwithstanding the terms in which the opinion was delivered, as settling a general principle which should apply to all contracts made in public paper. Yet there are in the case some particular circumstances which whether sufficient to be the motives for the decree or not were most probably of some weight.

Although the lowest price mentioned in the contract is in construction of law a penalty yet it was intended by Mr. Groves to avail himself of that penalty, he obtained a judgement at law for it, & his answer claimed the whole advantage of that judgement. ¶15

Even the actual price agreed upon was the lowest market price. Graves against whom the judgement was obtained was not himself the wrong doer, did not himself receive the money but was the security of Stockdell. ¶16

It is not impossible that these circumstances might have some weight in producing the opinion which was given. None of them exist in the case now under consideration. ¶17

The plfs. have cited a case from 2d. East 211 in which it was decided in the court of Kings bench that in a contract for replacing stock the price on the day was not the true measure of damages, but the subsequent rise ought to be taken into consideration.[10] The only peculiarity attending that case is that it appears to be a loan of stock & not a contract for its purchase. Between a loan & a contract to purchase at a fair price where the money is actually advanced by the purchaser, & no casualty prevents the seller from procuring the article, the court cannot distinctly perceive a difference. An agent misapplying the fund to his own use, does not appear in a more favorable point of view than a borrower. The case in 2d. East therefore appears to be directly in point, & in this case the court is of opinion that the defendent is accountable in certificates for the money remaining in his hands.[11] ¶18

Perhaps in strictness that money ought to be converted into certificates at the price taken by the commissioner. But the disposition to ¶19 diminish so excessive a loss as the defendent would sustain by this rigid application of the rule will induce the court to lay hold of any principle or fact which the case affords to effect this diminution.

¶20   If the money in the hands of Mr. Skipwith had been placed in the hands of Mr. Brown in the spring of 1789, altho this would have been a tardy execution of the trust it would have satisfied the court. Had the money been placed in Mr. Browns hands it is not clear that it would have been invested in a paper to more advantage than the money which was placed in his hands. Upon this part of the case then it is the opinion of the court that the money remaining in Mr. Skipwiths hands ought to be converted into certificates at the same rate that other monies were converted into paper in the year 1789 it is presumed by Mr. Brown.[12] The same train of reasoning which rejects the admission of compound interest, will induce the court to direct that these certificates shall be accounted for with only their legal interest & to set aside so much of the report as charges the defendent with the certificates into which the interest might annually have been converted.

¶21   The next point to be considered is the money placed in the hands of Colo. Kennon & invested by him in certificates.[13]

¶22   As this was a transaction of the defendent himself, it was his duty either to have collected this debt or to have transferred the claim to Mr. Brown & have put it in his power to collect it. To have omitted to do either is such an excessive negligence as in a case of the character of that before the court cannot be tolerated. By holding up this claim after the agency had passed into other hands, Mr. Skipwith must be considered as having taken it upon himself & made himself responsible for its amount to Mr. Short. But, pursuing the principle which was observed in regard to the money applied to his own use, the court will consider him as accountable only for the certificates & interest.

¶23   The 3d. exception to the report respects the debt which was due from Colo Harvie.[14]

¶24   The transaction relative to Harvies bond is in some important particulars distinguishable from those parts of the case which have been already noticed. This money does not appear to have been used by Colo. Skipwith in virtue of the general agency but in consequence of a loan. Previous to the letters of Jany. & Feby. 1786 a communication concerning the lending & borrowing of that debt had taken place between P: S.[15] & the deft. Altho the nature of this communication does not appear to be accurately recollected by either of the parties it is sufficiently apparent that the deft. wished to borrow the money & that the plf. was willing he should receive it on loan.[16] Altho the letter of July 3d. 1786 shows that Colo. Skipwith had relinquished any right to the money which might be given by the conversation with P: S. yet the proposition made to the plf. in that letter has relation to the original contract & seeks to renew it. It is true that at the time of obtaining the bond from Edmonds, the defendent did not take it upon himself. He seems at that time to have been equally apprehensive of paper money & of the abolition of certificates & not to have chosen to expose his friend to the one casualty or himself to the other. It was only after the debt was collected that he was willing to consider it as his own. His letter of March 1787 announces his collection of the debt & his determination to hold it at 6 percent. The plfs letter of the 20th. Decr: 87 manifests his satisfaction with this employment of the fund.

From a review of all the circumstances which preceded the completion of this transaction it results that the money was collected by the deft in his character as agent, & applied to his own use in consequence of a contract to that effect which was made before his agency commenced, which contract was sanctioned by the plf. in the letter of appointment, & which application was afterwards approved by him. ¶25

Where in different parts of the same transaction the same person acts in different capacities it is often difficult to assign to each part its distinct character. Indeed it will often happen that the two characters are so intermingled that each will impart something of itself to the transaction. ¶26

The question made in this case is whether Mr. Skipwith held the money collected from Colonel Harvie as a common debtor or as the agent of Mr Short. ¶27

So far as respects an ability to avail himself of any penalty to which Mr. Short might be exposed there can be no doubt but that he ought to be subjected to all the restraints of an agent or trustee. But in other respects his character seems to be rather that of an ordinary debtor. He appropriated the money to his own use not meerly in virtue of his authority as agent; but with the previous & subsequent approbation of the plf.; and he paid interest upon the money so appropriated. ¶28

It is true that an express promise was made to hold the money subject to the orders of the plf. but the loan does not appear to have been made on this *condition*; & in point of fact every sum payable on demand is held on the same terms. ¶29

Yet it is a question of some intricacy whether this money is not to be considered as being in Mr. Skipwiths hands as agent & not as a debtor in consequence of the letters of the plf directing its investment in certificates, & the promise of the deft. to comply with that direc-

tion, & whether Mr. Skipwith is not liable to the extent of his promise. With some hesitation the court has decided this question in the
negative.

¶31   The original appropriation of this money to his own use having
been an act which was perfectly rightful, Mr Skipwith has been already stated to have been so far an ordinary debtor & it would be
going a great way to subject a debtor who promises to pay a debt to all
the loss consequent on his failure to comply with his engagement.
The general policy of the law does not admit of such strictness; and
although in morals a man may justly charge himself as the cause of
any loss occasioned by the breach of his engagements yet in the
course of human affairs such breaches are so often occasioned by
events which were unforeseen & not easily prevented that interest is
generally considered as the compensation which must content the
injured. Mr. Skipwith therefore will be decreed to account for Harvies debt in specie not in certificates.

¶32   There is another part of this claim which the court touches with
real reluctance. The contract of loan being for an interest of 6 per
cent when the legal interest was only five, is evidently usurious. The
court cannot decree a greater interest than the law will authorize
whatever may be the contract of parties. But the person who drew the
plf. into this contract having been himself the agent it would be
against conscience that he should derive any advantage to the prejudice of the plf. from this circumstance. The court therefore allows the
legal interest of five per cent.[17]

¶33   Had the court approved the conversion of this debt into certificates
the commission upon its collection & upon its investment would undoubtedly be approved also. But the change of this essential principle
produces corresponding changes in minor parts which are connected
with it. The defendent having collected this money for himself is not
entitled to a commission on the collection; and as he is not chargeable
with certificates he can have no claim to commissions on such investment. Another slight change to be made in the account is in the
allowance of expenses as well as commissions on the business actually
transacted. That reasonable expenses ought to be allowed if commissions were withheld is unquestionable but when commissions are allowed it is supposed to be usual to admit no other charge on the
business.

¶34   The court has felt some difficulty respecting Griffins note.[18] It is
unquestionable that the orders of Mr. Short did not authorize the
purchase of note & that it was an indiscreet exercise of his powers as
agent to purchase the bond of any person for certificates instead of

the certificates themselves. This indiscretion is enhanced by taking an assignment without recourse on the assignor. It is answered by the defendent that Mr. Short was well satisfied with a similar contract made with Mr. Giles.[19] But upon examining the letter of Colo. Skipwith which announces this purchase, he states the acquisition to have been of certificates themselves, nor does he allude to the real state of the fact until his letter of June 16th. 1788. In that letter he gives some account of his investments & states himself to have paid Mr. Giles £30 for £200 in military notes. There are several reasons for not considering the non appearance of a disapprobation of this proceeding as an implied permission to deal in private bonds instead of public securities. The expressions used are ambiguous & might be misunderstood by Mr. Short. After a positive statement given by Colo. Skipwith that he had actually purchased public securities, the term military notes might well have been understood by a person in the situation of Mr. Short as a species of public paper not as a private note for public paper. The same letter too promises a detailed statement of the situation of the plfs affairs which was not given till 1791, long after this contract with Mr. Shore[20] was made. The letters of Mr. Short subsequent to June 88 press continually for this statement & urge the investment of all his funds according to the explicit instructions which were given in his letters of Decr. 87 & Feby. 1788. Those letters certainly contain nothing which can mend the defendents case.

The circumstances of the contract also deserve consideration. It is ¶35 remarkable that Colo. Skipwith purchased this note partly on credit. In march 1788 when the contract was made he paid £29.15.4 & in the Decr following £120.4.8. The argument that he purchased a bond instead of certificates themselves for the sake of the credit, is scarcely to be resisted. He ought not to have required credit. He would then have been in cash from the interest warrants of the plf. had he retained that fund for the object to which it was appropriated. What the opinion of the court on this point might have been had this bond been purchased for ready money need not be stated. It would certainly have presented the question under an aspect less unfavorable to the defendents cause; but circumstanced as the case is the court cannot admit this item to the defendents credit. This opinion is not formed on the situation of the obligor. The testimony of the case induces the opinion that his ability to pay the debt might have been confided in. But the defendent ought not to have purchased any bond, & the probability that this improper measure was occasioned by having made use of the funds of the plf. in his hands seems decisive of his liability for this sum. But as he has actually paid for the bond, &

has not in this respect retained in his hands the money of the plf. but has sought to invest it in certificates, there is a distinction between this part of the case & that in which the court held the defendent responsible for the amount of the money retained in certificates themselves. For this sum therefore the Deft. will be chargeable only in specie.

¶36   For the reasons given in the report the defendent is not chargeable with Randolphs bond.[21]

¶37   For the mare the deft is accountable[22] but the commissioner possessed no testimony which would enable him to introduce that item into the account. Unless it can be arranged by the parties it must be settled by a jury & for that purpose an issue will be directed.

¶38   Upon these principles the court has formed the following order & decree.

[Decree][23]

Short
   v   } in chancery
Skipwith

This cause came on to be heard at the last term on the bill answer exhibits, depositions, the report of the commissioner the exceptions to that report & the arguments of counsel all which being fully considered, the court is of opinion that the instructions given by the plf. to the deft. in his letters of Decr. 1787 & Feby. 88 to convert the money in his hands into public securities of some description were positive & ought not to have been disregarded, & that therefore the defendent is accountable in certificates at the rate at which they appear by the receipt of James Brown which is one of the exhibits to have been purchased in 1789, for so much money arising from the interest on the plfs certificates as was retained by the defendent & applied to his own use, but that he is accountable only for simple interest on those certificates at the rate of 6 per cent per annum. The court is also of opinion that the defendent having not only neglected to furnish the plf. or the agent who succeeded to the management of his affairs with any documents which could enable him to recover the debt due from Richard Kennon must be considered as having collected that debt or as having made himself responsible for it, & is therefore chargeable with the sum in certificates which the said Kennon stated himself to have purchased.

The court is further of opinion that the debt due from John Harvie in the proceedings mentioned was placed in the hands of the defendent on loan & is to be accounted for in specie with interest at the rate of five per centum per annum, that being the interest which when the debt was contracted it was lawful to receive; but the defendent is not entitled to the commissions with which he is credited in the report for collecting this debt, he having received it on loan.

The court is further of opinion that the defendent was instructed to purchase public securities & not empowered to buy private bonds for public securities, & that therefore he is not entitled to a credit in account for Griffins bond, the more especially as that bond was purchased on credit at a time when the money of the plf was in his hands. But as the sum given for this bond appears to have laid out with the intention to benefit the plf. & not for his own advantage the defendent is only to be charged with the sum in specie with interest thereon at the rate of 5 per cent.

The deft. is not chargeable with Randolphs bond. The court is further of opinion that the credits given to the defendent on account of expenses ought to be disallowed, the commission on his transactions as agent being a sufficient & proper compensation for those transactions.

There being no testimony sufficient to guide a commissioner in estimating the value of the mare in the proceedings mentioned the court directs an issue to be made up & tried at the bar for the purpose of ascertaining that value.

The report is remanded to the commissioner to be reformed forthwith according to the directions herein given in order to a final decree.[24]

AD, Marshall Judicial Opinions, PPAmP; printed, John W. Brockenbrough, *Reports of Cases Decided by the Honourable John Marshall . . .* , I (Philadelphia, 1837), 105–18. Edge of MS frayed. Decree, AD, Short v. Skipwith, U.S. Cir. Ct., Va., Ended Cases (Restored), 1806, Vi. For JM's deletions and interlineations, see Textual Notes below.

1. A native of Virginia, William Short since 1786 had lived mainly abroad, first as Thomas Jefferson's secretary, then as holder of a succession of diplomatic posts in France, the Netherlands, and Spain. His suit for an equitable accounting originated in transactions undertaken twenty years earlier, soon after he joined Jefferson in Paris. Short commissioned Henry Skipwith, his uncle, as agent to invest Short's funds in public securities. The substance of the complaint was Skipwith's alleged failure to perform this agency according to Short's positive instructions. Short was able to bring suit in the federal court because he was then nominally a resident of New York. The bill was filed in June 1803, followed by the answer, depositions, exhibits, commissioner's report, and exceptions to the report—proceedings that required more than three years to complete. JM delivered his opinion and decree on 2 Dec. 1806 (U.S. Cir. Ct., Va., Ord. Bk. IV, 327, 380, 440; V, 66–67, 264; VI, 36–38; bill in chancery, Short v. Skipwith).

2. Henry Skipwith resided at Hors du Monde, his estate on the Appomattox River in Cumberland County. Visiting there in 1796, Benjamin Latrobe wrote: "This place has

a name very appropriate: *Horsdumonde*. No possibility of communication by letter or visit, but by riding half a dozen miles *into* the world" (Edward C. Carter II, ed., *The Virginia Journals of Benjamin Henry Latrobe, 1795–1798*, I [New Haven, Conn., 1977], 142).

3. The public securities Short wished to purchase were known as "military certificates," issued by the state of Virginia to cover the army's back pay and depreciation losses. They bore an interest of 6 percent (*PJM*, V, 207 n. 6).

The originals and copies of all the correspondence between Short and Skipwith on this business were filed as exhibits in the suit. The report of the chancery commissioner William Hay, 27 Nov. 1805, embodied pertinent extracts of this correspondence (Short v. Skipwith).

4. James Brown, a Richmond merchant, was also involved in the case of Waddington v. Banks (see Opinion, 13 Dec. 1805). Brown's receipt for the certificates, bonds, interest warrants, and notes placed in his hands by Skipwith is in the case papers (Short v. Skipwith).

5. Report of commissioner, 27 Nov. 1805, 25, Short v. Skipwith.

6. A warrant is an order on the treasury to pay a specified sum of money—in this instance, the warrants were for interest on the military certificates. These warrants circulated at a discount until the interest accrued.

7. An action for money had and received to the plaintiff's use was one of the "common counts" in general assumpsit. On general and special assumpsit, see *PJM*, V, 22–23, 358–59, 361 n. 5.

8. Groves v. Graves, 1 Wash. 1 (1790), a case JM had argued in the Virginia Court of Appeals (*PJM*, II, 406 n. 20).

9. President Pendleton stated that the verdict of the jury was wrong "in the measure of damages, taking for that measure the value of certificates at the time of the trial when, under the peculiar circumstances of this case, the value at the time they should have been delivered, ought to be the rule" (1 Wash. 3).

In Reynolds v. Waller, 1 Wash. 165 (1793) and Morris v. Alexander, 3 Call 102 (1801), Pendleton distinguished Groves v. Graves. That case, he said, "was a contract to deliver, on a fixed day, certificates of a certain description, but no specific paper; and the principal reason for fixing the value at that day, was, that Groves was not afterwards obliged to take the paper if depreciated; and, therefore, ought not to have the gain by their rise" (3 Call 102).

10. Shepherd v. Johnson, 2 East 211, 102 Eng. Rep. 349 (K.B., 1802). The court held that damages should be assessed at the stock's price on the day of the trial, not at the price on the day the stock was to be replaced. "The true measure of damages in all these cases," said Judge Grose, "is that which will completely indemnify the plaintiff for the breach of the engagement. If the defendant neglect to replace the stock at the day appointed, and the stock afterwards rise in value, the plaintiff can only be indemnified by giving him the price of it at the time of the trial" (2 East 212, 102 Eng. Rep. 350).

11. The defendant had objected to being made liable for the amount in military certificates that the fifty-two pounds remaining in his hands might have purchased (defendant's exceptions to report of commissioner, Short v. Skipwith).

12. James Brown's receipt showed that £290 had purchased £1,040 in military certificates in the spring of 1789, a rate of approximately 5s. 6d. in the pound. Commissioner Hay used the rate 6s. in the pound in converting the £52 into certificates (receipt of James Brown; report of commissioner, 27 Nov. 1805, 25, 26, Short v. Skipwith).

13. Richard Kennon (1759–1805) served in the Virginia line of the Continental Army and later represented Mecklenburg County in the General Assembly (*VMHB*, XXXI [1923], 186). In his answer, Skipwith stated that he gave £25 to Kennon (then

attending the House of Delegates in Richmond) to buy military certificates. Commissioner Hay charged Skipwith with the amount of certificates stated by Kennon to have been purchased at 4s. 6d. in the pound—£113. Skipwith protested this charge, contending that there was no proof that certificates supposedly bought by Kennon had come into his hands or that the money had actually been invested in certificates (answer of Skipwith; report of commissioner, 27 Nov. 1805, 23; defendant's exceptions to report of commissioner, Short v. Skipwith).

14. In 1785 Short sold slaves and other property to John Harvie, taking his bond, to be paid either in specie or in military certificates. Short claimed in his bill that he instructed Skipwith to collect Harvie's bond in certificates, or, if in money, to invest the money in certificates. If the money arising on Harvie's bond was not invested in certificates, then Skipwith's "neglect was voluntary and fraudulent." The commissioner held Skipwith liable for the amount in certificates that £514 (the amount due on Harvie's bond at the time) might have purchased—that is, £2058 at 5s. to the pound (bill in chancery; report of commissioner, 27 Nov. 1805, 25; defendant's exceptions to report of commissioner, Short v. Skipwith).

15. Peyton Short (1761–1815), brother of William Short, at the time of this case a resident of Woodford County, Ky.

16. Peyton Short testified that he held Harvie's bond on behalf of his brother and that some time in 1785 Henry Skipwith proposed to take the amount of the bond when collected on loan, offering to pay 6 percent interest. Then about to move to Kentucky, Peyton Short declined to enter such a negotiation and turned the bond over to Thomas Edmunds of Sussex for collection. Soon thereafter Skipwith wrote him in Kentucky, informing him that he was now William Short's agent and requesting that Harvie's bond be turned over to him. Skipwith, in his answer, referred to a letter of Feb. 1786, in which William Short stated that his brother had directed the money from Harvie's bond to be placed in Skipwith's hands and to remain there at interest until called for. Skipwith stated that he turned the bond over to a William Hendrick for collection in Oct. 1786, at which time he debited himself with the amount of the bond and interest at 6 percent (deposition of Peyton Short, 30 Aug. 1803; answer of Skipwith, Short v. Skipwith).

17. The court presumably could have voided the contract or disallowed interest. The legal rate of interest in Virginia was raised to 6 percent in 1796 (Shepherd, *Statutes*, II, 27). JM here deleted a lengthy passage that is reproduced in the textual notes below.

18. The commissioner credited Skipwith with the purchase of a note by Dr. John Tayloe Griffin for payment of £400 in military certificates. This note, payable to Thomas Shore, was purchased by Skipwith from Shore in Mar. 1788 for £150, of which £30 was paid down and the balance the following December. The plaintiff insisted that Skipwith had no claim to a credit for purchasing Griffin's note. Peyton Short testified that he did not consider the purchase of this note as passing to Skipwith's credit in his account with William Short. Skipwith, he said, must have been aware of Griffin's "tottering credit" at the time (report of commissioner, 27 Nov. 1805, 20–21, 23; plaintiff's exceptions to report of commissioner; deposition of Peyton Short, 30 Aug. 1803, Short v. Skipwith).

19. Skipwith had paid thirty pounds to William B. Giles in purchase of a promissory note for two hundred pounds in military certificates (report of commissioner, 27 Nov. 1805, 23, Short v. Skipwith).

20. Thomas Shore (see n. 18).

21. Short claimed that Skipwith should be liable for a bond for sixty-two pounds given by Richard Randolph, Jr., having failed to collect it while Randolph was still solvent. Commissioner Hay disallowed this charge, stating that the collection of Ran-

dolph's debt had originally been entrusted to someone else; that Skipwith had possession of the bond only briefly before turning it over to James Brown; and that Ran
dolph's circumstances were good at the time Skipwith relinquished the bond and for
some years afterwards (bill in chancery; report of commissioner, 27 Nov. 1805, 20;
plaintiff's exceptions to report of commissioner, Short v. Skipwith).

22. Short directed his agent to sell a mare and invest the proceeds in public securities
(bill in chancery, Short v. Skipwith).

23. The decree, also in JM's hand, is a separate document in the case file of Short v.
Skipwith.

24. Commissioner Hay submitted a revised report on 10 Dec. upon which the court
rendered a final decree on 17 Dec. Skipwith was ordered to pay Short seventeen
hundred pounds Virginia currency in specie and three hundred pounds in military
certificates (report of commissioner, 10 Dec. 1806, Short v. Skipwith; U.S. Cir. Ct., Va.,
Ord. Bk. VI, 106–7).

Textual Notes:

¶ 1	l. 1	counsel ↑for↓ both
¶ 2	l. 4	owner, & ↑in the commencement↓ manifests
	l. 5	funds ↑& after some time expressly orders that investment.↓ The
¶ 3	l. 3	celerity ↑& adroitness↓ of
	l. 3	in ~~paper~~ certificates;
	l. 4	expected ~~, & the remote situation of the plf~~ that
¶ 4	l. 1	except ~~as to~~ as
	ll. 2–3	debts, ↑which will form an object of particular consideration↓ was
	ll. 3–4	certificates of ~~the plf~~[?] ↑his principal,↓ &
	ll. 9–10	submits ~~it~~ ↑it↓ to the ~~judgement~~ ↑discretion↓ of the agent
	l. 11	according to ~~circumstances & the dict~~[?] ~~the judgement~~ ↑the opinion↓ he should
	ll. 22–23	public ~~faith~~ ↑debt↓ would ~~be violated~~ ↑not be placed on solid funds,↓ could
	ll. 23–24	in ↑the postscript of↓ that letter.
	l. 24	latitude↓ ↑given↓ to
	l. 27	which ~~would justify~~ ↑might↓ render
¶ 5	ll. 1–2	defendent ~~was~~ ↑became↓ disposed to relinquish ~~his agency, at least~~ the active part of ~~it~~ ↑his agency,↓ & thereup↑on↓ he
	l. 3	Brown. ~~The certificates At this time the~~ ↑The↓ whole
	l. 4	not ↑at this time↓ accounted for.
	l. 5	that £~~77.4.9~~ ↑51.16.10↓ were
	ll. 6–7	manner. [erasure] ↑The↓ court know not ~~how otherwise~~ what
	l. 8	appropriated ↑by the deft↓ to his
¶ 6	ll. 5–7	it. ↑Had this money been placed in the hands of Mr. Brown it might have been & would have been, so far as any facts can authorize such a conclusion, converted into certificates.↓

¶ 7 l. 2   who ~~voluntary~~ ↑voluntarily↓ disobeys
¶ 8 l. 2   making ↑personally↓ the
    ll. 4–5   warrants to ~~James~~ Mr. Brown.
¶ 9 l. 5   is ~~probable.~~ ↑perhaps equally true.↓
¶10 ll. 2–3   is ↑viewed with↓ ~~to~~ ↑more↓ ~~to be~~ favored ~~than~~ that
    l. 3   gain. ~~This~~ ↑The↓ influence
    l. 6   its [erasure] ↑influence↓ must be
    l. 7   to ~~overrule~~ ↑overcome↓ the mild
    ll. 9–10   wrong doer ↑is the person who↓ ought
    l. 11   His ~~orders~~ ↑instructions↓ are
    l. 12   hands of ~~the defendent;~~ ↑Mr. Skipwith;↓ ~~& it cannot be alleged~~ and it
    l. 13   observe ↑them↓ is
    ll. 14–15   ascribed to ~~him~~ Mr. Short. ~~That Mr. Skipwith is entirely to blame~~ ↑the blame whatever it may be, rests entirely with Mr. Skipwith↓ seems
    l. 18   such a ~~principle~~ ↑decision↓ would
    ll. 20–21   in ~~many~~ ↑every↓ instances ~~to violate trusts~~ where
¶11 l. 1   that ~~imaginary~~ ↑extravagant↓ calculations
    ll. 5–6   have ~~made~~ ↑employed the produce of the sales↓ advantageously.
    l. 6   such ~~possibility~~ ↑possibilities↓ are
    l. 7   certainly ~~a~~ ↑where a↓ single
    l. 8   article ~~becomes more~~ of
    ll. 10–11   denominated ↑the result of↓ ~~as[?]~~ ↑an↓ extravagant
    l. 11   imaginary ~~damages.~~ ↑profits.↓ A ↑Suppose a↓ contract
    ll. 16–17   that ~~his prin~~ the remedy
    l. 17   should ↑be↓ limitted
    l. 18   is ~~certainly~~ to be
    l. 20   action ~~on the case~~ for money
    l. 26   fund. [erasure] ~~Indeed~~
¶12 l. 1 beg.   ~~If we reason~~ ↑In reasoning↓ by
    l. 5   But ~~on both sides~~ ↑by each party↓ an
¶13 l. 2   as ~~fin[?]~~ ↑a↓ direct
¶14 l. 2   contract ~~is broken~~ [erasure] ↑ought to be performed is↓ the
    l. 3   damages, ~~is~~ ↑was↓ not
    l. 3   rule ~~which is~~ to govern
    l. 4   but ~~it~~ ↑is↓ stated
    l. 7   them. ~~Indeed~~ That
    l. 8   weight ~~must~~ ↑ought to↓ be
    l. 9   peculiar [erasure] ↑circumstances.↓ If
    ll. 10–11   find ~~only~~ ↑no other testimony than↓ the
    l. 12   contract. ~~Neither of these would seem to furnish The Chancellor, in the~~ The ~~opinion delivered by him has~~ The decree

ll. 18 19   therefore ↑did not↓ exhibited ~~no~~ ↑those peculiar↓ circum-
                    stances ↑on↓ which

ll. 20–21   not ~~be such a cir~~ change the ~~correct~~ nature

l. 21   gave. [erasure] ↑In↓ fact

l. 25   case ~~no~~ ↑some↓ particular

¶15 l. 1   contract [erasure] ↑is↓ in

¶16 l. 3   wrong doer, ~~bu~~ ↑did↓ not

¶17 l. 3   case ~~before the court~~ now

¶18 l. 1   2d. East ~~111~~ ↑211↓ in which

l. 3   not the ↑true↓ measure

l. 6   Between ↑a loan↓ & a

l. 8   the seller~~s~~ from

l. 9   difference. ~~In the The case of an~~ ↑An↓ agent

ll. 11–12   borrower. ↑The case in 2d. East therefore appears to be di-
                   rectly in point, [erasure] & in↓ ~~In~~ this case ~~therefore~~ the
                   court

¶20 l. 3   court. ~~It is~~ Had

ll. 9–10   1789 ↑it is presumed↓ by

l. 13   as ~~charges~~ charges

l. 14   with the ~~annual~~ certificates

¶22 l. 1   was ~~certainly~~ his

l. 3   it. ~~The court must consider hi~~ To have

ll. 5–6   tolerated. ↑By holding up this claim after the agency had
                   passed into other hands,↓ Mr.

l. 7   taken ↑it↓ upon himself ~~the claim on Colo. Kennon~~ & ~~have~~
                   made

l. 9   money ~~placed in his hands~~ ↑applied to his own use,↓ the
                   court

¶23 l. 1   respects ~~Harvies~~ ↑the↓ debt

l. 2   from ↑Colo↓ Harvie. ~~To decide on this~~

¶24 ll. 3–4   money [erasure] ↑does↓ not appear to have ~~come to the hands
                   of~~ ↑been used by↓ Colo.

ll. 4–5   but ~~to have been received~~ ↑in consequence↓ [erasure] ↑of a↓
                   loan.

l. 7   deft. ~~The wish of Colo. Skipwith to borrow this debt is appar-
                   ent~~ Altho

ll. 14–15   of ~~taking possession of~~ ↑obtaining↓ the bond

l. 21   debt & ~~of~~ his

l. 23   fund. [erasure]

¶25 l. 5   commenced, & ↑which contract↓ was

l. 6   appointment~~.~~ ↑, & which application was afterwards approved
                   by him.↓

¶26 l. 2   part ~~of the transaction~~ its

¶29 l. 4   held ~~in~~ ↑on↓ the same ~~manner~~ terms.

¶30 ll. 3–4   investment ~~of~~ in

ll. 4–6   to ~~obs~~ comply with that direction, ↑& whether Mr. Skipwith is

		not liable to the extent of his promise.↓ With
¶31	ll. 4–5	all the ~~injury~~ ↑loss↓ consequent
	l. 8	of ↑his↓ engagements
	l. 11	the ~~only~~ compensation
	l. 13	debt ~~incl~~[?] in specie & not in certificates.
¶32	l. 9	interest [*erasure*] ↑of five↓ per cent. ~~Whether upon the~~ ~~change of legal interest from five to 6 per cent the interest~~ ~~on this debt ought to be changed also was a question on~~ ~~which the court entertained considerable doubt. The gen-~~ ~~eral principle is clear, but there are strong circumstances in~~ ~~this case to take it out of the general principle. The~~ ~~defendents promise to rep~~ ↑pay↓ ~~6 per cent has probably~~ ~~retained the money in his hands much longer than he~~ ~~might otherwise have been permitted to keep it, & his ex-~~ ~~press undertaking to convert the money into an article~~ ~~which carried an interest of 6 per cent also deserves con-~~ ~~sideration. These circumstances induce the court, in oppo-~~ ~~sition to a general principle to direct that int. of~~ ↑at↓ ~~the~~ ~~rate of 6 per cent shall be calculated on this debt from the~~ ~~time that rate of interest became lawful. The correctness of~~ ~~this part of the opinion however is greatly doubted.~~
¶33	l. 1	Had ~~the~~ [*erasure*] ~~decree of~~ the court
	ll. 2–3	undoubtedly ~~have~~ be
	l. 3	But ~~this essential~~ ↑the↓ change
	l. 4	parts [*erasure*] ↑which↓ are
	l. 5	The [*erasure*] ↑defendent↓ having
	l. 10	That ↑reasonable↓ expenses
	l. 12	usual to ~~make~~ ↑admit↓ no
¶34	ll. 5–6	themselves. ↑This indiscretion is enhanced by taking an as-signment without recourse on the assignor.↓ It
	l. 9	purchase, [*erasure*] ↑the↓ states
	l. 12	Mr. ~~Short~~ ↑Giles↓ £30
	l. 13	are ~~severa~~ several
	ll. 13–14	considering ~~this~~ the [*erasure*] non appearance
	ll. 15–16	securities. ~~In the first~~ The
	l. 22	the ↑plfs↓ affairs
	ll. 26–27	letters certain ↑ly↓ contain
¶35	l. 1 beg.	~~Th~~[?] ↑The circumstances↓ of the ~~purchase~~ ↑contract↓ also
	ll. 2–3	credit. ~~He paid~~ In
	ll. 3–4	made ↑the paid↓ £29.15.4 & in the ~~Novr~~ ↑Decr↓ following
	ll. 4–5	purchased ~~notes~~ ↑a bond↓ instead of certificates ↑themselves↓ for
	ll. 5–6	credit. ↑, is scarcely to be resisted.↓ He
	l. 6	credit. ~~The~~ He
	ll. 7–8	he ~~not~~ retained
	l. 12	but ~~in~~ ↑circumstanced↓ as
	l. 20	hands ↑the↓ money

l. 44   the p̶ ↑Defi,↓ will
¶36 l. 1 beg. ~~The For~~
¶37 l. 1   the ↑deft↓ is
¶38 l. 1 beg. ~~The report must be res~~ Upon
l. 1   formed ~~an~~ ↑the following↓ order

Martin v. Weekly
Bill and Answer in Chancery
U.S. Circuit Court, Virginia, December 1806

To[1] the Honble the Judges of the court of the United States for the   Circuit in the district of Virginia humbly complaining showeth unto your honors your orator Philip Martin a subject of the King of Great Britain.

That the late Thomas Lord Fairfax proprietor of the northern neck of Virginia had in his life time established a land office for the purpose of granting to individuals in conformity with certain rules prescribed by himself the vacant lands which lay within his propri:etary. It was the custom of the said Thomas Lord Fairfax to set apart from the mass of lands offered for sale on these general terms such particular portions as he chose to retain for his own private use. These tracts of land so to be retained were usually set apart by survey. In some instances he granted the land so surveyed to one of his friends & took back a conveyance to himself, in others he made no grant of the lands but held them to his own private use under the survey. The estate of Lord Fairfax in the northern neck of Virginia was an estate tail with power to grant in fee simple and it is presumed that this circumstance occasioned the adoption of the two modes which have been stated of appropriation to private use, or rather of exempting the lands from being acquired by others in conformity with the rules of the office. When Lord Fairfax wished to liberate lands from the entail it was necessary to grant them to others, while he was content to hold them subject to the entail it was unnecessary to grant them. Be this as it may property set apart in either way was incapable of being acquired by any individual in the common mode, & was known to be withdrawn from the general mass of lands which was for sale as waste & vacant by warrant.

Your orator further states that at different times Lord Fairfax caused to be surveyed several tracts of land for his private use adjoining each other which he denominated the Manor of Leeds, a great part of which he rented out to different tenents. In March 1747–8 he caused a large survey to be made on Gooney run as an addition to the manor of Leeds.[2] This survey in part joins the previous surveys for the manor of Leeds; but after running together for some distance the lines separate, &, diverging from each other leave an acute angle consisting of about 1500 acres which for a considerable time remained in the situation commonly denominated vacant & was consequently capable of being acquired by any individual who would purchase according to the rules of the office. About the commencement of the war of the revolution Lord Fairfax determined to unite the two parts of the manor by adding to it this unappropriated angle; and in pursuance of this determination he caused it to be surveyed by Robert Rutherford for his private use to be annexed to & become a part of the said Manor. The survey was accordingly made & after the death of Lord Fairfax or about the time of his death was returned to his office. That this survey was made & that the land it contained was thus annexed to the manor of Leeds & consequently set apart by Lord Fairfax for his private use were facts of notoriety. In the various removals which have been made of the papers of Lord Fairfax since his decease this survey has been lost.[3]

Your orator further states that Thomas Lord Fairfax departed this life some time in or about the year 1781 having first made his last will in writing wherein he devised sundry estates in Virginia comprehending the Manor of Leeds including the land herein mentioned to Denny Martin afterwards called Denny Martin Fairfax of the Kingdom of Great Britain who complied with the conditions of the devise. Afterwards, to wit in or about the month of February in the year 1793 an agreement was entered into between the said Denny Martin Fairfax & James M. Marshall a citizen of Virginia whereby the said Denny Martin Fairfax for a consideration therein mentioned agreed to sell the said Manor of Leeds to the said James M. Marshall who also became the purchaser of all the other lands lying in the Commonwealth of Virginia which were devised by the said Thomas Lord Fairfax to the said Denny Martin Fairfax. Your orator further estates that after the contract & purchase abovementioned the Commonwealth of Virginia claimed the said lands as being escheated & forfeited to this commonwealth because the said Denny Martin Fairfax was an alien & a British subject & caused inquests of office to be held thereon for the purpose of seizing the same into the hands of the commonwealth. At length in one of these inquests a verdict was obtained for the Commonwealth to which a traverse claiming the said land for Denny Martin Fairfax to whom the same was secured by the treaty of peace between the United States & Great Britain was filed in the court held for the district of Dumfries where a judgement was rendered in favor of the Commonwealth from which judgement the said Denny Martin

Fairfax appealed to the court of appeals where the cause depended for a considerable time & was repeatedly argued without being determined.[4]

Your orator further states that in pursuance of certain acts of the legislature of Virginia the government had granted certain parts of the land within the northern neck which were claimed by Denny Martin Fairfax as devisee of Thomas Lord Fairfax & as being also secured by the treaty of peace from being seized by the Commonwealth either by a legislative act or by an inquest of office. For one of these tracts which was held by David Hunter the said Denny Martin fairfax instituted a suit in this Honble court & obtained a judgement therefor to which the said David Hunter sued forth a writ of error from the supreme court of the United States which was afterwards dismissed.[5]

Your orator further states that while the said appeal from the district court of Dumfries was depending & undetermined in the court of appeals a compromise was entered into between the commonwealth of Virginia & John Marshall who was authorised to act for the benefit of the purchasers of the estate of Denny Martin Fairfax & also for the said Denny Martin Fairfax in pursuance of which the legislature passed an act intitled 'an act[6]   to which your orator refers as part of this his bill. All the conditions of the said act of compromise which were to be performed on the part of the said Denny Martin Fairfax or the purchasers of his estate have been performed, & the judgement aforesaid rendered in the district court of Dumfries was reversed & the inquest of office quashed & the right to the said lands adjudged to be in the said Denny Martin Fairfax as by the judgement of the court of appeals will more fully appear.

Your orator further shows that a certain   Weekly has laid a warrant purchased from the land office of Virginia on the land surveyed by Thomas Lord Fairfax as herein before mentioned & thereby annexed to the Manor of Leeds & has obtained a patent for the same. Your orator humbly states that in consequence of the treaty of peace and of the compromise aforesaid, the right of the devisees of Thomas Lord Fairfax & of those claiming under them by purchase is incapable of being defeated by the title obtained by the said   Weekly from the Commonwealth. Your orator concieves it to be immaterial whether the said Weekly had or had not notice of the survey annexing the said land to the Manor of Leeds, but as it is a fact that he had notice thereof, he avers it to be true.

Sundry persons to wit the said   Weekly himself & Thomas Buck   Claig   Williamson   Weekly   Weekly and   are in possession of the said land & hold the same under the title of the said   Weekly to whom the patent issued

as your orator understands, from the land office of the Commonwealth.[7]

Your orator further states that in the year   the said Denny Martin Fairfax departed this life having first made his last will & testament in writing whereby he devised his estate in the commonwealth
of Virginia which include the premises to your orator as by the said
will will appear. Your orator is ready & willing to convey the said
land to the said James M. Marshall but he is advised that the courts
of Virginia have construed a conveyance to be absolutely void which
is made during the existence of an adversary possession & the said
James therefore refuses to receive the said deed & to execute fully
the contract on his part.[8] He has required the persons in possession
to relinquish the same that he may execute the contract made by his
testator which they refuse to do. In tender consideration whereof &
as your orator is remediless by the rules of the common law   To
the end therefore that the said   Weekly Thomas Buck
          Claig   Williamson   Weekly   Weekly
&   and the said James M. Marshall may be made defendants hereto & may on oath true answer make to the premises, and
that the other defendants may be decreed to deliver up possession of
the premises to the said James M. Marshall & account with him for
the profits thereof & to convey to him & that the said James May be
decreed to receive a title from your orator & to execute his contract
with the said Denny M. Fairfax by paying to your orator who is also
exr. of the said Denny M. Fairfax the small balance of purchase
money amounting to   which he retains in his hands in consequence of the pretended title of the other defendents herein men-
tion⟨ed⟩ ⟨. . .⟩ ⟨th⟩at your orator may have such other relief as is
proper ⟨. . .⟩t please your Honor &c

[Answer]

The answer in chancery of James M Marshall to the bill of complaint exhibited against himself & other[s] in this Honble court by
Philip Martin

He admits the several allegations in the complainants bill to be true
& will cheerfully execute h⟨is⟩ ⟨ . . .⟩ ⟨that?⟩ ⟨ . . . ⟩ portion ⟨of the
purchase money⟩ ⟨which? . . .⟩ ⟨ . . . ⟩ in consideration of the property
withheld from ⟨ . . . ⟩ the other defendants so soon as the plf. shall
be enabled to put him in possession thereof & to secure his title
by obtaining a conveyance of the title set up by & under the said
Weekly.[9]

JS MARSHALL

AD, Martin v Weekly, U.S. Circuit Court, Va., Ended Cases (Unrestored), 1808, Vi. Answer of James M. Marshall, on verso of last sheet, also in JM's hand, except for signature. MS torn.

1. This case began and ended at the rules in the office of the clerk. According to the clerk's summary on the wrapper, the bill and the answer of James M. Marshall were filed at the Dec. 1806 rules (Martin v. Weekly).

2. On the creation of Leeds Manor and the addition of the Gooney Run tract (in present-day Warren County), see H. C. Groome, *Fauquier during the Proprietorship* . . . (Richmond, Va., 1927), 74–77; Josiah Look Dickinson, *The Fairfax Proprietary* . . . (Front Royal, Va., 1959), 28–29. For a map of the Fairfax manors, see *PJM*, II, 142.

3. In his answer to the bill, Weekly called for proof of such loss, contending that the books from Lord Fairfax's land office were understood to be "generally complete" (answer of Jacob Weekly, 24 Nov. 1807, Martin v. Weekly).

4. On the escheat proceedings against the Fairfax manors, see *PJM*, II, 143–48; V, 230–31.

5. For the case of Fairfax v. Hunter, which JM brought in the U.S. circuit court in 1795, see *PJM*, V, 228–56.

6. The act of 1796 "concerning certain lands lying in the Northern Neck," by which the purchasers of the Fairfax estate relinquished their claim to the waste and ungranted lands and the commonwealth relinquished its claim to the Fairfax manor lands (Shepherd, *Statutes*, II, 22–23).

7. Thomas Buck and William Williamson were also named as defendants in this suit. Buck put in his answer, stating that he had purchased land from Weekly in 1798 on the understanding that the claimants under Fairfax had given up their claim to this tract because the survey had been lost (answer of Thomas Buck, 18 Nov. 1807, Martin v. Weekly).

8. A deed from Philip Martin to JM, James Marshall, and Rawleigh Colston for Leeds Manor was executed on 18 Oct. 1806 ([copy], record of Marshall's Lessee v. Foley, Fauquier County Land Causes, III, 1833–50, 40–44 [microfilm], Vi). Edmund Randolph, attorney for the defendant Weekly, objected that making Philip Martin the complainant in this suit was a stratagem "to withdraw the cause from the cognizance of the state-courts of Virginia" (answer of Jacob Weekly, 24 Nov. 1807, Martin v. Weekly).

9. Weekly traced his title back to the purchase of rights acquired by others during the time of the proprietorship. He contended that these rights were to lands designated at the time as vacant and denied any notice of an appropriation by Lord Fairfax until long after he had acquired title (answer of Jacob Weekly, 24 Nov. 1807, Martin v. Weekly). The suit never came on the trial docket for a hearing and was dismissed at the rules in June 1808.

From William Wirt

Dear Sir   Richmond Feby. 12. 1807

Yours of the 3d. Int has been duly received.[1] The opinions which you give touching the case of Lee & Coulson have been always mine, ever since I examined the case. I now enclose you a Copy of Murdocks deposition. The application to the court for the delivery of the new powers, which you propose, is now renderd unnecessary—if, as I apprehend, the powers of which you have heard are nothing more, than an instrument by which the executors of Ann Gordon renounce and refuse the probate and execution of her will, and appoint a proctor of the Arches Court of Canterbury to have their renunciation received and recorded in the prerogative Court. Three instruments of this sort, the same to a letter, have been put into my hands by Mr. Sample the Attorney for the Plff: as murdock does not specify the defects which existed in the former powers, I am not able to say how this instrument of renunciation acts upon the case; I send you a Copy of it, and you will perhaps see and be able to explain to me what their effect is intended to be & will be. The Chancery term at Williamsburg commences on the first of April. You can furnish me with the deeds of Conveyance that I may be prepared to tender them, if such tender, at any stage of the cause will avail us. Why should we not have compleat powers drawn, tender them for execution in open Court, & tender the deeds as the condition of that execution. It seems to me that this would end the contest.[2] I am, Dear Sir, Very respectfully, Your obt Ser

WM WIRT

ALS (letterbook copy), William Wirt Papers, MdHi. Inside address to "The Honble John Marshall City of Washington."

1. Letter not found. A prominent lawyer who later became U.S. attorney general and achieved fame as the biographer of Patrick Henry, Wirt (1772–1834) was then practicing law in Richmond.

2. No subsequent surviving correspondence sheds additional light on the subject of this letter. "Murdock" was possibly William Murdock, the agent who acted for the Marshalls in executing the final contract for Leeds Manor with Philip Martin (JM to James M. Marshall, 13 Feb. 1806 and n. 6). "Mr. Sample" may have been James Semple (sometimes pronounced "Sample") of Williamsburg (1768–1831), who later served as judge of the General Court and as a professor of law at the College of William and Mary (WMQ, 1st ser., XXVI [1918], 174 and n.). As Wirt indicated, the case in question took place in the Superior Court of Chancery at Williamsburg. The records and papers of that court were destroyed by fire in 1911.

Ex Parte Bollman and Ex Parte Swartwout
Opinion
U.S. Supreme Court, 13 February 1807

EDITORIAL NOTE

The cases arising from the so-called "Burr Conspiracy" monopolized Marshall's judicial attention between February and October 1807. The habeas corpus proceedings in the Supreme Court on behalf of Erick Bollman and

CHARLES LEE

Oil on canvas by Cephas Thompson, 1807. *Courtesy of the National Portrait Gallery, Smithsonian Institution, Gift of Mrs. A. D. Pollock Gilmour*

Samuel Swartwout served as the overture to the spectacular trial for treason of Aaron Burr, which began that summer in the U.S. circuit court at Richmond.

In the fall of 1806 revelations of Burr's proposed plans to lead an expedition to the southwest, with the apparent intention of fomenting war with Spain and separating the western states from the Union, created a public sensation, particularly in the capital at Washington. Acting on evidence supplied by General James Wilkinson, governor of the Louisiana Territory, President Jefferson in November formally proclaimed the existence of a conspiracy and in January communicated to Congress the information he had received and the steps that had been taken to thwart the allegedly treasonous enterprise. Among these steps was Wilkinson's arrest of several of the alleged conspirators, including Bollman, a German adventurer whose mercantile business had failed, and Swartwout, a young member of a prominent New York family. Wilkinson sent Bollman and Swartwout to Washington under military guard. Late in January the U.S. Circuit Court for the District of Columbia ordered them to be committed without bail on a charge of treason. Charles Lee and Robert Goodloe Harper, counsel for the prisoners, then applied to the Supreme Court for writs of habeas corpus.

These judicial proceedings took place in a highly charged political atmosphere. The Senate reacted to the crisis by hastily adopting a bill temporarily suspending the privilege of the writ of habeas corpus in certain instances. Although the House subsequently defeated this bill by a large majority, the subject again came before the House in the form of a resolution "to make further provision by law, for securing the privilege of the writ of habeas corpus." Partisan debate on this motion occurred simultaneously with the Supreme Court's hearing the cases of Bollman and Swartwout.[1]

Charles Lee opened the argument on the motion for a habeas corpus with a brief speech on 9 February. U.S. Attorney General Caesar Rodney declined to speak to the motion, stating that if the court determined to issue the writ, "he should cheerfully submit to it." The next day Harper requested a chance to be heard as counsel for Bollman, having understood that "the court had some difficulty on certain points, which had not been so fully examined by Mr. Lee as their importance merited." On Wednesday, 11 February, Harper presented an elaborate argument lasting an hour and a half. The court postponed giving an opinion until Friday the thirteenth, the chief justice acknowledging that "there was some contrariety of sentiment among the members of the court."[2]

The first of the two opinions delivered by Marshall dealt solely with the abstract question of whether the Supreme Court could issue writs of habeas corpus. In addition to the chief justice, the judges present during the delivery of this opinion were Washington, Johnson, and Brockholst Livingston, who had just joined the court at this term. Justices Cushing and Chase were absent on account of illness. Washington and Livingston joined Marshall in the majority. Johnson dissented, noting that the absent Chase concurred with his sentiments.[3]

1. *Annals of Congress*, XVI, 102–25, 502–90.
2. *National Intelligencer*, 11 Feb., 13 Feb. 1807.
3. Ibid., 16 Feb. 1807.

OPINION

As preliminary to any investigation of the merits of this motion, this court deems it proper to declare that it disclaims all jurisdiction not given by the constitution, or by the laws of the U. States.

Courts which originate in the common law possess a jurisdiction which must be regulated by their common law until some statute shall change their established principles; but courts which are created by written law, and whose jurisdiction is defined by written law, cannot transcend that jurisdiction. It is unnecessary to state the reasoning on which this opinion is founded because it has been repeatedly given by this court; and with the decisions heretofore rendered on this point, no member of the bench has, even for an instant, been dissatisfied. The reasoning from the bar, in relation to it, may be answered by the single observation, that for the meaning of the term *Habeas Corpus*, resort may unquestionably be had to the common law; but the power to award the writ by any of the courts of the U. States, must be given by written law.[1]

This opinion is not to be considered as abridging the power of courts over their own officers, or to protect themselves, and their members, from being disturbed in the exercise of their functions. It extends only to the power of taking cognizance of any question between individuals, or between the government and individuals.

To enable the court to decide on such question, the power to determine it must be given by written law.

The enquiry therefore on this motion will be, whether by any statute, compatible with the constitution of the U.S. the power to award a writ of *Habeas Corpus*, in such a case as that of Erick Bollman and Samuel Swartwout, has been given to this court.

The 14th section of the judicial act,*[2] has been considered as containing a substantive grant of this power.

It is in these words: "That all the before mentioned courts of the United States shall have power to issue writs of *scire facias*, *Habeas Corpus*, and all other writs, not specially provided for by statute, which may be necessary for the exercise of their respective jurisdictions and agreeable to the principles and usages of law. And that either of the justices of the Supreme Court, as well as judges of the district courts shall have power to grant writs of *Habeas Corpus* for the purpose of an enquiry into the cause of commitment. *Provided* that

*Laws U.S. Vol. 1. p. 58.

writs of *Habeas Corpus* shall in no case extend to prisoners in goal unless where they are in custody under or by color of the authority of the U.S. or are committed for trial before some court of the same, or are necessary to be brought into court to testify."

The only doubt of which this section can be susceptible is whether the restrictive words of the first sentence limit the power to the award of such writs of *Habeas Corpus* as are necessary to enable the courts of the United States to exercise their respective jurisdictions in some cause which they are capable of finally deciding.

It has been urged that in strict grammatical construction these words refer to the last antecedent, which is, "all other writs not specially provided for by statute."[3]

This criticism may be correct, and is not entirely without its influence; but the sound construction, which the court thinks it safer to adopt, is, that the true sense of the words is to be determined by the nature of the provision and by the context.

It may be worthy of remark that this act was passed by the first Congress of the United States, sitting under a constitution which had declared "that the privilege of the writ of *Habeas Corpus* should not be suspended unless when in cases of rebellion or invasion the public safety might require it."[4]

Acting under the immediate influence of this injunction, they must have felt, with peculiar force, the obligation of providing efficient means by which this great constitutional privilege should receive life and activity; for if the means be not in existence, the privilege itself would be lost, although no law for its suspension should be enacted. Under the impression of this obligation they give, to all the courts, the power of awarding writs of *Habeas Corpus*.

It has been truly said that this is a generic term and includes every species of that writ.[5] To this it may be added that when used singly—when we say *the writ of Habeas Corpus*, without addition—we most generally mean that great writ which is now applied for; and in that sense it is used in the constitution.

The section proceeds to say that "either of the justices of the Supreme Court, as well as judges of the District Courts, shall have power to grant writs of *Habeas Corpus* for the purpose of an enquiry into the cause of commitment."

It has been argued that congress could never intend to give a power of this kind, to one of the judges of this court which is refused to all of them when assembled.[6]

There is certainly much force in this argument, and it receives additional strength from the consideration that if the power be denied to this court, it is denied to every other court of the United States; the right to grant this important writ is given, in this sentence, to every judge of the circuit, or district, court, but can neither be exercised by the circuit nor district court. It would be strange if the judge, sitting on the bench, should be unable to hear a motion for this writ where it might be openly made, and openly discussed, and might yet retire to his chamber and in private receive and decide upon the motion. This is not consistent with the genius of our legislation, nor with the course of our judicial proceedings. It would be much more consonant with both, that the power of the judge at his chambers should be suspended during his term, than that it should be exercised only in secret.

Whatever motives might induce the legislature to withhold from the *Supreme* court the power to award the great writ of *Habeas Corpus*, there could be none which would induce them to withhold it from *every* court in the U. States: and as it is granted to *all* in the *same sentence* and by the *same words*, the sound construction would seem to be, that the first sentence vests this power in all courts of the United States; but as those courts are not always in session, the second sentence vests it in every justice or judge of the United States.

The doubt which has been raised on this subject may be further explained by examining the character of the various writs of *Habeas Corpus*, and selecting those to which this general grant of power must be restricted, if taken in the limited sense of being merely used to enable the court to exercise its jurisdiction in causes which it is enabled to decide finally.

The various writs of *Habeas Corpus* as stated and accurately defined by judge Blackstone, (3 *Bl. Com.* 129)[7] are 1st. The writ of *Habeas Corpus ad respondendum* "when a man hath a cause of action against one who is confined by the process of some inferior court; in order to remove the prisoner and charge him with this new action in the court above."

This case may occur when a party having a right to sue in this court, (as a state at the time of the passage of this act, or a foreign minister) wishes to institute a suit against a person who is already confined by the process of an inferior court. This confinement may be either by the process of a court, of the *United States*, or of a *state* court. If it be in a court of the United States, this writ would be inapplicable, because perfectly useless, and consequently could not be contemplated by the legislature. It would not be required, in such case, to bring the body of the defendant actually into court, and he would already be in the charge of the person who, under an original writ from this court would be directed to take him into custody, and would already be confined in the same jail in which he would be confined under the process of this court if he should be unable to give bail.

If the party should be confined by process from a state court, there are many additional reasons against the use of this writ in such a case.

The state courts are not, in any sense of the word, *inferior* courts, except in the particular cases in which an appeal lies from their judgment to this court; and in these cases the mode of proceeding is particularly prescribed and is not by *Habeas Corpus*. They are not inferior courts because they emanate from a different authority, and are the creatures of a distinct government.

2d. The writ of *Habeas Corpus ad satisfaciendum*, "when a prisoner hath had judgment against him in an action, and the plaintiff is desirous to bring him up to some superior court to charge him with process of execution."

This case can never occur in the courts of the United States. One court never awards execution on the judgment of another. Our whole juridical system forbids it.

3d. *Ad prosequendum, testificandum, deliberandum*, &c. "which issue when it is necessary to remove a prisoner, in order to prosecute, or bear testimony, in any court, or to be tried in the proper jurisdiction wherein the fact was committed."

This writ might unquestionably be employed to bring up a prisoner to bear testimony in a court, consistently with the most limited construction of the words in the act of Congress; but the power to bring a person up that he may be tried in the proper jurisdiction is understood to be the very question now before the court.

4th and last. "The common writ *ad faciendum et recipiendum*, which issues out of any of the courts of Westminster-hall, when a person is sued in some inferior jurisdiction, and is desirous to remove the action into the superior court, commanding the inferior judges to produce the body of the defendant, together with the day and cause of his caption and detainer (whence the writ is frequently denominated an *habeas corpus cum causa*) to *do and receive* whatever the king's court shall consider in that behalf. This writ is grantable of common right, without any motion in court, and it instantly supercedes all proceedings in the court below."

Can a solemn grant of power to a court to award a writ be considered as applicable to a case in which that writ, if issuable at all, issues by law without the leave of the court?

It would not be difficult to demonstrate that the writ of *Habeas Corpus cum causa* cannot be the particular writ contemplated by the legislature in the section under consideration; but it will be sufficient to observe generally that the same act prescribes a different mode for bringing into the courts of the U. States, suits brought in a state court against a person having a right to claim the jurisdiction of the courts of the United States. He may, on his first appearance, file his petition and authenticate the fact, upon which the cause is *ipso facto* removed into the courts of the United States.[8]

The only power then, which on this limited construction would be granted by the section under consideration, would be that of issuing writs of *Habeas Corpus ad testificandum*. The section itself proves that this was not the intention of the legislature. It concludes with the following *proviso*, "That writs of *habeas corpus*, shall in no case extend to prisoners in goal, unless where they are in custody under or by color of the authority of the United States, or are committed for trial before some court of the same, or are necessary to be brought into court to testify."

This proviso extends to the whole section. It limits the powers previously granted to the courts, because it specifies a case [in which][9] it is particularly applicable to the use of the power by courts;—where the person is necessary to be brought into court to testify. That construction cannot be a fair one which would make the legislature except from the operation of a proviso, limiting the express grant of a power, the whole power intended to be granted.

From this review of the extent of the power of awarding writs of *habeas Corpus*, if the section be construed in its restricted sense; from a comparison of the nature of the writ which the courts of the United States would, on that view of the subject, be enabled to issue; from a comparison of the power, so granted, with the other parts of the section, it is apparent that this limited sense of the term cannot be that which was contemplated by the legislature.

But the 33d section throws much light upon this question. It contains these words "And upon all arrests in criminal cases, bail shall be admitted, except where the punishment may be death; in which cases it shall not be admitted *but by the supreme*, or a circuit *court*, or by a justice of the supreme court, or a judge of a district court, who shall exercise their discretion therein, regarding the nature and circumstances of the offence, and of the evidence, and of the usages of law."[10]

The appropriate process of bringing up a prisoner, not committed by the court itself, to be bailed, is by the writ now applied for. Of consequence, a court, possessing the power to bail prisoners not committed by itself, may award a writ of *Habeas Corpus* for the exercise of that power. The clause under consideration obviously proceeds on the supposition that this power was previously given, and is explanatory of the 14th section.

If by the sound construction of the act of Congress the power to award writs of *Habeas Corpus* in order to examine into the cause of commitment is given to this court, it remains to enquire whether this be a case in which the writ ought to be granted.

The only objection is, that the commitment has been made by a court having power to commit and to bail.

Against this objection the argument from the bar has been so conclusive that nothing can be added to it.[11]

If then this were *res integra*, the court would decide in favor of the motion. But the question is considered as long since decided. The case of Hamilton is expressly in point in all its parts; and although the question of jurisdiction was not made at the bar, the case was several days under advisement, and this question could not have escaped the attention of the court. From that decision the court would not lightly depart. (*U. S. v. Hamilton*, 3 *Dallas* 17.)[12]

If the act of Congress gives this court the power to award a writ of *Habeas Corpus* in the present case, it remains to enquire whether that act be compatible with the constitution.

In the *mandamus* case† it was decided that this court would not exercise original jurisdiction except so far as that jurisdiction was given by the constitution. But so far as that case has distinguished between original and appellate jurisdiction, that, which the court is now asked to exercise, is clearly *appellate*. It is the revision of a decision of an inferior court by which a citizen has been committed to jail.

It has been demonstrated at the bar that the question brought forward on a *Habeas Corpus*, is always distinct from that which is involved in the cause itself. The question whether the individual shall be imprisoned is always distinct from the question whether he shall be convicted or acquitted of the charge on which he is to be tried, and therefore these questions are separated, and may be decided in different courts.

The decision that the individual shall be imprisoned must always precede the application for a writ of *Habeas Corpus*, and this writ must always be for the purpose of revising that decision, and therefore appellate in its nature.

But this point also is decided in Hamilton's case and in Burford's case.‡[13]

If at any time the public safety should require the suspension of the powers vested by this act in the courts of the United States, it is for the legislature to say so.

That question depends on political considerations, on which the legislature is to decide. Until the legislative will be expressed, this court can only see its duty, and must obey the laws.

The motion, therefore, must be granted.[14]

---

† 1. *Cranch's reports, Marbury v. Madison.*

‡ At Feb. term, 1806, *in this court.*

Printed, *National Intelligencer, and Washington Advertiser* (Washington, D.C.), 23 February 1807.

1. JM alluded to Harper's contention that the power to issue writs of habeas corpus was one of the "incidental powers" deriving from the common law that belonged to all superior courts of record in England and the U.S. (4 Cranch 79–83).

2. *U.S. Statutes at Large*, I, 81–82.

3. Both Lee and Harper made this point (4 Cranch 78, 83–84).

4. Art. I, sec. 9.

5. Harper's argument (4 Cranch 84).

6. Harper's argument (4 Cranch 84).

7. For Blackstone's discussion of the writ of habeas corpus, see *Commentaries*, III, 129–38.

8. Judiciary Act of 1789, sec. 12 (*U.S. Statutes at Large*, I, 79–80).

9. Words in brackets supplied from text in 4 Cranch 99.

10. *U.S. Statutes at Large*, I, 91.

11. Harper's discussion of this point had strong partisan overtones. The U.S. Circuit Court, District of Columbia, had committed Bollman and Swartwout without bail. Judges Duckett and Fitzhugh, Jefferson's appointees, were in favor of the commitment; Judge William Cranch, a Federalist, opposed it. Harper strenuously opposed the principle that commitment by an inferior federal court, a court that was the creature of Congress and whose judges were more likely to be "the most servile tools of those in power for the moment," could prevent the issuance of a writ of habeas corpus by the Supreme Court: "Let it be once established by the authority of this court, that a commitment on record by such a tribunal, is to stop the course of the writ of *habeas corpus*, is to shut the mouth of the supreme court, and see how ready, how terrible, and how irresistible an engine of oppression is placed in the hands of a dominant party, flushed with victory, and irritated by a recent conflict; or struggling to keep down an opposing party which it hates and fears" (4 Cranch 90).

12. This case, decided in Feb. 1795, was a motion for a habeas corpus on behalf of a prisoner committed for treason for his part in the Whiskey Rebellion. The Supreme Court, "after holding the subject for some days under advisement," admitted the prisoner to bail. Although there was no reported inquiry into the jurisdictional issue, JM assumed the judges must have discussed it.

13. Ex parte Burford, 3 Cranch 448 (1806). This case also brought into issue the Supreme Court's jurisdiction. In a brief opinion, JM noted that there was "some obscurity in the act of congress, and some doubts were entertained by the court as to the construction of the constitution. The court, however, in favour of liberty, was willing to grant the *habeas corpus*." Moreover, he added, U.S. v. Hamilton was a decisive precedent for granting the writ (3 Cranch 449).

14. Dissenting, Justice Johnson contended that the Supreme Court had no authority to issue the writ in this case on the ground that it was an exercise of original jurisdiction not granted by the Constitution (4 Cranch 101–7).

Ex Parte Bollman and Ex Parte Swartwout
Opinion
U.S. Supreme Court, 21 February 1807

EDITORIAL NOTE

Arguments on a motion to discharge Bollman and Swartwout commenced on Monday, 16 February, and continued throughout the week. Lee opened with a speech of three and a half hours in favor of the motion, followed by Francis Scott Key for another hour. The next day Attorney General Rodney and U.S. Attorney Walter Jones, Jr., each spoke for two hours against the motion. They were followed by Harper (an hour and a half) on behalf of the prisoners. Luther Martin, also for the prisoners, consumed four and a half hours delivering his argument on Wednesday the eighteenth.

On Thursday the nineteenth the chief justice announced that the court had not been able to come to a decision and that in the meantime the prisoners could be bailed. The court, he added, "felt considerable difficulty with regard to the admissibility" of Wilkinson's affidavit, which reported the substance of Burr's incriminating "cipher letter" of 29 July 1806. Was an affidavit stating the substance of an original letter in possession of the person making the affidavit admissible evidence? Unable "to find any authorities on this point," the court invited counsel to submit any precedents they could find. The researches of Rodney and Martin proved unavailing, and the court postponed its opinion until Saturday the twenty-first. Sitting with the chief justice in this case were Chase, Washington, and Johnson. Livingston had taken leave to attend his ailing daughter.[1]

1. *National Intelligencer*, 18, 20, 23 Feb. 1807.

OPINION

The prisoners having been brought before this court on a writ of *Habeas Corpus*, and the testimony on which they were committed having been fully examined and attentively considered, the court is now to declare the law upon their case.

This being a mere enquiry which, without deciding upon guilt, precedes the institution of a prosecution, the question to be determined is whether the accused shall be discharged or held to trial, and if the latter, in what place they are to be tried, and whether they shall be confined, or admitted to bail. "If," says a very learned and accurate commentator, "upon this enquiry it manifestly appears that no such crime has been committed, or that the suspicion entertained of the prisoner was wholly groundless, in such cases only it is lawful totally to discharge him. Otherwise he must either be committed to prison or give bail."[1]

The specific charge brought against the prisoners is treason in levying war against the U. S.

As there is no crime which can more excite and agitate the passions of men than treason, no charge demands more from the tribunal before which it is made a deliberate and temperate enquiry. Whether this enquiry be directed to the fact or to the law, none can be more solemn, none more important to the citizen or to the government— none can more affect the safety of both.

To prevent the possibility of those calamities which result from the extension of treason to offences of minor importance, that great fundamental law which defines and limits the various departments of our government has given a rule on the subject both to the legislature and the courts of America which neither can be permitted to transcend.

"Treason against the U. S. shall consist only in levying war against them, or in adhering to their enemies giving them aid and comfort."[2]

To constitute that specific crime for which the prisoners now before the court have been committed, war must be actually levied against the U. States. However flagitious may be the crime of conspiring to subvert by force the government of our country, such conspiracy is not treason. To conspire to levy war, and actually to levy war, are distinct offences. The first must be brought into open action[3] by the assemblage of men for a purpose treasonable in itself, or the fact of levying war cannot have been committed. So far has this principle been carried that, in a case reported by Ventris, and mentioned in some modern treatises on criminal law, it has been determined that the actual enlistment of men to serve against the government does not amount to levying war.[4] It is true that in that case the soldiers enlisted were to serve without the realm, but they were enlisted within it, and if the enlistment for a treasonable purpose could amount to levying war, then war had been actually levied.

It is not the intention of the court to say that no individual can be guilty of this crime who has not appeared in arms against his country. On the contrary, if war be actually levied, that is, if a body of men be actually assembled for the purpose of effecting by force, a treasonable purpose, all those who perform any part, however minute or however remote from the scene of action, and who are actually leagued in the general conspiracy, are to be considered as traitors. But there must be an actual assembling of men for the treasonable purpose, to constitute a levying of war.

Crimes so atrocious as those which have for their object the subversion by violence of those laws and those institutions which have been ordained in order to secure the peace and happiness of society, are not to escape punishment because they have not ripened into treason. The wisdom of the legislature is competent to provide for the case; and the framers of our constitution who not only defined and limited the crime, but with jealous circumspection attempted to protect their limitation by providing that no person should be convicted of it, unless on the testimony of two witnesses to the same overt act, or on confession in open court, must have conceived it more safe that punishment in such cases should be ordained by general laws formed upon deliberation, under the influence of no resentments, and without knowing on whom they were to operate, than that it should be inflicted under the influence of those passions which the occasion seldom fails to excite, and which a flexible definition of the crime, or a construction which would render it flexible, might bring into operation. It is therefore more safe as well as more consonant to the principles of our constitution that the crime of treason should not be extended by construction to doubtful cases; and that crimes not clearly within the constitutional definition should receive such punishment as the legislature in its wisdom may provide.

To complete the crime of levying war against the U. S. there must be an actual assemblage of men for the purpose of executing a treasonable design. In the case now before the court, a design to overturn the government of the U. S. in New Orleans by force, would have been unquestionably a design which if carried into execution would have been treason, and the assemblage of a body of men for the purpose of carrying it into execution, would amount to levying of war against the U. S. but no conspiracy for this object, no enlisting of men to effect it, would be an actual levying of war.

In conformity with the principles now laid down have been the decisions heretofore made by the judges of the U. States.

The opinions given by judge Paterson and judge Iredell in cases before them imply an actual assembling of men though they rather designed to remark on the purpose to which the force was to be applied than on the nature of the force itself. Their opinions however contemplate the actual employment of force.[5]

Judge Chase in the trial of Fries was more explicit.[6]

He stated the opinion of the court to be "that if a body of people conspire and meditate an insurrection to resist or oppose the execution of any statute of the U. S. by force, they are only guilty of a high misdemeanor; but if they proceed to carry such intention into execution by force, that they are guilty of the treason of levying war; and the *quantum* of the force employed, neither lessens nor increases the crime: whether by one hundred, or one thousand persons, is wholly immaterial.["] "The court are of opinion," continued Judge Chase, on that occasion, "that a combination or conspiracy to levy war against the U. S. is not treason, unless combined with an attempt to carry such combination or conspiracy into execution; some actual force or violence must be used in pursuance of such design to levy war; but it is altogether immaterial whether the force used is sufficient to effectuate the object; any force connected with the intention, will constitute the crime of levying war."

The application of these general principles to the particular case before the court will depend on the testimony which has been exhibited against the accused.

The first deposition to be considered is that of general Eaton.[7] This gentleman connects in one statement the purpose of numerous conversations held with col. Burr throughout the last winter. In the course of these conversations were communicated various criminal projects which seem to have been revolving in the mind of the projector. An expedition against Mexico seems to have been the first and most matured part of his plan, if indeed it did not constitute a distinct and separate plan, upon the success of which other schemes still more culpable, but not yet well digested might depend. Maps and other information preparatory to its execution, and which would rather indicate that it was the immediate object, had been procured, and for a considerable time, in repeated conversations the whole efforts of Col. Burr were directed to prove to the witness who was to have held a high command under him, the practicability of the enterprise, and in explaining to him the means by which it was to be effected.

This deposition exhibits the various schemes of col. Burr, and its materiality depends on connecting the prisoners at the bar in such of those schemes as were treasonable. For this purpose the affidavit of general Wilkinson comprehending in its body the substance of a letter from Col. Burr has been offered and was received by the circuit court.[8] To the admission of this testimony great and serious objections have been made. It has been urged that it is a voluntary, or rather an extra-judicial affidavit made before a person not appearing to be a magistrate, and contains the substance only of a letter, of which the original is retained by the person who made the affidavit.

The objection that the affidavit is extrajudicial resolves itself into the question whether one magistrate may commit on an affidavit taken before another magistrate.[9] For if he may, an affidavit made as the foundation of a commitment, ceases to be extrajudicial, and the person who makes it would be as liable to a prosecution for perjury as if the warrant of commitment had been issued by the magistrate before whom the affidavit was made.

To decide that an affidavit made before one magistrate would not justify a commitment by another might in many cases be productive of great inconvenience, and does not appear susceptible of abuse if the verity of the certificate be established. Such an affidavit seems admissible on the principle that before the accused is put upon his trial, all the proceedings are ex parte. The court therefore over-rule this objection.

That which questions the character of the person who has on this occasion administered the oath is next to be considered.

The certificate from the office of the department of state has been deemed insufficient by the counsel for the prisoners, because the law does not require the appointment of magistrates for the territory of New Orleans to be certified to that office, because the certificate is in itself informal, and because it does not appear that the magistrate had taken the oath required by the act of Congress.[10]

The first of these objections is not supported by the law of the case, and the second may be so readily corrected that the court has proceeded to consider the subject as if it were corrected, retaining however any final decision, if against the prisoners, until the correction shall be made. With regard to the third, the magistrate must be presumed to have taken the requisite oaths, since he is found acting as a magistrate.

On the admissibility of that part of the affidavit which purports to be as near the substance of the letter from Colonel Burr to General Wilkinson as the latter could interpret it, a division of opinion has taken place, in the court. Two judges are of opinion that as such testimony delivered in the presence of the prisoner on his trial would be totally inadmissible, neither can it be considered as a foundation for a commitment. Although in making a commitment the magistrate does not decide on the guilt of the prisoner, yet he does decide on the probable cause, and a long and painful imprisonment may be the consequence of his decision. This probable cause therefore ought to be proved by testimony in itself legal, and which, though from the nature of the case it must be ex parte, ought, in most other respects to be such as a court and jury might hear.

Two judges are of opinion that in this incipient stage of the prosecution an affidavit stating the general purport of a letter may be read, particularly where the person in possession of it is at too great a distance to admit of its being obtained, and that a commitment may be founded on it.

Under this embarrassment it was deemed necessary to look into the affidavit for the purpose of discovering whether if admitted, it contains matter which would justify the commitment of the prisoners at the bar on the charge of treason.

That the letter from Col. Burr to general Wilkinson relates to a military enterprise meditated by the former has not been questioned. If this enterprise was against Mexico, it would amount to a high misdemeanor, if against any of the territories of the United States, or if in its progress the subversion of the government of the United States in any of their territories was a mean clearly and necessarily to be employed, if such mean formed a substantive part of the plan, the assemblage of a body of men to effect it would be levying war against the United States.

The letter is in language which furnishes no distinct view of the design of the writer.[11] The co-operation, however, which is stated to have been secured, points strongly to some expedition against the territories of Spain. After making these general statements the writer becomes rather more explicit and says, "Burr's plan of operations is to move down rapidly from the falls on the 15th of November with the first 500 or 1000 men in light boats now constructing for that purpose to be at Natchez between the 5th and 15th of December, there to meet Wilkinson; then to determine whether it will be expedient in the first instance to seize on or to pass by Baton Rouge. The people of the country to which we are going are prepared to receive us. Their agents now with Burr say that if we will protect their religion and will not subject them to a foreign power, in three weeks all will be settled."

There is no expression in these sentences which would justify a suspicion that any territory of the U. S. was the object of the expedition.

For what purpose seize on Baton Rouge; why engage Spain against this enterprize, if it was designed against the United States?

"The people of the country to which we are going are prepared to receive us." This language is peculiarly appropriate to a foreign country. It will not be contended that the terms would be inapplicable to a territory of the United States, but other terms would more aptly convey the idea, and Burr seems to consider himself as giving information of which Wilkinson was not possessed. When it is recollected that he was the governor of a territory adjoining that which must have been threatened, if a territory of the United States was threatened, and that he commanded the army, a part of which was stationed in that territory, the probability that the information communicated related to a foreign country, it must be admitted, gains strength.

"Their agents now with Burr say that if we will protect their religion and will not subject them to a foreign power, in three weeks all will be settled."

This is apparently the language of a people who, from the contemplated change of their political situation, feared for their religion, and feared that they would be made the subjects of a foreign power. That the Mexicans should entertain these apprehensions was natural and would readily be believed. They were, if the representation made of their dispositions be correct, about to place themselves much in the power of men who professed a faith different from theirs, and who by making them dependent on England, or the United States would subject them to a foreign power.

That the people of New Orleans as a people, if really engaged in the conspiracy, should feel the same apprehensions, and require assurances on the same points, is by no means so obvious.

There certainly is not in the letter delivered to general Wilkinson, so far as that letter is laid before the court, one syllable which has a necessary or a natural reference to an enterprise against any territory of the United States.

That the bearer of this letter must be considered as acquainted with its contents, is not to be controverted. The letter and his own declarations evince the fact.

After stating himself to have passed through New York and the western states and territories, without insinuating that he had performed on his route any act whatever which was connected with the enterprise, he states their object to be "to carry an expedition to the Mexican provinces."[12]

This statement may be considered as explanatory of the letter of col. Burr, if the expressions of that letter could be thought ambiguous.

But there are other declarations made by Mr. Swartwout, which constitute the difficulty of this case. On an enquiry from general Wilkinson, he said "this territory would be revolutionized where the people were ready to join them, and that there would be some seizing, he supposed, at New Orleans."

If these words import that the government established by the United States in any of its territories, was to be revolutionized by force, although merely as a step to, or a mean of executing some greater projects, the design was unquestionably treasonable, and any assemblage of men for that purpose would amount to a levying of war. But on the import of the words a difference of opinion exists. Some of the judges suppose they refer to the territory against which the expedition was intended, others to that in which the conversation was held. Some consider the words if even applicable to a territory of the United States, as alluding to a revolution to be effected by the people rather than by the party conducted by col. Burr.

But whether this treasonable intention be really imputable to the plan or not, it is admitted that it must have been carried into execution by an open assemblage of men for that purpose, previous to the arrest of the prisoner, in order to consummate the crime as to him; and a majority of the court is of opinion that the conversation of Mr. Swartwout affords no sufficient proof of such assembling.

The prisoner stated that "col. Burr with the support of a powerful association extending from New York to New Orleans, was levying an armed body of 7000 men from the state of New York and the western states and territories, with a view to carry an expedition to the Mexican territories."

That the association, whatever may be its purpose, is not treason, has been already stated. That levying an army may or may not be treason, and that this depends on the intention with which it is levied, and on the point to which the parties have advanced, has been also stated. The mere enlisting of men without assembling them is not levying war. The question then is whether this evidence proves col. Burr to have advanced so far in levying an army as actually to have assembled them.

It is argued that since it cannot be necessary that the whole 7000 men should have assembled, their commencing their march by detachments to the place of rendezvous, must be sufficient to constitute the crime.[13]

This position is correct, with some qualification. It can not be necessary that the whole army should assemble, and that the various parts which are to compose it should have combined. But it is necessary that there should be an actual assemblage, and therefore the evidence should make the fact unequivocal.

The travelling of individuals to the place of rendezvous would perhaps not be sufficient. This would be an equivocal act, and has no warlike appearance. The meeting of particular bodies of men and their marching from places of partial to a place of general rendezvous would be such an assemblage.

The particular words used by Mr. Swartwout are that col. Burr was levying an armed body of 7000 men. If the term levying in this place imports that they were assembled, then such fact would amount, if the intention be against the United States, to levying war. If it barely imports that he was enlisting or engaging them in his service, the fact would not amount to levying war.

It is thought sufficiently apparent that the latter is the sense in which the term was used. The fact alluded to, if taken in the former sense, is of a nature so to force itself upon the public view, that if the army had then actually assembled either together or in detachments, some evidence of such assembling, would have been laid before the court.

The words used by the prisoner in reference to seizing at New Orleans, and borrowing perhaps by force from the bank, though indicating a design to rob, and consequently importing a high offence, do not designate the specific crime of levying war against the United States.

It is therefore the opinion of a majority of the court, that in the case of Samuel Swartwout, there is not sufficient evidence of his levying war against the United States to justify his commitment on the charge of treason.

Against Erick Bollman there is still less testimony. Nothing has been said by him to support the charge that the enterprise in which he was engaged had any other object than was stated in the letter of col. Burr. Against him, therefore, there is no evidence to support a charge of treason.

That both of the prisoners were engaged in a most culpable enterprise against the dominions of a power at peace with the United States, those who admit the affidavit of general Wilkinson cannot doubt. But that no part of this crime was committed in the district of Columbia, is apparent. It is therefore the unanimous opinion of the court that they cannot be tried in this district.

The law read on the part of the prosecution is understood to apply only to offences committed on the high seas, or in any river, haven, bason or bay, not within the jurisdiction of any particular state.[14] In those cases there is no court which has particular cognizance of the crime, and therefore the place in which the criminal shall be apprehended, or, if he be apprehended where no court has exclusive jurisdiction, that to which he shall be first brought, is substituted for the place in which the offence was committed.

But in this case, a tribunal for the trial of the offence wherever it may have been committed, had been provided by Congress; and at the place where the prisoners were seized by the authority of the commander in chief, there existed such a tribunal.[15] It would too be extremely dangerous to say, that because the prisoners were apprehended, not by a civil magistrate, but by the military power, there could be given by law a right to try the persons so seized in any place which the general might select, and to which he might direct them to be carried.

The act of Congress which the prisoners are supposed to have violated, describes as offenders those who begin or set on foot, or provide or prepare the means for any military expedition or enterprise to be carried on from thence against the dominions of a foreign prince or state, with whom the United States are at peace.[16]

There is a want of precision in the description of the offence which might produce some difficulty in deciding what cases would come within it. But several other questions arise which a court consisting of four judges finds itself unable to decide, and therefore as the crime with which the prisoners stand charged has not been committed, the court can only direct them to be discharged. This is done with the less reluctance because the discharge does not acquit them from the of-tence which there is probable cause for supposing they have committed, and if those whose duty it is to protect the nation by prosecuting offenders against the laws shall suppose those who have been charged with treason to be proper objects for punishment, they will, when possessed of less exceptionable testimony, and when able to say at what place the offence has been committed, institute fresh proceedings against them.

Printed, *National Intelligencer, and Washington Advertiser* (Washington, D.C.), 25 February 1807.

1. Blackstone, *Commentaries*, IV, 293.

2. Art. III, sec. 3. The section continues: "No Person shall be convicted of Treason unless on the Testimony of two Witnesses to the same overt Act, or on Confession in open Court."

3. In the newspaper the phrase reads "brought into operation." It was so rendered in the first edition of Cranch (4 Cranch 126) but corrected in the list of "Errata" (xii).

4. JM apparently referred to Patrick Harding's Case, 2 Vent. 315, 86 Eng. Rep. 461 (K.B., 1690), which was also summarized in Edward Hyde East, *Pleas of the Crown* (2 vols.; 1803; London, 1972 reprint), I, 77.

5. JM referred to Paterson's charge in U.S. v. Mitchell, 2 Dall. 355–56, one of the cases arising from the Whiskey Rebellion, tried in the U.S. Circuit Court, Pennsylvania, in 1795; and to Iredell's charge in the first trial of John Fries, U.S. Circuit Court, Pennsylvania, 1799. See Wharton, *State Trials of the U.S.*, 182–83, 588–90.

6. Judge Chase's charge to the jury in the second trial of John Fries, U.S. Circuit Court, Pennsylvania, 1800 (ibid., 634–35).

7. William Eaton, formerly consul at Tunis, gave his deposition in the U.S. Circuit Court, District of Columbia, on 26 Jan. 1807. According to Eaton, Burr approached him the previous winter with plans for a military expedition against Mexico, offering him second in command. Eaton stated that Burr gradually began "to unveil" himself, revealing his design to detach the western country and set up a separate government (4 Cranch 463–67).

8. Wilkinson gave two affidavits, dated 14 and 26 Dec. 1806, both embodying the substance of Burr's cipher letter (4 Cranch 455–63).

9. Both Lee and Harper objected that the affidavits were not made before the judicial officer who was to issue the warrant of arrest or commitment (4 Cranch 111, 120).

10. Key objected that the affidavits had not been properly authenticated so as to constitute legal evidence. He further contended that the certificate of the secretary of state merely stated the appointment of the magistrates before whom Wilkinson gave his affidavits but did not show that they had taken the oaths necessary to qualify them to act (4 Cranch 112–13).

11. Whether Burr actually wrote this famous letter is a matter of scholarly doubt. The editors of his papers conclude that the real author was Jonathan Dayton, Burr's close associate in the enterprise. See Mary-Jo Kline and Joanne Wood Ryan, eds., *Political Correspondence and Public Papers of Aaron Burr* (2 vols.; Princeton, N.J., 1983), II, 973–90.

12. The references are to Wilkinson's record of his conversation with Samuel Swartwout, which is embodied in his second affidavit (4 Cranch 461–62).

13. 4 Cranch 118–19 (Jones).

14. 4 Cranch 116. Jones recited sec. 8 of the 1790 act "for the Punishment of certain Crimes against the United States" (*U.S. Statutes at Large*, I, 113–14).

15. The act of 1804 creating the territory of Orleans provided (sec. 8) for the establishment of a district court (ibid., II, 285–86).

16. "An Act in addition to the act for the punishment of certain crimes against the United States," enacted in 1794, sec. 5 (ibid., I, 384).

To Robert Alexander

Dear Sir: Richmond, March 16th, 1807.[1]

I received your letter written at Washington but have mislaid it.[2] I believe however that I recollect its contents sufficiently to answer it.

My engagement is that Mr. Colston, my [bro]ther & myself will not pursue further the decree obtained in the name of Mr. Morris against your Father provided I can receive two thousand pounds.[3] When I spoke of the time which would be given for the sale of lands & houses, I certainly supposed & presume was so understood, that this sum would in the meantime carry interest. The credit otherwise could not have been a matter of indifference. The interest may commence of the first of January next.

I really can devise no means by which the slaves settled in the marriage contract can be certainly secured but by taking out an execution & serving it on them. This may be done immediately & you may make any arrangement you can with the sheriff on the subject. I hereby authorize you to take out an execution & authorize the sheriff to return it in the usual way leaving in your hands the money you may bid which I shall consider as received. The commission however you must arrange with him on such terms as you can make. You may I presume make the transaction as private as the law will permit & by doing so the disagreeableness of a sale will be diminished & a large collection of people prevented. By selling the slaves in families too you may avoid competition & purchase them at a low rate, a thing certainly to be desired as the record would represent me as receiving all the money for which they sell. After purchasing them it will be in your power to make a settlement in conformity with the marriage agreement the validity of which can never be questioned.

As to the land & lotts you mention I can assent to the sale that will secure them to the purchaser. The ⟨*illegible*⟩ that the bonds are transferred to me will be sufficient. With much respect & esteem, I am dear Sir your obedt

J. MARSHALL

1. Albert Beveridge received a copy of this letter in 1917 from William E. Dodd, who in turn obtained it from a judge of the Kentucky Supreme Court in Frankfort (William E. Dodd to Albert Beveridge, 31 Jan. 1917, Beveridge Papers, DLC).

2. Letter not found. Alexander (1767–1841) was the son of William Alexander, whose dealings with Robert Morris in the 1780s gave rise to complex litigation. Although William Alexander lived until 1819, he had turned over the management of his affairs to his son. The elder Alexander had acquired Woodburn, an estate in Woodford County, Ky., where Robert settled in the 1790s. Robert Alexander represented the county in the legislature from 1795 to 1802 and later served as the first president of the Bank of Kentucky (William E. Railey, *History of Woodford County, Kentucky* [1938; Baltimore, 1975 reprint], 27–29, 207–8).

3. See JM to James M. Marshall, 1 Apr. 1804 and n. 5.

To David Daggett

Sir   Richmond March 30th. 1807

Your letter of the 21st. inst. reached me today.[1] With great pleasure I answer the enquiry you make.

I have not seen the opinion of the supreme court as published in the national intelligencer but I have seen it in other gazettes taken from that paper. It is substantially correct. If there be any errors they are meerly of the press & consequently unimportant.[2]

Judge Livingstone was on the bench when the writ of Habeas Corpus was awarded, but a melancholy occasion called him from us before the opinion to which you allude was formed.[3] With great respect, I am Sir Your Obedt. Servt

J MARSHALL

ALS, CtY. Addressed by JM to Daggett at New Haven, Conn.; postmarked Richmond, 31 Mar. Endorsed by Daggett.

1. Letter not found. Daggett (1764–1851), a prominent Connecticut lawyer, later served as a U.S. senator, as professor of law at Yale, and as chief justice of Connecticut.

2. JM referred to the second opinion in the case of Bollman and Swartwout, which was delivered on 21 Feb. and published in the *National Intelligencer* on 25 Feb.

3. Brockholst Livingston joined the Supreme Court at the Feb. 1807 term, succeeding William Paterson. He sat through 16 Feb., when he returned home on account of the illness of his daughter (U.S. Sup. Ct. Minutes, 16 Feb. 1807; *National Intelligencer*, 23 Feb. 1807).

APPENDICES

Appendix I
Calendar of Correspondence
1 November 1800–14 March 1806

Beginning with this volume, the editors have adopted a policy of presenting calendar summaries of letters in a separate appendix. Any inconvenience that may arise from this separation is more than offset, they believe, by keeping the main body of the volume reserved for documents selected for printing in full.

The calendar consists largely of Marshall's routine diplomatic and domestic correspondence as secretary of state, most of which falls into one of the following classifications: (1) Dispatches from U.S. ministers Rufus King (London), William Vans Murray (The Hague), David Humphreys (Madrid), William Smith (Lisbon), and John Quincy Adams (Berlin). These are calendared up to 15 December 1800; dispatches written after that date were received too late for consideration by Marshall and have therefore only been listed (see Appendix II). (2) Letters from the secretary of state to U.S. consuls or agents pertaining to impressments, seizures of vessels, or other matters requiring representations to foreign governments. (3) Notes from foreign diplomats resident in the United States. (4) Miscellaneous correspondence with the president, heads of departments, inferior officers (collectors, marshals, etc.), and members of Congress. (5) Correspondence with the purveyor of public supplies (Israel Whelen) concerning the loading of vessels bound for Algiers and Tunis in fulfillment of treaty obligations with the Barbary states. (6) Letters from private citizens requesting intervention by the State Department. (7) Letters from the commissioners of the District of Columbia addressed to heads of departments. (8) Letters of application and recommendation. (9) Letters not found whose contents are at least partly known from extracts or summaries in the catalogs of auction houses and autograph dealers. Most of the letters in this last group, if extant, would have been printed in full.

All calendar entries begin with the dateline in italics, followed by information (in parentheses) describing the document and its location. The contents of the document are then stated in summary style; however, extracts from letters not found are quoted in full. Where necessary, footnotes have been subjoined to calendar entries.

From William Vans Murray

1 November 1800, The Hague (LS, RG 59, DNA; received 24 Feb. 1801). In no. 118 writes that Ellsworth and Davie left Paris on 3 Oct. and sailed from

Havre de Grace for U.S. on 19 Oct. After reporting European news, states he has two executed copies of convention with French republic, one of which will be sent by first safe hand. His colleagues also have convention and journal, "which it is hoped may throw some light upon each stage of the negociation."[1]

1. See American Envoys to JM, 4 Oct. 1800 (*PJM*, IV, 315–19).

From Joshua Johnson

3 November 1800, Washington (LS, RG 59, DNA). Transmits account against U.S. and requests copy of Pickering's report concerning his expenditures as consul in London. Asks for advance of eight hundred dollars against his claim.[1]

1. Johnson, of Maryland, was the father of Louisa Catherine Johnson, wife of John Quincy Adams. After serving as U.S. consul in London, he was appointed in May 1800 to the newly created position of superintendent of stamps (*Senate Executive Journal*, I, 54, 350–51; Boyd, *Papers of Jefferson*, XVI, 522–23).

From Israel Whelen

3 November 1800, Philadelphia (letterbook copy, RG 45, DNA). Has received check for $3,543.23 from Treasury, which he assumes was issued on State Department's account in payment of award to John Murray & Son.[1]

1. Whelen was purveyor of public supplies. See Whelen to JM, 15 Aug., 18 Aug., 16 Oct. 1800 (*PJM*, IV, 221, 227, 329).

From John Quincy Adams

7 November 1800, Berlin (ALS, RG 59, DNA). In no. 170 notes he has received JM's no. 1 dated 24 July. Encloses copy of his note to Swedish minister Engeström. Reports advanced state of negotiations leading to revival of armed neutrality.

From John M. Pintard

7 November 1800, New York (ALS, RG 59, DNA). In reply to JM's 22 Oct. letter, responds at length to complaints about his conduct as consul at Madeira.[1]

1. See *PJM*, IV, 218 and nn., 265, 280–81, 327–29, 331–32.

From David Humphreys

7 November 1800, Madrid (ALS, RG 59, DNA; duplicate received 26 Feb. 1801). In no. 256 acknowledges receipt of duplicate of JM's letter of 2 Aug., accompanied by President Adams's letter to king of Spain. In 20 Nov. postscript (to duplicate) says he has conferred with acting first minister on quarantining vessels coming from U.S. Transmits copies of letters from Consul Richard O'Brien (Algiers) and Capt. William Bainbridge of *George Washington*.

From William Smith

7 November 1800, Lisbon (LS, RG 59, DNA; received 26 Jan. 1801). In no. 40 encloses correspondence with Pignatelli, Neapolitan minister at Lisbon, and with Pinto, Portuguese foreign minister, concerning misconduct of certain Portuguese officers of justice in aiding British press gang to seize American seamen. Has reported incident to Rufus King, who promises to apply for discharge of seamen impressed here. King proposes suspending order for procuring jewels for bey of Tunis until further advice from Eaton. Concludes with news of British expedition against Cádiz and plague epidemic at Seville.

To Israel Whelen

8 November 1800, Washington (ALS, CSmH). Advises that articles for Algiers should be placed on board merchantmen under convoy rather than on frigate *General Greene*. Requests information on this subject.

From William Vans Murray

10 November 1800, The Hague (ALS, RG 59, DNA; received 3 Mar. 1801). In no. 119 reports that Batavian government will probably order restitution for sale of *Mary*, lately condemned at Curaçao.[1] Council of prizes at Paris has recommenced trials. Encloses printed copy of convention with France.

1. On the case of the *Mary*, see JM to Murray, 16 June 1800 (*PJM*, IV, 166–67 and n. 2), and 11 Jan. 1801 (App. I, Cal.).

From Joseph Yznardy

10 November 1800, Philadelphia (LS, RG 59, DNA). Encloses lengthy defense of charges against him as acting consul at Cádiz.[1]

1. See Pickering to JM, 15 Jan. 1801 and n. 2.

From John Quincy Adams

11 November 1800, Berlin (ALS, RG 59, DNA; received 28 Feb 1801). In no. 171 encloses copy of declaration (dated 16 Aug. 1800) delivered by Russian ministry to envoys of Sweden, Denmark, and Prussia, proposing revival of armed neutrality. Also encloses copy of Swedish government's answer to Spain's complaint about capture of two Spanish armed vessels at Barcelona.

From Carlos Martinez de Yrujo

12 November 1800, Philadelphia (LS [in Spanish], RG 59, DNA; received 17 Nov. 1800). Complains of French ship *La Fortune*'s capture by U.S. ship *Ganges*, Capt. John Mullowny, outside port of Mantanzas, Cuba, on 28 July 1800. Circumstances of capture—at dusk, near Morro Castle, and wounding and killing of several crewmen—are contrary to U.S. principles and insulting to Spanish government.

From Joseph Yznardy

12 November 1800, Philadelphia (LS, RG 59, DNA). Encloses letter from John M. Pintard, which he omitted in 10 Nov. letter to JM.

From Commissioners of the District of Columbia

13 November 1800, Washington (letterbook copy, RG 42, DNA; addressed to secretaries of state, treasury, war, and navy; signed by Gustavus Scott and Alexander White). Request that unexpended funds allotted for paving footways be applied to enlarging drains and raising low parts of Pennsylvania Avenue.

From Israel Whelen

13 November 1800, Philadelphia (LS, RG 59, DNA). Acknowledges receipt of JM's letters of 28 Oct. and 8 Nov. Enough supplies are on hand to send vessel loaded with timber from Philadelphia to Algiers. There will not be sufficient quantity to load vessel at Portsmouth until spring. Vessel for Tunis can be dispatched from New York without delay.

To Frederick H. Wollaston

13 November 1800, Washington (letterbook copy, RG 59, DNA). In answer to Wollaston's letter of 27 June, JM encloses letter of introduction to government of Genoa to enable him to exercise his functions as consul.

From William Lee

14 November 1800, Boston (copy, RG 59, DNA). Applies for consulate at Bordeaux. Will accept appointment there or at Havre and Rouen.[1]

1. See *PJM*, III, 397 and n. 2.

From John Quincy Adams

15 November 1800, Berlin (ALS, RG 59, DNA). In no. 172 reports extensively on continental diplomacy, in particular on Austrian and French policies. "The policy of France upon this occasion, continues to be . . . to treat with each of her enemies separately and to avoid all general negotiations."

From Stephen Girard

15 November 1800, Philadelphia (letterbook copy, Girard Papers, PPAmP). Recommends Martin Bickham as consul for Isle of France (Mauritius).

From Commissioners of the District of Columbia

17 November 1800, Washington (letterbook copy, RG 42, DNA; addressed to secretaries of state, treasury, war, and navy; signed by Gustavus Scott, William Thornton, and Alexander White). Report that bridge over Rock Creek will soon be passable to foot passengers and to carriages. Advise continuing pavement on Pennsylvania Avenue.

From Joseph Yznardy

17 November 1800, Philadelphia (ALS, RG 59, DNA). Much afflicted by news of yellow fever epidemic at Cádiz. Has empowered certain persons to perform consular functions in case of accident to Vice-Consul Anthony Terry. Uncertain whether he will be able to return.

From Ebenezer Stevens

18 November 1800, New York (ALS, RG 59, DNA). Has been collecting remaining part of cargo for Tunis. Wrote Whelen requesting remittance of five thousand dollars; he says he wrote you on subject but had received no directions. Needs this remittance because has agreed to pay cash for lumber. Requests settlement of account with late purveyor (Tench Francis). Encloses list of stores remaining to be shipped to Tunis.

To Thomas Bulkeley

21 November 1800, Washington (letterbook copy, RG 59, DNA). Informs consul at Lisbon that "there is no legal provision to enable the President to form permanent hospital establishments, for the reception of our seamen in foreign countries." Sees no objection to making contributions to Royal Hospital of St. Joseph "in proportion to the benefit we receive from it." More information needed before making decision on this matter. Also tells consul to notify King if it is true that American vessels carried by British into Lisbon are adjudicated at Gibraltar. Concludes by saying that it is inexpedient to send any more commissions for armed vessels to be issued abroad.

From David Humphreys

21 November 1800, Madrid (ALS, RG 59, DNA). In no. 257 transmits additional copies of letters from O'Brien and Bainbridge sent in letter of 7 Nov., together with letter from Bainbridge to Stoddert. These show that Bainbridge and his ship *George Washington* have been obliged to go to Constantinople on service of dey of Algiers. Recommends that John Bulkeley & Son be appointed marine agents for U.S. at Lisbon. Agrees with O'Brien and Bainbridge on necessity of U.S. having small naval force in Mediterranean.

From John Quincy Adams

22 November 1800, Berlin (ALS, RG 59, DNA; duplicate received 28 Feb. 1801). In no. 173 reports revival of war between France and Austria, consequence of which is that latter "will be finally compelled to make her peace separately, and that Great-Britain will once more be left to contend alone against France." Great Britain will be more isolated than before because of northern powers' hostility to her naval force. Recounts recent incident in which Prussian government ordered troops to take possession of Cuxhaven, neutral port at mouth of Elbe, after British ship with its Prussian prize took shelter there during storm. This incident may be prelude to revival of armed neutrality. Concludes by speculating on negotiations between France and England. Encloses exchange of notes between English and Prussian ministers concerning occupation of Cuxhaven.

From Rufus King

22 November 1800, London (LS, RG 59, DNA; received 20 Feb. 1801; triplicate received 26 Jan. 1801). In no. 89 writes that soon after receiving JM's letter of 23 Aug., he informed Lord Grenville he was ready to resume discussions upon sixth article of Jay Treaty (relating to claims of British merchants for prewar American debts). Also reports progress of European negotiations, observing that France prefers to treat separately while England desires to negotiate jointly with Austria. In reply to JM's letter of 20 Sept. promises to bring forward once again subject of British seizures of American ships and impressment of American seamen. In partly coded passage observes that at present British government "has no animosity nor unusual prejudice against us."

From Charles Lee

23 November 1800, Alexandria (ALS, Adams Papers, MHi). Forwards recommendation from John Steele, secretary of Mississippi Territory, of James Campbell as U.S. attorney.

From William Vans Murray

25 November 1800, The Hague (ALS, RG 59, DNA; letterbook copy, NNPM). In private letter requests JM to speak to the president about his outfit as one of ministers plenipotentiary to France. Has had no intimation on this subject from government. Has always traveled and lived in France under persuasion he could expect emoluments equal to those of colleagues—a full outfit.

From William Smith

25 November 1800, Lisbon (ALS, RG 59, DNA). In private letter reports news of voyage of *George Washington* to Constantinople. Negotiations between France and Austria have resumed at Lunéville.

From Benjamin Stoddert

25 *November 1800, [Washington]* (LS, RG 59, DNA). Secretary of navy returns papers concerning capture of *Mercator* by Lt. William Maley and recapture of *Charming Betsey* by Capt. Alexander Murray. Maley is "a very ignorant illiterate man, & has been dismissed."[1]

1. This letter is printed in full in *Naval Documents: Quasi-War*, VI, 548. See JM to Lendemenn, 20 Nov. 1800 and n. 1; JM to Richard Söderström, 26 Nov. 1800.

To Edward Stevens

26 *November 1800, [Washington]* (letterbook copy, RG 59, DNA). Presumed that convention with France will mean entire restoration of trade and that U.S. merchants will be permitted to send their vessels to any St. Domingo port. To prevent misunderstanding, instructs Stevens to open this subject to General Toussaint. Requests Stevens to deliver enclosed letter of this date to Toussaint.

From David Humphreys

27 *November 1800, Madrid* (ALS, RG 59, DNA). In no. 258 transmits extracts of letter from William Eaton, U.S. consul at Tunis, and encloses copy of his letter to Bainbridge. In 28 Nov. postscript encloses answer of king of Sweden to Spanish minister in regard to *Catherine* of Baltimore, which he reported in letter of 30 Sept. 1800.

From Charles Cotesworth Pinckney

29 *November 1800, Columbia* (printed extract, *Aurora General Advertiser* [Philadelphia], 15 December 1800). "Contrary to my former advices to you and all my expectations, and owing to the absence of ten federal members of our legislature, by sickness, double returns, and other casualties, I am sorry to inform you that the anti-federalists will have a *small* majority in our legislature, though sufficiently strong to carry their ticket for electors, which every man is pledged to support for Jefferson and Burr. So far therefore as rests on South-Carolina the election is settled."[1]

1. This extract is from a letter to the editor of the Philadelphia *Aurora*, dated 10 Dec. 1800, which begins: "This morning the secretary of state, general Marshall, received a letter from gen. C. C. Pinckney, dated Columbia 29th Nov. 1800, which says."

From Rufus King

29 November 1800, London (LS, RG 59, DNA; received 26 Feb. 1801; duplicate received 20 Feb. 1801).[1] In no. 90 encloses note from Danish legation secretary announcing appointment of Danish minister to U.S. Also encloses other correspondence on this subject.

1. Another copy of this dispatch, now missing, was received in late Jan. 1801. See JM to King, 30 Jan. 1801 (App. I, Cal.).

From Commissioners of the District of Columbia

2 December 1800, Washington (letterbook copy, RG 42, DNA; signed by Gustavus Scott, William Thornton, and Alexander White). In reply to JM's letter of 28 Nov. (not found), have made inquiries concerning accommodation of Supreme Court. Suggest committee room in Capitol; if this inconvenient for Congress, then court could occupy rooms in new Executive or War Office.

From Israel Whelen

2 December 1800, Philadelphia (ALS, RG 59, DNA). In reply to JM's letter of 25 Nov., doubts vessel can be loaded in time before river is closed by ice. Also discusses timber to be shipped to Algiers and recommends sending new carriages for eight cannon borrowed from dey of Algiers.

From William Vans Murray

4 December 1800, The Hague (LS, RG 59, DNA; received 3 Mar. 1801). In no. 120 discusses case of *Wilmington Pacquet*, which had been condemned at St. Martin in Sept. 1793. Encloses copy of bill of exchange for twenty thousand guilders, by which Dutch government is discharged from all claims arising from condemnation.[1]

1. For an account of this case, see Peter P. Hill, *William Vans Murray, Federalist Diplomat: The Shaping of Peace with France, 1797–1801* (Syracuse, N.Y., 1971), 49–52.

From Commissioners of the District of Columbia

5 December 1800, Washington (letterbook copy, RG 42, DNA; signed by Gustavus Scott, William Thornton, and Alexander White). Request that plates from which city maps struck and maps still remaining in State Department be delivered to William Brent.

To Willink, Van Staphorst & Hubbard

5 December 1800, Washington (letterbook copy, RG 59, DNA). Encloses bills of exchange amounting to twenty-two thousand guilders. Requests proceeds be placed to State Department's credit.

From William Smith

7 December 1800, Lisbon (ALS, RG 59, DNA, received 10 Mar. 1801). In no. 41 encloses correspondence with Portuguese secretary for foreign affairs (Pinto) on subject of American ship *Factor*, taken into Lisbon to be turned over to British consul. Also encloses dispatches from Barbary. Has received letter from Eaton at Tunis (dated 26 Oct.) complaining about lack of communication from State Department. Has received no direct answer from Eaton about jewels for bey of Tunis. Will probably have to comply with this demand to preserve peace. Encloses communications from Bainbridge and O'Brien—these should strengthen motives for American show of naval force in Mediterranean.

From John Quincy Adams

8 December 1800, Berlin (LS, RG 59, DNA). In no. 174 writes that armistice between Austria and France has expired and that hostilities have recommenced. Relations between Great Britain and Russia are approaching state of open war, which may "impede the firm establishment of the armed neutrality." Prussia, too, is hostile to Great Britain. Prussia and Russia wish to use armed neutrality as instrument "to effect more than one purpose." Also reports recent proceedings of French legislative assembly, including announcement of convention with U.S. in terms reflecting moderation. Has received no letter from JM since that of 24 July and worries whether his own dispatches are reaching their destination.

From Ebenezer Stevens

8 December 1800, New York (ALS, RG 59, DNA). Has received JM's letter of 25 Nov. (not found) advising remittance of five thousand dollars on account of cargo he is procuring for Tunis. Annexes statement of cargo that can be shipped in four weeks.

From Israel Whelen

8 December 1800, Philadelphia (LS, RG 59, DNA). Ebenezer Stevens at New York informs Whelen that cargo of lumber for Tunis will be loaded in four weeks. Recommends postponing chartering vessel from Philadelphia to Algiers. Will not procure pine timber and plank without more particular directions.

To Theodore Sedgwick

9 December 1800, Washington (LS, RG 233, DNA). Lays before House of Representatives abstracts of impressments returned by port collectors and communications received by agents employed for protection of American seamen in foreign countries, pursuant to act "for the relief and protection of American seamen."[1]

1. The letter and abstracts are printed in *ASP, Foreign Relations,* II, 292–94. The same letter was also sent to John E. Howard, president of Senate (JM to Howard, 9 Dec. 1800, MdHi).

To Oliver Wolcott

10 December 1800, Washington (LS, RG 233, DNA). Returns papers relating to Arnold Henry Dohrman's claim to township in Northwest Territory.[1]

1. See Wolcott to JM, 3 Sept. 1800 (*PJM,* IV, 256 and n. 6); JM to Samuel Dexter, 16 Jan. 1801.

From Rufus King

10 December 1800, London (LS, RG 59, DNA; received 27 Feb. 1801). In no. 91 acknowledges receipt of bills of exchange, amounting to £9,821.1.7 sterling, to be applied to reimbursing sums borrowed by King from Sir Francis Baring & Co. to defray expenses of suits in court of prizes.

From William Smith

10 December 1800, Lisbon (ALS, RG 59, DNA). In private letter reports speculations on significance of missions of Napoleon's brothers at Madrid, Lunéville, and Berlin. One rumor is that Napoleon intends to restore Bourbon monarchy in France.

To George C. Morton

11 December 1800, Washington (letterbook copy, RG 59, DNA). Requests Morton apply to governor of Havana on behalf of Baltimore merchant John Hollins for permission to visit city safe from arrest. Hollins's business in Havana is to settle lawsuit with one Lewis Gonet.[1]

1. Morton was acting consul in place of his brother John. He wrote to JM's successor, James Madison, in the spring of 1801 that the governor had granted Hollins permission to visit Havana (Rutland, *Papers of Madison: Sec. of State*, I, 107–8 and n. 1, 231).

From Rufus King

12 December 1800, London (LS, RG 59, DNA; received Mar. 1801). In no. 92 predicts that hostilities will resume between France and Austria. France's manifest policy is to treat with her enemies separately. After dealing with Austria, France will then be free to act in concert with countries of northern Europe against England.

From Joseph Yznardy

12 December 1800, Philadelphia (LS, RG 59, DNA). Has heard rumors that new appointments are to be made in district of Cádiz, where he is consul. Wishes to be informed of any action taken by State Department in this matter.

To Collectors of Customs

12 December 1800, Washington (L[S], RG 36, DNA). Encloses additional list of impressed seamen's names, to be disposed of in same manner as that sent on 30 Oct.[1]

1. JM to Benjamin Lincoln, 30 Oct. 1800 (*PJM*, IV, 335). The same letter is also at CSmH and in Byron Reed Collection, NbO.

From William R. Davie

13 December 1800, Washington (ALS, RG 59, DNA). Encloses letter from Talleyrand, presumably covering transmission of packet to Létombe (French consul general to U.S.). Also encloses letter for Létombe covering copy of convention with his instructions.

From Rufus King

13 December 1800, London (LS, RG 59, DNA; received Mar. 1801). In no. 93 writes that England's dependence on America for food supplies makes present favorable moment to negotiate differences between two governments. Encloses copy of proposition to Lord Grenville for lump-sum payment in settlement of British creditors' claims.[1]

1. The letter and enclosure are printed in *ASP, Foreign Relations*, II, 399–400, and in King, *Life and Correspondence of Rufus King*, III, 345–50.

From David Humphreys

16 December 1800, Madrid (ALS, RG 59, DNA). In no. 259 reports that Don Pedro de Cevallos is new Spanish first minister of state and encloses copy of notes exchanged between Cevallos and Humphreys. Requests permission to retire to Portugal in case contagious fever presently raging in Spain should extend to Madrid. Forwards two letters from Richard O'Brien.

To John Gavino

17 December 1800, Washington (letterbook copy, RG 59, DNA). Requests Gavino, U.S. consul at Gibraltar, to demand release of Hercules Whitney, who had been impressed by British ship *Minotaur* at Leghorn.

To David Lenox

17 December 1800, Washington (LS, MH). Encloses proof of U.S. citizenship of six American seamen impressed by British ships of war. Requests Lenox, U.S. agent at London, to take particular notice of Hercules Whitney's case.

To William Savage

17 December 1800, Washington (letterbook copy, RG 59, DNA). Encloses proof of U.S. citizenship of six American seamen impressed by British ships of war on Jamaica station. Instructs Savage, U.S. agent at Kingston, to apply for their release.

From Joseph Yznardy

17 December 1800, Philadelphia (ALS, RG 59, DNA). Reports that John M. Pintard has commenced suit against him in federal court, in which he seeks damages for detention of his ship at Cádiz (where Yznardy was acting consul) in 1797. Encloses copy of Timothy Pickering's 31 Oct. 1797 letter to him, approving Yznardy's conduct in this affair. Requests JM to order federal attorney for Pennsylvania district to appear for him "in behalf of the Government as a cause of the United States."

From Stephen Girard

18 December 1800, Philadelphia (letterbook copy, Girard Papers, PPAmP). Referring to 15 Nov. letter, again recommends Martin Bickham to be U.S. consul at Isle of France (Mauritius). Offers to convey any dispatch JM may want to send to there.

To Turell Tufts

19 December 1800, Washington (letterbook copy, RG 59, DNA). Acknowledges several letters from Tufts, U.S. consul at Paramaribo, Surinam. Commends Tufts's conduct but cautions him to maintain respectful manner in communications with government officials. "Every thing beyond temperate remonstrance must be left for arrangement between the two governments." Concludes by requesting consul's "vigilant attention to detect any of our citizens engaging directly or indirectly in the slave trade."[1]

1. JM had not yet received Tufts's letter of 4 Dec. (App. II, List), complaining of his "irksome and vexatious" residence at Paramaribo and soliciting the consulship at Bordeaux or at some other suitable place in France.

To Elias Backman

22 December 1800, Washington (letterbook copy, RG 59, DNA). Informs Backman, U.S. consul at Göteborg, Sweden, that President Adams cannot make representation to Congress on his claim. Backman's demand for expenses of his journey to Stockholm has been suspended, but remainder of claim will be paid with interest.[1]

1. See *PJM*, IV, 184 and n. 5, 304 and n. 3.

From Samuel and Miers Fisher

23 December 1800, Philadelphia (ALS, RG 76, DNA). Renew request that U.S. demand recompense from Spain for capture and condemnation of their ship *Sussex*.[1]

1. See *PJM*, IV, 252–53 and n. 3, 266, 301–2; David Humphreys to JM, 24 Feb. 1801 (App. II, List).

From Charles DeWolfe

24 December 1800, Bristol, R.I. (LS, RG 76, DNA). Requests assistance in procuring restoration of his sloop *Little Charlotte* and cargo, together with costs, charges, and damages arising from her capture and detention. Encloses copy of vice-admiralty court's proceedings at Nova Scotia, where vessel had been condemned.

From James Swan

25 December 1800, Paris (ALS, RG 59, DNA). Seeks appointment as consul general in Paris.[1]

1. On Swan, see Howard C. Rice, "James Swan: Agent of the French Republic, 1794–1796," *New England Quarterly*, X (1937), 464–86.

From Stephen Girard

26 December 1800, Philadelphia (letterbook copy, PPAmP). Again urges JM's attention to case of his brig *Sally*, condemned by vice-admiralty court at Halifax. Encloses documents to establish his claim and copy of letter from Richard Peters, judge of Pennsylvania federal district court, to whom he had shown opinion of judge at Halifax.[1]

1. See *PJM*, IV, 326 and n. 2, 332, 333; Girard to JM, 29 Dec. 1800 (App. I, Cal.).

From Israel Whelen

27 December 1800, Philadelphia (LS, RG 59, DNA). Has received letter from Richard O'Brien complaining of quality of cotton cloth, oak and pine timber, walnut boards, and coffee shipped to Algiers on *George Washington*. Defends quality of articles and suggests O'Brien was under pressure from dey and his ministry to pass along these complaints. "It appears that the Government he resides with, wish to make the annuity spread over every thing their rapacity prompts them to require, and the continual irritation to which his mind is exposed by their demands & complaints, naturally diffuses itself through his communications."

From Benjamin Williams

27 December 1800, Raleigh (letterbook copy, Nc-Ar). Governor of North Carolina encloses copy of state legislature's resolution respecting extension of boundary line between that state and Indians. Urges necessity of fixing this boundary and expresses hope that this matter will not be neglected, as it was by preceding secretary of state.[1]

1. See JM to Williams, 5 Jan. 1801.

To John Hall

28 December 1800, Washington (copy, RG 233, DNA). President has refused his claim for compensation for extra services as marshal. Suggests he petition Congress.[1]

1. Hall, U.S. marshal for the district of Pennsylvania, sought reimbursement for an additional number of deputies hired during the trials of participants in Fries's Rebellion. This copy of the letter is filed with Hall's petition to Congress and other supporting papers (RG 233, DNA).

To Joseph Létombe

28 December 1800, Washington (printed extract of ALS, Sotheby Parke Bernet Auction Catalog, 25 Nov. 1975, item #411). "I have laid your two letters of the 18th of October & 22d Dec. before the Secretary of the Navy whose answer I enclose to you."

From Stephen Girard

29 December 1800, Philadelphia (letterbook copy, Girard Papers, PPAmP). Encloses letter received from Martin Bickham, whom he previously recommended for consulship of Isle of France. Adds that his agent for prosecuting his appeal in case of Sally will depart for England immediately upon receiving dispatches from State Department. Requests JM write Rufus King for aid in appeal.

From Benjamin Stoddert

29 December 1800, Washington (letterbook copy, RG 45, DNA). Seventy-eight French prisoners sent from Boston to New York on 14 Dec. to be delivered to Létombe. One hundred fifty prisoners still remain there but not proper during winter season to remove them to any other port for embarkation.

To John Adams

31 December 1800, [Washington] (ALS, Adams Papers, MHi). Encloses two copies of Mississippi Territory laws enacted since 30 June 1799.

From Henry Preble

2 January 1801, Washington (ALS, RG 76, DNA). Presents papers and documents relating to capture and detention of his ship *Eliza* by Spanish privateer in 1797. Protests that capture was direct violation of treaty between Spain and U.S. and complains that Joseph Yznardy, consul at Cádiz, neglected to protect and defend his rights.[1]

1. In Feb. 1801 Preble was appointed to succeed Yznardy as consul at Cádiz (*Senate Executive Journal*, I, 381, 385).

From Carlos Martinez de Yrujo

2 January 1801, Philadelphia (LS [in Spanish] and accompanying translation, RG 59, DNA; received 11 Jan. 1801). Spanish minister to U.S. protests incident involving American ship *Cataline* of Baltimore, James Mills master, in Barcelona harbor.

To Governor of Campeachy

2 January 1801, Washington (ALS, RG 76, DNA; letterbook copy, RG 59, DNA). American sloop *Commerce*, belonging to Abner and Christopher Griffing of Connecticut, has been captured by Spanish privateer and carried into Campeachy, where vessel and cargo sold. Requests proceeds of sale be paid immediately to owners.[1]

1. This letter is filed with other papers in support of Christopher Griffing's claim, which was presented to a commission appointed under the treaty of 1819 with Spain (Spanish Claims, XIX, RG 76, DNA). Campeachy (Campeche) is a city on the Yucatan peninsula.

To Stephen Girard

3 January 1801, Washington (ALS, Girard Papers, PPAmP). Encloses copy of letter to King of 3 Jan.

To Robert Ritchie

3 January 1801, Washington (letterbook copy, RG 59, DNA). Informs Ritchie, U.S. consul at Port-au-Prince, that Bartholomew Dandridge has been appointed consul for southern part of St. Domingo and that Ritchie's consular functions in that district will accordingly cease.

To Frederick Jacob Wichelhausen

4 January 1800 [1801], Washington (letterbook copy, RG 59, DNA). Approves conduct of U.S. consul at Bremen concerning arrest of Frederick Schaeffer, Baltimore merchant. If proceeding against Schaeffer in Bremen is usual in civil actions, then U.S. has no right to complain but if ordinary mode departed from, U.S. will consider it unfriendly act.

From Joseph Yznardy

8 January 1801, Philadelphia (LS, RG 59, DNA). Acknowledges JM's letters of 11 Dec. and 17 Dec. 1800 (not found). Discusses at length suit brought against him by Pintard, which he first reported in letter of 17 Dec. Proceedings against him unjust; does not owe a farthing and has broken no law. Is disappointed with President Adams's opinion that U.S. government cannot interfere in this business.

To William Vans Murray

11 January 1801, Washington (letterbook copy, RG 59, DNA). Concerning case of ship *Mary*, owned by Jeremiah Yellott of Baltimore, captured by French privateer and carried into Curaçao, JM has received papers in which French admit injustice done. These should remove all doubts on part of Batavian government in yielding to justice of this case.

To Job Wall

12 January 1801, Washington (letterbook copy, RG 59, DNA). Informs U.S. consul at St. Bartholomew that his bills cannot be accepted by State Department and are all protested. Indispensably necessary that he settle accounts.[1]

1. See *PJM*, IV, 204.

From Commissioners of the District of Columbia

13 January 1801, Washington (letterbook copy, RG 42, DNA; signed by William Thornton and Alexander White). Wish to have president's directions with regard to finding house for holding Supreme Court.

From Commissioners of the District of Columbia

15 January 1801, Washington (letterbook copy, RG 42, DNA; addressed to secretaries of state and navy; signed by William Thornton, Alexander White, and William Cranch). Have no objection to Fenwick's using clay to be removed from around War Office for making bricks.

From Richard Söderström

16 January 1801, Washington (LS, RG 59, DNA). Swedish consul general announces appointment of Francis S. Taylor as Swedish vice-consul at Norfolk in place of John Cowper.

From Jedidiah Leeds

16 January 1801, Charleston (ALS, DLC). Owns ship captured by French privateer on 28 June 1800. Ship carried to Mantanzas, Cuba, and sold along with perishable articles. Has papers that prove vessel and cargo must be delivered up upon application of U.S. government to Spanish government. Capture and sale are violation of U.S. treaty with Spain.

From Joseph Yznardy

16 January 1801, Philadelphia (LS, RG 59, DNA). Encloses copy of his attorney's letter advising him to obtain from secretary of state certified copy of letter from emperor of Morocco to U.S. consul James Simpson, in which

emperor threatened war if U.S. vessels were caught trading in Moroccan
ports not in allegiance to him.[1]

1. See *Naval Documents: Barbary Wars*, I, 181, 186.

To Israel Whelen

16 January 1801, Washington (LS, Collection of Mr. and Mrs. Morris Login,
New York, N.Y.). Anxious to know progress Colonel Stevens has made in
procuring vessel to carry third cargo to Tunis.

From George Thacher

17 January 1801, Washington (ALS, RG 59, DNA). Requests compensation
for William Savage, U.S. agent at Kingston, for services on behalf of American commerce and American sailors in West Indies region.[1]

1. Thacher was a member of the Massachusetts delegation in Congress.

From Chandler Price

20 January 1801, Philadelphia (ALS, RG 76, DNA; received 26 Jan. 1801).
Transmits copies of letters showing "flimsey pretences" upon which American vessels are intercepted by British cruisers and then condemned and detained by British courts of admiralty in New Providence, Halifax, and Jamaica. Calls particular attention to case of his brig *Ruby*, bound for New
Orleans when captured. Insists that his vessel carried no contraband articles
and that cargo is entirely native American and owned by him.[1]

1. Price was a Philadelphia merchant. On the case of the *Ruby*, see Price to JM, 28
Jan. (App. I, Cal.); JM to Thornton, 3 Feb., 24 Feb.; Thornton to JM, 4 Feb., 20 Feb.
1801.

From Commissioners of the District of Columbia

21 January 1801, Washington (letterbook copy, RG 42, DNA; addressed to
secretaries of state, treasury, war, and navy; signed by William Thornton,
Alexander White, and William Cranch). Enclose an order of board and request approval to carry it into effect.

From Israel Whelen

21 January 1801, Philadelphia (ALS, RG 59, DNA). Encloses copies of letter from Ebenezer Stevens, dated 13 Jan., and of his reply, dated 15 Jan., concerning freight charge for ship to Tunis.

To John Elmslie, Jr.

22 January 1801, Washington (letterbook copy, RG 59, DNA). Informs U.S. consul at Cape of Good Hope that State Department has received four letters from him—22 Sept., 7 Dec. 1799, 9 Sept., 18 Oct. 1800. Expresses surprise that consul has not received any communications from State Department, except by *Essex*. Again transmits copies of his commission and instructions, along with another copy of laws.

From William Hunter

23 January 1801, Frankfort (ALS, RG 59, DNA). Offers to publish session laws in his newspaper, Frankfort (Ky.) *Palladium*, which "circulates very generally throughout the State, & upwards of 600 Copies are distributed every Week."

From Benjamin Stoddert

23 January 1801, Washington (letterbook copy, RG 45, DNA). Sixty or seventy French prisoners at New York. Wrote Létombe they would be delivered to his order to be sent to France or islands.

From Arthur St. Clair

26 January 1801, Cincinnati (ALS, RG 59, DNA). Transmits recommendations for appointments as general officers of militia in Ohio Territory. These recommendations communicated in letter of 30 Mar. 1800 to former Secretary of State Pickering, which he is informed has been mislaid. Encloses copy of that letter.[1]

1. This letter and enclosure are published in full in Clarence E. Carter, ed., *The Territorial Papers of the United States: The Territory Northwest of the River Ohio, 1787–1803*, III (Washington, D.C., 1934), 80, 120.

From Chandler Price

28 January 1801, Philadelphia (ALS, RG 76, DNA). Sends copies of papers that will be sent to New Providence (Bahamas) for trial of *Ruby*, lately captured by British on voyage from Philadelphia to New Orleans. Requests official communication from U.S. government to assist in pressing his claim. In 29 Jan. postscript acknowledges JM's reply (not found) to letter of 20 Jan. Expresses disappointment with suggestion that he pursue appeal in case of condemnation. Thought that government would not hesitate to furnish him letter "remonstrating against or at least contradicting the Right of any power on Earth to Carry In & Condemn American property when in an Honest & Lawfull Trade, because it is the growth or produce of a power happening to be the Enemy of the Captor." Reminds JM that his predecessor had intervened with effect on similar occasion.

To William Savage

28 January 1801, Washington (letterbook copy, RG 59, DNA). Encloses proofs of U.S. citizenship of six seamen impressed on Jamaica station and instructs U.S. agent at Kingston to apply for their release. Requests him in future to send monthly returns of seamen who have been released through his agency.

To David Lenox

28 January 1801, Washington (LS, PHi). Encloses proofs of U.S. citizenship of four seamen impressed and detained by British ships of war. Also transmits to U.S. agent at London similar proofs of another seaman who is detained on board ship expected to return to England.

From John & Isaac Laurence and Others

29 January 1801, New York (ALS, RG 76, DNA). Narrate case of schooner *Nymph*, captured by Spanish privateer in Apr. 1797 and taken to Cuba. Although vessel and proceeds of cargo's sale were eventually turned over to ship's master, considerable losses were incurred in prosecuting claim and vessel was completely ruined. Not having received any information on this matter since last year, they request U.S. government to intervene on their behalf with court of Spain.[1]

1. JM had forwarded the papers concerning the *Nymph* in his letter to Humphreys of 23 Sept. 1800 (*PJM*, IV, 301).

To Rufus King

30 January 1801, Washington (letterbook copy, RG 59, DNA). In no. 11 acknowledges receipt of no. 90 (29 Nov. 1800) reporting appointment of Danish minister resident to U.S. Letter has been laid before the president, who "regards this nomination as a mark of the friendly dispositions of his Majesty the King of Denmark."

To Samuel A. Otis

1 February 1801, Washington (printed extract of DS, *The Collector* [June 1948], 138). Requests secretary of Senate "to cause the enclosed summons' to be delivered to the Members of the Senate to whom they are addressed, personally."

To Thomas T. Gantt

3 February 1801, Washington (letterbook copy, RG 59, DNA). Gives instructions to Gantt, new navy agent at St. Kitts, concerning procedures for obtaining relief for captured American seamen.

From Benjamin Booth

5 February 1801, Charleston (LS, DLC). Writes that he is agent for underwriters and others concerned in case of schooner *Nancy*, which had been captured by French privateer and carried to Matanzas, Cuba. Transmits memorial and other papers and adds that "spirited interference on the part of the government of the United States would secure to the interested full and complete restitution of their property."

From Samuel Bradford

7 February 1801, Boston (letterbook copy, DLC). U.S. marshal at Boston has received JM's letter of 19 Jan. (not found), enclosing president's pardon of John Salter and others. Requests instructions concerning fines and costs of prosecution that had been paid on behalf of prisoners.

To John & Isaac Laurence

8 February 1801, Washington (ALS, RG 76, DNA). Has received letter of 29 Jan. U.S. minister at Madrid has been instructed to seek compensation from Spanish government for depredations committed on U.S. commerce.

From Henry Lee and Others

10 February 1801, Washington (ALS, Adams Papers, MHi). Lee and other members of Virginia delegation in Congress—Leven Powell, Robert Page, Josiah Parker, Samuel Goode, and Thomas Evans—recommend George Keith Taylor and Charles Magill as circuit judges under new judiciary act.

From William Cocke and Others

16 February 1801, Washington (ALS, Adams Papers, MHi). Cocke and Joseph Anderson, Tennessee senators, and William C. C. Claiborne, Tennessee's representative, recommend Charles T. Porter as U.S. marshal for district of East Tennessee.

From William Cocke and Others

16 February 1801, Washington (ALS, Adams Papers, MHi). Cocke, Joseph Anderson, and William C. C. Claiborne recommend Thomas Gray as U.S. attorney for district of East Tennessee.

From William Barry Grove

16 February 1801, Washington (ALS, Adams Papers, MHi). Representative from North Carolina recommends John Sitgreaves as circuit court judge.

From Harrison G. Otis

16 February 1801, [Washington] (ALS, Adams Papers, MHi). Passes on letter from John Lowell indicating wish to be circuit judge under new judiciary act and intention to resign present office as federal district judge.

From Nathaniel Chipman

17 February 1801, Washington (ALS, Adams Papers, MHi). Senator from Vermont applies to be federal district judge.

From William Cocke and Others

17 February 1801, Washington (ALS, Adams Papers, MHi). Cocke, Joseph Anderson, and William C. C. Claiborne recommend Archibald Roane of Tennessee as judge of sixth circuit. If president desires that appointment should fall to resident of Kentucky, then they recommend William McClung of that state.

From Jesse Franklin

17 February 1801, Washington (ALS, Adams Papers, MHi). North Carolina senator recommends Samuel Johnston as federal court judge.

From Thomas Davis and John Fowler

18 February 1801, Washington (ALS, Adams Papers, MHi). Representatives from Kentucky recommend Buckner Thruston as judge of sixth circuit.

To Rufus King

21 February 1801, Washington (ALS, King Papers, NHi). Introduces Mr. Cooper, "a gentleman of respectable connections & character in Virginia."[1]

1. According to King's endorsement the spelling of the bearer's name was "Cowper." This could possibly be Wills Cowper, a Portsmouth merchant, or his son John Cowper, Jr. JM had represented Wills Cowper in a British debt case in the 1790s (*PJM*, II, 248–49).

From Henry Glen

22 February 1801, Washington (ADf, NSchHi). New York representative recommends nephew Jacob Glen as consul at Cowes, Isle of Wight.

From William McMillan

25 February 1801, Washington (ALS, Adams Papers, MHi). Delegate to Congress from Northwest Territory recommends Arthur St. Clair, Jr., as U.S. attorney and James Smith as U.S. marshal for Ohio district.

From Michael Jenifer Stone

25 February 1801 (ALS, Adams Papers, MHi). Maryland judge recommends Thomas Dyson as U.S. marshal for District of Columbia.

From Robert Page and Leven Powell

26 February 1801, Washington (ALS, Adams Papers, MHi). Recommend Charles Simms as chief judge of court of the District of Columbia, Thomas Swann as U.S. attorney, and Cleon Moore as register of wills.

From George Dent

27 February 1801, Washington (ALS, Adams Papers, MHi). Representative from Maryland recommends Thomas Dyson as U.S. marshal for District of Columbia.

From Leven Powell and Henry Lee

27 February 1801, Washington (ALS, Adams Papers, MHi). Recommend Charles Turner as U.S. marshal for District of Columbia.

From Leven Powell

27 February 1801, Washington (ALS, Adams Papers, MHi). Recommends John Herbert as judge of Orphan's Court for Alexandria County in District of Columbia. Also recommends following as justices of peace for Alexandria County: Charles Alexander, Sr., George Gilpin, Jonah Thompson, Dennis Ramsay, Simon Somers, Charles Alexander, Jr., Abram Faw, George Taylor, Jacob Houghman, Francis Peyton, Cuthbert Powell, and William Harper.

From Augustus Woodward

27 February 1801, Washington (ALS, Adams Papers, MHi). Applies for judgeship on court for District of Columbia. Identifies himself as author of "Considerations on the Government of the Territory of Columbia," written under the signature of "Epaminondas."[1]

1. On Woodward, see *Records of the Columbia Historical Society*, IV (1901), 39–42, 114–27.

From Thomas Dyson

28 February 1801, Washington (ALS, Adams Papers, MHi). Former sheriff of Charles County, Md., applies for office of U.S. marshal in District of Columbia.

From Richard Söderström

4 March 1801, Baltimore (ALS, RG 59, DNA). Requests return of papers concerning Danish schooner *Mercator*, which may be needed in case of trial.[1]

1. See JM to Söderström, 26 Nov. 1800 and n. 4.

From William Bainbridge

20 April 1801, U.S. Frigate George Washington, Delaware River (ALS, ICHi). Has arrived this day and forwards dispatches from Richard O'Brien concerning affairs of Algiers.[1] Many demands of sultan of Turkey on dey of Algiers, "and his compliance to the greater part, will in my opinion only tend to Irritate his capricious mind against Neutrals, trading in the Mediterranean Sea." Predicts that Algerine cruisers will soon have orders to capture American vessels.

1. On Bainbridge's mission, see Rutland, *Papers of Madison: Sec. of State*, I, 82 n. 4.

To LeRoy, Bayard, & McEvers

14 May 1801, Richmond (printed extract of ALS, Howard S. Mott, Inc., Autograph Catalog [Sheffield, Mass., 1975], 7). He is "entirely unacquainted with the whole transaction relative to the bank stock. . . ." He will get in touch with his brother in Alexandria, asking him to take care of matter.[1]

1. JM wrote to his brother James Marshall, ca. 14 May, enclosing a letter from LeRoy, Bayard, & McEvers (New York merchants) to JM, dated 19 Apr. These letters have not

been found but are mentioned in James Marshall to LeRoy, Bayard, & McEvers, 20 May 1801 (Gratz Collection, PHi). James Marshall explained that the bank stock in question probably was "part of about sixty shares which I sold in London in March 1794," adding that his power to receive dividends and to transfer the stock had been given to William Constable at that time. Apparently the New York merchants were attempting to determine if a dividend had been mistakenly paid to James Marshall.

To William Alexander

1 June 1801, Richmond (printed extract of ALS, John Heise, Catalog No. 3355 [Syracuse, N.Y., 1927], item #100). "I inclose you a letter from Mr. Means relative to some paper which I delivered to you in the winter 1800. I hope it will be entirely agreeable to you to return them to him after striking out your own signature. He resides at . . . ."[1]

1. This letter was addressed to Alexander in Carlisle, Pa.

Power of Attorney

21 September 1801 (ADS, Collection of Mrs. John Tyssowski, Delaplaine, Va.). JM empowers James Marshall to draw his salary as chief justice.

To James M. Marshall

7 February 1803 (summary, Irwin S. Rhodes, *The Papers of John Marshall: A Descriptive Calendar*, I [Norman, Okla., 1969], 489–90).[1] "Has considered bill, copy of which sent to James by Fitzsimmons; amendments proposed 'by our counsel.' Agrees 'our claim' should be introduced in present suit as proposed, expeditiously. Discretion allowed counsel to adopt ideas, hints J.M. gave. Discusses whether Gouverneur Morris not necessary party; hopes not, but believes so. Whole interest of Morris in New York property is equity of redemption in 1,500,000 acres; other land undisposed of when deed under which 'we' claim executed subject to judgment transferred to Gouverneur Morris before 'our lands' contribute. Suggests claim be made in bill; Holland Company should have satisfied judgment equity of redemption in lands to which they have legal title; injunction lies against sale of land conveyed to others to secure debt where held property in own hands sufficient to satisfy. Mason deposition must be taken."[2]

1. Rhodes cites the Hay Collection, Yale University, as the location of this document. According to the chief research archivist at Yale, however, the letter has been missing from that institution for some years and efforts to track it down have been unavailing (Judith Ann Schiff to Charles F. Hobson, 25 Aug. 1988, Editorial Office, Papers of John Marshall). It is evidently the same letter offered for sale in 1950 by Walter and Mary Benjamin Autographs. The sale catalog describes the document as a three-page

copy of a letter from JM, dated 7 Feb. 1803, in the hand of Thomas FitzSimons, in which JM gives his opinion on a suit involving Robert Morris's lands in New York (see n. 2). The description does not identify the recipient of the letter (*The Collector*, LXIII, No. 693 [1950], item #D 237).

2. The subject of this letter is the suit of FitzSimons v. Ogden, which was ultimately decided by the Supreme Court in 1812 (7 Cranch 2). See JM to FitzSimons, 28 Nov. 1800 and nn.

To Robert G. Harper

16 March 1803, Richmond (printed extract of ALS, John Heise, Catalog No. 94 [Syracuse, N.Y., 1914], item #156). "'Unquestionably the decision of the superior courts of Maryland, if they have settled the construction of the act on which the case depended, would have been considered as conclusive & I lament exceedingly that the decisions were unknown to us & that we have determined in opposition . . . I am surprised that neither Judge Chase,' etc."[1]

1. The reference is to the case of Wood v. Owings and Smith, in which JM had delivered the opinion of the Supreme Court on 1 Mar. Harper argued the case as counsel for the defendants in error (1 Cranch 239–52).

Certificate

22 December 1803 (ADS, Legislative Petitions, Box X, Vi). JM states he knew Capt. Jesse Davies very well during Revolutionary War and served for some time in same regiment. Gives history of Davies's service from 1775 to 1778.[1]

1. On Davies (Davis), see *PJM*, I, 21, 22; John Frederick Dorman, comp., *Virginia Revolutionary Pension Applications*, XXVII (Washington, D.C., 1977), 65–69.

To William Paterson

8 January 1804, Richmond (printed extract of ALS, Walter R. Benjamin Autographs, Inc., *The Collector*, LII [June 1938], 88). "'. . . I lament very sincerely the cause which will deprive us of your aid and your society at the ensuing term of the supreme court. I must however entreat that you will not permit your anxiety respecting your duties to expose you to the hazards which must result from your removal from home before your health shall be perfectly confirmed,' etc."[1]

1. The full date of this letter is supplied by the entry in Parke-Bernet Catalog, 11 May 1938, item #40, 24.

Thomas Jefferson to the Justices of the Supreme Court

29 March 1804, Washington (letterbook copy, Ð(+ 59, DNA). President communicates official allotment of justices to circuits in consequence of William Johnson's appointment to succeed Alfred Moore. Same allotment is continued, with Johnson assigned to sixth circuit.[1]

1. The Judiciary Act of 1802 stipulated that on every new appointment the justices were to allot themselves among the circuits. If they failed to do so at the session following the appointment, then the president was authorized to make the allotment, which was to "be binding until another *allotment* shall be made" (*U.S. Statutes at Large*, II, 158). This allotment was transmitted to the justices by Secretary of State Madison on 30 Mar. (letterbook copy, RG 59, DNA).

From Philip Schuyler

6 August 1804 (summary of ALS, Edward Eberstadt & Sons, Catalog No. 131 [New York, 1953], item #94). "A tragic letter expressing the grief of Hamilton's wife and father-in-law at the terrible outcome of the duel. Schuyler tells of his daughter's emotions on seeing friends whom 'her Hamilton loved'; and eulogizes him as 'my Hamilton.'"[1]

1. Alexander Hamilton died on 12 July, the day after his duel with Aaron Burr.

To Thomas FitzSimons

28 April 1805, Richmond (summary of ALS, Thomas F. Madigan, Inc., Catalog [New York, 1939], item #129). Discusses suit of FitzSimons v. Ogden. Mentions settlement of an annuity on wife of Robert Morris, which secured Morris's release from debtors' prison.[1]

1. See JM to FitzSimons, 28 Nov. 1800 and nn.

To Henry Potter

23 May 1805, Richmond (printed extract of ALS, Paul C. Richards Autographs, Catalog No. 28, Issue No. 19 [1968], item #463). Addressed to Judge Potter in Raleigh. "'As it is a part of the common law of North Carolina to do nothing on the first day, I hope to stand excused for postponing my departure from home. To get into Raleigh on Thursday & wait till Monday before we can enter on the docket would be perfectly useless....' Marshall will arrive on Saturday. He concludes: 'I think I shall not give an opinion in the great cause of Granville's heirs. I mention it that you may be prepared to decide it alone. . . .'" [1]

1. See Remarks, 18 June 1805 and nn. The first day of the term of the U.S. circuit court at Raleigh was Saturday, 15 June. JM was in court on Monday, 17 June.

To William Paterson

14 March 1806, Richmond (summary of ALS, Parke-Bernet Catalog No. 40 [11 May 1938], 24). Discusses "Money warrants."[1]

1. This may be the same letter offered for sale in July 1939 by Walter R. Benjamin Autographs, Inc. The catalog listed the date as "1806" and summarized the letter as JM's reply to a legal matter raised by Paterson (*The Collector*, LIII [July 1939], 106). Paterson died on 9 Sept. 1806.

Appendix II
Miscellaneous Diplomatic Dispatches
1 November 1800–2 March 1801

Listed below are dispatches from U.S. diplomats abroad, mainly routine reports of affairs within their respective jurisdictions. The list includes all dispatches from consuls addressed to Marshall as secretary of state between November 1800 and March 1801 and also those dated 15 December 1800 and after from ministers residing in European capitals. (Letters from ministers dated before 15 December are summarized in Appendix I, Calendar of Correspondence, 1 November 1800–14 March 1806.) Because these dispatches were received by the State Department after or at the very end of Marshall's tenure, responsibility for acting on them fell to his successor, James Madison.

The information in the list includes the date of the dispatch, the name of the correspondent, his title, and place of residence, the date the letter was received (if known), and a description of the document (ALS, LS, or letterbook copy). Most of these dispatches belong to Record Group 59 in the National Archives. If a letter is not in this record group, information concerning its location is provided after the description.

1 November 1800, James L. Cathcart, U.S. consul, Tripoli, received 15 April 1801, LS.

1 November 1800, William Eaton, U.S. consul, Tunis, received 27 April 1801, ALS (duplicate).

1 November 1800, William Savage, U.S. agent, Kingston, received May 1801, LS.

3 November 1800, Joseph Pitcairn, U.S. consul, Hamburg, received 28 February 1801, ALS.

5 November 1800, Benjamin H. Phillips, U.S. consul, Curaçao (Netherlands Antilles), letterbook copy, RG 84.

6 November 1800, Bird, Savage & Bird, bankers, London, received 3 January 1801, LS.

9 November 1800, Samuel Snow, U.S. consul, Canton, received 12 March 1801, ALS.

15 November 1800, William Eaton, U.S. consul, Tunis, received 29 April 1801, ALS.

15 November 1800, James Simpson, U.S. consul, Tangier, ALS.

16 November 1800, William Eaton, U.S. consul, Tunis, received 29 April 1801, ALS.

16 November 1800, Turell Tufts, U.S. consul, Paramaribo (Surinam), received 15 January 1801, ALS.

19 November 1800, John Gavino, U.S. consul, Gibraltar, received 14 February 1801, AL (duplicate).

21 November 1800, William Eaton, U.S. consul, Tunis, received 29 April 1801, ALS.

29 November 1800, Samuel Williams, U.S. consul, London, ALS.

4 December 1800, Turell Tufts, U.S. consul, Paramaribo (Surinam), received 29 February 1801, ALS.

6 December 1800, John Leamy, Philadelphia, ALS.

8 December 1800, William Eaton, U.S. consul, Tunis, ALS.

8 December 1800, Joseph Pitcairn, U.S. consul, Hamburg, received 28 February 1801, ALS.

13 December 1800, Thomas Appleton, U.S. consul, Leghorn (Italy), letterbook copy, RG 84.

14 December 1800, John Gavino, U.S. consul, Gibraltar, ALS.

15 December 1800, Rufus King, U.S. minister, London, received 19 May 1801, LS.

15 December 1800, William Kirkpatrick, U.S. consul, Malaga (Spain), copy.

17 December 1800, Elias Vanderhorst, U.S. consul, Bristol, received 10 April 1801, ALS.

18 December 1800, Rufus King, U.S. minister, London, received 11 March 1801, ALS.

18 December 1800, Fulwar Skipwith, commercial agent, Paris, received 18 March 1801, ALS.

19 December 1800, David Humphreys, U.S. minister, Madrid, received 16 March 1801, ALS (duplicate).

20 December 1800, John Quincy Adams, U.S. minister, Berlin, ALS.

20 December 1800, William Eaton, U.S. consul, Tunis, received 7 September 1801, ALS.

20 December 1800, Anthony Terry, vice-consul, Cádiz, ALS.

23 December 1800, Henry Hammond, U.S. consul, Cape François (Haiti), ALS.

23 December 1800, Robert Ritchie, U.S. consul, Port Republicain (Port-au-Prince, Haiti), received 29 January 1801, ALS.

24 December 1800, Turell Tufts, U.S. consul, Paramaribo (Surinam), ALS.

28 December 1800, William Eaton, U.S. consul, Tunis, LS.

28 December 1800, William Vans Murray, U.S. minister, The Hague, ALS (duplicate).

28 December 1800, Robert Ritchie, U.S. consul, Port Republicain (Port-au-Prince, Haiti), copy.

3 January 1801, Rufus King, U.S. minister, London, received 3 April 1801, ALS.

4 January 1801, James L. Cathcart, U.S. consul general, Tripoli, received 25 June 1801, ALS (duplicate).

4 January 1801, William Vans Murray, U.S. minister, The Hague, ALS.

5 January 1801, William Kirkpatrick, U.S. consul, Malaga (Spain), ALS.

5 January 1801, James Maury, U.S. consul, Liverpool, LS.

5 January 1801, Robert Ritchie, U.S. consul, Port Republicain (Port-au-Prince, Haiti), ALS (copy).

6 January 1801, John Quincy Adams, U.S. minister, Berlin, ALS.

6 January 1801, Sylvanus Bourne, U.S. consul general, Amsterdam, LS.

6 January 1801, Edward Stevens, U.S. consul general, Cape François (Haiti), ALS.

7 January 1801, Richard O'Brien, U.S. consul general, Algiers, received 29 April 1801, ALS (duplicate).

8 January 1801, William Vans Murray, U.S. minister, The Hague, received 4 April 1801, ALS.

8 January 1801, William Savage, U.S. agent, Kingston (Jamaica), received 28 April 1801, ALS (copy).

9 January 1801, William Smith, U.S. minister, Lisbon, LS.

10 January 1801, William Smith, U.S. minister, Lisbon, ALS (private).

10 January 1801, Edward Stevens, U.S. consul general, Cape François (Haiti), received 26 March 1801, ALS.

12 January 1801, Thomas Appleton, U.S. consul, Leghorn (Italy), letterbook copy, RG 84.

12 January 1801, Benjamin H. Phillips, U.S. consul, Curaçao (Netherlands Antilles), ALS.

13 January 1801, David Humphreys, U.S. minister, Madrid, ALS.

14 January 1801, William Kirkpatrick, U.S. consul, Malaga (Spain), received 2 May 1801, ALS.

15 January 1801, Rufus King, U.S. minister, London, LS.

15 January 1801, David Lenox, U.S. agent, London, letterbook copy, RG 233.

16 January 1801, William Kirkpatrick, U.S. consul, Malaga (Spain), ALS.

16 January 1801, William Vans Murray, U.S. minister, The Hague, received 30 April 1801, ALS.

16 January 1801, Robert Ritchie, U.S. consul, Port Republicain (Port-au-Prince, Haiti), received 2 March 1801, ALS.

16 January 1801, Edward Stevens, U.S. consul, Cape François (Haiti), ALS.

17 January 1801, John Quincy Adams, U.S. minister, Berlin, ALS.

17 January 1801, Rufus King, U.S. minister, London, received 13 April 1801, LS (duplicate).

19 January 1801, Joseph Pitcairn, U.S. consul, Hamburg, received 20 May 1801, ALS.

19 January 1801, Robert Ritchie, U.S. consul, Port Republicain (Port-au-Prince, Haiti), received 19 February 1801, ALS.

19 January 1801, Frederick J. Wichelhausen, U.S. consul, Bremen, received 24 May 1801, ALS.

20 January 1801, William Smith, U.S. minister, Lisbon, ALS (private).

22 January 1801, Robert W. Fox, U.S. consul, Falmouth, ALS.

22 January 1801, Rufus King, U.S. minister, London, received 13 April 1801, LS (duplicate).

23 January 1801, Rufus King, U.S. minister, London, received 3 April 1801, LS (duplicate).

24 January 1801, Bird, Savage & Bird, bankers, London, ALS.

24 January 1801, William Smith, U.S. minister, Lisbon, ALS (duplicate).

24 January 1801, Samuel Snow, U.S. consul, Canton, received 9 June 1801, LS.

27 January 1801, John Quincy Adams, U.S. minister, Berlin, ALS.

27 January 1801, William Vans Murray, U.S. minister, The Hague, ALS.

28 January 1801, James C. Mountflorence, U.S. agent, Paris, ALS.

28 January 1801, Samuel Snow, U.S. consul, Canton, received 2 July 1801, ALS.

29 January 1801, Anthony Terry, vice-consul, Cádiz, received 28 March 1801, ALS.

30 January 1801, William Vans Murray, U.S. minister, The Hague, received 16 April 1801, ALS.

31 January 1801, John Quincy Adams, U.S. minister, Berlin, ALS.

1 February 1801, Wilhem van Willink, banker, Amsterdam, LS.

1 February 1801, William Eaton, U.S. consul, Tunis, ALS (duplicate).

1 February 1801, John Gavino, U.S. consul, Gibraltar, received 2 April 1801, ALS.

1 February 1801, Turell Tufts, U.S. consul, Paramaribo (Surinam), received April 1801, LS.

5 February 1801, James L. Cathcart, U.S. consul, Tripoli, ALS.

6 February 1801, Rufus King, U.S. minister, London, received 2 April 1801, LS.

7 February 1801, William Vans Murray, U.S. minister, The Hague, received 30 May 1801, ALS.

8 February 1801, Thomas W Fox (for Robert W. Fox, U.S. consul, Falmouth), ALS.

9 February 1801, Rufus King, U.S. minister, London, received 28 April 1801, ALS.

10 February 1801, John Quincy Adams, U.S. minister, Berlin, ALS.

10 February 1801, Rufus King, U.S. minister, London, received 27 April 1801, ALS.

10 February 1801, William Smith, U.S. minister, Lisbon, ALS (private).

10 February 1801, Samuel Williams, U.S. consul, London, received 10 April 1801, ALS.

15 February 1801, William Kirkpatrick, U.S. consul, Malaga (Spain), ALS.

16 February 1801, Hans R. Saabye, U.S. consul, Copenhagen, received 6 July 1801, ALS (duplicate).

17 February 1801, John Quincy Adams, U.S. minister, Berlin, ALS.

17 February 1801, Rufus King, U.S. minister, London, ALS.

18 February 1801, William Vans Murray, U.S. minister, The Hague, ALS.

19 February 1801, John Gavino, U.S. consul, Gibraltar, received 26 May 1801, AL (duplicate).

19 February 1801, Robert Montgomery, U.S. consul, Alicante (Spain), received 10 May 1801, LS.

20 February 1801, William E. Hülings, vice-consul, New Orleans, ALS.

21 February 1801, John Quincy Adams, U.S. minister, Berlin, ALS.

24 February 1801, David Humphreys, U.S. minister, Madrid, LS.

24 February 1801, William Smith, U.S. minister, Lisbon, received 14 April 1801, LS.

25 February 1801, James L. Cathcart, U.S. consul, Tripoli, received 12 August 1801, ALS (triplicate).

25 February 1801, Rufus King, U.S. minister, London, LS.

28 February 1801, John Quincy Adams, U.S. minister, Berlin, ALS.

1 March 1801, Elias Backman, U.S. consul, Göteborg (Sweden), received 24 May 1801, ALS.

1 March 1801, James C. Mountflorence, U.S. agent, Paris, received 10 May 1801, ALS.

2 March 1801, David Humphreys, U.S. minister, Madrid, received 27 May 1801, ALS.

Appendix III
Opinions Delivered by Chief Justice John Marshall
in the U.S. Supreme Court
1801–1807

The calendar below lists in chronological order all the opinions delivered by Chief Justice Marshall from the August 1801 through the February 1807 term of the Supreme Court. Of the total number of seventy-three opinions, four were cases of original jurisdiction and sixty-nine were appellate jurisdiction. In addition to the date of the opinion and the name of the case, the calendar provides the following information: the citation to the printed report; the type of appeal; the name of the court below; the appellate case number; and the date(s) of arguments by counsel. This information has been compiled from the printed reports, and the Supreme Court minutes, dockets, and appellate case files belonging to Record Group 267 in the National Archives. The style of the case is that used by the reporter William Cranch, unless other sources indicate that he was mistaken.

Under the Judiciary Act of 1789, the only way to bring a case to the Supreme Court on appeal was by writ of error. Writ of error was used not only to reverse judgments at law but also to revise decrees of admiralty and equity courts. At common law the appellate court on a writ of error was confined to reviewing alleged errors of law appearing in the record of the case as heard below. The act of 1789 accordingly provided that in admiralty and equity causes the "facts" on which the decree was founded were to be stated upon the record. Thus federal appellate practice in its earliest phase assimilated the traditional "appeal" in admiralty and equity—essentially a rehearing of the whole case, facts as well as law—to the common law writ of error.[1]

This practice remained in effect until the Judiciary Act of 1801, which provided for equity and admiralty causes to be reviewed by appeal rather than by writ of error. The new law broadened the Supreme Court's review by requiring not simply a statement of facts but "a transcript of the libel, bill, answer, depositions, and all other proceedings of what kind soever in the cause" to be sent up. Moreover, although the 1801 act was repealed, this provision was reenacted by Congress in 1803 and extended by allowing new evidence to be submitted in appeals of admiralty cases. Procedurally, there was little practical difference between an appeal and writ of error; the former remedy was simply the name given to appeals of admiralty and equity cases, the latter that given to appeals of cases at law. "Appeals" were "subject to the same rules, regulations and restrictions as are prescribed in law in case of writs of error."[2]

Another means of bringing a case from a circuit court to the Supreme Court was by a certificate of a division of opinion of the circuit court judges. This procedure became necessary in 1802, when the circuit courts were set up to consist of two judges—a justice of the Supreme Court and the judge of the district court. When a division of opinion arose, "the point upon which the disagreement shall happen, shall, during the same term, upon the request of either party, or their counsel, be stated under the direction of the judges, and certified under the seal of the court, to the supreme court."[3]

1. *U.S. Statutes at Large*, I, 83; Goebel, *Antecedents and Beginnings*, 686–87, 696–702.
2. *U.S. Statutes at Large*, II, 99, 244.
3. Ibid., II, 159.

1801

11 August	Talbot v. Seeman, 1 Cranch 26–45. Error to U.S. Circuit Court, N.Y. Appellate Case No. 89. Argued 12 Aug. 1800, 7 Aug. 1801.
15 December	Wilson v. Mason, 1 Cranch 87–103. Error to U.S. District Court, Ky. Appellate Case Nos. 90 and 91. Argued 8, 10 Aug. 1801.
21 December	United States v. Schooner Peggy, 1 Cranch 108–10. Error to U.S. Circuit Court, Conn. Appellate Case No. 93. Argued 14, 17 Dec. 1801.
21 December	Turner v. Fendall, 1 Cranch 129–37. Error to U.S. Circuit Court, D.C., Alexandria. Appellate Case No. 95. Argued 10–11 Dec. 1801.

1803

10 February	Lloyd v. Alexander, 1 Cranch 366. Error to U.S. Circuit Court, D.C., Alexandria. Appellate Case No. 125. Not argued.
17 February	Clark v. Young, 1 Cranch 190–94. Error to U.S. Circuit Court, D.C., Alexandria. Appellate Case No. 110. Argued 10–11 Feb. 1803.
23 February	Hooe & Co. v. Groverman, 1 Cranch 229–39. Error to U.S. Circuit Court, D.C., Alexandria. Appellate Case No. 114. Argued 16 Feb. 1803.
23 February	United States v. Simms, 1 Cranch 256–59. Error to U.S. Circuit Court, D.C., Alexandria. Appellate Case No. 111. Argued 17 Feb. 1803.
24 February	Marbury v. Madison, 1 Cranch 153–80. Argued 11 Feb. 1803.

26 February   Wilson v. Lenox and Maitland, 1 Cranch 211. Error to U.S. Circuit Court, D.C., Alexandria. Appellate Case No. 113. Argued 12, 22 Feb. 1803.

26 February   Mandeville & Jameson v. Riddle & Co., 1 Cranch 298–99. Error to U.S. Circuit Court, D.C., Alexandria. Appellate Case No. 129. Argued 23 Feb. 1803.

28 February   Hepburn and Dundas v. Auld, 1 Cranch 330–32. Error to U.S. Circuit Court, D.C., Alexandria. Appellate Case No. 130. Argued 25–26 Feb. 1803.

28 February   Hamilton v. Russell, 1 Cranch 314–18. Error to U.S. Circuit Court, D.C., Alexandria. Appellate Case No. 132. Argued 24 Feb. 1803.

28 February   Abercrombie v. Dupuis, 1 Cranch 343. Error to U.S. Circuit Court, Ga. Appellate Case No. 134. Not argued.

1 March   Wood v. Owings and Smith, 1 Cranch 250–52. Error to U.S. Circuit Court, Md. Appellate Case No. 99. Argued 17 Feb. 1803.

2 March   Hodgson v. Dexter, 1 Cranch 363–65. Error to U.S. Circuit Court, D.C. Appellate Case No. 137. Argued 28 Feb. 1803.

1804

14 February   Faw v. Marsteller, 2 Cranch 22–33. Appeal from U.S. Circuit Court, D.C., Alexandria. Appellate Case No. 152. Argued 8–9 Feb. 1804.

22 February   Murray v. Schooner Charming Betsey, 2 Cranch 115–26. Appeal from U.S. Circuit Court, Pa. Appellate Case No. 115. Argued 1 Mar. 1803, 9–10, 13–15 Feb. 1804.

22 February   Pennington v. Coxe, 2 Cranch 51–64. Error to U.S. Circuit Court, Pa. Appellate Case No. 147. Argued 11, 13 Feb. 1804.

25 February   Head & Amory v. Providence Insurance Co., 2 Cranch 163–69. Error to U.S. Circuit Court, R.I. Appellate Case No. 142. Argued 15–17 Feb. 1804.

27 February   Little v. Barreme, 2 Cranch 176–79. Appeal from U.S. Circuit Court, Mass. Appellate Case No. 97. Argued 16, 19 Dec. 1801.

28 February   Dunlop & Co. v. Ball, 2 Cranch 184–85. Error to U.S. Circuit Court, D.C., Alexandria. Appellate Case No. 167. Argued 27 Feb. 1804.

5 March   Church v. Hubbart, 2 Cranch 232–39. Error to U.S. Circuit Court, Mass. Appellate Case No. 166. Argued 22–23 Feb., 29 Feb.-2 Mar. 1804.

6 March   Mason v. Ship Blaireau, 2 Cranch 263–71. Error to U.S. Circuit Court, Md. Appellate Case No. 175. Argued 28–29 Feb., 2–3 Mar. 1804.

1801

19 February   Adams v. Woods, 2 Cranch 340–42. Certified from U.S. Circuit Court, Mass. Appellate Case No. 144. Argued 6 Mar. 1804.

19 February   Reily v. Lamar, 2 Cranch 356–57. Appeal from U.S. Circuit Court, D.C. Appellate Case No. 169. Argued 6, 13 Feb. 1805.

21 February   United States v. Fisher, 2 Cranch 385–97. Error to U.S. Circuit Court, Pa. Appellate Case No. 148. Argued 7–9, 11–12 Feb. 1805.

25 February   Hepburn and Dundas v. Ellzey, 2 Cranch 452–53. Certified from U.S. Circuit Court, Va. Appellate Case No. 149. Argued 5, 13 Feb. 1805.

25 February   Graves and Barnewall v. Boston Marine Insurance Co., 2 Cranch 438–44. Appeal from U.S. Circuit Court, Mass. Appellate Case No. 174. Argued 13–15 Feb. 1805.

25 February   Telfair v. Stead's Executors, 2 Cranch 418. Error to U.S. Circuit Court, Ga. Appellate Case No. 85. Argued 14 Feb. 1803.

27 February   United States v. Hooe, 3 Cranch 88–92. Appeal from U.S. Circuit Court, D.C., Alexandria. Appellate Case No. 170. Argued 23, 25 Feb. 1805.

27 February   Peyton v. Brooke, 3 Cranch 96. Error to U.S. Circuit Court, D.C., Alexandria. Appellate Case No. 194. Not argued.

27 February   Huidekoper's Lessee v. Douglass, 3 Cranch 65–72. Certified from U.S. Circuit Court, Pa. Appellate Case No. 208. Argued 19–22 Feb. 1805.

2 March   Hodgson v. Butts, 3 Cranch 155–58. Error to U.S. Circuit Court, D.C., Alexandria. Appellate Case No. 171. Argued 25, 27 Feb. 1804, 28 Feb. 1805.

2 March   United States v. More, 3 Cranch 172–74. Error to U.S. Circuit Court, D.C. Appellate Case No. 172. Argued 6 Feb. 1805.

2 March   Faw v. Roberdeau's Executor, 3 Cranch 177–78. Error to U.S. Circuit Court, D.C., Alexandria. Appellate Case No. 193. Argued 27 Feb. 1805.

4 March   Levy v. Gadsby, 3 Cranch 186. Error to U.S. Circuit Court, D.C., Alexandria. Appellate Case No. 195. Argued 2 Mar. 1805.

5 March   Ray v. Law, 3 Cranch 179–80. Appeal from U.S. Circuit Court, D.C. Not argued.

6 March   Milligan v. Milledge, 3 Cranch 228. Error to U.S. Circuit Court, Ga. Appellate Case No. 188. Argued 5 Mar. 1805.

6 March   Hallett v. Jenks, 3 Cranch 218–19. Error to N.Y. Court for Trial of Impeachments and Correction of Errors. Appellate Case No. 189. Argued 5 Mar. 1805.

6 March   Wilson v. Codman's Executor, 3 Cranch 206–10. Error to

U.S. Circuit Court, D.C., Alexandria. Appellate Case No. 196. Argued 28 Feb.-1 Mar. 1805.

6 March   Cooke v. Graham's Administrator, 3 Cranch 235. Error to U.S. Circuit Court, D.C., Alexandria. Appellate Case No. 200. Argued 5 Mar. 1805.

1806

13 February   Hannay v. Eve, 3 Cranch 247–49. Error to U.S. Circuit Court, Ga. Appellate Case No. 177. Argued 10 Feb. 1806.

13 February   Silsby v. Young and Silsby, 3 Cranch 261–66. Error to U.S. Circuit Court, Ga. Appellate Case No. 184. Argued 10–11 Feb. 1806.

13 February   Strawbridge v. Curtiss, 3 Cranch 267–68. Appeal from U.S. Circuit Court, Mass. Appellate Case No. 190. Argued 12 Feb. 1806.

13 February   Gordon v. Caldcleugh, 3 Cranch 269–70. Error to Equity Court of S.C. Appellate Case No. 215. Not argued.

14 February   Wilson v. Speed, 3 Cranch 290–93. Error to U.S. District Court, Ky. Appellate Case No. 232. Argued 13 Feb. 1806.

14 February   M'Ferran v. Taylor and Massie, 3 Cranch 280–82. Error to U.S. District Court, Ky. Appellate Case No. 224. Argued 12 Feb. 1806.

17 February   Douglass & Mandeville v. M'Allister, 3 Cranch 300. Error to U.S. Circuit Court, D.C., Alexandria. Appellate Case No. 228. Argued 13 Feb. 1806.

19 February   Simms and Wise v. Slacum, 3 Cranch 306–9. Error to U.S. Circuit Court, D.C., Alexandria. Appellate Case No. 229. Argued 13–14 Feb. 1806.

19 February   Harris v. Johnston, 3 Cranch 317–19. Error to U.S. Circuit Court, D.C., Alexandria. Appellate Case No. 234. Argued 14 Feb. 1806.

19 February   Dixon's Executors v. Ramsay's Executors, 3 Cranch 323–24. Error to U.S. Circuit Court, D.C., Alexandria. Appellate Case No. 235. Argued 15 Feb. 1806.

19 February   Scott v. Negro London, 3 Cranch 329–31. Error to U.S. Circuit Court, D.C., Alexandria. Appellate Case No. 236. Argued 15 Feb. 1806.

19 February   Wise v. Withers, 3 Cranch 335–37. Error to U.S. Circuit Court, D.C., Alexandria. Appellate Case No. 237. Argued 17 Feb. 1806.

22 February   United States v. Grundy and Thornburgh, 3 Cranch 349–56. Error to U.S. Circuit Court, Md. Appellate Case No. 243. Argued 18–19 Feb. 1806.

26 February   Manella, Pujals & Co. v. Barry, 3 Cranch 439–48. Error to U.S. Circuit Court, Md. Appellate Case No. 244. Argued 21–22 Feb. 1806.

1 March   Buddicum v. Kirk, 3 Cranch 297–98. Error to U.S. Circuit
Court, D.C., Alexandria. Appellate Case No. 213. Argued 28
Feb. 1806.

3 March   Maley v. Shattuck, 3 Cranch 487–92. Appeal from U.S. Circuit Court, Pa. Appellate Case No. 242. Argued 1 Mar. 1806.

4 March   Sands v. Knox, 3 Cranch 503. Error to N.Y. Court for Trial
of Impeachments and Correction of Errors. Appellate Case
No. 251. Argued 3 Mar. 1806.

4 March   Ex Parte Burford, 3 Cranch 449. Motion for habeas corpus.
Argued 4 Mar. 1806.

4 March   Lawrason v. Mason, 3 Cranch 495–96. Error to U.S. Circuit
Court, D.C., Alexandria. Appellate Case No. 227. Argued 3
Mar. 1806.

1807

11 February   Jennings v. Carson, 4 Cranch 20–29. Appeal from U.S. Circuit Court, Pa. Appellate Case No. 205. Argued 2, 4–5, 9
Feb. 1807.

11 February   Rhinelander v. Insurance Co. of Pennsylvania, 4 Cranch 41–
46. Certified from U.S. Circuit Court, Pa. Appellate Case
No. 285. Argued 6–7 Feb. 1807.

12 February   Montalet v. Murray, 4 Cranch 47. Error to U.S. Circuit
Court, Ga. Appellate Case No. 180. Argued 12 Feb. 1807.

13 February   Ex Parte Bollman and Ex Parte Swartwout, 4 Cranch 93–
101. Motion for habeas corpus. Argued 9, 11 Feb. 1807.

14 February   United States v. Willings & Francis, 4 Cranch 55–59. Error to
U.S. Circuit Court, Pa. Appellate Case No. 206. Argued 7,
9–10 Feb. 1807.

14 February   Oneale v. Long, 4 Cranch 62. Error to U.S. Circuit Court,
D.C. Appellate Case No. 209. Argued 12 Feb. 1807.

16 February   Smith v. Carrington, 4 Cranch 69–73. Error to U.S. Circuit
Court, R.I. Appellate Case No. 246. Argued 12–13 Feb.
1807.

19 February   Wood v. Lide, 4 Cranch 181. Error to U.S. Circuit Court, Ga.
Appellate Case No. 256.

21 February   Ex Parte Bollman and Ex Parte Swartwout, 4 Cranch 125–
37. Motion for discharge. Argued 16–20 Feb. 1807.

23 February   French's Executrix v. Bank of Columbia, 4 Cranch 153–64.
Error to U.S. Circuit Court, D.C. Appellate Case No. 210.
Argued 14 Feb. 1807.

28 February   Sthreshley and Obannon v. United States, 4 Cranch 171. Error to U.S. District Court, Ky. Appellate Case No. 252. Argued 27 Feb. 1807.

28 February   United States v. Cantril, 4 Cranch 168. Certified from U.S.
Circuit Court, Ga. Appellate Case No. 263. Argued 27 Feb.
1807.

Appendix IV
The Sale of South Branch Manor

In 1801 and 1802 John Marshall sold off most of South Branch Manor, consisting of 56,000 acres situated in the counties of Hardy and Hampshire (now West Virginia). From the time they contracted with Denny Martin Fairfax in February 1793 to purchase the Fairfax manor lands, Marshall and his brother James intended to sell South Branch Manor for revenue needed to obtain the richer prize: Leeds Manor, 160,000 acres in the counties of Fauquier, Loudoun, Frederick, and Shenandoah. The total purchase price for the Fairfax manors was twenty thousand pounds, of which the Marshalls paid six thousand in February 1797 to gain title to South Branch. Another ten years would pass before they were able to pay the final installment on the fourteen thousand pounds for Leeds.[1]

As early as August 1793, six months after the contract with Denny Fairfax, the Marshalls entered into a contract with numerous tenants of South Branch Manor, who at the time held their lands by long-term leases that were perpetually renewable. The Marshalls agreed to convey these lands in fee simple in return for payment of all rents then due and the further sum of twenty-five pounds for every hundred acres (five shillings per acre). For this purpose, the tenants executed their bonds payable to James Marshall.[2] Most of the deeds later executed by John Marshall for South Branch lands originated in this transaction. As the tenants or their assignees paid off their bonds, they obtained conveyances from Marshall.

Because Denny Fairfax had conveyed South Branch Manor in February 1794 to John Marshall (the deed was not finally executed until February 1797 on payment of the purchase money), his name alone appears on these deeds as seller.[3] James Marshall was then in London and expected to be in Europe for some time. He arranged for Denny Fairfax to convey South Branch to John Marshall so that the latter could execute deeds to those tenants who paid off their bonds. In the summer of 1795 John Marshall traveled to South Branch to make such conveyances but found a "general unwillingness" on the part of the tenants to discharge their bonds—at the time the Commonwealth of Virginia was asserting title to the Fairfax estate. After the commonwealth relinquished its claim to the manor lands by the compromise act of 1796, the South Branch tenants began to make payments and obtain deeds.[4]

Sixty percent of the deeds listed below represent conversions of leaseholds to fee simple ownership.[5] All the deeds were recorded in the district court at the town of Moorefield in Hardy County, which was then the superior court for the counties of Hardy, Hampshire, and Pendleton Rawleigh Colston and Charles Magill acted as Marshall's agents in these transactions, though he and his brother did attend the court at Moorefield on one occasion to acknowledge a deed in person. This was on 7 September 1802, when the Marshalls sold the smaller of the two tracts comprising the South Branch Manor—the so-called "resurvey" tract of 1,150 acres—to Isaac and Jacob Vanmeter. In December 1802 the Marshalls conveyed the unsold remainder of South Branch Manor (consisting of 11,000 acres) to Abel Seymour. The handful of deeds bearing Marshall's name after that date represent contracts entered into before 1 October 1802, which were specifically exempted from the sale to Seymour.

The deeds are recorded in Hardy County Deed Books A (1797–1802), B (1802–5), C (1804–11), and Deed Book 5 (1800–1806), in the clerk's office at Moorefield. These deed books are also available on microfilm at the West Virginia Department of Archives and History, Charleston. In the list below, the editors have rounded off fractions of acres to the nearest whole number.

1. See *PJM*, II, 140–49.
2. Bond, 15 Aug. 1793, Simpson v. Marshall, Clerk's Office, Augusta County Circuit Court, Staunton, Va.
3. *PJM*, II, 254–58.
4. Answer of James M. Marshall, 25 Aug. 1800, Simpson v. Marshall.
5. For sales of South Branch lands previous to Nov. 1800, see *PJM*, II, 148–49; III, 382, 464–65, 475, 477, 523; IV, 5, 8, 9, 13, 22, 29, 43, 52, 82, 109, 111, 128, 148, 176.

Date	Purchaser	Acres
14 November 1800	George Harness, Jr., and Jacob Vanmeter, Jr.	92
1 December 1800	Michael Hyer	154
7 February 1801	William Renick	718
8 March 1801	Thomas McClung	8
12 March 1801	Jesse Welton	34
1 May 1801	Patrick Lynch	205
1 June 1801	Adam Sea and others	216
	James Cunningham	325
	James Machir	359
8 June 1801	William Cunningham	597
	William Cunningham	630
15 August 1801	William Renick, Jr.	496
5 September 1801	Henry Pringle	79
8 September 1801	William Cunningham	1,110
	William Cunningham	455
	Andrew Byrns	58
9 September 1801	Adam Fisher and John Fisher	74

Date	Purchaser	Acres
	Richard Seymour	236
	Thomas Jones	—
	Adam Fisher	40
	Jacob Fisher	95
	James Cunningham	196
	Job Welton	53
10 September 1801	Peter Higgins	352
	William D. Lucas	118
	Joseph Inskeep	534
	Job Welton	55
	Job Welton	6
	John Harness, Sr.	50
30 September 1801	Henry Pringle	23
5 March 1802	Andrew Byrns and Morgan Byrns	48
12 March 1802	Rudolph Shobe	16
5 May 1802	Job Welton	—
	Valentine Powers	41
	Frederick Sellars	95
6 May 1802	John Welton	45
	Andrew Byrns and Morgan Byrns	25
12 August 1802	Job Welton	5
7 September 1802	Conrod Carr	17
	Conrod Carr	49
	Isaac Vanmeter and Jacob Vanmeter	1,550
8 September 1802	Edward Williams	20
	Philip P. Yoakam	265
13 December 1802	Abel Seymour	11,000
11 March 1803	William Cunningham	340
	William Cunningham	11
	Joseph Inskeep	136
17 March 1803	Peter Higgins	848
9 May 1803	Joseph Obannon	137
9 May 1803	Moses Welton	105
	Strother McNeill	130
12 August 1803	Alexander Simpson	97
10 May 1806	Adam Fisher	117
13 May 1806	Jacob Fisher	117
	William Cunningham	125

Appendix V
A Note on the 1804 and 1805 Impressions of the *Life*

In the fall of 1804 Caleb P. Wayne, publisher of the *Life*, decided to reprint the first three volumes of the biography. This gave Marshall the opportunity to revise his text. Wayne incorporated these revisions in the second impression of those volumes, which appeared in the winter and spring of 1805.[1] To determine the extent of Marshall's alterations and whether all of his changes were included in the second impression, a comparison was made of five sets of the *Life* at the University of Virginia Library. Based on Marshall's extant notes and letters stipulating changes, the conclusion is that Wayne included all of Marshall's revisions in the second impression.[2] So extensive were they that line and page breaks vary from the beginning in each of the three volumes. Not only is there a different total number of pages but text on signature pages does not correspond in the two impressions.

Of the five sets examined, three are of the first impression and two are second impression, containing Marshall's corrections for volumes I–III. The sets are identified as follows, first impressions: copy 2 from the stacks, signed William Holliday (bookplate, Governor Holliday); from Rare Books, signed Jno. Coalter (bookplate, Laburnum Library/John Stuart Bryan); from Rare Books, signed C. S. G. Worthington (bookplate, Tracy W. McGregor); second impressions: from Rare Books, signed Jno. McClelland (bookplate, Laburnum Library/John Stuart Bryan); from Rare Books (card, Rev. T. Dabney Wellford). All three sets of the first impression have the same pagination, including two page numbers reversed in volume V (962/296 and 359/395). Worthington's set was trimmed in size. Of the two second impressions, McClelland's pagination varies for the first three volumes but matches that of the first impression for volumes IV and V.

In volumes I and II, Marshall's revisions actually increased rather than reduced the total number of pages of main text. The author did not correct volumes IV and V after initial publication, as he did volumes I–III. Although the two impressions of the last two volumes look identical page for page, on closer examination minor differences appear. In comparing volume IV, 375–76, McClelland contains two errors on pages that otherwise are identical with Holliday, indicating that either changes were made in that particular frame or they are in fact different impressions, in spite of a cursory comparison of signature pages in which they look the same. On p. 375 the first word in McClelland is "distant"; it should be "instant," as in Holliday. In McClelland the next page number is "326." In volume V, the reversed page numbers of Holliday are printed correctly as 296 and 395 in McClelland.

Wellford's set, the other second impression, is totally different in its pagination, except for volume V, which is the same as the other four sets. Wellford is printed on thinner paper; has smaller margins, more words per line, and fewer pages; and lacks the marginal notes run down the sides that all other sets contain. (The thickness of volume V, with the same number of pages, is one centimeter less than the other sets.) It is the cheap edition of which Weems complained.[3] It has the text corrected as in McClelland for volumes I–III but completely reset. The McClelland set represents the standard second impression to which Marshall referred. He noticed an error in revised volume II, 10, line 8, which corresponds exactly in McClelland but is found on p. 9, line 21, in Wellford.[4]

The following give publication date and pagination for prefatory material, text, and appendix of each volume in the different sets.

First Impressions

Volume	I	II	III	IV	V
	(1804)	(1804)	(1804)	(1805)	(1807)
Holliday	iii–xxii	v–viii	iii–viii	v–viii	iii–vii
	488	560	580	626	779
	45	72	28	16	36
Coalter	iii–xxii	v–viii	iii–viii	v–viii	iii–vii
	488	560	580	626	779
	45	72	28	16	36
Worthington	iii–xxii	v–viii	iii–viii	v–viii	iii–vii
	488	560	580	626	779
	45	72	28	16	36

Second Impressions

Volume	I	II	III	IV	V
	(1805)	(1805)	(1805)	(1805)	(1807)
McClelland	iii–xxii	iii–v	iii–vii	v–viii	iii–vii
	500	565	576	626	779
	43	67	28	16	36
Wellford	iii–xxii	v–vii	iii–vii	v–viii	iii–vii
	459	516	527	567	779
	43	67	28	16	36

In a "casual observation" of copies at the Library Company of Philadelphia, Edwin Wolf 2nd found five distinct printings of volume I published between 1804 and 1805, two "editions" of volumes II and III (1804 and 1805), three "editions" of volume IV (1805), and two "editions" of volume V (1807).[5] The five sets at the University of Virginia Library show that Wayne published at least three editions (totally reset type) of the *Life*, volumes I–III, between 1804 and 1805.

In terms of contents, though, the different editions consist only of one of two versions, that of the first (1804) or of the corrected second impression (1805). The second impression as represented by the McClelland set is the one that contains the author's final intentions until the second edition of 1832 was published.[6]

1. For an explanation of JM's writing and revising the *Life* and the distinction of impressions from editions, see *The Life of George Washington*, editorial note (preceding Preface, [ante 22 Dec. 1803]) and nn. 19, 21–23.

2. See JM to Noah Webster, 4 Oct. 1804 and nn. 4–6; JM to Wayne, [22 Oct.] and nn. 1, 4, 5, 7, 30 Oct. 1804 and nn. 1, 3, 4, 19 Feb. and nn. 3, 4, 1 Mar. 1805 and n. 1.

3. See JM to Wayne, 10 Jan. 1805 and n. 2.

4. See JM to Wayne, 8 June 1805.

5. Edwin Wolf 2nd, "Historical Grist for the Bibliographical Mill," *Studies in Bibliography*, XXV (1972), 30.

6. See *The Life of George Washington*, editorial note (preceding Preface, [ante 22 Dec. 1803]) and n. 23.

INDEX

In addition to persons and subjects, this index includes the titles of all cases mentioned in the documents and in the accompanying annotation. Identifications occur at or near the first mention of a person. If a person has been identified in an earlier volume, the volume number and page reference follow the name in parentheses. The editors prepared the index with the aid of NLCINDEX, a program developed by Charles T. Cullen of the Newberry Library in Chicago. NLCINDEX is an adaptation for microcomputer of CINDEX, a mainframe indexing program designed by David R. Chesnutt of the University of South Carolina.